Advanced RenderMan™

The Morgan Kaufmann Series in Computer Graphics and Geometric Modeling

Series Editor, Brian A. Barsky

Advanced RenderMan: Creating CGI for Motion Pictures
Anthony A. Apodaca, Larry Gritz

Curves and Surfaces in Geometric Modeling: Theory and Algorithms
Jean Gallier

Andrew Glassner's Notebook: Recreational Computer Graphics
Andrew S. Glassner

Warping and Morphing of Graphical Objects
Jonas Gomes, Lucia Darsa, Bruno Costa, and Luis Velho

Jim Blinn's Corner: Dirty Pixels
Jim Blinn

Rendering with Radiance: The Art and Science of Lighting Visualization
Greg Ward Larson and Rob Shakespeare

Introduction to Implicit Surfaces
Edited by Jules Bloomenthal

Jim Blinn's Corner: A Trip Down the Graphics Pipeline
Jim Blinn

Interactive Curves and Surfaces: A Multimedia Tutorial on CAGD
Alyn Rockwood and Peter Chambers

Wavelets for Computer Graphics: Theory and Applications
Eric J. Stollnitz, Tony D. DeRose, and David H. Salesin

Principles of Digital Image Synthesis
Andrew S. Glassner

Radiosity & Global Illumination
François X. Sillion and Claude Puech

Knotty: A B-Spline Visualization Program
Jonathan Yen

User Interface Management Systems: Models and Algorithms
Dan R. Olsen, Jr.

Making Them Move: Mechanics, Control, and Animation of Articulated Figures
Edited by Norman I. Badler, Brian A. Barsky, and David Zeltzer

Geometric and Solid Modeling: An Introduction
Christoph M. Hoffmann

An Introduction to Splines for Use in Computer Graphics and Geometric Modeling
Richard H. Bartels, John C. Beatty, and Brian A. Barsky

Advanced RenderMan™

Creating CGI for Motion Pictures

Anthony A. Apodaca
Larry Gritz

with additional material by
Ronen Barzel
Sharon Calahan
Clint Hanson
Scott Johnston

MORGAN KAUFMANN PUBLISHERS

AN IMPRINT OF ACADEMIC PRESS

A Harcourt Science and Technology Company

SAN FRANCISCO   SAN DIEGO   NEW YORK   BOSTON
LONDON   SYDNEY   TOKYO

Senior Editor	Diane Cerra
Director of Production and Manufacturing	Yonie Overton
Senior Production Editor	Robin Demers
Editorial Assistant	Belinda Breyer
Cover Design	Ross Carron Design
Text Design and Color Insert Design & Production	Side by Side Studios
Copyediting	Progressive Publishing Alternatives
Proofreader	Jennifer McClain
Composition	Windfall Software, using ZzTEX
Indexer	Ty Koontz
Printer	Courier Corporation

Cover image credits: "STUART LITTLE" © 1999 Global Entertainment Productions GmbH & Co. Medien KG. All Rights Reserved. Courtesy of Columbia Pictures, Sony Pictures Imageworks; *Toy Story* © Disney Enterprises, Inc.; *IRON GIANT* © 1999 Warner Bros. All Rights Reserved.

Designations used by companies to distinguish their products are often claimed as trademarks or registered trademarks. In all instances where Morgan Kaufmann Publishers is aware of a claim, the product names appear in initial capital or all capital letters. Readers, however, should contact the appropriate companies for more complete information regarding trademarks and registration.

ACADEMIC PRESS
A Harcourt Science and Technology Company
525 B Street, Suite 1900, San Diego, CA 92101-4495, USA
http://www.academicpress.com

Academic Press
Harcourt Place, 32 Jamestown Road, London, NW1 7BY, United Kingdom
http://www.academicpress.com

Morgan Kaufmann Publishers
340 Pine Street, Sixth Floor, San Francisco, CA 94104-3205
http://www.mkp.com

Library of Congress Cataloging-in-Publication Data

Apodaca, Anthony A.
    Advanced RenderMan : creating CGI for motion pictures / Anthony A. Apodaca, Larry
  Gritz, with additional material by Ronen Barzel . . . [et al.].
       p.   cm.
    Includes bibliographical references and index.
    ISBN 1-55860-618-1
    1. Cinematography—Special effects. 2. Computer animation. 3. Computer graphics. 4.
  RenderMan. I. Gritz, Larry. II. Barzel, Ronen. III. Title.
TR858 .A66 1999
778.5'345—dc21
                                                                        99-088455

This book is printed on acid-free paper.

This book is dedicated to the hundreds of hard-working and long-suffering CGI TDs who spend so much of their life and creative energy making motion pictures look so fabulously beautiful, exciting, awe-inspiring, and fun, and whose contributions are rarely recognized by the viewing public who are agape at their results. You are our customers, our colleagues, and our friends. We thank you all.

And in the end, the love you take is equal to the love you make.

—The Beatles

Foreword

Steve Upstill
Pixar Animation Studios

And about time, too.

The RenderMan Companion first appeared, 10 years ago, with several purposes behind it. First, we hoped to promote the RenderMan Interface as a standard for high-quality three-dimensional computer graphics, similar to the role PostScript plays in two dimensions. Second, and more importantly, we hoped to encourage and support the development of the field as a whole in both deed and word. Not only would the book's content enable people to do cool work with RenderMan, but its very existence would encourage subsequent publications that would continue to raise the platform of knowledge and technique.

On most of these counts, the effort must be considered a success. Today, RenderMan is the de facto standard for photorealistic 3D rendering in the digital effects industry. In fact, the revolution in digital effects began (with the "water weenie" of *The Abyss*) soon after Pixar's *PRMan* first entered the scene. Coincidence? We think not. And the interface has proven the equal of problems and dataset sizes that were laughable 10 years ago ("Ten million polygons? Don't be ridiculous."), supporting a revolution that continues to blow the minds of audiences the world over.

But still. For 10 years, *The RenderMan Companion* has been the only book available on the subject, complete with its thin spots, omissions, and obsolete view of the interface. Worse, although the art and practice of RenderMan continued to develop, somehow that progress never saw the ink that would allow the platform to rise and the field to move forward for the world at large. (The only time that people came together to deal with the real nitty-gritty of geometry and shaders was at the Advanced RenderMan courses of SIGGRAPH, organized and presented by many of the authors here.) This is a vacuum that has sorely needed filling, and now I'm delighted to see it being filled, and filled so well.

I have several reasons to be so delighted. First, it takes a longstanding monkey off my back—the need for a followup to the *Companion*. Second, it finally diverts attention and credit for the interface away from me and toward those who actually deserve it. We live in a world in which the messenger is easily mistaken for the message, and for 10 long years I have been far more closely identified with RenderMan than decency should allow. With this book the *real* wizards step out from behind the curtain so we can see what they're made of, and it's not a lot of smoke, mirrors, and subwoofers, either.

But the real reason this book is such a tonic is that I get to have it. I am sure that I am not alone in sometimes feeling a little lost and small in dealing with something as powerful as RenderMan. While I do believe that the *Companion* functions nicely as a field guide to the resources available, here at last are the maps to the territory, the signposts in the dark woods that can make the foreigner feel at home and enable her to make real progress. Here we have an august circle of expert guides to take you by the hand and show you what goes on inside the head of someone who knows their way around. With this book in hand, you may not be a wizard yourself, but you can play one on TV.

My warmest thanks go to Tony, Larry, and all of their contributors for sharing their light so generously and skillfully. But my real excitement is for you, the reader, who for so few dollars can get the benefit of so much hard-won experience in such a concentrated yet accessible form. As I said 10 years ago, and now say with even more reason: Happy Rendering!

Contents

Preface

This book explores the theory and the practice of using RenderMan to create computer graphics imagery (CGI) for use in motion pictures and animation. We have written many papers and taught many courses on the use of RenderMan, and this is the most advanced material we have presented yet. Readers are expected to understand the basics of using RenderMan. In this book, we will explore more advanced details on how to define scenes, discuss how to write truly excellent shaders, and will spend quite a bit of time revealing the tricks that are used in real motion picture production to create computer graphics animation and CGI special visual effects. Most importantly, we will explore topics that are beyond the scope of the only previously available reference book *The RenderMan Companion*.

Let us admit up front the primary bias of the authors of this book. We are the designers, implementers, and users of two specific RenderMan-compliant renderers: Pixar's *PhotoRealistic RenderMan* (referred to in this text as *PRMan*) and Blue Moon Rendering Tools' *rendrib* (referred to in this text as *BMRT*). These renderers are not the only renderers that have ever attempted to support the ambitious *RenderMan Interface Specification*, but they are the most well known and the most widely used. In fact, *PRMan* is so generally considered the "reference platform" for RenderMan that the word "RenderMan" is often used synonymously with *PRMan*. We recognize that by the time this book is in print, there may be a number of other RenderMan-compliant renderers available to our gentle readers. We believe that the vast majority of material in this book should apply equally well to any modern and fully RenderMan-compliant renderer—and in large measure to high-quality renderers that are not RenderMan, as well.

This book is designed primarily for beginning- to intermediate-level CG technical directors in the special effects industry, or those with equivalent backgrounds (such as graduate or advanced undergraduate students, or others with a strong interest in the technical aspects of computer graphics and animation). It is *not* assumed that you have years of production experience, or a Ph.D., or any other such exclusive prerequisites.

Nevertheless, to make this book possible, we are forced to assume that the reader brings to the table substantial background knowledge. Specifically, we assume that

- You have some background in programming, particularly in C (or a related programming language). You should be familiar with concepts such as data types and variables, conditionals and loops, subroutines and functions, parameter passing, and the basic mechanism of compiling programs. We will frequently explain concepts by merely pointing out the *differences* between Shading Language and C.

- You have a firm grasp of advanced high school math, including trigonometry, vector algebra, elementary functions, and analytic geometry. If you are comfortable with calculus and differential geometry, you'll be even more at home with the material.

- You are familar with the fundamental concepts of computer graphics. At the very least, the following phrases should be meaningful to you: shading and illumination models, texture mapping, geometric primitives (including polygons, patches, and NURBS), and image compositing. If you have extensively used any modeling package, animation package, or renderer, you are probably up to speed on the basic concepts of computer graphics.

In addition, there are a variety of other prerequisites that, though not strictly required, will certainly make this book much more useful to you:

- The value of some familiarity with physics, particularly with optics and material properties, cannot be overstated. A little intuition about how light behaves in the real world can be immensely helpful in understanding how renderers work.

- We tried not to leave anything out, but this book is more a discussion of advanced topics than a tutorial or a proper reference. Therefore we do recommend that you have *The RenderMan Companion* (Upstill, 1990) and the official *RenderMan Interface Specification* (Pixar, 1989) handy. (The RI Specification is available online at www.pixar.com.)

- It would certainly help if you had one of the several RenderMan-compliant renderers so that you can try out the examples. If you do not have *PRMan*, we partisanly recommend the *Blue Moon Rendering Tools,* which is free for noncommercial use, and can be downloaded from www.bmrt.org.

- Some knowledge of, and preferably experience with, the terminology and practice of composing and lighting of live-action and/or CG scenes is helpful. Chapter 13 provides some of this background and recommends several additional sources for this material.

A glance at the table of contents should reveal that this book is composed of very advanced material, hence the title. We have tried to provide as much context as possible by providing chapters giving introductory material on the APIs, Shading Language, and mathematical background. However, these chapters are designed more for quick reference, and while complete, they ramp up *very quickly* and assume substantial prior experience in certain areas. Moreover, because the material in the book is "advanced," much of it is interrelated, without a single linear path of progressing levels of difficulty. We tried to do our best to make few assumptions in earlier chapters, building on this material for later chapters, but this was not always possible.

Well, there it is. We don't want to scare anybody off, and we have tried to make this book as self-contained as practical. But we're writing about tools actually used to make films, and they do require a lot of detailed technical knowledge.

Acknowledgments

We would like to thank all of our alpha and beta readers, Dana Batali, Rob Cook, Tom Duff, Steve May, Chris Perry, Tom Porter, Guido Quaroni, Rick Sayre, Steve Upstill, Steve Westin, and Wayne Wooten, who added so much to the clarity and technical veracity of our prose. We are also indebted to Pixar Animation Studios, Walt Disney Feature Animation, Sony Pictures Imageworks, and Warner Brothers Feature Animation for their kind permission to use images from their work.

But we are especially thankful to Ed Catmull and the whole executive team at Pixar for creating and fostering an environment in which research and development of innovative rendering techniques is actively pursued, and where, while these techniques are developed to further our proprietary animation production systems, we are still allowed to publish our ideas and discoveries and share them with the graphics community at large.

Chapter 1 is adapted from "Photosurrealism," *Ninth Eurographics Workshop on Rendering*, Vienna, Austria, July 1998, published by Springer-Verlag, and is used with permission. Chapter 14 is adapted from "Lighting Controls for Computer Cinematography," *Journal of Graphics Tools*, Vol. 2, No. 1, and is used with permission. Much of the rest of the book was adapted from sections in various Siggraph course notes, particularly *Advanced RenderMan: Beyond the Companion* (Siggraph, 1998), *Writing RenderMan Shaders* (Siggraph, 1992), and *Pixel Cinematography: A Lighting Approach for Computer Graphics* (Siggraph, 1996).

RenderMan is a registered trademark of Pixar. *PhotoRealistic RenderMan* is a trademark of Pixar. The *RenderMan Interface Specification* and the documentation for *The RenderMan Toolkit* are copyrighted by Pixar, and excerpts are used with permission. All product names are trademarked by the companies that trademarked them.

About the Companion Web Site

Readers are encouraged to visit the companion Web site to this book at http://www
.mkp.com/renderman. At the Web site you will find all of the code in this book,
both library routines and full shaders. No need to type in any program listings—

moreover, the Web site's files will include any extensions and corrections that might be made after the book is printed. In addition, the Web site contains other examples, pointers to RenderMan-related URLs, and other resources, as well as an area where we can post additional examples and shaders, written and contributed by users, that are based on the material in the book.

Background

1 Photosurrealism

Over the last 25 years, a revolution has been taking place in the motion picture industry. It started slowly at first, faltered at times, but has been growing and building inexorably. What once was a mere curiosity used to obscure ends is now the basic paradigm of film production. Movies have gone digital.

There are many aspects to movie making, many processes and techniques where digital technology can and has made a difference in the way that movies are made—everything from text editors customized for script writing to digital soundtracks on the film (and eventually digital distribution replacing film itself). But perhaps none have been so revolutionary as the use of computer graphics to create imagery for motion pictures.

The first use of computer graphics in a feature film was in 1976 when *Futureworld* included a computer-animated simulation of a human hand and face. These animations, created by then graduate students Ed Catmull and Fred Parke at the University of Utah, started the computer graphics industry down the road that eventually led to the nearly ubiquitous use of computer graphics special effects in feature films.

The road was long, however. The first two films to make significant investments in computer-generated imagery (CGI), Disney's *Tron* and Universal's *The Last Starfighter*, were commercial flops. These failures made directors wary. Generally, CGI was limited to imagery that was clearly supposed to be from a computer (fancy displays on computer monitors, for example). It wasn't until 1990 that CGI scored its first real success: *The Abyss* won the Academy Award for Best Visual Effects, partially on the strength of the photorealistic CGI effects produced by Industrial Light and Magic.

Since 1990, everything has changed. Computer graphics has been used to create significant special effects for every film that has won the Academy Award for Best Visual Effects. Many Scientific and Technical Academy Awards have been awarded to the authors of computer graphics software, recognizing their contributions to the film industry. Presently, nearly all films that have any visual effects at all will have at least some effects that are computer generated. Most movie special effects houses in the United States have largely switched over from "practical" effects to CGI-based ones. Moreover, those visual effects are not limited to spaceships and monsters. Main characters with significant screen time can now be created with computer animation, as was seen in *Star Wars: Episode 1—The Phantom Menace*.

Or we can dispense with live-action footage entirely. The first full-length completely computer-generated feature film, Pixar's *Toy Story*, was released in 1995 and was a huge commercial success. As this book goes to press in 1999, three more successful all-CG films have already been released, and we are aware of at least 10 more that are in some stage of production.

Computer graphics has carried the day.

1.1   Making Movies

For more than 20 years, one of the stated goals of the computer graphics research community has been to solve the problem of making truly *photorealistic* images. We have strived to make the CG image, as much as possible, look exactly like a photograph of the scene, were that virtual scene to actually exist. Much of this work was done very specifically so that CGI could be used in films. Solving such problems as accurate light reflection models, motion blur, depth of field, and the handling of massive visual complexity was motivated by the very demanding requirements of the film industry.

Movies, however, are illusions. They show us a world that does not exist, and use that world to tell a story. The goal of the filmmaker is to draw the audience into this world and to get the audience to *suspend its disbelief* and watch the story unfold. Every element of the movie—the dialog, costumes and makeup, sets, lighting, sound and visual effects, music, and so on—is there to support the story and must help lead the viewer from one story point to the next. In order for the audience to understand and believe the movie's world, it clearly must be realistic. It cannot have arbitrary, nonsensical rules, or else it will jar and confuse the viewers and make them drop out of the experience. However, movie realism and physical realism are two different things. In a movie, it is realistic for a 300-foot-tall radioactive hermaphroditic lizard to destroy New York City, as long as its skin looks like lizard skin we are familiar with. Some things we are willing to suspend our disbelief for, and some things we are not!

There are two people who are primarily responsible for determining what the audience sees when they watch a movie. The director is responsible for telling the story. He determines what message (or "story point") the audience should receive from every scene and every moment of the film. The cinematographer (cinema photographer) is responsible for ensuring that the photography of the film clearly portrays that message.

Over time, filmmakers have developed a visual language that allows them to express their stories unambiguously. This language helps the filmmaker to manipulate the imagery of the film in subtle but important ways to focus the audience's attention on the story points. Distracting or confusing details, no matter how realistic, are summarily removed. Accenting and focusing details, even if physically unrealistic, are added in order to subtly but powerfully keep the audience's attention focused on what the director wants them to watch. The job and the art of the cinematographer is to arrange that this is true in every shot of the film. The result is that live-action footage does not look like real-life photography. It is distilled, focused, accented, bolder, and *larger than life*. In short, film images manipulate reality so that it better serves the story.

Our computer graphics images must, therefore, also do so. Perhaps even more than other parts of the filmmaking process, CGI special effects are there specifically to make a story point. The action is staged, lit, and timed so that the audience is guaranteed to see exactly what the director wants them to see. When a CG special effect is added to a shot, the perceived realism of the effect is more influenced by how well it blends with the existing live-action footage than by the photorealism of the element itself. What the director really wants are images that match as closely as possible the other not-quite-real images in the film. They are based in realism, but they bend and shape reality to the will of the director. Computer graphics imagery must be *photosurrealistic*.

1.2   Altered Reality

In a CG production studio, the job of the cinematographer is often divided among several CG artists whose jobs include geometric modeling, camera placement, material modeling, lighting, and renderer control. These digital cinematographers are collectively known as *technical directors*. They are the users of image synthesis software.

Computer graphics gives technical directors a whole host of new tools, removes restrictions, and provides an interesting and growing bag of tricks with which to manipulate reality. Jim Blinn once called these tricks "The Ancient Chinese Art of Chi-Ting" (Blinn, 1985). Technical directors now call them "getting work done."

1.2.1   Nonphysical lighting

One of the best cheats is to alter the physics of light. Chapter 14 discusses a light model used in computer graphics cinematography that was specifically designed for this type of flexibility. This work is based on the observation that movie viewers generally do not know where the lights are located in a scene, and even if they do, their limited 2D view does not allow them to reason accurately about light paths. Therefore, there is no requirement that the light paths behave realistically in order to ensure that an image is believable.

This situation is exploited by the live-action cinematographer in the placement of special-purpose lights, filters, bounce cards, and other tricks to illuminate objects unevenly, kill shadows, create additional specular highlights, and otherwise fudge the lighting for artistic purposes. Everyone who has ever seen a movie set knows that even in the middle of the day, every shoot has a large array of artificial lights that are used for a variety of such purposes.

However, the live-action cinematographer, despite his best tricks, cannot alter the physics of the light sources he is using. Computer graphics can do better. Creating objects that cast no shadow, having lights illuminate some objects and not others, and putting invisible light sources into the scene near objects are all de rigueur parlor tricks. Things get more interesting when even more liberties are taken. Consider, for example,

- a light that has negative intensity, and thus dims the scene
- a light that casts light brightly into its illuminated regions but into its "shadowed" regions casts a dim, blue-tinted light
- a spotlight that has at its source not simply 2D barndoors to control its shape, but instead has full 3D volumetric control over the areas it illuminates and doesn't illuminate, and at what intensities
- a light that contributes only to the diffuse component of a surface's bidirectional reflection distribution function (BRDF), or only to the specular component
- a light that has independent control over the direction of the outgoing beam, the direction toward which the specular highlight occurs, and the direction that shadows cast from the light should fall

In fact, such modifications to light physics in CGI are so common that the production community does not think of them as particularly special or noteworthy tricks. They are standard, required features of their production renderers. Other, even more nonphysical cheats, such as curved light rays, photons that change color based on what they hit, lights that alter the physical characteristics of the objects they illuminate, or even lights that alter the propagation of other lights' photons, are all plausible requirements in the production setting. Their use is only limited by their predictability. If the light model is so nonphysical that the technical directors cannot reason accurately about the lighting situation, cannot form a mental model with which to predict what their final rendered images will look like, and cannot get the renderer to emit the image they desire, *only then* will they not desire a feature.

This is exactly the situation with purely physical photon simulation as well. Remember, the goal of lighting a scene is primarily to accent the action and secondarily to make a beautiful artistic setting within which to stage the action. Energy conservation, truly accurate diffuse and specular interreflection, and other such goals are useful only insofar as they give the technical director (TD) a firmer, more intuitive mental model with which to manipulate the photons. Even if perfect, they will only leave the TD with the same situation that the live-action cinematographer has, with lights that they must finesse and sometimes fight to give them the image they desire.

1.2.2   Nonphysical optics

Another interesting cheat is to alter the physics of optics, or more generally all reflection and refraction, to create images with the appropriate emphasis and impact.

Much of the trickery involving manipulating optical paths is descended, at least in part, from limitations of early rendering systems and the techniques that were invented to overcome these limitations. For example, for over 20 years, most CGI was created without the benefit of ray tracing to determine the specular interreflection of mirrored and transparent objects. Even today, ray tracing is generally considered by the production community to be computationally too expensive to use except in particular extreme circumstances. However, mirrored and transparent surfaces still exist, and ways must be found to render them.

As before, the limited knowledge of the viewer comes to our rescue. Because the viewer cannot estimate accurately the true paths of interreflection in the scene, approximations generally suffice. In place of exact reflection calculations, texture maps are used: environment maps are accurate only from a single point in space (the center of their projection) but work on all surface types and in all directions; planar reflection maps are accurate everywhere on a planar surface but only when viewed from a particular camera location. Use of environment maps "near" the projection point and use of planar reflection maps on "almost" flat objects lead to slight imperfections. Refraction is handled similarly, using an environment map indexed by the refracted ray direction, and here the fudging of object thickness causes the largest imperfections.

Experience has shown that viewers have so little intuition about the reflection situation that almost any approximation will do. Only glaring artifacts, such as constant-colored reflections, inconsistency from frame to frame, or the failure of mirrors to reflect objects that touch them, will generally be noticed. In fact, experience has shown that viewers have so very, very little intuition about the reflection situation that wildly and even comically inaccurate reflections are perfectly acceptable. For example, it is common for production studios to have a small portfolio of "standard reflection images" (such as someone's house or a distorted photo of someone's face) that they apply to all objects that are not perfect mirrors.

This insensitivity to nonphysical optics gives rise to possibilities for storytelling. The objects that are actually visible in a reflection, the intensity and blurriness of the reflection of each object, and the size and location of the reflection of each object are all generally controlled independently. In *Toy Story*, for example, Buzz Lightyear's plastic helmet reflected only three objects of note:

- a prerendered image of the room he was in, quite blurry
- Woody's face when he was near, sharply
- the TV set during the commercial, very brightly and sharply

Just enough blurry room reflection was present to give Buzz the appearance of being in the room and to remind the viewer that Buzz's helmet was down, but it is only seen near the periphery, so that it never obscured Buzz's face and lip movements (Figure 1.1). A reflection of Woody was used when the director wanted to emphasize that they were close together and their fates were intertwined. The key reflection of the TV commercial in the helmet was carefully crafted to be large, bright, and sharp, so that the audience could easily watch it, but does not obscure Buzz's crucial facial expression at discovering the truth of his origins (which, of course, marked the turning point of the film).

Even more nonphysically, viewers are generally unaware of the difference between a convex and a concave mirror, to the director's delight. Convex mirrors are generally more common in the world, such as automobile windshields, computer monitors, metal cans, pens, and so on. However, mirrors that magnify are generally more interesting objects cinematographically. They help the director focus attention on some small object, or small detail, onto which it would otherwise be difficult to direct the viewers' attention. Unfortunately for the live-action cinematographer, magnifying mirrors are concave and are extremely difficult to focus. But this is no problem in CGI. Because the reflection is generally a texture map anyway (and even if it is not, the reflected rays are under the control

Figure 1.1 *Toy Story*—Buzz Lightyear's helmet reflection is carefully crafted to not obscure his winning features. (© Disney Enterprises, Inc.) See also color plate 1.1.

of the technical director), it is quite simple (and even quite common) for a convex (minifying) mirror to have a scaling factor that is not merely arbitrarily independent of its curvature, but actually *magnifying*—completely inverted from reality.

Similarly, refractions are extremely difficult for viewers to intuit, and they generally accept almost anything as long as it is vaguely similar to the background, distorted, and more so near the silhouette of the refracting object. They typically are blissfully unaware of when a real refraction would generate an inverted image and are certainly unable to discern if the refraction direction is precisely in the right direction. For example, in Pixar's short film *Geri's Game* (Pixar, 1997), there is a shot where the director asked for Geri to appear innocent and angelic after having just tricked his opponent into losing. This is accomplished by having Geri's eyes magnified large by his glasses, with pupils widely dilated (Figure 1.2). Even careful inspection of the frame by trained professionals fails to expose the fact that the image that we would see through Geri's glasses from this camera angle would not magnify nor frame his eyes this way. (Never mind the fact that he actually has flat lenses.) The refraction is actually zoomed, reoriented, and slightly rotated in order to give the director the image he desired.

Figure 1.2 *Geri's Game*—Geri's large eyes give him an angelic appeal. (© Pixar Animation Studios.) See also color plate 1.2.

1.3   Production Requirements

Once a production studio has made the choice to use CGI, for an effect or an entire film, it starts to make very specific demands on the rendering software developers. Films are very expensive to make, and a lot is riding on the studio's success in using the renderer. Failure is not an option when tens of millions of dollars are on the line.

1.3.1   Feature Set

The most obvious production requirement is feature set. The studio requires that the renderer do everything they could ever want or need. The features that are required to do a particular film are obviously different from one film to the next, and one year to the next, but there are certain constants.

For example, a production renderer must handle motion blur. One of the easiest ways for a viewer to detect that an object was filmed independently and added to the scene (i.e., an effect) is for the object to strobe when the background blurs. Audiences simply will not accept a return to the days of stop motion.

Production renderers must accept a wide variety of input geometry. It is not enough for the rendering algorithm to have just polygons. NURBS and other parametric curved surfaces are standard today, and various fads such as primitives for rendering hair, implicit surfaces, and other special-purpose models must be handled in a timely fashion.

Production renderers must make a wide variety of tricks available to the technical director. Everything from shadows, texture mapping of all varieties, atmospheric and volumetric participating-media effects, depth-of-field, lens flare, and control information for post-rendering compositing and manipulation of images must be provided for.

1.3.2   Flexibility

Related, yet perhaps even more important, requirements are flexibility and controllability. The studio requires that the renderer be user-programmable so that it can be made to do everything that no one ever knew would be needed.

For example, every production renderer now contains some sort of shading language (Hanrahan and Lawson, 1990) with which the users can redefine the shading model in almost arbitrary ways. It is hard to overstate how critical this one feature of a renderer is to a production environment. Technical directors will not accept the standard Phong shading model on all objects, no matter how many knobs and dials it has. As we have seen, they must be able, on a detailed object-by-object basis, to change surface properties and material characteristics, reactivity to light, and even the physics of light and optics itself to generate the compelling photosurrealistic image for each shot. The director of a film generally has very little sympathy for limitations of the software environment. They want their image to look a certain way, and the technical directors must find a way to make it happen.

The best proof of flexibility is the use of a renderer for purposes not envisioned by the software developer. For example, "photorealistic" renderers are now commonly used in traditional cel-animation studios to create distinctly nonphotorealistic imagery that blends with artwork. Cartoon realism is very distinct but easily accommodated if the rendering architecture is flexible enough.

Similarly, programmability in other parts of the rendering pipeline is becoming more important. Procedurally defined geometric primitives are coming back into style as data amplification is exploited to increase the visual complexity of images with minimal human work. Reprogrammable hidden-surface algorithms and easy access to other renderer "internal state" are also valuable.

A production renderer also has a powerful set of speed/quality and speed/memory trade-offs, which are intuitive and easily controllable. Production deadlines often require that compromises be made, and the variety of hardware to which the studios have access (often some of several different generations of hardware) makes it difficult to effectively utilize all available resources when only the "factory settings" are available.

1.3.3   Robustness

A key requirement for any large software package is robustness and reliability. A full-length computer-animated feature film has over 100,000 frames to render (and probably many times that number after counting test frames, rerenders for artistic changes, separate elements for compositing, and rendered texture maps), so the technical directors cannot slave over each one individually. A production renderer absolutely cannot crash, must have vanishingly few bugs, and must reliably generate the correct image each and every time it is executed. If the renderer could guess the intentions of the user even when he gave it the wrong input, that would be a requirement, too.

The renderer should, for all practical purposes, have no limits. Arbitrary limits on number of lights, number of texture maps, number of primitives, image resolution, and so on will all be exceeded by production studios in short order.

Moreover, the feature set of the renderer should be orthogonal. If the renderer can do motion blur on spheres and then a new primitive type is implemented, production will require motion blur on the new primitive on day 2. Every feature must interoperate with every other feature, unless it is clearly nonsensical to do so, and perhaps even then.

1.3.4   Performance

Another obvious production requirement is performance. Those 100,000 frames have to be computed in a matter of months on machines that the production studio can afford to buy. Movies cost a lot to make, but, in fact, very little of that money is actually allocated to the computer hardware necessary to make the effects. This means that the time to render a frame must be reasonable, the memory used to render the frame must be limited, and the database that holds the scene description must be compact. For this reason alone, global illumination is rarely used in production rendering, because it cannot generally fulfill these requirements.

And the software developers must not count on Moore's law[1] to solve this problem. While it is true that computers get faster and memory gets cheaper, seemingly without end, there is a countermanding observation that we call Blinn's law, which states that regardless of hardware, all renderings take the same amount of time. As computers get faster, all that happens is that the appetites of the users get greater, and their requirements get more demanding. In some studios, the appetite grows even faster than Moore allows!

Another aspect of performance that is often overlooked is predictability. A technical director should be able to guess, with some accuracy, how long a frame will take to render based on information that they know (such as the number of objects

---

[1] "Computing power doubles every 18 months."

in the scene, resolution, etc.). Frames that take nonlinearly more time because a small thing was added are unacceptable when the studio is trying to make budgets, allocate resources, and complete work by totally inflexible delivery dates.

1.3.5   Image Quality

Perhaps the most subtle, and yet in many ways the most important, production requirement is image quality. Production studios require images of the highest possible quality. Those images are going to be projected onto the *big screen*, and every bad pixel will be huge and ugly in front of millions of viewers. Artifacts of any and all varieties are to be eliminated with extreme prejudice. High-quality antialiasing in all dimensions, texture and shader filtering, pixel filtering, and accurate geometric approximations are all required features. Polygonal approximation artifacts, patch cracks, intersection mistakes, shadow acne, visible dithering patterns, Mach bands, and any other image-generation errors are unacceptable.

Because these images are going to be used in animations, frame-to-frame consistency is an important but subtle point. Objects that don't move shouldn't shimmer, and objects that move slowly shouldn't pop. Antialiasing of shading, lighting, and geometry must work consistently at all scales and all distances from the camera.

1.4   Enter RenderMan

In case it isn't obvious, for the last several pages we've really been talking about our pride and joy, Pixar's *PhotoRealistic RenderMan*. There are other production renderers available to the film production community, of course, but *PRMan* is currently the most widely used.

So, just what is RenderMan? The RenderMan Interface is a standard communications protocol between modeling programs and rendering programs capable of producing photorealistic-quality images. Its goal is to provide a standard mechanism for modeling and animation software to send data to rendering systems in a device-independent way and with minimal regard to the actual rendering algorithms being used. In this way, RenderMan is similar to PostScript™, but for 3D primitives. By creating input for a RenderMan-compliant renderer, you and your modeling or animation system can concentrate on making a beautiful image, largely without concern for the details of the exact rendering methods used. A particular RenderMan implementation may use scanline methods (z-buffer, Reyes), ray tracing, radiosity, or other methods (and indeed, implementations exist that support all of these). Because RenderMan's capabilities were designed for the very high end of animation production, you can be assured that nearly any fully compliant renderer will produce output of outstanding quality.

The RenderMan Interface specifies an ambitious list of features for compliant renderers, including a complete hierarchical graphics state, high-quality pixel filtering and antialiasing, a programmable Shading Language for describing lights and surfaces, and support of a wide array of high-level geometric primitives, including quadrics, bicubic patch meshes, and trimmed NURBS. In addition, RenderMan-compliant renderers may support CSG, level of detail, various types of texture mapping (including reflection, environment, shadow, and displacement mapping), motion blur, depth-of-field, volume shading, ray tracing, area lights, and radiosity effects. Many of these features are very advanced, and some rendering algorithms simply cannot support certain features, so the availability will tend to vary from implementation to implementation.

Pixar developed and published the *RenderMan Interface Specification* in 1988, with the goal that it would contain enough descriptive power to accommodate advances in modeling, animation, and rendering technologies for several years. It has done a remarkably good job, and even after 11 years, it is still the only open specification for scene description that includes concepts such as motion blur and user-definable appearance characteristics. This means that RenderMan renderers will generate very high-quality images, both in their simulation of objects in their environment and in their simulation of the camera.

Of course, the past 11 years have seen a lot of changes as well. The original dream that the RenderMan Interface would be an open standard that all renderer vendors would embrace, giving the industry a family of compatible renderers that each excelled at different effects, quite simply never came to pass. Instead, the name "RenderMan" colloquially came to refer only to Pixar's *PhotoRealistic RenderMan* product (referred to in this book as *PRMan*), and "RenderMan compatibility" came to mean being compatible with *PRMan*. Once it became clear that RenderMan was destined to be a proprietary interface after all, strict "standards conformance" was abandoned, and since then many new and very interesting features have been added to the RenderMan renderers that greatly increase their power and utility.

The result of this strength, both the strength of the specification and the strength of the flagship renderer that carries its name, is that studios throughout the world have made *RenderMan* their rendering platform of choice for doing work that demands images of the highest quality. Most visibly, major players in the motion picture industry have chosen RenderMan to generate 3D computer graphics special effects for films as diverse as *Jurassic Park*, *Mulan*, and, of course, *A Bug's Life*. The striking results that these and other films have achieved through the use of RenderMan is why we are writing this book.

Of course, nowadays more than one implementation of RenderMan is available. The most robust and widely used is still Pixar's *PRMan* product, of course. Another popular implementation is Blue Moon Rendering Tools' *rendrib* (referred to in this book as *BMRT*), which provides both a ray tracing/radiosity hybrid renderer and a fast previewer that runs atop OpenGL. Other vendors have, at various times, announced their own RenderMan-compatible renderers. The widespread availability of many different RenderMan renderers, with different algorithms, speed/quality trade-offs, and special capabilities, and yet with a consistent file format, API, and Shading Language, will make it ever more valuable to be fluent with RenderMan.

1.5   Sign Me Up!

How should a new technical director learn to use RenderMan? How should an experienced TD keep up-to-date on the state-of-the-art tricks? How should writers of competitive renderers (yes, we know you're out there!) learn what features they should be emulating in their software? Prior to this book, there was only one published source. Written in 1990, *The RenderMan Companion* (Upstill, 1990) is still excellent as a first course in using RenderMan, but it has at least two limitations. First, it is only an introductory course. There are a lot of topics of technical interest (and technical necessity) that are simply not covered, such as shader antialiasing techniques. Second, it is 10 years old. The fact that it doesn't discuss RIB is only the first of its anachronisms. Although the things that it does say are generally still true, some of the most interesting features of the modern RenderMan renderers are simply not there.

In those 10 years, the industry has changed as well. We've seen the rise of CGI from a curiosity used on a few unpopular movies to the dominant paradigm for generating special effects. The CGI community has three blockbuster all-CG movies and a bushel of Academy Awards to its credit, and now owns the mind-set of both the viewing public and the film directors who trust us to realize their most outlandish visions.

During this period of explosive growth, we've all learned a tremendous amount about how to create CGI, how to use CGI, how to run studios, and how to write resumes. The tricks we thought were so clever in 1992 are high school stuff nowadays. The beast needs new food, and that's really why we have written this book. We have amassed a large amount of material from several authors who will present to you some of what they know about making beautiful images. We've attempted to codify a large nebulous body of knowledge that has come out of our experiences creating CGI for motion pictures at a variety of motion picture and special effects studios. An uncountable number of individuals have added to this lore: immediate colleagues of the authors, our devoted customers, and the computer graphics industry at large. We thank you all for your fabulous ideas.

We hope the techniques and tricks we present in this book, and their results, will inspire you to make even more beautiful images, and realize even more outlandish visions, than any we've yet seen. After all, we're in the audience, too, and we love this stuff! Dazzle us!

2 Review of Mathematics and Computer Graphics Concepts

Let's face it. Before we get started writing RenderMan models and shaders in earnest, let's acknowledge that we just don't have *quite* as much background in math, physics, or even long-standing computer graphics concepts as we know we should have. There are plenty of reasons: didn't get to take the right courses in college, the professor was too boring to sit through, got into computer graphics by way of a mechanical engineering degree, or, hey, I'm an artist, not a programmer. It doesn't matter. Read this chapter in the privacy of your own home, while no one is looking, and no one ever need know that you skipped that lecture on matrix multiplication.

This chapter is a summary and review of a few important topics with which advanced RenderMan users should be fluent. It is in no way a complete treatise on these subjects. Readers who are interested in studying these topics in more depth are referred to any of the very excellent math, physics, and computer graphics textbooks that were written specifically to teach them. A few such texts are mentioned at the end of this chapter.

2.1   Trigonometry and Vector Algebra

Trigonometry is the mathematics of angles. Vector algebra is the manipulation of variables that have more than one number in them. Trigonometry and vector algebra are widely used to describe and implement computer graphics algorithms that manipulate geometric data because they are easy ways to put geometric concepts into the form of equations. These topics are, of course, very large fields of mathematics, but fortunately for RenderMan users, much of the day-to-day utility of these subjects can be summarized in a few simple concepts.

2.1.1   Trigonometry

Trigonometry is a vast and time-honored field, from the genesis of mathematics in Egypt to the dreaded high school math course where we had to do those horrible proofs. Fortunately, we use very few of those equations every day, even as full-time RenderMan shader writers.

As is common in ancient fields of study, angles can be measured in a variety of different units, and in RenderMan two of these appear: degrees and radians. Degrees are probably very familiar to everyone. There are 360 degrees in a circle, a right angle is 90 degrees. Degrees are used whenever angles are needed in the geometric scene description part of RenderMan as in RenderMan Interface Bytestream (RIB) commands, for example. Radians, on the other hand, are familiar to mathematicians and programmers. There are 2π radians in a circle, a right angle is $\frac{\pi}{2}$ radians. Radians are used whenever angles are needed in the Shading Language. Of course, it is simple to convert between them because we know that 360 degrees equals 2π radians.

radians = degrees $* \pi/180$

degrees = radians $* 180/\pi$

The three most important trigonometric functions are *sine*, *cosine*, and *tangent*. These functions are defined by the relationships among the lengths of the sides of a right triangle. A right triangle, of course, is one that has a right angle in it. The left side of Figure 2.1 shows a standard right triangle. The marked angle θ is made by two of the sides of the triangle, denoted as the *adjacent* side (which goes towards the right angle) and the *hypotenuse*, which is the longest side of the right triangle. The famous Pythagorean theorem (sing it with me now, "$a^2 + b^2 = c^2$") tells us that the square of the length of the hypotenuse (c) is equal to the sum of the squares of the other two sides. We'll call the third side the *opposite* side, for relatively obvious reasons. Because the opposite and adjacent sides have a right angle between them, they are perpendicular to each other.

The sine function is defined as the ratio of the length of the opposite side to the length of the hypotenuse. The cosine function is the ratio of the length of the adjacent side to the length of the hypotenuse. The tangent function is the ratio of

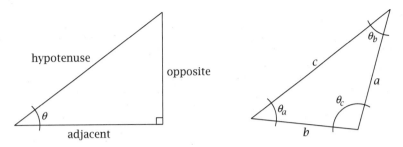

Figure 2.1 A simple right triangle and another triangle with three unremarkable angles.

the length of the opposite side to the length of the adjacent side. Three easy to remember equations:

■ *sin* is $\frac{\text{opposite}}{\text{hypotenuse}}$

■ *cos* is $\frac{\text{adjacent}}{\text{hypotenuse}}$

■ *tan* is $\frac{\text{opposite}}{\text{adjacent}}$

Of course, if we know the lengths of the sides, or even just the ratio of the lengths of any two of the sides, we can compute the angle by using one of the inverse functions, *arcsine*, *arccosine*, or *arctangent*, which are generally abbreviated *asin, acos,* and *atan.*

Quickly glancing at the graphs of the *sin* and *cos* functions (Figure 2.2) tells us some interesting things about them. *sin* and *cos* have the same graph, just offset by 90 degrees. They are periodic, repeating every 360 degrees, and they always stay within the range of −1.0 to 1.0. *tan* is also periodic, repeating every 180 degrees, but it runs from −∞ to ∞ on each cycle.

Interestingly, trigonometricians note that for small angles, less than about 15 degrees, the values of $radians(\theta)$, $tan(\theta)$, and $sin(\theta)$ are all nearly equal (to within a couple percent). For this reason, they sometimes refer to the *small angle approximation*, where the tangent and sine can be approximated by the angle itself.

Sometimes, we have the length of two sides of a triangle and need the third, but the triangle isn't a right triangle so we can't apply the Pythagorean theorem. Never fear, there are two useful trigonometric formulas to our rescue (but we do need to know at least one of the angles, too). As illustrated on the right side of Figure 2.1, we'll use the notation that the angle opposite a side a is θ_a. If we know the length of two sides, a and b, and the angle between those sides, θ_c, we can compute the length of the third side using the *law of cosines*:

$$c^2 = a^2 + b^2 - 2ab\cos(\theta_c)$$

You'll recognize this as a generalization of the Pythagorean theorem, since $\cos(90°)$ is 0.0. Alternatively, if we know the length of a and b and one of the opposing

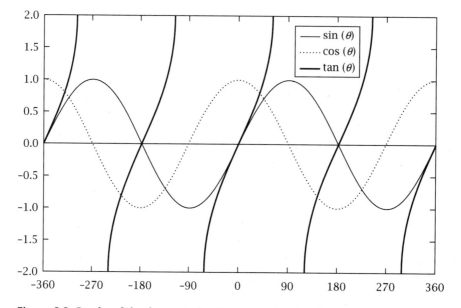

Figure 2.2 Graphs of the three standard trigonometric functions.

angles, our tool is the *law of sines*:

$$a/\sin(\theta_a) = b/\sin(\theta_b) = c/\sin(\theta_c)$$

Given this, and the fact that the angles of every triangle add up to 180°, we can derive both of the other angles, and hence the length of the third side.

2.1.2   Vectors 101

In computer graphics, we use vectors to represent many important concepts: positions, directions, tangents, surface normals, colors, and so on. Therefore, a working knowledge of vector algebra, the manipulation of vectors, is quite important.

A *vector* is an array of numbers. When we want to emphasize the fact that a single individual number is used in a particular calculation, we use the term *scalar*. Positions in 3D are represented by vectors known as *points*. Points have three coordinates, which refer to the distances from the origin to that location in each of the three dimensions (by convention known as *x*, *y*, and *z*). Directions in 3D are represented by *direction vectors*. Direction vectors are often loosely just called *vectors*, which inevitably leads to certain confusion. Fortunately, it is usually obvious from context whether *vector* means general mathematical vectors or direction vectors specifically.

Direction vectors also have three coordinates, which refer to the distance they represent in each of the three dimensions. Notice that vectors have both "direction" and "length," where the length of a vector is computed as the square root of the

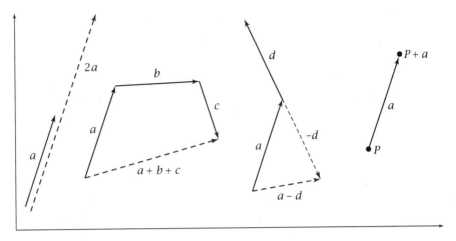

Figure 2.3 Scaling, adding, and subtracting direction vectors.

sum of the squares of the coordinates (there's that Pythagorean theorem again) and is denoted by writing the vector between vertical bars.

$$|V| = \sqrt{V_x{}^2 + V_y{}^2 + V_z{}^2}$$

There are an infinite number of vectors that point in the same direction but have different lengths. In situations where only the direction matters, any of those vectors could be used, but it is common to refer to the unique vector that has the right direction and has length equal to 1.0. Such a vector is said to be *normalized*. This is often noted by printing the name of the vector with a bar above it, such as $\overline{N}$. Note that by convention, direction vectors that have *negative* length are considered to be pointing in the opposite direction.

Certain mathematical operations are considered to be "legal" on points and direction vectors. For example, it is legal to multiply a vector by a scalar. To do so, you simply multiply each vector coordinate by that number. The result of this is to multiply the length of the vector by that same number, without changing the direction, and so is said to *scale* the vector. Negating a vector makes it point in the opposite direction.

Vectors can be added together by adding the corresponding coordinates. We can visualize this as chaining the vectors together, the end of one attached to the start of the next. The resulting vector is identical to the vector that runs from the start of the first to the end of the last (see Figure 2.3). Subtracting vectors is also legal; it is just like adding the negated vector. A vector can also be added to a point, again by adding the matching coordinates, which creates a new point that is displaced from the first by the distance and direction of the vector.

It is not generally considered "legal" to add two points, because there is no geometrically logical result. Interestingly, it *is* possible to subtract two points, which creates a vector that is the distance between the points. Similarly, points cannot be scaled, as vectors can; however, it is acceptable to take the weighted average of a set of points, such as computing the midpoint or the centroid.

There are two other operations on vectors that are useful and that correspond to different types of multiplication. The first is *dot product*. This is computed by adding together the products of the corresponding components. The resulting value is a scalar that equals the cosine of the angle between the vectors times the length of each of the vectors.

$$V_1 \cdot V_2 = V_{1x}V_{2x} + V_{1y}V_{2y} + V_{1z}V_{2z}$$
$$= |V_1||V_2| \cos(\theta_{1 \rightarrow 2})$$

If used on normalized vectors, of course, the lengths of the vectors are both 1.0, so the result is just the bare cosine.

This function is really useful because it converts directions into relative angles. Notice that $\cos(90°)$ is 0.0. This means that dot product can be used to quickly test whether two vectors are perpendicular to each other, regardless of their magnitude (that is, as long as the vectors do not have 0 length to start with). Moreover, because $\cos(\theta)$ is positive for angles between −90 and 90 degrees, and negative for angles outside that range, the dot product can be used to quickly determine if two vectors point roughly in the same direction or roughly oppositely. If the dot product is positive, the angle between them is less than 90 degrees, and they can be said to point roughly in the same direction. If the dot product is negative, the angle between them is more than 90 degrees, and they can be said to point roughly in opposite directions.

The other version of vector multiplication is the *cross product*. The equation for the cross product is somewhat complicated, but the result is very useful. The cross product creates a new vector that is perpendicular to both of the original vectors. The length of the new vector is the product of the sine of the angle between the vectors and the lengths of the vectors.

$$|V_1 \times V_2| = |V_1||V_2| \sin(\theta_{1 \rightarrow 2})$$

Usually, we don't care about the length so much as the direction—creating a perpendicular vector is very useful in computer graphics for such things as rotation axes and surface normals.

Notice on the graphs in Figure 2.2 that $\sin(0°) = \sin(180°) = 0.0$, so the cross product can be used to quickly identify whether two vectors are parallel, regardless of length.

2.1.3   Coordinate System Transformations

At the beginning, we noted that positions and direction vectors measure distances and directions from the "origin" but never mentioned where the origin was. Who legislated that the origin of the universe ought to be east of San Francisco and not north of Los Angeles? No one, in fact. To misquote Einstein, "Everything is relative."

In computer graphics, we often use a plethora of 3D *coordinate systems*, each of which has its own origin and three primary direction axes. A point that is $(1, 2, 3)$ in one coordinate system could easily be $(14, -97.2, 3.94)$ in a different coordinate system. They are the same point, but the values of the coordinates are different because they are each specified relative to the origin of a different coordinate system. The relationship between one coordinate system and another, and therefore the mathematical formula for converting one representation of a point or vector into the other representation, is embodied in a *coordinate transformation*. Because it is easy to convert from one coordinate system to another, it is common to have a number of utility coordinate systems that are relative to interesting features in the 3D environment, such as relative to the camera position, to each light source, to key objects in the scene, and so on.

There are many useful and important coordinate transformations that fall into two categories: those that map points, vectors, and parallel lines into unique equivalent versions in the other space, called *affine mappings*; and those that compress a dimension out of the space, called *projections*.[1] Affine mappings include the familiar transformations of *translation, scaling,* and *rotation*. Projective mappings include perspective and orthographic projection, as well as any other mapping that takes 3D coordinates and turns them into 2D coordinates (such as a spherical projection).

Translations are simple offsets of one coordinate system from another. Translating a point from one coordinate system to the other is done by adding a particular direction vector to the point. Translation leaves the old and new axes parallel to each other and doesn't change the size of anything. Scaling changes the size of the distance units of a coordinate system without moving the origin. Scaling is most often done uniformly, scaling all dimensions equally. If the dimensions are not scaled the same, it is called *nonuniform scaling*. This transformation converts a cube into a rectangular box. Rotation spins the coordinate system without moving the origin or changing size. Rotations can be specified in several different equivalent ways, but RenderMan specifies rotation by an angle around an arbitrary axis, not restricting rotations to be around one of the primary axes.

2.1.4   Matrices 101

Matrices are rectanglar arrays of $n \times m$ numbers (called *elements*), arranged as n rows with m elements in each row (or, equivalently, m columns with n elements in each column). In 3D computer graphics, it is very common to use 4-row, 4-column (4×4) matrices for a variety of purposes. A 4×4 matrix therefore has 16 values, arranged in a square. There are only a small number of mathematical operations

---

[1] In the wider world of mathematics, other transformations exist that don't do either of these things, but we don't use them too often in computer graphics.

that make sense on matrices and are useful to us, but these turn out to be very important.

First, let's identify one very important special matrix, known as the *identity matrix*. The elements on the diagonal of the identity matrix are all 1.0, and all of the other elements are 0.0. For example, the 4×4 identity matrix is

$$\begin{pmatrix} 1.0 & 0.0 & 0.0 & 0.0 \\ 0.0 & 1.0 & 0.0 & 0.0 \\ 0.0 & 0.0 & 1.0 & 0.0 \\ 0.0 & 0.0 & 0.0 & 1.0 \end{pmatrix}$$

Now to work. A vector (that is, any mathematical vector type) can be multiplied by a matrix, $V \times M$. The result is a vector, which is calculated by computing the dot products of the vector with each column of the matrix. Notice that the dot product computation requires two vectors that are the same length. This means that the number of elements in the original vector must equal the number of rows in the matrix. The number of elements in the result vector is equal to the number of columns in the matrix.

Conversely, you can multiply a matrix by a vector, $M \times V$, resulting in a vector that is calculated by computing the dot products of the vector with each row of the matrix. In that case, the number of elements in the original vector must equal the number of columns in the matrix, and the number of elements in the result is equal to the number of rows.

The first type of vector-matrix multiply, $V \times M$, is called *premultiplying* the vector by the matrix, because the vector appears before the matrix. By convention, vectors that premultiply matrices are written horizontally, as rows, and are therefore known as *row vectors*. The second type of multiply, $M \times V$, is called *postmultiplying* the vector by the matrix, because the vector appears after the matrix. By convention, vectors that postmultiply matrices are written vertically, as columns, and are therefore known as *column vectors*.

Two matrices can be combined in an operation we call *matrix multiplication*, $M_1 \times M_2$. The actual process of multiplying the two matrices together is somewhat complicated. It is not simply multiplying the corresponding elements together, but is actually computing every possible dot product of rows of M_1 with columns of M_2. The resulting "product" matrix is the combination of the two matrices. Using it (such as in vector-matrix, multiplication) is equivalent to sequentially using the first matrix, then the second. That is, $(V \times M_1) \times M_2 = V \times (M_1 \times M_2)$.

Multiplying a matrix by the identity matrix leaves the matrix unchanged. Similarly for a vector. This is the reason that the identity matrix is called the *identity*. It is important to note that in matrix multiplication, the order of the matrices matters. Reversing the order of the matrices changes the result. That is, $M_1 \times M_2 \neq M_2 \times M_1$.

Another useful operation is taking the *inverse* of a matrix. The inverse matrix does the opposite of the original matrix and is often denoted M^{-1}. This is because multiplying a matrix by its inverse always results in the identity matrix, just as multiplying a number by its multiplicative inverse (the reciprocal) always yields 1.0.

There are, of course, many other useful operations on matrices, such as computing the transpose or the determinant of a matrix. We don't need these to discuss the computer graphics topics that we want to cover in this book, so we'll skip over them. Consult your friendly neighborhood mathematics textbook for details.

2.1.5   Vectors 201

One of the reasons that vectors and matrices are important in discussions of computer graphics is that quite a few years ago, some of the early researchers in computer graphics demonstrated that a 4×4 matrix was a very convenient way to represent a 3D transformation. For example, there is a standard way to represent scaling, translation, and rotation as a 4×4 matrix. We call this a *transformation matrix*. At first, it may seem wasteful to represent a simple translation, which requires only 3 values, with a 16-element matrix, but there is a mathematical elegance that makes it worthwhile. For example, the transformation matrix that represents any combination of transformations is identical to the result of multiplying the simple transformation matrices together.

Similarly, transforming a point or a vector through any of these transformations, or any combination of these transformations, is easily computed by merely multiplying the vector by the transformation matrix. It turns out that all of the other interesting 3D transformations, such as shears and even perspective, can also be represented by 4×4 matrices. This means that any series of standard computer graphics transformations, no matter what order and no matter how complex, can be represented as a single matrix. Thus, it is now commonplace for graphics systems to use matrices to represent all of their transformations, because far from being wasteful, it is the most compact and elegant method of storing that data.

Recall from the previous discussion that vector by matrix multiplication imposes certain restrictions on the dimensions of the data, and, in particular, it seems illegal to multiply points and direction vectors (which have three elements) by a 4×4 matrix. However, there is an explanation. When transforming a point by a transformation matrix, the required "fourth element" is assumed to be 1.0. When transforming a direction vector by a transformation matrix, the required fourth element is assumed to be 0.0.

$$P' = (P_x P_y P_z 1) \times M$$
$$V' = (V_x V_y V_z 0) \times M$$

When points and vectors are written in this 4D notation, they are in *homogeneous coordinates*. Similarly, the 4×4 arrays that operate on them are known as *homogeneous transformation matrices* (to distinguish them from other matrices that might be 4×4 for other reasons).

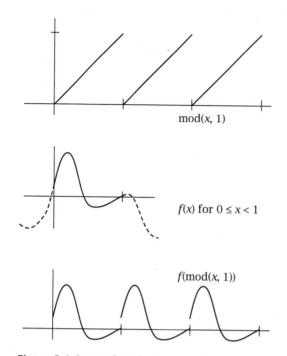

mod(x, 1)

$f(x)$ for $0 \le x < 1$

$f(\text{mod}(x, 1))$

Figure 2.4 Sawtooth and other periodic functions can be created by modulo arithmetic.

The intrepid reader might notice that this also explains why adding and subtracting vectors is legal, adding vectors to points is legal, and subtracting two points yields a vector, while adding points is illegal. But we won't dwell on those pieces of trivia.

When using vectors to represent points and direction vectors, and matrices to represent transformations, the values you place in the matrix depend on whether you are going to premultiply row vectors or postmultiply column vectors. The results are equivalent either way, but it is important to be consistent about your notation. Unfortunately, some of the popular computer graphics textbooks use one notation, and others use the other. In RenderMan texts and documentation, we always premultiply row vectors by transformation matrices.

2.1.6   Periodic Functions

Some mathematical functions are naturally *periodic*, meaning that their values repeat at regular intervals. More specifically, $f(x) = f(x + n \cdot period)$ for all integers n. Two examples are sine and cosine: $\sin(\theta) = \sin(\theta + 2\pi n)$ for all integers n.

Not all functions are periodic, of course, but sometimes it is very handy to create periodic versions of a segment of a function. For example, consider the sawtooth wave in Figure 2.4. Periodically repeating functions such as these are easy to create using the *modulo* function. Because modulo is itself a simple periodic function (in fact, it *is* the sawtooth function), using it to create the argument to any other function creates a periodic version of that function. For example, $f(\mathrm{mod}(x, period))$ repeats the section of f from 0.0 through *period*.

2.2   Geometry

The geometric primitives that RenderMan handles are 2D surfaces. They are thin sheets, like pieces of paper, or perhaps more like sheets of rubber, that are deformed and transformed into the 3D coordinate system that we intrinsically think of as being our modeling space. RenderMan does not have any 1D drawing or annotation primitives, nor a 2D drawing surface on which to place them. Therefore, we will not spend too much time describing 1D or 4D surfaces, which, while interesting in themselves, have nothing to do with the task at hand.

2.2.1   Primitive Equations

The curves and surfaces that are used in computer graphics are all derived from various types of mathematical equations. Plug values into the variables of the equations, and they identify which points are on the object, and all the rest are not. There are three types of equations that provide the basis for (most) computer graphics geometric primitives: *explicit*, *implicit*, and *parametric*.

An explicit equation is one that evaluates one coordinate of the position of the object from the values of the other coordinates. For example, $z = 2x + y$ is the explicit equation for a plane. One of the features of the explicit equation is that it is mathematically a *function*, meaning that it only has one result value for each set of input coordinates. This means that it cannot layer over itself like, for example, a circle does.

An implicit equation is one in which certain values of input coordinates satisfy an equation: $\mathrm{surface}(x, y, z) = 0$. Points that satisfy the equation are "on" the primitive, while others that do not are "not on" the primitive. For example,

$$x^2 + y^2 + z^2 - 1 = 0$$

is the implicit equation for a sphere. The point (0.6,0,0.8) is on the sphere because it satisfies the equation, whereas the point (0.4,0.8,0.2) is not because it does not. The points that are generated by complex implicit equations are not always connected—there can be isolated points or small isolated regions that satisfy the equation. This makes it tricky to find them all.

A *parametric surface* is a surface generated by an equation with two variables: $P = \mathrm{surface}(u, v)$. For example, a sphere can be generated by the parametric equations

$$x = \cos(\theta) \cos(\phi)$$
$$y = \sin(\theta) \cos(\phi)$$
$$z = \sin(\phi)$$

Other valuable parametric surfaces include planes, all of the quadric surfaces, bilinear and bicubic patches, ruled surfaces, and NURBS.

Generally, we are not interested in infinite parametric surfaces, but rather that subset of the surface that is generated for values of the parameters within a certain range, typically between 0.0 and 1.0. Notice that it is simple to reparameterize equations with other parametric ranges by a simple replacing of variables, so this choice doesn't actually cause any restrictions. For example, rather than have the sphere in the preceding equations parameterized for θ between 0 and 2π and ϕ between $-\frac{\pi}{2}$ and $\frac{\pi}{2}$, we can change to equations of this form:

$$x = \cos(2\pi u) \cos(\pi v - \frac{\pi}{2})$$

for values of u and v between 0.0 and 1.0. Some surfaces, such as spheres, can be defined implicitly as well as parametrically, but most parameteric equations cannot be easily implicitized.

Parametric surfaces have two interesting properties that make them useful in computer graphics. First, because the parametric equation can be evaluated directly, you can compute any point that is on the object by plugging in values for the parameters. It is easy to generate a few points that are on the surface and then approximate the rest of the surface by linear approximation. We call this technique *tesselation*. Second, because we have an equation that converts a 2D pair of *parametric coordinates* into 3D, the surface has a natural 2D coordinate system. This makes it easy to map other 2D data onto the surface, the most obvious example being texture maps.

2.2.2   Tangents and Normals

Having mathematical equations for our geometric primitives allows us to use the machinery of analytic geometry and calculus to compute important properties of the equations, which in turn are important properties of the geometric primitives. Two of the most important of these are tangents and normals.

The tangent at a point on an object is a flat object that just touches the object at that point but doesn't cross or penetrate the object (at least, not in the immediate neighborhood of the point). It just skims the surface at that point. In two dimensions, the tangent to a curve is a line and is unique. The slope of the tangent line is considered to be the slope of the curve at that point. Generally, we are not interested in the tangent line per se, but in a direction vector that has the same slope. We call this the *tangent vector*. The value of the slope is computed by evaluating the *derivative* of the curve at that point, generally a very simple operation if we have an explicit, implicit, or parametric equation for the curve.

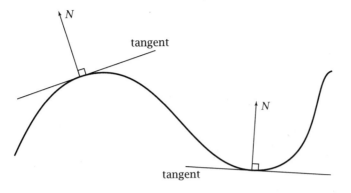

Figure 2.5 Tangent lines and normal vectors to a curve at two points.

In three dimensions, the tangent to a surface is a plane and is also unique. Any vector that lies in the tangent plane is tangent to the surface, so there are infinitely many tangent vectors, radiating from the point at all angles. Generally, it is quite easy to find two of the tangent vectors that lie on the tangent plane: take the partial derivatives of the surface equations with respect to a couple of the variables. For example, consider a parametric equation of two variables, u and v. The partial derivative of the equation with respect to u, $\partial P/\partial u$, will give us one such tangent vector, as will the partial derivative with respect to v, $\partial P/\partial v$.

Another important concept (that is probably obvious if we think about it for just a moment) is that there is a unique direction that is perpendicular, or "normal," to a plane. This unique vector is called the plane's *normal vector*. Of particular interest to us is the vector that is normal to the tangent plane at the particular point on the surface. For obvious reasons, we call it the point's normal vector and usually denote it N (see Figure 2.5).

This relationship between planes and normals means that you can derive one from the other. Any vector that is perpendicular to the normal must be in the tangent plane, while the normal is perpendicular to *all* vectors in the tangent plane. It takes two vectors to define a plane (for example, the partial derivatives defining the tangent plane), so the unique vector that is perpendicular to both vectors *must* be the plane normal. Recall from Section 2.1.2 that the main tool for computing perpendicular vectors is the cross product, so we can immediately say that $(\partial P/\partial u) \times (\partial P/\partial v) = N$. Conversely, if you have a normal vector at a point, you immediately know the tangent plane at that point.

We mentioned earlier that points and direction vectors transform differently. Normal vectors transform in yet a third way—they use a different matrix! Normal vectors transform through the *inverse transpose* matrix, that is, the transpose of the inverse of the matrix, which is denoted M^{-1^T}. For many matrices, including most of the matrices that we see in common cases in computer graphics, the inverse of a matrix and the transpose of it are identical, so they cancel and $M^{-1^T} = M$. For this reason, a common mistake is to transform normal vectors just like direction vectors. In fact, you should always use the inverse transpose.

$$N' \neq (N_x N_y N_z 0) \times M$$

$$N' = (N_x N_y N_z 0) \times M^{-1^T}$$

Just to be complete in our confusion, tangent vectors *do* transform just like direction vectors. Sigh!

2.2.3 Curvature

The next, more abstract concept beyond the tangent at a point is the *curvature*. Just as the tangent measures the slope of a line that touches the object without crossing it (at least, locally), the curvature measures the radius of a circle that hugs the object without crossing it. If the circle is very small, the surface has high curvature; and if the circle is very large, the surface has low curvature. As you might expect by now, the curvature is computed by taking the second derivative of the surface equations. Note that curvature is a signed quantity. Positive curvature means the surface curves up, cupping the surface normal. Negative curvature means the surface curves down, drooping away from the surface normal. Zero curvature means the surface is flat.

Just as there are infinitely many tangent vectors at a point on a surface, all radiating at different angles, so too there are infinitely many curvatures, corresponding to all the circles oriented at different angles around the point. Of these, a few in particular are interesting. On a parametric surface, the curvatures in the two parametric directions are interesting because they are easy to compute. However, these values are not necessarily the "most curved" directions on the surface. If we are interested in those, we need values known as the *principal curvatures*, κ_{max} and κ_{min}. The equations for computing κ are somewhat complex and scary, so persons wearing Math-Sensitive Sunglasses™ will see a large blank space next:

$$\kappa_u = \frac{\partial^2 P / \partial u^2}{|\partial P / \partial u|^2}$$

$$\kappa_v = \frac{\partial^2 P / \partial v^2}{|\partial P / \partial v|^2}$$

$$\kappa_{uv} = \frac{\partial^2 P / \partial u \partial v}{|\partial P / \partial u||\partial P / \partial v|}$$

$$\tan 2\phi = \frac{2\kappa_{uv}}{\kappa_u - \kappa_v}$$

$$\kappa_{max} \text{ and } \kappa_{min} = \kappa_u \sin^2 \phi + \kappa_v \cos^2 \phi \pm 2\kappa_{uv} \sin \phi \cos \phi$$

The curvature in the u and v directions are κ_u and κ_v, respectively. The curvature along the two principal axes are κ_{min} and κ_{max}. The angle between one principal axis and u is ϕ (as is the angle between the other principal axis and v), but without evaluating κ, you can't really know which is the axis of minimum curvature and which is the axis of maximum curvature.

For most surfaces, κ_{min} and κ_{max} are both the same sign, implying a bump or dent, or one of them is 0.0, implying it is flat in some direction, like a cylinder. Surfaces for which κ_{min} is negative and κ_{max} is positive are known as *saddles*, because in one direction they bend up and in the perpendicular direction they bend down, like a horse's saddle.

2.2.4   Continuity

When two primitives with different surface equations are set adjacent to each other, conceptually joined to become parts of the same object, we are often concerned about the *continuity* at the seam. The type of continuity that exists at the seam determines whether we consider the seam to be "smooth."

There are four types of continuity that are typically of interest to us:

- C^0: the surface is connected but could have sharp corners
- C^1: the first derivative has no abrupt changes—no corners—but could have abrupt curvature changes
- C^2: the second derivative, curvature, has no abrupt changes—surface *feels* smooth
- C^∞: no derivatives at any level have abrupt changes—mathematically smooth

For example, when two polygons share an edge but there is an angle between them, the seam has a *cusp*, a corner, and therefore the surface is C^1 discontinuous at the edge. Two semicircles that connect to form an *S*-shaped curve are C^1 continuous at the joint but are C^2 discontinuous there.

2.3   Physics and Optics

Many computer graphics algorithms, particularly shading algorithms, rely on the simulation of various aspects of the physics of materials and light to provide their realism. Sometimes the physical properties are duplicated exactly, sometimes they are approximated, sometimes ignored entirely and replaced by ad hoc rules. However, a little bit of physical intuition and a few simple equations will help you program RenderMan much more effectively.

2.3.1   Light Spectra

As everyone remembers from elementary physics, visible light is a wave of electromagnetic energy within a certain range of wavelengths (roughly 380 nanometers to 750 nanometers, or 790 to 400 teraHertz). In fact, most forms of visible light contain a continuum of frequencies, each at a different intensity. This function of intensities at various frequencies is called the light's *spectrum*. Each wavelength of light corresponds to a color in the rainbow, and light beams that are dominated by a particular color appear to our eyes to have that color. Light beams that have a spectrum like that of sunlight, roughly equal intensity over a broad range of colors but somewhat dominated by colors near 530 nm (green), appear "white" to us, and are called *white light*.

Most interactions between light and materials are *wavelength dependent*, meaning that they have different effects upon light of different wavelengths. For example, refraction of light through a prism separates the light into a rainbow of colors because light's refraction direction is dependent on wavelength. Blue wavelengths refract more than red, which spreads a white light beam apart into the visible spectrum.

When we look at an object, we see the spectrum of the light that is reflected from that object. The surface color of the object is due to the fact that each material absorbs more light at certain wavelengths and reflects more light at other wavelengths. This process, where the color is determined by the remaining light after certain portions of the spectrum have been removed, is called *subtractive color*. The filtering of transmitted light is another example of a subtractive process. The color of a filter, such as a piece of stained glass, is primarily based on the spectrum that remains after the light that is passing through has mostly been absorbed by the filter. A "red" filter is one that absorbs most of everything except red.

The complementary process, where the color is determined by adding together light emitted from various colored light sources, is called *additive color*. Television monitors are an example of an additive process. The color on a monitor is determined by the sum of the spectra that the phosphors emit (actually, this is a somewhat complex situation, due to a subtle interaction with our visual system described in Section 2.4.7).

2.3.2   Reflection and Refraction

When light reflects off of a mirrored surface, the direction of the reflected ray is easily computed due to the well-known maxim that "the angle of reflection equals the angle of incidence." This relationship is shown in Figure 2.6. In distilling this relationship into an equation, we take advantage of the fact that the normal vector describes the mirror plane. By looking at relationships of the vectors in the figure, it is pretty easy to tell just by looking that the reflection vector can be computed by $R = I + 2(\alpha N)$, for some constant α. Invoking a little trigonometry (and assuming that the vectors N and I are normalized), we can see that $\cos(\theta) = \alpha/1.0$. But remembering the dot product rule, we can say $\alpha = (-\bar{I} \cdot \overline{N})$. With a little algebra, we conclude that $R = \bar{I} - 2(\bar{I} \cdot \overline{N})\overline{N}$. It turns out the equation is the same even if I isn't normalized, but it's a little messier if N isn't normalized. And if you prefer the vectors to point in different directions, you might negate one term or other.

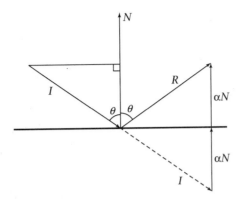

Figure 2.6 Computing reflection vectors.

Table 2.1: Indices of refraction for common materials.

Material	η
Vacuum	1
Air	1.0003
Water	1.33
Alcohol	1.36
Crown glass	1.52
Quartz	1.54
Flint glass	1.65
Ruby	1.77
Diamond	2.42

When light refracts through a transparent surface, the direction of the refracted vector is computed using a well-known equation called *Snell's law*. This law specifies how light is bent by using the indices of refraction for the material that the light is leaving and for the material that the light is entering. The index of refraction of a material, usually denoted η (eta), is a physical constant of the material and can be looked up in physics reference books such as the *CRC Handbook*. For most common materials, such as the ones listed in Table 2.1, the index of refraction is in the range of 1.0 to around 2.4. Vaguely speaking, as light enters a material that is more dense, it is bent towards the surface normal; and as it enters a material that is less dense, it is bent away from the surface normal (as illustrated on the top of Figure 2.7). The precise equation is: $\eta_{leave} \sin(\theta_{leave}) = \eta_{enter} \sin(\theta_{enter})$, where θ is the angle between surface normal and the light ray on that side.

There are several important subtleties about refraction that every good computer graphics artist should know. First, the index of refraction of material is actually

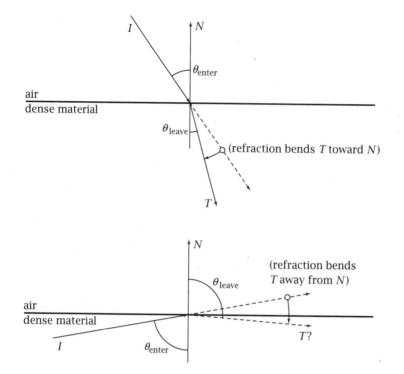

Figure 2.7 Computing refraction vectors and total internal reflection.

wavelength dependent. This means that as light travels through it, different colors get bent more than other colors. For some materials, this effect is minor, for other materials, this effect is usefully large. This is, of course, how prisms work.

Second, when light strikes an object, no matter how clear it is, not all the light enters the object and is refracted. Some light is absorbed, of course, but also some light is reflected. The *Fresnel equation* tells us the intensity of the light that will pass through (be transmitted and refracted) and the intensity of the light that will be reflected off the surface. The Fresnel equation is very dependent on incoming light angle because light that strikes perpendicular to the surface will transmit strongly, while light that strikes at a glancing angle reflects very strongly.

Third, it is interesting to consider the following situation. Light is inside the dense material, and it approaches the boundary at a glancing angle, quite a bit away from the surface normal. The bottom of Figure 2.7 shows the situation. Because refraction bends it even farther away from the surface normal, Snell's equation implies that the refraction angle should be more than 90 degrees. But that would put the refraction direction T *inside* the object! That would not be refraction, of course, so the light refuses to go in that direction. The refraction simply doesn't occur, and all of the light is reflected off the boundary instead. This situation is known as *total internal reflection*.

It is also useful to note that if light is passing through a flat solid with parallel walls (for example, a pane of glass), the final light direction on the far side will be the same as the original direction. The light gets bent to the side and then gets bent exactly back again, the difference being that it was simply shifted to the side a little.

2.3.3   Light Interacting with Surfaces

When light strikes the surface of an object, some portion of the light is absorbed by the object and some portion of the light reflects off the object in various directions. The spectrum that it reflects strongly is seen as the object's "color." The exact directions and colors of the reflections depend on many factors, such as the direction of the incoming light, the chemical makeup and electrical properties of the material, the macroscopic and microscopic geometry of the surface, and even physical effects, such as diffraction and interference. Materials that appear smooth tend to reflect light primarily in the direction of the reflection vector, with some light reflected in directions near the reflection vector and almost no light reflected in other directions far from the reflection vector. Materials that appear rough tend to reflect light strongly in a wide range of directions. Transparent materials, such as plastic and glass, refract some light based on angle-dependent Fresnel equations, so they reflect more strongly at glancing angles and therefore appear glossy. Iridescent materials reflect different colors at different angles due to destructive interference in the reflection.

In fact, these light reflection properties are actually components of a more comprehensive characteristic of the material known as the *bidirectional reflection distribution function* or *BRDF*. The BRDF determines the intensity of reflection in every direction and at every wavelength, based on the incoming light direction. There are no good general-purpose techniques for predicting the exact BRDF of a material based on its chemical composition and manufacturing process, so tables of the BRDF for various materials are almost always created by careful examination of a sample of the material.

It is often the case that at the microscopic level, the surface of a material is actually a complex composite of different types of materials mixed together or layered on top of each other, each of which has a different BRDF. For example, common plastic is a mixture of a pure-white transparent base material with tiny flecks of opaque paint particles suspended in it. Human skin, on the other hand, is a complex layering of translucent cells, some dead, some living, some brown, some red, covered with thin layers of oil and moisture, which together have a very complicated composite interaction with light that strikes it.

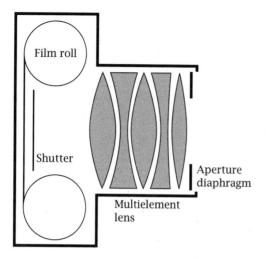

Figure 2.8 Diagram of a typical camera.

2.3.4   Cameras and Depth of Field

Physical cameras have three important parts, a lens system, a lens diaphragm with an adjustable aperture, and film to record the image. The lens system in modern cameras is usually relatively complicated—it magnifies, is typically adjustable in several ways, compensates for certain types of optical distortion, and so on. However, at any given zoom and focus setting, the multielement lens system is effectively equivalent to a single perfect converging lens at some position in the lens barrel. The lens system focuses light onto the film, which lies flat on a plane in the back of the camera, behind the shutter (see Figure 2.8). Because of the way the lenses work, the image on the film plane is upside down. Narrowing the lens aperture blocks some light from reaching the film, and therefore dims the image.

The primary characteristic of a lens is its *focal length*, which is the distance from the center of the lens to the point where light from an infinitely distant object will focus. The focal length of a simple lens is determined solely by how it is manufactured, the material, and the curvature of the lens, and so it is a constant. However, light that does not come from an infinitely distant object will focus at a different distance, as determined by the *thin lens equation*:

$$\frac{1}{d_{\text{object}}} + \frac{1}{d_{\text{image}}} = \frac{1}{\text{focal length}}$$

Notice from this equation that as an object comes closer to the camera, the image focuses farther back. A camera focuses on those closer objects by moving the lens back and forth so that the distance to the film plane matches the d_{image} for that object.

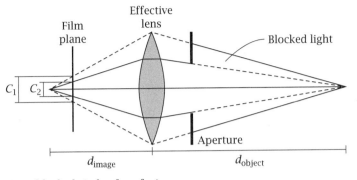

C_1: unblocked circle of confusion
C_2: blocked circle of confusion

Figure 2.9 An object whose image distance does not match the film plane appears out of focus. C_1 and C_2 are the circles of confusion before and after the aperture has been used to shrink the effective lens diameter.

When the film plane is not adjusted correctly for a given object, it will be out of focus. As we can see from Figure 2.9, the light streaming toward the focus has the shape of a cone, and the misaligned film plane cuts the cone in a large disk-shaped region. We call this region the *circle of confusion*, and its size depends on two things: the amount of the misalignment of the focus and the diameter of the lens. Notice that a smaller lens would have a narrower light cone, and all circles of confusion would be smaller.

The interesting feature of the circle of confusion is that if it is smaller than a certain size—say, smaller than the resolving power of the film or of our eyes—we can't really notice it, and the object appears to still be in focus. For this reason, even though there is only one unique distance that the lens focuses exactly, there is a range of distances for which objects are only so slightly out of focus that the circle of confusion is not objectionable. This range of distances is known as *the depth of the camera's field* or simply *depth of field*.

The final piece of this puzzle is to see that the aperture in the lens diaphragm has the effect of shrinking lens diameter without changing the other physical characteristics of the lens. By making the aperture smaller, it cuts off the sides of the focusing cones, which has the dual effect of making the image dimmer and shrinking the circles of confusion. Smaller circles mean more objects are in focus, there is more depth in the field. The measure of the size of the aperture is known in physics literature as the *f-number* and in camera literature as the *f-stop*. Because *f*-number is defined as focal length divided by aperature diameter, smaller apertures have bigger *f*-numbers. If the aperture shrank down to nearly zero (an *f*-number approaching infinity), nothing would have a noticeable circle of confusion, and all objects would appear to be in focus. This is why the pinhole camera has infinite depth of field.

2.4   Computer Graphics

In the 30 years that computer graphics has been studied, many algorithms, techniques, and tricks of the trade have been invented. Over the years, many have been refined, put onto a firm theoretical basis, and studied extensively. Others are hacks that are used because they look good. Often, it is not easy to tell (or remember) which is which. But having a good working vocabulary of these techniques is vital to doing good work with RenderMan, a system that was specifically designed to promote the development of new techniques.

2.4.1   Antialiasing

Aliasing is perhaps the most reviled artifact to plague computer graphics images. Also known as "stair-stepping" or "jaggies," aliasing is a term we borrow from signal processing theory to describe artifacts that come from inadequate sampling of the underlying scene.

A scene is continuous, meaning that the scene description provides sufficient information for there to be a color at every infinitesimal point on the image plane. The pixels of an image are regularly spaced discrete samples of the colors of the scene. The few discrete pixels we decide to put into the frame buffer are therefore only representative of the continuously varying colors underneath. If you were to graph the continuous colors (in one dimension along a scanline, or in two dimensions over the whole image), you would have an oscilloscope-like signal. Such signals, be they heartbeats or audio waveforms or scene colors, all have various frequencies in them; signals that move up and down fast have higher frequencies than those that change slowly. One of the most important theories of signal processing (known as the Nyquist theorem) says that representing a signal accurately takes twice as many regularly spaced discrete samples as the highest frequency in the signal. Rarely do computer graphics images have such high spatial resolution. Without enough samples, we get aliasing. The interesting high-frequency data is lost and is replaced by inconsistent and visually upsetting low-frequency aliases that were not really part of the scene (see Figure 2.10).

There are two ways around this conundrum. First, our samples can be nondiscrete. That is, they can represent not the specific colors at particular points in the scene, but instead some average color over a region of the scene. Supersampling, where each pixel is a weighted average of many samples that are close together, and area sampling, where each pixel is the weighted average of the regions of color in some area covered by that pixel, are both techniques that can be used to reduce aliasing. When these techniques are used well, the high-frequency data is still

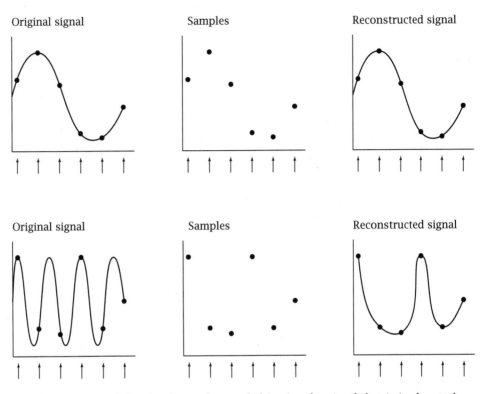

Figure 2.10 A signal that is adequately sampled (top) and a signal that is inadequately sampled, which therefore aliases (bottom).

lost, but no low-frequency aliases are added in their place, and the image appears slightly blurry. Keep in mind, however, that supersampling only raises the bar—it does not entirely eliminate the problem. Frequencies even higher than the super-sampling rate may still exist, and those will still alias even with the supersampling.

The second way around the conundrum is for our samples to be irregularly spaced, a technique known as *stochastic sampling*. Supersamples are still used, but the fact that they are not regularly spaced helps them weed out higher-than-representable frequencies in an interesting way. Using this technique, high-frequency data is still lost, but it is replaced by a constant low-intensity white noise that makes images look grainy. This is not better than aliasing in a quantitative way, but due to certain perceptual tricks of the human visual system, this white noise is often a "less objectionable artifact" than the aliasing. This process only works well when many supersamples are available to make up the final regularly spaced discrete pixel.

Once we have the required samples of the image "signal," the second critical phase of the antialiasing process is reconstructing the signal. In loose terms, this

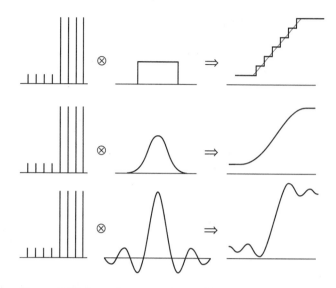

Figure 2.11 Several reconstruction filters operating on identical samples creating very different reconstructions of the signal.

is the process wherein the supersamples are averaged together to create the final pixels. The weights that are applied to each sample in the "weighted average" mentioned earlier come from the *reconstruction filter*. In less loose terms, reconstruction creates a new continous signal that we deem to be the best representation of the true signal that we can guess, given the point samples that we have. We pluck our output samples (the final pixels) from this reconstructed signal. Reconstruction proceeds by the *convolution* of the filter with the known supersamples. Different reconstruction filters give different results (see Figure 2.11), introducing new artifacts into our image that we know as *blurring* (when sharp edges become visible ramps in the output) and *ringing* (when sharp edges create waviness in the output).

Actually, there is a third way to reduce aliasing, which is to construct the scene so that the high-frequency data never exists in the first place and therefore never needs to be removed. This technique is known as *prefiltering* the scene and is a quite useful technique in situations where the signal is constructed from functions of other signals, such as is described in Chapter 11.

It would be a mistake to think that renderers are only worried about the spatial, or geometric, aliasing that causes "jaggies." Aliasing can and does occur in any rendering process where sampling takes place. For example, rendering a moving scene at a moment in time causes *temporal aliasing*. Rendering by representing color spectra by only the three RGB color samples can cause *color aliasing*. Aliasing happens in a wide variety of dimensions, and the techniques for reducing or ameliorating the effects of aliasing are similar in all of them.

2.4.2   **Quantization and Gamma**

The physical equations of light transport, and the approximations that are used in computer graphics, compute light intensity and color values with real numbers. However, most output devices are controlled by integer pixel values. The process of converting the floating-point real values into integers is called *quantization*. There are three special details that must be taken into account during quantization—bit-depth, gamma correction, and dithering.

Quantization converts the floating-point intensity values into the appropriate integer values for the output display based on their bit-depth. Devices vary in their ability to re-create subtle differences in color. For example, most computer monitors have the ability to reproduce only 256 different color levels (per color component or *channel*), whereas film is much more sensitive and can reproduce several thousand color levels. As a result, images that are computed for display on standard monitors will typically be converted to 8 bits per channel, whereas images computed for film may be converted to 10 to 14 bits per channel. The original floating-point numbers are scaled so as to convert 1.0, which requests the maximum intensity that the output device can attain, into the integer pixel value that will attain that intensity (generally, $2^{bits} - 1$).

All physical display media, be they film, hard-copy prints, or computer monitors, have a nonlinear response to input intensity. Small increments in pixel values in the dark regions create a smaller change in output intensity than the same increments in pixel values in the lighter regions. One effect of this is that when a device is given a pixel value of 0.5, the visual result the device produces will not appear to be intensity 0.5, but actually something less. For this reason, when integer pixel values are displayed on the device, they are often *gamma corrected*. This means that the dark values are pumped up along a curve like the one shown in Figure 2.12 to compensate for the device's laggardness. This curve is generated by the function $out = in^{1/\gamma}$, where γ (gamma) is a constant chosen appropriately for the display. Typical computer monitors, for example, will have a gamma between 1.8 and 2.4. Gamma correction restores the linearity of the image, so that linear changes in the computed light intensity will result in linear changes in the device's emitted image intensity.

A side effect of the nonlinear response is that output devices have more available pixel values in the darks (that is, more than half of the input values will create output intensities less than 0.5). However, passing the pixel data through a gamma curve upon display will skip over a lot of these values, and we can often see the multilevel jumps. To compensate for this, some images will be stored with a few more bits per channel, so that there is some extra precision for use in the darks, or with gamma correction already applied to the pixel values, or in a logarithmic format like Kodak's Cineon, which concentrates its available pixel values at the low end.

However, it is important to notice that the appropriate γ is a function of the device that the image is being shown on, and the image needs to be recorrected if it

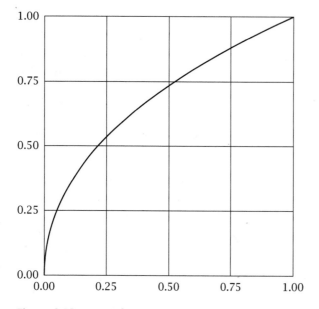

Figure 2.12 A typical gamma curve, with $y = 2.2$.

is shown on a different device. Moreover, the standard image processing calculations that might be applied to an image, such as blurring, resizing, or compositing,
all work best if the data is "linear," that is, has no built-in gamma correction. For
this reason, it is usually best for high-quality images to be stored with no gamma
correction and to apply correction as the image is being loaded into a display.

There are three ways to convert the floating-point intensity values to integers:
truncation, rounding, and dithering. Truncation is the easiest, just use the floor
function to drop the fractional bits after scaling. However, it is easy to see that
this will drop the overall intensity of the entire image by a tiny amount, so perhaps
rounding is better. Rounding means use floor if the fraction is less than 0.5 and
ceiling if the fraction is more than 0.5. However, even rounding has an unfortunate
effect on the appearance of the image because areas where the floating-point pixels
are nearly identical will form a large constant-colored block once quantized. At the
edge of this region, the color will abruptly change by one pixel level, and there will
be the appearance of color "stair-stepping" in a region that should be a continuous
gradient. These effects can be eliminated by *dithering*.

The term *dithering* is used confusingly in computer graphics to mean several
different algorithms that have one thing in common: raising and lowering pixel values in a constant-colored region to simulate more bit-depth in a device that has too
few output levels. *Halftone dither* and *ordered dither* describe algorithms that trade
off spatial resolution to get more apparent color depth in a device that has lots of
resolution but very few color levels. That's not the kind of dither we are referring

to. *Quantization dither* is a tiny random value added to floating-point pixel values just before they are truncated to integers. In a sense, it randomizes the choice between using `floor` and `ceiling` to do the conversion. This has the effect of breaking up these constant-colored blocks, making them less regular and almost fuzzy, so that on average the pixels in the region have the intended floating-point intensity. Another algorithm that accomplishes the same goal is *error-diffusion dither*, which computes the difference between the floating-point and integer versions of the image and makes sure that all of the image intensity is accounted for.

2.4.3   Mach Bands

The human eye is extremely sensitive to boundaries and edges. Our vision accentuates these boundaries—a perceptual trick that makes them more noticeable. In fact, any time dark and light areas abut, our vision perceives the dark area getting even darker near the boundary and the light area getting even lighter near its side of the boundary, so as to enhance the contrast between the abutting colors. This effect is often so strong that we actually appear to see bands outlining the edge several shades off from the true color of the region. These bands are called *Mach bands*, after the psychophysicist Ernst Mach who first studied them in the late nineteenth century.[2]

Unfortunately for computer graphics images, boundaries between large regions of constant or slowly changing colors are common, and the resulting Mach bands are noticeable artifacts (even though they aren't really there!). Mach bands are also visible when the slope of a color ramp changes suddenly along an edge; in other words, if there is a boundary in the *derivative* of the color. These effects are illustrated in Figure 2.13. In the figure, the graph below each image shows the actual and perceptual pixel values in the image. Notice that in the image on the right there is no discontinuity in the actual pixel values across the edge. The appearance of the lighter strip in the center is entirely perceptual.

2.4.4   Coordinate System Handedness

Three-dimensional coordinate systems come in two varieties, known as *left-handed* and *right-handed*. The difference between these varieties is based on the directions that the coordinate axes point relative to one another. For example, if the *x*-coordinate axis points right, and the *y*-coordinate axis points up, then there are two possibilities for orienting the *z*-coordinate axis: towards the viewer or away from the viewer. Hold one of your hands up, with thumb and forefinger extended

---

[2] This is the same Mach who defined the concept of Mach number for objects moving faster than the speed of sound.

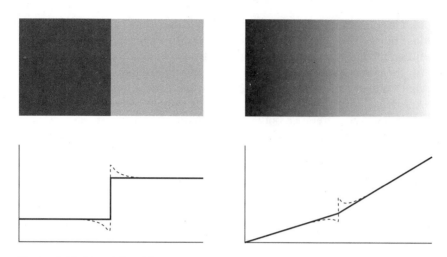

Figure 2.13 A Mach band between two constant-colored regions (left) and a Mach band delineating the change in color ramp slope (right). The graphs under the images illustrate the actual pixel values and the apparent pixel values.

like a capital L. The thumb points right along x, and the forefinger points up along y. If the z-axis points away from the viewer, this is termed "left-handed", because if you use your left hand, you can (somewhat uncomfortably) extend your middle finger (yes, that one) away from the viewer along the z-axis. If the z-axis points towards the viewer, this is termed "right-handed," because you need to use your right hand to extend your middle finger toward the viewer. Don't just sit there reading— try it! The physics students in the room perhaps recall a slightly different set of dexterous digit machinations from studying electromagnetic fields, where you hold your hand flat, fingers and thumb outstretched. With palm up, point your fingers right along x. You can then bend (curl) them to point up along y (we often say "rotate x into y"). The thumb then points along z. Same-handedness result: left hand gives you z away from the viewer, right hand gives you z toward the viewer.

Transformations that change the handedness of a coordinate system are called *mirror transformations.* Scaling by a negative value on one (or three) axes does this, as does exchanging any two axes.

Now we can answer the most baffling question in all of human history. Why do mirrors reflect left-right, but not top-bottom? You can turn sideways, spin the mirror, stand on your head, but it always does it. Is this because we have two eyes that are next to each other left-right? (No, obviously not, because it happens even if one eye is closed . . . .) Does it have something to do with the way our brains are wired, because we stand vertically, so our eyes are immune to top-bottom swaps? (No, it can't be simply perceptual, because we can touch our reflection and everything matches . . . .)

The answer is, a mirror doesn't reflect left-right. Point down the positive x-axis (right). Your mirror image also points down the positive x-axis. Right is still right.

Left is still left. Up is still up, down is still down. What is swapped is front-back! Our nose points away from the viewer (positive z), but the reflection's nose points toward the viewer (negative z). If it didn't swap front-back, we'd see the back of our heads. And guess what, the sole axis that is swapped, the z-axis, is the one that is perpendicular to the plane of the mirror—the one axis that doesn't change if you spin the mirror or yourself.

2.4.5   Noise

In his 1985 Siggraph paper, Perlin developed the concept that is commonly known today as *noise*. Image and signal processing theory, of course, had already studied many different types of noise, each with a name that indicated its frequency content (e.g., white noise, pink noise). But signal processing noises all share one important quality: they are intrinsically random. Perlin recognized that in computer graphics, we want functions that are repeatable, and thus pseudorandom. But even more, he discovered that we get more utility out of functions that are random at a selected scale but are predictable and even locally smooth if seen at a much finer resolution.

The noise functions that Perlin developed, and the ones that were later developed by other researchers, all have similar properties:

- deterministic (repeatable) function of one or more inputs
- roughly bandlimited (no frequency content higher than a chosen frequency)
- visually random when viewed at scales larger than the chosen frequency
- continuous and smooth when viewed at scales finer than the chosen frequency
- having a well-bounded range

These properties give Perlin noise two important capabilities when used in computer graphics—it can be antialiased and it can be combined in a manner similar to spectral synthesis. Antialiasing comes from the fact that noise has controlled frequency content, which makes it possible to procedurally exclude frequencies that would lead to aliasing later in the rendering process. *Spectral synthesis* is the technique of layering different frequencies at different intensities to create complex and interesting patterns. Many natural patterns have a similar kind of controlled random appearance, random over a set of frequencies but controlled at higher and lower ones. Perlin noise provides an interesting tool to simulate these and other patterns.

2.4.6   Compositing and Alpha

It is usually the case in image synthesis that the final image is made up of a combination of several images that each contain part of the data. For example, the image might be computed in layers, with the objects close to the camera rendered in one image and the images in the background rendered separately. In conventional special effects photography, optically combining the images is known as *matting* or *composite photography* and is done on a device called an *optical printer*. However, only three operations are available on an optical printer: adjusting the exposure or focus of an image, multiplying two images together (often used to cut a piece out of an image), and multiple exposure (adding two images together). Creating a multilayered effect requires multiple passes through the optical printer, with generation loss at each step.

Compositing of digital images, however, can do anything that can be programmed, to any number of images, and with no generation loss. The most common operation is layering two images on top of one another, with the "background" image showing through only where the "foreground" image is vacant—an operation called *over*. Determining where the image actually has data and where it is vacant is tricky for live-action footage and involves various combinations of rotoscoped mattes and blue/green-screen extraction, but for computer-generated footage it is quite easy. The renderer tells you, by storing this information in a separate image channel called the *alpha* (α) channel. In 1984, Porter and Duff described an algebra for combining images using the α channel of each image.

Modern paint packages often include the concept of mattes and matte channels, but α is a very specific version. First, painted mattes are often one bit deep, identifying if the pixel is in or out. In order to be useful in a world where synthetic pixels are well antialiased, the α channel usually has as many bits as the other color channels. Second, painted mattes with multiple bits (known as *fuzzy mattes*) are stored without modifying the actual color data. Extracting the intended image requires the program to multiply the color by the matte, using all of the image color where the matte is full-on, a fraction of the color in the fuzzy regions, and black where the matte is full-off. α, on the other hand, is stored *premultiplied* into the color channels. In places where the matte is full-on, the color channels hold the full-intensity color. In the fuzzy regions, the color channels themselves are predimmed. Where the matte is full-off, the color channels hold black. There are various advantanges in the rendering and compositing process that make this premultiplication scheme superior for encoding computer-generated images.

Digital images are now commonly stored in four channels—red, green, blue, and alpha, or RGBA. Of course, just having a fourth A channel does not guarantee that it contains α, as some software might store a matte value in the channel instead. In some sources, premultiplied alpha is called *associated alpha*, to distinguish it from matte data or other arbitrary data that might be stored in the fourth channel of an image.

2.4.7   Color Models

As mentioned in the previous section, light is a continuous phenomenon that can be accurately represented only as a complete spectrum. Color, on the other hand, is a psychophysical concept, because it refers to the way that we perceive light. Over the years, practitioners in the disparate fields of colorimetry, physiology, electrical engineering, computer graphics, and art have developed a variety of ways of representing color. With rare exceptions, these representations each have three numeric values. The human eye has three kinds of color sensors, the *cones*. Any light presented to the cones stimulates them each by some amount depending on their sensitivity to the frequency spectrum of that light. This acts to "convert" the continuous spectral representation of the light into three independent samples, so-called *tristimulus* values, that we perceive as the color of the light. Because we perceive light in this three-dimensional color space, it is perhaps not surprising that most other color spaces also require three dimensions to span the full range of visual colors.

Interestingly, though perhaps also not surprisingly, there are many subtleties in the psychophysical study of color perception. For example, there are often many different light spectra that will stimulate our cones with the same intensity, and so therefore are the same color perceptually. These spectra are called *metamers*, and without them, it would be impossible to re-create the appearance of color on a television display. Televisions (and computer monitors and laser displays, etc.) generate color using three guns with very specific (and sometimes very narrow) spectral output characteristics. These are made to look like a wide variety of colors because they create metamers for each light spectrum that the display needs to represent.

The most common representation of color in computer graphics is *RGB*: red, green, blue. This color scheme is simply the direct control of the colored guns of the television or computer monitor. The color channels range from 0.0, meaning the gun is off, to 1.0, meaning the gun is at maximum intensity. There are many other color models that are piecewise linear transformations of the RGB color model. Some of these color models, such as *HSL* (hue, saturation, lightness) and *HSV* (hue, saturation, value), were created because the triples were more intuitive to artists than the RGB tristimulus values. Other models, such as the television color models $Y'IQ$ (which obviously stands for luminance, in-phase, and quadrature) and $Y'UV$, were created because they model a specific color output device or an analog signal encoding. In each case, a simple linear equation or simple procedure converts any value in one color model to a value in the other color models.

Notice, however, that these models don't specify exact colors. They merely describe the intensity of the guns (or other color generators) of the output device. If the guns on one device generate a different "base color" than the guns on another device (a relatively common occurrence, actually), then the resulting colors will appear different on the two devices. There are some color models that attempt to solve this problem by tying specific color-model values to specific light spectra. For example, the CIE is an international standards organization whose purpose is to quantify color, and they have created several specific color models that lock down colors exactly. The most widely used of these is *CIE XYZ 1931. NTSC RGB 1953* attempted to solve the same problem for television by specifying the exact CIE values of the "standard phosphors."[3]

---

[3] Unfortunately, as technologies changed, these values quickly became obsolete.

Printing processes, which need color primaries in a subtractive color space, often specify ink or die colors in the *CMY* (cyan, magenta, yellow) color model. Descriptions of CMY often appeal to the idea that cyan is the "absence of red," and therefore CMY = (1,1,1) − RGB. In fact, printing is a much too subtle process to be captured by such a simplistic formula, and good transformations of RGB to CMY (or to the related *CYMK* color model, which is CMY augmented by a channel of black ink) are proprietary trade secrets of printing companies.

Other color models solve a different problem. Because the human eye is more sensitive to color changes in some parts of the spectrum than others, most color models do not have the property that a constant-sized change in the value of one channel has a constant-sized apparent change in the color. Models that take these nonlinearities of color perception into account are called *perceptual color spaces*. Artists appreciate these models, such as the Munsell color model, because it makes it easier to create visually smooth gradations and transitions in color. CIE *L*u*v** and CIE *L*a*b** try to perform the same function in a mathematically more rigorous way with nonlinear transformations of standard CIE coordinates. Recently, image compression engineers have started to study these models because they help determine which are the "important bits" to save and which bits won't ever be noticed by the audience anyway.

The *gamut* of a device refers to the range of colors that it can reproduce. For example, there are many colors displayable on a computer monitor that ink on paper cannot reproduce. We say that ink has a "smaller gamut" than monitors. Figure 2.14 shows the relationship between the gamuts of NTSC RGB and a typical dye sublimation printer. Anyone who is trying to faithfully reproduce an image from one medium in another medium needs to be aware of the limitations of the gamuts of the two media and have a strategy for approximating colors that are outside of the new color gamut.

2.4.8   Hierarchical Geometric Models

When we are building geometric models of complicated objects, it is often the case that one part of the model is connected to another part through some type of joint or other mechanism. For example, the shoulder, elbow, and wrist connect rigid body sections with joints that limit motion to particular rotations. This leads to *hierarchical* motion of the body parts, where rotating the shoulder joint causes the whole arm and hand to move in unison, whereas rotating the elbow causes only the lower arm and hand to move, and rotating the wrist moves only the hand. Each body part's position is always relative to the positions of the higher body parts.

Rather than model each body part separately, and make complex calculations to refigure the position of the hand every time any of the arm joints move, it is significantly simpler to encode the model's motion hierarchy directly into a tree-structured *hierarchical geometric model*. Each body part lives at a node in the hierarchy, and the transformation stored at the node is relative to the immedi-

Color gamut

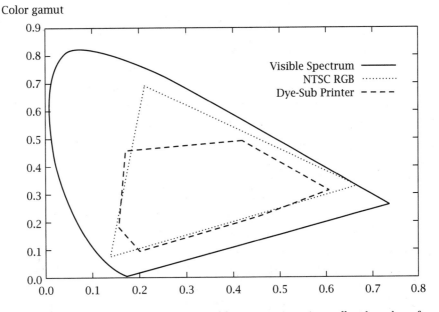

Figure 2.14 The gamut of a typical dye sublimation printer is smaller than that of an NTSC RGB monitor, which itself is a subset of all of the visible colors. This plot is a slice of the 3D CIE XYZ color space.

ate parent node, not relative to the world coordinate system. Thus, a change to the transformation at a particular node automagically modifies the position of all geometry below that node in the tree without having to modify any of those nodes' specific transformations. This makes modeling complex jointed objects much easier.

This concept of parts with subparts that are generally the same, but which may differ in a minor way relative to the nodes above them, can be expanded to include more than simply the transformations that control their position and orientation. It is quite common for hierarchies of material attributes to be just as useful. For example, the paint color of a small part on a car will generally be the same as the color of the structure above it. Another way of looking at this scheme is that nodes lower in the hierarchy generally inherit their basic characteristics from their parent nodes but can modify them as necessary.

The obvious data structure for manipulating hierarchical trees is a stack. At each node of the tree, the state of the hierarchy is pushed onto the stack for safekeeping. The node is allowed to make whatever modifications to the state that are required to fulfill its purpose and to supply the appropriate state to its child subnodes. When the node is completed, the state stack is popped and thus the state is restored to the state of the parent. Sibling subnodes can then start their processing with the same state that the first subnode had.

A geometric model can have a variety of different useful hierarchies—transformation hierarchies, attribute hierarchies, illumination hierarchies, dynamics hierarchies, even manufacturer and cost hierarchies. However, complex interrelationships often form data structures more complex than simple tree hierarchies (such as groups or directed graphs), and rendering systems are interested in a small subset of this list anyway. For this reason, RenderMan describes models in terms of a single unified attribute and transformation hierarchy.

2.4.9   Shading Models

The process that a renderer uses to determine the colors of the objects in a scene is known as *shading*. As mentioned in Section 2.3.3, the BRDF of an object, and hence the color of the object as seen from any particular viewpoint, is a complex interaction of light with the microscopic structure of the material at the surface (and sometimes beneath the surface) of the object. Fortunately for computer graphics, it is usually not necessary to model this interaction with exact physical correctness in order to get a good-looking or believable appearance for our images. In fact, a wide variety of materials can be effectively simulated with a small number of approximations that have been developed over the years. The popular approximations to the BRDFs are typically *empirical* models (based on experiment and observation without relying on scientific theory), although many slightly more complex models exist that are better grounded in materials physics (and these really should be used instead).

Two of computer graphics' most venerable empirical models of light reflection are Lambert shading and Phong lighting,[4] which are illustrated in Figure 2.15. Lambert shading captures the idea of an ideal *diffuse* reflector, an extremely rough surface. Such an object reflects light equally in all directions. The only difference in the appearance of such an object relates to the angle that it makes with the light source direction. An object that is lit edge-on covers a smaller area as seen from the light source, so it appears dimmer, than an object that presents itself full-on to the light. This difference is captured by the cosine of the illumination angle, which can be computed as the dot product of the surface normal and the light source direction, $\overline{N} \cdot \overline{L}$.

Phong lighting simulates the appearance of the bright white spots that are visible on shiny objects. These spots are caused when smooth objects reflect light preferentially in a direction near the reflection direction and are known as *specular*

---

[4] In 1975, Bui Tuong Phong actually described in a single research paper three related but distinct ideas that are often confused with one another and are rarely given separate names. Phong *shading* refers to computing the color at every pixel rather than only at the corners of large polygons, Phong *interpolation* refers to linearly interpolating normal vectors to get the appearance of continuous curvature on the flat polygonal surface, and Phong *lighting* refers to the popular specular highlight equation he developed. By the way, Phong was his given name, Bui was his surname.

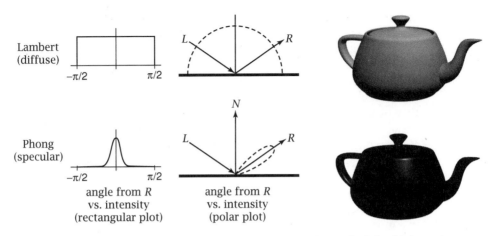

Figure 2.15 Lambert shading and Phong lighting. The graphs on the left plot intensity as a function of the angle between R and the viewing direction. The center graphs show the same plot as presented in many graphics textbooks: polar plots where intensity is read as distance from the origin at any viewing angle around R. The images on the right show the effect of the light reflection models.

highlights. Phong noticed that the specular highlight on many objects he examined appeared to be a fuzzy white circle, brighter in the center and fading at the edges. He recognized that this shape was similar to cosine raised to a power and created the popular $\cos(\overline{R} \cdot \overline{L})^{\text{roughness}}$ equation. Other specular highlight models have been suggested through the years, some more physically motivated, others purely phenomenological. One of the biggest advances was the recognition that the primary difference between metallic appearances and plastic appearances was the color of the specular highlight—metals reflecting specularly with the same color as the diffuse reflection, plastic reflecting pure white specularly (Cook and Torrance, 1981).

Shading is almost always done in the RGB color space, even though it is clear that most reflection calculations are wavelength dependent and therefore should more properly be done in the continuous spectral space. However, experiments with spectral shading calculations, such as with 9 or 20 spectral samples for each color, have rarely shown significant improvements in image quality except for contrived examples using prisms or iridescent materials. For this reason, we rarely worry that wavelength-dependent calculations are being ignored and usually use some form of color filtering as an approximation in any situation where it is obvious.

2.4.10 Ray Tracing

One of the most common methods of explaining the process of image synthesis is to appeal to our intuition about the actual physical process of photography: light rays are emitted from light sources, bounce around in a scene, reflecting off objects and picking up their color, and eventually strike the film in a camera. This paradigm of following the paths of photons as they meander through a scene is called *ray tracing*. In practice, ray tracing renderers do not follow rays forward from the light sources in hopes that some of them will eventually make their way to the camera. The vast majority of rays do not, and it would take a long time to render a picture. Instead, ray tracers follow rays backwards from the camera, until they eventually reach a light. (Interestingly, the ancient Greeks believed that what we saw was dependent on where "vision beams" that came out of our eyes landed. Modern physicists say that the simulation result is the same because a path of light is reversible—light can go equally well in either direction and follows the same path both ways.)

Because ray tracing simulates the propagation of light, it is capable of creating realistic images with many interesting and subtle effects. For example, reflections in a mirror and refractions through glass are very simple because they require only minor changes to the ray path that are easily calculated with the reflection and refraction laws discussed earlier. Techniques have been developed to simulate a variety of optical effects, such as fuzzy reflections (reflections in rough surfaces where the image is blurred because the reflected rays don't all go in the same direction) and *participating media* (also known as *volumetric*) effects (light interacts with a material that it is passing through, such as scattering off smoke in the air). One of the most interesting of these effects is the *caustic*, the phenomenon of light being focused by the reflective and refractive objects in the scene, which causes bright (or dark) spots on objects nearby, such as on the table under a wine glass.

The fundamental operation of a ray tracing algorithm is finding the intersection of a line with a geometric object. The semi-infinite line represents the ray of light. (We use a "semi-infinite" line because we are interested only in that region of the line in front of the ray's origin, not behind it.) If several objects intersect the ray, the desired intersection is the one that is closest to the origin of the ray. Depending on the type of geometric primitive (sphere, polygon, NURBS, and so on), anything from a simple mathematical equation to a complex geometric approximation algorithm may be necessary to calculate the intersection of the ray with that primitive type. Practical ray tracers have elaborate algorithms for trivially rejecting objects that are nowhere near the ray, in order to economize on expensive intersection calculations. The process of intersecting a single ray with a set of geometric primitives is properly known as *ray casting*. *Ray tracing* properly refers to the technique of recursively casting reflection, refraction, or other *secondary rays* from the point of intersection of the primary ray, in order to follow the path of light as it bounces through the scene.

It is not uncommon for renderers that do not use ray tracing as their basic algorithm to nonetheless require the occasional intersection of a ray with a single or a few geometric objects. In common usage, the phrases "trace a ray" or "cast a ray" are used to describe any such intersection calculation.

2.4.11 Other Hidden-Surface Algorithms

Because ray tracing is intuitive and captures a wide variety of interesting optical effects, it is one of the most common ways to write a renderer. In some circles, the terms *ray tracing* and *rendering* are naively used synonymously. However, ray tracing is a computationally expensive process, and there are other image synthesis algorithms that take computational shortcuts in order to reduce the overall rendering time.

One of the main operations that a renderer performs is to determine which objects are visible in the scene and which objects are hidden behind other objects. This is called *hidden-surface elimination.* Many algorithms exist that examine the objects in the scene and determine which are visible from a single point in the scene—the camera location. Scanline, z-buffer, and Reyes algorithms are examples of these. Objects are typically sorted in three dimensions: their x and y positions when projected onto the camera's viewing plane and their z distance from the camera. The differences among the many algorithms are based on factors such as the order of the sorting, the data structures that are used to maintain the geometric database, the types of primitives that can be handled, and the way that the hidden-surface algorithm is interleaved with the other calculations that the renderer needs to do (such as shading) to create the final image.

The primary computational advantage of these algorithms is that they only handle each object in the scene once. If it is visible from the camera, it is only visible at one location on the screen and from that one angle. It cannot appear in other parts of the screen at different angles or at different magnifications. Once an object has been rendered, it can be discarded. If it is not visible in a direct line of sight from the camera, it can be discarded up front, as there is no other way to see it. Ray tracers, on the other hand, must keep all of the objects in the scene in memory for the entire rendering, as mirrors or a complex arrangement of lenses in the image can cause any object to appear multiple times in the scene at different sizes and from different angles.

Notice, however, that because these hidden-surface algorithms compute visibility only from a single point, it is not generally possible to calculate information about what other points in the scene can see, such as would be necessary to do true reflection and refraction calculations. We lose the ability to simulate these optical effects. Ray tracing, on the other hand, keeps the data structures necessary to generate visibility information from between any two points in the scene. For this reason, we say that ray tracing is a *global visibility* algorithm, and lighting calculations that make use of this facility are called *global illumination* calculations. Renderers without global visibility capabilities must simulate global illumination effects with tricks, such as texture maps that contain images of the scene as viewed from other angles.

Further Reading

There are any number of great textbooks on math, physics, and computer graphics, and to leave any of them out would be a disservice to their authors. However, we aren't the Library of Congress index, so we'll pick just a handful that we find useful, informative, and easy to read. If we left out your favorite (or the one you wrote!), we apologize profusely.

For a very gentle introduction to mathematics as it applies to computer graphics, we've recently discovered *Computer Graphics: Mathematical First Steps* by Egerton and Hall. The next step up is *Mathematical Elements for Computer Graphics* by Rogers and Adams, but be comfortable with matrix math before you dig in. For those wanting to brush up on the calculus, Martin Gardner's rewrite of Thompson's classic text *Calculus Made Easy* wins high praise from everyone who reads it.

On basic physics and optics, the one on our shelves is still Halliday and Resnick's *Fundamentals of Physics*, now in its fifth edition and still a classic. Pricey, though. For a more gentle introduction, it's hard to go wrong with Gonick's *Cartoon Guide to Physics*. If you're interested in cool optical effects that happen in nature, two of the best books you'll ever find are Minnaert's *Light and Color in the Outdoors* and Lynch and Livingston's *Color and Light in Nature*.

Modern computer graphics algorithms are not well covered in most first-semester textbooks, so we recommend going straight to Watt and Watt, *Advanced Animation and Rendering Techniques*. It's diving into the deep end, but at least it doesn't burn 50 pages on 2D line clipping algorithms, and it gets bonus points for mentioning RenderMan in one (short) chapter.

Scene Description

3 Describing Models and Scenes in RenderMan

RenderMan is divided into two distinct but complementary sections: scene modeling and appearance modeling. The placement and characteristics of objects, lights, and cameras in a scene, as well as the parameters of the image to be generated, are described to a RenderMan renderer through the RenderMan Interface. The details of the appearance for those objects and lights are described to a RenderMan renderer through the RenderMan Shading Language.

3.1 Scene Description API

The RenderMan Interface (RI) is a scene description API. *API* stands for "Applications Programming Interface," but what it really means is the set of data types and function calls that are used to transmit data from one part of a system to another—in this case, from a "modeler" to the "renderer."

Users of RenderMan often find themselves initially separated into two camps: users of sophisticated modeling programs that communicate the scene description directly to the renderer and who therefore never see the data, and users who write scene descriptions themselves (either manually or, hopefully, by writing personal, special-purpose modeling programs) and who need to be fluent in the capabilities of RI API. Over time, however, these groups tend to blend, as modeler users learn to "supplement" the scene description behind the back of the modeler and thus become RI programmers themselves.

The next two chapters describe the RenderMan Interface API and try to show how it is typically used so that users in both groups will be able to create more powerful customized scene descriptions. It is a summary and will skimp on some of the specific details. Those details can be found in the *RenderMan Interface Specification*; recent extensions are usually documented extensively in the documentation sets of the RenderMan renderers themselves.

3.1.1   Language Bindings

In computer science parlance, an API can have multiple *language bindings*—that is, versions of the API that do basically the same tasks but are customized for a particular programming language or programming system. The RenderMan Interface has two official language bindings, one for the C programming language and another that is a metafile format (the RenderMan Interface Bytestream, or RIB). Details of both of these bindings can be found in Appendix C of the *RenderMan Interface Specification*. Bindings to other programming languages, such as C++, Lisp, Tcl, and recently Java have been suggested, but none have yet been officially blessed by Pixar.

Early descriptions of the RenderMan Interface concentrated on the C binding, because it was felt that most users of the API would actually be the programmers of modeling systems—users would never actually see RI data. The RIB metafile binding was not finalized and published until after the *RenderMan Companion* had been written, so the *Companion* unfortunately does not contain any reference to RIB.

We call RIB a metafile format because of its specific nature. Metafiles are datafiles that encode a log of the calls to a procedural API. RIB is not a programming language itself. It does not have any programming structures, like variables or loops. It is simply a transcription of a series of calls to the C API binding into a textual format. In fact, the syntax of RIB was designed to be as close to the C API as possible without being silly about it. For example, the C RenderMan calls to place a sphere might be

```
RiAttributeBegin ( );
RiTranslate ( 0.0, 14.0, -8.3 );
RiSurface ( "plastic", RI_NULL );
RiSphere ( 1.0, -1.0, 1.0, 360.0, RI_NULL );
RiAttributeEnd ( );
```

while the RIB file version of this same sequence would be

```
AttributeBegin
Translate 0.0 14.0 -8.3
Surface "plastic"
Sphere 1 -1 1 360
AttributeEnd
```

Every RIB command has the same name (minus the leading Ri) and has parameters of the same types, in the same order. In the few cases where there are some minor differences, it is due to the special situation that C calls are "live" (the modeling program can get return values back from function calls), whereas RIB calls are not. For this reason, examples of RI calls in RIB and in C are equivalent and equally descriptive. In this book, we will present all examples in RIB, because it is generally more compact than C.

RIB has a method for compressing the textual datastream by creating binary tokens for each word, and some renderers also accept RIB that has been compressed with gzip to squeeze out even more space. We won't worry about those details in this book, as those files are completely equivalent but harder to typeset. Again, see the *RenderMan Interface Specification*, Appendix C, if you are interested in the particulars.

3.1.2   Modeling Paradigm

RenderMan is a rich but straightforward language for describing the objects in a scene. Like other computer graphics APIs (such as PHIGS+, OpenGL, and Java3D), it contains commands to draw graphics primitives in certain places, with certain visual attributes. Unlike those APIs, RenderMan is intended to be a high-level description, in that modeling programs would describe *what* was to be rendered without having to describe in detail *how* it was to be rendered. As such, it contains commands for high-level graphics primitives, such as cubic patches and NURBS, and abstract descriptions of visual attributes, such as Shading Language shaders. It was also specifically designed to contain a rich enough scene description that it could be used by photorealistic renderers, such as ray tracers, whereas most other APIs deal specifically with things that can be drawn by current-generation hardware graphics accelerators.

However, the designers also realized that over time, graphics hardware would grow in speed and capability and that eventually features that were once the sole domain of high-end renderers (such as texture mapping, shadows, and radiosity) would eventually be put into hardware. RenderMan was designed to bridge the gap between fast rendering and photorealistic rendering, by considering the constraints of each and removing things that would make it impossible to efficiently do one or the other.

There are several basic rules that RenderMan follows, which determine the overall outline of how it describes scenes. Understanding these sets the stage for understanding the details of the individual API commands and why they have both the power and restrictions they have.

RenderMan allows no forward references of any kind

In a RenderMan scene description, everything that is needed to process a command is defined before that command. For example, the color and other visual attributes of a primitive object, such as a sphere, are defined *before* the sphere is defined. Moreover, if there are several lights that are supposed to be shining on the sphere, those lights must also be defined before the sphere. This is true of every facet of the scene description.

In this way, RenderMan accommodates (and is very much like) immediate-mode graphics hardware rendering. Because every primitive is literally drawn the moment the primitive command is executed, there is no opportunity for lights later on in the description to somehow say " . . . and I also shine on that sphere that was drawn a few seconds ago." Too late. That sphere is already drawn, and its color cannot be revised.

For this reason, the structure of a RenderMan scene description is very predictable. First, parameters of the image itself are defined. Next, parameters of the camera model are defined, including the position of the camera in the 3D space. Next, lights and other global attributes of the scene are defined. Then, and only then, do the primitives start appearing, with their private attributes individually preceding them.

RenderMan employs a strict hierarchical graphics state for transformations and object attributes

Attributes of primitives are stored in a database (also known as the *graphics state*) that is manipulated as a stack. The set of attributes that are at the top of the stack when a primitive is created are the ones that describe that primitive and are attached to it as it is rendered. Attributes can be changed and new primitives created with the new state, or the entire graphics state can be pushed onto the stack, where it is remembered and can be later restored by popping the stack. In this way, it is extremely easy to create hierarchical models such as robots or articulated characters by pushing the stack at each joint. Notice that this means the RenderMan scene description is not a DAG (directed acyclic graph), as many modelers use to describe their scenes, but a simple tree.

Pushing and popping the graphics state machine is considered to be a very inexpensive and common operation. For this reason, RenderMan assumes that it is easy to push the state, set a short-term attribute, call a command that uses the attribute, and then pop the state.

The RenderMan scene description also has several useful "modes" that will be discussed as they come up. Each of these modes is also embedded in the hierarchy so that entering and leaving the mode is equivalent to pushing and popping the state machine.

The RenderMan API is extensible by both renderer designers and renderer users

The designers of the RenderMan Interface recognized that technology travels fast, and a graphics API that was locked into a particular set of primitives, visual attributes, and algorithms would either quickly become obsolete or else would need to be augmented by an unending set of extensions. Instead, RenderMan was designed with extensible mechanisms built in, which took the burden off of the designers to anticipate every use and in fact allows the API to be extended as each individual frame is rendered.

Chief among these extensibility mechanisms is the concept of the parameter list. Rather than have every possible parameter to every possible call predefined, most calls to RenderMan have only the most fundamental parameters defined specifically and then also take a variable-length argument list of additional parameters. These additional parameters are generically known as the *parameter list* and are specified by name-value pairs, much like keyword parameters in interpreted languages like Lisp. Each name is a string, which ideally is at least somewhat descriptive of its purpose, like "width" or "compression", and the value is an array of data. Many commands have predefined parameter list entries, and renderer implementations often predefine additional entries to create datapaths for their extensions. One thing that makes RenderMan unique is that users can also define additional parameter list entries and supply corresponding data in ways that will extend the model's descriptive power. This unifying syntax enables the predefined, renderer-defined, and user-defined data types to coexist in a scene description with no syntactic incompatibilities.

RenderMan also provides a few specific extension back doors, which renderer implementations can use to add controls over features that are not in other renderers.

3.1.3   Compatibility

Version 3.1 of the *RenderMan Interface Specification*, published in 1989, spends some not-inconsiderable verbiage describing what it means to be "compatible" with the RenderMan Interface. It also divides features of a renderer into "Required Features" and "Optional Capabilities" and specifies what the default behavior should be in cases where the renderer does not implement any given "Optional Capability." The *RenderMan Companion* describes the RenderMan Interface generically, without specifying or describing features of particular renderer implementations. All of this was done with an eye towards the day when RenderMan would be a de facto industry standard for high-end computer graphics.

However, RenderMan is not an industry standard. It is the interface definition of a popular, but proprietary, renderer. As changes are made to its interface, no new public documents are published to proclaim "the new and improved version 9 of the *RenderMan Interface Specification.*" Compatibility with RenderMan Interface now means being compatible with *PRMan*. *BMRT* is considered compatible not because it follows a particular book, but rather because it has been painstakingly checked with a wide variety of input to determine that it behaves identically to *PRMan* or, where the algorithmic differences require it, in a way that users can easily understand the differences. As new RenderMan renderers appear, there is no compatibility suite or test bed to exhaustively check them, and renderer developers and users are left to their own devices to determine if a particular code base is compatible enough for their own liking.

For that reason, in this book we will not discuss strict standards conformance, Optional versus Required Capabilities, or pretend that we are discussing RenderMan renderers generically. We will discuss RenderMan as it exists today, embodied in two compatible but very different renderer implementations.

3.2   Structure of a Scene Description

RenderMan scene descriptions have a particular structure, embodied in the tree of the hierarchical graphics state. There are actually several calls that manipulate the hierarchical graphics state stack, some that change the mode of the graphics state and others that push a subset of the attributes onto the stack. We describe the subtree of the hierarchy inside of a balanced pair of these commands as being a *block*. Being "in" a particular block means that one of the ancestors of that level of the hierarchy was created by that particular API call.

3.2.1   Outline

The scene description is divided into two phases: describing the *viewer* and describing the *world*. The RenderMan viewer description includes various parameters of the camera as well as parameters of the image file that is being generated. These parameters are called *options* and are global to the entire rendered image. The RenderMan world description includes all of the geometry in the scene, with their material descriptions and other parameters that can be specific to individual objects in the scene. These parameters are called *attributes*. The division between describing "the viewer" and describing "the scene" occurs at WorldBegin, which starts a *world block*.

Rendering an animation can include the rendering of large numbers of frames, and each frame might require prerendering a certain number of images for use as texture maps or for other purposes. The scene description API allows for these logical divisions of the work to be specified as well.

A RenderMan scene description therefore proceeds as a series of nested blocks, in the following order:

Options global to the entire animation

Frame block
  Image options
  Camera options
  World block
    Attributes, lights, primitives
  Changed options
  Another world block
Next frame block

These blocks are divided by the following RenderMan API calls:

WorldBegin

WorldBegin starts the scene description of a single image. The current transformation matrix is stored as the camera-to-world matrix, and the new object-to-world matrix is initialized with the identity matrix (see Section 3.2.4). As a side effect, the entire attribute state is also pushed. World blocks cannot be nested.

WorldEnd

Ends the scene description for a single image and causes the image to be rendered.

FrameBegin *frameno*

FrameBegin begins the description of a single frame to be rendered. A frame can contain any number of world blocks that can generate texture maps, shadow maps, background elements, or any other renderings required to make the "real image" (which is presumably rendered last). The frame number *frameno* is descriptive only.

FrameBegin pushes both the attribute and the option state. It cannot be nested (there is a single frame block).

FrameEnd

Ends the description of a frame. Pops the attribute and option state.

An *attribute block* is all of the scene description between matching Attribute-Begin and AttributeEnd calls. That block inherits the attribute state of the parent block, manipulates it, presumably assigns it to some geometric primitives, and then restores the state to the parents' version. The attribute state contains all of the visual attributes of the geometric primitives in the scene, such as the color and shaders attached to the objects, as well as the transformation matrices. The transformation matrix stack can also be pushed and popped independently of the rest of the attribute state using TransformBegin and TransformEnd (creating a *transform block*), but those stack calls must be made in a way that is completely nested within its attribute block.

AttributeBegin

> AttributeBegin pushes the entire graphics attribute state, including the transformation stack. Although attribute blocks are typically used inside the world block, it is perfectly legal to use them outside as well.

AttributeEnd

> Pops the attribute stack.

TransformBegin

> TransformBegin pushes the transformation stack but leaves all other attributes alone. Transform blocks can be nested within attribute blocks, and vice versa, but the stacking must always be balanced. That is, the sequence

```
AttributeBegin
TransformBegin
AttributeEnd
TransformEnd
```

> is *not* legal.

TransformEnd

> Pops the transformation stack.

3.2.2   Parameter Declarations

In Section 3.1.2, we mentioned parameter lists, which contain the majority of the interesting data that the modeler transmits to the renderer. An entry in a parameter list has two parts, the parameter name and an array of data values for the parameter. The name is a string, of course, whereas the data values can be many different things.

Of course, the renderer needs to know exactly what the data is and how many items are expected to be in the array. For this reason, the renderer maintains a symbol table, or *dictionary*, defining the *data type* and *storage class* of each parameter that the modeler will use to describe the scene. The choices for parameter data type include all of the types that are available for variables in the Shading Language (Chapter 7). Storage classes are used to define various styles of primitive variables (described in Section 4.1).

A reasonably large number of parameters are predefined, corresponding to those parameters that the renderer has built-in knowledge about. However, as we will see in future sections, most parameters to shaders and geometric primitives are data that the user or the modeler has created. These new parameters must be *declared* before use so that the RIB parser knows what kind and how much data to expect and so that the renderer can process it correctly.

Declare *name declaration*

Declare adds a new parameter name to the dictionary. The parameter *name* will be used as the identifier in subsequent parameter lists. The parameter *declaration* defines the storage class and data type of the data. The syntax is similar to, but not identical to, variable declarations in the Shading Language—"*class type*".

class can be any of the four storage classes constant, uniform, varying, or vertex. *class* is optional, because it is only relevant to primitive variables, and defaults to uniform if left out.

type can be any of the Shading Language data types float, point, vector, normal, color, string, or matrix or can be a fixed-length array of any of those types by providing a trailing integer array length inside square brackets.

In addition, two data types that are specific to the RenderMan API (that don't appear in the Shading Language) can be declared. The first data type, hpoint, refers to homogeneous points, such as the standard vertex data type "Pw". Such data have four coordinates when specified but revert to the standard three-coordinate point type when accessed by the Shading Language. The second data type, integer, refers (naturally enough) to integer data. Integer data is not useful to shaders, but may be useful to declare parameter list data types for other RenderMan API calls that have parameter lists (such as Attribute and Display).

For example, here are several valid parameter declarations:

```
Declare "Kd" "uniform float"
Declare "m1" "matrix"
Declare "N" "varying normal"
Declare "specularcolor" "color"
Declare "st" "varying float[2]"
Declare "texturenames" "uniform string[3]"
Declare "Pw" "vertex hpoint"
```

The parameter dictionary is global to the scene; that is, it is not stacked as part of the hierarchical attribute state. If a parameter name is redeclared, the new value will replace the old value for the rest of the RIB stream, and the old value will be permanently lost. Therefore, it is best if each parameter name is unique. If this cannot be ensured, the modeler will have to keep track of whether each usage of a parameter name is consistent with the current declaration of that name, and if not, be prepared to redeclare it each time it is used a different way.

Newer versions of *PRMan* and *BMRT* have addressed this issue by creating a new *in-line* declaration style. In this style, a parameter name can be declared during its use in a particular RIB command, and its dictionary definition is neither referenced nor updated for the scope of this one command. In-line declarations look even more like Shading Language declarations because of their form—"*class type name*". For example, here is the use of an in-line declaration to temporarily override but not clobber the standard dictionary definition of the parameter "Kd".

```
Declare "Kd" "uniform float"          # standard definition
Surface "plastic" "Kd" [.2]           # standard usage
Surface "carpetfloss" "Ka" [.05]      # normal, but...
       "uniform color Kd" [.3 .2 .4]  # special usage
Surface "plastic" "Kd" [.5]           # standard usage again
```

3.2.3   Transformations

Internally, RenderMan represents all transformations as transformation matrices—in particular, as 4×4 matrices that are premultiplied by row vectors. In other words, points are transformed as $P \cdot M$, and the translation component is on the bottom, in elements 12 through 14.

A note on confusing terminology: the transformation matrix that appears on the top of the transformation stack is known as the *current transformation matrix*. The coordinate system that this matrix represents is confusingly called the *local coordinate system*, the "object" coordinate system, or the *current coordinate system*, depending on context. The latter is the worst because it is easily mistaken with the "current" coordinate system as defined in the Shading Language, which is a different thing entirely. Moreover, in the *RenderMan Interface Specification*, various pieces of renderer documentation, the *RenderMan Companion*, and even in this book, the authors often use the word "space" as a shorthand for "coordinate system" (e.g., "transform "P" to "world" space"), and "coordinates" as shorthand for "as expressed in the (blank) coordinate system" (e.g., "examine the x component of "P" in "world" coordinates"). The current authors have striven to be consistent in both naming and typesetting so as to minimize the confusion.

It is often convenient for modeling programs to describe changes to the local coordinate systems in terms of simple transformations rather than whole transformation matrices. For this reason, RenderMan has a generous set of API calls that apply transformations to the local coordinate system:

Translate *dx dy dz*

    Translate the local coordinate system by (*dx,dy,dz*).

Rotate *angle vx vy vz*

> Rotate the local coordinate system by *angle* degrees around axis given by the direction vector (*vx,vy,vz*)

Scale *sx sy sz*

> Scale the local coordinate system by *sx* in the *x*-axis, *sy* in the *y*-axis, *sz* in the *z*-axis.

Skew *angle vx vy vz ax ay az*

> The Skew call shears everything parallel to a plane. Everything moves along a vector parallel to the axis vector $A = (ax,ay,az)$, the amount of the shift being proportional to the distance from the plane defined by A and $A \times V$. The exact amount is calculated based on the desire for the vector $V = (vx,vy,vz)$ to rotate *angle* degrees, around the origin, toward A.

ConcatTransform *matrix*

> ConcatTransform premultiplies the supplied parameter *matrix* into the current transformation matrix. *matrix* is, of course, 16 floating-point numbers and encodes the transformation matrix that transforms points from the new coordinate system to the previous coordinate system.

Identity

> The Identity call replaces the current transformation matrix by the identity matrix. In effect, this call returns the local coordinate system to be identical to the world coordinate system when used inside a world block, and to the camera coordinate system when used outside a world block. However, see the newer CoordSysTransform call in the next section for a more general and explicit syntax.

Transform *matrix*

> The Transform call replaces the current transformation matrix by the supplied parameter *matrix*. This is equivalent to Identity followed by ConcatTransform *matrix*.

3.2.4   Special Coordinate Systems

The RenderMan Interface has a few distinguished coordinate systems, which are important enough to both the modeling process and the rendering process that they have predefined names and relationships. The first of these is "camera" space. This is the coordinate system that exists around the virtual camera. The camera is at the origin of this coordinate system, where the positive *z*-axis extends in front of the camera, the positive *x*-axis is to the right, and the positive *y*-axis is up (a left-handed coordinate system). This coordinate system is critical due to the fact that the RenderMan modeling paradigm builds the scene from the camera out—the camera coordinate system is the center of the visual universe. All other coordinate systems are relative to this in some way. Camera space is created when `Projection` is called, and at that point the current transformation matrix is set to the identity. From then on, until `WorldBegin`, changes to the current transformation matrix are actually building up the eventual `world-to-camera` matrix.

The next important coordinate system is "`world`" space. This is the coordinate system that the modeler generally thinks of as being the canonical coordinate system for scene description. In RenderMan, however, it is placed relative to "`camera`" space, not vice versa. World space is initialized when `WorldBegin` is called. The current transformation matrix at that time is stored with the other now-fixed options as the official `world-to-camera` matrix, and the current transformation matrix is reset to the identity. From then on, until `WorldEnd`, changes to the current transformation matrix create coordinate systems that are relative to "`world`" space. That is, the matrix transforms points from the local coordinate system into "`world`" space.

When geometric primitives are created, they take their positions from the current transformation matrix at the time. That coordinate system is also stored (for future reference) as the "`object`" space for that particular geometric primitive. Naturally, every geometric primitive has its own "`object`" space. Similarly, when shaders are created with `Surface` and other calls, the local coordinate system is stored as the "`shader`" space for that particular shader.

There are three other distinguished coordinate systems that are sometimes referred to in models or in shaders that relate to the projection of the 3D scene into the eventual 2D image:

- "`screen`": the 2D coordinate system on the $z = 1$ projection plane (after the projection occurs), in which `ScreenWindow` is defined. As with camera space, x is right and y is up. Depths are encoded so that the near and far clipping planes are projected to 0.0 and 1.0, respectively.
- "`NDC`" (normalized-device coordinates): the resolution-independent 2D coordinate system in the image, in which the upper-left corner is (0.0, 0.0) and the lower-right corner is (1.0, 1.0). `CropWindow` is defined in this space. Notice that y is *down* in this coordinate system.
- "`raster`": the resolution-dependent 2D pixel coordinates on the image, where the upper-left corner of the upper-left pixel is (0, 0) and the lower-right corner of the lower-right pixel is (`xres`, `yres`).

Of course, it wouldn't be RenderMan if the modeler were not able to extend the distinguished set of predefined coordinate systems:

`CoordinateSystem` *name*

> `CoordinateSystem` marks the local coordinate system and labels it with identifier *name*. Subsequent calls that refer to coordinate systems by their names can thereafter refer to this name in addition to any of the predefined names.

These named coordinate systems, both built in and user-defined, are most useful because they can be referred to by shaders. It is extremely common, and extremely easy, for shaders to transform points and vectors into various coordinate systems by using their names. In addition, geometric models can be placed into specific named coordinate systems, making them useful in the geometric scene description as well. The following API call allows you to use named coordinate systems in the RIB file:

CoordSysTransform *name*

> The CoordSysTransform call replaces the current transformation matrix with the matrix that forms the *name* coordinate system. This permits objects to be placed directly into special or user-defined coordinate systems by their names. For example, if an object needs to be placed on the near clipping plane (regardless of the position of the camera or the settings of Clipping), you can simply use CoordSysTransform "NDC" to make the local coordinate system "NDC"-space and then place the object at $z = 0$.

Modeler-defined coordinate system names, like the standard predefined coordinate system names, are global to the scene and are not part of the hierarchical attribute state. If a name is reused, the old matrix is lost permanently. This can have unintended effects on the renderer, as shading and modeling operations may desire to refer to the old matrix long after it has been destroyed and will unknowingly get the new matrix instead.

3.3   Rendering Options

As described above, the RenderMan scene description is generally divided into phases. The first phase describes parameters of the image to be rendered and of the camera. These parameters are called *options* because they must hold true for the entire process of image generation and therefore might be considered global to the scene. For example, the resolution of the image being rendered, or the position of the camera, are obviously global parameters. The following RIB listing contains a typical option setup for a single frame of an animation:

```
FrameBegin 14
    # Image options
    Display "joe27.s9.14.tif" "tiff" "rgba"
    Format 1880 800 1
    Exposure 1.0 1.0
    Quantize "rgba" 255 0 255 0.5
    PixelSamples 3 3
    PixelFilter "sinc" 4 4
```

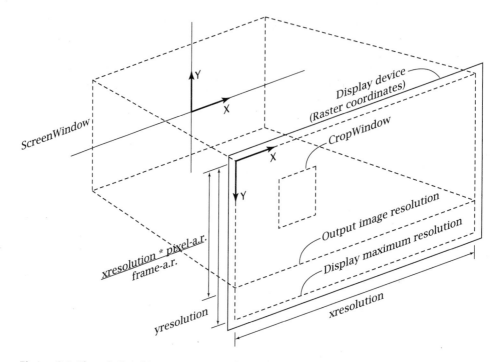

Figure 3.1 The relationship among parts of the image description.

```
        # Camera options
        Clipping 0.4 1200
        Projection "perspective" "fov" [30]
        ConcatTransform [1 0 0 0  0 0 1 0  0 1 0 0  0 0 0 1]
        Translate [-20 -8 10]
        Rotate 40  0 .6 1
        WorldBegin
             # Scene Description
             ...
        WorldEnd
   FrameEnd
```

3.3.1   Image Description

The first requirement of the scene description is to specify the image to be made. Several parameters of the image must be determined before any rendering of any kind can be done. These parameters of the image (some of which are illustrated in Figure 3.1) are specified by eight RI API calls.

Display *filename fileformat imagetype parameterlist*

> Display sets the name and file format of the output image. The *fileformat* could be one of any number of specific file formats that the renderer knows, such as "tiff" or "cineon", or the generic names "file" or "framebuffer", where the renderer uses some default format of the appropriate type. The *parameterlist* specifies optional parameters that are meaningful to the particular image file format, such as compression parameters.
>
> *imagetype* specifies the type of data (color, depth, etc.) that is to be put into the file. For example, "rgb" and "rgba" request three- and four-channel color images, respectively. The various types of data that a renderer can emit into a file is very dependent on both the capabilities of the renderer and the flexibility of the file format.
>
> Recent versions of *PRMan* permit multiple images to be created from a single scene description, using multiple calls to Display. In that case, each output image would generally have a different output type.

Format *xresolution yresolution pixelaspectratio*

> Format specifies the resolution of the image to be generated. The *pixelaspectratio* parameter defines whether the pixels of the image should be square (as they are for most computer monitors) by specifying 1.0, or some other rectangular shape (such as 0.9 for televisions).

FrameAspectRatio *ratio*

> FrameAspectRatio specifies exactly the aspect ratio of the final rendered frame. This can be important if the image is being generated for some anamorphic format, such as 2.35 for Cinemascope frames.

You might notice that these calls redundantly specify certain image parameters, and that might lead to their being inconsistent. For example, the parameter to the FrameAspectRatio call and the frame aspect ratio implied by the Format call can easily be inconsistent. It was intended that the user specify only the most important one, and a reasonable default value would be guessed for the unspecified ones. If incompatible settings are specifically requested, the renderer compromises as best it can.

Exposure *gain gamma*

> Exposure controls the gamma correction (see Section 2.4.2) of the output image. By default, the renderer writes files with no gamma correction (also known as linear gamma). By specifying a floating point *gamma* value, a gamma appropriate for a particular display or printing device can be set. The floating point *gain* parameter simply scales all output values uniformly, a function

that is useful to punch up dark scenes without modifying all of the lights. RenderMan does not have any "automatic gain control."

Quantize *imagetype one min max dither*

> Quantize controls the way that floating point data computed by the renderer is converted into the integer data that is required by most file formats. The parameter *one* specifies the integer value that corresponds to floating-point 1.0. *min* and *max* specify the minimum and maximum values that the file format will accept. Generally, these are 0 and *one*, but some file formats can store values that are out of range, either negative intensities or *superwhite* values. If all three of these parameters are set to 0.0, quantization is turned off and full floating point values are presented to the display.

> *dither* controls the dithering of floating point values as they are quantized, as described in Section 2.4.2. A random number between 0.0 and *dither* is added to each floating point number before it is truncated to create integer values. Generally, this is set to either 0.0, to turn dither off, or 0.5, to set dithering to round up or down equally often.

> The *imagetype* parameter specifies which type of data this Quantize call refers to. It is common for different types of data to be quantized differently, such as quantizing "rgba" to 8-bit integers while leaving "z" depth values in floating point.

PixelSamples *nx ny*

> Most modern renderers do antialiasing via supersampling. The PixelSamples call controls the level of antialiasing by specifying the number of samples per pixel in the *x* and *y* directions. Typical values for PixelSamples range from 2 by 2 when simple antialiasing is needed, through 8 by 8 or higher when more stochastic sampling is needed to support motion blur or depth of field (Section 3.8).

PixelFilter *filtername xwidth ywidth*

> High-quality antialiasing requires full control over the reconstruction of the individual pixel samples into the final pixel color. PixelFilter specifies the type and width of the pixel reconstruction filter that is to be used. Filter width is the diameter of the filter kernel, so a filter with *xwidth* of 3.0 covers a full pixel to the right and to the left of the center of a pixel. Different filters have different qualities, and it is not always obvious which is the right filter for particular applications. For example, most would agree that "box" 1 1 is a pretty poor filter. Some would argue that the windowed "sinc" 4 4 is a great filter, while others would complain about its "negative lobes." The default

filter, "gaussian" 2 2, is a pretty good filter with no negative lobes but is a little blurry for some people's tastes.

CropWindow *xmin xmax ymin ymax*

CropWindow specifies that only a portion of the image should be rendered. The parameters are floating point numbers that specify a box that is the fractional region of the image that is desired (using "NDC" coordinates). Because the values are floating point, they are resolution independent. For example, you can always request the upper-left quarter of the image by specifying CropWindow 0 .5 0 .5. The floating point values are specifically rounded by the renderer into pixel values so that if the user renders several images with crop windows that tile the unit square in floating point, then every image pixel will be rendered exactly once. Images tiled together from these separately rendered crop windows are dependably free of stitching artifacts.

3.3.2   Camera Description

The second requirement of the scene description is to describe the exact parameters of the camera. These include both the position of the camera and the projection of the camera view onto the image.

The position of the camera in the world is specified, as described above, with standard transformation commands that create the transformation matrix that relates "world" space to "camera" space. In particular, "world" space is specified relative to the camera rather than specifying the camera as a position in "world" space. In other words, the camera is not an object in the scene. This is often confusing to first-time users, but it is consistent with the first paradigm requirement that the camera be fixed before any objects are placed in front of it.

The parameters of the projection (illustrated in Figure 3.2) are specified with three API calls.

Projection *type parameterlist*

The fundamental job of the camera is to transform objects in 3D onto the 2D projection (or film) plane. In RenderMan, the default projection plane is at $z = 1$ in "camera" space. Projection specifies the type of camera projection, which then determines where on the projection plane objects in the scene will appear. RenderMan renderers all support at least "orthographic" projection, which is sometimes called a *planar* or *flat* projection, and the "perspective" projection.

The *parameterlist* provides additional projection-specific parameters. The most common example is the perspective field of view, specified with the "fov" parameter. "fov" takes the full angle (in degrees) of the perspective

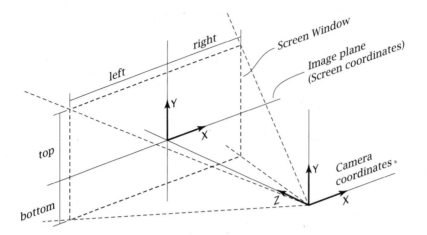

Figure 3.2 The relationship among parts of the camera description.

projection, which defaults to 90 degrees. Specifying a different "fov" is equivalent to moving the projection plane (to the position $z = 1/\tan(fov/2)$), which zooms the image.

ScreenWindow *xmin xmax ymin ymax*

The projection determines where on the projection plane objects in the scene will appear. ScreenWindow specifies the rectangular region of the projection plane that should appear in the image. There is no requirement that the screen window be centered (although it usually is). If it is not, we get an off-center view, such as the ones seen by view cameras. Similarly, there is no requirement that the shape of the screen window match the shape of the frame aspect ratio (although it usually does). If it does not, there will be some anamorphic squashing of the image as it is scaled to fit into the requested output resolution.

The default value for ScreenWindow, if one is not set, is to fit the narrower dimension of the image resolution into the -1.0 to 1.0 range, and center the wider dimension while respecting the frame aspect ratio.

Notice that zooming a perspective camera can be equivalently done by either lowering the perspective "fov" or by narrowing the ScreenWindow. It is best to choose one, as using both simultaneously is confusing.

Clipping *nearplane farplane*

Clipping sets the near and far clipping planes. Setting the clipping planes is not required but is friendly to the renderer. Clipping planes are commonly used by renderers to optimize their perspective projections, as the math involved in perspective divides tends to waste floating point precision if the scene is not well bounded in depth. In particular, the default values of Clipping (nearly zero through infinity) are very bad and really should be overridden by any modeler that has even rough bounds on the overall depth of scene.

3.3.3   Renderer Control

In addition to the image and camera parameters, the RenderMan API provides the opportunity for the user to set various other options that control the way the renderer is to create the image. Some of these options control details of advanced rendering features and are described with them in following sections. Other parameters are very renderer specific and are passed into the renderer through the generic extension backdoors like Option.

Hider *type parameterlist*

> The Hider call controls the way that the hidden-surface elimination calculation is done. The value *type* can take the predefined names "hidden", for a normal depth-based hidden-surface algorithm, or "paint", for the rarely used painter's algorithm (the last primitive is on top). Additionally, the renderer might define other names for renderer-specific algorithms. The *parameterlist* provides the method for giving the renderer any renderer-specific parameters to control the chosen hidden-surface algorithm.

Option *type parameterlist*

> Option provides the entry point for renderer-specific data that is global to the scene or image-generation process and therefore falls into the category of options. For example, both *PRMan* and *BMRT* have options that control memory usage, arbitrary limits on various calculations that are theoretically unbounded, rendering mode settings, and so on. These options are generally very algorithm specific, and as a result renderers tend to have non-overlapping sets. Renderers ignore options they do not understand, so it is possible to write RIB files that contain parameters appropriate for multiple renderers.

RiSynchronize("abort")

> This special function is available only in the C binding of the RI API. RiSynchronize("abort") causes the current rendering to be stopped immediately. Whatever pixels have already been generated, if any, are flushed, and the interface returns to the point in the hierarchical state immediately outside the world block. If called prior to RiWorldEnd(), it pops the attribute stack to the appropriate level. If called while rendering, that is, during the execution of the RiWorldEnd() call (for example, by an interrupt handler or in an application subroutine that was supplied to RiProcedural() or RiErrorHandler()), it immediately exits RiWorldEnd().

3.4   Primitive Attributes

RenderMan has a rich set of visual attributes that can be applied to the geometric primitives in the scene description. In many ways, the predefined attribute set is very extensive, and yet in many ways it is quite limited. This is because rather than define all possible attributes and give RenderMan hundreds of API calls to set each one independently (as many graphics APIs have), RenderMan was instead defined to have a completely extensible set of primitive attributes. Only a few of the most important attributes were made part of the predefined set. All other attributes were made part of the open-ended shader and generic attribute systems. For complete flexibility, two different methods of specifying attributes were created: attributes in the graphics state that are inherited by primitives and attributes that are part of the geometric description itself. As we will see, these two complementary styles make RenderMan very powerful. The following section of a RIB file contains a typical attribute block for a single object in a scene:

```
AttributeBegin
    # Hemispherical wooden dome in a dense fog
    Declare "density" "uniform float"
    Color [.2 .45 .8]
    Opacity [1 1 1]
    Sides 2
    ShadingRate 1.0
    Surface "paintedplastic" "texturename" ["wood.tx"]
    Atmosphere "myfog" "density" [1.48]
    Sphere 1.0 0.0 1.0 360.0
    Disk 0.0 1.0 360.0
AttributeEnd
```

3.4.1   Color Attributes

It is hard to imagine a graphics API that doesn't have specific support for a visual attribute as fundamental as the *color* of each object, and RenderMan doesn't disappoint.

Color *color*

> Color sets the default color of geometric primitives. The parameter *color* is an array of three floating point numbers that specify the red, green, and blue components of the color.[1]

---

[1] There is a very advanced way to change the number and interpretation of components that RenderMan expects from its colors (ColorSamples), but it is so rarely used that we'll just ignore it. See the RI Spec for details if you're interested.

Opacity *color*

> Opacity sets the default opacity of geometric primitives. RenderMan does not consider opacity to be a single value, but rather a color filter, so requires a value for each of the three color channels. Therefore, the parameter *color* is an array of three floating point numbers. Opacity must fall between 0.0 (totally transparent) and 1.0 (completely opaque) for the renderer to work correctly.

These color and opacity values are the ones that will appear in the Shading Language as Cs and Os, unless they are overridden by primitive variable data as defined in Section 4.1.

Matte *flag*

> RenderMan can create images with 3D holdout mattes (see Section 2.4.6 for a discussion of compositing with mattes). Matte objects do not appear in the final rendered frame, and they also remove all objects behind them from the frame as well. As a result, they leave a "hole" in the alpha channel of the final frame, which will undoubtedly be filled later by compositing in some other image. This technique is used when another image must be composited into the middle of a rendered image. Matte objects are used to create an image hole at the appropriate depth, so that objects in front of the matte are rendered normally (and therefore obscure portions of the other image normally), but objects behind the matte are missing to leave room for the image.

> The parameter *flag* is a Boolean value: 1 means the geometric primitive is a matte object; 0 means the primitive is not a matte object. The color matte objects do not matter, as they will not be visible nor have any other visible effect on the image, but opacity is used by some renderers to modulate the transparency of the hole.

3.4.2   Shaders

The most important attributes of a geometric primitive are the Shading Language shaders that are attached to it. Other references on RenderMan imply that renderers might not have a Shading Language and describe the "default" shaders that every RenderMan renderer must have. Let's get real. Over the last decade we have learned that the Shading Language is one of the most important features that RenderMan has to offer, and it is really not optional. Every existing RenderMan renderer has a Shading Language, and it is certain that future ones will as well, so we'll drop the pretense and just assume that shaders are being used.

Because shaders completely control the calculation of the color of the objects in the scene, various attributes that are familiar and common in other graphics APIs (such as the diffuse coefficient or specular color) do not appear in RenderMan. They are really just parameters of some predefined shading model. Instead, each shader has parameters that are necessary to its shading model, and rather than store them independently in the graphics state, they are simply given in the parameter list of the shader call.

Most shaders have many parameters. In particular, in shaders that are written somewhat generically, there may be many parameters to control subtle variations of that shader. It is quite often the case that many of these parameters may be superfluous to a particular instance of the shader on a particular object. For this reason, every parameter has a default value, and only those parameters that are different from the default need be listed in the parameter list of a particular call. Therefore, the parameter list of each shader call may have different numbers of arguments, perhaps even none. Shader parameters are given in the call's parameter list as a name-value pair of arguments: the parameter name as a string and the parameter value as an array of data of the appropriate type.

There are three key attributes of geometric primitives that are specified as shaders: *surface*, *displacement*, and *atmosphere*. The surface shader is the main shader on any geometric primitive. It is responsible for computing the color and opacity of the primitive. As will be described in detail in later chapters, the surface shader uses the geometric information of the primitive, the parameters of the shader, and light emitted from light source shaders to compute this color (Ci) and opacity (Oi).

Surface *shadername parameterlist*

> Surface specifies that the surface shader named *shadername* should be used to compute the color and opacity of the geometric primitive.

Displacement mapping is a perturbation of the surface, often used to provide pits, dents, embossing, or other small-scale surface position changes that are too small to worry about in the geometric model itself. Displacement mapping literally moves the surface and changes where it will appear on-screen. *PRMan* can do this in both surface and displacement shaders. *BMRT*, on the other hand, can only do true displacement mapping in displacement shaders, with attempts to displace in surface shaders resulting in bump mapping. Bump mapping is a visual trick that modifies the surface normal to make it appear as though the surface has small-scale shape distortions without actually moving the surface itself. Of course, a displacement shader could simply compute a bump map without displacement if that is desired.

The displacement shader on a geometric primitive is run prior to the surface shader on that primitive. The function of the displacement shader is to modify the Shading Language global variables "P" and "N" prior to the surface shader being run, so that the surface shader operates on the new data.

Displacement *shadername parameterlist*

> Displacement specifies that the displacement shader named *shadername* should be used to compute surface perturbations on the geometric primitive.

When doing true displacements, in either surface or displacement shaders, the renderer needs to know the maximum possible distance that any point might be displaced in order to correctly bound the primitive. See Section 8.2.4 for a complete discussion of specifying the displacement bounds of primitives that have displacement.

RenderMan also provides a shader type whose job is to modify the apparent color of primitives in the scene to simulate atmospheric effects such as fog or distance-related hue shifts. This shader is known as the atmosphere shader, and it runs after the surface shader has finished. The atmosphere modifies Ci and Oi to account for the visual changes caused by the volumetric effects of the atmosphere between the primitive and the camera.

Atmosphere *shadername parameterlist*

> Atmosphere specifies that the volume shader named *shadername* should be used to compute the atmospheric contributions to the color of the geometric primitive.

As we will see in Chapter 7, the Shading Language syntax has the flexibility to accept shader parameters that are uniform (the same on all parts of the primitive) and that are varying (different on different parts of the surface). Parameters passed to shader calls require exactly one value, regardless of parameter storage class. Section 4.1 will discuss how variables attached to geometric primitives can also be used to provide different amounts of data to uniform and varying shader parameters. Notice that such primitive variables always override any parameters which appear in these shader calls.

When "point", "vector", "normal", or "matrix" data (any of the geometric data types) is supplied as a parameter of a shader call, the data is assumed to be expressed in the current coordinate system—that is, in "shader" coordinates. However, as we will see in Section 7.2.3, Shading Language calculations do not happen in "shader" space. Therefore, there is an implied coordinate transformation that brings this "shader" space data into the Shading Language's "current" space before the shader starts execution. If raw, untransformed coordinate values are desired, the easiest way to provide them is through an array of three floats.

3.5   Other Shading Attributes

We have just seen how to specify which Shading Language programs should be attached to a geometric primitive to calculate its color. Those shaders are run at many points on the surface of the primitive, depending on where the renderer needs to know that information. There are two attributes that determine how often this calculation is made.

ShadingRate *area*

> ShadingRate specifies how often shaders are run on the surface of the geometric primitive. This is done by specifying a maximum distance between shading samples. If the shader on a primitive is not run frequently enough—that is, the runs (samples) of the shader are spaced too far apart—then a large region of the surface will have the same color, and a lot of the subtle detail of the texture will be lost. If the shader on a primitive is run too frequently—that is, the shader samples are unnecessarily close together—then most shader samples return the same color as neighboring samples, and this redundant calculation wastes a lot of valuable compute cycles.

> For historical reasons, shading rate is specified as an area rather than a frequency (that is, a rate). The parameter *area* is a floating point number that gives the area in pixels of the largest region on the primitive that any given shader sample may represent. Typically, a shading rate of 1.0, meaning one unique shading sample on each pixel, is used in high-quality renderings. Preview renderings, or renderings that don't require calculation of the surface color (for example, depth-only images), could set the shading rate significantly sparser (4.0 or 8.0) and still get an acceptable image.

ShadingInterpolation *style*

> Occasionally, the renderer needs to know a primitive's color at some point between the shading samples. That point is too close to the existing samples to warrant another whole run, so the renderer simply interpolates between the existing values. The string parameter *style* controls the type of interpolation. If *style* is "constant", then the renderer simply reuses one of the neighboring shader samples (creating a small region with constant color). If *style* is "smooth", then the renderer does a bilinear interpolation between the neighboring values to get a smooth approximation of the color. This technique is often called *Gouraud shading*.

3.5.1 Sidedness

As with most graphics APIs, RenderMan's geometric primitives are thin sheets. That is, they are 2D (no thickness) objects that have been placed and generally bent into the third dimension. While it is convenient to think of them as being like sheets of paper floating in 3D, a sheet of paper has one very important property that RenderMan primitives do not have. Paper has two sides. RenderMan primitives have only one.

That is to say, the natural method for defining RenderMan's geometric primitives includes the definition of the surface normal, which points away from the surface perpendicularly. And it points in only one direction, which we call the *front*. The direction that it doesn't point, we call the *back*. Primitives whose front sides are visible from the camera position we call *front facing*, and naturally those whose back sides are visible from the camera position we call *back facing*.

For two reasons, it is common for renderers to care about the difference between back facing and front facing sections of the primitive. First, most shading equations are sensitive to the direction of the surface normal and will generally create black (or otherwise incorrectly shaded) images of any objects that are back facing. This is generally repaired by reversing the direction of the bad normals whenever they are visible (in the Shading Language, this is done by the `faceforward` routine). Second, many objects being modeled are solid objects, completely enclosed with no holes and no interiors visible. It should be obvious that any back facing primitives would be on the far side of the object and as such would never be seen (they will be covered up by front facing primitives on the near side). The renderer can save time by throwing those never-visible primitives away, a process called *backface culling*. However, this should not be done on objects that have holes or are partially transparent, because if we can see "inside" the object, we will intentionally see the back facing primitives in the rear.

For these reasons, the modeler should explicitly state whether an object is intended to be seen from both sides, or only the front. And if only from the front, it is convenient to be able to explicitly state which side *the modeler* considers the front to be! RenderMan has calls that control both of these attributes.

Sides *n*

> Sides is a very simple call. If the integer parameter *n* is 1, the object is one-sided. The renderer can assume that the primitive will be seen only from the front and can backface cull it or any portion of it that is seen from the back. If *n* is 2, the object is two-sided. The renderer must assume it can legally be seen from both sides. The renderer will *not* automatically flip surface normals on the back facing portions of a two-sided primitive—the shader must do this if it is appropriate.

Orientation *direction*

> Orientation is also a very simple call, although many RenderMan users find it very confusing. Given that the standard mathematics of each primitive defines which way the default surface normal will face, Orientation simply controls whether we use that default definition or whether we should instead flip the normal around and "turn the primitive inside out." If *direction* is "outside", the default normal is used, and the primitive is outside out. If *direction* is "inside", the normal is flipped, and the primitive is considered to be inside out.

> Figuring out the standard mathematics of each primitive is the confusing part. This is because the transformation matrix influences the mathematics. Transformation matrices are either *right-handed* or *left-handed*, depending on their data (see Section 2.4.4). Geometric primitives that are created in a

right-handed coordinate system use the "right-hand rule" (sometimes called the *counterclockwise rule*) to find the default ("outside") surface normal. Geometric primitives that are created in a left-handed coordinate system use the "left-hand rule" (also known as the *clockwise rule*) to find it.

ReverseOrientation

ReverseOrientation flips the value of Orientation. It's there because it is sometimes handy for modelers to use.

3.5.2 Renderer Control

In addition to the visual appearance parameters, the RenderMan API provides the opportunity for the modeler (or user) to set various other attributes that control the way that the renderer handles geometric primitives. Some of these attributes control details of advanced rendering features and are described with them in the following sections. Other parameters are very renderer specific—they are passed into the renderer through the generic extension backdoors like Attribute.

GeometricApproximation *type value*

The GeometricApproximation call provides a way for modelers to control the way that the renderer approximates geometric primitives when it tessellates them or otherwise converts them into simpler representations for ease of rendering. The predefined *type* of "flatness" specifies an error tolerance so that tessellations do not deviate from the true surface by more than *value* pixels. Renderers can define additional *type* metrics that apply to their particular algorithm.

Attribute *type parameterlist*

Attribute provides the entry point for renderer-specific data that are potentially different in each of the geometric primitives or individual lights and therefore fall into the category of attributes. For example, both *PRMan* and *BMRT* have attributes that control tessellation styles, set arbitrary limits on various calculations that are theoretically unbounded, determine special light characteristics, and so on. These options are generally very algorithm specific, and as a result renderers tend to have non-overlapping sets. Renderers ignore attributes they do not understand, so it is possible to write RIB files that contain the appropriate sets of parameters for multiple renderers.

ErrorHandler *style*

The ErrorHandler call determines what the renderer should do if it detects an error while reading a scene description or rendering it. There are several choices for *style* that determine how paranoid the renderer should be about various problems, which come in three severities: warnings, which say the renderer found something wrong but tried to correct it, so it may or may not affect the final image; errors, which say the image will probably have clear flaws; and severe errors, where the renderer's internal state is badly trashed, and an image probably cannot even be generated. The exact severity of an individual problem is up to the renderer to determine, of course.

The three built-in error handlers are:
- □ "ignore": ignore all errors, continue to render regardless
- □ "print": print warning and error messages, but continue to render
- □ "abort": print warning messages, but print and terminate on any error

In the C binding, the user can supply an error-handling subroutine that is called when errors are encountered, and this subroutine will then have to make a determination of what to do based on the error's type and severity.

3.6   Lights

Most shaders will not generate a very interesting color in the dark. RenderMan, like all graphics APIs, has virtual light sources that are modeled as objects in the scene. The light sources emit light, which is then reflected toward the camera by the surface shaders on the objects, giving them color.

The RenderMan Interface defines two types of light sources: *point lights* and *area lights*. Point lights usually refer to light sources that emit light from a single point in space; area lights usually refer to light sources that emit light from some or all points in a specific (but finite) region of space. In RenderMan, of course, the exact details of the way that light emanates from a light source, and then interacts with the surface, is under the complete control of the Shading Language shaders that are associated with them. For this reason, it is probably more descriptive to call RenderMan light sources either nongeometric or geometric.

Nongeometric lights are light sources for which there is a single "ray" of light from the light source to any given point on the surface. The origins of the rays of light might not be coincident (since they could be under shader control), but regardless, no geometric primitive shapes are needed in the RIB file to describe the sources of the rays.

LightSource *shadername handle parameterlist*

LightSource creates a nongeometric light source. The exact manner that light is emitted from the light source is described by the Shading Language shader *shadername*. The parameters for the shader are in the *parameterlist*. In order to refer to this specific light source later, the light source is given a unique identifier, the integer *handle*. It is an error to reuse a light handle, because the modeler will lose the ability to refer to the original light source.

In the C binding for RiLightSource, the routine does not take a handle parameter, but instead returns a handle value to the modeling program (which is guaranteed to be unique).

Geometric lights are light sources for which there are multiple rays of light, emanating from independent positions, streaming toward each point on the surface. The easiest way to describe those positions is to associate some geometric shape with the light source. In RenderMan, that geometric shape is specified with normal geometric primitives in the RIB file. Those primitives might be considered to be the actual body of the emissive object, like a light bulb or a light panel.

AreaLightSource *shadername handle parameterlist*

AreaLightSource starts the definition of a geometric (area) light source. The exact manner in which light is emitted from the light source is described by the Shading Language shader *shadername*, but the region of space that will be used to generate the multiple light source emission positions is defined by the standard RenderMan geometric primitives that follow this call. The area light stops accumulating new primitives when a new (or a "null") area light is started or when the current attribute block is ended.

As with LightSource, an AreaLightSource is identified by the integer *handle* in RIB and by the return value of RiAreaLightSource in C.

Not all rendering algorithms can handle area light sources, as computing them with enough visual quality to be believable is a difficult problem. Of the RenderMan renderers, *BMRT* can do so, but *PRMan* cannot. If an area light is requested of *PRMan*, a point light is generated instead, at the origin of the current coordinate system.

3.6.1 Illumination List

Light sources are handled in a slightly more complex manner than you might first guess, for two reasons. First, we would like to place light sources in their "obvious" place in the geometric transformation hierarchy (for example, the headlights of a car would be easiest to describe while we are describing the car's front-end grill area). However, we must abide by the RenderMan requirement that all attributes that affect objects must appear before those objects (so the headlights must be defined before the asphalt road they shine on is defined). This puts significant (and sometimes contradictory) restrictions on the timing of LightSource calls versus geometry in the scene description. Second, because this is computer graphics, we would like some flexibility about which objects are illuminated by which lights. In fact, it is almost required that any subset of the lights in the scene can shine on any subset of the geometric primitives in the scene. In this sense, the light sources that illuminate an object should be part of the visual attributes of that object.

Both of these problems are solved by the concept of an illumination list. The light sources themselves are not attributes of the primitive, they are independent objects in the scene description. However, the graphics state has an attribute that is the list of all lights currently illuminating geometric primitives. This list can be modified as an attribute, adding or deleting lights from the list. Equivalently, you might think of light sources as having an attribute in the graphics state that says whether they are "on" or "off." In either case, because the list is an attribute, pushing the attribute stack allows you to modify the lights temporarily and then restore them to their previous state by popping the stack.

Illuminate *handle state*

> Illuminate turns a light source on or off. The light source to be modified is specified by *handle*, the light source handle that was given to the light source when it was created. *state* is an integer, which is either 1 for on or 0 for off.

A light source is on when it is defined. It then illuminates all subsequent geometric primitives. It can be turned off and back on by using the Illuminate call. When the attribute stack where the light source was created is finally popped, the light source is turned off. However, the light sources themselves are global to the scene—it is only the light list that is an attribute. Therefore, popping the stack does not destroy the light, it only turns it off. Later, it can then be turned back on at any point in the scene description, even outside the hierarchical tree where it was originally defined. This is how we permit lights to illuminate objects outside their hierarchy, such as the car headlights illuminating the road.

Some modeling systems have the idea of "local lights" and "global lights." Local lights are specific to particular objects, whereas global lights are available to shine on any objects. RenderMan doesn't have those specific concepts, as they are subsets of the more flexible illumination lists. Local lights are merely buried in the geometric hierarchy of a particular object and are never turned on for other objects. Global lights are emitted early in the model (usually immediately after WorldBegin, before all of the real geometric primitives) and then are turned on and off as appropriate.

3.7   External Resources

In addition to the scene description, which is provided to the renderer through one of the RenderMan APIs (either C or RIB), the renderer needs access to several types of external data sources in order to complete renderings. These files—texture maps, Shading Language shaders, and RIB archives—are identified in the scene description by a physical or symbolic filename, and the renderer finds and loads them when it needs the data.

3.7.1   Texture Maps

Texture maps are relatively large data files, and it is quite common to use a lot of them in a high-quality scene. Of course, images come in a wide variety of file formats, and not all of these are necessarily appropriate for loading on demand by the renderer. In fact, over the years, computer graphics researchers have sometimes found it valuable to preprocess image data into some prefiltered form (such as *mip-maps*) in order to save computation or speed data access during the rendering phase. *PRMan*, for example, *requires* all image data to be converted into a private format that was specifically designed for fast access and low memory footprint. Similarly, while *BMRT* is able to read ordinary TIFF files directly during rendering, it benefits greatly from converting the file into a mip-map prior to rendering.

The RenderMan Interface provides for the situation where a renderer cannot, or chooses not to, read arbitrary image file formats as textures. There are four entry points for converting "arbitrary" image files into *texture files*, specialized to the particular texturing functions defined in the Shading Language. These functions provide the ability to filter the pixels during this conversion process. Therefore, several of the calls have parameters that specify a filtering function and texture wrapping parameters.

The filter functions for texture are the same ones used by `PixelFilter` and have filter kernel width parameters measured in pixels. Texture wrapping refers to the value that should be returned when the texture is accessed beyond the range of its data (that is, with texture coordinates outside the unit square). The texture's wrap mode can be "black", returning 0 outside of its range; "periodic", repeating (tiling) itself infinitely over the 2D plane; or "clamp", where the edge pixels are copied to cover the plane. The texture filtering code takes the wrapping behavior into account in order to correctly filter the edges of the texture. Both filtering and wrapping are independently controllable in the *s* (horizontal) and *t* (vertical) directions on the texture.

`MakeTexture` *imagename texturename swrap twrap filter swidth twidth parameterlist*

> A simple texture map is an image that is accessed by specifying a 2D rectangle of coordinates on the map. It will typically be a single-channel (monochrome) map or a three-channel or four-channel (color or RGBA) map, although a fancy shader might use the data for something other than simple object color, of course.

`MakeLatLongEnvironment` *imagename texturename filter swidth twidth parameterlist*

> An environment map is an image that is accessed by specifying a direction vector. The map is assumed to wrap around and enclose the origin of the vector, and the value returned is the color where the ray hits the map. A *latitude-longitude* environment map wraps around the origin like a sphere, so

it must wrap periodically in the *s* direction and it "pinches" at the poles in the *t* direction. Typically, painted environment maps will be made in this format.

MakeCubeFaceEnvironment *pximage nximage pyimage nyimage pzimage nzimage texturename fov filter swidth twidth parameterlist*

A *cube-face* environment map wraps around the origin as a box. It requires six input images, one for each face of the box, identified by their axial direction (positive *x*, negative *x*, etc.). Typically, rendered environment maps will be made in this format, by placing the camera in the center and viewing in each direction.

For better filtering, the images can be wider than the standard 90-degree views so that they overlap slightly. The floating point *fov* parameter identifies the field of view of the cameras that rendered the images.

MakeShadow *imagename texturename parameterlist*

A shadow map is an image that contains depth information and is accessed by specifying a position in space. The value returned identifies the occlusion of that position by the data in the map. Typically, the map is a rendered image from the point of view of a light source, and the lookup asks if that position can be seen by the light source or if it is hidden behind some other, closer object. Because it makes no sense to filter depth images, there are no filtering parameters to this particular call.

The shadow map also contains information about the position and parameters of the shadow camera, which are used by the Shading Language shadow call to compute the shadow occlusion of objects in the scene. For this reason, it is not possible to create a shadow map out of any random image, but only from those images that have stored this important camera information with the depth information.

3.7.2   Shaders

Shaders are written in the RenderMan Shading Language. Every renderer that supports the Shading Language has a compiler that converts the Shading Language source code into a form that is more easily read and manipulated by the renderer. The object code of the compile is usually some form of byte code representation, for a virtual machine that is implemented by the renderer (though some renderers may compile to machine code). Shader object code is not generally portable between renderer implementations, but is often portable between machine architectures.

Interestingly, unlike texture maps, the RenderMan Interface does not have an API call for converting Shading Language shader source code into shaders. It is assumed that this process will be done off-line. The names of shaders that are provided in Surface and other calls are symbolic, in that the renderer has some algorithm for finding the right shader object code based on a relatively simple name. Typically, the name refers to the prefix of a filename, where the suffix is known (in *PRMan* it is .slo), and the renderer has some type of search path mechanism for finding the file in the directory structure.

3.7.3   RIB Archive Files

RIB files are referred to as *archive* files in the *RenderMan Interface Specification* document because as metafiles their function was to archive the calls to the C procedural interface. When it was recognized that RIB files might be used as containers of more abstract scene descriptions, rather than merely the log of a session to render a particular frame, some small accommodation was made in the file format for facilitating that.

RIB files may have comments, started by # characters and ending at the following end-of-line. These comments are ignored by the renderer as it is reading the RIB file, but it is possible to put data into these comments that is meaningful to a special RIB parsing program. Such a program could read these comments and act on them in special ways. For this reason, the comments are called *user data records*. Appendix D of the *RenderMan Interface Specification* discusses special data records that can be supplied to a hypothetical "render manager" program. The predefined commands to this program are called *structure comments*, because they mostly deal with nonrendering information that describes the structure of the model that was contained in the RIB file. Such structure comments are denoted by a leading ##. Other comments, random user comments, get a single #.

The C interface has a call for putting such a data record into the scene description (under the assumption that the calls are being recorded in an archive). Moreover, the C interface can read these data records back, giving the application developer a way to put private data into the file and then interpret and act on them when the file is read back in.

RiArchiveRecord(RtToken *type*, char **format*, ...);

>   This call writes arbitrary data into the RIB file. The parameter *type* denotes whether the record is a regular "comment" or a "structure" comment. The rest of the call is a printf-like list of parameters, with a string *format* and any number of required additional parameters.

ReadArchive *filename*

>   The ReadArchive call will read the RIB file *filename*. Each RIB command in the archive will be parsed and executed exactly as if it had been in-line in the referencing RIB file. This is essentially the RIB file equivalent of the C language #include mechanism.

>   In the C API version of this routine, there is a second parameter that is a modeler function that will be called for any RIB user data record or struc-

ture comment found in the file. This routine has the same C prototype as RiArchiveRecord. Supplying such a callback function allows the application program to notice user data records and then execute special behavior based on them while the file is being read.

3.8   Advanced Features

The RenderMan Interface has specific API calls to enable and control many advanced image synthesis features that are important for the highest-quality images, such as those used in feature-film special effects. Some of these features have been part of the computer graphics literature for decades, but RenderMan is still the only graphics API that supports them.

3.8.1   Motion Blur

In any computer-generated animation that is supposed to mesh with live-action photography, or simulate it, one extremely important visual quality is the appearance of motion blur. In order to adequately expose the film, live-action camera shutters are open for a finite length of time, generally on the order of 1/48 of a second per frame. Fast-moving objects leave a distinctive blurry streak across the film. Rendered images that don't simulate this streak appear to strobe because the image appears sharply and crisply at one spot in one frame and then at a different spot in the next frame. Any computer graphics imagery that does not have the same motion blur streak as a real photograph will be instantly recognizable by audiences as "fake." Stop-motion photography had this strobing problem, and when mechanisms for alleviating it (such as motion control cameras and ILM's "go-motion" armatures) were invented in the mid-1970s and early 1980s, the increased realism of miniature photography was stunning.

Specifying motion in a RenderMan scene requires the use of three API calls.

Shutter *opentime closetime*

> Shutter is a camera option; that is, it must be called during the option phase of the scene description while other parameters of the camera (such as its position) are being set up. The two floating point parameters specify the time that the virtual camera's shutter should open and close. If *opentime* and *closetime* are identical (or if no Shutter statement was found at all), the rendered image will have no motion blur.

> The scale of the times is arbitrary—users can choose to measure time in frames, seconds from the beginning of the scene, minutes from the beginning of the movie, or any other metric that is convenient for the modeling system. The choice only matters for one reason: MotionBegin calls have times with the same time scale, as does the Shading Language global variable time.

MotionBegin *times*

> MotionBegin initiates a *motion block*. A motion block contains two or more RI API calls that are *time samples*—versions of the same call at different points in time. The parameter *times* is an array of floating point numbers that specifies the times that each of the following time samples correspond to. Naturally, the number of samples in the block must match the number of values in the *times* array.

MotionEnd

> The MotionEnd call ends a motion block. The renderer will validate that the renderer can correctly interpolate (through time) between the motion samples provided. If there are errors in the block, such as incorrect matching of API calls or topological inconsistencies, the entire motion block will typically be discarded.

For example, a sphere that is inflating from a radius of 1.0 to a radius of 1.5 can be specified with the following snippet of RIB:

```
MotionBegin [ 0.0 1.0 ]
Sphere 1 -1 1 360
Sphere 1.5 -1.5 1.5 360
MotionEnd
```

RenderMan is very particular about the data that appears in a motion block. In particular, each time sample

- must be the same API call
- must be on the short list of API calls that are amenable to motion blur
- must differ only in parameter data that can be interpolated through time

This is because the renderer must be able to generate interpolated versions of the calls at any other point in time that it needs data. Not all API calls and not all parameters can be interpolated, so time samples are restricted to the set that can.

PRMan and *BMRT* implement motion blur on slightly different sets of data. Both can handle two-sample motion blur of all transformation calls (such as Rotate, Translate, or ConcatTransform). *PRMan* can motion blur primitive geometry calls (excepting Procedural) quite robustly, though *BMRT*'s ability to do so is restricted to only certain primitives. Both renderers also require that any primitive geometry so blurred must be "topologically equivalent." That is, the control points of the primitives can move, but the number of polyhedral facets, edge connectivity, or any other values that affect the topology of the primitive are not allowed to change between samples.

In addition, recent versions of *PRMan* permit motion blocks that are slightly more general, such as those with more than two time samples in the block or those with time samples that do not occur exactly at shutter times. *PRMan* also permits geometry to be created (or destroyed) during the frame time so that it can appear to "blink in" (or out). The instantaneous occurrence of a transformation is not permitted because it implies that objects have discontinuous motion.

Neither *PRMan* nor *BMRT* currently support motion blur on shading parameters, although this will probably be implemented by one or both eventually. This has three important consequences. First, shading and other attribute calls are not on the "short list" of motion-blurrable API calls. There is no way to specify that a primitive changes color during a frame. Second, as objects move, they do not correctly respond to the changing lighting environment around them. In *PRMan*, shading samples occur at some particular time (depending on several factors), and the moving geometry that inherits this color "drags" the color across the screen as it moves. If an object leaves a shadow, for example, the object drags its darkened in-shadow color with it out of the shadow. Note that *BMRT* only suffers this particular problem on the radiosity pass, not on the ray tracing pass. Third, as objects move, the lighting changes that they impart to neighboring objects do not occur. For example, the shadows cast by a moving object do not move because the shadow receiver is not sampling the shadow through time.

3.8.2   Depth of Field

Another effect that real cameras exhibit, but that most computer graphics cameras do not, is *depth of field*. Depth of field describes the photographic effect that occurs when a camera focuses at a particular distance. Objects that are nearly that distance from the camera appear to be in focus, while objects that are far from that distance are blurry. Most computer graphics cameras do not simulate out-of-focus objects, and this is equivalent to a pinhole camera, which has infinite depth of field (all distances are in focus, so there are no out-of-focus distances).

The depth of the field depends on three parameters: the length of the lens, the distance at which the camera is focused, and the diameter of the aperture, ex-pressed as its *f*-stop. RenderMan allows these camera parameters to be specified as part of the scene description, and RenderMan renderers then simulate the ap-propriate amount of blurriness for the objects in the scene.

DepthOfField *fstop focallength focaldistance*

The DepthOfField call is a camera option that sets the parameters of the virtual camera that determine the camera's depth of field. The *focallength* specifies the fundamental length of the camera's lens, which for most modern physical cameras is in the range of 30 to 300 mm. The *focaldistance* speci-fies the distance at which the camera is focused. Both of these distances are measured in the units of "camera" space. For example, if one unit in the "cam-era" coordinate system is 1 meter, then a reasonable number for *focallength* is 0.055, and *focaldistance* might be 5.0. On the other hand, if one unit in the "camera" coordinate system is 1 inch, a reasonable number for *focallength* is more like 2.2. The *fstop* specifies the camera's aperture f-stop in the normal way (a value between 2.8 and 16 is typical).

In order to turn off depth of field calculations, we specify the camera to be a pinhole camera. This is the default. A pinhole camera has an infinite f-stop and consequently has infinite depth of field. This can be done by specifying infinity for *fstop*, in which case the values of the other parameters are irrelevant. As a shortcut, specifying DepthOfField with no parameters will do the same thing.

Because depth of field requires a large amount of blurring of objects that are significantly out of focus, the stochastic sampling algorithms that compute it usually require extremely large numbers of samples in order to create an image with acceptable amounts of grain and noise. For this reason, accurate depth of field is quite expensive to compute. On the other hand, simple approximations of depth of field can be made with blurred composited layers. Although there are limits to the generality and the fidelity of this $2\frac{1}{2}$-D approximation, it is so much faster that it is often used instead of rendered DepthOfField.

3.9   The Rest of the Story

There are some options and attributes defined in the *RenderMan Interface Specification* that, with 20/20 hindsight, we think should not have been there and are rarely used. Perhaps they have never been implemented by any renderer, or perhaps they have been subsumed by more powerful mechanisms provided in a different part of the interface. Without spending too much space going into the details of unimportant calls, we will simply mention that the API has these calls and refer the curious to the *RenderMan Interface Specification* and/or renderer documentation to learn the details. These calls include

- TextureCoordinates: sets default texture coordinates on patches
- Deformation: sets the deformation shader to be used
- Perspective: pushes a perspective matrix onto the modeling transformation
- Exterior: sets the volume shader to be used on reflected rays
- Interior: sets the volume shader to be used on refracted rays
- Bound: provides a bounding box for subsequent primitives
- MakeBump: creates bump texture maps
- ObjectBegin/ObjectEnd: creates a piece of reusable geometry
- PixelVariance: provides an error bound for sampling algorithms that can compute error metrics
- Imager: sets the imager shader to be used on pixels prior to display
- RiTransformPoints: a C-only call that transforms data between named coordinate systems

4 Geometric Primitives

Probably the most important RI API calls are the ones that draw geometric primitives. The original specification had a wide variety of geometric primitives, and over the years, renderers have added new geometric primitive types to meet the evolving needs of the users.

Many graphics APIs support only a small number of "fundamental" primitives, such as triangle strips or perhaps polyhedra, under the assumptions that (1) any other primitive can always be tessellated into or approximated by these, and (2) it simplifies the renderer to optimize it for a few well-understood primitives. These primitives, which are chosen for their ease of rendering, might be considered to be "drawing" primitives.

RenderMan, on the other hand, supports a large variety of high-level curved-surface primitives, which we consider to be "modeling" primitives. It does so for three reasons. First, high-level primitives are a very compact way to represent an object. Tessellating primitives into large collections of simpler ones will clearly increase the size of the geometric database, and usually dramatically so. Second, they are more appropriate for a photorealistic renderer. Tessellated primitives usually show artifacts such as polygonal silhouettes, which need to be avoided in high-quality renderings. Third, a renderer with a different algorithm might find them significantly more efficient to process. A ray tracer, for example, can make short work of a single sphere, but it takes a lot of extra (wasted) computation to handle a tessellated version.

Of course, RenderMan doesn't try to implement every possible geometric primitive that has ever been suggested in the computer graphics literature. It also relies on the modeler approximating any other primitive types with some from the basic set. But the basic set has enough variety and spans enough computational geometry to handle almost anything.

4.1   Primitive Variables

On a few occasions now we have alluded to *primitive variables*, which are attached to the geometric primitives. Primitive variables refer to the geometric, appearance, and other data that the modeler provides on the parameter list of each geometric primitive.

As we will soon see, nearly every primitive is made up of vertices that are combined into strings of edges that outline facets, which are then joined to form the geometric primitive. The minimal data necessary to describe the shape and position of each geometric primitive is the vertex data itself. This is provided (on vertex-based primitives) with a parameter list entry for the variable "P" (or in some cases "Pw"). It is common for simple graphics APIs to provide for additional visual information at each vertex—for example, specifying the surface color at each vertex or putting a Phong normal vector at each vertex. The parameter list mechanism provides this functionality easily, as well, by specifying variables such as "Cs" or "N" for the primitive. Table 4.1 lists several of the useful predefined primitive variables that are commonly used.

RenderMan generalizes this simple concept in two powerful ways. First, RenderMan provides that *any* visual attribute or geometric parameter that might be interesting to the shaders on that surface can be provided on each vertex. This includes a relatively rich set of data that becomes the global variables of the shaders (see Chapter 7). But more powerfully and uniquely, it includes any or all of the parameters to the shaders themselves. This means that shader writers can define arbitrary interesting data as being parameters to the shader (perhaps geometric information, perhaps a new surface property, perhaps something completely unique),

Table 4.1: Commonly used primitive variables.

Name	Declared type	Description
"P"	vertex point	Position
"Pw"	vertex hpoint	Position in homogeneous coordinates
"N"	varying normal	Phong shading normals
"Cs"	varying color	Surface color (overrides RIB Color)
"Os"	varying color	Surface opacity (overrides RIB Opacity)
"st"	varying float[2]	Texture coordinates

and instruct the modeler to attach that data to the primitives—extending the attribute set of the renderer *at runtime*. Because primitive variables are for the benefit of the shaders that are attached to objects, they can be created using any data type that the Shading Language accepts.

Second, RenderMan provides that this data attached to the primitives can have a variety of different granularities, so data that smoothly changes over the surface can be described as easily as data that is identical over the whole surface. There are four such granularities, known as *storage classes*. Some RenderMan geometric primitives are individual simple primitives, whereas others are collections of other primitives connected in some way. The number of data values that is required for a particular class is dependent on the type and topology of the primitive.

- vertex: takes data at every primitive vertex. There are as many data values in a vertex variable as there are in the position variable "P", and the data is interpolated using the same geometric equations as "P" (bicubicly, with the basis matrix, etc.).
- varying: takes data at every parametric corner. For simple parametric primitives, there are obviously four such corners. For patch meshes and other collective parametric primitives, the number of corners is data dependent. varying data is interpolated bilinearly in the parametric space of the primitive.
- uniform: takes data at every facet and is identical everywhere on the facet. For individual primitives, there is a single facet, but for polyhedra and other collective primitives, the number of facets is data dependent.
- constant: takes exactly one piece of data, no matter what type of primitive, and so is identical everywhere on the primitive.

The formulas for determining exactly how many data values are required for each class on each primitive type is therefore dependent on the topology of the primitive, and will be mentioned with the primitives as they are discussed.

Notice that when primitive variable data is accessed inside the Shading Language, there are only two data classes, uniform and varying. All constant and uniform RI primitive variables become uniform Shading Language variables. All varying and vertex RI primitive variables become varying Shading Language variables.

When a primitive variable of type "point", "vector", "normal", or "matrix" (any of the geometric data types) is supplied for a primitive, the data are assumed to be expressed in the current coordinate system—that is, in "object" coordinates. However, as we will see in Section 7.2.3, shader calculations do not happen in "object" space. Therefore, there is an implied coordinate transformation that brings this "object" space data into the Shading Language's "current" space before the shader starts execution.

4.2   Parametric Quadrics

The simplest primitives to describe are the seven quadrics that are defined by RI. Each quadric

- is defined parametrically, using the trigonometric equation that sweeps it out as a function of two angles
- is created by sweeping a curve around the z-axis in its local coordinate system, so z is always "up." Sweeping a curve by a negative angle creates a quadric that is inside out
- has simple controls for sweeping a partial quadric, using ranges of z or the parametric angles
- is placed by using a transformation matrix, since it has no built-in translation or rotational controls
- has a parameter list that is used solely for applying primitive variables, and so does not affect the shape of the primitive;
- requires four data values for any vertex or varying parameter, one for each parametric corner, and one data value for any uniform or constant parameter.

The seven quadric primitives are illustrated in Figures 4.1 and 4.2. In each of the following descriptions, the parameters are floating-point values (with the exception of *point1* and *point2*, which are obviously points). Angles are all measured in degrees.

Sphere *radius zmin zmax sweepangle parameterlist*

Sphere creates a partial or full sphere, centered at the origin, with radius *radius*. *zmin* and *zmax* cut the top and bottom off of the sphere to make ring-like primitives. As with all the quadrics, *sweepangle* (denoted θ_{max} in this chapter's figures) controls the maximum angle of sweep of the primitive around the z-axis. With these controls, hemispheres can be made two different ways (around the z-axis or around the y-axis).

Cylinder *radius zmin zmax sweepangle parameterlist*

Cylinder creates a partial or full cylinder with radius *radius*. Because *zmin* and *zmax* are arbitrary, it can be slid up and down the z-axis to match the location of other quadric primitives.

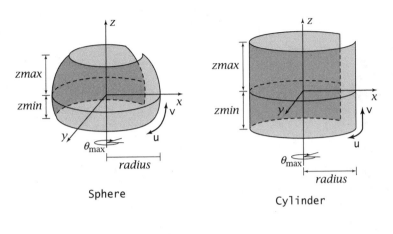

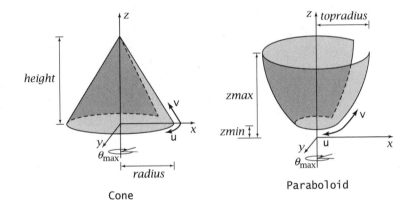

Figure 4.1 The parametric quadrics (part I).

Cone *height radius sweepangle parameterlist*

Cone creates a cone that is closed at the top (at the position (0.0, 0.0, *height*)) and open with radius *radius* at the bottom (on the *x-y* plane).

Paraboloid *topradius zmin zmax sweepangle parameterlist*

Paraboloid creates a partial paraboloid, swept around the *z*-axis. The paraboloid is defined as having its minimum at the origin and has radius *topradius* at height *zmax*, and only the portions above *zmin* are drawn.

Hyperboloid *point1 point2 sweepangle parameterlist*

The Hyperboloid (of one sheet) is perhaps the hardest quadric to visualize. It is created by rotating a line segment around the *z*-axis, where the segment is

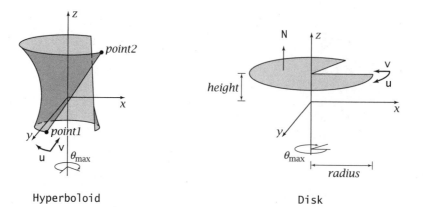

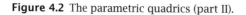

Torus

Figure 4.2 The parametric quadrics (part II).

defined by the two points *point1* and *point2*. If *point1* and *point2* are not both in an axial plane, it will generate a cooling-tower-like shape.

The hyperboloid is actually quite a flexible superset of some of the other primitives. For example, if these points have the same x- and y-coordinates, and differ only in z, this will create a cylinder. If the points both have the same z-coordinate, it will make a planar ring (a disk with a hole cut out of the center). If the points are placed so that they have the same angle with the x-axis (in other words, are on the same radial line if looked at from the top), they will create a truncated cone. In truth, some of these special cases are more useful for geometric modeling than the general case that creates the "familiar" hyperboloid shape.

Disk *height radius sweepangle parameterlist*

The Disk primitive is usually used to cap the tops or bottoms of partial quadrics such as cylinders, hemispheres, or paraboloids. For this reason, it has a *height* control, which allows it to be slid up and down the *z*-axis, but it stays parallel to the *x-y* plane. Partial sweeps look like pie segments.

Torus *majorradius minorradius phimin phimax sweepangle parameterlist*

Torus creates the quartic "donut" surface (so it isn't a quadric, but it is defined with two angles, so we let it go). The cross section of a torus is a circle of radius *minorradius* on the *x-z* plane, and the angles *phimin* and *phimax* define the arc of that circle. It will be swept around the *z*-axis at a distance of *majorradius* to create the torus. Thus, *majorradius* + *minorradius* defines the outside radius of the torus (its maximum size), while *majorradius* − *minorradius* defines the radius of the hole.

4.3   Polygons and Polyhedra

Compared to other graphics APIs, RenderMan appears to have less support for polygons and polyhedra. This is somewhat true because the RenderMan API was clearly optimized for parametric curved surfaces, and polygons are neither parametric nor curved. However, the major difference is that most graphics APIs consider polygons to be drawing primitives, whereas RenderMan considers polygons to be modeling primitives. As a result, those other graphics APIs have many variants of the same primitive based on hardware drawing efficiency constraints (for example, triangles, triangle meshes, triangle strips, etc.) or coloring parameters. RenderMan has only four polygon primitives, based on one modeling constraint and one packaging efficiency.

RenderMan recognizes that there are two types of polygons—convex and concave. Convex polygons are loosely defined as polygons where every vertex can be connected to every other vertex by a line that stays within the polygon. In other words, they don't have any indentations or holes. Concave polygons do. This difference matters because renderers can usually make short work of convex polygons by chopping them quickly into almost random small pieces, whereas concave polygons require careful and thoughtful segmentation in order to be cut into smaller chunks without losing or adding surface area. In either case, polygons must be planar in order to render correctly in all renderers at all viewing angles.

RenderMan calls convex polygons *polygons* and concave polygons *general polygons*. General polygons also include any polygons that have holes in them. Therefore, the description of a general polygon is a list of *loops*, the first of which specifies the outside edge of the polygon and all the rest describe holes cut out of the interior.[1] It is not an error to call a polygon "general" when it is actually not, just to be cautious. It is simply a little less efficient. However, if a general polygon is called

---

[1] Some modeling packages accept general polygons that have multiple disconnected "islands" as a single polygon. RenderMan does not permit this and considers these islands to be separate polygons.

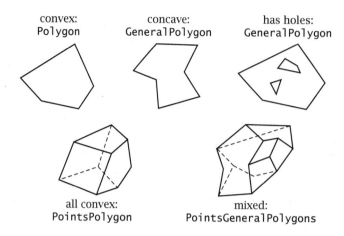

convex:
Polygon

concave:
GeneralPolygon

has holes:
GeneralPolygon

all convex:
PointsPolygon

mixed:
PointsGeneralPolygons

Figure 4.3 Examples of each of the four types of polygonal primitives.

convex, the renderer will probably draw it incorrectly (filling in holes or concavities, for example).

RenderMan also provides two packaging styles—individual polygons and polyhedra. Polyhedra are sets of polygons that share vertices, which makes for efficient database description because defining each such polygon individually would require large numbers of redundant vertex descriptions to be passed through. Polyhedra are described by first specifying all of the vertices and then specifying which vertices are linked together in which order to create each individual polyhedral face. Figure 4.3 shows examples of various types of polygonal primitives.

Polygons do not have a specific parameter that holds the positions of each vertex. Instead, every polygon primitive has a parameter list, which contains the vertex data. The primitive variable "P" denotes vertex information, an array of floating-point numbers that are the 3D vertex coordinates. For example, a triangle would have a "P" array with nine floating-point numbers.

Section 4.1 discussed the fact that additional data, known as primitive variables, can be attached to the vertices of polygons and other primitives. For every polygon type, primitive variables of type "vertex" and "varying" occur with the same frequency—one per polygon vertex. Primitive variables of type "uniform" happen once per facet—that is, exactly once on individual polygons and once per polyhedral face on polyhedra. Naturally, primitive variables of type "constant" appear exactly once regardless of primitive type.

The single onus that the other parameter list values can place on the geometric description of polygonal primitives concerns vertex uniqueness. A vertex is "shared" in a polygon only if all of the values associated with that vertex are identical. If a vertex has to have two different values for any parameter (say, color), depending on which of two faces it is part of, then those two faces don't actually share a common vertex, but have "different but coincident" vertices, and those vertices must be specified separately.

Polygon *parameterlist*

Polygon creates an individual convex polygon, with any number of vertices.

GeneralPolygon *loopverts parameterlist*

GeneralPolygon creates an individual concave polygon (or polygon with holes). The parameter *loopverts* is an array of integers that specifies how many vertices make up each loop of the general polygon. General polygons that are concave but have no holes would have just one loop, so the *loopverts* array would have one entry.

PointsPolygons *nverts vertids parameterlist*

PointsPolygons creates a polyhedron made up of many convex polygons. The parameter *nverts* is an array of integers that specifies how many vertices make up each polyhedral face. For example, a cube would have six entries, all saying 4.

The parameter *vertids* is a long array of integers that specifies the index number of the vertices that are connected to create each of the faces. Its length is equal to the sum of all the entries in the *nverts* array. In the cube example, it would have 24 entries, the first four listing the vertices in order for the top face, then four listing the vertices for a side, and so on. Vertex indices start at 0, which specifies the first vertex in the "P" array.

PointsGeneralPolygons *nloops loopverts vertids parameterlist*

PointsGeneralPolygons is the most complex and confusing of the four polygon calls because it is the superset of all of them. It creates a polyhedron made up of many general polygons, each with potentially several loops describing its holes. The parameter *nloops* is an array of integers that describes, for each general polygon face of the polyhedron, how many loops that face has. It is not uncommon for this array to be all 1s, specifying a polyhedron made of concave polygons that have no holes. The parameter *loopverts* is an array of integers that describes how many vertices are in each loop. Its length is obviously the sum of all the values in *nloops*.

The parameter *vertids* is a long array of integers that specifies the index number of each of the vertices that make up each loop. Its length is the sum of all the values in the *loopverts* array. As before, vertex indices start at 0.

Notice that for the two polyhedron primitives, the indirection provided by the vertex indices means that the order of the vertices in the "P" array is not critical. In fact, even the number of values in the "P" array is not critical. If some vertices are not referenced, there is no harm done, just a little database inefficiency.

4.4   Parametric Patches

The workhorse primitives of most RenderMan scenes are the parametric patch primitives. These primitives are topologically rectangular (they have four sides), and the two pairs of opposite sides are called their *parametric directions*, denoted *u* and *v*. Patches are curved, so they are useful in photorealistic renderings where they need to be seen at a wide range of sizes with no polygonal approximation artifacts. They can be connected with smooth continuity, so they are useful for approximating other primitives that RenderMan does not support directly, such as surfaces of revolution. They have easy-to-understand rectangular parametric spaces, so they are relatively intuitive to texture map.

Although there is a large set of potential choices for patch primitives, RenderMan has chosen three relatively general primitives that span a large range of functionality: bilinear patches, bicubic patches, and non-uniform rational B-splines (NURBS, discussed in the next section). Bilinear patches are quadrilaterals, where each edge is a straight line, but the patch is a smooth curved surface that connects the edges. It is an example of a ruled surface, so named because it can be created by sweeping a straight-edged "ruler." The set of points on the surface with one parametric coordinate identical is always a straight line.

Bicubic patches have cubic curves on each edge. Cubic curves can be characterized by their *basis function*. Cubic basis functions are equations that determine the shape of the curve, using four control points as parameters. Geometrically, some basis functions use their control points as locations; others use their control points as tangent directions. There are a wide variety of cubic basis functions available (Farin, 1990), each customized to manipulating the curve in a particular way. RenderMan has several common basis functions built in and also provides the capability for the modeler to define its own basis functions.

As with polygons, the vertex (also called *control point*) information is passed in an array in the parameter list. Patches can take two types of control-point data: standard 3D vertices, denoted by "P"; and rational or homogeneous 4D vertices, denoted by "Pw". This control-point information is used according to the basis function of the patch.

Basis *ubasis ustep vbasis vstep*

> Basis specifies the two cubic basis functions (one for each parameteric direction) that will be used to create bicubic Patch and PatchMesh primitives. The *ubasis* and *vbasis* parameters can be either a string, identifying one of the standard built-in basis functions, or can be a 16-element floating-point array, specifying the basis function in matrix notation. RenderMan's built-in set of basis functions include "bezier", "bspline", "catmull-rom", and "hermite".

> Every cubic basis function has a *step* value associated with it for use by the PatchMesh primitive. It specifies how many control points should be skipped to go from the first patch in a mesh to the second patch in the mesh, and

so on. The required basis steps for the standard bases are: three for Bezier, two for Hermite, and one for B-spline and Catmull-Rom. This means, for example, that a patch mesh with two Bezier patches in the u direction would have seven control points in that direction. A patch mesh with two B-spline patches would have only five control points in that direction. The designers of other basis matrices must determine the appropriate step value based on the mathematical details of the particular matrices.

Patch *type parameterlist*

Patch defines an individual parametric patch primitive. If *type* is "bilinear", the 2×2 control points define a bilinear patch. If *type* is "bicubic", the 4×4 control points define a bicubic patch, according to the basis functions specified by the preceding Basis call. The 16 control points are specified in *u*-major order; that is, the point at $(u, v) = (0, 0)$ first, $(1, 0)$ fourth, $(0, 0.25)$ fifth, and $(1, 1)$ last.

PatchMesh *type nu uwrap nv vwrap parameterlist*

PatchMesh creates a rectangular mesh of patches. Like a polyhedron, the patch mesh is more compact than a series of patches because it shares vertices. Patch meshes can be "bilinear" or "bicubic" depending on their *type*. *nu* and *nv* specify the number of control points in the u and v directions, respectively. Bicubic meshes use the basis functions and basis step values specified by the preceding Basis call, so the number of control points must be appropriate according to those values.

In addition, patch meshes can *wrap*. This means that they are connected together in one parametric direction or another, creating a cylinder, or even in both, creating a torus. This means that the mesh uses some control points from the "end of the line" followed by some control points from the "beginning of the line" to create a patch that connects the end to the beginning. If the *uwrap* or *vwrap* parameters are "periodic", they have this behavior in the respective parametric direction. If they are "nonperiodic", they do not.

When specifying primitive variables on bilinear or bicubic patches, variables of type "vertex" have the same frequency as the control points, 4 on bilinear and 16 on bicubic patches. Primitive variables of type "varying" occur at the parametric corners, so require 4 values on any patch. Primitive variables of type "uniform" or "constant" occur exactly once on a patch.

The situation with patch meshes is a bit more complex, for two reasons. First, there are many interior parametric corners (at the edges of each individual patch in the mesh). Second, the wrapping behavior determines the number of patches that the mesh has in each parametric direction. Because "uniform" variables occur once per patch, and "varying" variables occur once per parametric corner, the equations for computing the appropriate numbers for a given patch mesh are somewhat

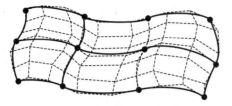

10 × 7 aperiodic Bezier bicubic patch mesh
3 × 2 subpatches
4 × 3 `varying` variable positions

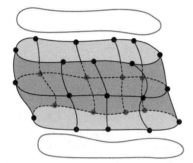

9 × 5 *U*-periodic Catmull-Rom bicubic patch mesh
9 × 2 subpatches
9 × 3 `varying` variable positions

Figure 4.4 Typical patch mesh primitives.

complex. However, as Figure 4.4 shows, it is not that difficult to understand the intent. The number of patches, and the number of varying data items, in the *u* parametric direction is

$$nupatches = \begin{cases} nu - 1 & \text{for nonperiodic bilinear meshes} \\ nu & \text{for periodic bilinear meshes} \\ \left(\frac{nu-4}{ustep}\right) + 1 & \text{for nonperiodic bicubic meshes} \\ \frac{nu}{ustep} & \text{for periodic bicubic meshes} \end{cases}$$

$$nuvarying = \begin{cases} nupatches + 1 & \text{for nonperiodic meshes} \\ nupatches & \text{for periodic meshes} \end{cases}$$

And similarly for the *v* direction. So the total number of data values on the whole mesh for variables of type "vertex" is *nu · nv*. The number of data values for variables of type "varying" is *nuvarying · nvvarying*. The number of data values for variables of type "uniform" is *nupatches · nvpatches*. There is always exactly one data value for any variable of type "constant". Whew!

4.5   NURBS

The most general type of parametric patch, and certainly the most complex, is the
NuPatch, RenderMan's version of the nonuniform rational B-spline patch or *NURBS*
patch.[2] A nu-patch is similar to a patch mesh, in that it has parametric curves in
each direction, which create a rectangular array of individual subpatches. However,
the mathematical equations that generate nu-patches are generalized over standard
patches to give more descriptive power and more detailed control of the shape of
the primitive.

4.5.1   NURBS Curves

Like B-spline curves, NURBS curves are parametric curves that are specified with
control points. The NURBS curves are divided into segments, with each segment
defined by a few of the control points. The control points overlap with a "step" of
one, meaning that adding one more control point to the list adds one more segment
to the curve.

The differentiating characteristic of a NURBS curve is the *knot vector*. The knot
vector is a nondecreasing series of numbers that controls the basis functions of
the curve, just as the basis matrix did for the cubic curves described previously.
The basis functions determine how much importance each of the control points
has in specifying the position of the curve. For example, in a Bezier cubic curve, the
curve passes through the first and fourth control point, whereas in a B-spline cubic
curve the curve only passes near them. In addition, the knot vector also controls the
parameterization of the curve, so curves that are geometrically identical can have
different parametric coordinates. For example, three typical knot vectors might be

$$(-3, -2, -1, 0, 1, 2, 3)$$
$$(0, 0, 0, 1, 1, 1)$$
$$(\frac{-1}{2}, \frac{-1}{2}, 0, \frac{1}{2}, 1, \frac{3}{2}, \frac{3}{2})$$

In the use of NURBS curves, one type of knot vector stands out as particularly
interesting. Any knot vector that is an increasing series of consecutive integers is
known as a *uniform knot vector*. It is notable because NURBS curves that use a uniform knot vector are the standard B-spline-basis curves with which we are already
familiar. Various other special forms of knot vectors are of interest as well, because
the knot vector can create the other familiar basis functions such as Bezier basis.
The more complex *nonuniform knot vectors,* from whence the NURBS gets its name,

---

[2] The word *NURBS* is commonly used as a singular adjective and as a plural noun—"a NURBS curve"
versus "NURBS are confusing."

generalize the basis functions so that individual control points can have Bezier-like qualities, or B-spline-like qualities, or various other styles, all within the same curve.

It turns out that the values in the knot vector can be uniformly offset or scaled without changing the curve geometrically. The only change in the curve is that the parametric coordinates of every point on the curve will be offset or scaled by the same amount. This means that a knot vector that is an increasing series of multiples of any number is uniform, too. We can use this feature to reparameterize a curve that used to run from $u = 0$ to $u = 5$ into a curve that runs from $u = -1$ to $u = 1$, if that turns out to be useful for any reason.

The second generalization of the NURBS curve over a standard cubic curve is the *degree* of the curve. The degree refers to the polynomial complexity of the curve's equation. A cubic curve, by definition, has degree three. This means that the equation for the curve includes a u^3 term somewhere and that this is the highest power of u that appears. A linear curve has degree one. RenderMan's NURBS curve can have any degree desired, so, for example, creating quadratic curves or quartic curves is easy.

Actually though, in RenderMan, we specify curves by their *order*, which is just the degree plus 1 (cubic curves are order 4). There is no additional complexity, no subtle cases, it's just a terminology thing. The order identifies how many control points it takes to make one segment. A cubic curve requires four control points. It also identifies how many knots are necessary to make a segment, that being $2 \cdot order$. As mentioned earlier, adding a segment to a NURBS curve requires adding one control vertex, and it also requires adding one knot. Therefore, the number of knots required to specify a curve is *ncvs* + *order*.

A key factor in the way that knot values are interpreted is called the *multiplicity* of the knot. In any nondecreasing knot sequence, several knots in a row might have the same value. This causes discontinuities in the curve description. A NURBS curve is $C^{degree-1}$ continuous at its normal knot values (e.g., a cubic NURBS curve is C^2 continuous at normal knots). If a knot value appears twice (doubled, or multiplicity 2), then one level of continuity vanishes, and a tripled knot makes two levels of continuity vanish. A cubic curve is only C^1 at doubled knots and C^0 (has a cusp) at tripled knots.

The final component of the name NURBS is *rational*. This means that the control points of the NURBS curve are homogeneous points, with four components. As with other homogeneous coordinate mathematics in computer graphics, this means that the parametric equations create functions to compute x, y, z, and the homogeneous coordinate w, and that at any place in the geometric pipeline when true 3D positions are required, x, y, and z are each divided by w to get those values. If the homogeneous coordinates of all of the control points are 1, the curve is called *polynomial*, and the w components of all of the other calculations are also 1. This means we can obviously ignore the w divide and can actually ignore the w component entirely. In RenderMan, nu-patches, standard patches, and patch meshes can

all have rational homogeneous coordinates for their control points, which is why
we don't single out nu-patches as "nur-patches."

4.5.2   NURBS Patches

RenderMan's nu-patches (NURBS) are relatively standard as far as CAD/CAE geometric modeling descriptions go. They are based on the NURBS support of PHIGS+,
which in turn is extremely similar to those in IGES and STEP, the main international
standards for NURBS.

Nu-patches can be any order in the u and v parametric directions, not necessarily
the same, and any uniform or nonuniform knot vector is acceptable. Some packages
enforce limits on the multiplicity of knots, because it makes little sense to have knot
multiplicity greater than the order, but RenderMan doesn't enforce that particular
restriction (it just skips the empty disconnected sections). Nu-patches can also
specify parametric clipping values, which allows the ends of the nu-patch to be
trimmed off without having to remodel it. It is unclear why this is important, but
we just go along with it.

NuPatch *nucvs uorder uknot umin umax nvcvs vorder vknot vmin vmax*

> The NuPatch call creates a nu-patch (also known as a NURBS patch). There are
> five parameters that control each parametric direction of the nu-patch: the
> parameters *nucvs* and *nvcvs* are integers that identify the number of control
> points in each direction; *uorder* and *vorder* are integers that specify the order
> of the NURBS curves in each direction; *uknot* and *vknot* are the floating-point
> arrays that contain the knot vectors in each parametric direction. The knot
> vectors must obey the standard rules of being nondecreasing sequences, and
> each is *ncvs* + *order* in length. The parameters *min* and *max* clip the nu-
> patch to the parametric range [*min, max*] in each parametric direction. The
> math requires that this range not extend outside of the range *knot*[*order* − 1]
> to *knot*[*ncvs*].

For specifying primitive variables, nu-patches are handled as though they were
nonperiodic B-spline patch meshes. The key is that the number of segments in each
NURBS curve is *ncvs* − *order* + 1. Multiplying values for the two parametric curves
together gets the number of "subpatches" in the nu-patch. For primitive variables of
class "vertex", there are *nucvs* · *nvcvs* data items. For primitive variables of class
"varying", there is one data value per segment corner, which is (*nusegments* + 1) ·
(*nvsegments* + 1) values. For primitive variables of class "uniform", there is one
data value per segment, or *nusegments* · *nvsegments* values. For primitive variables
of class "constant", there is exactly one data value.

Two good books for understanding the details of NURBS are Piegl and Tiller's *The NURBS Book* and Farin's *NURB Curves and Surfaces*. In the terminology of Piegl's book, our *ncvs* is $n + 1$, *order* is $p + 1$, and *nknots* is $m + 1$.

4.5.3   Trim Curves

RenderMan supports *trim curves*, which are NURBS curves drawn in the parameter space of a nu-patch, which "cuts a hole" in the surface. This is typically used for "trimming" the edges of the patch so that it doesn't have a rectangular shape but still maintains a rectangular parametric coordinate system (for the convenience of texturing and other parametric operations). One example of this is when two NURBS patches intersect to form a joint. It is rarely the case that they join at a nice clean isoparametric line on both of the patches. Instead, each NURBS patch is trimmed at the line of intersection. Notice that trim curves are defined in the parameter space of the patch, not in 3D. This make some uses of trim curves more convenient and makes other uses more difficult. Trim curves operate *only* on NuPatch primitives. If quadrics, patch meshes, or other primitives need to be trimmed, they must first be reformulated as nu-patches.

Trim curves resemble GeneralPolygons in the way that they are defined. The trim "curve" is actually a set of loops, and each loop is a series of NURBS edge curves, connected head-to-tail, which must be explicitly closed (e.g., by repeating vertices). A trimming loop draws a line on the surface.

The *RenderMan Interface Specification* says that the part of the surface that is "kept" and the part that is "thrown away" are dependent on the direction that the loop is wound. But both *PRMan* and *BMRT* simply perform a "crossing" test, without regard to the actual directions of the loops. The inside or outside of the trim region to be kept or thrown away can be selected with Attribute "trimcurve" ["inside"] or Attribute "trimcurve" ["outside"]. The default is "inside", indicating that the renderer should keep the part of the patch on the *inside* of the trim curve and throw away the part of the patch on the *outside* of the trim curve (obviously, "outside" keeps the outside and throws away the inside of the trim region).

Trim curves are attributes in the hierarchical graphics state. This means that multiple nu-patch primitives can be trimmed with the same curve—for example, if it is valuable to rubber-stamp a large number of identically shaped items. Removing the trim curve from the state can be done by AttributeEnd, or by specifying a new TrimCurve with 0 loops.

TrimCurve *nloops ncurves order knot min max n u v w*

> The TrimCurve call specifies the multiple loops that will trim nu-patch prim-
> itives. The integer parameter *nloops* specifies the number of loops that will
> cut the primitive. Each loop is made up of multiple edge curves, specified in
> the integer array *ncurves*. The order and number of knots in each edge curve
> are specified in the integer arrays *order* and *n*, respectively. The knots them-

selves are specified in the floating-point array *knots*. The knot values for all the edges are concatenated into one long array. Each edge curve can be clipped to a particular parametric range with the floating-point *min* and *max* arrays.

For reasons that are lost in time, trim curve control points are not specified with the standard parameter list syntax that every other primitive uses. Instead, the homogeneous *u*, *v*, and *w* coordinates of the trim curve control points are specified in individual floating-point arrays.

4.6   Subdivision Meshes

Perhaps the most interesting new primitive that has been added to the RenderMan family is *subdivision mesh* (also called "subdivision surface"). The great motivation for using subdivision meshes is that they simultaneously capture the most desirable properties of several of the different surface types that we currently use. A subdivision mesh, as with patch primitives, is described by its mesh of control points. The surface itself interpolates this mesh and is piecewise smooth. However, unlike NURBS or patch mesh primitives, its mesh is not constrained to be rectangular, a major limitation of parametric patches. It can have arbitrary topology and arbitrary vertex valence. In this respect, the mesh is analogous to a polyhedral description. No longer do you have to painstakingly model a smooth surface as a quilt of rectangular patches.

But where a polyhedral surface requires a large number of data points to approximate a smooth surface, a subdivision mesh is always smooth and needs far fewer points to produce the same quality of smooth surface fit (see Figure 4.5). This significantly reduces the time necessary to create the model, reduces the amount of data necessary to hold the model, and gives the model significantly more flexibility in terms of the range of model distances and image resolutions at which the model will look good. There is no point at which the rendering of the model betrays its underlying polygonal basis.

For animation, the subdivision surface also shares another important feature with polyhedra: adding detail is a local operation. There is no need to add large "isoparams" that extend far beyond the area of interest. And because there are no topology restrictions, edges can follow character features (such as skin folds) more directly. This leads to better isolation of one part of the mesh from another, such as when model articulation requires "muscles" that drag vertices along lines that traverse the surface in arbitrary directions. Adding vertices to the mesh along these lines leads to fewer problems with unintentional muscle effects on distant parts of the surface.

The RenderMan API for subdivision meshes is extremely powerful and permits the specification of variable sharpness creases along a surface, holes, and other enhancements as described in recent literature (DeRose, Kass, and Truong, 1998).

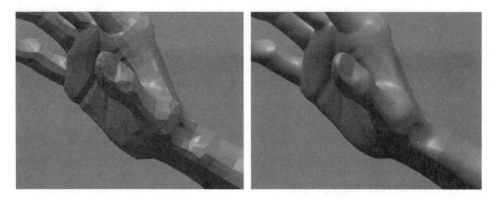

Figure 4.5 Polygon mesh and subdivision mesh renderings of the same object.

This gives subdivision meshes the ability to model fillets, rounds, and blends, and to do other modeling tasks often associated with trim curves.

These enhancements are specified by *component tags*. A component of a subdivision mesh is either a face, a vertex, or a chain of edges. Components of the subdivision mesh may be tagged to have various user-defined properties. Each tag has four parts: a command name, a pair of numbers that identify the number of integer and floating-point arguments to the tag (some tags have fixed numbers of arguments, others have variable-length argument lists), followed by the zero or more actual integer arguments, and the zero or more floating-point arguments. Several tags are currently defined, and more may be added over time.

SubdivisionMesh *scheme nverts vertids tags nargs intargs floatargs parameterlist*

The string parameter *scheme* specifies the mathematical subdivision scheme to be used by the primitive. There are several such schemes defined in the literature, but currently *PRMan* only implements "catmull-clark". The subdivision mesh itself is made up of faces, very similar to the facets in PointsPolygons, with an integer *nverts* array that contains the number of vertices in each face and an integer *vertids* array containing the index of each vertex.

The string array *tags* contains the list of tags that are associated with this mesh. The number of integer and floating-point arguments provided for each tag is listed as a pair in the integer *nargs* array. The *intargs* and *floatargs* arrays contain the actual integer and floating-point argument data for the tags. The currently defined tags include:

□ "hole": specifies that certain faces are holes. This tag has one integer argument for each face that is a hole and no floating-point arguments.

□ "corner": specifies that certain vertices are semisharp corners. This tag has one integer argument for each vertex that is a semisharp corner and equally many floating-point arguments specifying a sharpness at each such corner.

The sharpness of a vertex (or of an edge) ranges from completely smooth at 0.0 to essentially infinitely sharp (C^1 discontinuous) at values exceeding 10.0.

☐ "crease": specifies that a certain chain of edges should be a crease. This tag has any number of integer arguments, listing the vertices that make up the chain of edges, and one floating-point argument, specifying a sharpness for the edges in the crease. There may be multiple "crease" tags on a subdivision mesh that form independent creases on the primitive. It is an error to specify two sequential vertices in an edge chain that do not form an edge of one or more of the mesh faces.

☐ "interpolateboundary": specifies that the subdivision mesh should interpolate all boundary faces to their edges. This tag has no integer arguments and no floating-point arguments.

The parameterlist must include at least position ("P") information. As with polygons, subdivision mesh primitive variables of type "vertex" and "varying" occur with the same frequency—one per mesh vertex. Primitive variables of type "uniform" happen once per face. Naturally, primitive variables of type "constant" appear exactly once.

Any subdivision face that is a quadrilateral, and whose four corners each touch four faces (as if it were a vertex in a standard rectangular patch mesh) is, in fact, equivalent to a B-spline patch. However, despite this, subdivision meshes are not parametric surfaces. After a single subdivision step, every face that is not already quadrilateral becomes a set of quadrilateral subfaces. Each of these subfaces then has a locally consistent internal biparametric space. However, there is no guaranteed parametric continuity across faces, so the (u, v) parameters seen by shaders can change abruptly across geometrically smooth face edges.

4.7   Reference Geometry

Every geometric primitive (except Procedural, of course) has a parameter list with which it can identify primitive variables that are interesting to the shaders attached to it. The most obvious examples of primitive variables, such as per-vertex color ("Cs") or per-vertex normals ("N"), have special meaning to the shaders because they provide data for the Shading Language's global variables that are used to override the default values of those variables. But the system was designed to be extensible by the modeler, to add new types of data that the renderer did not already know about. And while it might seem like modeler-extensible variables are "interesting," perhaps it is not at all clear exactly what they are for. One of the best examples is the concept of *reference geometry*.

Imagine this situation: A character in the scene is modeled using patches or subdivision surfaces with many skin and clothing control points, subtly placed, to get a complex, interesting, continuous surface geometry. The shaders for the character are also relatively complex and use significant amounts of texture mapping to get color, surface properties, displacements, dirt, and other features onto the character. Some textures might be 2D parametric maps, others 3D solid procedural textures or 3D projected texture maps.

Then the character animates. As the character's skeleton moves, the skin and clothing move to conform. As the skin and clothing control points are animated, these surfaces stretch and fold, in order to appear natural. This type of control-point animation is sometimes called *deformation*. Notice, however, that the texture mapping, which is dependent on either the 3D position of the surface or the 2D parametric lengths of the patches, will change. Unless the animation is done extremely carefully, and sometimes even then, parametric textures will stretch in unnatural ways as the surface moves. 3D textures have no chance of staying put, because they depend on the positions of the vertices in object (or perhaps shader) space, and the control points are moving in those spaces. What is needed is a fixed, unmoving frame of reference, that can be used as the parameters for the texture mapping, regardless of how the character deforms. This is exactly what reference geometry provides.

Reference geometry is implemented through the use of primitive variables. We define a primitive variable, often called "Pref", as a "vertex point". This means that it has exactly the same type as "P". For every value of "P" on every primitive, there will be a corresponding "Pref". We create a static version of the model in some reference pose, and those same control-point positions will be given as the "Pref" data *on every frame* of the animation. Shading proceeds as normal, except that it uses "Pref" as the source of texture coordinates instead of using "P". This way, the shading on every frame operates on the same data, and the textures will appear the same on every frame. The texture will *stick* to the character.

The advantage of using a "vertex" point instead of a "varying" point in this application is that "vertex" points interpolate identically to the position (using cubic or nonrational or subdivision math, as appropriate). In this way they track the surface in the way that people expect that something embedded in the surface would track. "varying" points are interpolated bilinearly in parametric space, which in this application is like a polygonal approximation of the surface. The texture wavers as the bilinear approximation deviates from the true surface.

Of course, on a NURBS or other primitive where the vertices are defined by homogeneous point data "Pw", the reference position will also want to be of type "vertex hpoint", rather than "vertex point", so that they undergo the same homogeneous transformations that the vertices undergo.

4.8 Constructive Solid Geometry

Some modelers use a technique for modeling objects known as *constructive solid geometry* (CSG). In the CSG modeling paradigm, all objects are solid—they have

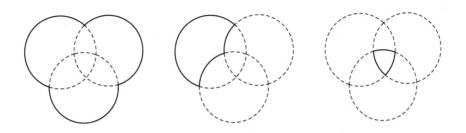

Figure 4.6 The three basic CSG operations: union, difference, and intersection.

volume as opposed to being shells that surround volume. Specifically, CSG categorizes a certain region of space as being "inside" the solid, and the rest of space is "outside," by the obvious definition. Complex solid objects are created as Boolean combinations of simpler solid objects. Boolean operators define the new insides and outsides by combining volumes. For example, a pipe might be defined by subtracting a thin solid cylinder from a slightly thicker solid cylinder. CSG is often used in mechanical modeling because of its obvious relationship with manufacturing processes by which real-world parts are constructed.

CSG modeling systems have several Boolean operators that work on solid objects the same way that mathematical set operators work on Venn diagrams. Solid objects can be fused together with the "union" operator. One can be cut out of another with the "difference" operator. The "intersection" operator is a spatial AND operation. These operators are illustrated in Figure 4.6. Complex CSG objects—say, an internal combustion engine—are created by complex hierarchical trees of Boolean CSG operations.

In RenderMan, CSG trees are defined by using a special form of attribute hierarchy that identifies the Boolean operator to be applied at each node of the tree and specifically identifies the leaf nodes. The leaf node is a set of geometric primitives that fit together to define the boundary of a single simple solid object.

SolidBegin *operation*

SolidBegin starts a *solid block*, which is a node in a CSG tree. The parameter *operation* is a string that defines the relationship among the children of this node. Four CSG operations are defined:

- "primitive": defines a CSG tree leaf node. All primitives inside this node define a single solid object
- "union": points are inside the result if they are inside any of the children
- "difference": points are inside the result if they are inside the first child and are outside all of the rest of the children

□ "intersection": points are inside the result if they are inside all of the children

RenderMan CSG trees can have any fan-out (that is, a node can have any number of children nodes). For the difference operator, the second and subsequent children are subtracted from the first child. For other operators, the order of the children is not important.

SolidEnd

SolidEnd ends a *solid block* and closes that node in the CSG tree.

It is extremely important that every "primitive" (leaf) object in the Boolean hierarchy be "closed." That is, it has a definite inside and definite outside, and there are no "holes" in the definition that make it ambiguous whether certain points are in the interior or in the exterior. In RenderMan, few individual geometric primitives have this property of closure, so RenderMan allows a CSG primitive to be created out of a *set* of geometric primitives, which, when taken together, create a closed region.

It is important to notice that, even though CSG operates on "solid objects," and in theory exposes the inner mass of these objects by cutting their surfaces away with other objects, the reality is that there are no inner masses to expose. After all, RenderMan primitives are thin sheets, which means that they are just the shells that surround some empty space. Instead, the surface of the "exposed cutaway" is actually just a section of the *cutting* object. In the pipe example described earlier, the inner surface of the pipe is not the exposed interior of the large cylinder, but is actually the inside-out surface of the smaller cylinder. In fact, every point on the final surface of a CSG object is actually some part of one of the original leaf geometric primitives. RenderMan renders CSG primitives so that the visible attributes of every point on the final object are the attributes of the geometric primitive that caused that surface. This can be confusing when complex CSG trees are involved, but there is interesting descriptive power in making the cutting and the cut objects have different appearance parameters, so that the holes appear to have different properties than the bulk exterior. For example, the cutting object can be made of metal to represent the inside of a block of steel, while the cut object is given the properties of a painted coating.

5 Handling Complexity in Photorealistic Scenes

One defining characteristic of photorealistic images is extreme visual complexity. The real world is a very complex and visually interesting place, and the photographs that record it contain the subtleties that help you recognize it as real. Computer graphics simulations of that world need to be of equal visual complexity, or it will be patently obvious to the most casual observer that they are not real. This visual complexity can arise from three sources: complicated geometric models, detailed surface material properties, and subtle lighting calculations. A RenderMan scene created for feature-film special effects usually has all three of these. Later chapters will examine shading and lighting. This chapter will examine the problems we encounter creating scene databases with enormous amounts of geometry and will provide a few solutions.

5.1   Procedural Primitives

RenderMan procedural primitives are user-defined extensions to the scene description capability of the RenderMan Interface. They provide a simple but powerful
mechanism for the modeler to state that a piece of geometry exists at a particular position in the scene, without immediately specifying the complete dataset for
that object.

The main advantage that this presents is to support *data amplification*. The idea
behind data amplification is that a simple data description acts as input to a process
that creates large amounts of data. That output data might be partially random or
completely deterministic. However, it is generally most interesting when the process
that creates the output data does so late in the game, with some cognizance of the
amount of data that is necessary to fulfill the purpose. In other words, it tailors
its quantity of output to the specific need. This makes data amplification more
powerful than simply accessing a gigantic pregenerated dataset.

The classic example of a procedural primitive is a fractal mountain. A procedure
takes as arguments a triangle and a few simple parameters and recursively subdi-
vides the triangle into smaller and smaller triangles with perturbed vertex positions
and orientations, eventually generating a mountain range. Importantly, because the
procedure creates objects that are self-similar, this process only needs to run until
the individual triangles are too small to be seen. Below the threshold of visual acu-
ity, there is no benefit to creating more data. The process therefore runs for a short
time and produces a compact dataset when the mountain is at the horizon in the
background of a scene and runs for a long time generating very complex data when
we are on the mountain examining the ground at our feet. Figure 5.1 shows how the
visible size on-screen can be used to control this data generation process.

From the modeler's point of view, there are two great advantages to using procedural primitives. First, the modeler can create whole objects or simple geometric
primitives that the renderer does not already understand and effectively extend the
renderer. RenderMan doesn't have a built-in notion of a Mountain primitive, but
with a small bit of coding, one can be created in this way. Second, the modeler can
hide a tremendous amount of geometric complexity behind a simple data structure,
using data amplification to create exactly the right amount of data at the right time,
rather than precomputing a huge and potentially overspecified dataset during the
original scene-description generation.

When trying to render complex scenes for feature-film special effects or similar
projects, this second advantage is the more important one. The complete scene
description for such scenes often includes large-scale sets, large numbers of highly
detailed objects, and great depth complexity, not all of which are actually onscreen
and visible in any given frame. Delaying the generation and loading of these large-
scale models until the renderer has determined that they are visible saves enormous
amounts of CPU time, memory, and disk space. The initial placeholder descriptions
are extremely small but provide enough data to determine if the model is necessary
or not and even give an estimate as to the size of the model on-screen. This way,

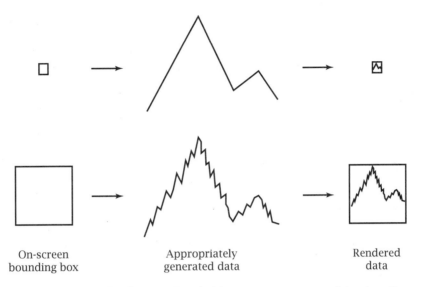

On-screen   Appropriately   Rendered
bounding box   generated data   data

Figure 5.1 A procedural mountain primitive can generate more data when the on-screen view is large than when it is small, speeding the rendering while still providing enough visual detail in the image.

model generation is delayed until the object is confirmed as necessary and the required amount of detail is known.

5.1.1   The C Procedural Interface

In the C API, RenderMan procedural primitives are implemented by having the modeling application provide subroutines that manipulate a private data structure that the renderer knows nothing about. This data contains geometry descriptions that are manipulated solely by the procedural primitive subroutines. The procedural primitive subroutines do whatever they want to that data (often following the lead of the other primitives in the renderer and recursively subdividing it into smaller, simpler primitives of the same type), the only caveat being that ultimately it must be converted into normal RenderMan API calls.

There are two entry points for each procedural primitive, the *subdivide* method and the *free* method. Each instance of a procedural primitive contains three important pieces of data: pointers to the appropriate methods, a blind (to the renderer) data pointer that points at data allocated by (and meaningful to) the methods, and a bounding box that completely contains any geometry of the primitive.

When the renderer reaches the bounding box of a particular instance of a procedural primitive, it calls the subdivide method, passing in the blind data pointer and a floating-point number that indicates the number of pixels that the bounding box covers (called the *detail size*). The subdivide method splits the primitive into smaller primitives. It can either generate standard RenderMan primitives, or it can generate more instances of procedural primitives with their own blind data pointers and (presumably smaller) bounding boxes, or some combination.

The renderer is permitted to subdivide the same blind pointer multiple times if it needs to (for example, if it had to discard the results and then needs them back again). The subdivision method should return identical results each time, or the renderer could become extremely confused. Or it may never call subdivide on that blind pointer, if it recognizes that the primitive is irrelevant to the current rendering. In any case, at some point the renderer will know that it will never need a particular blind pointer again. It will then call the free method to destroy that blind pointer. This signals the procedural primitive that it may release any data structure that the blind pointer refers to.

Because procedural primitives need their methods in order to function, they were originally only defined for the C version of the API. An application program that contained such procedural primitive methods would need to be linked with a linkable library version of the renderer in order to use them. The original C version of this API is as follows:

RiProcedural(RtPointer *blinddata*, RtBound *boundingbox*, void (*subdivide) (),
void (*free)());

> This RenderMan C API call creates a procedural primitive. The pointer *blinddata* contains any data that the modeler knows "describes" the procedural primitive. The renderer does not examine this data, but only gives it to the *subdivide* method when the renderer discovers (by virtue of the *boundingbox*) that it needs to know the details of the geometry inside the procedural primitive. When the renderer has determined that the primitive is no longer needed (because it has been subdivided, culled, or for any other reason), it will call the *free* method on the *blinddata* pointer.
>
> The prototypes for the method calls are:
> □ void *subdivide* (RtPointer *blinddata*, RtFloat *detailsize*)
> □ void *free* (RtPointer *blinddata*)
> *detailsize* is the approximate size in pixels of the projection of the bounding box onto the screen, or *infinity* (1.0e30) if that size cannot be determined for any reason.

The limitation of having access to procedural primitives only from the C API made procedural primitives mostly uninteresting. To restore their utility and unleash their power, modern RenderMan renderers now provide three built-in procedural primitives that can be used from the stand-alone renderer executable via simple RIB directives. These are

■ **Delayed Read-Archive**: read a RIB file as late as possible
■ **Run Program**: run a program to generate the subdivided data
■ **Dynamic Load**: load object code that contains the required subroutines

5.1.2   Delayed Read-Archive

The simplest of the new RIB procedural primitives is *delayed read-archive*. The existing interface for "including" one RIB file into another is `ReadArchive`. Delayed read-archive operates exactly like `ReadArchive` except that the reading is delayed until the procedural primitive bounding box is reached, unlike `ReadArchive`, which reads RIB files immediately during parsing. The advantage of the new interface is that because the reading is delayed, memory for the read primitives is not used until the bounding box is actually reached. In addition, if the bounding box proves to be offscreen, the parsing time of the entire RIB file is saved. The disadvantage is that an accurate bounding box for the contents of the RIB file is now required.

The RIB syntax for the delayed read-archive primitive is

`Procedural "DelayedReadArchive"` *filename boundingbox*

> The parameter *filename* is a string array with a single element, the name of a partial RIB file. The file can contain any amount of valid RIB, although it is suggested that it either be "flat" (have no hierarchy) or have some balanced hierarchy (matching `Begin-End` calls). As with all RIB parameters that are bounding boxes, the *boundingbox* is an array of six floating-point numbers, which are *xmin, xmax, ymin, ymax, zmin, zmax* in the current object space.

5.1.3   Run Program

A more dynamic method of generating procedural primitives is to call a helper program that generates geometry on-the-fly in response to procedural primitive requests in the RIB stream. As will be seen, each generated procedural primitive is described by a request to the helper program, in the form of an ASCII data block that describes the primitive to be generated. This data block can be anything that is meaningful and adequate to the helper program, such as a sequence of a few floating-point numbers, a filename, or a snippet of code in an interpreted modeling language. In addition, the renderer supplies the *detail size* of the primitive's bounding box, so that the generating program can decide what to generate based on how large the object will appear on-screen.

The generation program reads the request data blocks on its standard input stream and emits RIB commands on its standard output stream. These RIB streams are read into the renderer as though they were read from a file (as with `ReadArchive` above) and may include any standard RenderMan attributes and primitives (including procedural primitive calls to itself or other helper programs). As long as any procedural primitives exist in the rendering database that require the same helper program for processing, the socket connection to the program will remain open. This means that the program should be written with a loop that accepts any number of requests and generates a RIB "snippet" for each one.

The RIB syntax for specifying a RIB-generating program procedural primitive is

Procedural "RunProgram" *generator boundingbox*

> *generator* is a string array with two elements. The first element is the name of the helper program to execute and may include command line options. The second element is the generation-request data block. It is an ASCII printable string that is meaningful to the helper program and describes the children to be generated. The *boundingbox* is an array of six floating-point numbers, which is *xmin, xmax, ymin, ymax, zmin, zmax* in the current object space.

Notice that the data block is a quoted string in the RIB file, so if it is a complex description that contains quote marks or other special characters, these must be escaped in the standard way (similar to C, using backslash metacharacters like \" and \n). You might be inclined to try to pack a binary data structure into the data block, but these quoting issues make that nearly impossible.

5.1.4   Procedural Primitive DSO

A more efficient method for accessing subdivision routines is to write them as dynamic shared objects (DSOs)[1] and *dynamically load* them into the renderer executable at run-time. In this case, you write your subdivision and free routines in C, exactly as you would if you were writing them to be linked into the renderer using the C RiProcedural() interface. DSOs are compiled with special compiler options to make them run-time loadable and are specified in the RIB file by the name of the shared object file. The renderer will load the DSO the first time that the subdivision routine must be called, and from then on, it is called as if (and executes as fast as if) it were statically linked. DSOs are more efficient than external programs because they avoid the overhead of interprocess communication.

When writing a procedural primitive DSO, you must create three specific public subroutine entry points, named Subdivide, Free, and ConvertParameters. Subdivide is a standard RiProcedural() primitive subdivision routine, taking a blind data pointer to be subdivided and a floating-point detail to estimate screen size. Free is a standard RiProcedural() primitive free routine, taking a blind data pointer to be released. ConvertParameters is a special routine that takes a string and returns a blind data pointer. It will be called exactly once for each Dynamic-Load procedural primitive in the RIB file, and its job is to convert a printable string version of the progenitor's blind data (which must be in ASCII in the RIB file) into something that the Subdivide routine will accept.

The C prototypes for these functions are as follows:

```
RtPointer ConvertParameters(char *initialdata);
void Subdivide(RtPointer blinddata, RtFloat detailsize);
void Free(RtPointer blinddata);
```

---

[1] on some systems called dynamically linked libraries (DLLs)

The RIB syntax for specifying a dynamically loadable procedural primitive is

Procedural "DynamicLoad" *generator boundingbox*

> *generator* is a string array with two elements. The first element is the name of the shared object file that contains the three required entry points and has been compiled and prelinked as described earlier. The second element is the ASCII printable string that represents the initial data to be sent to the ConvertParameters routine. The *boundingbox* is an array of six floating-point numbers, which is *xmin, xmax, ymin, ymax, zmin, zmax* in the current object space.

Note that if the DSO Subdivide routine wants to recursively create child procedural primitives of the same type as itself, it should specify a direct recursive call to itself, with RiProcedural(newdata,newbound,Subdivide,Free), *not* call itself as a DynamicLoad procedural. The latter would eventually just call the former after wasting time checking for and reloading the DSO.

5.2   Lightweight Primitives

Recent versions of the RenderMan renderers support two new lightweight geometric primitives that were designed to solve the problems of dealing with massive complexity in modeling scenes for feature-film special effects and animation, specifically, situations where there are huge numbers of very small primitives. The primitives, Points and Curves, are very compact in the geometric database because they are defined using line-oriented instead of surface-oriented vertex data. They are shaded but take advantage of the fact that they are intended to be small on the screen. As a result, the renderer can generally process much larger numbers of these primitives than it can of the standard surface-oriented primitives, even when those primitives are small on the screen.

5.2.1   Point Clouds

The new Points primitive is intended to be used for small particles such as sparks, snowflakes, or raindrops (see Figure 5.2). RenderMan points are intended to be fast and very efficient primitives for use where hundreds of thousands or millions of tiny spots are required, such as for particle systems or stars. They are optimized for the case where the intended particle is small, taking up at most a couple of pixels on the screen.

Points *parameterlist*

> Points draws a set of flat-shaded points, individual dots with no derivatives. Position is specified in the standard way, with 3D vertex data in the "P" array. Size is specified with an array of floating-point "width" values. Width is

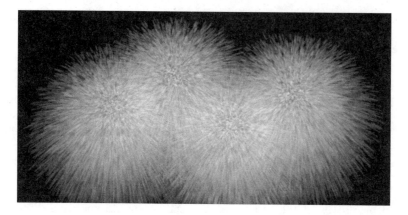

Figure 5.2 Moving Points creating fireworks. See also color plate 5.2.

measured as diameter in object space, not in raster space as you might expect of annotation or 2D drawing primitives. If all of the "width" values for a complex primitive are identical, there is a special shorthand version, "constantwidth", which takes a single floating-point value for use with the entire primitive. Each point can have an independent "width" value, or providing a single "constantwidth" value for the set will make all points the same size.

Points are much cheaper, in terms of both memory and shading time, than small bilinear patches or small spheres. In *PRMan*, each point is only shaded once, and generates only two micropolygons that always face the camera (to form a little hexagon, which should be too small to distinguish from a disk). You can efficiently render very large point clouds using the point primitive.

There are some disadvantages of this lightweight primitive, however. Because points are only shaded at a single point, they have no access to derivative information. If you want your particle to have differing shading across its surface, or if the particle takes up multiple pixels, you might want to use bilinear patches or spheres. Points may be motion blurred; however, you must be aware that when a very small object is motion blurred, the process of stochastic sampling tends to make individual objects vanish into a peppering of dim dots.

The widths of Points are defined in the current object coordinate system and default to 1.0. You can either give each point an individual width by using the "varying float" variable "width" or give a single width value for all points using the "constantwidth" parameter, which is defined as a "constant float". Notice that the rendered size of points is *not* specified in raster coordinates. This choice was made because Points were intended to be a rendering primitive, not an annotation primitive. If widths were specified in raster space, they would be the same size independent of distance from the camera and independent of resolution. This would look very wrong in animation, particularly in situations where the points are moving rapidly past the camera.

Points will often be used to create fire or explosion effects. For example, consider the original particle systems of the *Star Trek Genesis Sequence* done by Bill Reeves in 1982. In those renderings, particle opacities were set to 0.0, so that in each pixel, by virtue of the compositing algebra, the intensity of all of the particles in the pixel would add rather than having the front particles obscure underlying ones. At the center of an explosion where many particles overlap, this gives the illusion of a glowing hot center.

In situations where point primitives are not appropriate (such as when stochastically sampled motion blur doesn't give the correct look) but enormously large quantities of particles are still necessary, special-purpose particle rendering programs may be required (for example, consider Reeves and Blau, 1985).

5.2.2   Curves

The Curves primitive models objects that are long and thin enough to appear visually as mere 3D curves. You may think of this primitive as a ribbon or a string of spaghetti. RenderMan curves are intended to be fast and efficient primitives, for use where hundreds of thousands or millions of thin strokes are required, such as for hair and grass. As such, they are flat ribbons that are defined only by a single curve, which is their spine.

Curves *type nvertices wrap parameterlist*

> Curves draws a set of 3D ribbons. The Curves primitive can contain any number of individual curves, and the parameter *nvertices* is an array of integers that specifies the number of control points in each curve.

> Curves are very much like 1D patch meshes. If the *type* is "linear" (*not* "bilinear"), each curve is piecewise linear. If the *type* is "cubic" (*not* "bicubic"), each curve is a cubic curve that responds to the *v* basis function and step defined by the Basis call. The *u* parameter changes across the width of the curve, whereas the *v* parameter changes along the length of the curve (i.e., the direction specified by the control vertices). Curves can also wrap in the *v* direction if the *wrap* parameter is "periodic".

The number of data items required for primitive variables on curves is somewhat reminiscent of those required for patch meshes, only in one dimension. Three of the storage classes are very simple. Primitive variables of class "vertex" have one value per control point, just as "P" has. This is the sum of the values in the *nvertices* array. Primitive variables of class "uniform" have one value per curve. This is the number of elements in the *nvertices* array. Primitive variables of class "constant" have exactly one value.

The only complex class is primitive variables of class "varying", which have one value at each segment boundary. Like patch meshes, curves obey the basis matrix and basis step. Therefore, the number of segments in an individual curve with nv vertices, and therefore the number of varying data items on that curve, is

$$nsegments = \begin{cases} nv - 1 & \text{for nonperiodic linear curves} \\ nv & \text{for periodic linear curves} \\ \left(\frac{nv-4}{vstep}\right) + 1 & \text{for nonperiodic cubic curves} \\ \frac{nv}{vstep} & \text{for periodic cubic curves} \end{cases}$$

$$nvarying = \begin{cases} nsegments + 1 & \text{for nonperiodic curves} \\ nsegments & \text{for periodic curves} \end{cases}$$

The number of "varying" data items on a composite Curves primitive is obviously the sum of the number of "varying" items on the individual curves.

The width along the curve may be specified with either a "width" parameter, which is a "varying float" argument, or a "constantwidth" parameter, which is a "constant float" (one value for the entire Curves). Widths are specified in object space units of the curve. If no "width" vector or "constantwidth" value is given, the default width is 1.0 unit in object space. Again, the choice to use object space to define curve widths instead of raster space seems wrong until you consider using them as hair on the head of a character. Imagine the character walking away from the camera. As he recedes into the distance his head gets smaller but his hair stays the same thickness on-screen. Eventually each hair would be a sizable fraction of the width of his whole head! This is clearly incorrect, so raster space is not used.

Each curve generates a flat ribbon but the control vertices only specify the direction of the "spine"; the rotation of the flat ribbon about the spine is ambiguous. In the standard case, the ribbon will always rotate to be as parallel to the view plane as possible. In other words, it will twist to face the camera. This is a good way to simulate a thin tube, because the silhouette of the ribbon will match that of the tube but is perhaps hundreds of times more efficient to render (in both time and memory) than an equivalent surface of circular cross section. Figure 5.3 shows such tubes used as hairs on a mythical creature.

Alternatively, if "N" values are supplied, the normals will be used to guide the ribbon so that it stays perpendicular to the supplied normals, thus allowing user-controlled rotation of the ribbon. To summarize, if you need to model something like grass, which is a ribbon, and the twistiness is important, give "N" values to control the twist. If you are modeling something like hair, which is tubular and so the twist is irrelevant, you do not need to supply "N" values.

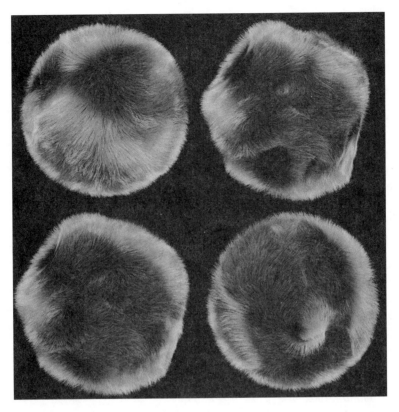

Figure 5.3 Tribbles very simply described with a large number of curves and a tube-like appearance. See also color plate 5.3.

5.3   Level of Detail

The traditional model-based special effects industry has a long tradition of building multiple models of the same object to satisfy various shot requirements. Shots of objects in the distance can utilize relatively small and coarse models, but close-ups often use very large and detailed models. In computer graphics, we can benefit by adopting a similar methodology, because simpler models require less time and memory to render than their large and complex versions, and the renderer will waste a lot of time (and memory) if it is forced to deal with the excess. Nevertheless, very often it is inconvenient for the modeling system, or the user, to customize the amount of detail that is specified for every rendering individually. Instead, modelers can provide multiple versions, or *representations*, of an object, which are intended to be used when the object appears at different sizes. The renderer can then choose which representation is appropriate for the particular rendering, using that representation and ignoring all others. This optimizes image generation without compromising image quality. This technique is known as *level of detail*.

RenderMan provides a set of level of detail commands that permits the renderer to take advantage of these multiple model versions. The beneficial features are

- the user may specify multiple versions of a particular object in a RIB file
- the renderer automatically selects the version appropriate for the final size of the object on the screen
- *PRMan* can make a smooth transition between multiple versions of a model
- this transition can be very smooth despite radical changes in topology, shading model, or even color of the different versions
- memory and time can be drastically cut compared to not using level of detail
- models with appropriate complexity are far easier to antialias, leading to fewer artifacts in animation

5.3.1   Specifying Level of Detail

In RenderMan, there are two attributes that control the renderer's level of detail choices. The first attribute is known as the *detail size* (also sometimes confusingly called *current detail*). This is the size of the object on the screen—small objects will want to use low-detail representations and large objects will want to use high-detail ones. The user specifies a bounding box around the object, and the renderer calculates the detail size based on number of pixels it covers in the final image.

Detail *boundingbox*

> The Detail call defines a bounding box whose size is used to quantify the importance of the various representations that follow. The parameter *boundingbox* is an array of six floating-point numbers, in the order *xmin, xmax, ymin, ymax, zmin, zmax*.

The *detail size* is specified by giving an axis-aligned bounding volume in the current coordinate system. Notice that the modeler provides the bounding box in object space and then the renderer computes the actual detail size, which is the raster space area of the projection of the specified bounding volume onto the image plane.

The second attribute is known as the *detail range*. This attribute says, for each representation, in which range of detail sizes that representation should be used. This is how the modeler identifies to the renderer which representation actually *is* the low-detail representation and which is the high-detail one.

DetailRange *start low high end*

> The DetailRange call specifies the range of detail sizes at which the particular representation that follows should be used. Each of the four parameters is a floating-point number that represents a size of the detail bounding box in pixels. They plot out a graph describing the relative importance of each

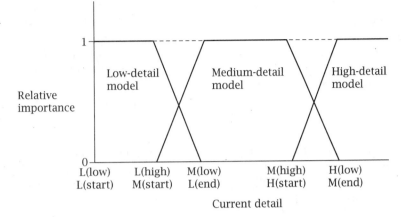

Figure 5.4 The relative importance, at various detail sizes, of three representations of a model that have increasing amounts of visual detail.

representation of the model. Each geometric primitive in the representation will be used, or not used, depending on the following rules:

☐ If the *detail size* is outside the range (less than *start* or greater than *end*), the importance is 0, so all primitives in that representation will be discarded without rendering them

☐ If the detail size is in the center region between *low* and *high*, the importance is 1, and the primitives will be rendered normally

☐ If the detail size lies in the rising region between *start* and *low* or in the falling region between *high* and *end*, known as the *transition regions*, the model is changing from this representation to another representation. The renderer is instructed to make some pleasant blending between the representations, weighted by their relative importance

Figure 5.4 shows the relative importance of each of three models over a range of detail sizes as specified by the following RIB commands:

```
AttributeBegin                  # push the graphics state
Detail [-1 1 -2 2 0 8]          # setup a "ruler" for detail calcs
DetailRange [0 0 1 4]
    #... primitives for the low-detail model (< 4 pixels)
DetailRange [1 4 256 400]
    #... primitives for the medium-detail model
DetailRange [256 400 1e38 1e38]
    #... primitives for the high-detail model
AttributeEnd                    # pop the graphics state, LOD object done
```

You may use as few or as many representations as desired, but the sum of all model importances should be 1.0 over the entire range of potential detail values in order to keep objects from being accidentally over- or underrepresented in any particular image. In practice, this means that each representation's transition regions should exactly match the next-higher and next-lower representation, as shown in Figure 5.4. The sole exception to this rule is that it may be valuable to underrepresent the lowest complexity representation, to allow the object to fade out as it falls below some minimum size.

The modeler has a control for globally scaling all detail size calculations:

RelativeDetail *scale*

> RelativeDetail is an image option that specifies a scale factor to be applied to the reported size of every detail box in the scene. This is a quick way of globally scaling all detail sizes up or down by a certain ratio, usually as a way to control rendering speed for preview renders.

5.3.2   Simple Level of Detail Example

The top image in Figure 5.5 shows three different models of a chair. The most detailed model has nicely sculpted surfaces for all of the boards and spindles. The second has several patches and some simple cylinders for the spindles. The simplest is only two bilinear patches. A RIB file was created specifying appropriate detail levels for each representation, and chairs at different distances were rendered. The most detailed model's RIB description is over 250 Kbytes. The middle model's RIB description is approximately 40 Kbytes. The trivial model's RIB description is less than 300 bytes.

In the bottom image of Figure 5.5, we see them rendered with level of detail. Notice that as the chair gets smaller in the frame, the transitions to simpler versions are smooth and extremely difficult to detect. Even when animated, the transitions between these models occur smoothly. The smallest rendition does indeed take almost no time or memory, because the complex models are completely ignored by the renderer.

It may be useful to fade between representations of a model in a still frame, but it is far more interesting to use level of detail in animation. In animation, the raster size of a model will change as the model or camera moves, and therefore each frame will typically have different contributions by the various representations.

5.3.3   Choosing Detail Ranges

There are many techniques for building models with multiple complexity levels. In addition to the obvious replacement of complex (high vertex count) surfaces with simpler (smoother, low vertex count) versions, these techniques also include shader tricks, such as replacing displacements with bumps and replacing complex procedural shaders with texture map approximations, and even eliminating features when they become too thin or too small for the renderer to antialias reasonably. Choos-

Figure 5.5 Three levels of detail for a chair (top), and a smooth blend between them (bottom). See also color plate 5.5.

Figure 5.6 High (top) and low (bottom) detail levels for tree branches and leaves. See also color plate 5.6.

ing detail ranges that appropriately remove complexity when it is too small to see is also a bit of an art. A good renderer (like *PRMan*) can do an excellent job of blending based on relative importance, but, nevertheless, the smoothness of transitions in animation largely depends on how carefully the models are constructed. If silhouettes change radically, or surface coloration changes drastically, it may be possible to see the changes, even if they occur smoothly.

Once carefully crafted models are created, the remaining issue is to carefully compute the transition ranges so that the appropriate model is visible at the appropriate size. This is sometimes tricky because the metric, the detail size, is computed in a relatively simplistic way. It is the raster size of the bounding box provided to the Detail call, and this will change as the bounding box rotates or is seen from different angles, even if the distance from the camera is the same. It must be considered the "worst-case" raster size of the object and may differ significantly from the number of pixels that the object actually appears in.

Notice, however, that while we have mentioned that the detail size is calculated from a bounding box in object space, there are no calculations that actually depend on the object being entirely within the box. The box is not a *bound* in the classical sense, such as being part of a culling or clipping calculation. In fact, the only thing that the Detail bound is being used for is as a size metric and, indirectly, an importance metric. Once we have realized that this is true, it becomes clear that we should consider the argument to Detail to be a ruler, not a bounding box. And with this ruler we can measure whatever we like to determine the importance.

For example, consider a multiresolution model of a tree. One model might be the entire tree in full glory, with detailed twigs and leaf shapes. A second model might have square leaves and no twigs at all. A third model might be a cylinder trunk and some spheres with texture maps representing the leaf canopy. (See Figure 5.6 for an illustration of the first two of these models.) Because trees often have long trunks and sprawling branches, it is easy to imagine that the bounding box around the entire tree is very large and yet very sparsely covered. If the tree grows or bends in the wind, an accurate bounding box would change sizes even though the "importance" of the various models doesn't really change.

Alternatively, consider placing the Detail ruler around a single leaf. If the leaf is large, we need the most detailed model. If the leaf is subpixel, we can't see individual leaves, so we can just use the canopy. This is tantamount to saying that the most relevant indicator of the required amount of visual detail is how big the leaf is on the screen. The visual perception of the leaf becomes the ruler with which we judge the entire model. A taller tree or a bushier tree gets the same importance because the leaves are the same size on each. Figure 5.7 shows a forest scene where this metric was used to measure the importance of a variety of trees at different distances from the camera.

Once the detail ruler is used in this way, surrounding some visual complexity indicator rather than the entire model, it becomes significantly easier to quantify the required transition ranges on models. Detail sizes are tighter and less prone to undesired "angle-dependent" oscillation. Models can be changed significantly, or

Figure 5.7 A forest composed of level-of-detail trees. See also color plate 5.7.

instanced in slightly different versions, without having to recompute the `Detail-Range` every time. And good values for `DetailRange` are quite simply easier for the TD to estimate and finalize in the first place, as they actually measure whatever geometric or shading element is providing the relevant visual complexity and not any irrelevant overall structure or bulk.

5.3.4 Using Level of Detail with Procedural Primitives

In some productions that have attempted to use models with varying complexity, but without the advantage of this level of detail feature, it has been incumbent on some (unlucky) TD to painstakingly determine for every shot (or even for every frame of every shot) which representation of each model was the best to use for that particular rendering. It is easy to see that this is a tedious, error-prone, and unglorious task. With level of detail, the renderer is able to determine with very little computation which representations will be used in a particular image and which will have zero importance and can be trivially rejected. This means that there is often no reason not to put all representations of the model in the RIB file of every frame.

However, in those situations where it is very undesirable for any of the too complex representations to exist in the RIB file (for example, when RIB file size or RIB file-generation time are serious issues), these issues can be ameliorated by combining level of detail with procedural primitives. When used in combination with the procedural primitive functions, the detailed object descriptions need never be loaded, or even created, if they aren't used. As an example, suppose we have three versions of a particular object, stored in three RIB files named small.rib, medium.rib, and big.rib that represent the underlying object at various levels of detail.

```
AttributeBegin                          # push the graphics state
Detail [-1 1 -1 1 -1 1]                 # set up a "ruler" for detail calcs
DetailRange [0 0 1 4]
    Procedural "DelayedReadArchive" [ "small.rib" ] [-1 1 -1 1 -1 1]
DetailRange [1 4 256 400]
    Procedural "DelayedReadArchive" [ "medium.rib" ] [-1 1 -1 1 -1 1]
DetailRange [256 400 1e38 1e38]
    Procedural "DelayedReadArchive" [ "big.rib" ] [-1 1 -1 1 -1 1]
AttributeEnd
```

The Procedural "DelayedReadArchive" geometric primitive acts as a place-holder. The corresponding RIB file is only read when the bounding box given is determined to be potentially visible. If the box is determined to be outside the version's detail range (or otherwise invisible), it will never be read at all. This means that you can create RIB files that include large amounts of geometry for use when necessary, without incurring any expense if those high-detail models are not drawn.

Similarly, you could create a modeling system that created RIB representations of objects "on demand," where Procedural "RunProgram" primitives are executed to generate their RIB only when those primitives are discovered to have some relevance in the current frame.

© Pixar Animation Studios

6 How PhotoRealistic RenderMan Works

. . . and What You Can Do about It

6.1   History

Pixar's *PhotoRealistic RenderMan* renderer is an implementation of a scanline rendering algorithm known as the *Reyes* architecture. Reyes was developed in the mid-1980s by the Computer Graphics Research Group at Lucasfilm (now Pixar) with the specific goal of creating a rendering algorithm that would be applicable to creating special effects for motion pictures. The algorithm was first described by Cook et al. in their 1987 Siggraph paper "The Reyes Image Rendering Architecture." They developed this novel rendering algorithm because they felt that the other algorithms generally in use at the time (polygon *z*-buffer algorithms, polygon scanline algorithms, and ray tracers) had various flaws and constraints that really limited their use in this venue.

Images used in motion picture special effects need to be photorealistic — that is, appear of such high quality that the audience would believe they were filmed with a real camera. All of the image artifacts that computer graphics researchers had to live with up to this point were unacceptable if the images were going to fool the critical eyes of the movie-going masses. In particular, Reyes was designed to overcome the following problems with existing rendering algorithms:

- **Vast visual complexity**: Photographs of the real world contain millions of objects, and every object has minute details that make it look real. CG images must contain the same complexity if they are to blend seamlessly with live camera work.
- **Motion blur**: Photographs of moving objects naturally exhibit a blur due to the camera shutter being open for a period of time while the object moves through the field of view. Decades of stop-motion special effects failed to take this into account, and the audience noticed.
- **Speed and memory limitations**: Motion pictures contain over 100,000 frames and are filmed in a matter of days or weeks. Fast computers are expensive, and there is never enough memory (particularly in retrospect). Implementability on special-purpose hardware was a clear necessity.

The resulting design brought together existing work on curved surface primitives and scanline algorithms with revolutionary new work in flexible shading and stochastic antialiasing to create a renderer that could produce images that truly looked like photographs. It was first used in a film titled *Young Sherlock Holmes* in 1985, drew rave reviews for its use in *The Abyss* in 1989, and in 1993 was given an Academy Award for contributions to the film industry.

6.2   Basic Geometric Pipeline

The Reyes algorithm is a geometric pipeline, not entirely unlike those found in modern-day hardware graphics engines. What sets it apart is the specific types of geometric operations that occur in the pipeline, and the way that, as the data streams through the system, it gains and retains enough geometric and appearance fidelity that the final result will have very high image quality. Figure 6.1 shows the basic block diagram of the architecture.

The first step, of course, is loading the scene description from the modeler. Typically, the scene description is in a RIB file, loaded from disk. In that case, the RIB file is read by a RIB parser, which calls the appropriate RI routine for each line of the RIB file. Notice that since the RIB file is a simple metafile of the RI API, it is extremely easy to parse. The only minor complexity arises from the handling of parameter list data, which is dependent on the parameter type declarations that appear earlier in the RIB file. Alternatively, a program that is linked to the renderer can call the RI API directly, in which case the parser is simply bypassed.

The second step is the processing of the RenderMan Interface calls themselves. This stage of the pipeline maintains the hierarchical graphics state machine. RI calls fall into two classes: attributes or options that manipulate the graphics state machine, and geometric primitives whose attributes are defined by the then-current version of the graphics state machine. The hierarchical graphics state machine

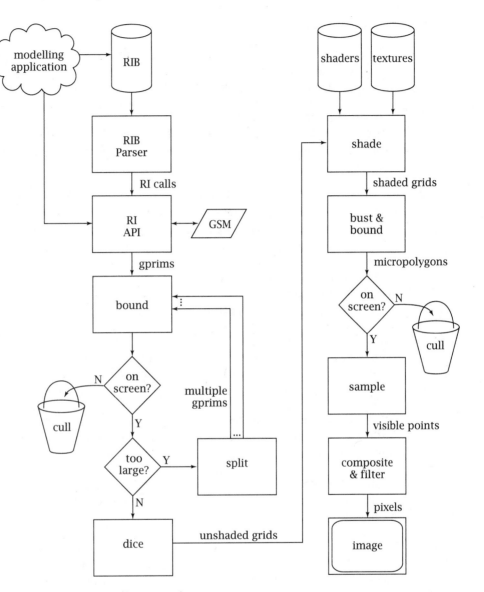

Figure 6.1 The Reyes rendering pipeline.

is kept in a stack-based data structure within the RI layer. Whenever a geometric primitive arrives, the current top-of-the-stack set of attributes is attached to the primitive before it proceeds into the main Reyes geometric processing engine.

6.2.1   Splitting Loop

The first thing that Reyes does to arriving primitives is *bound* them. The renderer computes a camera-space axis-aligned bounding box that is guaranteed to contain the entire primitive. RenderMan does not contain any unbounded primitives (such as infinite planes), so this is generally straightforward. Most RenderMan primitives have the convex-hull property, which means that the primitive is entirely contained within the volume outlined by the vertices themselves. Primitives that don't have this property (such as Catmull-Rom patches) are converted to equivalent primitives that do (such as Bezier patches).

Next, the bounding box is checked to see if the primitive is actually on-screen. The camera description in the graphics state gives us the *viewing volume*, a 3D volume of space that contains everything that the camera can see. In the case of perspective projections, this is a rectangular pyramid, bounded on the sides by the perspective projection of the screen window (sometimes called the *screen space viewport* in graphics texts) and truncated at front and back by the near and far clipping planes; for an orthographic projection this is a simple rectangular box. It is important to note at this point that Reyes does not do any global illumination or global intervisibility calculations of any kind. For this reason, any primitive that is not at least partially within the viewing volume cannot contribute to the image in any way and therefore is immediately culled (trivially rejected). Also, any one-sided primitives that are determined to be entirely back facing can be culled at this stage, because they also cannot contribute to the image.

If the primitive is (at least partially) on-screen, its size is tested. If it is deemed "too large" on-screen, according to a metric described later, it is *split* into smaller primitives. For most parametric primitives, this means cutting the primitive in two (or possibly four) along the central parametric line(s). For primitives that are containers of simpler primitives, such as polyhedra, splitting may mean roughly dividing into two containers each with fewer members. In either case, the idea is to create subprimitives that are simpler and smaller on-screen and more likely to be "small enough" when they are examined. This technique is often called "divide and conquer."

The resulting subprimitives are then dropped independently into the top of the loop, in no particular order, to be themselves bound, cull-tested, and size-tested. Eventually, the progeny of the original primitive will pass the size test and can move on to the next phase called *dicing*. Dicing converts the small primitive into a common data format called a *grid*. A grid is a tessellation of the primitive into a rectangular array of quadrilateral facets known as *micropolygons* (see Figure 6.2). (Because of the geometry of the grid, each facet is actually a tiny bilinear patch, but we call it a micropolygon nonetheless.) The vertices of these facets are the points that will be shaded later, so the facets themselves must be very small in order for the renderer to create the highly detailed, visually complex shading that we have come to expect. Generally, the facets will be on the order of one pixel in area. All primitives, regardless of original type, are converted into grids that look

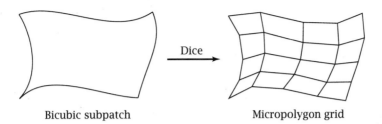

Bicubic subpatch   Micropolygon grid

Figure 6.2 A primitive that is small enough will be diced into a grid
of tiny bilinear facets known as micropolygons.

essentially the same to the remainder of the rendering pipeline. At this stage, each
grid retains all of the primitive's attributes, and any primitive vertex variables that
were attached to the primitive have been correctly interpolated onto every vertex in
the grid, but the vertices have not yet been shaded.

6.2.2   Shading

The grid is then passed into the shading system to be shaded. *PRMan* first evaluates
the displacement shader, which may move grid vertices and/or recompute shading
normals. Then the surface shader is evaluated. In a typical surface shader, there are
calls to `diffuse` or `illuminance` somewhere in the code. These routines require the
evaluation of all of the light shaders attached to the object. The light shaders run
as "coroutines" of the surface shader the first time that they are needed, but their
results are cached and reused if they are accessed again (for example, in a subsequent `specular` call). When the surface shader finishes, it has computed the color
and opacity of every grid vertex. Finally, the atmosphere shader is evaluated, making adjustments to the vertex color and opacity to simulate fog or other volumetric
effects. The end result of all of these evaluations is that the grid now has final color
and opacity assigned to each vertex, and the vertices themselves might be in different places than when originally diced. The other attributes of the original primitive
are now mostly superfluous.

The details of the method that the shading system uses to assign color and
opacity to each grid vertex are of very little consequence to the Reyes pipeline itself
but, of course, are of central importance to the users of *PRMan*. However, readers
who are not very familiar with the material in Chapters 7 and 11 will probably
want to review those chapters before spending too much time worrying about these
details.

PRMan's shading system is an interpreter for the RenderMan Shading Language,
which reads the byte-codes in the `.slo` file previously created by the Shading
Language compiler (Hanrahan and Lawson, 1990). Notice that the data structure
that the interpreter operates on, a grid, is a bunch of large rectangular arrays of
floating-point numbers. For this reason, it may not be surprising that the interpreter

actually executes as a virtual SIMD (single instruction, multiple data) vector math unit. Such vector pipelines were typical in 1980s-vintage supercomputers.

The run-time interpreter reads shader instructions one at a time and executes the operator on all grid vertices. It is important to contrast this scheme with the alternative, which would run the entire shader on the first grid vertex, then run it on the second grid vertex, and so on. The advantages of the breadth-first solution is efficiency. We are able to make near-optimal use of the pipelined floating-point units that appear in modern processors, and we have excellent cache performance due to strong locality of reference. In addition, for uniform variables, the grid has exactly one data value, not *nvertices* values. As a result, the interpreter is able to compute operations on uniform data exactly once on each grid, saving significantly over the redundant calculations that would be necessary in a depth-first implementation.

However, life is never all gravy. When a conditional or loop instruction is reached, the results may require that not all points on the grid enter the protected block. Because of this, the SIMD controller has *run flags*, which identify which grid vertices are "active" and which are "inactive" for the current instruction. For any instruction where the run-flag vector has at least one bit on, the instruction is executed, but only on those grid vertices that require it. Other operators such as else, break, and continue manipulate the run flags to ensure that the SIMD execution accurately simulates the depth-first execution.

Another advantage of the SIMD execution model is that neighborhood information is available for most grid vertices (except those on the grid edges), which means that differentials can be computed. These differentials, the difference between values at adjacent grid vertices, substitute for derivatives in all of the Shading Language operators that require derivative information. Those operators, known generically as *area operators*, include Du, calculatenormal, texture, and their related functions. Notice that grid vertices on edges (actually on two edges, not all four) have no neighbors, so their differential information is estimated. *PRMan* version 3.8 and lower estimated this poorly, which led to bad grid artifacts in second-derivative calculations. *PRMan* version 3.9 has a better differential estimator that makes many of these artifacts disappear, but it is still possible to confuse it at inflection points.

6.2.3   Texturing

The number and size of texture maps that are typically used in photorealistic scenes are so large that it is impractical to keep more than a small portion of them in memory at one time. For example, a typical frame in a full-screen CGI animation might access texture maps approaching 10 Gb in total size. Fortunately, because this data is not all needed at the highest possible resolution in the same frame, mip-maps can be used to limit this to 200 Mb of texture data actually read. However, even this is more memory than can or needs to be dedicated to such transient data. *PRMan* has a very sophisticated texture caching system that cycles texture data in as necessary, and keeps the total in-core memory devoted to texture to under 10

Mb in all but extreme cases. The proprietary texture file format is organized into 2D tiles of texture data that are strategically stored for fast access by the texture cache, which optimizes both cache hit rates and disk I/O performance.

Shadows are implemented using shadow maps that are sampled with *percentage closer* filtering (Reeves, Salesin, and Cook 1987). In this scheme, grid vertices are projected into the view of the shadow-casting light source, using shadow camera viewing information stored in the map. They are determined to be in shadow if they are farther away than the value in the shadow map at the appropriate pixel. In order to antialias this depth comparison, given that averaging depths is a nonsensical operation (because it implies that there is geometry in some halfway place where it doesn't actually exist), several depths from the shadow map in neighboring pixels are stochastically sampled, and the shadowing result is the percentage of the tests that succeeded.

6.2.4   Hiding

After shading, the shaded grid is sent to the hidden-surface evaluation routine. First, the grid is *busted* into individual micropolygons. Each micropolygon then goes through a miniature version of the main primitive loop. It is bounded, checked for being on-screen, and backface culled if appropriate. Next, the bound determines in which pixels this micropolygon might appear. In each such pixel, a stochastic sampling algorithm tests the micropolygon to see if it covers any of the several predetermined point-sample locations of that pixel. For any samples that are covered, the color and opacity of the micropolygon, as well as its depth, are recorded as a *visible point*. Depending on the shading interpolation method chosen for that primitive, the visible-point color may be a Gouraud interpolation of the four micropolygon corner colors, or it may simply be a copy of one of the corners. Each sample location keeps a list of visible points, sorted by depth. Of course, keeping more than just the frontmost element of the list is only necessary if there is transparency involved.

Once all the primitives that cover a pixel have been processed, the visible-point lists for each sample can be composited together and the resulting final sample colors and opacities blended together using the reconstruction filter to generate final pixel colors. Because good reconstruction kernels span multiple pixels, the final color of each pixel depends on the samples not merely in that pixel, but in neighboring pixels as well. The pixels are sent to the display system to be put into a file or onto a frame buffer.

6.2.5   Motion Blur and Depth of Field

Interestingly, very few changes need to be made to the basic Reyes rendering pipeline to support several of the most interesting and unique features of *PRMan*. One of the most often used advanced features is motion blur. Any primitive may be motion blurred either by a moving transformation or by a moving deformation (or both). In the former case, the primitive is defined as a single set of control points with multiple transformation matrices; in the latter case, the primitive actually contains multiple sets of control points. In either case, the moving primitive when diced becomes a moving grid, with positional data for the beginning and ending of the motion path, and eventually a set of moving micropolygons.

The only significant change to the main rendering pipeline necessary to support this type of motion is that bounding box computations must include the entire motion path of the object. The hidden-surface algorithm modifications necessary to handle motion blur are implemented using the *stochastic sampling* algorithm first described by Cook et al. in 1984. The hidden-surface algorithm's point-sample locations are each augmented with a unique sample time. As each micropolygon is sampled, it is translated along its motion path to the position required for each sample's time.

PRMan only shades moving primitives at the start of their motion and only supports linear motion of primitives between their start and stop positions. This means that shaded micropolygons do not change color over time, and they leave constant-colored streaks across the image. This is incorrect, particularly with respect to lighting, as micropolygons will "drag" shadows or specular highlights around with them. In practice, this artifact is rarely noticed due to the fact that such objects are so blurry anyway.

Depth of field is handled in a very similar way. The specified lens parameters and the known focusing equations make it easy to determine how large the circle of confusion is for each primitive in the scene based on its depth. That value increases the bounding box for the primitive and for its micropolygons. Stochastically chosen lens positions are determined for each point sample, and the samples are appropriately jittered on the lens in order to determine which blurry micropolygons they see.

6.2.6   Shading before Hiding

Notice that this geometric pipeline has a feature that few other renderers share: the shading calculations are done before the hidden-surface algorithm is run. In normal scanline renderers, polygons are depth-sorted, the visible polygons are identified, and those polygons are clipped to create "spans" that cover portions of a scanline. The end points of those spans are shaded and then painted into pixels. In ray tracing renderers, pixel sample positions are turned into rays, and the objects that are hit by (and therefore visible from) these rays are the only things that are shaded. Radiosity renderers often resolve colors independently of a particular viewpoint but nonetheless compute object intervisibility as a prerequisite to energy transfer. Hardware *z*-buffer algorithms do usually shade before hiding, as Reyes does; however, they generally only compute true shading at polygon vertices, not at the interiors of polygons.

One of the significant advantages of shading before hiding is that displacement shading is possible. This is because the final locations of the vertices are not needed by the hider until after shading has completed, and therefore the shader is free to move the points around without the hider ever knowing. In other algorithms, if the shader moved the vertices after the hider had resolved surfaces, it would invalidate the hider's results.

The biggest disadvantage of shading before hiding is that objects are shaded before it is known whether they will eventually be hidden from view. If the scene has a large depth complexity, large amounts of geometry might be shaded and then subsequently covered over by objects closer to the camera. That would be a large waste of compute time. In fact, it is very common for this to occur in z-buffer renderings of complicated scenes. This disadvantage is addressed in the enhanced algorithm described in Section 6.3.2.

6.2.7   Memory Considerations

In this pipeline, each stage of processing converts a primitive into a finer and more detailed version. Its representation in memory gets larger as it is split, diced, busted, and sampled. However, notice also that every primitive is processed independently and has no interaction with other primitives in the system. Even sibling subprimitives are handled completely independently. For this reason, the geometric database can be streamed through the pipeline just as a geometric database is streamed through typical z-buffer hardware. There is no long-term storage or buffering of a global database (except for the queue of split primitives waiting to be bounded, which is rarely large), and therefore there is almost no memory used by the algorithm. With a single exception: the visible point lists.

As stated earlier, no visible-point list can be processed until it is known that all of the primitives that cover its pixel have, in fact, been processed. Because the streaming version of Reyes cannot know that any given pixel is done until the last primitive is rendered, it must store all the visible-point lists for the entire image until the very end. The visible-point lists therefore contain a point-sampled representation of the *entire* geometric database and consequently are quite large. Strike that. They are absolutely huge—many gigabytes for a typical high-resolution film frame. Monstrously humongous. As a result, the algorithm simply would not be usable if implemented in this way. Memory-sensitive enhancements are required to make the algorithm practical.

6.3   Enhanced Geometric Pipeline

The original Reyes paper recognized that the memory issue was a problem, even more so in 1985 than it is now. So it provided a mechanism for limiting memory use, and other mechanisms have been added since, which together make the algorithm much leaner than most other algorithms.

6.3.1   Bucketing

In order to alleviate the visible-point memory problem, a modified Reyes algorithm recognizes that the key to limiting the overall size of the visible-point memory is to know that certain pixels are done before having to process the entire database. Those pixels can then be finished and freed early. This is accomplished by dividing the image into small rectangular pixel regions, known as *buckets*, which will be processed one by one to completion before significant amounts of work occur on other buckets.

The most important difference in the pipeline is in the bounding step, which now also sorts the primitives based on which buckets they affect (that is, which buckets the bounding box overlaps). If a primitive is not visible in the current bucket of interest, it is put onto a list for the first bucket where it will matter and is thereby held in its most compact form until truly needed.

After this, the algorithm proceeds in the obvious way. Buckets are processed one at a time. Objects are removed from the list for the current bucket and either split or diced. Split primitives might be added back to the list or might be added to the lists of future buckets, depending on their bounding boxes. Diced primitives go through the normal shading pipeline and are busted. During busting, the micropolygons are bound and similarly bucket-sorted. Micropolygons that are not in the current bucket of interest are not sampled until the appropriate bucket is being processed. Figure 6.3 shows four primitives whose disposition is different. Primitive A will be diced, shaded, and sampled in the current bucket. Primitive B needs to be split, and half will return to the current bucket while half will be handled in a future bucket. Primitive C is in the current bucket because its bounding box touches it (as shown), but once split, you can see that both child primitives will fall into future buckets. Primitive D will be diced and shaded in the current bucket, but some of the micropolygons generated will be held for sampling until the next bucket is processed.

Eventually, there are no more primitives in the current bucket's list, because they all have either been sampled or transferred to future buckets. At that point, all of the visible-point lists in that bucket can be resolved and the pixels for that bucket displayed. This is why *PhotoRealistic RenderMan* creates output pixels in little blocks, rather than in scanlines like many algorithms. Each block is a bucket. The algorithm does not require that the buckets be processed in a particular order, but in practice the implementation still uses a scanline-style order, processing buckets one horizontal row at a time, left to right across the row, and rows from top to bottom down the image.

The major effect of this pipeline change is the utilization of memory. The entire database is now read into memory and sorted into buckets before any significant amount of rendering is done. The vast majority of the geometric database is stored in the relatively compact form of per-bucket lists full of high-level geometric primitives. Some memory is also used for per-bucket lists of micropolygons that have already been diced and shaded but are not relevant to the current bucket. The

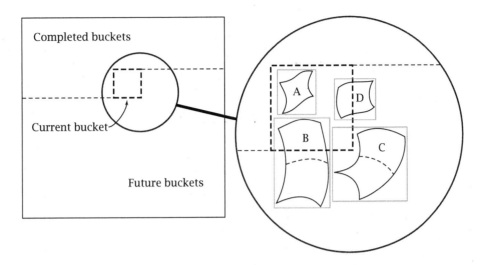

Figure 6.3 When the renderer processes the primitives that are on the list for the currrent bucket, their size and positions determine their fates.

visible-point lists have been reduced to only those that are part of the current bucket, a small fraction of the lists required for an entire image. Thus we have traded visible-point list memory for geometric database memory, and in all but the most pathological cases, this trade-off wins by orders of magnitude.

6.3.2   Occlusion Culling

As described so far, the Reyes algorithm processes primitives in arbitrary order within a bucket. In the preceding discussion, we mentioned that this might put a primitive through the dicing/shading/hiding pipeline that will eventually turn out to be obscured by a later primitive that is in front of it. If the dicing and shading of these objects takes a lot of computation time (which it generally does in a photorealistic rendering with visually complex shaders), this time is wasted. As stated, this problem is not unique to Reyes (it happens to nearly every z-buffer algorithm), but it is still annoying. The enhanced Reyes algorithm significantly reduces this inefficiency by a process known as *occlusion culling*.

The primitive bound-and-sort routine is changed to also sort each bucket's primitives by depth. This way, objects close to the camera are taken from the sorted list and processed first, while farther objects are processed later. Simultaneously, the hider keeps track of a simple hierarchical data structure that describes how much of the bucket has been covered by opaque objects and at what depths. Once the bucket is completely covered by opaque objects, any primitive that is entirely behind that covering is occluded. Because it cannot be visible, it can be culled before the expensive dicing and shading occurs (in the case of procedural primitives, before they are even loaded into the database). By processing primitives in front-to-back order, we maximize the probability that at least some objects will be occluded and culled. This optimization provides a two- to ten-times speedup in the rendering times of typical high-resolution film frames.

6.3.3   Network Parallel Rendering

In the enhanced Reyes algorithm, most of the computation—dicing, shading, hiding, and filtering—takes place once the primitives have been sorted into buckets. Moreover, except for a few details discussed later, those bucket calculations are generally independent of each other. For this reason, buckets can often be processed independently, and this implies that there is an opportunity to exploit parallelism. *PRMan* does this by implementing a large-grain multiprocessor parallelism scheme known as *NetRenderMan*.

With NetRenderMan, a parallelism-control client program dispatches work in the form of bucket requests to multiple independent rendering server processes. Server processes handle all of the calculation necessary to create the pixels for the requested bucket, then make themselves available for additional buckets. The overall multiprocessor efficiency is limited to about 70–80% on typical frames, due to factors such as serial sections of the code (particularly in database sorting), redundant work on primitives that overlap multiple buckets, and network latency. Nevertheless, the algorithm often shows linear speedup through 8–10 processors. Because these processes run independently of each other, with no shared data structures, they can run on multiple machines on the network, and in fact on multiple processor architectures in a heterogeneous network, with no additional loss of efficiency.

6.4   Rendering Attributes and Options

With this background, it is easy to understand certain previously obscure rendering attributes and options, and why they affect memory and/or rendering time, and also why certain types of geometric models render faster or slower than others.

6.4.1   Shading Rate

In the RenderMan Interface, the ShadingRate of an object refers to the frequency with which the primitive must be shaded (actually measured by sample area in pixels) in order to adequately capture its color variations. For example, a typical ShadingRate of 1.0 specifies one shading sample per pixel, or roughly Phong-shading style. In the Reyes algorithm, this constraint translates into micropolygon size. During the dicing phase, an estimate of the raster space size of the primitive is made, and this number is divided by the shading rate to determine the number of micropolygons that must make up the grid. However, the dicing tessellation is

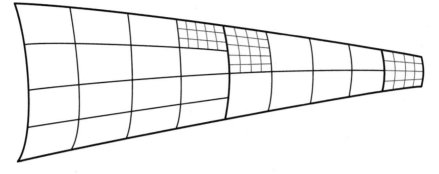

Figure 6.4 Adaptive parametric subdivision leads to adjacent grids that are different sizes parametrically and micropolygons that approximate the desired shading rate.

always done in such a manner as to create (within a single grid) micropolygons that are of identically sized rectangles in the parametric space of the primitive. For this reason, it is not possible for the resulting micropolygons in a grid to all be exactly the same size in raster space, and therefore they will only approximate the shading rate requested of the object. Some will be slightly larger, others slightly smaller than desired.

Notice, too, that any adjacent sibling primitive will be independently estimated, and therefore the number of micropolygons that are required for it may easily be different (even if the sibling primitive is the same size in parametric space). In fact, this is by design, as the Reyes algorithm fundamentally takes advantage of *adaptive subdivision* to create micropolygons that are approximately equal in size in raster space independent of their size in parametric space (see Figure 6.4). That way, objects farther away from the camera will create a smaller number of equally sized micropolygons, instead of creating a sea of inefficient nanopolygons. Conversely, objects very close to the camera will create a large number of micropolygons, in order to cover the screen with sufficient shading samples to capture the visual detail that is required of the close-up view. For this reason, it is very common for two adjacent grids to have different numbers of micropolygons along their common edge, and this difference in micropolygon size across an edge is the source of some shading artifacts that are described in Section 6.5.4.

In most other rendering algorithms, a shading calculation occurs at every hidden-surface sample, so raising the antialiasing rate increases the number of shading samples as well. Because the vast majority of calculations in a modern renderer are in the shading and hidden-surface calculations, increasing PixelSamples therefore has a direct linear effect on rendering time. In Reyes, these two calculations are decoupled, because shading rate affects only micropolygon dicing, not hidden-surface evaluation. Antialiasing can be increased without spending any additional time shading, so raising the number of pixel samples in a Reyes image will make a much smaller impact on rendering time than in other algorithms (often in the range of percentage points instead of multiplicative factors). Conversely, adjusting the shading rate will have a large impact on rendering time in images where shading dominates the calculation.

6.4.2   Bucket Size and Maximum Grid Size

The bucket size option obviously controls the number of pixels that make up a bucket and inversely controls the number of buckets that make up an image. The most obvious effect of this control is to regulate the amount of memory devoted to visible-point lists. Smaller buckets are more memory efficient because less memory is devoted to visible-point lists. Less obviously, smaller buckets partition the geometric database into larger numbers of shorter, sorted primitive lists, with some consequential decrease in sorting time. However, this small effect is usually offset by the increase in certain per-bucket overhead.

The maximum grid size option controls dicing by imposing an upper limit on the number of micropolygons that may occur in a single grid. Larger grids are more efficient to shade because they maximize vector pipelining. However, larger grids also increase the amount of memory that can be devoted to shader global and local variable registers (which are allocated in rectangular arrays the size of a grid). More interestingly, however, the maximum grid size creates a loose upper bound on the pixel area that a grid may cover on-screen—a grid is unlikely to be much larger than the product of the maximum grid size and the shading rate of the grid. This is important in relation to the bucket size because grids that are larger than a bucket will tend to create large numbers of micropolygons that fall outside of the current bucket and that must be stored in lists for future buckets. Micropolygons that linger in such lists can use a lot of memory.

In the past, when memory was at a premium, it was often extremely important to optimize the bucket size and maximum grid size to limit the potentially large visible-point and micropolygon list memory consumption. On modern computers, it is rare that these data structures are sufficiently large to concern us, and large limits are perfectly acceptable. The default values for bucket size, 16×16 pixel buckets, and maximum grid size, 256 micropolygons per grid, work well except under the most extreme situations.

6.4.3   Transparency

Partially transparent objects cause no difficulty to the algorithm generally; however, they can have two effects on the efficiency of the implementation. First, transparent objects clearly affect the memory consumption of the visible-point lists. Due to the mathematical constraints of the compositing algebra used by *PRMan*, it is not possible to composite together the various partially transparent layers that are held in the visible-point list of a sample until the sample is entirely complete. Notice that an opaque layer can immediately truncate a list, but in the presence of large amounts of transparency, many potentially visible layers must be kept around. Second, and more importantly, transparent layers do not contribute to the occlusion culling of future primitives, which means that more primitives are diced and shaded than usual. Although this should be obvious (since those primitives are probably going to be seen through the transparent foreground), it is often quite surprising to see the renderer slow down as much as it does when the usually extremely efficient occlusion culling is essentially disabled by transparent foreground layers.

6.4.4   Displacement Bounds

Displacement shaders can move grid vertices, and there is no built-in constraint on the distance that they can be moved. However, recall that shading happens halfway through the rendering pipeline, with bounding, splitting, and dicing happening prior to the evaluation of those displacements. In fact, the renderer relies heavily on its ability to accurately yet tightly bound primitives so that they can be placed into the correct bucket. If a displacement pushes a grid vertex outside of its original bounding box, it will likely mean that the grid is also in the wrong bucket. Typically, this results in a large hole in the object corresponding to the bucket where the grid "should have been considered, but wasn't."

This is avoided by supplying the renderer a bound on the size of the displacement generated by the shader. From the shader writer's point of view, this number represents the worst-case displacement magnitude—the largest distance that any vertex might travel, given the calculations inherent in the displacement shader itself. From the renderer's point of view, this number represents the padding that must be given to every bounding box calculation prior to shading, to protect against vertices leaving their boxes. The renderer grows the primitive bounding box by this value, which means that the primitive is diced and shaded in a bucket earlier than it would normally be processed. This often leads to micropolygons that are created long before their buckets need them, which then hang around in bucket micropolygon lists wasting memory, or primitives that are shaded before it is discovered that they are offscreen. Because of these computational and memory inefficiencies of the expanded bounds, it is important that the displacement bounds be as tight as possible, to limit the damage.

6.4.5   Extreme Displacement

Sometimes the renderer is stuck with large displacement bounds, either because the object really does displace a large distance or because the camera is looking extremely closely at the object and the displacements appear very large on-screen. In extreme cases, the renderer can lose huge amounts of memory to micropolygon lists that contain most of the geometric database. In cases such as these, a better option is available. Notice that the problem with the displacement bound is that it is a worst-case estimate over the primitive as a whole, whereas the small portion of the primitive represented by a single small grid usually does not contain the worst-case displacement and actually could get away with a much smaller (tighter) bound. The solution to this dilemma is to actually *run the shader* to evaluate the true displacement magnitude for each grid on a grid-by-grid basis and then store those values with the grid as the *exact* displacement bound. The disadvantage of this technique is that it requires the primitive to be shaded twice, once solely to determine the displacement magnitude and then again later to generate the color when the grid is processed normally in its new bucket. Thus, it is a simple space-time trade-off.

This technique is enabled by the `extremedisplacement` attribute, which specifies a threshold raster distance. If the projected raster size of the displacement bound for a primitive exceeds the extreme displacement limit for that primitive, the extra shading calculations are done to ensure economy of memory. If it does not, then the extra time is not spent, under the assumption that for such a small distance the memory usage is transient enough to be inconsequential.

6.4.6   Motion-Factor

When objects move quickly across the screen, they become blurry. Such objects are indistinct both because their features are spread out over a large region and because their speed makes it difficult for our eyes to track them. As a result, it is not necessary to shade them with particularly high fidelity, as the detail will just be lost in the motion blur. Moreover, every micropolygon of the primitive will have a very large bounding box (corresponding to the length of the streak), which means that fine tessellations will lead to large numbers of micropolygons that linger a long time in memory as they are sampled by the many buckets along their path.

The solution to this problem is to enlarge the shading rate of primitives if they move rapidly. It is possible for the modeler to do this, of course, but it is often easier for the renderer to determine the speed of the model and then scale the shading rates of each primitive consistently. The attribute that controls this calculation is a GeometricApproximation flag known as `motionfactor`. For obscure reasons, `motionfactor` gives a magnification factor on shading rate per every 16 pixels of blurring. Experience has shown that a motion-factor of 1.0 is appropriate for a large range of images.

The same argument applies equally to depth of field blur, and in the current implementation, `motionfactor` (despite its name) also operates on primitives with large depth of field blurs as well.

6.5   Rendering Artifacts

Just as an in-depth understanding of the Reyes pipeline helps you understand the reason for, and utility of, various rendering options and attributes, it also helps you understand the causes and solutions for various types of geometric rendering artifacts that can occur while using *PhotoRealistic RenderMan*.

6.5.1   Eye Splits

Sometimes *PhotoRealistic RenderMan* will print the error message "Cannot split primitive at eye plane," usually after appearing to stall for quite a while. This error message is a result of perhaps the worst single algorithmic limitation of the modified Reyes algorithm: in order to correctly estimate the shading rate required for a primitive, the primitive must first be projected into raster space in order to evaluate its size. Additionally, recall that the first step in the geometric pipeline is to bound the primitive and sort it into buckets based on its position in raster space, which requires the same projection. The problem is that the mathematics of perspective projection only works for positions that are in front of the camera. It is not possible to project points that are behind the camera. For this reason, the renderer must divide the primitive into areas that are in front of and areas that are behind the camera.

Most rendering algorithms, if they require this projection at all, would clip the primitive against the near clipping plane (hence the name) and throw away the bad regions. However, the entire Reyes geometric and shading pipelines require subprimitives that are rectangular in parametric space, which can be split and diced cleanly. Clipping does not create such primitives and cannot be used. Instead, Reyes simply splits the primitive hoping that portions of the smaller subprimitives will be easier to classify and resolve.

Figure 6.5 shows the situation. Notice that primitives that lie entirely forward of the eye plane are projectable, so can be accepted. Primitives that lie entirely behind the near clipping plane can be trivially culled. It is only primitives that span both planes that cannot be classified and are split. The region between the planes can be called the "safety zone." If a split line lies entirely within this zone (in 3D, of course), both children of the bad primitive are classifiable, which is the situation we are hoping for. If the split line straddles a plane, at least we will shave some of the bad primitive away and the remaining job, we hope, is slightly easier. Reyes splits as smartly as it can, attempting to classify subprimitives.

Unhappily, there are geometric situations where the splitting simply doesn't work in a reasonable number of steps. "Reasonable" is defined as a small integer because each split doubles the number of subprimitives, so even 10 attempts create $2^{10} = 1024$ primitives. If, after splitting the maximum permitted number of times, the primitive still cannot be classified, Reyes gives up and throws the primitive away and prints the "Cannot split" message. If that primitive was supposed to be visible, the lost section will leave a hole in the image.

Primitives that have large displacement bounds, or are moving rapidly toward the camera, will exacerbate the eye-splitting problem because the parametric splitting process will do very little to reduce the bounding box. Indeed, for primitives for which the camera is inside the displacement bound of part of the surface, or primitives whose motion path actually goes through the camera, splitting can never succeed.

In order to reduce the artifacts due to eye-split culling, the key is to give the renderer the largest possible safety zone. Place the near clipping plane as far forward

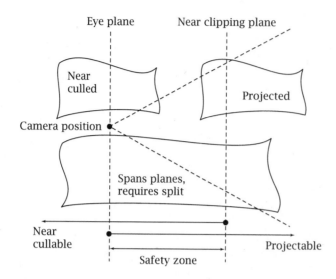

Figure 6.5 The geometric relationship of the near and eye planes gives rise to three categories of primitives: the cullable, the projectable, and the "spanners," which require splitting.

as is possible without otherwise affecting the image. The near clipping plane can be placed surprisingly far forward for most shots made with cameras that have reasonable fields of view. If you don't normally set the clipping plane, set it to some small but reasonable value immediately—the default value of 1e-10 is just about as bad as you could get! The number of splitting iterations that will be permitted can be controlled with a rendering option, and if you permit a few more, you can sometimes help handling of large but otherwise simple primitives. Beware, however, of the displacement and motion cases, because upping the limit will just let the renderer waste exponentially more time before it gives up.

Also, make sure that displacement bounds for primitives near the camera (for example, the ground plane) are as tight as possible and that the shader is coded so that the displacement itself is as small as possible. If you place the camera so close to some primitive that the displacement bound is a significant portion of the image size, there will be no end of trouble with both eye splits and displacement stretching (discussed later). In flyovers of the Grand Canyon, the canyon should be modeled, not implemented as a displacement map of a flat plane!

It will also help to keep the camera as high off the ground as possible without ruining the composition of the shot. Reyes simply has lots of trouble with worm's-eye views. And make sure that no object is flying through the camera (you wouldn't do that in live-action photography, would you?). Generally, if you pretend that the CG camera has a physical lens that keeps objects in the scene at least a certain distance away and respect that border, you will have fewer problems with eye splits.

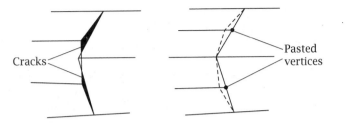

Figure 6.6 Tessellation differences result in patch cracks, but these can be repaired by moving binary-diced vertices.

6.5.2   Patch Cracks

Patch cracks are tiny holes in the surface of objects that are caused by various errors in the approximation of primitives by their tessellations (we'll use the term loosely to include tessellation-created cracks on primitives other than patches). Patch cracks usually appear as scattered pinholes in the surface, although they can sometimes appear as lines of pinholes or as small slits. Importantly, they always appear along parametric lines of primitives. They are recognizably different from other holes created by clipping, culling, or bucketing errors, which are usually larger, often triangular, and occur in view-dependent places (like on silhouettes or aligned with bucket boundaries).

Patch cracks occur because when objects are defined by sets of individual primitives, the connectedness of those primitives is only implied by the fact that they abut, that they have edges that have coincident vertices. There is no way in the RenderMan Interface to explicitly state that separate primitives have edges that should be "glued together." Therefore, as the primitives go through the geometric pipeline independently, there is a chance that the mathematical operations that occur on one version of the edge will deviate from those on the other version of the edge, and the vertices will diverge. If they do, a crack occurs between them.

The deviations can happen in several ways. One is for the tessellation of the edge by adjacent grids to be done with micropolygons of different sizes. Figure 6.6 shows that such tessellations naturally create intermediate grid vertices that do not match, and there are tiny holes between the grids. For many years, *PRMan* has had a switch that eliminated most occurrences of this type of crack. Known as *binary dicing*, it requires that every grid have tessellations that create a power-of-two number of micropolygons along each edge. Although these micropolygons are smaller than are required by shading rate alone, binary dicing ensures that adjacent grids have tessellations that are powers-of-two multiples of each other (generally, a single factor of two). Thus, alternating vertices will coincide, and the extra vertices on one side are easily found and "pasted" to the other surface.

Another way that patch cracks can happen is when the displacement shader that operates on grid vertices gets different results on one grid from another. If a common vertex displaces differently on two grids, the displacement literally rips the surface apart, leaving a crack between. One common reason for such differing results is displacement mapping using texture filter sizes that are mismatched (see Section 6.5.4). The texture call then returns a slightly different value on the two grids, and one grid displaces to a different height than the other. Another common reason is displacement occurring along slightly different vectors. For example, the results of `calculatenormal` are almost guaranteed to be different on the left edge of one grid and on the right edge of the adjacent grid. If displacement occurs along these differing vectors, the vertices will obviously go to different places, opening a crack. Unfortunately, only careful coding of displacement shaders can eliminate this type of cracking.

Notice that patch cracks cannot happen on the interiors of grids. Because grid micropolygons explicitly share vertices, it is not possible for such neighbor micropolygons to have cracks between them. For this reason, patch cracks will only occur along boundaries of grids, and therefore along parametric edges. In *PRMan* versions prior to 3.9, patch cracks could occur on any grid edge, including those that resulted from splitting a patch into subpatches. Later versions of *PRMan* have a crack-avoidance algorithm that glues all such subpatches together. Therefore, modern versions of *PRMan* will only exhibit patch cracks along boundaries of original primitives, not along arbitrary grid boundaries.

6.5.3   Displacement Stretching

Another problem that displacement shaders might create is stretching of micropolygons. This is caused when displacement shaders move the vertices of a micropolygon apart, so that it no longer obeys the constraint that it is approximately the size specified by the shading rate.

In the process of dicing, the renderer estimates the size of the primitive on-screen and makes a grid that has micropolygons that approximately match the shading rate. Shading then occurs on the vertices of the grid (the corners of the micropolygons). Displacement shaders are permitted to move grid vertices, but there is no constraint on where they are moved. If two adjacent grid vertices are moved in different directions (wildly or subtly), the area of the micropolygon connecting them will change. Generally, this change is so small that the micropolygon is still safely in the range expected of shading rate. However, if the displacement function has strong high frequencies, adjacent grid vertices might move quite differently. For example, an embossing shader might leave some vertices alone while moving vertices inside the embossed figure quite a distance. The micropolygons whose corners move very differently will change size radically, and sometimes will be badly bent or twisted (see Figure 6.7).

Twisted micropolygons have unusual normal vectors, and this alone may be enough to cause shading artifacts. For example, highly specular surfaces are very sensitive to normal vector orientation, so a micropolygon that is twisted in an unusual direction may catch an unexpected highlight.

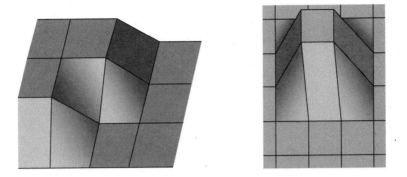

Figure 6.7 Displacement stretching leads to micropolygons that are bent, twisted, or significantly larger than anticipated.

More common, however, is that the stretching of the micropolygons will it-self be visible in the final image. An individual flat-shaded micropolygon creates a constant-colored region in the image. With a standard shading rate of around a pixel, every pixel gets a different micropolygon and the flat shading is not visible. But large stretched or long twisted micropolygons will cover many pixels, and the constant-colored region will be evident. Sometimes this takes the form of alternating dark and light triangles along the face of a displacement "cliff." Corners of micropolygons that are shaded for the top of the plateau hang down, while corners of micropolygons that are shaded for the valley poke up, interleaved like teeth of a gear.

The visual artifacts of these problems can be somewhat ameliorated by using smooth shading interpolation, which will blur the shading discontinuities caused by the varying normals. However, the geometric problems remain. The primary solution is to lower the frequency content of the displacement shader so that adjacent micropolygons cannot have such wildly varying motion (see Chapter 11 on antialiasing shaders for hints). If this cannot be done, the brute-force approach is to reduce the shading rate to values such as 0.25 pixels or smaller so that even stretched micropolygons stay under one pixel in size. However, this will have significant performance impact, because shading time is inversely proportional to shading rate. Fortunately, shading rate is an attribute of individual primitives, so the extra expense can be limited to the part of the model that requires it.

6.5.4   Texture Filter Mismatches

As primitives are split, their subprimitives proceed through the rendering pipeline independently, and when the time comes to dice them, their own individual size on-screen determines the tessellation rate. As a result, it is often the case that the adjacent grids resulting from adjacent subprimitives will project to different sizes on the screen and as a result will tessellate at different rates during dicing. Tessellated micropolygons are rectangular in the parametric space of the original primitive, and all of the micropolygons in a single grid will be the same size in that parametric space, but due to the differing tessellation rates, the micropolygons that make up the adjacent grids will have different sizes in parametric space.

One of the artifacts that results from this difference is that filtering calculations based on parametric size will change discontinuously across a grid boundary. In Chapter 11 on shader antialiasing, various filtering techniques are discussed that use parametric size as part of the calculation of filter width. This type of size discontinuity will result in filtering discontinuities, which can be visible in the final image. For example, in simple texturing, the texture filter size defaults to the micropolygon size. The resulting texture can have visible changes in sharpness over the surface of an otherwise smooth primitive. If the result of a texture call is used as a displacement magnitude, a displacement crack can result (Section 6.5.2).

Recent versions of *PRMan* have significantly reduced problems such as these by the introduction of smooth derivatives. The derivatives and the parametric size values that are available to shaders now describe a smoothly varying idealized parametric size for the micropolygon. That is, the values do not exactly match the true size of the micropolygon in parametric space, but instead track closely the desired parametric size given the shading rate requested (in some sense compensating for the compromises that needed to be made to accommodate binary dicing or other tessellation constraints at the time of dicing). These smoothly varying parametric size estimates ameliorate texture filter size mismatches, both in built-in shading functions and in antialiased procedural textures. Generally, the fact that micropolygons are not exactly the size that they advertise is a small issue, and where it is an issue, it can be compensated for by minor modifications to the shader.

6.5.5   Conclusion

The Reyes rendering architecture is so general and flexible that new primitives, new graphics algorithms, and new effects features have been added modularly to the existing structure almost continously for over 15 years. The system has evolved from an experimental testbed with a seemingly unattainable dream of handling tens of thousands of primitives into a robust production system that regularly handles images a hundred times more complex than that. The speed and memory enhancements that have been added may appear to have been short-term requirements, as Moore's law allows us to run the program on computers that are faster and have more memory without any additional programming. However, this is shortsighted, for our appetite for complexity has scaled, too, as fast or faster than Moore's law allows. Undoubtedly, in 15 more years, when computers with a terabyte of main memory are common and optical processors chew up 1 billion primitives without flinching, we will still be using the Reyes architecture to compute our holofilms.

Shading

7 Introduction to Shading Language

This chapter provides a refresher on the RenderMan Shading Language. However, it is not a tutorial on programming in general, nor is it intended to be a substitute for *The RenderMan Companion* or the *RenderMan Interface Specification*. But rather it is meant to serve as a handy quick reference guide to Shading Language itself.

Shading Language is loosely based on the C programming language. We will use this to our advantage in this chapter by assuming that (1) you already know about general programming concepts such as variables, loops, and so on; (2) you are reasonably familiar with C; (3) your mathematical background is sufficient to allow casual discussion of trigonometry and vector algebra; (4) you have sufficient background in computer graphics to understand intermediate-level concepts related to illumination computations. If you are lacking in any of these areas, you should review the material in Chapter 2 and its references.

7.1 Shader Philosophy

Many renderers have a fixed shading model. This means that a single equation is used to determine the appearance of surfaces and the way that they respond to light. For example, many renderers use simple Phong illumination, which looks like this:

$$C_{\text{output}} = K_{\text{a}} C_{\text{amb}} + \sum_{i=1}^{\text{nlights}} (K_{\text{d}} C_{\text{diff}} (N \cdot L_i) Cl_i + K_{\text{s}} C_{\text{spec}} (R \cdot L_i)^n)$$

where

- L_i and Cl_i are the direction and color, respectively, of light number i
- K_{a}, K_{d}, K_{s}, n, C_{amb}, C_{diff}, and C_{spec} are user-specified parameters to the equation. By changing these parameters, the user can make different objects look as if they are made of different materials
- N is the surface normal and R is the mirror reflection direction from the point of view of the camera
- C_{output} is the resulting color of the surface

This particular equation is especially common and tends to make objects appear as though they are made of plastic if C_{spec} is white and somewhat like metal if both C_{spec} and C_{diff} are set to the same color.

Because a world made of flat-colored plastic would hardly be interesting, a common extension to this scheme is to allow the use of stored image files to determine the value of C_{diff} as it varies across the surface (this is called "texture mapping") or to modulate the surface normal N ("bump mapping"). Somewhat more sophisticated renderers may allow an image file to modulate any of the user-supplied parameters, but this still does not change the fundamental form of the shading equation, and therefore the resulting materials have a rather narrow range of appearances. Furthermore, even when using stored images to modulate the surface parameters, you are limited to the few kinds of modulations allowed by the renderer, and stored textures have a variety of limitations including limited resolution, obvious tiling and repetition artifacts, storage costs, and the problem of how the image textures get created in the first place.

7.1.1 Shading Language Overview

In contrast to this scheme, RenderMan-compliant renderers do not use a single shading equation. Rather, a programming language is used to describe the interactions of lights and surfaces. This idea was pioneered by Rob Cook (Cook, 1984), and further elaborated by Pat Hanrahan in the *RenderMan Specification* itself (Pixar, 1989; Hanrahan and Lawson, 1990) and by the *PRMan* product. The programs describing the output of light sources, and how the light is attenuated by surfaces and volumes, are called *shaders*, and the programming language that we use is known as *Shading Language*.

The *RenderMan Interface Specification* describes several types of shaders, distinguished by what quantities they compute and at what point they are invoked in the rendering pipeline:

Surface shaders describe the appearance of surfaces and how they react to the lights that shine on them.

Displacement shaders describe how surfaces wrinkle or bump.

Light shaders describe the directions, amounts, and colors of illumination distributed by a light source in the scene.

Volume shaders describe how light is affected as it passes through a participating medium such as smoke or haze.

Imager shaders describe color transformations made to final pixel values before they are output. (Programmable imager shaders are supported by *BMRT*, but not by *PRMan*.)

All shaders answer the question "What is going on at this spot?" The execution model of the shader is that you (the programmer) are only concerned with a single point on the surface and are supplying information about that point. This is known as an *implicit* model, as compared to an *explicit* model, which would be more of the flavor "draw feature *X* at position *Y*." The job of a surface shader is to calculate the color and opacity at a particular point on some surface. To do this, it may calculate any function, do texture map lookups, gather light, and so on. The shader starts out with a variety of data about the point being shaded but cannot find out about any other points.

The RenderMan Shading Language is a C-like language you can use to program the behavior of lights and surfaces. Shading Language gives you

- basic types useful for manipulating points, vectors, or colors
- mathematical, geometric, and string functions
- access to the geometric state at the point being shaded, including the position, normal, surface parameters, and amount of incoming light
- parameters supplied to the shader, as specified in the declaration of the shader or alternatively attached to the geometry itself

With this information, the goal of the surface shader is to compute the resulting color, opacity, and possibly the surface normal and/or position at a particular point.

The remainder of this chapter will give a quick introduction to the RenderMan Shading Language, with an emphasis on the basic functionality you will need to write surface and displacement shaders. The vast majority of shaders written for production are surface shaders. Although volume and light shaders are also important, they are more esoteric and less frequently written and so will be covered separately elsewhere in this book.

Listing 7.1 `plastic.sl`: The standard `plastic` shader. Note that we have modified the shader slightly from the RI spec in order to reflect more modern SL syntax and idioms. The line numbers are for reference only and are not part of the shader!

```
1    surface
2    plastic ( float Ka=1, Kd=1, Ks=0.5, roughness = 0.1;
3               color specularcolor = 1;
4            )
5    {
6        /* Simple plastic-like reflection model */
7        normal Nf = faceforward(normalize(N),I);
8        vector V = -normalize(I);
9        Ci = Cs * (Ka*ambient() + Kd*diffuse(Nf))
10             + Ks*specularcolor*specular(Nf,V,roughness);
11       Oi = Os;  Ci *= Oi;
12   }
```

7.1.2   Quick Tour of a Shader

Listing 7.1 is an example surface shader that roughly corresponds to the single built-in shading equation of many renderers. If you are an experienced C programmer, you will immediately pick out several familiar concepts. Shaders look rather like C functions.

Lines 1 and 2 specify the type and name of the shader. By convention, the source code for this shader will probably be stored in a disk file named `plastic.sl`, which is simply the shader name with the extension `.sl`. Lines 2-4 list the parameters to the shader and their default values. These defaults may be overridden by values passed in from the RIB stream. Lines 5-12 are the body of the shader. In lines 7-8, we calculate a forward-facing normal and a normalized "view" vector, which will be needed as arguments to the lighting functions. Lines 9-10 call several built-in functions that return the amount of ambient, diffuse, and specular reflection, scaling each by different weights, and summing them to give the final surface color `Ci`. Because surface shaders must set associated colors and opacities, line 11 sets the final opacity `Oi` simply to the default opacity of the geometric primitive, `Os`, and then multiplies `Ci` by `Oi`, in order to ensure that it represents *associated* color and opacity. Note that several undeclared variables such as `N`, `I`, and `Cs` are used in the shader. These are so-called *global* variables that the renderer precomputes and makes available to the shader.

Most surface shaders end with code identical to lines 7-11 of the example. Their main enhancement is the specialized computations they perform to select a base surface color, rather than simply using the default surface color, `Cs`. Shaders may additionally change the weights of the various lighting functions and might modify `N` and/or `P` for bump or displacement effects.

Table 7.1: Names of built-in data types.	
float	Scalar floating-point data (numbers)
point	Three-dimensional positions, directions, and surface orientations
vector	
normal	
color	Spectral reflectivities and light energy values
matrix	4×4 transformation matrices
string	Character strings (such as filenames)

7.2   Shading Language Data Types

Shading Language provides several built-in data types for performing computations inside your shader as shown in Table 7.1. Although Shading Language is superficially similar to the C programming language, these data types are not the same as those found in C. Several types are provided that are not found in C because they make it more convenient to manipulate the graphical data that you need to manipulate when writing shaders. Although float will be familiar to C programmers, Shading Language has no double or int types. In addition, SL does not support user-defined structures or pointers of any kind.

7.2.1   Floats

The basic type for scalar numeric values in Shading Language is the float. Because SL does not have a separate type for integers, float is used in SL in circumstances in which you might use an int if you were programming in C. Floating-point constants are constructed the same way as in C. The following are examples of float constants: 1, 2.48, -4.3e2.

7.2.2   Colors

Colors are represented internally by three floating-point components.[1] The components of colors are referent to a particular *color space*. Colors are by default represented as RGB triples ("rgb" space). You can assemble a color out of three

---

[1] Strictly speaking, colors may be represented by more than three components. But since all known RenderMan-compliant renderers use a three-component color model, we won't pretend that you must be general. It's highly unlikely that you'll ever get into trouble by assuming three color components.

Table 7.2: Names of color spaces.

`"rgb"`	The coordinate system that all colors start out in and in which the renderer expects to find colors that are set by your shader (such as Ci, Oi, and Cl).
`"hsv"`	hue, saturation, and value
`"hsl"`	hue, saturation, and lightness
`"YIQ"`	The color space used for the NTSC television standard.
`"xyz"`	CIE *XYZ* coordinates
`"xyY"`	CIE *xyY* coordinates

floats, either representing an RGB triple or some other color space known to the renderer. Following are some examples:

```
color (0, 0, 0)           /* black */
color "rgb" (.75, .5, .5)  /* pinkish */
color "hsv" (.2, .5, .63)  /* specify in "hsv" space */
```

All three of these expressions return colors in "rgb" space. Even the third example returns a color in "rgb" space—specifically, the RGB value of the color that is equivalent to hue 0.2, saturation 0.5, and value 0.63. In other words, when assembling a color from components given relative to a specific color space in this manner, there is an implied transformation to "rgb" space. The most useful color spaces that the renderer knows about are listed in Table 7.2.

Colors can have their individual components examined and set using the comp and setcomp functions, respectively. Some color calculations are easier to express in some color space other than "rgb". For example, desaturating a color is more easily done in "hsv" space. Colors can be explicitly transformed from one color space to another color space using ctransform (see Section 7.5 for more details). Note, however, that Shading Language does not keep track of which color variables are in which color spaces. It is the responsibility of the SL programmer to track this and ensure that by the end of the shader, Ci and Oi are in the standard "rgb" space.

7.2.3   Points, Vectors, Normals

Points, vectors, and normals are similar data types with identical structures but subtly different semantics. We will frequently refer to them collectively as the "point-like" data types when making statements that apply to all three types.

A point is a position in 3D space. A vector has a length and direction but does not exist in a particular location. A normal is a special type of vector that is *perpendicular* to a surface and thus describes the surface's orientation. Such a perpendicular vector uses different transformation rules from ordinary vectors, as we will discuss in this section. These three types are illustrated in Figure 7.1.

Figure 7.1 Points, vectors, and normals are all comprised of three floats but represent different entities—positions, directions, and surface orientations.

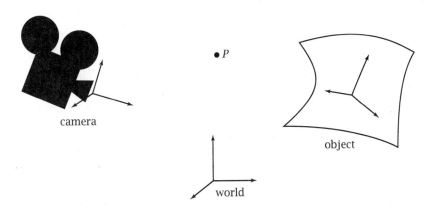

Figure 7.2 A point may be measured relative to a variety of coordinate systems.

All of these point-like types are internally represented by three floating-point numbers that uniquely describe a position or direction relative to the three axes of some coordinate system.

As shown in Figure 7.2, there may be many different coordinate systems that the renderer knows about ("world" space and a local "object" space, for example, were discussed in Chapter 3; others will be detailed later). Obviously, a particular point in 3D can be represented by many different sets of three floating-point numbers—one for each coordinate system. So which one of these spaces is the one against which your points and vectors are measured?

All points, vectors, and normals are described relative to some coordinate system. All data provided to a shader (surface information, graphics state, parameters, and vertex data) are relative to one particular coordinate system that we call the "current" coordinate system. The "current" coordinate system is one that is convenient for the renderer's shading calculations.

You can "assemble" a point-like type out of three floats using a constructor:

```
point (0, 2.3, 1)
vector (a, b, c)
normal (0, 0, 1)
```

These expressions are interpreted as a point, vector, and normal whose three components are the floats given, relative to "current" space. For those times when you really need to access or set these three numbers, SL provides the routines xcomp, ycomp, zcomp, comp, setxcomp, setycomp, setzcomp, setcomp (see Section 7.5).

As with colors, you may also specify the coordinates relative to some other coordinate system:

```
Q = point "object" (0, 0, 0);
```

This example assigns to Q the point at the origin of "object" space. However, this statement does *not* set the components of Q to (0,0,0)! Rather, Q will contain the "current" space coordinates of the point that is at the same location as the origin of "object" space. In other words, the point constructor that specifies a space name implicitly specifies a transformation to "current" space. This type of constructor also can be used for vectors and normals.

The choice of "current" space is implementation dependent. For *PRMan*, "current" space is the same as "camera" space; and in *BMRT*, "current" space is the same as "world" space. Other renderers may be different, so it's important not to depend on "current" space being any particular coordinate system.

Some computations may be easier in a coordinate system other than "current" space. For example, it is much more convenient to apply a "solid texture" to a moving object in its "object" space than in "current" space. For these reasons, SL provides built-in functions that allow you to transform points among different coordinate systems. The built-in functions transform, vtransform, and ntransform can be used to transform points, vectors, and normals, respectively, from one coordinate system to another (see Section 7.5). Note, however, that Shading Language does not keep track of which point variables are in which coordinate systems. It is the responsibility of the SL programmer to keep track of this and ensure that, for example, lighting computations are performed using quantities in "current" space.

Be very careful to use the right transformation routines for the right point-like types. As described in Chapter 2, points, direction vectors, and surface normals all transform in subtly different ways. Transforming with the wrong matrix math will introduce subtle and difficult-to-fix errors in your code. Therefore, it is important to always use transform for points, vtransform for vectors, and ntransform for normals.

Several coordinate systems are predefined by name in the definition of Shading Language. Table 7.3 summarizes some of the most useful ones. The RIB statement CoordinateSystem (or C API RiCoordinateSystem) may be used to give additional names to user-defined coordinate systems. These names may also be referenced inside your shader to designate transformations.

Table 7.3: Names of predeclared geometric spaces.

"current"	The coordinate system that all points start out in and the one in which all lighting calculations are carried out. Note that the choice of "current" space may be different on each renderer.
"object"	The local coordinate system of the graphics primitive (sphere, patch, etc.) that we are shading.
"shader"	The coordinate system active at the time that the shader was declared (by the Surface, Displacement, or LightSource statement).
"world"	The coordinate system active at WorldBegin.
"camera"	The coordinate system with its origin at the center of the camera lens, x-axis pointing right, y-axis pointing up, and z-axis pointing into the screen.
"screen"	The *perspective-corrected* coordinate system of the camera's image plane. Coordinate (0,0) in "screen" space is looking along the z-axis of "camera" space.
"raster"	The 2D projected space of the final output image, with units of pixels. Coordinate (0,0) in "raster" space is the upper-left corner of the image, with x and y increasing to the right and down, respectively.
"NDC"	Normalized device coordinates—like raster space but normalized so that x and y both run from 0 to 1 across the whole image, with (0,0) being at the upper left of the image, and (1,1) being at the lower right (regardless of the actual aspect ratio).

7.2.4   Matrices

Shading Language has a matrix type that represents the transformation matrix required to transform points and vectors between one coordinate system and another. Matrices are represented internally by 16 floats (a 4×4 homogeneous transformation matrix). Beware if you declare a matrix of storage class varying. That's going to be a lot of data!

A matrix can be constructed from a single float or 16 floats. For example:

```
matrix zero = 0;   /* makes a matrix with all 0 components */
matrix ident = 1;  /* makes the identity matrix */

/* Construct a matrix from 16 floats */
matrix m = matrix (m00, m01, m02, m03, m10, m11, m12, m13,
                   m20, m21, m22, m23, m30, m31, m32, m33);
```

Assigning a single floating-point number x to a matrix will result in a matrix with diagonal components all being x and other components being zero (i.e., x times the

identity matrix). Constructing a matrix with 16 floats will create the matrix whose
components are those floats, in row-major order.

Similar to point-like types, a matrix may be constructed in reference to a named
space:

```
/* Construct matrices relative to something other than "current" */
matrix q = matrix "shader" 1;
matrix m = matrix "world" (m00, m01, m02, m03, m10, m11, m12, m13,
                           m20, m21, m22, m23, m30, m31, m32, m33);
```

The first form creates the matrix that transforms points from "current" space to
"shader" space. Transforming points by this matrix is identical to calling trans-
form("shader",...). The second form prepends the current-to-world transforma-
tion matrix onto the 4×4 matrix with components $m_{0,0} \ldots m_{3,3}$. Note that although
we have used "shader" and "world" space in our examples, any named space is
acceptable.

Matrix variables can be tested for equality and inequality with the == and !=
Boolean operators. Also, the * operator between matrices denotes matrix multiplication, while m1 / m2 denotes multiplying m1 by the inverse of matrix m2. Thus, a
matrix can be inverted by writing 1/m. In addition, some functions will accept matrix variables as arguments, as described in Section 7.5.

7.2.5 Strings

The string type may hold character strings. The main application of strings is to
provide the names of files where textures may be found. Strings can be checked for
equality and can be manipulated with the format() and concat() functions. String
constants are denoted by surrounding the characters with double quotes, as in "I
am a string literal". Strings in Shading Language may be uniform only.

7.3 Shading Language Variables

There are three kinds of variables in Shading Language: global variables, local variables, and shader parameters. These correspond pretty much exactly to the globals,
locals, and parameters of a subroutine in a language like C. The one difference is
that variables in Shading Language not only have a data type (float, point, etc.) but
also a designated *storage class*. The storage class can be either uniform or varying
(except for strings, which can only be uniform). Variables that are declared as uniform have the same value everywhere on the surface. (Note that you may assign to,
or change the value of, uniform variables. Do not confuse uniform with the concept
of "read-only.") Variables that are declared as varying may take on different values
at different surface positions.

Table 7.4: Global variables available inside surface and displacement shaders. Variables are read-only except where noted.

`point P`	Position of the point you are shading. Changing this variable displaces the surface.
`normal N`	The surface shading normal (orientation) at `P`. Changing `N` yields bump mapping.
`normal Ng`	The true surface normal at `P`. This can differ from `N`; `N` can be overridden in various ways including bump mapping and user-provided vertex normals, but `Ng` is always the true surface normal of the facet you are shading.
`vector I`	The *incident* vector, pointing from the viewing position to the shading position `P`.
`color Cs, Os`	The default surface color and opacity, respectively.
`float u, v`	The 2D parametric coordinates of `P` (on the particular geometric primitive you are shading).
`float s, t`	The 2D texturing coordinates of `P`. These values can default to `u`, `v`, but a number of mechanisms can override the original values.
`vector dPdu` `vector dPdv`	The partial derivatives (i.e., tangents) of the surface at `P`.
`time`	The time of the current shading sample.
`float du, dv`	An estimate of the amount that the surface parameters `u` and `v` change from sample to sample.
`vector L` `color Cl`	These variables contain the information coming from the lights and may be accessed from inside `illuminance` loops only.
`color Ci, Oi`	The final surface color and opacity of the surface at `P`. Setting these two variables is the primary goal of a surface shader.

7.3.1 Global Variables

So-called *global variables* (sometimes called *graphics state variables*) contain the basic information that the renderer knows about the point being shaded, such as position, surface orientation, and default surface color. You need not declare these variables; they are simply available by default in your shader. Global variables available in surface shaders are listed in Table 7.4.

7.3.2 Local Variables

Local variables are those that you, the shader writer, declare for your own use. They are analogous to local variables in C or any other general-purpose programming language.

The syntax for declaring a variable in Shading Language is (items in brackets are optional)

[*class*] *type variablename* [= *initializer*]

where

- the optional *class* specifies one of `uniform` or `varying`. If *class* is not specified, it defaults to `varying` for local variables.
- *type* is one of the basic data types, described earlier.
- *variablename* is the name of the variable you are declaring.
- if you wish to give your variable an initial value, you may do so by assigning an *initializer*.

Recent renderers also support arrays, declared as follows:

class type variablename [*arraylen*] = { *init0* , *init1* . . . }

Arrays in Shading Language must have a constant length; they may not be dynamically sized. Also, only 1D arrays are allowed. Other than that, however, the syntax of array usage in Shading Language is largely similar to C. Some examples of variable declarations are

```
float a;         /* Declare; current value is undefined */
uniform float b; /* Explicitly declare b as uniform */
float c = 1;     /* Declare and assign */
float d = b*a;   /* Another declaration and assignment */
float e[10];     /* The variable e is an array */
```

When you declare local variables, you will generally want them to be `varying`. But be on the lookout for variables that take on the same value everywhere on the surface (for example, loop control variables) because declaring them as `uniform` may allow some renderers to take shortcuts that allow your shaders to execute more quickly and use less memory. (*PRMan* is a renderer for which `uniform` variables take much less memory and experience much faster computation.)

7.3.3 Shader Parameters

Parameters to your shader allow you to write shaders that are capable of simulating a family of related surfaces. For example, if you are writing a shader for a wood surface, you may wish to use parameters to specify such things as the grain color and ring spacing, rather than having them "hard-coded" in the body of the shader.

Parameterizing your shader not only allows you to reuse the shader for a different object later but also allows you to write the shader without knowing the value of the parameter. This is particularly useful if you are working in a production environment where an art director is likely to change his or her mind about the details of an object's appearance after you have written the shader. In this case, it is much easier to change the parameter value of the shader than to return to the source code and try to make deeper changes. For this reason, we strongly encourage parameterizing your shader to the greatest degree possible, eliminating nearly all hard-coded constants from your shader code, if possible. Well-written shaders for "hero" objects often have dozens or even hundreds of parameters.

Here is an example partial shader, showing several parameters being declared:

```
surface pitted ( float Ka=1, Kd=1, Ks=0.5;
                 float angle = radians(30);
                 color splotcolor = 0;
                 color stripecolor = color (.5, .5, .75);
                 string texturename = "";
                 string dispmapname = "mydisp.tx";
                 vector up = vector "shader" (0,0,1);
                 varying point Pref = point (0,0,0);
               )
{
  .
  .
  .
}
```

Note the similarity to a function declaration in C. The syntax for parameter declarations is like that for ordinary local variable declarations, except that shader parameters *must* be declared with default values assigned to them. If a storage class is not specifed, it defaults to uniform for shader parameters.

In the RIB file, you'll find something like

```
Declare "Kd" "float"
Declare "stripecolor" "color"
Surface "pitted" "Kd" [0.8] "stripecolor" [.2 .3 .8]
Sphere 1 -1 1 360
```

The Surface line specifies that the given shader should become part of the attribute state and hence be attached to any subsequent geometric primitives. That line not only specifies the name of the shader to use but also overrides two of its parameter values: Kd and stripecolor. Notice that prior to their use, those parameters are declared so that the renderer will know their types.

7.3.4   Declarations and Scoping

It is worth noting that a local variable declaration is just an ordinary program statement; a declaration may be placed anywhere that a statement would be allowed. In particular, it is not necessary to sharply divide your shader such that all variables are declared, then all statements are listed with no further variable declarations. Rather, you may freely mix variable declarations and other statements as long as all variables are declared prior (textually) to their first use. This is largely a stylistic choice, but many programmers feel that declaring variables near their first use can make code more readable.

Declarations may be scoped, as in C, by enclosing a group of statements inside curly braces. For example,

```
float x = 2;            /* outer declaration */
{
    float x = 1;        /* inner declaration */
    printf("%f\n", x);
}
    printf ("%f/n", x);
```

In this code fragment, the first `printf` statement will produce 1, but the second `printf` will produce 2. In other words, the variable x declared in the *inner* scope hides the similarly named but nevertheless separate variable x declared in the *outer* scope.

7.4   Statements and Control Flow

The body of a shader is a sequence of individual *statements*. This section briefly explains the major types of statements and control-flow patterns in Shading Language.

7.4.1   Expressions

The expressions available in Shading Language include the following:

- constants: floating point (e.g., `1.0`, `3`, `-2.35e4`), string literals (e.g., `"hello"`), and the named constant `PI`
- point, vector, normal, or matrix constructors, for example: `point "world" (1,2,3)`
- variable references
- unary and binary operators on other expressions, for example:

- expr	(negation)
expr + expr	(addition)
*expr * expr*	(multiplication)
expr - expr	(subtraction)
expr / expr	(division)
expr ∧ expr	(vector cross product)
expr . expr	(vector dot product)

The operators +, -, *, /, and the unary - (negation) may be used on any of the numeric types. For multicomponent types (colors, vectors, matrices), these operators combine their arguments on a component-by-component basis.

The ∧ and . operators only work for vectors and normals and represent cross product and dot product, respectively.[2]

The only operators that may be applied to the matrix type are * and /, which respectively denote matrix-matrix multiplication and matrix multiplication by the inverse of another matrix.

■ type casts, specified by simply having the type name in front of the value to cast:

```
vector P          /* cast a point to a vector */
point f           /* cast a float to a point */
color P           /* cast a point to a color! */
```

The three-component types (point, vector, normal, color) may be cast to other three-component types. A float may be cast to any of the three-component types (by placing the float in all three components) or to a matrix (which makes a matrix with all diagonal components being the float). Obviously, there are some type casts that are not allowed because they make no sense, like casting a point to a float or casting a string to a numerical type.

■ ternary operator, just like C: *condition* ? *expr1* : *expr2*
■ function calls

7.4.2   Assignments

Assignments are nearly identical to those found in the C language:

variable = *expression* ;

arrayvariable[*expression*] = *expression* ;

Also, just as in C, you may combine assignment and certain arithmetic operations using the +=, -=, *=, and /= operators. Examples of declarations and assignments follow:

```
a = b;            /* Assign b's value to a */
d += 2;           /* Add 2 to d */
e[5] = a;         /* Store a's value in element 5 of c */
c = e[2];         /* Reference an array element */
```

Unlike C, Shading Language *does not* have any of the following operators: integer modulus (%), bit-wise operators or assignments (&, |, ∧, &=, |=, ∧=), pre- and postincrement and decrement (++ and --).

---

[2] Because the vector and normal type are recent additions to SL (with point serving their purposes previously), most SL compilers will allow the vector operations to be performed on points but will issue a warning.

7.4.3   Decisions, Decisions

Conditionals in Shading Language work much as in C:

> `if ( condition )`
>   *truestatement*

and

> `if ( condition )`
>   *truestatement*
> `else`
>   *falsestatement*

The statements can also be entire blocks, surrounded by curly braces. For example,

```
if (s > 0.5) {
    Ci = s;
    Oi = 1;
} else {
    Ci = s+t;
}
```

In Shading Language, the condition may be one of the following Boolean opera-tors: ==, != (equality and inequality); <, <=, >, >= (less-than, less-than or equal, greater-than, greater-than or equal). Conditions may be combined using the logical operators: && (and), || (or), ! (not).

Unlike C, Shading Language has no implied cast from float to Boolean. In other words, the following *is not legal*:

```
float f = 5;
if (f) {   /* Not legal */
    ...
}
```

A C programmer may instinctively write this code fragment, intending that the conditional will evaluate to true if f is nonzero. But this is not the case in Shading Language. Rather, the shader programmer must write

```
float f = 5;
if (f != 0) {   /* OK */
    ...
}
```

7.4.4   Lather, Rinse, Repeat

Two types of loop constructs work nearly identically to their equivalents in C. Repeated execution of statements for as long as a condition is true is possible with a `while` statement:

```
while ( condition )
   truestatement
```

Also, C-like `for` loops are also allowed:

```
for ( init; condition; loopstatement )
   body
```

As with `if` statements, loop conditions must be relations, not floats. As with C, you may use `break` and `continue` statements to terminate a loop altogether or skip to the next iteration, respectively. As an enhancement over C, the `break` and `continue` statements may take an optional numeric constant, allowing you to efficiently exit from nested loops. For example,

```
for (i = 0;  i < 10;  i += 1) {
    for (j = 0;  j < 5;  j += 1) {
        if (...some condition...)
            continue 2;
    }
    ...
}
```

In this example, the numeral 2 after the `continue` indicates that under the appropriate conditions, execution should skip to the next iteration in the loop involving i—that is, the outer loop. If no number indicating a nesting level is given, it is assumed that 1 is intended—that is, that only the current loop should be exited or advanced.

As discussed in Chapter 6, *PRMan* shades entire grids at a time by simulating a virtual SIMD machine. This introduces extra overhead into keeping track of which points are executing inside the body of loops and conditionals that have varying conditions. Be sure to declare your loop control variables (the counters controlling the loop iteration, such as i and j in the example) as `uniform` whenever possible. Care that the conditions controlling `if`, `while`, and `for` statements are `uniform` can greatly speed up execution of your shaders. In addition, using `varying` variables in the condition of a loop or conditional is asking for trouble, because this can lead to jaggies on your surface and can even produce incorrect results if derivatives are calculated inside the body of the loop or conditional (see Chapter 11 for more details).

7.5   Simple Built-in Functions

Shading Language provides a variety of built-in functions. Many are described in this section. For brevity, functions that are identical to those found in the standard C library are presented with minimal elaboration, as are simple functions that are adequately explained in both *The RenderMan Companion* and *The RenderMan Interface* 3.1.

This section documents most of the everyday functions you will use for surface shaders but is not intended to be comprehensive. Many built-in functions are covered elsewhere in this book. Functions used for patterns are covered in Chapter 10. Derivatives (Du( ), Dv( ), area( )) are covered in Chapter 11. Lighting and environment mapping functions are covered in Chapter 9.

Note that some functions are *polymorphic*; that is, they can take arguments of several different types. In some cases we use the shorthand ptype to indicate a type that could be any of the point-like types point, vector, or normal. (Note that there is no actual type ptype—we are just using this as shorthand!)

Angles and Trigonometry

```
float radians (float d)
float degrees (float r)
```

```
float sin (float angle)
float cos (float angle)
float tan (float angle)
```

```
float asin (float f)
float acos (float f)
float atan (float y, x)
float atan (float y_over_x)
```

Angles, as in C, are assumed to be expressed in radians.

Exponentials, etc.

```
float pow (float x, float y)
float exp (float x)
float log (float x)
```

```
float log (float x, base)
```

Arbitrary base logarithm of x.

```
float sqrt (float x)
float inversesqrt (float x)
```

Square root and 1/sqrt.

Miscellaneous Simple Scalar Functions

```
float abs (float x)
```

Absolute value of x.

`float sign (float x)`

Returns 1 if $x > 0$, -1 if $x < 0$, 0 if $x = 0$.

`float floor (float x)`
`float ceil (float x)`
`float round (float x)`

Return the highest integer less than or equal to x, the lowest integer greater than or equal to x, or the closest integer to x, respectively.

`float mod (float a, b)`

Just like the *fmod* function in C, returns $a - b * \text{floor}(a/b)$.

type `min (`*type*` a, b, ...)`
type `max (`*type*` a, b, ...)`
type `clamp (`*type*` x, minval, maxval)`

The `min` and `max` functions return the minimum or maximum, respectively, of a list of two or more values. The `clamp` function returns

`min(max(x,minval),maxval)`

that is, the value x clamped to the specified range. The *type* may be any of `float`, `point`, `vector`, `normal`, or `color`. The variants that operate on colors or point-like objects operate on a component-by-component basis (i.e., separately for x, y, and z).

type `mix (`*type*` x, y; float alpha)`

The `mix` function returns a linear blending of any simple *type* (any of `float`, `point`, `vector`, `normal`, or `color`): $x * (1 - \alpha) + y * (\alpha)$

`float step (float edge, x)`

Returns 0 if $x < edge$ and 1 if $x \geq edge$.

`float smoothstep (float edge0, edge1, x)`

Returns 0 if $x \leq edge0$, and 1 if $x \geq edge1$ and performs a smooth Hermite interpolation between 0 and 1 when $edge0 < x < edge1$. This is useful in cases where you would want a thresholding function with a smooth transition.

Color Operations

`float comp (color c; float i)`

Returns the ith component of a color.

`void setcomp (output color c; float i, float x)`

Modifies color c by setting its ith component to value x.

```
color ctransform (string tospacename; color c_rgb)
color ctransform (string fromspacename, tospacename; color c_from)
```

Transform a color from one color space to another. The first form assumes that c_rgb is already an "rgb" color and transforms it to another named color space. The second form transforms a color between two named color spaces.

Geometric Functions

```
float xcomp (ptype p)
float ycomp (ptype p)
float zcomp (ptype p)
float comp (ptype p; float i)
```

Return the x, y, z, or simply the ith component of a point-like variable.

```
void setxcomp (output ptype p; float x)
void setycomp (output ptype p; float x)
void setzcomp (output ptype p; float x)
void setcomp (output ptype p; float i, x)
```

Set the x, y, z, or simply the ith component of a point-like type. These routines alter their first argument but do not return any value.

```
float length (vector V)
float length (normal V)
```

Return the length of a vector or normal.

```
float distance (point P0, P1)
```

Returns the distance between two points.

```
float ptlined (point P0, P1, Q)
```

Returns the distance from Q to the closest point on the line segment joining P0 and P1.

```
vector normalize (vector V)
vector normalize (normal V)
```

Return a vector in the same direction as V but with length 1—that is, V / length(V) .

```
vector faceforward (vector N, I, Nref)
vector faceforward (vector N, I)
```

If Nref . I < 0, returns N; otherwise, returns -N. For the version with only two arguments, Nref is implicitly Ng, the true surface normal. The point of these routines is to return a version of N that faces towards the camera—in the direction "opposite" of I.

To further clarify the situation, here is the implementation of `faceforward` expressed in Shading Language:

```
vector faceforward (vector N, I, Nref)
{
    return (I.Nref > 0) ? -N : N;
}

vector faceforward (vector N, I)
{
    extern normal Ng;
    return faceforward (N, I, Ng);
}
```

`vector reflect (vector I, N)`

For incident vector `I` and surface orientation `N`, returns the reflection direction $R = I - 2*(N.I)*N$. Note that `N` must be normalized (unit length) for this formula to work properly.

`vector refract (vector I, N; float eta)`

For incident vector `I` and surface orientation `N`, returns the refraction direction using Snell's law. The `eta` parameter is the ratio of the index of refraction of the volume containing `I` divided by the index of refraction of the volume being entered.

`point transform (string tospacename; point p_current)`
`vector vtransform (string tospacename; vector v_current)`
`normal ntransform (string tospacename; normal n_current)`

Transform a point, vector, or normal (assumed to be in "current" space) into the `tospacename` coordinate system.

`point transform (string fromspacename, tospacename; point pfrom)`
`vector vtransform (string fromspacename, tospacename; vector vfrom)`
`normal ntransform (string fromspacename, tospacename; normal nfrom)`

Transform a point, vector, or normal (assumed to be represented by its "fromspace" coordinates) into the `tospacename` coordinate system.

`point transform (matrix tospace; point p_current)`
`vector vtransform (matrix tospace; vector v_current)`
`normal ntransform (matrix tospace; normal n_current)`

`point transform (string fromspacename; matrix tospace; point pfrom)`

```
vector vtransform (string fromspacename; matrix tospace; vector vfrom)
normal ntransform (string fromspacename; matrix tospace; normal nfrom)
```

These routines work just like the ones that use the space names but instead use transformation matrices to specify the spaces to transform into.

```
point rotate (point Q; float angle; point P0, P1)
```

Returns the point computed by rotating point Q by angle radians about the axis that passes from point P0 to P1.

String Functions

```
void printf (string template, ...)
string format (string template, ...)
```

Much as in C, printf takes a template string and an argument list. Where the format string contains the characters %f, %c, %p, %m, and %s, printf will substitute arguments, in order, from the argument list (assuming that the arguments' types are float, color, point-like, matrix, and string, respectively).

The format function, like printf, takes a template and an argument list. But format returns the assembled, formatted string rather than printing it.

```
string concat (string s1, ..., sN)
```

Concatenates a list of strings, returning the aggregate string.

```
float match (string pattern, subject)
```

Does a string pattern match on subject. Returns 1 if the pattern exists anywhere within subject and 0 if the pattern does not exist within subject. The pattern can be a standard Unix expression. Note that the pattern does not need to start in the first character of the subject string, unless the pattern begins with the ^ (beginning of string) character.

Matrix Functions

```
float determinant (matrix m)
```

Returns the determinant of matrix m.

```
matrix translate (matrix m; point t)
matrix rotate (matrix m; float angle; vector axis)
matrix scale (matrix m; point t)
```

Return a matrix that is the result of appending simple transformations onto the matrix m. These functions are similar to the RIB Translate, Rotate, and Scale commands, except that the rotation angle in rotate() is in radians, not in degrees as with the RIB Rotate. There are no perspective or skewing functions.

7.6   **Writing SL Functions**

Even though Shading Language provides many useful functions, you will probably want to write your own, just as you would in any other programming language. Defining your own functions is similar to doing it in C:

returntype functionname (params)
{
　　⋮   *do some computations*

　　`return` *return_value* ;
}

However, in many ways SL function definitions are not quite like C:

- Only one `return` statement is allowed per function. The exception to this rule is for `void` functions, which have no return type and thus have no `return` statement.
- All function parameters are passed by reference.
- You may not compile functions separately from the body of your shader. The functions must be declared prior to use and in the same compilation pass as the rest of your shader (though you may place them in a separate file and use the `#include` mechanism).[3]

Valid return types for functions are the same as variable declarations: `float`, `color`, `point`, `vector`, `normal`, `matrix`, `string`. You may declare a function as `void`, indicating that it does not return a value. You may not have a function that returns an array.

In C, parameters are passed by value, which means that the function has a private copy that can be modified without affecting the variable specified when the function was called. SL function parameters are passed by *reference*, which means that if you modify it, it will actually change the original variable that was passed. However, any parameters you want to modify must be declared with the `output` keyword, as in the following example:

```
float myfunc (float f;        /* you can't assign to f */
              output float g;) /* but you can assign to g */
```

In the SL compilers of both *PRMan* and *BMRT*, functions are expanded in-line, not compiled separately and called as subroutines. This means that there is no overhead associated with the call sequence. The downside is increased size of compiled code and the lack of support for recursion.

---

[3] It's possible that other renderers will allow separate compilation, but as of the time of this writing, both *PRMan* and *BMRT* require functions to be compiled at the same time as the shader body.

Shading Language functions obey standard variable lexical scope rules. Functions may be declared outside the scope of the shader itself, as you do in C. By default, SL functions may only access their own local variables and parameters. However, this can be extended by use of an extern declaration—global variables may be accessed by functions if they are accessed as extern variables. Newer SL compilers also support *local* functions defined inside shaders or other functions—that is, defined anyplace where a local variable might be declared. In the case of local functions, variables declared in the outer lexical scope may be accessed if they are redeclared using the extern keyword. Following is an example:

```
float x, y;

float myfunc (float f)
{
    float x;         /* local hides the one in the outer scope */
    extern float y; /* refers to the y in the outer scope */
    extern point P; /* refers to the global P */
    ...
}
```

Further Reading

More formal documentation on the RenderMan Shading Language can be found in the *RenderMan Interface Specification* (Pixar, 1989) as well as Upstill (1990) and Hanrahan and Lawson (1990).

Discussions of color spaces can be found in Foley, van Dam, Feiner, and Hughes (1990), Hall (1989), or Glassner (1995).

8 Texture Mapping and Displacement

A common technique to make computer-generated imagery more realistic is to apply a scanned or painted image like a "decal" to a surface, thus providing fine color detail on an otherwise plain-looking surface. This is known as *texture mapping* (see Figure 8.1).

Figure 8.1 Texture mapping applies an image file "decal" to geometry. See also color plate 8.1.

Listing 8.1 `paintedplastic.sl`: the standard "painted plastic" shader.

```
surface
paintedplastic ( float Ka = 1, Kd = .5, Ks = .5, roughness = .1;
                 color specularcolor = 1;
                 string texturename = ""; )
{
    color Ct = Cs;
    if (texturename != "")
        Ct *= color texture (texturename);

    normal Nf = faceforward (normalize(N),I);
    vector V = -normalize(I);
    Ci = Ct * (Ka*ambient() + Kd*diffuse(Nf)) +
        specularcolor * Ks * specular(Nf,V,roughness);
    Oi = Os;  Ci *= Oi;
}
```

8.1   Texture Access in Shading Language

In Shading Language, basic texture mapping is accomplished with the `texture()`
function (items in curly braces are optional):

type `texture (` *filename* `{ [` *firstchannel* `] } {,` *coords* `} {,` *params* `} )`

The only required parameter is the *filename*, which is a string giving the name of the
disk file containing the texture. The following subsections will describe the various
optional parameters.

An example shader that uses the `texture()` function is `paintedplastic`, shown
in Listing 8.1. Notice that it is much like the `plastic.sl` shader shown in Listing 7.1.
Rather than using the default surface color `Cs` as the base color of the material,
`paintedplastic` "filters" the base color by the color looked up from the texture
map.

8.1.1   Texture Return Type

The return type of `texture()` may be either a `float` or a `color`. These return types
would indicate that either one or three channels, respectively, should be read from
the texture file. You could explicitly ask for a one- or three-channel texture lookup,
as in

```
f = float texture ("foo.tex");  /* explicit float lookup */
c = color texture ("bar.tex");  /* explicit color lookup */
```

Alternatively, if you do not explicitly specify the type, the SL compiler will try to
infer the type depending on how you are using the resulting data. This is inher-

ently ambiguous, dangerous, and strongly discouraged! For example, consider the following:

```
Ci = Cs * texture ("foo.tex");
```

Does this line read a single channel used to *scale* the surface color, or does it read three channels of texture to *filter* the surface color? There is no way that the SL compiler can tell what your intent was, so its best guess could be wrong. In addition, it's possible that different SL compilers could guess differently. For these reasons, let us again urge you to *always* use the explicitly cast texture calls, as in the preceding examples.

8.1.2   Selecting Channels

By default, `texture()` returns channel 0 (if cast to float) or channels 0, 1, and 2 (if cast to a color). It is also possible to request that the texture lookup begin with some other channel of the texture file. This can be done by specifying the channel number in square brackets immediately after the filename. For example,

```
f = texture ("foo.tex"[1]);
```

One use for this feature would be if you are texture-mapping a four-channel texture file—the first three channels are color, and the fourth channel is *alpha* (coverage). Consider the case where you want to *composite* the texture *over* the existing base color. In other words, an alpha of 0 should indicate that no paint is applied, not that black paint is applied. The following shader code fragment implements texture mapping with alpha compositing (assuming that the texture file colors are premultiplied by the alpha values):

```
/* Assuming Ct contains the base color of the object... */
C = texture (file);      /* color in channels 0-2 */
a = texture (file[3]);   /* alpha in channel 3 */
Ct = C + (1-a) * Ct;
/* Now Ct is the color of the object with paint applied */
```

Notice that the syntax for selecting texture channels looks suspiciously like the syntax for accessing array elements. This is because texture channels were in the language long before arrays were allowed, and so the potential confusion was overlooked. When arrays were added, it created a grammatical ambiguity. The SL compiler is pretty good at sorting out the difference but still can have difficulties if the name of the texture is an array variable, as in the following example:

```
string filenames[10];
Ci = float texture ((filenames[i])[1], s, t);
```

In this example, we have an array of strings, and we are accessing channel 1 from the *i*th filename. To avoid ambiguities, we have surrounded the filename specifier by parentheses, clearly delineating the array access (inside the parentheses) from the channel selection (outside the parentheses).

8.1.3   Texture Coordinates

Stored image file textures are fundamentally 2D and are thus indexed by a pair of numbers: horizontal and vertical offsets from the upper-left corner of the texture, indexed from 0 to 1, called *texture coordinates*. There are three forms of the `texture()` call. Channel selections, explicit return type casts, and optional texture arguments may be used with any of these forms. For simplicity, the examples of the three forms of `texture()` calls are shown unaugmented by these variations.

`texture (filename, q, r)`

> When two floating-point arguments are given as texture coordinates, these numbers are used as the texture lookup coordinates. Furthermore, the renderer will automatically figure out the range of q and r over the shading unit (pixel, micropolygon, sample, etc.) and return the average of the texture over the resulting area in texture space, thus giving you a filtered texture lookup. Chapter 11 will give more details on how you can antialias your own shaders and functions, but this form of the `texture()` call is one way in which the renderer will automatically perform antialiasing for you.

`texture (filename)`

> Geometric primitives have both 2D parametric coordinates u, v (typically ranging from 0 to 1 in each direction) and also standard texture coordinates s, t. By default, $s = u$ and $t = v$, but this can be overridden in the RIB file. In either case, for many primitives s, t already contains a well-defined 2D decal-like mapping on the primitive and thus can be used as a convenient source of texture coordinates.

> If no texture coordinates are supplied at all, the compiler will assume that you want to map based on the standard texture coordinates s, t. Texture filtering is performed as we have described, based on s, t.

`texture (filename, q0, r0, q1, r1, q2, r2, q3, r3)`

> If eight texture coordinates are supplied, they are taken to describe a quadrilateral in texture space over which the texture is filtered. Thus, in this form you are explicitly specifying the filter region, rather than allowing the renderer to compute it. (One explanation of the one-point version of `texture()` is that the renderer will figure out the appropriate four points given your center point and the derivatives of its coordinates.) This four-point version of `texture()` is more rarely used than the single-point version, but occasionally you will want its high degree of control.

Listing 8.2 `simpletexmap.sl`: texture mapping with some extremely basic texture placement.

```
surface
simpletexmap ( float Ka=1, Kd=1, Ks=0.5;
               float roughness = 0.1;
               color specularcolor = 1;
               string texturename = "";
               float sstart = 0, sscale = 1;
               float tstart = 0, tscale = 1; )
{
    /* Simple scaled and offset s-t mapping */
    float ss = (s - sstart) / sscale;
    float tt = (t - tstart) / tscale;

    /* Look up texture if a filename was given, otherwise use the
     * default surface color.
     */
    color Ct;
    if (texturename != "") {
        float opac = float texture (texturename[3], ss, tt);
        Ct = color texture (texturename, ss, tt) + (1-opac)*Cs;
    }
    else Ct = Cs;

    /* Simple plastic-like reflection model */
    normal Nf = faceforward(normalize(N),I);
    vector V = -normalize(I);
    Ci = Ct * (Ka*ambient() + Kd*diffuse(Nf))
         + Ks*specularcolor*specular(Nf,V,roughness);
    Oi = Os;   Ci *= Oi;
}
```

Listing 8.2 shows an example shader that performs slightly more flexible texture mapping than the standard `paintedplastic.sl` shader of Listing 8.1. The `simpletexmap` shader contains two extensions to `paintedplastic`: (1) rather than simply filtering the surface color by the texture color, it uses an alpha channel in the texture to properly composite the texture over the surface color; and (2) parameters allow the texture to be offset and scaled on the surface (though it remains aligned with the surface's s, t coordinates).

We have thus far shown techniques for simple s, t decal mapping where we simply filter the surface color by the texture lookup or apply the $RGB\alpha$ texture over the surface color. Not only do you have total freedom in mapping the texture onto the surface but you may use the resulting data from the texture files in any way you choose. Examples include the following:

Figure 8.2 Texture mapping with additive blur (compare to Figure 8.1): blur = 0.02 (left); blur = 0.1 (right). See also color plate 8.2.

- a shader parameter that swaps s and t for the mapping, rotates the texture on the surface, or even allows an arbitrary affine mapping from s, t space to texture lookup coordinates
- multiple, possibly overlapping, texture map files affecting the surface
- handling both associated and unassociated alpha texture files
- using texture maps to modify the surface color in ways other than filtering and simple compositing—for example, in addition to specifying a base color, texture maps could be used to control opacity, specularity, roughness, or other surface parameters
- using texture maps to modulate the transition between radically different surface types—for example, metal versus rust

8.1.4   Optional `texture()` Arguments

In addition to texture filename, channel selection, and texture lookup coordinates, individual renderers allow additional parameters for fine control over some aspects of texture lookups. These additional parameters are specified as additional token-value pairs passed to `texture()` after the texture coordinates. Each token is a string, and values are typically floating-point numbers.

Blurred Texture Lookup

At times, you may want to blur your texture lookup. This can be accomplished with an additive "blur" parameter, measured relative to the texture image size (see Figure 8.2). For example:

```
texture (filename, s, t, "blur", 0.01);
```

This example adds a blur of 1% of the image width, which is equivalent to *preblurring* the texture by a filter kernel that is 1% of the width of the image. The default additive blur value is 0, indicating that no preblurring should be done to the texture.

Filter Width Multiplier

We described earlier how texture lookups are automatically antialiased, either explicitly (by specifying all four corners of a quadrilateral in texture space) or implicitly (by giving a single s, t coordinate pair and letting the renderer deduce how much it changes from pixel to pixel). In the latter case, you may want to make the implicit texture lookups sharper or more blurry in order to achieve some particular effect. The filter width estimate can be scaled by multiplication using the "width" parameter, taking a floating-point multiplier as a value:

```
texture (filename, s, t, "width", 2);
texture (filename, s, t, "width", 0);
texture (filename, s, t, "swidth", 1, "twidth", 4);
```

The first example doubles the filter width. This results in antialiasing the texture lookup approximately as if the image resolution was cut in half (or the Shading-Rate was multiplied by 4). The middle example multiplies the filter width by zero, effectively point sampling the texture (or coming as close to point sampling as the renderer can). The third example shows how "swidth" and "twidth" parameters can be used to set the filter width multipliers differently for the s and t coordinates. Note that the default value for width multipliers is 1, meaning that the original estimates should be used unmodified.

Note the subtle difference between the additive "blur" and the multiplicative "width" parameters. The former is absolute (at least for fixed texture content), whereas the latter is relative, adapting to the shading rate and thus, indirectly, to the output image resolution and apparent object size. In general, if you want a blurry texture lookup, you should use "blur", but if you want to second-guess the renderer's filter size estimates, then you should use "width".

Texture Filter Selection

We have mentioned filtering of textures but have not specified which filter will be used. By default, a box filter is used by the renderer. However, for more fine control, you may specify which filter to use for the texture lookup:

```
texture (filename, s, t, "filter", "box");
texture (filename, s, t, "filter", "gaussian");
```

Note that the selection of valid filter names is implementation dependent; consult your renderer documentation for supported filters.

Fill Color for Missing Channels

What happens when you ask for color texture on a file that contains only a single channel, or when you ask for a channel number higher than exists in the file? In these cases, the renderer will "fill in" the missing channels for you with a constant value. The optional "fill" parameter takes a float argument that specifies the constant used to fill in missing channels.

The default fill value is 0. If you examine the `simpletexmap.sl` shader, you might become suspicious about what happens if the texture file does not contain an alpha channel. In that case, the `texture` call would return 0, indicating that the texture was transparent everywhere: exactly the opposite of what you want— it would be better for textures with missing alpha channels to appear to be fully opaque everywhere. This can be accomplished by changing a single line of the shader:

```
float opac = float texture (texturename[3], ss, tt, "fill", 1);
```

Note that the fill value applies to entire channels that are not present in the texture file and is unrelated to the issue of what happens when you address texture coordinates outside the [0, 1] range. The latter issue is handled separately at texture-generation time and is described in Section 8.1.6.

8.1.5   Texture Coordinates and Conditionals

Be careful with textures inside of conditionals, for example:

```
if (varying_condition) {
    ss = some formula ;
    tt = another formula ;
    Ci = texture ("foo", ss, tt);
}
```

If the condition is `varying` (able to take on different true/false values at different points on the surface), then this statement will have unpredictable results. This is because, as we mentioned earlier, the two-coordinate texture lookup tries to estimate how much the texture coordinates change over the shading unit (pixel, micropolygon, etc.) and will filter the texture accordingly. But consider a shading unit that straddles the *boundary* between where the condition is true and where it is false. The `ss` and `tt` variables are well defined only on one side of the boundary, because the assignments to `ss` and `tt` are *inside* the "true" clause of the `if` statement. They are uninitialized on the "false" side of the boundary. Thus, it is not possible for the renderer to determine how these variables change over the straddling shading element, and texture filtering will fail unpredictably.

Therefore, it is important to remember that the texture coordinates must be well defined on the entire surface. One solution is to simply move the definitions of the texture lookup coordinates *outside* the conditional itself. For example:

```
ss = some formula ;
tt = another formula ;
if (varying_condition) {
        Ci = texture ("foo", ss, tt);
}
```

In this example, even though the texture() function is called only at points where the condition is true, the texture *coordinates* are well defined everywhere, so there are no problems at the boundary conditions.

Note that the original idiom is completely safe if the condition consists only of uniform quantities (such as numerical constants and uniform variables). This guarantees that the condition is either always true or always false and, hence, that there is never a boundary between true and false regions. No boundary, no problem.

For similar reasons, all Shading Language functions that implicitly take derivatives or filter their results will have the same limitation. The environment, Du(), Dv(), filterstep(), area(), and calculatenormal() functions all should be avoided when inside varying conditionals or loops. (These functions are described in Sections 8.2, 9.2.1, and 11.2.)

8.1.6   Creating Texture Files

The format for texture files is not dictated by the *RenderMan Interface Specification*, so each renderer is likely to have its own idiosyncratic methods for texture generation and storage, often involving custom texture formats that are designed for efficient access. Thus, a preprocessing step may be necessary to turn your scanned or painted image into a texture file. This can be done from the procedural API or RIB by using the MakeTexture command described in Section 3.7.1. Alternatively, most renderers will come with a separate program that converts ordinary image files (say, in TIFF format) into texture files.

PRMan requires that all textures be in a special, proprietary texture format. The txmake program that comes with *PRMan* will convert a variety of image file formats into *PRMan* texture files:

txmake [*arguments*] *inputfile outputfile*

Several optional arguments are occasionally useful:

- -mode *modename*
    Determines the "wrap mode," or what value the texture takes on for values of *s* and *t* outside the range [0,1]. If the *modename* is black (the default), out-of-range texture lookups will return black for all channels. A *modename* of clamp treats out-of-range texture lookups as if they happened right on the border of the texture—in other words, the texture extends its border values to infinity. Finally, the *modename* periodic will cause the texture to simply wrap.
    The -mode flag specifies the wrapping behavior for both the *s* and *t* directions, but you could specify them separately using the -smode and -tmode flags.
- -resize *resizemode*
    The use of this flag is somewhat esoteric, but we strongly recommend that you use *resizemode* of up-. (Yes, that's "up dash.") The several other options are explained in the *PRMan* documentation.
- -short
    -float

By default, txmake creates 8-bit, unsigned textures, regardless of the input file. Therefore, if your input file is 16 bits per channel and you want to retain full precision, you must use the -short flag. Similarly, the -float flag will create a 32-bit floating-point texture if you have a floating-point input file.

Several other options exist for txmake, and you are encouraged to read the *PRMan User Manual* for more information.

BMRT, on the other hand, allows you to use TIFF files directly as textures, though this is not terribly efficient or flexible for ordinary scanline-oriented TIFF. However, *BMRT* comes with a utility called mkmip, which operates much like txmake, preprocessing your textures so that memory and time are greatly reduced for the renderer when using your textures. The texture files created by mkmip are still legal TIFF files—they just happen to be multiresolution, tile-oriented TIFF, which can be very efficiently accessed by *BMRT*. The mkmip program also takes the -mode/-smode/-tmode parameters to determine wrapping. There are no -short or -float options—mkmip will always create a texture file with the same bit depth and format of your original TIFF file. Consult the *BMRT User Manual* for details and other options.

8.2   Displacement and Bump Mapping

You now know that you can write shaders to modulate the surface color by a texture or function. Using RenderMan Shading Language, you can also add small geometric surface details, such as bumps, grooves, general crust, and roughness. Also, some details or shapes that are difficult to build into the model because they are too tedious, too fine, or need information only available at render time can be better implemented through displacements.

8.2.1   Basic Displacement

RenderMan actually allows you to modify the surface position from inside a Displacement[1] shader, using the following idiom:

```
P += offsetvector ;
N = calculatenormal(P);
```

---

[1] Current releases of *PRMan* can do true displacement inside Surface shaders as well as inside Displacement shaders. However, we still recommend using Displacement shaders whenever possible. Some renderers, such as *BMRT*, can do true displacement only when in a Displacement shader, whereas displacing inside Surface shaders will result in bump mapping only. Additionally, it is possible that *PRMan* will someday have additional capabilities or efficiencies that are possible only if displacements happen in their own shader.

Color Plates

Figure 1.1 *Toy Story* — Buzz Lightyear's helmet reflection is carefully crafted not to obscure his winning features. (© Disney Enterprises, Inc.)

Figure 1.2 *Geri's Game* — Geri's large eyes give him an angelic appeal. (© Pixar Animation Studios)

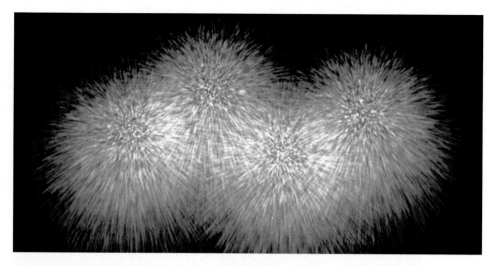

Figure 5.2 *(above)* Moving `Points` creating fireworks.
Figure 5.3 *(below)* Tribbles very simply described with a large number of curves and a tube-like appearance.

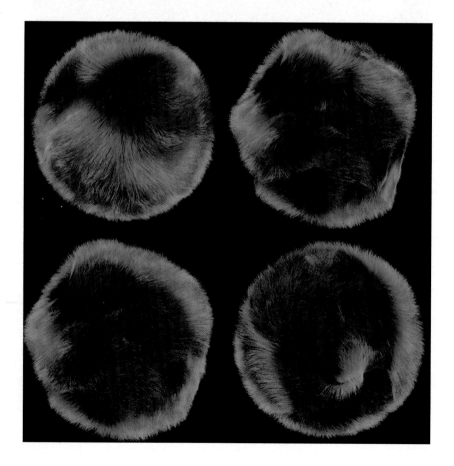

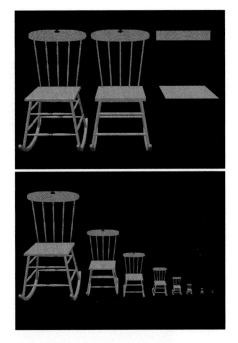

Figure 5.5 Three levels of detail for a chair (top), and a smooth blend between them (bottom).

Figure 5.6 High (top) and low (bottom) detail levels for tree branches and leaves.

Figure 5.7 A forest composed of level-of-detail trees.

Figure 8.1 Texture mapping applies an image file "decal" to geometry.

Figure 8.2 Texture mapping with additive blur (compare to Figure 8.1): blur = 0.02 (left); blur = 0.1 (right).

Figure 9.2 The finishes (left to right) `MaterialPlastic`, `MaterialRoughMetal`, and `MaterialMatte` applied to a vase.

Figure 9.3 *Geri's Game* — An example environment map. (© Pixar Animation Studios)

Figure 9.6 `MaterialShinyMetal` (left) and `MaterialShinyPlastic` (right).

Figure 9.7 When the light source is directly behind the viewer, the Oren/Nayar model (left) acts much more as a retroreflector, compared to the Lambertian mode (right).

Figure 9.8 Examples of the Ward anisotropic reflection model. Isotropic reflection with xroughness=yroughness=0.3 (top). Anisotropic reflection with xroughness=0.15, yroughness=0.5 (bottom left). Anisotropic reflection with xroughness=0.5, yroughness=0.15 (bottom right). In all cases, xdir=normalize (dPdu).

Figure 9.9 Comparing the glossy versus plastic specular illumination models.

Figure 12.7 The final `ceramictiles` shader.

Figure 12.10 Example uses the oak shader. Each object uses slightly different parameters to the shader, resulting in different looks and feels for the wood. (Trivia: the elephant is called "Gumbo" and was modeled by Ed Catmull.)

Figure 12.11 Example use of the oakplank shader.

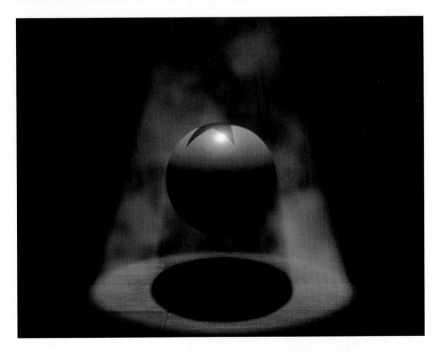

Figure 12.12 Volumetric smoke using the smoke shader.

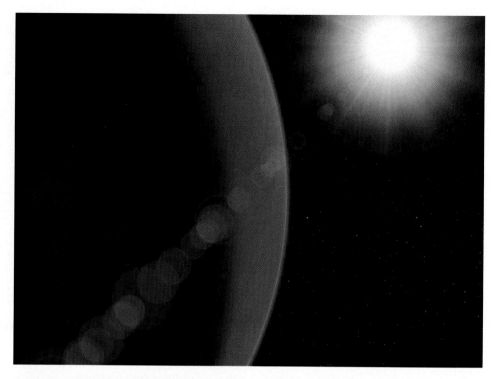

Figure 12.14 *(above)* Example use of the `lensflare` shader.

Figure 12.17 *(left) Tin Toy* — Our `cel` shader applied to a previously modeled 3D character. (© Pixar Animation Studios)

Figure 13.1 *(opposite page, top and middle) A Bug's Life* — Bunker with uniform lighting (top) and with controlled lighting (bottom). (© Disney Enterprises, Inc. and Pixar Animation Studios)

Figure 13.13 *(opposite page, bottom) A Bug's Life* — Implied line created by a row of ants. (© Disney Enterprises, Inc. and Pixar Animation Studios)

Figure 13.17 (bottom) *(opposite page, top) A Bug's Life* — An example of deep staging and lighting. (© Disney Enterprises, Inc. and Pixar Animation Studios)

Figure 13.18 *(opposite page, middle) A Bug's Life* — Reversing the usual value cues by making more distant objects brighter. (© Disney Enterprises, Inc. and Pixar Animation Studios)

Figure 13.20 *(opposite page, bottom) A Bug's Life* — Dot running from the grasshoppers. (© Disney Enterprises, Inc. and Pixar Animation Studios)

Figure 13.22 *(above) A Bug's Life* — This image is staged to remind the viewer of the true scale of tiny insects in the huge world. (© Disney Enterprises, Inc. and Pixar Animation Studios)

Figure 13.23 *(below) A Bug's Life* — This image emphasizes scale on the insect's level. (© Disney Enterprises, Inc. and Pixar Animation Studios)

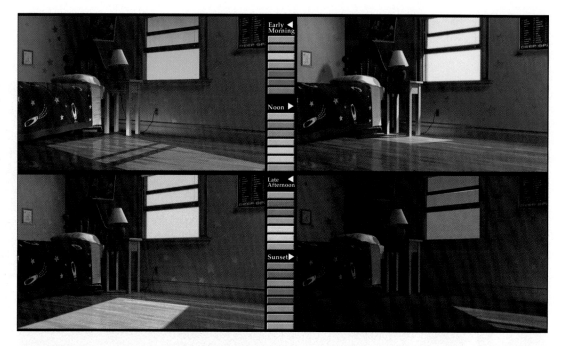

Figure 13.29 *Toy Story 2* — Andy's room at four different times of day, and the light color palettes for each setting. (© Disney Enterprises, Inc. and Pixar Animation Studios)

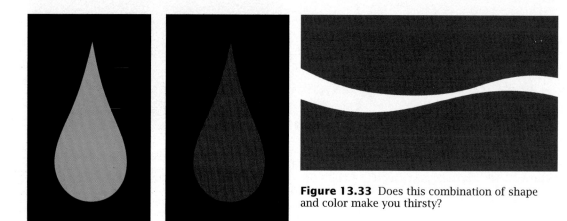

Figure 13.33 Does this combination of shape and color make you thirsty?

Figure 13.32 Water or blood? The same shape with different colors can evoke entirely different emotions. Color provides context for shape.

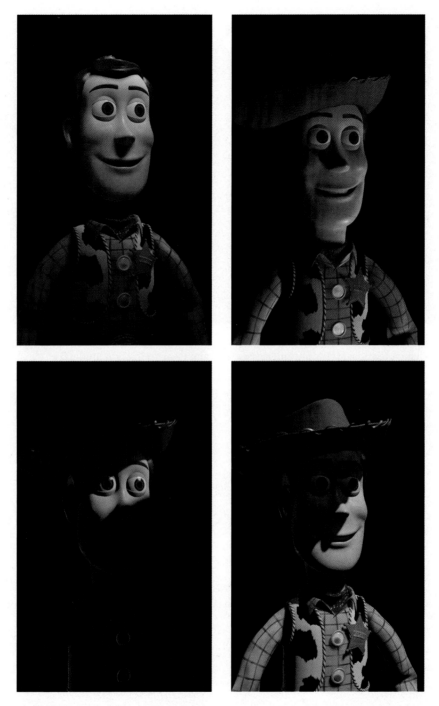

Figure 13.34 *Toy Story* — Lighting, direction, quality, and shaping are powerful tools to change the visual personality of a character. (© Disney Enterprises, Inc.)

Figure 13.35 *A Bug's Life* — An example of staging and lighting used to reveal personality of a character and to heighten tension. (© Disney Enterprises, Inc. and Pixar Animation Studios)

Figure 14.14 Example 1: *Toy Story* — A simple scene that illustrates the significance of light shape and placement. (© Disney Enterprises, Inc.)

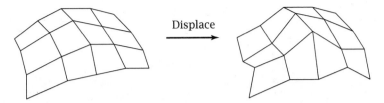

Figure 8.3 Displacements move surface positions.

Typically, *offsetvector* is along the normal vector, like this:

```
P += bumpheight * normalize(N);
N = calculatenormal(P);
```

Displacements work roughly in the following manner. First, surface primitives are turned into grids. The displacement (or surface) shaders are run at the grid vertices. The shader may move the actual grid points by altering P. This moves the vertices of the grid, shifting their positions, as shown schematically in Figure 8.3.

Once you have moved P to its new location, you must recalculate a new N based on the displaced surface position. This doesn't happen automatically, but you may do it quite simply with the function `calculatenormal`. The following line sets N to the normal of the surface given its new P values:

```
N = calculatenormal(P);
```

More generally, `calculatenormal()` will compute the normal to the surface "defined" by any point expression.

How can `calculatenormal()` work? We have an apparent paradox: normals are calculated by a cross product of the tangents (derivatives) of surface position, yet we've only specified how P moves at a single point. How can `calculatenormal()` know about the other points on the surface and where they displace to? The answer is that Shading Language requires that it will work somehow. In the case of *PRMan*, you're really shading grids in an SIMD fashion, so the P+=foo statement is executed everywhere at once, then the N=calculatenormal(P) statement is executed everywhere. So by the time you call `calculatenormal()`, its arguments are already known everywhere. Different renderers may use different strategies to make this work, but you can be assured that it will work somehow on any RenderMan-compliant renderer.

8.2.2   Bump Mapping

Consider the following code fragment:

```
N = calculatenormal(P + amp*normalize(N));
```

Figure 8.4 Lumpy teapot. Top row: plain (left), bump mapping (center), displacements (right). Bottom row: close-up. Note the difference between bumping and displacing apparent on the silhouette.

This sets N to the normal of the surface that you would have gotten *if* you had offset P but doesn't actually move P! This is basic *bump mapping*—moving the normals without actually displacing the surface.

Figure 8.4 shows the difference between bump mapping and true displacements. An object with displacements will have a ragged silhouette, and its dents and protuberances can self-shadow. Bumps may look just like displacements when viewed from the front, but a bump-mapped surface will still have a smooth silhouette. At certain scales bump mapping and displacing are virtually indistinguishable, and the self-shadowing and ragged silhouette are not significant visual features. Therefore, it is an empirical question whether bumping is sufficient or displacements are necessary. It largely depends on the size of the bumps and the scale at which you are viewing the object.

Bump mapping is less likely to suffer from artifacts or renderer errors such as cracking and may be faster to render. In addition, with bump mapping, you need not worry about displacement bounds, which are explained in Section 8.2.4. For these reasons, we suggest that you use bump mapping whenever possible and save true displacements for those times when they are really needed. In reality, there is little cost associated with starting out using bumps and only going to displacements when the need becomes clear.

The reader with a photographic memory may wonder about the RenderMan Interface's direct bump map support through the RIB MakeBump and SL bump( ) calls. These were never implemented in any RenderMan renderer (that we know of) because they turned out to be less powerful than the faked-displacement method just described. So now this functionality has been completely subsumed by the displacement mechanism, and with 20/20 hindsight we just ignore MakeBump/bump.

8.2.3   Scaling Displacements

The idiom: P += *amp* * normalize(N) displaces the surface *amp* units in the direction of N, but what coordinate space are these units measured in? Remember that N,
like all other variables passed to the shader, is represented in "current" space. So
the statement above pushes the surface *amp* units in the direction of N as measured
in "current" space. This is almost certainly *not* what you want, if for no other reason than that the definition of "current" space is implementation dependent and
may vary from renderer to renderer.

Instead, you probably want your displacements measured in "shader" space
units. That way, if you scale the overall size of your model, the bumps will scale
just as the rest of the geometry does. We could do this by transforming everything
to "shader" space, displacing, then transforming back:

```
vector Nshad = vtransform("shader", N);
point Pshad = transform("shader", P);
Pshad += amp * normalize(Nshad);
P = transform("shader", "current", Pshad);
N = calculatenormal(P);
```

This will work, and this idiom was commonly used in shaders for many years. But
there is another way to measure displacements in an arbitrary space that requires
fewer transforms and temporary variables (and is thus more compact and efficient).
Consider the following alternate idiom for displacing *amp* units in "shader" space:

```
vector Nn = normalize(N);
P += Nn * (amp / length(vtransform("shader",Nn)));
```

That statement may be tricky to decipher, so let's dissect it carefully.

1. By definition, normalize(N) has unit length in "current" space, but if any
   scaling has happened, it may have some other length in another space (such
   as "shader" space in this example).
2. Thus, vtransform("shader",normalize(N)) is the "shader" space representation of a vector that had unit length in "current" space.
3. So the length of that vector, let's call it ℓ, is a scaling factor such that a vector
   of length m in "current" space will have length $m\ell$ in "shader" space.
4. Conversely, a vector of length n in "shader" space will have length n/ℓ in
   "current" space.
5. Putting all this together, we see that the statement above will push P in the
   direction of N by an amount that is *amp* units in "shader" space.

In summary, the length() expression is a correction factor between "current"
space units and "shader" space units. Obviously, if you wanted to displace in
another space, you could simply substitute another space name where we have used
"shader" in the previous example. You might want to displace in "world" space
units if you knew that you wanted the bumps to have a particular amplitude in

Figure 8.5 Example use of the emboss shader.

absolute units, regardless of how you might want to scale your object model. Also, you don't *have* to displace along N, but you almost always want to.

Now we can construct a function that combines displacement, bump mapping, and the idioms for displacing relative to a particular coordinate space. This function is shown in Listing 8.3. Listing 8.3 also shows a simple displacement shader that allows a single-channel texture map to determine the amount of displacement on a surface, as if embossing an image into the surface. Notice how most of the smarts are inside the Displace function, so the emboss shader itself is implemented in very few lines of code. An example use of the shader is shown in Figure 8.5.

8.2.4   Displacement Bounds

Most renderers need to calculate spatial bounds for all primitives. The renderer knows how to bound each primitive, but the problem is that displacements can move the surface arbitrary amounts. Thus, displaced geometry may "poke out" of the bounding box that the renderer calculates for the primitive. This can cause the geometry to be incorrectly "clipped." These missing slivers of geometry tend to be aligned with scanlines (see Figure 8.6).

To avoid this artifact, you must tell the renderer, in advance, the maximum distance that any part of the primitive might displace so that the renderer can grow the bounds to accommodate the displacements. This can be done in RIB with the following line:

```
Attribute "displacementbound" "sphere" [radius]
            "coordinatesystem" ["space"]
```

> **Listing 8.3** Displace function that combines displacement and bumping, relative to a given coordinate system, and the emboss displacement shader.

```
/* Combine displacement and bump mapping, with units relative to
 * a particular space.  When truedisp != 0, this function modifies
 * P as a side effect.
 *
 * Inputs:
 *    dir        direction in which to push the surface, assumed to
 *                    already be in "current" space and normalized.
 *    amp        amplitude of the actual displacement or bumping.
 *    space      the name of the coordinate system against which the
 *                    amplitude is measured.
 *    truedisp   when 1, truly displace; when 0, just bump.
 * Return value: the normal of the displaced and bumped surface,
 *                    in "current" space, normalized.
 */
normal Displace (vector dir;  string space;
                 float amp; float truedisp;)
{
    extern point P;
    float spacescale = length(vtransform(space, dir));
    vector Ndisp = dir * (amp / spacescale);
    P += truedisp * Ndisp;
    return normalize (calculatenormal (P + (1-truedisp)*Ndisp));
}



displacement
emboss (string texturename = "";          /* Name of image */
        float   Km         = 1;           /* Max displacement amt */
        string dispspace  = "shader";    /* Space to measure in */
        float   truedisp   = 1;           /* Displace or bump? */
        float sstart = 0, sscale = 1;
        float tstart = 0, tscale = 1;
        float blur = 0; )
{
    /* Only displace if a filename is provided */
    if (texturename != "") {
        /* Simple scaled and offset s-t mapping */
        float ss = (s - sstart) / sscale;
        float tt = (t - tstart) / tscale;
        /* Amplitude is channel 0 of the texture, indexed by s,t. */
        float amp = float texture (texturename[0], ss, tt, "blur",
                                    blur);
        /* Displace inward parallel to the surface normal,
         * Km*amp units measured in dispspace coordinates.
         */
        N = Displace (normalize(N), dispspace, -Km*amp, truedisp);
    }
}
```

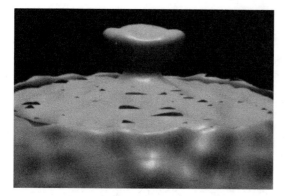

Figure 8.6 Missing slivers of geometry resulting from not supplying the correct `displacementbound`.

This line indicates that the shaders on subsequent objects may displace the surface up to (but no more than) *radius* units as measured in the coordinate system *space*. The parameter name `"sphere"` indicates that it could grow in any direction. It's currently the only option, but we imagine that someday it may be possible to indicate that the displacements will be only in a particular direction. Typical values for *space* might be `"shader"`, `"object"`, or `"world"`.

Specifying a displacement bound that is too small (or not specifying it when it is needed) results in a characteristic artifact where the top or left of the object is clipped along a vertical or horizontal boundary (see Figure 8.6). It's as if the object were stamped with a rectangular cookie cutter that wasn't quite large enough to miss the border of the object. On the other hand, if you give a displacement bound that is much larger than required by the shader, your rendering speed may suffer.

Unfortunately, it's up to you to make sure that the displacement bounds value in the RIB stream matches the behavior of the shader. You may recognize that it's sometimes tricky to correctly guess, in the model, what the biggest possible displacement in the shader may be. This task is much easier if your displacement shader is written with an explicit parameter giving the maximum amplitude for displacement and the space to measure against.

8.3   Texture Projections

8.3.1   Alternatives to *s,t* Mappings

The examples we have seen of texture and displacement mapping have all assumed that textures were somehow indexed based on the (s, t) coordinates of the surface. For example, both the `simpletexmap` shader in Listing 8.2 and the `emboss` shader in Listing 8.3 align the texture lookup with the surface geometry's s, t coordinates, allowing only for simple offsetting and scaling. However, it's likely that for many models and textures, this is not at all appropriate for a variety of reasons:

1. s, t may not be evenly distributed over a surface, and thus texture that is indexed by s, t will appear warped.
2. It is difficult for separate, but abutting, geometric primitives to have a continuous s, t mapping across the seams between them. Nevertheless, it is an entirely valid goal to have a seamless texture spanning several primitives.
3. Some primitives (such as subdivision surfaces) don't have a global s, t parameterization at all.

Luckily, the advantage of specifying surface appearances with a programming language is that you are not limited to such a simple texture coordinate mapping scheme, or even to one that was considered by the renderer authors. A typical method of dealing with these limitations is to eschew (s, t) mappings in favor of *projective* texture mappings. Such mappings may include spherical (like latitude and longitude on a globe), cylindrical, planar (simply using x, y of some coordinate system), or perspective projections. Listing 8.4 contains Shading Language function code for spherical and cylindrical projections. Both take points, assumed to be in an appropriate shading space, and produce `ss` and `tt` texture indices as well as derivative estimates `ds` and `dt`. Note that the derivative computations try to take into account the seams that inevitably result from these types of "wrapped" projections. (The background for and uses of derivatives will be discussed more thoroughly in Chapter 11.)

We may wish to keep our shader sufficiently flexible to allow any of these, including (s, t). This gives rise to the function `ProjectTo2D` in Listing 8.4, which takes a 3D point and the name of a projection type and computes the 2D texture coordinates and their estimated derivatives. For added flexibility, it also takes the name of a coordinate system in which to compute the mapping, as well as an additional 4×4 matrix for an added level of control over the mapping. The `ProjectTo2D` function supports the following projection types:

- `"st"` ordinary (s, t) mapping
- `"planar"`, which maps the (x, y) coordinates of a named coordinate system to (ss, tt) values
- `"perspective"`, which maps the (x, y, z) coordinates of a named coordinate system as $ss = x/z, tt = y/z$
- `"spherical"`, which maps spherical coordinates to (ss, tt) values
- `"cylindrical"`, which maps cylindrical coordinates to (ss, tt) values

8.3.2   Texture Application and `supertexmap.sl`

Now that we have a general mapping routine, we can complete our library of useful texture functions with routines that call `ProjectTo2D`, as in Listing 8.5. `GetColorTextureAndAlpha()` projects the input point, yielding 2D texture coordinates and derivatives, then performs an antialiased texture lookup to yield color and alpha

Listing 8.4 Shading Language functions for projecting 3D to 2D coordinates using one of several named projection types.

```
/* Project 3D points onto a unit sphere centered at the origin */
void spherical_projection (point p; output float ss, tt, ds, dt;)
{
    extern float du, dv;     /* Used by the filterwidth macro */
    vector V = normalize(vector p);
    ss = (-atan (ycomp(V), xcomp(V)) + PI) / (2*PI);
    tt = 0.5 - acos(zcomp(V)) / PI;
    ds = filterwidth (ss);
    if (ds > 0.5)
        ds = max (1-ds, MINFILTWIDTH);
    dt = filterwidth (tt);
    if (dt > 0.5)
        dt = max (1-dt, MINFILTWIDTH);
}


/* Project 3D points onto a cylinder about the z-axis between z=0 and z=1 */
void cylindrical_projection (point p; output float ss, tt, ds, dt;)
{
    extern float du, dv;     /* Used by the filterwidth macro */
    vector V = normalize(vector p);
    ss = (-atan (ycomp(V), xcomp(V)) + PI) / (2*PI);
    tt = zcomp(p);
    ds = filterwidth (ss);
    if (ds > 0.5)
        ds = max (1-ds, MINFILTWIDTH);
    dt = filterwidth (tt);
}


void ProjectTo2D (string projection;
                  point P;  string whichspace;
                  matrix xform;
                  output float ss, tt, ds, dt; )
{
    point Pproj;
    extern float du, dv;     /* Used by the filterwidth macro */
    if (projection == "st") {
        extern float s, t;
        Pproj = point (s, t, 0);
    } else {
        Pproj = transform (whichspace, P);
    }
    Pproj = transform (xform, Pproj);
    if (projection == "planar" || projection == "st") {
        ss = xcomp(Pproj);
        tt = ycomp(Pproj);
        ds = filterwidth (ss);
        dt = filterwidth (tt);
    }
```

▶

Listing 8.4 (continued)

```
    else if (projection == "perspective") {
        float z = max (zcomp(Pproj), 1.0e-6);  /* avoid zero division */
        ss = xcomp(Pproj) / z;
        tt = ycomp(Pproj) / z;
        ds = filterwidth (ss);
        dt = filterwidth (tt);
    }
    /* Special cases for the projections that may wrap */
    else if (projection == "spherical")
        spherical_projection (Pproj, ss, tt, ds, dt);
    else if (projection == "cylindrical")
        cylindrical_projection (Pproj, ss, tt, ds, dt);
}
```

(assuming full opacity if no alpha channel is present). `ApplyColorTextureOver()` calls `GetColorTextureAndAlpha` and then applies the texture over the existing base color using the usual alpha composition rule. Similar routines for single-channel textures can be easily derived.

Finally, with these functions we can write yet another refinement of a basic texture-mapping shader. The standard `paintedplastic.sl` scales the surface color by a simple (s, t) lookup of a color texture. The `simpletexmap.sl` (Listing 8.2 in Section 8.1) supports textures with alpha channels applying paint over a surface and also allows simple positioning and scaling of the texture pattern. Now we present `supertexmap.sl` (Listing 8.6), which uses the flexible texture routines of this section. This shader allows the use of texture maps for color, opacity, specularity, and displacement. Furthermore, each one may use a different projection type, projection space, and transformation.

When using `supertexmap.sl`, you position the textures on the surface by manipulating the named texture coordinate space and/or providing 4×4 transformation matrices. Note that the 4×4 matrices are passed to the shader as arrays of 16 floats rather than as a `matrix` type, in order to avoid the transformation of the matrix relative to "current" space.

Further Reading

Texture mapping was first developed in Ed Catmull's doctoral dissertation (Catmull, 1974). While countless papers have been written on texture mapping, an excellent overall survey of texture-mapping techniques can be found in Heckbert (1986).

Bump mapping was proposed by Blinn (1978), displacements by Cook (1984) and Cook, Carpenter, and Catmull (1987), and opacity maps by Gardner (1984).

Listing 8.5 Shading Language functions for `GetColorTextureAndAlpha` and `ApplyColorTextureOver`

```
color GetColorTextureAndAlpha (string texturename;
                               string projection;
                               point P;  string whichspace;
                               matrixxform;  float blur;
                               float alphachannel;
                               output float alpha; )
{
   float ss, tt, ds, dt;
   ProjectTo2D (projection, P, whichspace, xform, ss, tt, ds, dt);
   ds *= 0.5;  dt *= 0.5;
   color Ct = color texture (texturename, ss-ds, tt-dt, ss+ds,
                             tt-dt, ss-ds, tt+dt, ss+ds, tt+dt,
                             "blur", blur);
   alpha = float texture (texturename[alphachannel], ss-ds, tt-dt,
                          ss+ds, tt-dt, ss-ds, tt+dt, ss+ds, tt+dt,
                          "blur", blur, "fill", 1);
   return Ct;
}


color ApplyColorTextureOver (color basecolor;
                             string texturename;  string projection;
                             point P;  string whichspace;
                             matrix xform;  float blur; )
{
   float alpha;
   color Ct = GetColorTextureAndAlpha (texturename, projection, P,
                                       whichspace, xform, blur,
                                       3, alpha);
   return Ct + (1-alpha)*basecolor;
}
```

Listing 8.6 `supertexmap.sl` : perform color, opacity, specularity, and displacement mapping on a surface, each with a potentially different projection type, space name, and adjustment matrix. The helper function `array_to_mx` is also listed.

```
#include "project.h"

matrix array_to_mx (float m[16]) {
    return matrix (m[0], m[1], m[2], m[3], m[4], m[5],
                   m[6], m[7], m[8], m[9], m[10], m[11],
                   m[12], m[13], m[14], m[15]);
}
```

▶

Listing 8.6 (continued)

```
surface
supertexmap (float Ka = 1, Kd = .5, Ks = .5, roughness = .1;
              color specularcolor = 1;
              /* base color */
              string Csmapname = "", Csproj = "st",
              Csspace = "shader";
              float Csmx[16] = {1,0,0,0, 0,1,0,0, 0,0,1,0, 0,0,0,1};
              /* opacity */
              string Osmapname = "", Osproj = "st",
              Osspace = "shader";
              float Osmx[16] = {1,0,0,0, 0,1,0,0, 0,0,1,0, 0,0,0,1};
              /* specularity */
              string Ksmapname = "", Ksproj = "st",
              Ksspace = "shader";
              float Ksmx[16] = {1,0,0,0, 0,1,0,0, 0,0,1,0, 0,0,0,1};
              /* displacement */
              string dispmapname = "", dispproj = "st",
              dispspace = "shader";
              float dispmx[16] = {1,0,0,0, 0,1,0,0, 0,0,1,0, 0,0,0,1}; )
              float truedisp = 1;
{
    /* Start out with the regular plastic parameters,
       unless overridden */
    color Ct = Cs, Ot = Os;
    float ks = Ks, disp = 0;

    if (Csmapname != "")     /* Color mapping */
        Ct = ApplyColorTextureOver (Ct, Csmapname, Csproj, P,
                                    Csspace, array_to_mx (Csmx), 0);
    if (Osmapname != "")     /* Opacity mapping */
        Ot = ApplyColorTextureOver (Ct, Osmapname, Osproj, P,
                                    Osspace, array_to_mx (Osmx), 0);
    if (Ksmapname != "")     /* specularity mapping */
        ks = ApplyFloatTextureOver (Ks, Ksmapname, Ksproj, P,
                                    Ksspace, array_to_mx (Ksmx, 0);
    if (dispmapname != "") {     /* displacement mapping */
        disp = ApplyFloatTextureOver (disp, dispmapname, dispproj, P,
                                      dispspace, array_to_mx
                                      (dispmx), 0);
        N = Displace (normalize(N), dispspace, disp, truedisp);
    }

    /* Finish up with a plastic illumination model */
    normal Nf = faceforward (normalize(N),I);
    Ci = Ct * (Ka*ambient() + Kd*diffuse(Nf)) +
         specularcolor * ks*specular(Nf,-normalize(I),roughness);
    Oi = Ot;  Ci *= Oi;
}
```

9 Illumination Models and Lights

In the past two chapters we have glossed over exactly how shaders respond to light, as well as how light sources themselves operate, which of course are important aspects of the overall appearance of materials. These are the issues that will be addressed by this chapter. In doing so, we will build up a variety of library routines that implement different material appearances.

9.1 Built-in Local Illumination Models

In earlier chapters, all of our shaders have ended with the same three lines:

```
Ci = Ct * (Ka*ambient() + Kd*diffuse(Nf)) +
    specularcolor * Ks*specular(Nf,-normalize(I),roughness);
Oi = Os;  Ci *= Oi;
```

Three functions are used here that have not been previously described:

`color diffuse(vector N)`

Calculates light widely and uniformly scattered as it bounces from a light source off of the surface. Diffuse reflectivity is generally approximated by Lambert's law:

$$\sum_{i=1}^{\text{nlights}} Cl_i \max(0, N \cdot L_i)$$

where for each of the i light sources, L_i is the unit vector pointing toward the light, Cl_i is the light color, and N is the unit normal of the surface. The max function ensures that lights with $N \cdot L_i < 0$ (i.e., those *behind* the surface) do not contribute to the calculation.

`color specular(vector N, V; float roughness)`

Computes so-called *specular* lighting, which refers to the way that glossier surfaces have noticeable bright spots or highlights resulting from the narrower (in angle) scattering of light off the surface. A typical formula for such scattering might be the Blinn-Phong model:

$$\sum_{i=1}^{\text{nlights}} Cl_i \max(0, N \cdot H)^{1/\text{roughness}}$$

where H is the vector halfway between the viewing direction and the direction of the light source (i.e., `normalize(normalize(-I)+normalize(L))`). The equation above is for the Blinn-Phong reflection model, which is what is dictated by the *RenderMan Interface Specification*. PRMan actually uses a slightly different, proprietary formula for `specular()`. BMRT also uses a slightly non-standard formulation of `specular()` in order to more closely match *PRMan*. So beware—though the spec dictates Blinn-Phong, individual implementations can and do substitute other reflection models for `specular()`.

`color ambient()`

Returns the contribution of so-called *ambient* light, which comes from no specific location but rather represents the low level of scattered light in a scene after bouncing from object to object.[1]

---

[1] In most renderers, ambient light is typically approximated by a low-level, constant, nondirectional light contribution set by the user in a rather ad hoc manner. When renderers try to accurately calculate this interreflected light in a principled manner, it is known as *global illumination*, or, depending on the exact method used, as *radiosity*, *path tracing*, *Monte Carlo integration*, and others.

> **Listing 9.1** `MaterialPlastic` computes a local illumination model approximating the appearance of ordinary plastic.

```
/* Compute the color of the surface using a simple plastic-like BRDF.
 * Typical values are Ka=1, Kd=0.8, Ks=0.5, roughness=0.1.
 */
color MaterialPlastic (normal Nf;  color basecolor;
                       float Ka, Kd, Ks, roughness;)
{
    extern vector I;
    return basecolor * (Ka*ambient() + Kd*diffuse(Nf))
          + Ks*specular(Nf,-normalize(I),roughness);
}
```

Therefore, those three lines we had at the end of our shaders calculate a weighted sum of ambient, diffuse, and specular lighting components. Typically, the diffuse and ambient light is filtered by the base color of the object, but the specular contribution is not (or is filtered by a separate `specularcolor`).

We usually assign `Oi`, the opacity of the surface, to simply be the default surface opacity `Os`. Finally, we scale the output color by the output opacity, because RenderMan requires shaders to compute premultiplied opacity values.

When `specularcolor` is 1 (i.e., white), these calculations yield an appearance closely resembling plastic. Let us then formalize it with the Shading Language function `MaterialPlastic` (in Listing 9.1). With this function in our library, we could replace the usual ending lines of our shader with:

```
Ci = MaterialPlastic (Nf, V, Cs, Ka, Kd, Ks, roughness);
Oi = Os;  Ci *= Oi;
```

For the remainder of this chapter, functions that compute completed material appearances will be named with the prefix `Material`, followed by a description of the material family. Arguments passed will generally include a base color, surface normal, viewing direction, and a variety of weights and other knobs that select individual appearances from the family of materials.

The implementation of the `Material` functions will typically be to compute a weighted sum of several *primitive local illumination functions*. Before long, it will be necessary to move beyond `ambient()`, `diffuse()`, and `specular()` to other, more sophisticated local illumination functions. When we start writing our own local illumination functions, we will use the convention of naming them with the prefix `LocIllum` and will typically name them after their inventors (e.g., `LocIllumCook-Torrance`).

But first, let us see what effects we can get with just the built-in `specular()` and `diffuse()` functions.

Listing 9.2 MaterialMatte computes the color of the surface using a simple Lambertian BRDF.

```
color MaterialMatte (normal Nf;  color basecolor;  float Ka, Kd;)
{
    return basecolor * (Ka*ambient() + Kd*diffuse(Nf));
}
```

9.1.1 Matte Surfaces

The typical combination of the built-in diffuse() and specular() functions, formalized in MaterialPlastic(), is great at making materials that look like manufactured plastic (such as toys). But many objects that you model will not be made from materials that feature a prominent specular highlight. You could, of course, simply call MaterialPlastic() passing Ks = 0. However, that seems wasteful to call the potentially expensive specular() function only to multiply it by zero. Our solution is to create a separate, simpler MaterialMatte that only calculates the ambient and Lambertian (via diffuse()) contributions without a specular highlight, as shown in Listing 9.2.

9.1.2 Rough Metallic Surfaces

Another class of surfaces not well modeled by the MaterialPlastic function is that of metals. Deferring until the next section metals that are polished to the point that they have visible reflections of surrounding objects, we will concentrate for now on roughened metallic surfaces without coherent reflections.

Cook and Torrance (1981,1982) realized that an important difference between plastics and metals is the effect of the base color of the material on the specular component. Many materials, including paint and colored plastic, are composed of a transparent substrate with embedded pigment particles (see Figure 9.1). The outer, clear surface boundary both reflects light specularly (without affecting its color) and transmits light into the media that is permeated by pigment deposits. Some of the transmitted light is scattered back diffusely after being filtered by the pigment color. This white highlight contributes greatly to the perception of the material as plastic.

Homogeneous materials, including metals, lack a transparent outer layer that would specularly reflect light without attenuating its color. Therefore, in these materials, all reflected light (including specular) is scaled by the material's base color. This largely contributes to the metallic appearance. We implement this look in MaterialRoughMetal (Listing 9.3).

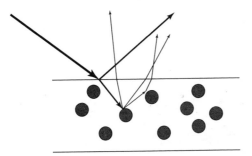

Figure 9.1 Cross section of a plastic-like surface.

Listing 9.3 `MaterialRoughMetal` calculates the color of the surface using a simple metal-like BRDF.

```
/* Compute the color of the surface using a simple metal-like BRDF.
 * To give a metallic appearance, both diffuse and specular
 * components are scaled by the color of the metal.  It is
 * recommended that Kd < 0.1, Ks > 0.5, and roughness > 0.15
 * to give a believable metallic appearance.
 */
color MaterialRoughMetal (normal Nf;  color basecolor;
                          float Ka, Kd, Ks, roughness;)
{
    extern vector I;
    return basecolor * (Ka*ambient() + Kd*diffuse(Nf) +
                        Ks*specular(Nf,-normalize(I),roughness));
}
```

9.1.3　Backlighting

So far, the materials we have simulated have all been assumed to be of substantial thickness. In other words, lights on the same side of the surface as the viewer reflect off the surface and are seen by the camera, but lights "behind" the surface (from the point of view of the camera) do not scatter light around the corner so that it contributes to the camera's view.

It is not by accident that such backlighting is excluded from contributing. Note that the `diffuse()` function takes the surface normal as an argument. The details of its working will be revealed in Section 9.3; let us simply note here that this normal parameter is used to exclude the contribution of light sources that do not lie on the same side of the surface as the viewer.

But thinner materials—paper, lampshades, blades of grass, thin sheets of plastic—do have appearances that are affected by lights behind the object. These

Figure 9.2 The finishes (left to right) `MaterialPlastic`, `MaterialRoughMetal`, and `MaterialMatte` applied to a vase. See also color plate 9.2.

objects are translucent, so lights shine *through* the object, albeit usually at a lower intensity than the reflections of the lights in front of the object.[2] Therefore, since

    `diffuse(Nf)`

sums the Lambertian scattering of lights on the viewer's side of the surface, then the lights from the *back side* should be described by

    `diffuse(-Nf)`

In fact, this works exactly as we might hope. Thus, making a material translucent is as easy as adding an additional contribution of `diffuse()` oriented in the backwards direction (and presumably with a different, and smaller, weight denoted by `Kt`). This is exemplified by the `MaterialThinPlastic` function of Listing 9.4.

9.2 Reflections

We have covered materials that are linear combinations of Lambertian diffuse and specular components. However, many surfaces are polished to a sufficient degree that you can see coherent reflections of the surrounding environment. This section will discuss two ways of simulating this phenomenon and show several applications.

People often assume that mirror-like reflections require ray tracing. But not all renderers support ray tracing (and, in fact, those renderers are typically much faster than ray tracers). In addition, there are situations where even ray tracing does not help. For example, if you are compositing a CG object into a live-action shot, you

---

[2] Note the difference between *translucency*, the diffuse transmission of very scattered light through a thickness of material, and *transparency*, which means you can see a coherent image through the object. Ordinary paper is translucent, whereas glass is transparent.

> **Listing 9.4** `MaterialThinPlastic` implements a simple, thin, plastic-like BRDF.

```
/* Compute the color of the surface using a simple, thin, plastic-like
 * BRDF. We call it _thin_ because it includes a transmission component
 * to allow light from the _back_ of the surface to affect the appearance.
 * Typical values are Ka=1, Kd=0.8, Kt=0.2, Ks=0.5, roughness=0.1.
 */
color MaterialThinPlastic (normal Nf;  vector V;  color basecolor;
                           float Ka, Kd, Kt, Ks, roughness;)
{
    return basecolor * (Ka*ambient() + Kd*diffuse(Nf) + Kt*diffuse(-Nf))
          + Ks*specular(Nf,V,roughness);
}
```

may want the object to reflect its environment. This is not possible even with ray tracing because the environment does not exist in the CG world. Of course, you could laboriously model all the objects in the live-action scene, but this seems like too much work for a few reflections.

Luckily, RenderMan Shading Language provides support for faking these effects with texture maps, even for renderers that do not support any ray tracing. In this case, we can take a multipass approach, first rendering the scene from the points of view of the reflectors, then using these first passes as special texture maps when rendering the final view from the main camera.

9.2.1   Environment Maps

Environment maps take images of six axis-aligned directions from a particular point (like the six faces of a cube) and allow you to look up texture on those maps, indexed by a direction vector, thus simulating reflection. An example of an "unwrapped" environment map is shown in Figure 9.3.

Accessing an environment map from inside your shader is straightforward with the built-in `environment` function:

type `environment (string filename, vector R, ...)`

The `environment` function is quite analogous to the `texture()` call in several ways:

- The return type can be explicitly cast to either `float` or `color`. If you do not explicitly cast the results, the compiler will try to infer the return type, which could lead to ambiguous situations.
- A `float` in brackets immediately following the filename indicates a starting channel (default is to start with channel 0).
- For environment maps, the texture coordinates consist of a direction vector. As with `texture()`, derivatives of this vector will be used for automatic filtering of

Figure 9.3 *Geri's Game*—An example environment map. (© Pixar Animation Studios.)
See also color plate 9.3.

the environment map lookup. Optionally, four vectors may be given to bound the
angle range, and in that case no derivatives will be taken.

■ The environment function can take the optional arguments "blur", "width", and
"filter", which perform the same functions as for texture().

Environment maps typically sample the mirror direction, as computed by the
Shading Language built-in function reflect(). For example,

```
normal Nf = normalize (faceforward (N, I));
vector R = normalize (reflect (I, N));
color Crefl = color environment (envmapname, R);
```

Note that the environment() is indexed by direction only, not position. Thus, not
only is the environment map created from the point of view of a single location
but all lookups are also made from that point. Alternatively, you can think of
the environment map as being a reflection of a cube of infinite size. Either way,
two points with identical mirror directions will look up the same direction in the
environment map. This is most noticeable for flat surfaces, which tend to have all
of their points index the same spot on the environment map. This is an obvious and
objectionable artifact, especially for surfaces like floors, whose reflections are *very*
sensitive to position.

We can partially overcome this difficulty with the following strategy:

1. We assume that the environment map exists on the interior of a sphere with a *finite* and known radius as well as a known center. Example: if the environment map is of a room interior, we choose a sphere radius representative of the room size. (Even if we have assembled an environment map from six rectangular faces, because it is indexed by direction only, for simplicity we can just as easily think of it as a spherical map.)
2. Instead of indexing the environment by direction only, we define a ray using the position and mirror direction of the point, then calculate the intersection of this ray with our aforementioned environment sphere.
3. The intersection with the environment sphere is then used as the environment lookup direction.

Thus, if a simple `environment()` lookup is like ray tracing against a sphere of infinite radius, then the scheme above is simply ray tracing against a sphere of a radius appropriate to the actual scene in the environment map.

As a subproblem, we must be able to intersect an environment sphere with a ray. A general treatment of ray/object intersections can be found in (Glassner, 1989), but the ray/sphere case is particularly simple. If a ray if described by end point E and unit direction vector I (expressed in the coordinate system of a sphere centered at its local origin and with radius r), then any point along the ray can be described as $E + It$ (for free parameter t). This ray intersects the sphere anyplace that $|E + It| = r$. Because the length of a vector is the square root of its dot product with itself, then

$$(E + It) \cdot (E + It) = r^2$$

Expanding the $x, y,$ and z components for the dot product calculation yields

$$(E_x + I_x t)^2 + (E_y + I_y t)^2 + (E_z + I_z t)^2 - r^2 = 0$$
$$E_x^2 + 2E_x I_x t + I_x^2 t^2 + E_y^2 + 2E_y I_y t + I_y^2 t^2$$
$$+ E_z^2 + 2E_z I_z t + I_z^2 t^2 - r^2 = 0$$
$$(I \cdot I)t^2 + 2(E \cdot I)t + E \cdot E - r^2 = 0$$

for which the value(s) of t can be solved using the quadratic equation. This solution is performed by the `raysphere` function, which in turn is used by our enhanced `Environment` routine (see Listing 9.5). Note that `Environment` also returns an `alpha` value from the environment map, allowing us to composite multiple environment maps together.

9.2.2   Creating Cube Face Environment Maps

The creation of cube face environment maps is straightforward. First, six reflection images are created by rendering the scene from the point of view of the reflective object in each of six orthogonal directions in "world" space, given in Table 9.1.

Listing 9.5 Environment function replaces a simple environment call, giving more accurate reflections by tracing against an environment sphere of finite radius.

```
/* raysphere - calculate the intersection of ray (E,I) with a sphere
 * centered at the origin and with radius r.  We return the number of
 * intersections found (0, 1, or 2), and place the distances to the
 * intersections in t0, t1 (always with t0 <= t1).  Ignore any hits
 * closer than eps.
 */
float
raysphere (point E; vector I;    /* Origin and unit direction of the ray */
           float r;              /* radius of sphere */
           float eps;            /* epsilon - ignore closer hits */
           output float t0, t1;  /* distances to intersection */
    )
{
    /* Set up a quadratic equation -- note that a==1 if I is normalized */
    float b = 2 * ((vector E) . I);
    float c = ((vector E) . (vector E)) - r*r;
    float discrim = b*b - 4*c;
    float solutions;
    if (discrim > 0) {              /* Two solutions */
        discrim = sqrt(discrim);
        t0 = (-discrim - b) / 2;
        if (t0 > eps) {
            t1 = (discrim - b) / 2;
            solutions = 2;
        } else {
            t0 = (discrim - b) / 2;
            solutions = (t0 > eps) ? 1 : 0;
        }
    } else if (discrim == 0) {  /* One solution on the edge! */
        t0 = -b/2;
        solutions = (t0 > eps) ? 1 : 0;
    } else {                        /* Imaginary solution -> no intersection */
        solutions = 0;
    }
    return solutions;
}


/* Environment() - A replacement for ordinary environment() lookups, this
 * function ray traces against an environment sphere of known, finite
 * radius.  Inputs are:
 *     envname - filename of environment map
 *     envspace - name of space environment map was made in
 *     envrad - approximate supposed radius of environment sphere
 *     P, R - position and direction of traced ray
 *     blur - amount of additional blur to add to environment map
 * Outputs are:
 *     return value - the color of incoming environment light
 *     alpha - opacity of environment map lookup in the direction R.
```

▶

```
 * Warning -  the environment call itself takes derivatives, causing
 * trouble if called inside a loop or varying conditional!  Be cautious.
 */
color Environment ( string envname, envspace;  uniform float envrad;
                    point P;  vector R;  float blur; output float alpha;)
{
    /* Transform to the space of the environment map */
    point Psp = transform (envspace, P);
    vector Rsp = normalize (vtransform (envspace, R));
    uniform float r2 = envrad * envrad;
    /* Clamp the position to be *inside* the environment sphere */
    if ((vector Psp).(vector Psp) > r2)
        Psp = point (envrad * normalize (vector Psp));
    float t0, t1;
    if (raysphere (Psp, Rsp, envrad, 1.0e-4, t0, t1) > 0)
        Rsp = vector (Psp + t0 * Rsp);
    alpha = float environment (envname[3], Rsp, "blur", blur, "fill", 1);
    return color environment (envname, Rsp, "blur", blur);
}
```

Table 9.1: The six view directions in an environment map.

Face view	Axis toward top	Axis toward right
px (positive x)	$+y$	$-z$
nx (negative x)	$+y$	$+z$
py	$-z$	$+x$
ny	$+z$	$+x$
pz	$+y$	$+x$
nz	$+y$	$-x$

Next, these six views (which should be rendered using a square 90° field of view to completely cover all directions) are combined into a single environment map. This can be done from the RIB file:

MakeCubeFaceEnvironment *px nx py ny pz nz envfile*

Here *px*, *nx*, and so on are the names of the files containing the individual face images, and *envfile* is the name of the file where you would like the final environment map to be placed.

Alternatively, most renderers will have a separate program that will assemble an environment map from the six individual views. In the case of *PRMan*, this can be done with the txmake program:

txmake -envcube *px nx py ny pz nz envfile*

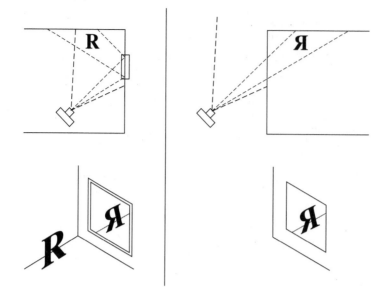

Figure 9.4 Creating a mirrored scene for generating a reflection map. On the top left, a camera views a scene that includes a mirror. Below is the image it produces. On the top right, the camera instead views the *mirror scene*. Notice that the image it produces (below) contains the required reflection.

9.2.3 Flat Surface Reflection Maps

For the special case of flat objects (such as floors or flat mirrors), there is an even easier and more efficient method for producing reflections, which also solves the problem of environment maps being inaccurate for flat objects.

For the example of a flat mirror, we can observe that the image in the reflection would be identical to the image that you would get if you put another copy of the room on the other side of the mirror, *reflected* about the plane of the mirror. This geometric principle is illustrated in Figure 9.4.

Once we create this reflection map, we can turn it into a texture and index it from our shader. Because the pixels in the reflection map correspond exactly to the reflected image in the same pixels of the main image, we access the texture map by the texture's pixel coordinates, not the s, t coordinates of the mirror. We can do this by projecting P into "NDC" space. This is done in the ReflMap function in Listing 9.6.

9.2.4 General Reflections and Shiny Surfaces

We would prefer to write our shaders so that we may use either reflection or environment maps. Therefore, we can combine both into a single routine, SampleEnvironment(), given in Listing 9.7.

Listing 9.6 `ReflMap` function performs simple reflection mapping.

```
color ReflMap ( string reflname; point P; float blur;
                output float alpha; )
{
    /* Transform to the space of the environment map */
    point Pndc = transform ("NDC", P);
    float x = xcomp(Pndc), y = ycomp(Pndc);
    alpha = float texture (reflname[3], x, y, "blur", blur, "fill", 1);
    return color texture (reflname, x, y, "blur", blur);
}
```

Listing 9.7 `SampleEnvironment` function makes calls to either or both of `Environment` or `ReflMap` as needed.

```
#define ENVPARAMS       envname, envspace, envrad

#define DECLARE_ENVPARAMS                               \
        string envname, envspace;  uniform float envrad

#define DECLARE_DEFAULTED_ENVPARAMS                     \
        string envname = "", envspace = "world";        \
        uniform float envrad = 100


color
SampleEnvironment (point P;  vector R;  float Kr, blur;
                   DECLARE_ENVPARAMS;)
{
    color C = 0;
    float alpha;
    if (envname != "") {
        if (envspace == "NDC")
            C = ReflMap (envname, P, blur, alpha);
        else C = Environment (envname, envspace, envrad, P, R, blur,
                              alpha);
    }
    return Kr*C;
}
```

A few comments on the source code in Listing 9.7. To allow easy specification of the many environment-related parameters, we define macros ENVPARAMS, DECLARE_ENVPARAMS, and DECLARE_DEFAULTED_ENVPARAMS, which are macros containing the parameter names, declarations, and declarations with default values, respectively. These macros allow us to succinctly include them in any shader, as we have done in shader shinymetal (Listing 9.8).

Listing 9.8 `MaterialShinyMetal` and the `shinymetal` shader.

```
/* Compute the color of the surface using a simple metal-like BRDF.  To
 * give a metallic appearance, both diffuse and specular components are
 * scaled by the color of the metal.  It is recommended that Kd < 0.1,
 * Ks > 0.5, and roughness > 0.15 to give a believable metallic appearance.
 */
color MaterialShinyMetal (normal Nf;  color basecolor;
                          float Ka, Kd, Ks, roughness, Kr, blur;
                          DECLARE_ENVPARAMS;)
{
    extern point P;
    extern vector I;
    vector IN = normalize(I), V = -IN;
    vector R = reflect (IN, Nf);
    return basecolor * (Ka*ambient() + Kd*diffuse(Nf) +
                    Ks*specular(Nf,V,roughness) +
                    SampleEnvironment (P, R, Kr, blur, ENVPARAMS));
}


surface
shinymetal ( float Ka = 1, Kd = 0.1, Ks = 1, roughness = 0.2;
            float Kr = 0.8, blur = 0;  DECLARE_DEFAULTED_ENVPARAMS; )
{
    normal Nf = faceforward (normalize(N), I);
    Ci = MaterialShinyMetal (Nf, Cs, Ka, Kd, Ks, roughness, Kr, blur,
                        ENVPARAMS);
    Oi = Os;  Ci *= Oi;
}
```

With this routine in our toolbox, we can make a straightforward shader that can be used for shiny metals like mirrors, chrome, or copper (see Listing 9.8). If you are using the shader for a flat object with a prepared flat reflection map, you need only pass "NDC" as the envspace parameter and the `SampleEnvironment` function will correctly access your reflection map.

9.2.5   Fresnel and Shiny Plastic

All materials are more reflective at glancing angles than face-on (in fact, materials approach 100% reflectivity at grazing angles). For polished metals, the face-on reflectivity is so high that this difference in reflectivity with angle is not very noticeable. You can convince yourself of this by examining an ordinary mirror—it appears nearly equally shiny when you view your reflection head-on versus when you look at the mirror at an angle. So we tend to ignore the angular effect on reflectivity, assuming for simplicity that polished metals are equally reflective in all directions (as we have in the previous section).

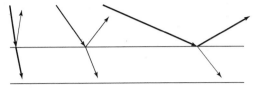

Figure 9.5 The ratio of reflected to transmitted light at a material boundary changes with the angle of the incident light ray.

Dielectrics such as plastic, ceramics, and glass are much less reflective than metals overall, and especially so when viewed face-on. Therefore, their higher reflectivity at grazing angles is a much more significant visual detail (see Figure 9.5). The formulas that relate angle to reflectivity of such materials are known as the *Fresnel equations*.

A function that calculates the Fresnel terms is included in Shading Language:

```
void fresnel (vector I; normal N; float eta;
            output float Kr, Kt; output vector R, T);
```

According to Snell's law and the Fresnel equations, fresnel computes the reflection and transmission direction vectors R and T, respectively, as well as the scaling factors for reflected and transmitted light, Kr and Kt. The I parameter is the normalized incident ray, N is the normalized surface normal, and eta is the ratio of refractive index of the medium containing I to that on the opposite side of the surface.

We can use fresnel() to attenuate the relative contributions of environmental and diffuse reflectances. This is demonstrated in the MaterialShinyPlastic and shinyplastic, both shown in Listing 9.9. Figure 9.6 compares the appearance of MaterialShinyMetal and MaterialShinyPlastic.

The index of refraction of air is very close to 1.0, water is 1.33, ordinary window glass is approximately 1.5, and most plastics are close to this value. In computer graphics, we typically assume that 1.5 is a reasonable refractive index for a very wide range of plastics and glasses. Therefore, a reasonable value for the eta parameter passed to fresnel() is 1/1.5. Nearly any optics textbook will list the indices of refraction for a variety of real materials, should you wish to be more physically accurate.

Of course, for real materials the refractive index is wavelength dependent. We tend to ignore this effect, since we have such an ad hoc approach to spectral sampling and color spaces anyway. Although metals also have wavelength-dependent indices of refraction, Fresnel effects, and angle-dependent spectral reflectivities, they are much less visually noticeable in most metals, so we usually just pretend

Listing 9.9 shinyplastic shader is for highly polished plastic and uses
fresnel(IN, Nf, 1/ior, fkr, fkt, R, T) so that reflections are stronger at
grazing angles.

```
color
MaterialShinyPlastic (normal Nf;  color basecolor;
                      float Ka, Kd, Ks, roughness, Kr, blur, ior;
                      DECLARE_ENVPARAMS;)
{
    extern vector I;     extern point P;
    vector IN = normalize(I), V = -IN;
    float fkr, fkt;  vector R, T;
    fresnel (IN, Nf, 1/ior, fkr, R, T);
    fkt = 1-fkr;
    return  fkt * basecolor * (Ka*ambient() + Kd*diffuse(Nf))
                + (Ks*fkr) * specular(Nf,V,roughness)
                + SampleEnvironment (P, R, fkr*Kr, blur, ENVPARAMS));
}


surface
shinyplastic ( float Ka = 1, Kd = 0.5, Ks = .5, roughness = 0.1;
             float Kr = 1, blur = 0, ior = 1.5;
             DECLARE_DEFAULTED_ENVPARAMS; )
{
    normal Nf = faceforward (normalize(N), I);
    Ci = MaterialShinyPlastic (Nf, Cs, Ka, Kd, Ks, roughness, Kr,
                               blur, ior,  ENVPARAMS);
    Oi = Os;  Ci *= Oi;
}
```

Figure 9.6 MaterialShinyMetal (left) and MaterialShinyPlastic (right). See also color
plate 9.6.

that shiny metals reflect uniformly. You are, of course, perfectly free to go to the extra effort of computing the wavelength and angle dependency of metals!

Important note: in MaterialShinyPlastic we set fkt=1-fkr, overriding the value returned by fresnel(). The reasons for this are extremely subtle and well beyond the scope of this book. Suffice it to say that the value that fresnel() is supposed to return for Kt assumes a more rigorous simulation of light propagation than either *PRMan* or *BMRT* provides. In light of these inaccuracies, the intuitive notion that Kt and Kr ought to sum to 1 is about as good an approximation as you might hope for. We will therefore continue to use this oversimplification.

9.3   Illuminance Loops, or How diffuse() and specular() Work

We have seen classes of materials that can be described by various relative weightings and uses of the built-in diffuse() and specular() functions. In point of fact, these are just examples of possible illumination models, and it is quite useful to write alternative ones. In order to do that, however, the shader needs access to the lights: how many are there, where are they, and how bright are they?

The key to such functionality is a special syntactic structure in Shading Language called an illuminance loop:

```
illuminance ( point position ) {
    statements;
}
```

```
illuminance ( point position; vector axis; float angle ) {
    statements;
}
```

The illuminance statement loops over all light sources visible from a particular *position*. In the first form, all lights are considered, and in the second form, only those lights whose directions are within *angle* of *axis* (typically, *angle*=$\pi/2$ and *axis*=N, which indicates that all light sources in the visible hemisphere from P should be considered). For each light source, the *statements* are executed, during which two additional variables are defined: L is the vector that points to the light source, and Cl is the color representing the incoming energy from that light source.

Perhaps the most straightforward example of the use of illuminance loops is the implementation of the diffuse() function:

```
color diffuse (normal Nn)
{
    extern point P;
    color C = 0;
    illuminance (P, Nn, PI/2) {
```

```
        C += Cl * (Nn . normalize(L));
    }
    return C;
}
```

Briefly, this function is looping over all light sources. Each light's contribution is computed using a Lambertian shading model; that is, the light reflected diffusely is the light arriving from the source multiplied by the dot product of the normal with the direction of the light. The contributions of all lights are summed and that sum is returned as the result of diffuse().

9.4   Identifying Lights with Special Properties

In reality, surfaces simply scatter light. The scattering function, or BRDF (which stands for bidirectional reflection distribution function) may be quite complex. Dividing the scattering function into diffuse versus specular, or considering the BRDF to be a weighted sum of the two, is simply a convenient oversimplification. Many other simplifications and abstractions are possible.

In the physical world, light scattering is a property of the surface material, not a property of the light itself or of its source. Nonetheless, in computer graphics it is often convenient and desirable to place light sources whose purpose is solely to provide a highlight, or alternatively to provide a soft fill light where specular highlights would be undesirable. Therefore, we would like to construct our diffuse() function so that it can ignore light sources that have been tagged as being "nondiffuse"; that is, the source itself should only contribute specular highlights. We can do this by exploiting the *message passing* mechanism of Shading Language, wherein the surface shader may peek at the parameters of the light shader.

float lightsource (string paramname; output *type* result)

> The lightsource() function, which may only be called from within an illuminance loop, searches for a parameter of the light source named paramname. If such a parameter is found and if its type matches that of the variable result, then its value will be stored in the result and the lightsource() function will return 1.0. If no such parameter is found, the variable result will be unchanged and the return value of lightsource will be zero.

We can use this mechanism as follows. Let us assume rather arbitrarily that any light that we wish to contribute only to specular highlights (and that therefore should be ignored by the diffuse() function) will contain in its parameter list an output float parameter named __nondiffuse. Similarly, we can use an output float parameter named __nonspecular to indicate that a particular light should not contribute to specular highlights. Then implementations of diffuse() and specular(), as shown in Listing 9.10, would respond properly to these con-

> **Listing 9.10** The implementation of the built-in `diffuse()` and `specular()` functions, including controls to ignore nondiffuse and nonspecular lights.

```
color diffuse (normal Nn)
{
    extern point P;
    color C = 0;
    illuminance (P, Nn, PI/2) {
        float nondiff = 0;
        lightsource ("__nondiffuse", nondiff);
        C += Cl * (1-nondiff) * (Nn . normalize(L));
    }
    return C;
}


color specular (normal Nn; vector V; float roughness)
{
    extern point P;
    color C = 0;
    illuminance (P, Nn, PI/2) {
        float nonspec = 0;
        lightsource ("__nonspecular", nonspec);
        vector H = normalize (normalize(L) + V);
        C += Cl * (1-nonspec) * pow (max (0, Nn.H), 1/roughness);
    }
    return C;
}
```

trols. In both *PRMan* and *BMRT*, the implementations of `diffuse()` and `specular()` respond to __nondiffuse and __nonspecular in this manner (although as we explained earlier, the implementation of `specular()` is not quite what is in Listing 9.10).

This message passing mechanism may be used more generally to pass all sorts of "extra" information from the lights to the surfaces. For example, a light may include an output parameter giving its *ultraviolet* illumination, and special surface shaders may respond to this parameter by exhibiting fluorescence.

There is an additional means of controlling `illuminance` loops with an optional *light category* specifier:

```
illuminance ( string category; point position )
    statements;
```

```
illuminance ( string category; point position;
              vector axis; float angle )
    statements;
```

Ordinary illuminance loops will execute their body for every nonambient light source. The named category extension to the illuminance syntax causes the *statements* to be executed only for a subset of light sources.

Light shaders can specify the categories to which they belong by declaring a string parameter named __category (this name has two underscores), whose value is a comma-separated list of categories into which the light shader falls. When the illuminance statement contains a string parameter *category*, the loop will only consider lights for which the *category* is among those listed in its comma-separated __category list. If the illuminance *category* begins with a - character, then only lights *not* containing that category will be considered. For example,

```
float uvcontrib = 0;
illuminance ("uvlight", P, Nf, PI/2) {
    float uv = 0;
    lightsource ("uv", uv);
    uvcontrib += uv;
}
Ci += uvcontrib * uvglowcolor;
```

will look specifically for lights containing the string "uvlight" in their __category list and will execute those lights, summing their "uv" output parameter. An example light shader that computes ultraviolet intensity might be

```
light
uvpointlight (float intensity = 1, uvintensity = 0.5;
              color lightcolor = 1;
              point from = point "shader" (0,0,0);
              output varying float uv = 0;
              string __category = "uvlight";)
{
    illuminate (from) {
        Cl = intensity * lightcolor / (L . L);
        uv = uvintensity / (L . L);
    }
}
```

Don't worry too much that you haven't seen light shaders yet: before the end of this chapter, this example will be crystal clear.

9.5   Custom Material Descriptions

We have seen that the implementation of diffuse() is that of a Lambertian shading model that approximates a rough surface that scatters light equally in all directions. Similarly, specular() implements a Blinn-Phong scattering function (according to the RI spec). As we've seen, different weighted combinations of these two functions can yield materials that look like a variety of plastics and metals. Now that we understand how they operate, we may use the `illuminance` construct ourselves to create custom primitive local illumination models. Past ACM SIGGRAPH proceedings are a treasure trove of ideas for more complex and realistic local illumination models. In this section we will examine three local illumination models (two physically based and one ad hoc) and construct shader functions that implement them.

9.5.1   Rough Surfaces

Lambert's law models a perfectly smooth surface that reflects light equally in all directions. This is very much an oversimplification of the behavior of materials. In the proceedings of SIGGRAPH '94, Michael Oren and Shree K. Nayar described a surface scattering model for rough surfaces. Their model (and others, including Beckman, Blinn, and Cook/Torrance) considers rough surfaces to have microscopic grooves and hills. This is modeled mathematically as a collection of microfacets having a statistical distribution of relative directions. Their results indicated that many real-world rough materials (like clay) could be more accurately modeled using the following equation:

$$L_r(\theta_r, \theta_i, \phi_r - \phi_i, \sigma) = \frac{\rho}{\pi} E_0 \cos\theta_i (A + B \max[0, \cos(\phi_r - \phi_i)] \sin\alpha \tan\beta),$$

where

$$A = 1.0 - 0.5 \frac{\sigma^2}{\sigma^2 + 0.33}$$

$$B = 0.45 \frac{\sigma^2}{\sigma^2 + 0.09}$$

$$\alpha = \max[\theta_i, \theta_r]$$

$$\beta = \min[\theta_i, \theta_r],$$

and the terms mean

- ρ is the reflectivity of the surface (Kd*Cs).
- E_0 is the energy arriving at the surface from the light (Cl).
- θ_i is the angle between the surface normal and the direction of the light source.
- θ_r is the angle between the surface normal and the vector in the direction the light is reflected (i.e., toward the viewer).
- $\phi_r - \phi_i$ is the angle (about the normal) between the incoming and reflected light directions.
- σ is the standard deviation of the angle distribution of the microfacets (in radians). Larger values represent more rough surfaces; smaller values represent smoother surfaces. If $\sigma = 0$, the surface is perfectly smooth, and this function reduces to a simple Lambertian reflectance model. We'll call this parameter "roughness."

Listing 9.11 LocIllumOrenNayar implements a BRDF for diffuse, but rough, surfaces.

```
/*
 * Oren and Nayar's generalization of Lambert's reflection model.
 * The roughness parameter gives the standard deviation of angle
 * orientations of the presumed surface grooves.  When roughness=0,
 * the model is identical to Lambertian reflection.
 */
color
LocIllumOrenNayar (normal N;  vector V;  float roughness;)
{
    /* Surface roughness coefficients for Oren/Nayar's formula */
    float sigma2 = roughness * roughness;
    float A = 1 - 0.5 * sigma2 / (sigma2 + 0.33);
    float B = 0.45 * sigma2 / (sigma2 + 0.09);
    /* Useful precomputed quantities */
    float  theta_r = acos (V . N);          /* Angle between V and N */
    vector V_perp_N = normalize(V-N*(V.N)); /* Part of V perpendicular to N
*/

    /* Accumulate incoming radiance from lights in C */
    color  C = 0;
    extern point P;
    illuminance (P, N, PI/2) {
        /* Must declare extern L & Cl because we're in a function */
        extern vector L;  extern color Cl;
        float nondiff = 0;
        lightsource ("__nondiffuse", nondiff);
        if (nondiff < 1) {
            vector LN = normalize(L);
            float cos_theta_i = LN . N;
            float cos_phi_diff = V_perp_N . normalize(LN - N*cos_theta_i);
            float theta_i = acos (cos_theta_i);
            float alpha = max (theta_i, theta_r);
            float beta = min (theta_i, theta_r);
            C += (1-nondiff) * Cl * cos_theta_i *
                (A + B * max(0,cos_phi_diff) * sin(alpha) * tan(beta));
        }
    }
    return C;

}
```

These equations are easily translated into an illuminance loop, as shown in Listing 9.11.

Figure 9.7 shows a teapot with the Oren/Nayar reflectance model. The left teapot uses a roughness coefficient of 0.5, while the right uses a roughness coefficient of 0, which has reflectance identical to Lambertian shading. Notice that as roughness

Figure 9.7 When the light source is directly behind the viewer, the Oren/Nayar model (left) acts much more as a retroreflector, compared to the Lambertian model (right). See also color plate 9.7.

increases, a strong backscattering effect is present. The object begins to act as a retroreflector, so that light that comes from the same direction as the viewer bounces back at a rate nearly independent of surface orientation.

It is this type of backscattering that accounts for the appearance of the full moon. Everyone has noticed that a full moon (when the viewer and sun are nearly at the same angle to the moon) looks like a flat disk, rather than like a ball. The moon is not Lambertian—it is more closely modeled as a rough surface, and this reflection model is a good approximation to the behavior of lunar dust.

9.5.2   Anisotropic Metal

The `MaterialRoughMetal` function described earlier does an adequate job of simulating the appearance of a metal object that is rough enough that coherent reflections (from ray tracing or environment maps) are not necessary. However, it does make the simplifying assumption that the metal scatters light only according to the angular relationship between the surface normal, the eye, and the light source. It specifically does not depend on the orientation of the surface as it spins around the normal vector.

To help visualize the situation, consider the following diagram:

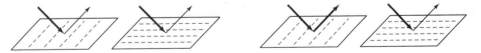

Imagine rotating the material around the normal vector. If the reflectivity in a particular direction is independent of the surface orientation, then the material is said to be *isotropic*. On the other hand, if the material reflects preferentially depending on surface orientation, then it is *anisotropic*.

Anisotropic materials are not uncommon. Various manufacturing processes can produce materials with microscopic grooves that are all aligned to a particular direction (picture the surface being covered with tiny half-cylinders oriented in parallel or otherwise coherently). This gives rise to anisotropic BRDFs. A number of papers have been written about anisotropic reflection models, including Kajiya (1985) and Poulin and Fournier (1990).

Greg Ward Larson described an anisotropic reflection model in his SIGGRAPH '92 paper, "Measuring and Modeling Anisotropic Reflection" (Ward, 1992). In this paper, anisotropic specular reflection was given as

$$\frac{1}{\sqrt{\cos \theta_i \cos \theta_r}} \frac{1}{4\pi \alpha_x \alpha_y} \exp\left[-2 \frac{\left(\frac{\hat{h} \cdot \hat{x}}{\alpha_x}\right)^2 + \left(\frac{\hat{h} \cdot \hat{y}}{\alpha_y}\right)^2}{1 + \hat{h} \cdot \hat{n}}\right],$$

where

- θ_i is the angle between the surface normal and the direction of the light source.
- θ_r is the angle between the surface normal and the vector in the direction the light is reflected (i.e., toward the viewer).
- $\hat{x}$ and $\hat{y}$ are the two perpendicular tangent directions on the surface.
- α_x and α_y are the standard deviations of the slope in the $\hat{x}$ and $\hat{y}$ directions, respectively. We will call these xroughness and yroughness.
- $\hat{n}$ is the unit surface normal (normalize(N)).
- $\hat{h}$ is the half-angle between the incident and reflection rays (i.e., H = normalize (normalize(-I) + normalize(L))).

Listing 9.12 lists the function LocIllumWardAnisotropic, which implements the anisotropic specular component of Larson's model.[3] This function can be used instead of an ordinary specular() call. It differs from specular() in that it takes *two* roughness values: one for the direction aligned with surface tangent xdir, and the other for the perpendicular direction. Figure 9.8 shows this model applied to a teapot.

9.5.3 Glossy Specular Highlights

The previous subsections listed Shading Language implementations of two local illumination models that are physically based simulations of the way light reflects

---

[3] When comparing the original equation to our Shading Language implementation, you may wonder where the factor of $1/\pi$ went and why there appears to be an extra factor of $L \cdot N$. This is not an error! Greg Ward Larson's paper describes the BRDF, which is only part of the kernel of the light integral, whereas shaders describe the result of that integral. This is something that must be kept in mind when coding traditional BRDFs in illuminance loops.

Listing 9.12 `LocIllumWardAnisotropic`: Greg Ward Larson's anisotropic specular illumination model.

```
/*
 * Greg Ward Larson's anisotropic specular local illumination model.
 * The derivation and formulae can be found in:  Ward, Gregory J.
 * "Measuring and Modeling Anisotropic Reflection," ACM Computer
 * Graphics 26(2) (Proceedings of Siggraph '92), pp. 265-272, July, 1992.
 * Notice that compared to the paper, the implementation below appears
 * to be missing a factor of 1/pi, and to have an extra L.N term.
 * This is not an error!  It is because the paper's formula is for the
 * BRDF, which is only part of the kernel of the light integral, whereas
 * shaders must compute the result of the integral.
 *
 * Inputs:
 *   N - unit surface normal
 *   V - unit viewing direction (from P toward the camera)
 *   xdir - a unit tangent of the surface defining the reference
 *          direction for the anisotropy.
 *   xroughness - the apparent roughness of the surface in xdir.
 *   yroughness - the roughness for the direction of the surface
 *          tangent perpendicular to xdir.
 */
color
LocIllumWardAnisotropic (normal N;  vector V;
                         vector xdir;  float xroughness, yroughness;)
{
    float sqr (float x) { return x*x; }

    float cos_theta_r = clamp (N.V, 0.0001, 1);
    vector X = xdir / xroughness;
    vector Y = (N ^ xdir) / yroughness;

    color C = 0;
    extern point P;
    illuminance (P, N, PI/2) {
        /* Must declare extern L & Cl because we're in a function */
        extern vector L;  extern color Cl;
        float nonspec = 0;
        lightsource ("__nonspecular", nonspec);
        if (nonspec < 1) {
            vector LN = normalize (L);
            float cos_theta_i = LN . N;
            if (cos_theta_i > 0.0) {
                vector H = normalize (V + LN);
                float rho = exp (-2 * (sqr(X.H) + sqr(Y.H)) / (1 + H.N))
                    / sqrt (cos_theta_i * cos_theta_r);
                C += Cl * ((1-nonspec) * cos_theta_i * rho);
            }
        }
    }
    return C / (4 * xroughness * yroughness);
}
```

Figure 9.8 Examples of the Ward anisotropic reflection model. Isotropic reflection with xroughness=yroughness=0.3 (top). Anisotropic reflection with xroughness=0.15, yroughness=0.5 (bottom left). Anisotropic reflection with xroughness=0.5, yroughness=0.15 (bottom right). In all cases, xdir=normalize(dPdu). See also color plate 9.8.

off certain material types. Many times, however, we want an effect that achieves a particular look without resorting to simulation. The look itself may or may not match a real-world material, but the computations are completely ad hoc. This subsection presents a local illumination model that achieves a useful look but that is decidedly not based on the actual behavior of light. It works well for glossy materials, such as finished ceramics, glass, or wet materials.

We note that specular highlights are a lot like mirror reflections of the light source. The observation that they are big fuzzy circles on rough objects and small sharp circles on smooth objects is a combination of the blurry reflection model and the fact that the real light sources are not infinitesimal points as we often use in computer graphics, but extended area sources such as light bulbs, the sun, and so on.

For polished glossy surfaces, we would like to get a clear, distinct reflection of those bright area sources, even if there isn't a noticeable mirror reflection of the rest of the environment (and even if we aren't really using true area lights). We

Listing 9.13 LocIllumGlossy function: nonphysical replacement for specular() that makes a uniformly bright specular highlight.

```
/*
 * LocIllumGlossy - a possible replacement for specular(), having
 * more uniformly bright core and a sharper falloff.  It's a nice
 * specular function to use for something made of glass or liquid.
 * Inputs:
 *   roughness - related to the size of the highlight, larger is bigger
 *   sharpness - 1 is infinitely sharp, 0 is very dull
 */
color LocIllumGlossy ( normal N;  vector V;
                        float roughness, sharpness; )
{
    color C = 0;
    float w = .18 * (1-sharpness);
    extern point P;
    illuminance (P, N, PI/2) {
        /* Must declare extern L & Cl because we're in a function */
        extern vector L;   extern color Cl;
        float nonspec = 0;
        lightsource ("__nonspecular", nonspec);
        if (nonspec < 1) {
            vector H = normalize(normalize(L)+V);
            C += Cl * ((1-nonspec) *
                    smoothstep (.72-w, .72+w,
                            pow(max(0,N.H), 1/roughness)));
        }
    }
    return C;
}
```

propose that we could achieve this look by thresholding the specular highlight. In other words, we modify a Blinn-Phong specular term (c.f. Listing 9.10) from

```
Cl * pow (max (0, Nn.H), 1/roughness);
```

to the thresholded version:

```
Cl * smoothstep (e0, e1, pow (max (0, Nn.H), 1/roughness));
```

With an appropriately chosen e0 and e1, the specular highlight will appear to be smaller, have a sharp transition, and be fully bright inside the transition region. Listing 9.13 is a full implementation of this proposal (with some magic constants chosen empirically by the authors). Finally, Figure 9.9 compares this glossy specular highlight to a standard plastic-like specular() function. In that example, we used roughness=0.1, sharpness=0.5.

Figure 9.9 Comparing the glossy versus plastic specular illumination models. See also color plate 9.9.

9.6   Light Sources

Previous sections discuss how surface shaders respond to the light energy that arrives at the surface, reflecting in different ways to give the appearance of different types of materials. Now it is time to move to light shaders, which allow the shader author similarly detailed control over the operation of the light sources themselves.

9.6.1   Nongeometric Light Shaders

Light source shaders are syntactically similar to surface shaders. The primary difference is that the shader type is called `light` rather than `surface` and that a somewhat different set of built-in variables is available. The variables available inside light shaders are listed in Table 9.2. The goal of a light shader is primarily to determine the radiant energy Cl and light direction L of light impinging on Ps from this source. In addition, the light may compute additional quantities and store them in its output variables, which can be read and acted upon by `illuminance` loops using the `lightsource` statement.

The most basic type of light is an ambient source, which responds in a way that is independent of position. Such a shader is shown in Listing 9.14. The `ambientlight` shader simply sets Cl to a constant value, determined by its parameters. It also explicitly sets L to zero, indicating to the renderer that there is no directionality to the light.

For directional light, although we could explicitly set L, there are some syntactic structures for emitting light in light shaders that help us do the job efficiently. One such syntactic construct is the `solar` statement:

> **Table 9.2:** Global variables available inside light shaders. Variables are read-only except where noted.
>
> | | |
> |---|---|
> | point Ps | Position of the point *on the surface* that requested data from the light shader. |
> | vector L | The vector giving the direction of outgoing light from the source to the point being shaded, Ps. This variable can be set explicitly by the shader but is generally set implicitly by the illuminate or solar statements. |
> | color Cl | The light color of the energy being emitted by the source. Setting this variable is the primary purpose of a light shader. |

> **Listing 9.14** Ambient light source shader.

```
light
ambientlight (float intensity = 1;
              color lightcolor = 1;)
{
    Cl = intensity * lightcolor;   /* doesn't depend on position */
    L = 0;                         /* no light direction */
}
```

```
solar ( vector axis; float spreadangle ) {
    statements;
}
```

The effect of the solar statement is to send light to every Ps from the same direction, given by *axis*. The result is that rays from such a light are parallel, as if the source were infinitely far away. An example of such a source would be the sun.

Listing 9.15 is an example of the solar statement. The solar statement implicitly sets the L variable to its first argument; there is no need to set L yourself. Furthermore, the solar statement will compare this direction to the light gathering cone of the corresponding illuminance statement in the surface shader. If the light's L direction is outside the range of angles that the illuminance statement is gathering, the block of statements within the solar construct will not be executed.

The *spreadangle* parameter is usually set to zero, indicating that the source subtends an infinitesimal angle and that the rays are truly parallel. Values for *spreadangle* greater than zero indicate that a plethora of light rays arrive at each Ps from a range of directions, instead of a single ray from a particular direction. Such lights are known as *broad solar lights* and are analogous to very distant but very large area lights. (For example, the sun actually subtends a 1/2 degree angle when seen from Earth.) The exact mechanism for handling these cases may be implementation dependent, differing from renderer to renderer.

> **Listing 9.15** `distantlight`, a light shader for infinitely distant light sources with parallel rays.

```
light
distantlight ( float intensity = 1;
               color lightcolor = 1;
               point from = point "shader" (0,0,0);
               point to = point "shader" (0,0,1); )
{
    solar (to-from, 0) {
        Cl = intensity * lightcolor;
    }
}
```

> **Listing 9.16** `pointlight` radiates light in all directions from a particular point.

```
light
pointlight (float intensity = 1;
            color lightcolor = 1;
            point from = point "shader" (0,0,0);)
{
    illuminate (from) {
        Cl = intensity * lightcolor / (L . L);
    }
}
```

For lights that have a definite, finitely close position, there is another construct to use:

```
illuminate ( point from ) {
    statements;
}
```

This form of the `illuminate` statement indicates that light is emitted from position *from* and is radiated in all directions. As before, `illuminance` implicitly sets L = Ps − *from*. Listing 9.16 shows an example of a simple light shader that radiates light in all directions from a point `from` (which defaults to the origin of light shader space[4]). Dividing the intensity by L.L (which is the square of the length of L) results in what is known as $1/r^2$ falloff. In other words, the energy of light impinging on a surface falls off with the square of the distance between the surface and the light source.

---

[4] In a light shader, "shader" space is the coordinate system that was in effect at the point that the `LightSource` statement appeared in the RIB file.

Listing 9.17 spotlight radiates a cone of light in a particular direction.

```
light
spotlight ( float intensity = 1;
            color lightcolor = 1;
            point from = point "shader" (0,0,0);
            point to = point "shader" (0,0,1);
            float coneangle = radians(30);
            float conedeltaangle = radians(5);
            float beamdistribution = 2; )
{
    uniform vector A = normalize(to-from);
    uniform float cosoutside = cos (coneangle);
    uniform float cosinside  = cos (coneangle-conedeltaangle);
    illuminate (from, A, coneangle) {
        float cosangle = (L . A) / length(L);
        float atten = pow (cosangle, beamdistribution) / (L . L);
        atten *= smoothstep (cosoutside, cosinside, cosangle);
        Cl = atten * intensity * lightcolor;
    }
}
```

A second form of illuminate also specifies a particular cone of light emission, given by an axis and angle:

```
illuminate ( point from; vector axis; float angle ) {
    statements;
}
```

An example use of this construct can be found in the standard spotlight shader, shown in Listing 9.17. The illuminate construct will prevent light from being emitted in directions outside the cone. In addition, the shader computes $1/r^2$ distance falloff, applies a cosine falloff to directions away from the central axis, and smoothly fades the light out at the edges of the cone.

Both forms of illuminate will check the corresponding illuminance statement from the surface shader, which specified a cone axis and angle from which to gather light. If the *from* position is outside this angle range, the body of statements inside the illuminate construct will be skipped, thus saving computation for lights whose results would be ignored.

The lights presented here are very simple examples of light shaders, only meant to illustrate the solar and illuminate constructs. For high-quality image generation, many more controls would be necessary, including more flexible controls over the light's cross-sectional shape, directional and distance falloff, and so on. Such controls will be discussed in detail in Chapter 14.

Table 9.3: Global variables available inside area light shaders. Variables are read-only except where noted.

`point Ps`	Position of the point *on the surface* that requested data from the light shader.
`point P`	Position of the point *on the light*.
`normal N`	The surface normal of the light source geometry (at P).
`float u, v, s, t`	The 2D parametric coordinates of P (on the light source geometry).
`vector dPdu` `vector dPdv`	The partial derivatives (i.e., tangents) of the light source geometry at P.
`vector L`	The vector giving the direction of outgoing light from the source to the point being shaded, Ps. This variable can be set explicitly by the shader but is generally set implicitly by the `illuminate` or `solar` statements.
`color Cl`	The light color of the energy being emitted by the source. Setting this variable is the primary purpose of a light shader.

9.6.2   Area Light Sources

Area light sources are those that are associated with geometry (see Section 3.6). Table 9.3 lists the variables available inside area light sources. Many of the variables available to the area light shader describe a position *on the light* that has been selected by the renderer as the point at which the light shader is sampled. You need not worry about how this position is selected—the renderer will do it for you.

Positions, normals, and parameters on the light only make sense if the light is an area light source defined by a geometric primitive. If the light is an ordinary point source rather than an area light, these variables are undefined. Note that *PRMan* does not support area lights. Therefore, in that renderer the light geometry variables are undefined and should not be trusted to contain any meaningful data.

An example light shader that could be used for a simple area light source is given in Listing 9.18. Note the similarity to the `pointlight` shader—the main difference is that, rather than using a `from` parameter as the light position, we illuminate from the position P that the renderer chose for us by sampling the area light geometry. This shader illuminates only points on the *outside* of the light source geometry. It would also be fine to simply use `pointlight`, if you wanted the area light geometry to illuminate in all directions.

9.6.3   Shadows

Notice that light shaders are strictly "do-it-yourself" projects. If you want color, you have to specify it. If you want falloff, you need to code it (in the case of `distantlight` we have no distance-based falloff; for `spotlight` and `pointlight` we

Listing 9.18 arealight is a simple area light shader.

```
light
arealight (float intensity = 1;
           color lightcolor = 1;)
{
    illuminate (P, N, PI/2) {
        Cl = (intensity / (L.L)) * lightcolor;
    }
}
```

used $1/r^2$ falloff). Similarly, if you want the lights to be shadowed, that also needs to be in the shader.

A number of shadowing algorithms have been developed over the years, and their relative merits depend greatly on the overall rendering architectures. So as not to make undue demands on the renderer, the RenderMan standard provides for the "lowest common denominator": shadow maps. Shadow maps are simple, relatively cheap, very flexible, and can work with just about any rendering architecture.

The shadow map algorithm works in the following manner. Before rendering the main image, we will render separate images *from the vantage points of the lights*. Rather than render RGB color images, these light source views will record depth only (hence the name, *depth map*). An example depth map can be seen in Figure 9.10.

Once these depth maps have been created, we can render the main image from the point of view of the camera. In this pass, the light shader can determine if a particular surface point is in shadow by comparing its distance to the light against that stored in the shadow map. If it matches the depth in the shadow map, it is the closest surface to the light in that direction, so the object receives light. If the point in question is *farther* than indicated by the shadow map, it indicates that some other object was closer to the light when the shadow map was created. In such a case, the point in question is known to be in shadow. Figure 9.10 shows a simple scene with and without shadows, as well as the depth map that was used to produce the shadows.

Shading Language gives us a handy built-in function to access shadow maps:

```
float shadow ( string shadowmapname;  point Ptest; ... )
```

The shadow() function tests the point Ptest (in "current" space) against the shadow map file specified by shadowmapname. The return value is 0.0 if Ptest is unoccluded and 1.0 if Ptest is occluded (in shadow according to the map). The return value may also be between 0 and 1, indicating that the point is in partial shadow (this is very handy for soft shadows).

Like texture() and environment(), the shadow() call has several optional arguments that can be specified as token/value pairs:

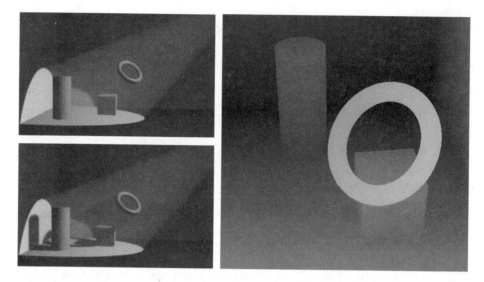

Figure 9.10 Shadow depth maps. A simple scene with and without shadows (left). The shadow map is just a depth image rendered from the point of view of the light source (right). (To visualize the map, we assign white to near depths, black to far depths.)

- "blur" takes a float and controls the amount of blurring at the shadow edges, as if to simulate the penumbra resulting from an area light source. (See Figure 9.11.) A value of "blur=0" makes perfectly sharp shadows; larger values blur the edges. It is strongly advised to add some blur, as perfectly sharp shadows look unnatural and can also reveal the limited resolution of the shadow map.
- "samples" is a float specifying the number of samples used to test the shadow map. Shadow maps are antialiased by supersampling, so although having larger numbers of samples is more expensive, they can reduce the graininess in the blurry regions. We recommend a minimum of 16 samples, and for blurry shadows it may be quite reasonable to use 64 samples or more.
- "bias" is a float that *shifts the apparent depth of the objects from the light*. The shadow map is just an approximation, and often not a very good one. Because of numerical imprecisions in the rendering process and the limited resolution of the shadow map, it is possible for the shadow map lookups to incorrectly indicate that a surface is in partial shadow, even if the object is indeed the closest to the light. The solution we use is to add a "fudge factor" to the lookup to make sure that objects are pushed out of their own shadows. Selecting an appropriate bias value can be tricky. Figure 9.12 shows what can go wrong if you select a value that is either too small or too large.
- "width" is a float that multiplies the estimates of the rate of change of Ptest (used for antialiasing the shadow map lookup). This parameter functions analogously to the "width" parameter to texture() or environment(). Its use is

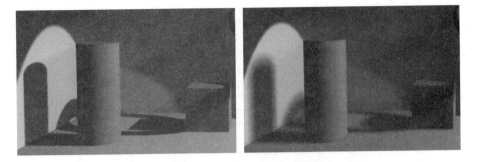

Figure 9.11 Adding blur to shadow map lookups can give a penumbra effect.

Figure 9.12 Selecting shadow bias. Too small a bias value will result in incorrect self-shadowing (left). Notice the darker, dirtier look compared to Figures 9.11 or 9.10. Too much bias can also introduce artifacts, such as the appearance of "floating objects" or the detached shadow at the bottom of the cylinder (right).

largely obsolete and we recommend using "blur" rather than "width" to make soft shadow edges.

The Ptest parameter determines the point at which to determine how much light is shadowed, but how does the renderer know the point of origin of the light? When the renderer creates a shadow map, it also stores in the shadow file the origin of the camera at the time that the shadow map was made—in other words, the emitting point. The shadow() function knows to look for this information in the shadow map file. Notice that since the shadow origin comes from the shadow map file rather than the light shader, it's permissible (and often useful, see Section 14.2.3) for the shadows to be cast from an entirely different position than the point from which the light shader illuminates. Listing 9.19 shows a modification of the spotlight shader that uses a shadow map. This light shader is still pretty simple, but the entirety of Chapter 14 will discuss more exotic features in light shaders.

Here are some tips to keep in mind when rendering shadow maps:

Listing 9.19 shadowspot is just like spotlight, but casts shadows using a shadow depth map.

```
light
shadowspot ( float   intensity = 1;
             color   lightcolor = 1;
             point   from = point "shader" (0,0,0);
             point   to = point "shader" (0,0,1);
             float   coneangle = radians(30);
             float   conedeltaangle = radians(5);
             float   beamdistribution = 2;
             string  shadowname = "";
             float   samples = 16;
             float   blur = 0.01;
             float   bias = 0.01; )
  {
    uniform vector A = normalize(to-from);
    uniform float cosoutside = cos (coneangle);
    uniform float cosinside  = cos (coneangle-conedeltaangle);

    illuminate (from, A, coneangle) {
        float cosangle = (L . A) / length(L);
        float atten = pow (cosangle, beamdistribution) / (L . L);
        atten *= smoothstep (cosoutside, cosinside, cosangle);
        if (shadowname != "") {
            atten *= 1 - shadow (shadowname, Ps, "samples",
                                 samples, "blur", blur, "bias",
                                 bias);
        }
        Cl = atten * intensity * lightcolor;
    }
}
```

- Select an appropriate shadow map resolution. It's not uncommon to use 2k × 2k or even higher-resolution shadow maps for film work.
- View the scene through the "shadow camera" before making the map. Make sure that the field of view is as small as possible, so as to maximize the effective resolution of the objects in the shadow map. Try to avoid your objects being small in the shadow map frame, surrounded by lots of empty unused pixels.
- Remember that depth maps must be one unjittered depth sample per pixel. In other words, the RIB file for the shadow map rendering ought to contain the following options:

```
PixelSamples 1 1
PixelFilter "box" 1 1
Hider "hidden" "jitter" [0]
Display "shadow.z" "zfile" "z"
ShadingRate 4
```

- In shadow maps, only depth is needed, not color. To save time rendering shadow maps, remove all `Surface` calls and increase the number given for `ShadingRate` (for example, as above). If you have surface shaders that displace significantly and those bumps need to self-shadow, you may be forced to run the surface shaders anyway (though you can still remove the lights). Beware!
- When rendering the shadow map, only include objects that will actually cast shadows on themselves or other objects. Objects that only receive, but do not cast, shadows (such as walls or floors) can be eliminated from the shadow map pass entirely. This saves rendering time when creating the shadow map and also eliminates the possibility that poorly chosen bias will cause these objects to incorrectly self-shadow (since they aren't in the maps anyway).
- Some renderers may create shadow map files directly. Others may create only "depth maps" (or "z files") that require an additional step to transform them into full-fledged shadow maps (much as an extra step is often required to turn ordinary image files into texture maps). For example, when using *PRMan*, z files must be converted into shadow maps as follows:

```
txmake -shadow shadow.z shadow.sm
```

This command invokes the `txmake` program (*PRMan*'s texture conversion utility) to read the raw depth map file `shadow.z` and write the shadow map file `shadow.sm`.

It is also possible that some renderers (including *BMRT*, but not *PRMan*) support automatic ray-cast shadows that do not require shadow maps at all. In the case of *BMRT*, the following RIB attribute causes subsequently declared `LightSource` and `AreaLightSource` lights to automatically be shadowed:

```
Attribute "light" "shadows" ["on"]
```

There are also controls that let you specify which geometric objects cast shadows (consult the *BMRT* User's Manual for details). Chapter 17 also discusses extensions to Shading Language that allow for ray-cast shadow checks in light shaders.

Further Reading

Early simple local illumination models for computer graphics used Lambertian reflectance. Bui Tuong Phong (Phong, 1975) proposed using a specular illumination model $(L \cdot R)^n$ and also noted that the appearance of faceted objects could be improved by interpolating the vertex normals. Phong's reflection model is still commonly used in simple renderers, particularly those implemented in hardware. Blinn reformulated this model as $(N \cdot H)^n$, with H defined as the angle halfway between L and N. This gives superior results, but for some reason few renderers or graphics boards bother to use this improved version.

The fundamentals of environment mapping can be found in Greene (1986a, 1986b).

The anisotropic specular illumination model that we use came from Ward (1992). The reader is directed to that work for more information on the derivation, details, and use of Greg Ward Larson's model. Additional anisotropic local illumination models can be found in Kajiya (1985) and Poulin and Fournier (1990). Oren and Nayar's generalization of Lambert's law can be found in Oren and Nayar (1994). A similar reflection model for simulation of clouds and dusty and rough surfaces can be found in Blinn (1982). Treatments of iridescence can be found in Smits and Meyer (1989) and Gondek, Meyer, and Newman (1994).

An excellent overall discussion of surface physics, including refraction and the Fresnel equations (derived in all their gory detail), can be found in Hall (1989). This book contains equations and pseudocode for many of the more popular local illumination models. Unfortunately, it has come to our attention that this book is now out of print. Glassner's book (1995) also is an excellent reference on BRDFs.

Additional papers discussing local illumination models include Blinn and Newell (1976), Blinn (1977), Cook and Torrance (1981), Whitted and Cook (1985, 1988), Hall (1986), Nakamae, Kaneda, Okamoto, and Nishita (1990), He, Torrance, Sillion, and Greenberg (1991), Westin, Arvo, and Torrance (1992), Schlick (1993), Hanrahan and Krueger (1993), Lafortune, Foo, Torrance, and Greenberg (1997), and Goldman (1997).

Shadow maps are discussed in Williams (1978) and Reeves, Salesin, and Cook (1987).

10 Pattern Generation

10.1 Proceduralism versus Stored Textures

One advantage of having a full programming language to specify the behavior of lights and surfaces is that you can perform arbitrary computations to determine appearances. Not only can you compute new texture coordinates, as we've already seen, but you can even compute entire patterns without any texture file access at all. This is known as *procedural texturing*.

There are many potential advantages of procedural textures over stored image textures:

- Stored image textures need to come from somewhere—either by meticulously painting or being scanned from a photograph or a real object. Painting obviously requires a lot of work by a skilled artist. Scanning is not always convenient either. Real objects with the desired pattern may not be flat enough to be easily scanned, or it may be hard to acquire a large enough area of material. Furthermore, the scanning process itself will capture the illumination on the object at the time of the scan, which is generally not what is desired. Procedural textures do not suffer from these problems.

- Any stored texture has limited resolution. If you zoom in too closely, you will see a lack of detail or even signs of the original pixels in the texture. But procedural patterns can have detail at all scales (for example, by introducing new high-frequency detail as you zoom in).

- Similarly, if you zoom out on a stored texture, you will eventually have problems related to its covering only a finite area. What happens if your object is larger than your scanned sample? You will have to tile the texture, which can result in seams or noticeable repetition. On the other hand, a procedural texture can be written to cover arbitrarily large areas without seams or repetition.
- Painted textures created for a specific object are usually one-of-a-kind works that cannot be practically used in other situations or for other objects (unless you truly want an exact duplicate). In contrast, a good procedural texture can often be used for many different objects of related material types or can make different instances of an object each appear slightly different with no more difficulty than adjusting parameters.
- Stored image textures can take lots of disk space, whereas procedural textures only require the space of the compiled shaders themselves, which are much smaller than texture files.

But, of course, there are also many reasons why scanned or painted textures can be much more convenient than proceduralism:

- You have to write a program to generate a procedural texture. This is not always easy. It can often take longer for a programmer to write a procedural shader than it would to have an artist paint a texture and simply use `paintedplastic`. Some patterns are difficult for even the most experienced shader writer to reproduce procedurally.
- What happens if your carefully crafted procedural texture isn't quite what is desired? Imagine the art director pointing at the screen and saying, "Change the color of *that* plank, and add another big gouge *here*." Particularly with stochastic patterns, it can be difficult or impossible to fine-tune the exact appearance. With a painting, it is trivial to add, subtract, or edit particular features at the whim of your art director.
- Procedural textures are notoriously hard to antialias (see Chapter 11, which only touches on the basics). You can easily spend more time trying to antialias your shader than it took you to generate the pattern in the first place. On the other hand, anything you can shove into a stored texture map will be *automatically* antialiased by the texture system in the renderer (assuming, of course, that the texture was created in the first place without any aliasing).

Ultimately, the proceduralism versus stored texture debate is a false dichotomy. At Pixar, we used to have a macho attitude about proceduralism, thinking that only artwork (like a product label) should be painted or scanned but everything else should be done procedurally if at all possible. This position has fallen out of favor, yielding a more pragmatic attitude.

Obviously, what would be artwork in the real world (product labels, paintings, signs, etc.) are painted and used as texture maps. The textures for "hero objects" (character faces or other objects that are important for plot points) are almost always painted for maximum flexibility, editability, and potential to please the art director. Almost none of the shaders that we write for production are either simple RGB texture maps or purely procedural textures. Rather, most shaders combine the two techniques in various ways. For example, a painted texture may be used to compute the underlying color of an object, but a procedural noise function may supply the lumpy displacement.

Stored texture is often used to control proceduralism. Consider the task of creating a rusty metal object. It would be too much trouble for an artist to paint the individual rust grains all over the object. Making a procedural rust pattern may look convincing but it would be hard to direct exactly where on the object had more or less rust (something that may be very important for aesthetic or plot reasons). A hybrid approach may be for the artist to paint a simple grey map that specifies which areas of the object are rusty (black representing no rust, white full rust). The shader may read the texture and use the value to modulate between a procedural rust grain pattern and the unrusted surface.

Patterns that must cover large areas seamlessly or must be detailed over large ranges of scale, and would therefore be impractical or exhaustive to paint, are done procedurally. An example of this is the ground plane shader on Ant Island in the film *A Bug's Life*, created over the course of several months by Chris Perry. In some shots you can see hundreds of square meters of the island at once; in other shots a few square millimeters fill an entire theater movie screen. No artist could ever paint so much texture at so fine a detail (at least, not in a single lifetime and not without going insane) or get it to follow all the nooks and crannies of the island geometry. As we have described, this shader did use texture maps under the control of procedures and, in turn, to control the proceduralism.

10.2   Regular Patterns

This section will describe some more built-in Shading Language functions that are useful for building regular patterns.

10.2.1   Thresholding

float step (float edge, x)

> The built-in step() function returns 0 if $x < edge$ and 1 if $x \geq edge$.

float smoothstep (float edge0, edge1, x)

> The smoothstep() function returns 0 if $x \leq edge0$, returns 1 if $x \geq edge1$, and performs a smooth Hermite interpolation between 0 and 1 when $edge0 < x < edge1$. This is useful in cases where you would want a thresholding function with a smooth transition.

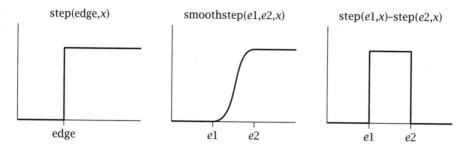

Figure 10.1 A comparison of the built-in step( ) and smoothstep( ) functions and a pulse function made from the difference of two steps.

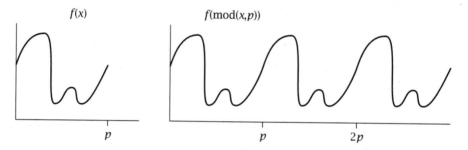

Figure 10.2 Using mod( ) to construct periodic functions.

Figure 10.1 shows graphs of the built-in step( ) and smoothstep( ) functions, as well as a pulse( ) function that can be constructed from the difference of two steps.

10.2.2 Constructing Periodic Functions

Recall the mod(x, $period$) function, which returns the remainder of $x/period$. An interesting use of mod( ) is to make periodic functions. Suppose you have an arbitrary function $f(x)$ defined on $[0, p]$. Then

    f (mod(x,p))

will give a periodic version of $f(x)$. Naturally, you must beware of any discontinuity at p. (See Figure 10.2.)

10.2.3 Arbitrary Spline Interpolation

A handy feature of Shading Language is a built-in spline interpolation function:

    type spline (float x; *type* val1, ..., valn)

As x varies from 0 to 1, spline returns the value of a cubic interpolation of val1...valn. Knots are assumed to be evenly spaced. The *type* may be any of float, color, point, or vector. By default, the interpolating spline uses a Catmull-Rom basis (that's why you want val1=val2 and val(n-1)=valn). However, you can specify other interpolation bases by name with an optional first parameter:

> *type* spline (string basis; float x; *type* val1, val2, ... valn)

Valid bases include "catmull-rom" (the default), "bspline", and "linear", indicating a piecewise-linear interpolation. In the case of linear interpolation, val1 and valn are effectively ignored. In other words, when x = 0, the linear spline returns val2; and when x = 1, the spline returns val(n-1). This is for the sake of symmetry to the cubic case. In addition, you have the option of supplying an array instead of a list of individual values. For example,

> *type* spline (float x; *type* vals[])

10.3   Irregular Patterns: noise()

It is also very useful to build *irregular* patterns, and Shading Language provides a number of built-in functions to facilitate this. Most of these are based on variations of the noise() function.

10.3.1   The noise() Function

Shading Language provides a primitive function called noise() that can be used as a basis for irregular patterns. (In this book, noise() refers to the variety described in the RenderMan spec.) Noise is a variant of a function described by Perlin (1985). The noise() function looks a little like a sine wave but with the bumps not all the same height. Figure 10.3 shows a plot of 1D noise.

Noise has the following useful properties:

- noise() is *repeatable*, in the sense that multiple calls to noise with the same arguments will always return the same values. In other words, it is not a random number generator, which would return a different value every time it is called.
- noise() comes in varieties that are defined on 1D, 2D, 3D, and 4D domains:

```
noise (float)
noise (float, float)
noise (point)              /* also vector or normal */
noise (point, float)
```

- The return value of noise() ranges from 0–1, with an overall average of 0.5. The return value of noise is exactly 0.5 whenever its input coordinates are exactly integer values. While noise() is guaranteed not to stray outside the [0,1] range, in fact it tends to spend the vast majority of its time within [0.3, 0.7].

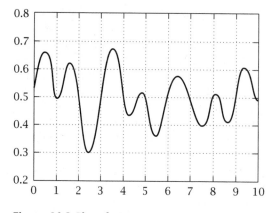

Figure 10.3 Plot of 1D noise.

- noise() is C^1 continuous everywhere, meaning that its first derivative is continuous. Most places it is also C^2 (i.e., the derivative changes smoothly) but not everywhere—in particular, the second derivative is discontinuous at the integer lattice points. (You may occasionally see artifacts related to this.)
- noise() is bandlimited, with its peak frequencies in the range of 0.5–1.
- noise() is approximately isotropic (has no preferred direction) and is effectively nonperiodic. (This is not quite true. The implementations of noise() that we know of all have a surprisingly short period. Nonetheless, very few situations crop up in which this is a problem.)

Noise that varies over three dimensions is often called *solid noise* because when used on a surface it makes the object look like it was carved out of a solid block of the material, as opposed to simply having a 2D decal applied to it. Figure 10.4 shows the difference between 2D noise and 3D noise when applied to a teapot. More recent renderers also support a 4D noise: noise (point, float). The intent of this function is to allow a solid noise to vary with time.

Different varieties of noise also exist that have different return types. We have thus far discussed noise() as if it always returned a float; for example,

```
float f = float noise (P);
```

But noise can also return a point, vector, or color, regardless of the input domain, as in the following examples:

```
color C = color noise (s,t);
vector offset = vector noise (P, time);
```

The return type is denoted by type casting, just as we did with texture(). Also as with texture(), if you don't explicitly cast the return type for noise(), it does not default to float—rather, the compiler tries to deduce what you want from the context. This is often not what you intended, as the context is often ambiguous. It is therefore good practice to *always* explicitly cast noise().

Figure 10.4 Teapots with 2D noise on (s, t) (left) and 3D noise on P (right). The teapot with 3D noise seems "solid," while the 2D noise appears to vary considerably depending on how the s, t space is stretched on each piece of geometry.

10.3.2 cellnoise()—A Discrete Pseudorandom Value

Sometimes, rather than a continuous noise value, you may want a repeatable pseudorandom discrete value. Example uses include coloring each flower petal differently, each brick, each wood plank, and so on. The standard noise() call is undesirable because it's expensive (partly due to its interpolation, which is unnecessary in this application) and its values hang out too close to 0.5.

For this purpose, there is a built-in function called cellnoise() that has the following desirable properties:

- cellnoise() is pseudorandom but repeatable (same inputs yield same outputs). Although most implementations are periodic, its period is long enough to not be noticeable.
- The return value of cellnoise() is *constant* between integer input values (i.e., within each "cell") but discontinuous just before integer values. In other words, cellnoise(x) ≡ cellnoise(floor(x)).
- The range of cellnoise(x) is uniformly distributed on (0,1). It is not biased to have a tendency to stay close to 0.5, as noise() does.
- Like noise(), cellnoise() has varieties with 1, 2, 3, and 4D domains, as well as float, color, or point, or vector return values:

```
type   cellnoise (float x)
type   cellnoise (float x, y)
type   cellnoise (point p)
type   cellnoise (point p, float t)
```

where *type* may be any of float, color, or point, or vector.

The cellnoise(x) function is much cheaper to compute than regular noise().

10.3.3 Periodic Noise

Sometimes you want noise that is periodic—that repeats at a particular interval. An example would be if you wanted to wrap a cylindrical projection, like a banana. Such a function is provided by pnoise(). The domain of pnoise() is like noise, 1–4 dimensions, and its range is also any of float, color, point, vector:

```
type pnoise (float f; uniform float period)
type pnoise (float s, t; uniform float speriod, tperiod)
type pnoise (point P; uniform point Pperiod)
type pnoise (point P; float t; point Pperiod; uniform float
             tperiod)
```

10.3.4 Ideas for Using Noise

How can noise() be manipulated and used? Here are some ideas for experimentation.

- amplitude modulation: amp * noise(x)
- frequency modulation: noise (freq * x)
- using an offset to "push" noise() around: noise (x + offset)
- remapping noise() to the range $(-1,1)$, also called *s*igned noise:

```
#define snoise(x) (2*noise(x)-1)
#define vsnoise(x) (2*(vector noise(x))-1)
```

This is useful because it gives you a function whose average value is zero, rather than 0.5.

- making anything lumpy and irregular:

```
foo += noise(P);
```

- using noise() to perturb otherwise regular patterns by changing

```
foo = func(x);
```

into

```
foo = func(x + amp*snoise(freq*x));
```

or

```
foo = amp * noise(freq * func(x));
```

or even into

```
foo = func(x);
foo += amp * snoise(freq*foo));
```

In particular, this can be used to perturb the lookup coordinates of a texture access, giving a warped appearance:

```
float ss = s + amp * noise(freq*s,freq*t);
float tt = t + amp * noise(freq*s-12.2,freq*t+100.63);
color C = color texture (texturename, ss, tt);
```

Notice that this example offsets the texture lookup by separate noise() values in each of s and t. We add large offsets to the second noise() lookup in order for s and t to appear uncorrelated.

■ adding detail to surfaces:

```
Ct = mix (basecolor, dirtcolor,
          smoothstep(0.2,0.8,noise(freq*P)))
```

■ adding bumps to keep a surface from looking totally smooth:

```
P += snoise(freq*P) * amp * normalize(N);
N = calculatenormal(P);
```

■ making each discrete part of a pattern look different:

```
woodcolor *= cellnoise(plankx, planky)
```

■ thresholding noise():

```
step(thresh, noise(x))
```

which gives an irregularly spaced kind of pulse. (*Note*: after you read Chapter 11, you will know that you should be using filterstep() rather than step.)

■ taking an iso-value set of noise():

```
n = noise(x);
f = step(iso-0.05, n) - step(iso+0.05, n)
```

We hope this will give you some taste for how noise might be used. We're not providing explicit examples at this point, though, because noise has the tendency to alias, and we don't want to encourage you even a little bit to write shaders that alias. The following chapter will cover the basics of shader antialiasing. With those new tools in our arsenal, we will later return to the task of writing beautiful procedural shaders.

10.4   Fractional Brownian Motion and Turbulence

What happens when we add together several copies of noise at different frequencies, weighted so that lower frequencies are stronger? As you can see in Figure 10.5, the big wiggles of the low frequency add with the smaller, closer wiggles of the higher frequencies, until we get a net effect of a rough curve reminiscent of the profile of a mountain range. Such patterns turn up frequently (no pun intended) in nature, and not just in the way that mountains are shaped. We will formalize this summation of noise octaves as shown in the fBm() function in Listing 10.1. (Note that this version will tend to alias at high frequencies. See Section 11.4 for an antialiased fBm.)

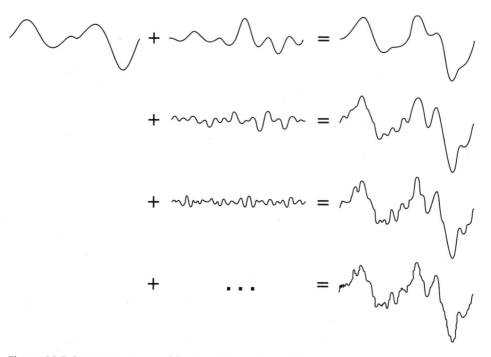

Figure 10.5 Summing octaves of fractional Brownian motion.

You can see that fBm adds several copies of noise() together, and each copy has a different frequency and amplitude. The frequencies and amplitudes of successive additions of noise() are related by factors of lacunarity and gain, respectively. Notice that it is "self-similar"—in other words, it is summing different copies of itself at different scales. This function is called "fractional Brownian motion." (**Not** *fractal* Brownian motion! That is a common mispronunciation, though this function does happen to be a fractal as long as you sum more than two octaves.) Fractional Brownian motion just happens to have a nice, complex, natural-looking pattern that mimics many things in nature. Typical parameters are lacunarity = 2 and gain = 0.5. Any time that gain = 1/lacunarity, the function is what is known as "1/f noise," indicating that the amplitude of successive additions of noise is inversely proportional to its frequency. Figure 10.6 explores some of the parameter space of the fBm function, by varying one of the parameters at a time.

A relative of fBm is a function that Perlin called *turbulence*. The only difference between turbulence and fBm is the presence of the absolute value call. This roughly doubles the effective frequency and makes everything positive. The result is a more "billowy" appearance, like clouds. (*Warning*: the sharp corner produced by the abs() also introduces a small amount of arbitrarily high frequencies, which

Listing 10.1 fBm: shader code for fractional Brownian motion.

```
float fBm (point p;  uniform float octaves, lacunarity, gain)
{
    varying float sum = 0, amp = 1;
    varying point pp  = p;
    uniform float i;

    for (i = 0;  i < octaves;  i += 1) {
        sum += amp * snoise(pp);
        amp *= gain;  pp *= lacunarity;
    }
    return sum;
}


vector vfBm (point p; uniform float octaves, lacunarity, gain)
{
    uniform float amp = 1;
    varying point pp = p;
    varying vector sum = 0;
    uniform float i;

    for (i = 0;  i < octaves;  i += 1) {
        sum += amp * vsnoise (pp);
        amp *= gain;  pp *= lacunarity;
    }
    return sum;
}


float turbulence (point P; uniform float octaves, lacunarity, gain)
{
    varying float sum = 0, amp = 1;
    varying point pp  = p;
    uniform float i;

    for (i = 0;  i < octaves;  i += 1) {
        sum += amp * abs (snoise(pp));
        amp *= gain;  pp *= lacunarity;
    }
    return sum;
}
```

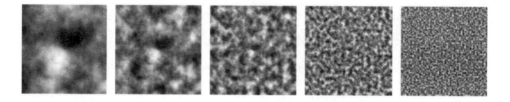

Changing the frequency. Going from left to right, each successive image doubles the base frequency of the previous one.

Maximum numbers of octaves, left to right: 1, 2, 3, 4, 5.

Adjusting the lacunarity, left to right: 0.5, 1, 2, 4, 8.

Adjusting the gain, left to right: 0.2, 0.5, 0.75, 1, 1.5. The gain parameter changes the mix of frequencies, with larger gain emphasizing higher frequencies.

Figure 10.6 Exploring the parameter space of the fBm function. For all examples, parameters that did not vary were assigned oct = 6, lac = 2, gain = 0.5.

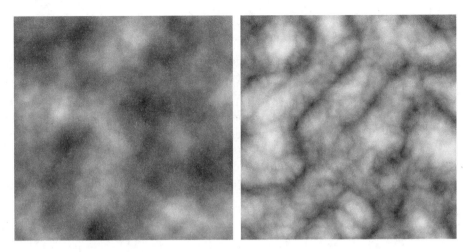

Figure 10.7 fBm (left); turbulence (right). Notice that the turbulence function appears more "billowy."

may be particularly tricky to antialias.) Figure 10.7 shows a comparison of fBm and turbulence in 2D.

10.5   Cellular Patterns

Section 10.4 explains fractional Brownian motion and "turbulence" in detail. These functions are useful because they may be used as basis functions for procedural texture synthesis. In other words, they are not in and of themselves final patterns but are very useful as building blocks for procedural textures. Steve Worley introduced another basis function in Worley (1996). Worley's texture basis functions can be used to generate patterns that resemble cellular divisions—cobblestone patterns, lizard scales, and so on. The gist of Worley's technique is to picture space as containing a random distribution of "feature points." Knowing which of these feature points is closest to your shading position (and possibly knowing about the 2nd- or 3rd-closest points) yields information that turns out to be surprisingly useful for generating natural-looking patterns. Let us then develop a Shading Language implementation of such a function.

First, let's suppose that space is divided up into $1 \times 1 \times 1$ cells, with a "feature point" somewhere in each cell. Thus, for any point P, the center of the cell P occupies is at

```
point cellcenter = point (floor(xcomp(P))+0.5, floor(ycomp(P))+0.5,
                          floor(zcomp(P))+0.5);
```

To randomly place a feature point inside the cell, we will add an offset to the center point using `cellnoise()`:

```
point featurepos = cellcenter +
                 (vector cellnoise(cellcenter) - 0.5);
```

Remember that the `vector cellnoise()` function will return a vector that is constant over a single cell (whose boundaries are the integers) but will differ from cell to cell. The range of `cellnoise()` is such that each component is on $(0, 1)$; we subtract 0.5 so that the offset is in the range $(-0.5, 0.5)$.

The following figure illustrates the jittering of feature positions. The unjittered grid is shown on the left; the features in their jittered positions are shown on the right.

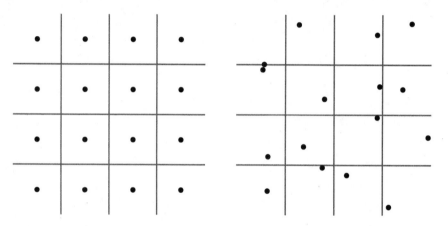

Now that we can compute the feature position within any individual cell, we want to figure out which feature is nearest to us. Since the jittered points stay within their original cells (i.e., the jitter amounts are in the range $(-0.5, 0.5)$), we can simply loop over the neighboring cells, computing the feature position for each of those cells and comparing each one's distance to P:

```
point thiscell = point (floor(xcomp(P))+0.5, floor(ycomp(P))+0.5,
                    floor(zcomp(P))+0.5);
dist_to_nearest = 1000;    /* initialize to too large */
for (i = -1;  i <= 1;  i += 1) {
    for (j = -1;  j <= 1;  j += 1) {
        for (k = -1;  k <= 1;  k += 1) {
            point testcell = thiscell + vector(i,j,k);
            point pos = testcell +
                       vector cellnoise (testcell) - 0.5;
            float dist = distance(pos,P);
            if (dist < dist_to_nearest) {
```

```
        dist_to_nearest = dist;
        nearestfeature = pos;
      }
    }
  }
}
```

This code fragment stores the position of the feature nearest to P in nearest-feature and the distance to that feature in dist_to_nearest.

Listing 10.2 formalizes this code, giving the complete shader function that returns both the nearest and second-nearest features. It also contains a "jitter" parameter that scales the amount of possible jitter in the feature positions within their cells. Outputs include the distances to the closest and second-closest features (f1 and f2) and the positions of those two features (pos1 and pos2). Note that you can also create a version that is optimized for the 2D case.

Now that we have this magic function, what can we do with it? Let us summarize some potential uses:

■ Because each feature exists in a unique cell, a cellnoise() lookup for the feature position will also be unique. For example, consider the following code fragment:

```
voronoi_f1f2_3d (P, 1, f1, pos1, f2, pos2);
Ci = color cellnoise (pos1 + vector(10,0,0));
```

This will assign a surface color to P that depends on the closest feature. The effect is shown in Figure 10.8(a) and is the basis for forming cellular patterns. This figure alone should provide adequate explanation for why we call this function "Voronoi." (Examining the code reveals why we don't call it "Worley"—we differ

---

Listing 10.2 voronoi_f1f2_3d function computes the distances and positions of the two nearest features in 3D space.

```
/* Voronoi cell noise (a.k.a. Worley noise) -- 3D, 1- and 2-feature version.
 * Inputs:
 *      P - the domain point
 *      jitter - how much (in the range 0-1) to jitter feature positions
 * Outputs:
 *      f1 - distance between P and the closest feature point
 *      f2 - distance between P and the second-closest feature point
 *      pos1, pos2 - positions of the closest and 2nd-closest feature points
 */

void
voronoi_f1_3d (point P;  float jitter;
               output float f1;  output point pos1;)
{
    point thiscell = point (floor(xcomp(P))+0.5, floor(ycomp(P))+0.5,
                            floor(zcomp(P))+0.5);
```
▶

Listing 10.2 (continued)

```
        f1 = 1000;
        uniform float i, j, k;
        for (i = -1;  i <= 1;  i += 1) {
            for (j = -1;  j <= 1;  j += 1) {
                for (k = -1;  k <= 1;  k += 1) {
                    point testcell = thiscell + vector(i,j,k);
                    point pos = testcell +
                                jitter * (vector cellnoise (testcell) - 0.5);
                    vector offset = pos - P;
                    float dist = offset . offset; /* actually dist^2 */
                    if (dist < f1) {
                        f1 = dist;  pos1 = pos;
                    }
                }
            }
        }
        f1 = sqrt(f1);
}


void
voronoi_f1f2_3d (point P;
                float jitter;
                output float f1;  output point pos1;
                output float f2;  output point pos2;)
{
    point thiscell = point (floor(xcomp(P))+0.5, floor(ycomp(P))+0.5,
                            floor(zcomp(P))+0.5);
    f1 = f2 = 1000;
    uniform float i, j, k;
    for (i = -1;  i <= 1;  i += 1) {
        for (j = -1;  j <= 1;  j += 1) {
            for (k = -1;  k <= 1;  k += 1) {
                point testcell = thiscell + vector(i,j,k);
                point pos = testcell +
                            jitter * (vector cellnoise (testcell) - 0.5);
                vector offset = pos - P;
                float dist = offset . offset; /* actually dist^2 */
                if (dist < f1) {
                    f2 = f1;  pos2 = pos1;
                    f1 = dist;  pos1 = pos;
                } else if (dist < f2) {
                    f2 = dist;  pos2 = pos;
                }
            }
        }
    }
    f1 = sqrt(f1);  f2 = sqrt(f2);
}
```

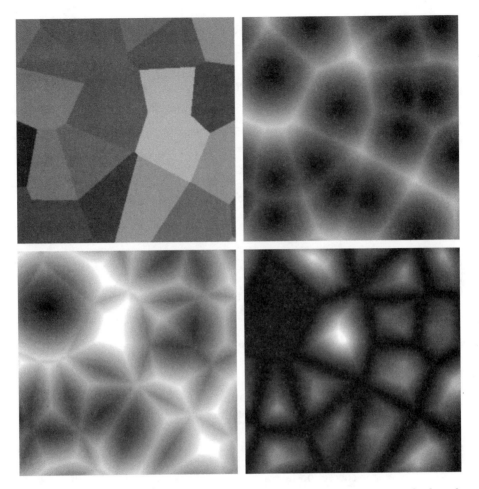

Figure 10.8 Basis functions of the Voronoi cellular function. (a) assigning a color based on the position of the nearest feature (top left); (b) the value of f1, the distance to the nearest feature (top right); (c) the value of f2, the distance to the second-closest feature (bottom left); (d) the difference of f2 – f1 (bottom right).

in implementation from Worley's description and take several shortcuts.) We add an integer offset to our cellnoise lookup because the feature position within the cell was determined by a cellnoise lookup based on that point. We do not want any correlations between the color and feature position, so it's wise to use a different offset for each effect that is being keyed off of the feature position.

- The values of f1 and f2 themselves make interesting patterns. Figure 10.8b and c show these raw outputs, respectively.
- The difference f1 – f2, as shown in Figure 10.8d.

Figure 10.9 Thresholding Voronoi f2 - f1 to find cell boundaries. From left to right:
(a) naive thresholding of f2 - f1; (b) more careful thresholding of f2 - f1 to produce
evenly wide strips; (c) using fBm to make the borders jagged.

■ Notice that f1 - f2 is zero exactly on the boundaries of two cells because on the
  boundaries we are equally distant from two features. We can apply a threshold
  to this value, as shown in Figure 10.9a and embodied by the following code
  fragment:

```
voronoi_f1f2_3d (P, 1, f1, pos1, f2, pos2);
Ci = step (0.05, f2-f1);
```

But as you can see from Figure 10.9a, this naive thresholding approach has
the unfortunate property that the separator lines are unequal in width. This is
because the features themselves are unevenly spaced, and therefore a particular
threshold will represent a different width for each feature pair. We can correct for
this, as shown in Figure 10.9b and in the code fragment below (deducing exactly
why this correction factor works is left as an exercise for the reader).

```
voronoi_f1f2_3d (P, 1, f1, pos1, f2, pos2);
float scalefactor = distance(pos1,pos2) /
                    (distance(pos1,P)+distance(P,pos2));
Ct = step (0.05*scalefactor, f2-f1);
```

■ We can make the borders more ragged by adding fBm to the input position, as
  shown in Figure 10.9c:

```
point PP = P + 0.15 * vfBm(2*P, 4, 2, 0.5);
voronoi_f1f2_3d (PP, 1, f1, pos1, f2, pos2);
float scalefactor = distance(pos1,pos2) /
                    (distance(pos1,P)+distance(P,pos2));
Ct = step (0.05*scalefactor, f2-f1);
```

Further Reading

Other sources for algorithms and applications of noise can be found in Lewis (1989) and Perlin and Hoffert (1989). Readers interested in computation and uses of noise are especially encouraged to read Ebert, Musgrave, Peachey, Perlin, and Worley (1998).

11 Shader Antialiasing

Everybody has experienced it: sharp jaggies, pixellation artifacts, creepy-crawlies as the camera moves, horrible twinkling, or just plain weirdness when you pull back from your favorite procedural texture. It's aliasing, and it's a fact of life when writing shaders. This chapter is designed to make the problem seem less scary and to give you the conceptual tools to attack the problem on your own. It's not the complete compendium of antialiasing techniques, but it should get you started.

11.1 Sources of Aliasing in Shading

What is aliasing, really? The heart of the problem lies in the domain of signal processing. Fundamentally, our conceptual model is that there is a continuous *image function* in front of the camera (or alternatively, impinging on the film plane). But we need to represent this function using a raster of discrete pixels in our image,

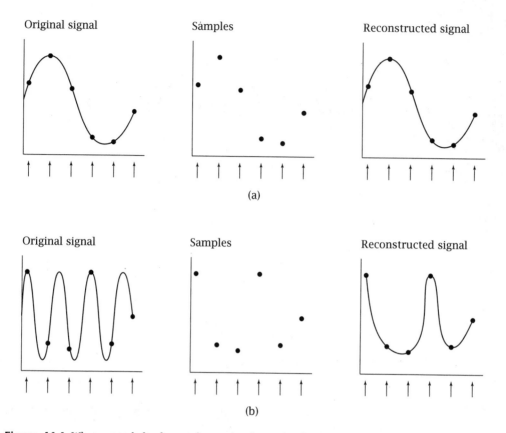

Figure 11.1 When sampled adequately, a signal can be faithfully reconstructed (a). Frequencies in the signals above the Nyquist limit will not be reconstructed correctly (b).

so we must somehow *sample* the image function with an eye to how it will later be *reconstructed* for display.

Conceptually, we want each pixel value to represent some kind of weighted average measure of the image function in the area "behind" the entire pixel. But renderers aren't terribly good at computing that directly, so they tend to use *point sampling* to measure the scene at a finite number of places, then use that information to reconstruct an estimate of the image function. When the samples are spaced much closer than the distance between the "wiggles" of the image function as shown in Figure 11.a, this reconstructed signal is an accurate representation of the real image function. But when the samples aren't spaced closely enough as we see in Figure 11.b, then the trouble begins. As illustrated below, if the wiggles in the signal are spaced too closely (compared to the spacing of the samples), the wrong signal will be reconstructed.

Specifically, the highest frequency that can be adequately sampled is half the frequency of the samples themselves. This is known as the Nyquist limit. To put it another way, the samples must be at least twice the highest frequency present in the signal, or it will not adequately sample the signal. The energy of frequencies in the original signal that were higher than the Nyquist limit will appear in, or *alias* to, lower frequencies.

There are potentially two different sampling processes going on: the screen space samples and the shading samples on the surface of the geometric primitive. Either one could cause aliasing if it is sampling a signal with frequencies above the Nyquist limit. In screen space, most renderers avoid aliasing by sampling geometry in a jittered fashion rather than with regularly spaced samples. Jittering replaces the aliasing with noise, which is a less objectionable artifact than aliasing, but it is still an artifact that can be avoided if we ensure that the image function itself has limited frequency content. But in *PRMan* the situation is worse, because by the time we are stochastically sampling in screen space, we have already taken regularly spaced samples in parametric space. In other words, the shader aliasing happens before the stochastic sampling can help. But even in a stochastic ray tracer, it would be better to sample an image function that didn't have frequencies beyond the Nyquist limit. We would like to *prefilter* the pattern.

The key is that these evils are all the result of point sampling the pattern. A single shader execution will be used to assign a color to an entire micropolygon or to color an entire pixel (or subpixel). "Prefiltering" the texture means estimating the integral that is the *convolution* of the texture function and the filter kernel that the sample represents. This convolution is, in plain terms, a weighted average of the texture function in the neighborhood of the point sample, with the size and weighting of the neighborhood given by the filter kernel. In other words, we do not want to point sample the texture function, but rather we want some kind of average value underneath the pixel that contains the point being shaded.

There are two trivial methods for estimating the average texture value under a region. First, you could use brute force to point sample several places underneath the filter kernel and average those samples. This approach is poor because it merely replaces one point sample with many, which are still likely to alias, albeit at a higher frequency. Also, the cost of shading is multiplied by the number of samples that you take, yet the error decreases only as the *square root* of the number of samples. So you would have to do a huge amount of extra shading in order to eliminate the aliasing.

The second trivial approach would be to generate the texture as an image map, a stored texture. RenderMan automatically antialiases texture lookups and does a pretty good job at it. So once a texture map is made (assuming that the generation of the texture map itself did not have aliasing artifacts), further use of the texture is guaranteed to antialias well with no need for you to worry about it in your shader. The problems with this approach mirror the downsides to texture mapping in general, discussed extensively in Section 10.1.

So assuming that we want to antialias a truly procedural texture, and don't feel that a valid option is to subsample the texture by brute force, we are left searching for more clever options. Sections 11.3 and 11.4 will explain two prefiltering strategies: analytic solutions to the integral and frequency clamping methods. But first, Section 11.2 will review the Shading Language facilities that are needed for these approaches.

11.2 Facilities for Filter Estimation

We have now recast the problem as estimating the average value of the texture function over an area represented by a sample (either a micropolygon or a pixel—it hardly matters which from here on, so we will sometimes interchange the terms). Pictorially in 1D, we have some function f that we are sampling at location x, as shown in Figure 11.2. But while we are supplied a single x value, we really want to average f over the range of values that x will take on underneath the entire pixel with width w. The question is, how big should w be in order to cover a pixel? Luckily, Shading Language provides us with methods for estimating the filter size w. In particular, there are two useful built-in functions, and two built-in variables, that do the job for us:

- Du(x) returns the derivative of arbitrary expression x with respect to surface parameter u.
- du is the change in surface parameter u between adjacent samples being shaded.
- Dv(x) returns the derivative of arbitrary expression x with respect to surface parameter v.
- dv is the change in surface parameter v between adjacent samples being shaded.

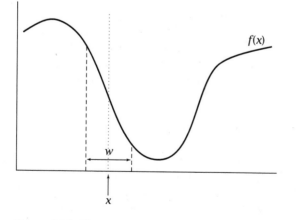

Figure 11.2 The pixel represented by this sample covers a width of w.

Du(x) is the amount that x changes per unit change of u, and du is the amount that u changes between adjacent shading samples. Therefore, **the amount that x changes between adjacent shading samples** (moving in the direction of changing u) is given by

Du(x) * du

And similarly, the amount that x changes between adjacent shading samples (moving in the direction of the v parameter) is

Dv(x) * dv

Not only can we take these derivatives explicitly, but there are also some other built-in Shading Language functions that implicitly make use of derivatives:

- calculatenormal(p) returns the cross product of the surface tangent vectors in each direction—that is, the surface normal vector at p:

  Du(p) ∧ Dv(p)

- area(p) returns the area of the sample, related to the cross product of the partial derivatives of p in u and v:

  length (Du(p)*du ∧ Dv(p)*dv)

  If p = P, this is loosely interpreted as the area of the microfacet that we are shading (if the tangents are approximately perpendicular, which they usually are).

- texture($filename,s,t$) implicitly takes the derivatives of coordinates s and t to decide how large an area of texture to filter.

Incidentally, because these functions all make implicit use of derivatives, it is dangerous to put them inside of varying conditionals or loops, for the same reason you should not put texture() commands inside conditionals or loops (see Section 8.1.5).

How can we use these functions to estimate filter size? Recalling the expressions above for estimating how much x changes as we move one sample over in either u or v, a fair estimate of the amount that x will change as we move one sample over in any direction might be

abs(Du(x)*du) + abs(Dv(x)*dv)

Informally, we are just summing the potential changes in each of the parametric directions. We take absolute values because we don't care if x is increasing or decreasing; we only are concerned with *how much* it changes between where we are and the neighboring sample. The geometric interpretation of this formula is shown in Figure 11.3.

That formula works great if x is a float expression. But if x is a point, its derivative is a vector, and so the rest of the formula doesn't make much sense. But recall the definition of the built-in area() function:

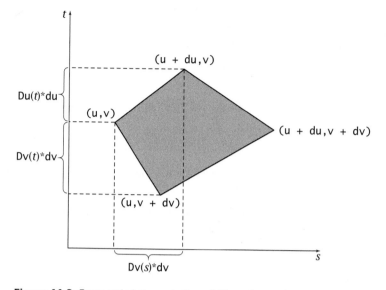

Figure 11.3 Geometric interpretation of filter size estimates.

$$\text{area}(p) \equiv \text{length}((\text{Du}(p)\text{*du}) \wedge (\text{Dv}(p)\text{*dv}))$$

The cross product of the two tangent vectors ($\text{Du}(p)\text{*du}$ and $\text{Dv}(p)\text{*dv}$) is another vector that is mutually perpendicular to the other two and has length equal to the "area" of the parallelogram outlined by the tangents—hence the name of the function. The square root of area is a length, the geometric mean of the lengths of the tangent vectors. Thus, $\text{sqrt}(\text{area}(p))$ is a decent estimate of the amount that point p changes between adjacent samples (expressed as a scalar), assuming that the parametric directions of a surface primitive are nearly perpendicular (which is generally a good approximation).

With this knowledge, we can write macros that are useful for filter width estimates for either float or point functions:

```
#define MINFILTWIDTH 1.0e-6
#define filterwidth(x) max (abs(Du(x)*du)+abs(Dv(x)*dv), MINFILTWIDTH)
#define filterwidthp(p) max (sqrt(area(p)), MINFILTWIDTH)
```

The filterwidth and filterwidthp macros can be used to estimate the change of its parameters from sample to sample for float or point-like arguments, respectively. We impose a minimum filter size in order to avoid math exceptions if we divide by the filter size later. With these macros, we can move on to specific antialiasing techniques.

11.3 Analytic Antialiasing

Recall Figure 11.2 illustrating the function f, which we are trying to sample at x. We really want some metric of the "average" value of f in the region surrounding x with width w. More technically, we want the *convolution* of function f and some filter kernel k having support of width w. Convolution is defined as

$$F(x) = (f \otimes k)(x) = \int_{-\infty}^{\infty} f(\delta)k(x - \delta)d\delta$$

Convolution amounts to taking a weighted average of the input signal over some interval (called the *support* of the kernel). If we could use our knowledge of f to analytically (i.e., exactly, symbolically) derive the convolution $F = f \otimes k$, then we could replace all references to f in our shader with F, and that function would be guaranteed not to alias.

In the formula above, the kernel's support is infinite in extent. Consider the simple case of averaging the input signal over the interval $(x - w/2, x + w/2)$. That is equivalent to convolving the input signal with a box filter, which has some serious problems but reduces the convolution to a simple definite integral of the signal. For simplicity in the following examples, we will often assume a box filter for our convolution kernel.

11.3.1 Example: Antialiasing a Step Function

As an example, consider the built-in step (*edge, val*) function. This function returns 0 when *val* $\le$ *edge* and 1 when *val* > *edge*. If we make such a binary decision when we are assigning colors to a micropolygon, the entire micropolygon will be "on" or "off." This will tend to produce "jaggies," a form of aliasing, as shown in Figure 11.4. Can we construct a function, *filteredstep*, that is the convolution of step() with an appropriate filter kernel? Then we could use *filteredstep* in place of step() in our shaders and eliminate the resulting jaggies.

As usual for these problems, we must choose an appropriate filter kernel. For simplicity, let's just choose a box filter because it is so easy to analyze. (Of course, if we wished a more robust but more difficult solution, we could derive a version of *filteredstep* that uses, say, a Catmull-Rom filter.) An intuitive way of looking at this problem is: for a box filter of width w centered at value x, what is the convolution of the filter with step(e, x)? This problem is easy to analyze, as shown in Figure 11.5. If $(x + w/2) < e$, then the result of *filteredstep* is 0, because the box filter only overlaps the part of step that is zero. Similarly, if $(x - w/2) > e$, then *filteredstep* should return 1, because the filter only overlaps the portion of step that is 1. If the filter overlaps the transition e, then *filteredstep* should return the fraction of the filter that is greater than e. For our box filter, this is a simple ramp, described by the equation $(x + w/2 - e)/w$. As a further optimization, note that we can express this in Shading Language very compactly:

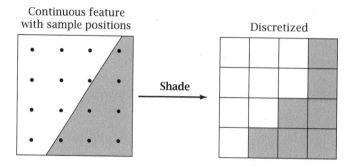

Figure 11.4 A feature, such as an edge, will tend to make "jaggies" when sampled discretely.

```
float filteredstep (float edge, float x, float w)
{
    return clamp ((x+w/2-edge)/w, 0, 1);
}
```

Can you convince yourself that this is correct? Of course, the w you supply to this function is properly the filter width returned by the macros we discussed earlier.

Note that we made a compromise for simplicity: We generated the antialiased version of `step()` by convolving with a box filter. It would be better to use a Catmull-Rom, or other higher-quality filter, and for a function as simple as `step()`, that wouldn't be too hard. But for more difficult functions, it may be very tricky to come up with an analytic solution to the integral when convolved with a nontrivial kernel. But we can often get away with simplifying the integration by assuming a simple kernel like a box filter.

As an aside, there's now a built-in SL function, `filterstep`, that does exactly what we've described:

```
float filterstep (float edge, s; ...)
float filterstep (float edge, s0, s1; ...)
```

The `filterstep` function provides an analytically antialiased step function. In its two-argument form, it takes parameters identical to `step` but returns a result that is filtered over the area of the surface element being shaded. In its three-argument form, the step function is filtered in the range between the two values s0 and s1 (i.e., s1-s0 = w). This low-pass filtering is similar to that done for texture maps. In both forms, an optional parameter list provides control over the filter function and may include the following parameters: `"width"` (also known as `"swidth"`), the amount to "overfilter" in s; and `"filter"`, the name of the filter kernel to apply. The filter may be any of the following: `"catmull-rom"` (the default), `"box"`, `"triangle"`, or `"gaussian"`.

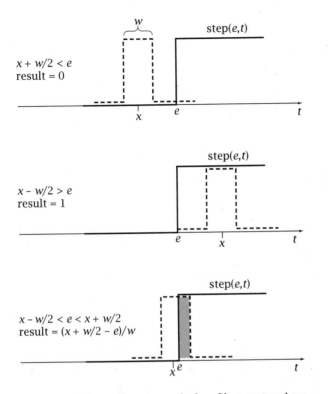

Figure 11.5 A step function and a box filter centered on x. What is the convolution?

11.3.2   More Complex Examples

Pulse

As another example, consider the function

```
float pulse (float edge0, edge1, x)
{
     return step(edge0,x) - step(edge1,x);
}
```

This is a useful function that returns 1 when edge0 $\leq$ x $\leq$ edge1 and 0 otherwise. Like step, it aliases horribly at any sampling rate because it has infinite frequency content. And here is its antialiased (box-filtered) version:

```
float filteredpulse (float edge0, edge1, x, dx)
{
     float x0 = x - dx/2;
```

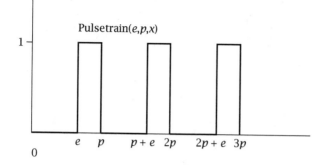

Figure 11.6 A pulsetrain function

```
        float x1 = x0 + dx;
        return max (0, (min(x1,edge1)-max(x0,edge0)) / dx);
}
```

Pulsetrain

Another, less trivial, example of analytic antialiasing involves antialiasing a pulse-train. Such a function is shown in Figure 11.6. You might imagine using such a function as the basis for a striped pattern. Here is this function expressed in Shading Language:

```
/* A pulsetrain: a signal that repeats with a given period and is
 * 0 when 0 <= mod(x,period) < edge, and 1 when mod(x,period) > edge.
 */
float pulsetrain (float edge, period, x)
{
    return pulse (edge, period, mod(x,period));
}
```

Attacking this function is more difficult. Again, we will assume a box filter, which means that `filteredpulsetrain(edge,period,x,w)` is

$$\frac{1}{w}\int_{(x-w/2)}^{(x+w/2)} \text{pulsetrain}(e, p, y)dy$$

This integral is actually not hard to solve. First, let's divide x and w by *period*, reducing to a simpler case where the period is 1. A graph of the *accumulated* value of the function between 0 and x is shown in Figure 11.7. This function is given by $F(x) = (1 - e)\text{floor}(x) + \max(0, x - \text{floor}(x) - e)$. The calculus experts in the crowd will recognize that $F(x)$, the accumulated sum of $f(x)$, is known as the *indefinite*

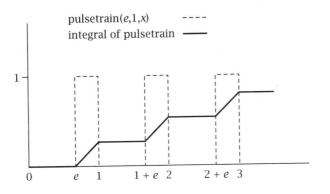

Figure 11.7 The pulsetrain function and its integral (accumulated value).

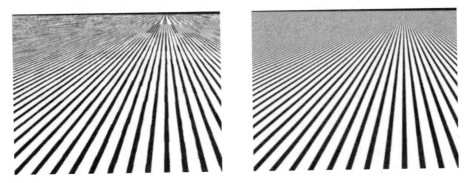

Figure 11.8 A pattern based on `pulsetrain`, aliasing (left), and using `filteredpulse-train` (right).

integral. To compute our desired result, the *definite integral*, we evaluate this at two points and subtract:

$$\int_{x_0}^{x_1} f(x)\,dx = \int_{-\infty}^{x_1} f(x)\,dx - \int_{-\infty}^{x_0} f(x)\,dx = F(x_1) - F(x_0)$$

The code in Listing 11.1 implements a filtered pulsetrain. This code works well even when the filter size is larger than the pulse period. Figure 11.8 shows an example of a pattern based on `pulsetrain` (left) versus the filtered version using the function in Listing 11.1 (right). Note that there is still some bad ringing. This is a result of our use of a box filter—it's not very good at clamping frequencies. A better filter would have less ringing but would have a more difficult integral to solve. Nonetheless, the most egregious aliasing is gone.

Listing 11.1 The `filteredpulsetrain` function.

```
/* Filtered pulsetrain: it's not as simple as just returning the mod
 * of filteredpulse -- you have to take into account that the filter may
 * cover multiple pulses in the train.
 * Strategy: consider the function that is the integral of the pulse-
 * train from 0 to x. Just subtract!
 */
float filteredpulsetrain (float edge, period, x, dx)
{
    /* First, normalize so period == 1 and our domain of interest
       is > 0 */
    float w = dx/period;
    float x0 = x/period - w/2;
    float x1 = x0+w;
    float nedge = edge / period;    /* normalized edge value */

    /* Definite integral of normalized pulsetrain from 0 to t */
    float integral (float t) {
        extern float nedge;
        return ((1-nedge)*floor(t) + max(0,t-floor(t)-nedge));
    }

    /* Now we want to integrate the normalized pulsetrain over
       [x0,x1] */
    return (integral(x1) - integral(x0)) / w;
}
```

Listing 11.2 The `filteredabs` function: a filtered version of abs.

```
/* Antialiased abs(): the box filter of abs(t) from x-dx/2 to x+dx/2.
 * Hinges on the realization that the indefinite integral of abs(x) is
 * sign(x) * x*x/2;
 */
float filteredabs (float x, dx)
{
    float integral (float t) {
        return sign(t) * 0.5 * t*t;
    }

    float x0 = x - 0.5*dx;
    float x1 = x0 + dx;
    return (integral(x1) - integral(x0)) / dx;
}
```

Absolute Value

Another built-in function that can be trouble is abs(). Because abs(x) produces a discontinuity at $x = 0$, it can introduce infinite frequency content, which will alias badly. Luckily, it is not hard to convolve abs() with a box filter. As with pulsetrain(), we will approach the problem by graphing the integral of abs():

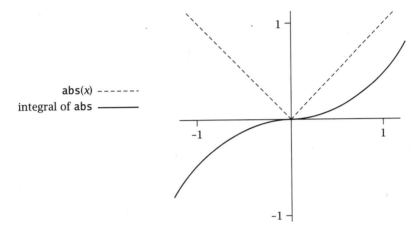

abs(x) -------
integral of abs ———

It's not hard to see that since

$$\int_0^x t \, dt = x^2/2$$

then

$$\int_0^x \mathrm{abs}(t) \, dt = \mathrm{sign}(x) \, x^2/2$$

Therefore, we can express a filtered version of abs(), as shown in Listing 11.2.

11.4   Antialiasing by Frequency Clamping

You will find that your favorite Shading Language functions fall into three categories: (1) functions for which you can easily derive the convolution with a filter kernel, probably a box filter; (2) functions that are *really hard* to integrate analytically—lots of work, some integral tables, and maybe a session with *Mathematica* will help; and (3) functions that don't have an analytic solution, or whose solution is just too hard to derive.

Many useful functions fall into the third category. Don't worry, just try another strategy. In general, the next best thing to an analytic solution is frequency clamping. The basis of this approach is to decompose your function into composite functions with known frequency content and then to only use the frequencies that are low enough to be below the Nyquist limit for the known filter size.

The general strategy is as follows. Suppose you have a function $g(x)$ that you wish to antialias, and your computed filter width is w. Suppose further that you know the following two facts about your function g:

1. Function g has no features (the "wiggles" of the function) smaller than width f.
2. The average value of $g(x)$, over large ranges of values, is a.

We know that when $w \ll f/2$, we are sampling areas of g much smaller than its smallest wiggles, so we will not alias. If $w \gg f/2$, then the signal frequency is too high for our sampling rate, so we will alias. But we know the average value of g, so why not substitute this average value when the filter is too wide compared to the feature size? In between those extremes, we can use a smoothstep to fade between the true function and its average:

```
#define fadeout(g,g_avg,featuresize,fwidth) \
        mix (g, g_avg, smoothstep(.2,.6,fwidth/featuresize))
```

This simple macro does just what we described. When the filter width is small compared to the feature size, it simply returns g. When the filter width is too large to adequately sample the function with that feature size, it returns the known average value of g. And in between it fades smoothly between these values.

As an example, let's look at the noise() function. We use it in shaders all the time. It will alias if there are fewer than two samples per cycle. We know that it has a limited frequency content—the frequency is approximately 1. We also know that its average value is 0.5. But noise() is often less useful than its cousin, snoise (for signed noise). We usually define snoise as follows (for float and vector cases):

```
#define snoise(x) (2*(float noise(x))$-$1)
#define vsnoise(x) (2*(vector noise(x))-1)
```

Regular noise() has a range of (0,1), but snoise ranges on $(-1,1)$ with an average value of 0. Consider the following macros:

```
#define filteredsnoise(x,w)  fadeout(snoise(x), 0, 1, w)
#define filteredvsnoise(p,w) fadeout(vsnoise(x), 0, 1, w)
```

This macro takes a domain value x and a filter width w and returns an (approximately) low-pass filtered version of snoise. We can extend this to make filtered versions of the fractional Brownian motion functions given in Section 10.4. These filtered functions are shown in Listing 11.3 (compare to the aliasing-prone versions in Section 10.4).

Note that this is not really low-pass filtering—each octave fades to the average value just as the frequency gets high enough. To see that this is different, think about a noise octave where the key frequency is twice the Nyquist limit. This will be attenuated severely by fadeout. But in fact, this noise octave has power at all frequencies from 0 to the key frequency. Real low-pass filtering would completely eliminate the high frequencies and leave the low frequencies intact. Frequency clamping

Listing 11.3 Antialiased fBm, vfBm, and turbulence.

```
/* fractional Brownian motion
 * Inputs:
 *    p, filtwidth    position and approximate interpixel spacing
 *    octaves         max # of octaves to calculate
 *    lacunarity      frequency spacing between successive octaves
 *    gain            scaling factor between successive octaves
 */
float fBm (point p; float filtwidth;
           uniform float octaves, lacunarity, gain)
{
    varying float sum = 0;
    varying point pp  = p;
    varying float fw  = filterwidth;
    uniform float amp = 1;
    uniform float i;

    for (i = 0;  i < octaves;  i += 1) {
        sum += amp * filteredsnoise(pp, fw);
        amp *= gain;  pp *= lacunarity;  fw *= lacunarity;
    }
    return sum;
}


vector vfBm (point p; float filtwidth;
             uniform float octaves, lacunarity, gain)
{
    uniform float amp = 1;
    varying point pp = p;
    varying vector sum = 0;
    varying float fw = filtwidth;
    uniform float i;

    for (i = 0;  i < octaves;  i += 1) {
        sum += amp * filteredvsnoise (pp, fw);
        amp *= gain;  pp *= lacunarity;  fw *= lacunarity;
    }
    return sum;
}


float turbulence (point P; float dP;
                  uniform float octaves, lacunarity, gain)
{
    varying float sum = 0;
    varying point pp  = p;
    varying float fw  = dP;
    uniform float amp = 1;
    uniform float i;
```

▶

Listing 11.3 (continued)

```
for (i = 0;  i < octaves;  i += 1) {
    sum += amp * filteredabs (filteredsnoise(pp, fw), 2*fw);
    amp *= gain;
    pp *= lacunarity;  fw *= lacunarity;
}
return sum;
}
```

---

attenuates them all equally, leaving in too much of the high frequencies and removing too much of the low frequencies. This can lead to artifacts, particularly when
the filter width is so large that even the lowest frequencies (the first octave) of the
fBm will fade to their average value of 0—in other words, the entire function will
fade to a flat color with no detail.

11.5 Conclusions and Caveats

This chapter has outlined three methods for antialiasing your procedural shaders:
(1) putting your pattern into an image file and accessing it using texture( ), thus
letting the system antialias it for you; (2) constructing an analytically antialiased
"filtered" version of your pattern; and (3) eliminating or fading out high-frequency
patterns as they approach the Nyquist limit. Unfortunately, even with these methods, antialiasing your shaders is still a hard task. And these methods, even when
they work fine, are not without their share of problems:

- Using the renderer's automatic filtering of texture map lookups is guaranteed
  not to alias, provided that you created the texture without aliasing in the first
  place. However, this method is subject to all the usual limitations and downsides
  of texture mapping (see Section 10.1).
- Although analytic integration yields exact antialiased results, only a few (generally simple) functions have analytic solutions that exist and are easy to derive.
- Frequency clamping and global fading are applicable to more complex functions, but they are not really the same as low-pass filtering, and artifacts may
  result. (But those clamping artifacts are probably less objectionable than horrible
  aliasing.)
- Both methods do not necessarily hold across the *composition* of functions—
  that is, using the output of one function as the input to another, such as
  step(0.6,snoise(P)). For functions f and g and filtering kernel k, if you want
  the low-pass-filtered composition of $f(g(x))$ and all you know are the low-pass-

filtered versions $F = f \otimes k$ and $G = g \otimes k$, you should be aware that in general

$$((f(g)) \otimes k)(x) \neq F(G(x))$$

In other words, filtering the composition of functions is not always the same as prefiltering each function and then composing their results. What this means is that you cannot blindly replace all your step calls with filterstep and your snoise calls with filteredsnoise and expect thresholded noise to properly antialias. This is intrinsically unsatisfying because it means that we cannot always use the functions we just learned about and expect them to work. The practical result, luckily, is not quite so dismal. Sometimes composition works fine. Other times, the answer is somehow incorrect but acceptable because the error is not jaggy, sparkling, or otherwise recognized as aliasing. And sometimes, of course, you just need to spend more time at the whiteboard deriving the correct antialiased composition.

- Versions of *PRMan* prior to 3.8 had du and dv estimates that were constant across each grid. That meant that any filter size estimates that depended on derivatives (as all the ones discussed in this chapter do) potentially had discontinuities at grid boundaries. This was a particularly evil problem when dealing with displacements, as discontinuities of displacement amounts across grid boundaries can result in cracking. This derivative discontinuity issue was never a problem with *BMRT* and is now fixed in *PRMan*, but it's an additional bugaboo to watch out for if you are using an earlier version of *PRMan*.

- We've been restricting our discussion to color; however, displacement is even trickier. Consider a surface that is displaced with a noise field. If we use the filtered noise to antialias the bumps, what happens as we approach the Nyquist limit and the bumps fade down? A flat surface catches and reflects light much differently than a rough surface, so you may notice a light or color shift that you didn't want. This is a common problem when antialiasing bumps or displacements. A more correct solution would probably replace the "too-small-to-be-seen" bumps with some surface roughness in the BRDF. We have yet to see a satisfactory solution that works in the general case.

- Small amounts of aliasing will often be completely masked by noise or other factors in a still image. But in animation, the resulting twinkling of the texture will be very apparent. In addition, in animations objects are seen over a wider variety of scales, often changing size dramatically within a single shot. This forces you to write your shaders so that they both appear sufficiently detailed and also correctly antialias over a wide range of scales.

These are only the basics, but they're the bread and butter of antialiasing, even for complex shaders. Watch out for high frequency content, conditionals, and so on, in your shaders. Always try to calculate what's happening under a filter area, rather than at a single point. Don't be afraid to cheat—after all, this is computer graphics.

Further Reading

Section II of Glassner (1995) and Chapters 4-6 of Wolberg (1990) provide a good in-depth coverage of signal processing, sampling and reconstruction, and antialiasing issues.

12 A Gallery of Procedural Shaders

This chapter will present several more complex shaders that simulate particular kinds of surfaces or effects that you might find in many scenes. Most of these shaders lean toward the completely procedural, in spite of the complex trade-offs discussed earlier. This is simply because procedural shaders are trickier and take specific advantage of RenderMan Shading Language, whereas almost any renderer can do fairly trivial texture mapping without the need for any programming language. Procedural shaders are also much more interesting to discuss in this context; there's really not much to say about a painting. At least, not in a technical book like this. There's no doubt that the painters' work is as magical and important as ours, but we write about what we know. Perhaps another author will write a book for artists revealing tips for painting killer textures. Still, we do not wish to downplay the importance of scanned or painted textures, so the concluding discussion for each shader will often suggest various ways that paintings could substitute for, augment, enhance, or otherwise control the shaders we present.

We have tried to present several shaders for materials that the average user may actually want to use and to construct them with emphasis on high visual quality, flexibility, modularity, efficiency, and reusability. We have attempted to present shaders in their full and complete detail, as would be necessary for shaders that would be used in a production setting. But while we would be thrilled if people used these shaders unmodified in their work, that is not our goal. Rather, we are hoping that these shaders provide examples and insights into the shader-writing process as well as components that can be reused, cloned, copied, and cannibalized to make new shaders that we haven't even thought about.

12.1   Shader Strategy

When modeling the shape of an object, we don't try to skimp by using exactly the model that was used for some previous similar object (unless it's intentionally a clone of the earlier object). Rather, we create a new shape for the new object to the exacting specifications of the art director or other designers. Similarly, we are not satisfied to reuse a shader that is moderately close, but will instead create a new shader for that particular object. If the object merits additional work to create a custom shape, shouldn't it also have a custom pattern and appearance?

For these reasons, we tend to write a custom shader for *every* object. Of course, we don't actually start with a totally blank page on every shader. We shamelessly steal code and techniques from other similar shaders. We have extensive function libraries filled with routines such as those in Chapters 7-11. Nonetheless, a considerable effort goes into getting the shaders just right for each object.

Every shader programmer probably has his or her own specific strategy for approaching the shader-writing process. Use whatever approach works best for you, but below is a strategy that has worked for us.

Before you start, make sure you understand the problem.

What does the object look like? If you are matching the appearance of a real-world object, get reference materials such as photographs or, if possible, a real object. Try to get multiple references so that you can understand the natural variation of the objects. If the object doesn't exist in the real world, make sure you get as complete a description as possible from the art director. Sketches, textual descriptions, pastels, paintings, and photographs of similar objects are helpful. Try to force your art director to provide any quantifiable parameters, such as RGB values for a base color.

How big will the object appear on-screen, and for how long? Try to budget your shader development time proportionally to the total number of pixels on which it will appear. An object in a dimly lit area in the background for one shot can probably be plastic or have a very simple shader that you can write in an hour. A main character face that will fill a movie screen at times of major plot points could easily justify several months of development.

Build appearance theories and construct the shader in layers.

Study the object carefully. Hypothesize about materials that comprise the object and the physical processes that contributed to its construction and current appearance. Guess about the material characteristics of the object. What is its average color and specularity? Does it have wrinkles? If so, at what amplitude and frequency? Is it a mixture of materials?

Make a list of the top four or five features that make the object recognizable, ranked in order of their importance. For example, the ceramic tiles in my bathroom are arranged in a regular rectangular pattern, have a yellowish-brown mottled color, are darker near their borders, and are slightly reflective. An apple is reddish with high-frequency yellowish streaks, occasional brown bruises, dark spots, some low-frequency lumpiness, and has bright specular highlights but does not reflect a mirror image of its surroundings.

Go down your list in order, translating the perceived features into modular shader code. It is often helpful to think of the features as occurring in layers, composited atop one another. Think first of the lowest level of detail (overall color, for example) and work toward the finer levels until you achieve sufficient realism.

Test the shader and get constant feedback.

When you are viewing only still images, it's easy to lull yourself into complacency about antialiasing, scale, and other animation issues. Obviously, you should be using antialiased pattern-generation techniques as we have discussed in earlier chapters. You should also be producing test images at different distances and resolutions. As early as possible, test the shader in animation. Slow zooms reveal aliasing tendencies with frustrating efficiency.

Make sure your shader looks good at all scales at which it will appear and then some. Much as civil engineers design bridges to withstand ten times their projected loads, it may be worth the investment to make your shader look good even at an order of magnitude closer and farther away than originally called for (this can save lots of time if the script changes after you have completed the shader).

Try to get early feedback from whoever originally specified the appearance of your object. It's better to have a tight review cycle than to get too far along in your shader only to have to abandon the code later. If you don't have an art director, get another objective third party to give feedback.

Remember that it's only in rare circumstances that your shader must exactly match a real object. Usually, the goal is for your shader to *read* as the correct object given the constraints of size and time that your object will appear. Oddly enough, a slightly simplified or stylized look will often read more clearly than a photorealistic replica. Sometimes people's mental model of an object will be quite different from the way a real object appears, and your shader must cater to those expectations.

Remember efficiency.

It is important to remember that your shaders execute in the *innermost loop* of the renderer. If you are writing complex shaders with texture, noise, rich lighting, and so on, they can be quite expensive to execute and constitute the majority of the cost of rendering a scene. This is particularly true for *PRMan*, which can process large amounts of geometry very cheaply. In fact, we have found that shader execution can account for upwards of 90% of total rendering time. Thus, the frugality of your shader has a proportional effect on the overall cost of rendering your scene.

Most operations are fairly inexpensive, but not all shadeops are created equal. The things worth watching out for:

- Moderately expensive shadeops include `normalize()` and `cellnoise()`.
- Significantly expensive shadeops include `noise()`, `texture()`, `environment()`, `shadow()`, `transform()` (all varieties), matrix multiplies and inversions, and point/vector constructors with space names (because they imply a transformation).
- Some common operations can be *arbitrarily* expensive or otherwise hard to predict: `diffuse()`, `specular()`, and `illuminance` loops (because they can trigger execution of large numbers of lights), and `fBm` loops (because they involve many `noise` calls).
- Remember that `uniform` variables and expressions are much less expensive than `varying` computations. Try to declare your local variables as `uniform` wherever possible.

We would never imply that you should sacrifice quality just to speed up a shader. The shaders in this book are quite expensive, but we feel it's worth it for shaders that achieve superior visual quality and have many useful controls. That being said, we have tried to make the shaders as efficient as possible and urge you to do the same in your shaders.

12.2 Aside: Shading Spaces and Reference Meshes

In Chapter 7 we discussed that points, vectors, and normals may be expressed in a variety of coordinate spaces. However, not all of these coordinate systems are equally valuable for expressing shading and texturing calculations. Choosing a good coordinate system for these calculations is an important part of implementing them well.

12.2.1 Don't Shade in "current" Space

Consider the following fragment of shader code, which computes texture using `P` as an index into a "solid noise" function, thresholds the result, and mixes between two colors:

Figure 12.1 A torus with thresholded fBm indexed in "current" space will appear to be moving "through" the texture pattern as the object moves (top). If the fBm is calculated in "shader" space, the pattern will stick to the surface as the object moves rigidly (bottom).

```
float f = float noise (P);
color Ct = mix (C1, C2, filterstep(.5, f));
Ci = Ct * (Ka*ambient() + Kd*diffuse(Nf)) +
     specularcolor * Ks * specular(Nf,V);
```

P, the position of the point being shaded, is expressed in "current" space. What happens if the object is moving and you render several frames in a row? Figure 12.1 shows such a situation. The texture lookups are happening in "current" space (which is probably a "fixed" coordinate system such as "world" space or "camera" space). Because the object is moving relative to "current" space, it will appear to be traveling *through* the texture! This is almost certainly not the desired effect.

Although "current" space is necessary for lighting and certain other calculations, it is extremely inconvenient for texturing calculations. In addition, the exact nature of "current" space is renderer dependent and may vary among implementations. For these reasons, we never texture in "current" space.

12.2.2 Texture Spaces Rigidly Connected to the Geometry

If the object is moving rigidly—that is, its movement is due to changing its transformation—then the relationship between "world" space and "object" space changes from frame to frame. But the geometry is in a fixed position relative to its local or "object" space. The following shader fragment indexes the noise field using the "object" space coordinates of P:

```
point Pobj = transform ("object", P);
float f = float noise (Pobj);
```

```
color Ct = mix (C1, C2, filterstep(.5, f));
    .
    .
    .
```

As a further refinement, we observe that it may be convenient to rotate, translate, or scale the texture relative to the object geometry. Luckily, there is another coordinate system that can be structured to be rigidly connected to "object" space, yet can be independently transformed: "shader" space. Recall that "shader" space is the coordinate system that was active when the shader was declared. Below is a RIB fragment showing how "shader" space can be transformed relative to "object" space.

```
AttributeBegin
  ConcatTransform [...]       # Translate, rotate, scale the object
  TransformBegin
    ConcatTransform [...]     # Move shader relative to object
    Surface "noisy"           # Specify the shader
  TransformEnd                # Restore the object transformation
  PatchMesh ...               # Make some geometry
AttributeEnd
```

In this example, we have inserted an additional transformation after the object-placing transform but before the shader is declared (and then we restore the object transformation before declaring the geometry). This gives us an additional control over the placement and scaling of the texturing that is built into the model, provided we look up our texture in "shader" space:

```
point Pshad = transform ("shader", P);
float f = float noise (Pshad);
    .
    .
    .
```

Another reason for preferring "shader" space over "object" space is that your model may be comprised of different geometric primitives that have different object transformations. Yet you may prefer a single coordinate system for texturing that is independent of the individual object systems for each primitive. As a case in point, suppose your model contains (perhaps among other things) a number of spheres. Because spheres are always centered on their object coordinate spaces, shading in "object" space would result in each sphere having the *same* pattern on them. This is almost certainly not desired; rather, if texturing were performed in a single "shader" space, each sphere would be sampling a different part of the texture space. Furthermore, all of the primitives in the model would appear to be carved from the same block of texture. This is illustrated in Figure 12.2.

Figure 12.2 All spheres are centered at the origin of their local coordinate systems, so shading in "object" space will make spheres with identical patterns (left). Using "shader" space allows you to vary the pattern on identical primitives by making each one index texture from a different area of the pattern space (right).

12.2.3 Deformations and Reference Geometry

Using "shader" space for indexing 3D patterns prevents the texture from sliding along the surface but only as long as the object is undergoing *rigid* transformations—in other words, translation and rotation. But if your object is *deforming*, then its points are moving around within "shader" space. This is illustrated in Figure 12.3 (left and center), which shows a soda can with a solid grid texture applied in "shader" space. If the can is deformed by moving the control vertices of its mesh, then its points will move nonrigidly through "shader" space, and again we will be faced with the pattern sliding around on the geometry.

How can we attach texture to the deforming object in a way that will cause the pattern to stick to the surface? Recall that RenderMan allows you to attach arbitrary data to geometric meshes, with the renderer interpolating the data across the surface and providing it to the shader. What if the data being interpolated is the original, undeformed geometric positions of the mesh? We can use those coordinates as the basis for texturing, secure in the knowledge that they will "track" the surface regardless of what wacky deformations the surface undergoes. The solution to our sliding texture problem, then, is to construct the model with both the deformed position and an *undeformed reference mesh* used for texturing (see Section 4.7).

Because any shaders that create patterns based in some way on P will almost certainly want to transform to a shading space (generally, "shader" space), and often will want a reference mesh if the geometry may deform, let us create some reusable code that simplifies the process for us. There are two steps involved. First, the shader must include parameters for the name of the shading space and for Pref (if a reference mesh is provided). Second, we must transform either P or Pref

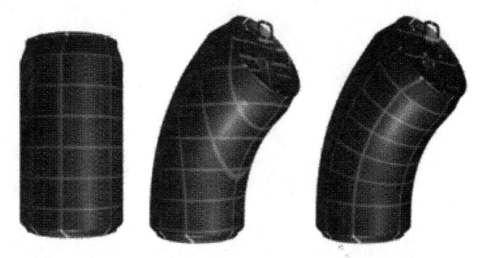

Figure 12.3 Deforming the control mesh of an object will result in the texture sliding over
the surface if the geometry moves nonrigidly (left and center). Using a reference mesh for
texturing makes the texture "stick" to the deforming mesh (right). (Example and images
courtesy of Shaun Oborn, Pixar Animation Studios.)

(depending on whether a reference mesh is provided) into the appropriate shading
space. Listing 12.1 shows a header file that provides macros that perform these
operations.

Listing 12.1, which lists pshad.h, defines three useful macros. PSHAD_PARAMS
and DEFAULT_PSHAD_PARAMS both declare the necessary parameters shadingspace,
which gives the name of the space in which to perform shading calculations, shad-
ingfreq, which provides an additional means of scaling the frequency of the pattern, and Pref, the reference mesh position. You should write one of these macro
names somewhere in the parameter list for your shader. While DEFAULT_PSHAD_
PARAMS uses "shader" as the shading space and a frequency multiplier of 1, PSHAD_
PARAMS takes two parameters that let you specify those defaults. Remember that in
either case, the model may override these defaults by passing an explicit parameter
to the shader declaration.

The GET_PSHAD macro sets the value of Pshad to the shading space coordinates
of either P or Pref. Pref is used if it exists and appears to have data; otherwise, P
is used. We pick an unlikely default value for Pref so that we can easily recognize
if this value was overridden, indicating that the RIB stream contained Pref data for
this geometric primitive. For good measure, the GET_PSHAD macro also declares and
computes dPshad as an estimate of the amount that Pshad changes between adjacent shading samples. This can be used for antialiasing of your pattern-generation
operations.

Finally, to eliminate the extra Pref storage and computation that is unnecessary
for a rigid mesh, we use the preprocessor symbol USE_PREF. You should #define

Listing 12.1 pshad.h: a header file that provides the PSHAD_PARAMS and
GET_PSHAD macros.

```
/**********************************************************************
 * pshad.h - define macros for easy use of reference meshes and texture
 *           spaces:
 * PSHAD_PARAMS(space,freq) - put this macro in the parameter list of
 *                 your shader to declare a shadingspace parameter (and
 *                 optionally Pref, if USE_PREF is nonzero).  Takes as
 *                 arguments the default shading space name and frequency.
 * DEFAULT_PSHAD_PARAMS - calls PSHAD_PARAMS with default space "shader"
 *                 and default frequency 1.
 * GET_PSHAD     - put this in the body of your shader, near the top.
 *                 It sets Pshad to the shading coordinates of P (or Pref,
 *                 if provided), and sets dPshad to the expected change
 *                 in Pshad between adjacent shading samples.
 * This file expects that the .sl file #define's the symbol USE_PREF
 * _prior_ to inclusion of this header file.
 **********************************************************************/

/* If USE_PREF is not defined, assume that Pref will not be used. */
#ifndef USE_PREF
#define USE_PREF 0
#endif

#if (USE_PREF)

/* Pick an unlikely value to let us recognize an uninitialized Pref */
#define UNINITIALIZED_PREF point (-1e10, -1e10, -1e10)

#define PSHAD_PARAMS(spacedefault,freqdefault)                       \
                varying point Pref = UNINITIALIZED_PREF;             \
                string shadingspace = spacedefault;                 \
                float shadingfreq = freqdefault;

#define GET_PSHAD     varying point Pshad;                           \
                if (Pref != UNINITIALIZED_PREF)                      \
                    Pshad = transform (shadingspace, Pref);         \
                else Pshad = transform (shadingspace, P);           \
                Pshad *= shadingfreq;                               \
                float dPshad = filterwidthp(Pshad);

#else /* if (USE_PREF) */

#define PSHAD_PARAMS(spacedefault,freqdefault)                       \
                string shadingspace = spacedefault;                 \
                float shadingfreq = freqdefault;                   ▶
```

Listing 12.1 (continued)

```
#define GET_PSHAD    varying point Pshad;                  \
                     Pshad = shadingfreq
                     * transform (shadingspace, P);        \
                     float dPshad = filterwidthp(Pshad);

#endif /* USE_PREF */

#define DEFAULT_PSHAD_PARAMS PSHAD_PARAMS("shader",1)
```

this symbol *prior* to where you #include the pref.h file. If USE_PREF is nonzero, the PSHAD_PARAMS and GET_PSHAD macros will include the Pref declarations and operations. If USE_PREF is zero, these extra computations will be avoided in favor of somewhat simpler implementations of PSHAD_PARAMS and GET_PSHAD that do not consider Pref.

Following is an example of a shader that uses these macros:

```
#define USE_PREF 1
#include "filterwidth.h"
#include "noises.h"
#include "pshad.h"

surface
splotch (float Ka = 1, Kd = 0.5, Ks = .65, roughness = .1;
         color specularcolor = 1;
         float octaves = 4, lacunarity = 2, gain = 0.5;
         DEFAULT_PSHAD_PARAMS )
{
   GET_PSHAD;
   float f   = fBm (Pshad, dPshad, octaves, lacunarity, gain);
   color Ct  = mix (color 1, color (.8, .1, 1), filterstep (0, f));
   normal Nf = faceforward (normalize(N),I);
   Ci = Ct * (Ka*ambient() + Kd*diffuse(Nf)) +
        specularcolor * Ks*specular(Nf,-normalize(I),roughness);
   Oi = Os;  Ci *= Oi;
}
```

The overriding lesson of this section is: forget "current" space, it is quite undependable. It is better to always take steps to work in something dependable like "shader" space. Furthermore, if your object is undergoing nonaffine transformations or deformations, you will need to provide a reference mesh and use the interpolated reference positions for your pattern generation.

12.3   **Ceramic Tiles**

For our first shader, we will create a procedural texture that resembles ceramic tiles, like the kind you often see lining the walls and other surfaces of bathrooms or kitchens.

After long contemplation in the shower, this author made a list of the main features of the tiles:

- The tiles are square and arranged in a regular rectilinear pattern.
- The tiles themselves are ceramic, and slightly reflective, while the space between adjacent tiles is filled with dirty mortar.
- The tiles are slightly raised (or is the mortar pushed in?) and the corners of the tiles are rounded.
- The individual tiles tend to have a mottled appearance in the interior, shifting between different colors. There often seems to be another, usually darker, color around the outer border of each tile. Tiles also seem to have little dark specks occasionally.
- Each tile is different, with noticeable shifts in the overall color from tile to tile.

The basic structure of our shader will simply implement these features roughly in order. We will use comments to indicate where the features will be implemented. Notice that we are already considering both the visual appearance and the shader implementation to be organized in steps or layers.

```
surface
ceramictiles ( /* parameters */ )
{
    /* Step 0: Get 2D texture coordinates for the texturing */

    /* Step 1: Find out where in the pattern we are: whether we're in
     * a tile section or a mortar section, which tile we're on,
     * and the coordinates within our individual tile.
     */

    /* Step 2, displacement: the edges of the tile displace down a bit,
     * as do the grooves between tiles.  Also, add just a little bit of
     * per-tile normal variation to break up reflections.
     */

    /* Step 3: Set the color of the mortar between tiles and/or the color
     * of our spot of tile (the tile texture itself, that is).
     */

    /* Step 4: vary the color on a per-tile basis so that every tile
     * looks a little different.
     */
```

```
/* Step 5: Illumination model */
Ci = MaterialCeramicTiles (...);
Oi = Os;  Ci *= Oi;
}
```

For Step 0, we can make use of the ProjectTo2D routine that we presented in Section 8.3 to give the user great flexibility in defining texture projection spaces based on parameters to the shader. ProjectTo2D will set 2D texture coordinates ss and tt and their filter widths dss and dtt. All the routines that follow can probably be greatly simplified if we assume that tiles are one unit square (counting the mortar). So our preamble will "normalize" the texture coordinates in this manner. Thus, we have

```
float ss, tt, dss, dtt;
ProjectTo2D (projection, P, textureprojspace, array_to_mx(mx),
            ss, tt, dss, dtt);
ss /= stilespacing;
dss /= stilespacing;
tt /= ttilespacing;
dtt /= ttilespacing;
```

where projection, textureprojspace, mx, stilespacing, and ttilespacing are all parameters to our shader. Typical real-life tiles have a spacing of about 10 cm, with groove width of about 0.5 cm.

Now we turn to finding our place in the pattern. Recall the pulsetrain routine we discussed in Section 11.3.2. We can extend it to 2D by multiplying a pulse train in s with a pulse train in t,

```
pulsetrain (groovewidth, 1, ss+groovewidth/2) *
    pulsetrain (grooveheight, 1, tt+grooveheight/2);
```

where groovewidth and grooveheight are the widths of the mortar grooves between tiles, expressed as a fraction of the tile-to-tile spacing (which we have assumed has been normalized to 1.0). This gives us the pattern in Figure 12.4 (left). Notice the bad aliasing—this results from the high frequencies of the infinitely sharp pulses. In some cases, the dark lines disappear altogether when they are so narrow that they fall "between" shading samples.

We can remedy this aliasing by using the filteredpulsetrain function instead (Figure 12.4, right). We must also compute which tile we are on (indexed by a 2D integer) and where in our particular tile we are shading:

```
swhichtile = floor (ss);
twhichtile = floor (tt);
stile = ss - swhichtile;
ttile = tt - twhichtile;
intile = filteredpulsetrain (groovewidth, 1, ss+groovewidth/2, ds)
        * filteredpulsetrain (grooveheight, 1, tt+grooveheight/2, dt);
```

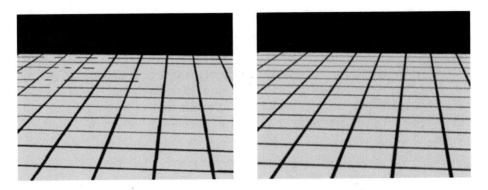

Figure 12.4 Criss-crossing pulsetrains provide the basic structure of the tile pattern but alias badly (left). Using `filteredpulsetrain` serves to antialias the groove/tile pattern (right).

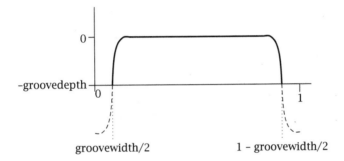

Figure 12.5 Profile of a tile displacement.

Next we want to make the tiles appear displaced. Rather than displacing the tiles up, we will displace the grooves *down*, which will avoid any strange intersection artifacts. Furthermore, we can probably get away with bump mapping, as the groove depth (typically only a couple millimeters) is probably very small in screen space. Figure 12.5 shows our desired tile profile. The mortar areas drop down to -groovedepth, the centers of the tile stay where they were, and we can use a smoothstep to round the corner of the tile. Note that we offset the smoothstep so that the tile corner is rounded, but we have a sharper transition where the tile meets the mortar. Here is the implementation of the displacement strategy:

```
float smoothpulse (float e0, e1, e2, e3, x) {
    return smoothstep(e0,e1,x) - smoothstep(e2,e3,x);
}


float tiledisp = smoothpulse (0, .075, 0.925, 1, stile);
```

```
tiledisp *= smoothpulse (0, .075, 0.925, 1, ttile);
normal Nf = faceforward (normalize(N), I);
normal Ntile = Displace (P, Nf, 0, groovedepth*(tiledisp-1), "shader");
```

We notice that in real life, every tile is oriented slightly differently than every other, thus causing reflected images to break up a bit at tile boundaries. We can simulate this effect by adding a very small amount of per-tile noise to the surface normal, using the vector cellnoise function:

```
float tileindex = swhichtile + 13*twhichtile;
Ntile += 0.05 * (vector cellnoise (tileindex+5) - 0.5);
Nf = normalize (mix (Nf, Ntile, intile));
```

Moving on to the texture *within* each tile, we can observe that the tiles have a complex and pleasing mottling of color. We can use fBm from Section 10.4 for this purpose:

```
color C = Cbase;
float dst = max(ds,dt);
point noisep = mottlefreq*point(stile,ttile,tileindex);
float mottle = .2+.6*fBm(noisep, mottlefreq*dst, 4, 2, 0.65);
C = mix (C, Cmottle, clamp(mottling*mottle,0,1));
```

We have computed fBm on 3D points constructed from the stile and ttile coordinates (scaled by an appropriate frequency) and a per-tile index. This causes the pattern to be looking at a different slice of fBm space for every tile so that each tile will not have the identical mottling pattern.

Frequently there is another, usually darker, color close to the edges of the tile and with a ragged boundary:

```
float sedgeoffset = .05*fBm(point(stile*10, ttile*10, tileindex+10),
                           10*dst, 2, 2, 0.5);
float tedgeoffset = .05*fBm(point(stile*10, ttile*10, tileindex-3),
                           10*dst, 2, 2, 0.5);
float edgy = 1 - (smoothpulse (.05, .15, .85, .95, stile+sedgeoffset) *
                  smoothpulse (.05, .15, .85, .95, ttile+tedgeoffset));
C = mix (C, Cedge, edgy);
```

Here we have used fBm to *offset* the stile and ttile values before being passed through smoothpulse. Figure 12.6 shows the variable edgy with and without the noise warping.

To add speckles, we will threshold a medium-frequency noise by running it through a smoothstep that ramps up from 0.55 to 0.7. Most noise "bumps" will be lower than the threshold, thus falling out. Some will be large enough and will show up as a speckle.

```
float speckfreq = 7;
point noisep = point(stile*speckfreq, ttile*speckfreq, tileindex+8);
```

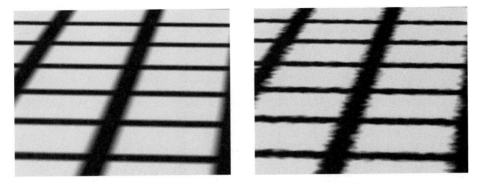

Figure 12.6 Close-up of the edgy variable, which mixes between the base mottled color and the special tile edge color (small values of edgy are shown in white, large values in black). Just using the smoothpulse to define the shape of the edge region (left). Using fBm to warp the domain gives a ragged edge (right).

```
float specky = filteredsnoise (noisep, speckfreq*dst);
specky = smoothstep (0.55, 0.7, specky);
C = mix (C, Cspeck, specky);
```

We notice that in real life, the colors aren't the same on each tile—they can differ quite a bit in the base color. Therefore, we will add a function that, given the computed color of the tile, will tweak it on a per-tile basis. For flexibility, we will allow user controls over the per-tile variation, separately for each of hue, saturation, and luminance (using the variables varyhue, varysat, and varylum). We do this by transforming Ctile into "hsl" space, where it can more conveniently have variation added to its hue, saturation, and lightness. Before returning, we clamp to reasonable values and convert back to "rgb" space:

```
color varyEach (color Cin; float index, varyhue, varysat, varylum;)
{
    /* Convert to "hsl" space, it's more convenient */
    color Chsl = ctransform ("hsl", Cin);
    float h = comp(Chsl,0), s = comp(Chsl,1), l = comp(Chsl,2);
    /* Modify Chsl by adding Cvary scaled by our separate h,s,l
       controls */
    h += varyhue * (cellnoise(index+3)-0.5);
    s *= 1 - varysat * (cellnoise(index-14)-0.5);
    l *= 1 - varylum * (cellnoise(index+37)-0.5);
    Chsl = color (mod(h,1), clamp(s,0,1), clamp(l,0,1));
    /* Clamp hsl and transform back to rgb space */
    return ctransform ("hsl", "rgb", clamp(Chsl,color 0, color 1));
}
```

We're nearly done. The mortar can simply be a diffuse fBm pattern:

```
color Cmortar = mortarcolor;
point Q = 20*point(ss,tt,0);
float dQ = filterwidthp (Q);
if (intile < 1.0)
    Cmortar *= smoothstep (0, 1, (.5 + .4 * fBm (Q, dQ, 3, 2, .6)));
```

And now the only thing left is the illumination model. We will make an appropriate ceramic reflection model with components for diffuse, the glossy specular of Section 9.5.3, and some Fresnel-based reflection. We multiply kr and ks by intile in order to get rid of highlights and reflections for the mortar parts:

```
color basecolor = mix (Cmortar, Ctile, intile);
float ks = Ks * intile;
float kd = mix (Kdmortar, Kdtile, intile);
vector IN = normalize(I), V = -IN;
float fkr, fkt;  vector R, T;
fresnel (IN, Nf, 1/eta, fkr, fkt, R, T);
fkt = 1-fkr;
float kr = fkr * Kr * intile;
Ci =    fkt * basecolor * (Ka*ambient() + kd*diffuse(Nf))
        + ks * LocIllumGlossy (Nf, V, roughness/10, specsharpness)
        + kr * SampleEnvironment (P, R, blur, ENVPARAMS);
```

Figure 12.7 shows the final tile shader in action, and Listing 12.2 lists the complete shader source code. Notice how we have modularized the shader, moving each of the major pieces of functionality into a separate function.

There are a number of enhancements that could be made to this shader. We will leave these modifications as exercises for the reader, but here are some suggestions:

- Add the ability to use texture maps to control some of the procedural aspects of the shader, including:
  - □ the mortar/tile division and in-tile coordinates; one way to do this might be to have a three-channel texture specify the intile with channel 0, and stile and ttile in channels 1 and 2, respectively
  - □ the pattern of mottling and specks within each tile
  - □ the base color of each tile; this would allow you to lay out tiles in patterns, as is often done in real life

    For any of these features for which texture maps are not specified, the shader can fall back on the purely procedural code.
- By increasing the tile and groove sizes, changing the type of illumination model to a rough diffuse appearance rather than a ceramic appearance, and modifying the mottling pattern, you could easily modify this shader into one for those orange terra-cotta tiles that line walkways.
- We may reuse the technique of dividing into rectilinear tiles with very different "in-tile" patterns. For example, by replacing the mottling tiletexture function with a marble appearance, we could make a floor of tiled marble slabs.

Listing 12.2 Final shader for procedural ceramic tiles.

```
/****************************************************************
 * ceramictiles.sl
 *
 * Description: Ceramic tiles (like you'd find in a bathroom)
 *
 * Parameters for pattern placement and size:
 *   projection, textureprojspace, mx - define the projection used to
 *     establish a basic 2D coordinate system for the pattern.
 *   stilespacing, ttilespacing - tile-to-tile spacing (separate controls
 *     for s and t directions)
 *   groovewidth, grooveheight - width of the spacing between tiles,
 *     expressed as a fraction of the tile-to-tile spacing.
 *   groovedepth - displacement amount for the grooves (expressed in
 *     shader space units)
 *   truedisp - 1 for true displacement, 0 for bump mapping
 *
 * Parameters for tile color and pattern:
 *   Cbase, Cmottle - base color and mottle color of the tile
 *   mottlefreq - frequency of the mottling between Cbase & Cmottle
 *   Cedge - separate edge color for the tiles
 *   Cspeck - color of the occasional specks in the tiles
 *   edgevary, mottling, speckly - individual scalar controls over
 *     edge variation, mottling, and speckles.  Setting any to zero will
 *     turn that feature off.
 *   varyhue, varysat, varylum - individual controls for the per-tile
 *     color variation (0 means don't vary in that way, larger values
 *     cause more tile-to-tile variation).
 *
 * Parameters for illumination model:
 *   Ka - the usual meaning
 *   Kdmortar - Kd for the mortar between tiles
 *   mortarcolor - base color of the mortar
 *   Kdtile - diffuse component weighting of the tile
 *   Ks, roughness, specsharpness - glossy specular controls of the tile
 *   Kr, blur, eta - reflection parameters for the tile
 *   envname, envspace, envrad - environment mapping controls
 *   rayjitter, raysamples - ray tracing controls
 *
 ****************************************************************/


#include "project.h"
#include "material.h"
#include "noises.h"
#include "displace.h"
#include "patterns.h"
```

▶

Listing 12.2 (continued)

```
/* Given 2D texture coordinates ss,tt and their filter widths ds, dt,
 * and the width and height of the grooves between tiles (assuming that
 * tile spacing is 1.0), figure out which (integer indexed) tile we are
 * on and what coordinates (on [0,1]) within our individual tile we are
 * shading.
 */
float
tilepattern (float ss, tt, ds, dt;
             float groovewidth, grooveheight;
             output float swhichtile, twhichtile;
             output float stile, ttile;)
{
    swhichtile = floor (ss);
    twhichtile = floor (tt);
    stile = ss - swhichtile;
    ttile = tt - twhichtile;

    return filteredpulsetrain (groovewidth, 1, ss+groovewidth/2, ds)
            * filteredpulsetrain (grooveheight, 1, tt+grooveheight/2, dt);
}


/* Given coordinates (stile,ttile) and derivatives (ds,dt) *within* a
 * single tile, calculate the color of the tile at that point.  Major
 * features include (1) mottling of the color; (2) darkening or shifting
 * to a different color near the border of the tile (with a ragged edge
 * to the color transition); (3) occasional dark specks.
 */
color
tiletexture (float tileindex;
             float stile, ttile, ds, dt;
             float edgevary, mottling, speckly;
             float mottlefreq;
             color Cbase, Cedge, Cmottle, Cspeck)
{
    color C = Cbase;
    float dst = max(ds,dt);
    if (mottling > 0) {
        point noisep = mottlefreq*point(stile,ttile,tileindex);
        float mottle = .2+.6*fBm(noisep, mottlefreq*max(ds,dt), 4, 2, 0.65);
        C = mix (C, Cmottle, clamp(mottling*mottle,0,1));
    }
    if (edgevary > 0) {
        float sedgeoffset = .05*fBm(point(stile*10, ttile*10, tileindex+10),
                                    10*dst, 2, 2, 0.5);
```
▶

Listing 12.2 (continued)

```
        float tedgeoffset = .05*fBm(point(stile*10, ttile*10, tileindex-3),
                                    10*dst, 2, 2, 0.5);
        float edgy = 1 - (smoothpulse (.05, .15, .85, .95,
                              stile+sedgeoffset) *
                          smoothpulse (.05, .15, .85, .95,
                              ttile+tedgeoffset));
        C = mix (C, Cedge, edgevary*edgy);
    }
    if (speckly > 0) {
        float speckfreq = 7;
        point noisep = point(stile*speckfreq, ttile*speckfreq,
                             tileindex+8);
        float specky = filteredsnoise (noisep, speckfreq*dst);
        specky = smoothstep (0.55, 0.7, specky);
        C = mix (C, Cspeck, speckly*specky);
    }
    return C;
}


/* Compute the color of a ceramic object.  Like plastic, but use a
 * "glossy" specular term.  We're actually blending between a purely
 * diffuse model for the mortar and a ceramic model for the tiles,
 * depending on the variable intile.  When in the mortar area, we turn
 * off highlights and reflections.
 */
color MaterialCeramicTiles (normal Nf;  color Cmortar, Ctile;
                            float intile;
                            float Ka, Kdmortar, Kdtile, Ks;
                            float roughness, specsharpness, Kr, blur, eta;
                            DECLARE_ENVPARAMS)
{
    extern vector I;
    extern point P;
    color basecolor = mix (Cmortar, Ctile, intile);
    float ks = Ks * intile;
    float kd = mix (Kdmortar, Kdtile, intile);
    vector IN = normalize(I), V = -IN;
    float fkr, fkt;  vector R, T;
    fresnel (IN, Nf, 1/eta, fkr, fkt, R, T);
    fkt = 1-fkr;
    float kr = fkr * Kr * intile;
    return   fkt * basecolor * (Ka*ambient() + kd*diffuse(Nf))
           + ks * LocIllumGlossy (Nf, V, roughness/10, specsharpness)
           + kr * SampleEnvironment (P, R, blur, ENVPARAMS);
}
```
▶

Listing 12.2 (continued)

```
surface
ceramictiles ( float Ka = 1, Ks = .75, roughness = 0.1;
               float Kr = 1, blur = 0, eta = 1.5;
               float specsharpness = 0.5;
               float Kdtile = 0.5;
               float Kdmortar = 0.8;
               color mortarcolor = color (.5, .5, .5);
               DECLARE_DEFAULTED_ENVPARAMS;
               float stilespacing = 10, ttilespacing = 10;
               float groovewidth = 0.06, grooveheight = 0.06;
               float groovedepth = 0.2, truedisp = 0;
               string projection = "st";
               string textureprojspace = "shader";
               float mx[16] = {1,0,0,0, 0,1,0,0, 0,0,1,0, 0,0,0,1};
               float edgevary = 1, mottling = 1, speckly = 1;
               float mottlefreq = 7;
               color Cbase   = color(.05, .075, .6);
               color Cedge   = color(.025, .025, .2);
               color Cmottle = color(.2, .2, .7);
               color Cspeck  = color(.015, .015, .015);
               float varyhue = 0.025, varysat = 0.4, varylum = 0.5;
    )
{
    /*
     * Get a 2D texture coordinate for the texturing, then
     * Normalize everything so that the tiles are 1 x 1 units
     */
    float ss, tt, dss, dtt;
    ProjectTo2D (projection, P, textureprojspace, array_to_mx(mx),
                 ss, tt, dss, dtt);
    ss /= stilespacing;
    dss /= stilespacing;
    tt /= ttilespacing;
    dtt /= ttilespacing;

    /*
     * Find out where in the pattern we are: which tile we're on, and
     * the (stile,ttile) coordinates (both on [0,1]) within our tile.
     */
    float swhichtile, twhichtile, stile, ttile;
    float intile = tilepattern (ss, tt, dss, dtt,
                                groovewidth, grooveheight,
                                swhichtile, twhichtile, stile, ttile);
    float tileindex = swhichtile + 13*twhichtile;
```
▶

Listing 12.2 (continued)

```
/*
 * Displacement: the edges of the tile displace down a bit, as do
 * the grooves between tiles.  Also, add just a little bit of
 * per-tile normal variation to break up reflections.
 */
float tiledisp = smoothpulse (0, .075, 0.925, 1, stile);
tiledisp *= smoothpulse (0, .075, 0.925, 1, ttile);
normal Nf = faceforward (normalize(N), I);
normal Ntile = Displace (Nf, "shader", groovedepth*(tiledisp-1),
truedisp);

Ntile += 0.05 * (vector cellnoise (tileindex+5) - 0.5);
Nf = normalize (mix (Nf, Ntile, intile));


/*
 * Here's the exciting part -- calculate the color of the spot we're
 * in within the tile.  Then use the tile index to vary its color
 * so every tile looks a little different.
 */
color Ctile = tiletexture (tileindex, stile, ttile, dss, dtt,
                           edgevary, mottling, speckly,
                           mottlefreq,
                           Cbase, Cedge, Cmottle, Cspeck);
Ctile = varyEach (Ctile, tileindex, varyhue, varysat, varylum);


/*
 * Set the color of the mortar between tiles, make it look good by
 * scaling it by some high-frequency fBm.
 */
color Cmortar = mortarcolor;
point Q = 20*point(ss,tt,0);
float dQ = filterwidthp (Q);
if (intile < 1.0)
    Cmortar *= smoothstep (0, 1, (.5 + .4 * fBm (Q, dQ, 3, 2, .6)));


/*
 * Illumination model
 */
Ci = MaterialCeramicTiles (Nf, Cmortar, Ctile, intile, Ka, Kdmortar,
                           Kdtile, Ks, roughness, specsharpness,
                           Kr, blur, eta, ENVPARAMS);

    Oi = Os;  Ci *= Oi;
}
```

Figure 12.7 The final `ceramictiles` shader. See also color plate 12.7.

12.4   Wood Grain

Our "theory" of wood is as follows:

- The wood is composed of light and dark wood alternating in concentric cylinders surrounding a central axis. We will call the dark bands *rings*.
- The rings are not, of course, perfect cylinders; they are warped in a variety of interesting ways.
- Throughout the wood there is a high-frequency "grain" pattern of dark streaks. These grains are darker than the surrounding wood.
- The grains are darker and more prevalent in the dark areas of the rings than in the light wood area.

For simplicity, the central axis of the rings will be taken to be the *z*-axis in "shader" space. To position the ring pattern relative to an object, the user should manipulate the "shader" space coordinate system.

```
/* Calculate the radius from the center. */
float r2 = sqr(xcomp(Pshad)) + sqr(ycomp(Pshad));
```

```
float r = sqrt(r2) * ringfreq;
float inring = smoothpulsetrain (.1, .55, .7, .95, 1, r);
color Cwood = mix (Clightwood, Cdarkwood, inring);
```

We have calculated a radius from the z-axis, multiplied by a ringfreq, and then alternated between light and dark wood colors according to a pulse train. We set up the pulse train so that we ramp from light to dark more slowly, then we drop from dark back down to light (this is purely for aesthetic reasons). The smoothpulsetrain function is analogous to the pulsetrain function from Section 11.3.2, but with smoothstep:

```
float smoothpulse (float e0, e1, e2, e3, x)
{
    return smoothstep(e0,e1,x) - smoothstep(e2,e3,x);
}


/* A pulsetrain of smoothsteps: a signal that repeats with a given
 * period and is 0 when 0 <= mod(x/period,1) < edge, and 1 when
 * mod(x/period,1) > edge.
 */
float smoothpulsetrain (float e0, e1, e2, e3, period, x)
{
    return smoothpulse (e0, e1, e2, e3, mod(x,period));
}
```

This results in a perfectly regular pattern of concentric rings, as shown in Figure 12.8. Because we are philosophically opposed to regular patterns, we will "noise it up" in a variety of ways:

- Warp the domain by using vector-based fBm to offset Pshad:

```
vector offset = vfBm(Pshad*ringnoisefreq,dPshad*ringnoisefreq,
        2, 4, 0.5);
point Pring = Pshad + ringnoise*offset;
```

- Add some low-frequency noise() of z to simulate the tree trunk not being quite aligned with the z-axis:

```
Pring += trunkwobble *
            vsnoise(zcomp(Pshad)*trunkwobblefreq) * vector(1,1,0);
```

The final multiply by $(1,1,0)$ squashes the z component of the vsnoise, thus offsetting only the x, y components, based on noise of the z component.

- Add some noise() of the angle about the z-axis, to simulate rings that are not quite round:

```
r += angularwobble * smoothstep(0,5,r)
        * snoise (angularwobblefreq*(Pring)*vector(1,1,0.1));
```

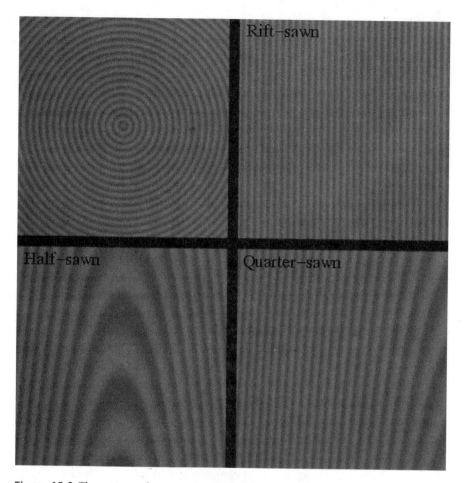

Figure 12.8 The pattern of concentric rings of dark and light wood.

■ Add `noise(r)` to r to prevent all rings from being equally spaced:

```
float dr = filterwidth(r);
r += 0.5*filteredsnoise(r,dr);
```

The resulting ring structure is shown in Figure 12.9. This is getting closer to the large-scale structure, but we still need the fine grain for close-ups. First, we must find a domain for our noise grain. We will use our original Pshad scaled by a high-frequency `grainfreq`. Furthermore, we want our grains to be long and thin, stretched out in the z-direction, which we achieved by multiplying the domain by `vector(1,1,0.05)` (remember that multiplication of vectors is done component by component, so this squashes the domain by a factor of 20 in the z-direction):

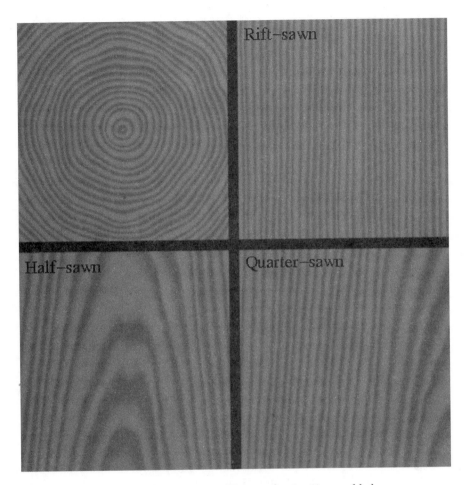

Figure 12.9 The ring pattern after several layers of noise() are added.

```
point Pgrain = Pshad*grainfreq*vector(1,1,.05);
float dPgrain = dPshad*grainfreq;
```

At this point, just calculating noise(Pshad) does not quite give the look we wanted. Instead, after a couple hours of trial and error, this author hit on the following unrolled fBm loop:

```
float grain = 0;
float i, amp=1;
for (i = 0;  i < 2;  i += 1) {
    float grain1valid = 1-smoothstep(.2,.6,dPgrain);
    if (grain1valid > 0) {
        float g = grain1valid * snoise (Pgrain);
```

```
        g *= (0.3 + 0.7*inring);
        g = pow(clamp(0.8 - (g),0,1),2);
        g = smoothstep (0.5, 1, g);
        if (i == 0)
            inring *= (1-0.4*grain1valid);
        grain = max (grain, g);
    }
    Pgrain *= 2;
    dPgrain *= 2;
    amp *= 0.5;
}
return mix (inring, 1, grain);
```

There is little apparent rhyme or reason to this code. Like much shader pattern generation, it is simply the result of trial and error, and a little intuition about the shape of these functions. However, you should be able to extract some meaning from the loop: it adds two octaves of grain; it attempts to antialias by fading out the grain at the Nyquist limit; it makes the grain stronger in the dark sections of the rings; it uses smoothstep and pow to sharpen the grain appearance; and for the lower frequency of grain, it scales down the inring value. Our reason for scaling inring is that for close-ups, the grain is the dominant feature. For far shots, the grains visually merge to contribute to the ring look.

We combine inring (which is 1 when in the dark portion of the rings) with grain (which is 1 inside a grain) to form the final blending value between the light and dark woods:

```
return mix (inring*ringy, 1, grain);
```

The meaning of the mix is that when grain==0, we return the ring value, but when grain==1, we return the dark wood, regardless of the ring. Finally, we present the completed shader (Listing 12.3), which modularizes the wood pattern into a reusable function, uses the result to blend between light and dark wood as well as to displace down slightly in the grains, and uses a basic plastic illumination model (as this is for unfinished wood). The results are shown in Figure 12.10.

Listing 12.3 The oak.sl shader implements a simple, unfinished oak wood grain.

```
/**********************************************************************
 * oak.sl
 *
 * Description: makes procedural solid texture that looks very much like
 *    wood grain.  The rings surround the z-axis, so to position the
 *    pattern, one should translate the shadingspace (which defaults to
 *    "shader").  This makes a fairly plain, unfinished wood that looks
 *    very much like oak.                                           ▶
```

Listing 12.3 (continued)

```
* Parameters for the coordinate mapping:
*    shadingspace - space in which the pattern is laid out
*    shadingfreq - overall scaling factor for the pattern
*    Pref - if supplied, gives the reference pose
*
* Parameters for the color and pattern:
*    Clightwood - the light, "background" wood color
*    Cdarkwood - the darker color in the ring/grain
*    ringfreq - mean frequency of ring spacing
*    ringunevenness - 0=equally spaced rings, larger is unequally spaced
*    grainfreq - frequency of the fine grain
*    ringnoise, ringnoisefreq - general warping of the domain
*    trunkwobble, trunkwobblefreq - controls noise that wobbles the
*        axis of the trunk so that it's not perfectly on the z-axis.
*    angularwobble, angularwobblefreq - warping indexed by angle about
*        the z-axis.
*    ringy, grainy - overall scale on the degree to which rings and
*        grain are weighted.  0 turns one off; 1 makes full effect.
*    divotdepth - depth (in shader units) of the displacement due to
*        ring or grain.
*    truedisp - 1 for true displacement; 0 for bump mapping
*
* Parameters for illumination model:
*    Ka, Kd, Ks, roughness - the usual meaning
************************************************************************/

#include "project.h"
#include "pshad.h"
#include "material.h"
#include "displace.h"

float
oaktexture (point Pshad;  float dPshad;
            float ringfreq, ringunevenness, grainfreq;
            float ringnoise, ringnoisefreq;
            float trunkwobble, trunkwobblefreq;
            float angularwobble, angularwobblefreq;
            float ringy, grainy;)
{
    /* We shade based on Pshad, but we add several layers of warping: */
    /* Some general warping of the domain */
    vector offset = vfBm(Pshad*ringnoisefreq,dPshad*ringnoisefreq,
                         2, 4, 0.5);
    point Pring = Pshad + ringnoise*offset;
    /* The trunk isn't totally steady xy as you go up in z */
    Pring += trunkwobble *
                vsnoise(zcomp(Pshad)*trunkwobblefreq) * vector(1,1,0);

    /* Calculate the radius from the center. */
    float r2 = sqr(xcomp(Pring)) + sqr(ycomp(Pring));
```

▶

Listing 12.3 (continued)

```
    float r = sqrt(r2) * ringfreq;
    /* Add some noise around the trunk */
    r += angularwobble * smoothstep(0,5,r)
            * snoise (angularwobblefreq*(Pring)*vector(1,1,0.1));

    /* Now add some noise so all rings are not equal width */
    extern float du, dv;
    float dr = filterwidth(r);
    r += 0.5*filteredsnoise(r,dr);

    float inring = smoothpulsetrain (.1, .55, .7, .95, 1, r);

    point Pgrain = Pshad*grainfreq*vector(1,1,.05);
    float dPgrain = filterwidthp(Pgrain);
    float grain = 0;
    float i, amp=1;
    for (i = 0;  i < 2;  i += 1) {
        float grain1valid = 1-smoothstep(.2,.6,dPgrain);
        if (grain1valid > 0) {
            float g = grain1valid * snoise (Pgrain);
            g *= (0.3 + 0.7*inring);
            g = pow(clamp(0.8 - (g),0,1),2);
            g = grainy * smoothstep (0.5, 1, g);
            if (i == 0)
                inring *= (1-0.4*grain1valid);
            grain = max (grain, g);
        }
        Pgrain *= 2;
        dPgrain *= 2;
        amp *= 0.5;
    }

    return mix (inring*ringy, 1, grain);
}
surface
oak ( float Ka = 1, Kd = 1, Ks = .25, roughness = 0.2;
        DEFAULT_PSHAD_PARAMS;
        float ringfreq = 8, ringunevenness = 0.5;
        float ringnoise = 0.02, ringnoisefreq = 1;
        float grainfreq = 25;
        float trunkwobble = 0.15, trunkwobblefreq = 0.025;
        float angularwobble = 1, angularwobblefreq = 1.5;
        float divotdepth = 0.05;
        color Clightwood = color (.5, .2, .067);       /* light wood color */
        color Cdarkwood = color(0.15, 0.077, 0.028);
        float ringy = 1, grainy = 1;
        float truedisp = 0;
    )
```

▶

Listing 12.3 (continued)

```
{
    GET_PSHAD;
    normal Nf = faceforward(normalize(N),I);

    float wood;
    wood = oaktexture (Pshad, dPshad, ringfreq, ringunevenness, grainfreq,
                       ringnoise, ringnoisefreq, trunkwobble,
                       trunkwobblefreq, angularwobble,
                       angularwobblefreq, ringy, grainy);
    color Cwood = mix (Clightwood, Cdarkwood, wood);
    Nf = faceforward(Displace (Nf, "shader", -wood*divotdepth,
                     truedisp), I);

    /* Illumination model - just use plastic */
    Ci = MaterialPlastic (Nf, Cwood, Ka, Kd, Ks*(1-0.5*wood), roughness);
    Oi = Os;  Ci *= Oi;
}
```

Figure 12.10 Example uses of the oak shader. Each object uses slightly different parameters to the shader, resulting in different looks and feels for the wood. (Trivia: the elephant is called "Gumbo" and was modeled by Ed Catmull.) See also color plate 12.10.

12.5 Wood Planks

The shader from the previous section is adequate to shade an object that is presumed to be carved from a single block of wood. An obvious extension is to make finished planks, as you would see on a floor. One strategy would be to divide up the 2D domain into individual planks, then simply reference the oak pattern using a different "per-plank" offset into the texture function. We will divide ss and tt space into planks using a method reminiscent of the tilepattern function that we used in Section 12.3. First, we find which "plank column" we're in:

```
swhichplank = floor (ss/plankwidth);  /* integer selector */
splank = ss - swhichplank*plankwidth; /* relative place within the
    strip */
```

Instead of doing exactly the same thing for t, we shift the t coordinate by a different amount for every plank column, prior to taking the combination of perpendicular pulse trains:

```
float newt = tt + planklength*cellnoise(swhichplank);
twhichplank = floor (newt/planklength);
    tplank = newt - twhichplank*planklength;
    return filteredpulsetrain (groovewidth, plankwidth,
        ss+groovewidth/2, ds)
        * filteredpulsetrain (grooveheight, planklength,
                              newt+grooveheight/2, dt);
```

Knowing which plank we are on, we can call oaktexture with a different offset for every plank (again using cellnoise). We can shift the color of each plank independently, also reusing the varyEach function from Section 12.3. (Are you noticing the trend? Once we hit on a good idea, we put it in our library and reuse it as frequently as we can get away with it.)

```
point Ppat = point(splank-0.5,height-0.01*tplank,tplank)
        + vector(1,5,10)* (vector cellnoise(swhichplank,
                            twhichplank) - 0.5);
float wood = oaktexture (Ppat, dPshad, ringfreq, ringunevenness,
                         grainfreq, ringnoise, ringnoisefreq,
                         trunkwobble, trunkwobblefreq,
                         angularwobble, angularwobblefreq,
                         ringy, grainy);
color Cwood = mix (Clightwood, Cdarkwood, wood);
Cwood = varyEach (Cwood, plankindex, varyhue, varysat, varylum);
```

Also reused from earlier sections are the techniques for displacing the grooves and rounding the corners of the planks. We throw in some low-amplitude noise to simulate lumpy varnish and use the MaterialShinyPlastic illumination model (not an entirely bad approximation to varnished wood). See Figure 12.11 and Listing 12.4.

Figure 12.11 Example use of the oakplank shader. See also color plate 12.11.

Listing 12.4 The oakplank.sl shader implements varnished oak planks.

```
/*********************************************************************
 * oakplank.sl
 *
 * Description: makes procedural varnished wood planks.  The planks
 *    are projected onto the x-y plane, with the length aligned with
 *    the y-axis.  The subpattern within each individual plank is just
 *    a shifted version of the oaktexture function from oak.h.
 *
 * Parameters for the coordinate mapping:
 *    shadingspace - space in which the pattern is laid out
 *    shadingfreq - overall scaling factor for the pattern
 *    Pref - if supplied, gives the reference pose
 *
 * Parameters for the pattern of the plank structure:
 *    plankwidth, planklength - size of the planks
 *    groovewidth, grooveheight - width of the grooves between planks
 *    Cgroove - color of the grooves between the planks
 *    groovedepth - how far down do the grooves displace?
 *    edgewidth - how close to the plank border does the wood start to curl?
 *    varyhue, varysat, varylum - control plank-to-plank color variation   ▶
```

Listing 12.4 (continued)

```
 * Parameters for the color and pattern of the wood grain:
 *    Clightwood - the light, "background" wood color
 *    Cdarkwood - the darker color in the ring/grain
 *    ringfreq - mean frequency of ring spacing
 *    ringunevenness - 0=equally spaced rings, larger is unequally spaced
 *    grainfreq - frequency of the fine grain
 *    ringnoise, ringnoisefreq - general warping of the domain
 *    trunkwobble, trunkwobblefreq - controls noise that wobbles the
 *        axis of the trunk so that it's not perfectly on the z-axis.
 *    angularwobble, angularwobblefreq - warping indexed by angle about
 *        the z-axis.
 *    ringy, grainy - overall scale on the degree to which rings and
 *        grain are weighted.  0 turns one off; 1 makes full effect.
 *    divotdepth - depth (in shader units) of the displacement due to
 *        ring or grain.
 *    truedisp - 1 for true displacement; 0 for bump mapping
 *
 * Parameters for illumination model:
 *    Ka, Kd, Ks, roughness - the usual meaning
 *    Kr, blur, eta - reflection parameters for the tile
 *    envname, envspace, envrad - environment mapping controls
 *    rayjitter, raysamples - ray tracing controls
 *    varnishlump, varnishlumpfreq - amp & freq of lumpiness in the varnish
 *******************************************************************/
#include "project.h"
#include "pshad.h"
#include "material.h"
#include "noises.h"
#include "displace.h"
#include "patterns.h"

#include "oak.h"


/* Given 2D texture coordinates ss,tt, filter widths ds, dt, and the
 * width and height of the grooves between tiles, figure out which
 * (integer indexed) plank we are on and what coordinates within our
 * individual plank we are shading.
 */
float
plankpattern (float ss, tt, ds, dt;
              float plankwidth, planklength;
              float groovewidth, grooveheight;
              output float swhichplank, twhichplank;
              output float splank, tplank;)
{
    /* Find which s plank we're on and our s coordinate within it */
    swhichplank = floor (ss/plankwidth);
    splank = ss - swhichplank*plankwidth;
```

►

Listing 12.4 (continued)

```
     /* Shift in t a random amount for each plank column */
     float newt = tt + planklength*cellnoise(swhichplank);
     /* Find which t plank we're on and our t coordinate within it */
     twhichplank = floor (newt/planklength);
     tplank = newt - twhichplank*planklength;
     /* Calculate our "in-plank" value by multiplying two perpendicular
      * filtered pulsetrain functions.
      */
     return filteredpulsetrain (groovewidth, plankwidth,
                                ss+groovewidth/2, ds)
        * filteredpulsetrain (grooveheight, planklength,
                              newt+grooveheight/2, dt);
}


surface
oakplank ( float Ka = 1, Kd = 1, Ks = .75, roughness = 0.1;
           float Kr = 1, blur = 0, eta = 1.5;
           DECLARE_DEFAULTED_ENVPARAMS;
           DEFAULT_PSHAD_PARAMS;
           float ringfreq = 8, ringunevenness = 0.5;
           float ringnoise = 0.02, ringnoisefreq = 1;
           float grainfreq = 25;
           float trunkwobble = 0.15, trunkwobblefreq = 0.025;
           float angularwobble = 1, angularwobblefreq = 1.5;
           float divotdepth = 0.012, truedisp = 0;
           color Clightwood = color (.5, .2, .067);      /* light wood color
*/
           color Cdarkwood = color(0.15, 0.077, 0.028);
           color Cgroove = color(0.02, 0.02, 0.02);
           float ringy = 1, grainy = 1;
           float plankwidth = 2, planklength = 30;
           float groovewidth = 0.05, grooveheight = 0.05;
           float varyhue = 0.015, varysat = 0.1, varylum = 0.5;
           float groovedepth = 0.03, edgewidth = 0.1;
           float varnishlump = 0.01, varnishlumpfreq = 0.5;
       )
{
    GET_PSHAD;
    float ss = xcomp(Pshad), tt = ycomp(Pshad), height = zcomp(Pshad);
    float dss = filterwidth(ss), dtt = filterwidth(tt);

    /*
     * Find out where in the pattern we are: which plank we're on, and
     * the (splank,tplank) coordinates (both on [0,1]) within our tile.
     */
    float swhichplank, twhichplank, splank, tplank;
    float inplank = plankpattern (ss, tt, dss, dtt, plankwidth,
                                  planklength, groovewidth, grooveheight,
                                  swhichplank, twhichplank, splank,
                                  tplank);                              ▶
```

Listing 12.4 (continued)

```
float plankindex = swhichplank + 13*twhichplank;

point Ppat = point(splank-0.5,height-0.01*tplank,tplank)
        + vector(1,5,10)* (vector cellnoise(swhichplank,twhichplank)
                 - 0.5);

float wood = oaktexture (Ppat, dPshad, ringfreq, ringunevenness,
                     grainfreq, ringnoise, ringnoisefreq,
                       trunkwobble, trunkwobblefreq, angularwobble,
                       angularwobblefreq, ringy, grainy);
color Cwood = mix (Clightwood, Cdarkwood, wood);
Cwood = varyEach (Cwood, plankindex, varyhue, varysat, varylum);
Cwood = mix (Cgroove, Cwood, inplank);

/* Displacement: the edges of the planks displace down a bit, as do
 * the grooves between planks.
 */
float edgedisp = smoothpulse (0, edgewidth, plankwidth-edgewidth,
                          plankwidth, splank);
edgedisp *= smoothpulse (0, edgewidth, planklength-edgewidth,
                     planklength, tplank);
normal Nf = faceforward (normalize(N), I);
float disp = -wood*divotdepth + groovedepth*(edgedisp-1);
disp += varnishlump * filteredsnoise (Pshad*varnishlumpfreq,
                              dPshad*varnishlumpfreq);
Nf = faceforward(Displace (Nf, "shader", disp, truedisp), I);

/* Illumination model
 * Less specular in the grooves, more specular in the dark wood.
 */
float specadjusted = 1 + .3*wood - 0.8*(1-inplank);
Ci = MaterialShinyPlastic (Nf, Cwood, Ka, Kd, specadjusted*Ks,
                       roughness, specadjusted*Kr,
                       blur, eta, ENVPARAMS);
Oi = Os;   Ci *= Oi;
}
```

12.6   Smoke: A Volume Shader

There is only one important shader type that we have not yet covered: volume
shaders. Just as each geometric primitive may have a surface and a displacement
shader bound to it, so too may each primitive have an "atmosphere." Because
atmosphere shaders bind to geometric primitives, just like surface or displacement
shaders do, you must have an object in the background for the atmosphere shader
to run. In other words, pixels with no geometry at all "behind" them will not run
any atmosphere shaders.

Table 12.1: Global variables available inside volume shaders.	
point P	Position on the surface we are shading (at one end of the incident ray).
vector I	The *incident* vector through the volume. For atmosphere shaders, I points from the camera (or viewing position) toward P.
color Ci, Oi	The surface color and opacity of the viewing ray. Modifying these two variables is the primary goal of a volume shader.

Listing 12.5 The fog volume shader implements a simple exponential fading with distance.

```
volume
fog (float distance = 1;
     color background = color(.5,.5,.5);)
{
    float d = 1 - exp (-length(I)/distance);
    Ci = mix (Ci, background, d);
    Oi = mix (Oi, color(1,1,1), d);
}
```

Such an atmosphere, implemented by a volume shader, may modify Ci and Oi due to the volume between the camera position and P. Table 12.1 shows the limited global variables available inside volume shaders.

A simple volume shader suitable to being an atmosphere is the fog shader shown in Listing 12.5. This shader implements a simple exponential absorption model of atmosphere by fading to a background color with distance.

The fog shader has a major deficiency: it does not take into consideration the actual light scattered by the volume into the camera (which should be affected by light intensities and shadows). More sophisticated atmospheric effects are possible if we *ray march* along the incident ray I, sampling illumination and accounting for atmospheric extinction. Typically, this is done with the following algorithm:

> Choose an appropriate step size for marching along the ray.
> $len = $ length(I)
> $P_{cur} = $ P-I;
> while ($len > 0$) {
>   sample the smoke density and light at P_{cur}
> C_{vol} += $(1 - O_{vol})$ + *stepsize* * (scattered light) ;
> O_{vol} += $(1 - O_{vol})$ + *stepsize* * (local density) ;
> P_{cur} += *stepsize* * normalize(I) ;
> len -= *stepsize* ;
> }

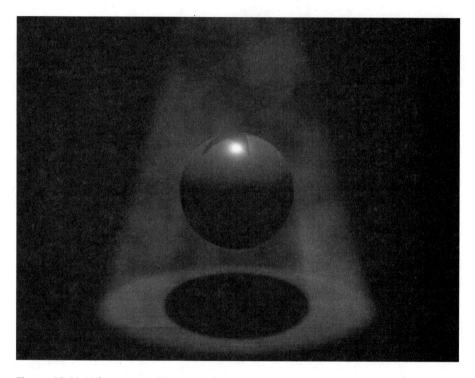

Figure 12.12 Volumetric smoke using the smoke shader. See also color plate 12.12.

Thus, we are taking equal steps through the volume along the viewing ray. At each step, we sample the density of the smoke and the illumination arriving from the light sources at that point. Some light reflects from the smoke particles and scatters toward the viewer. Also, the density of the volume obscures the light coming from behind the volume (including other parts of the volume behind the current point).

Listing 12.6 is a shader that implements such a ray marching algorithm to simulate smoke. If the light sources in the scene cast shadows, you should be able to see the shadows in the smoke. (See Figure 12.12.)

Careful examination of the smoke shader will reveal several useful subtleties and areas for improvement (left as potential exercises):

- *Trapezoidal integration* is used. The volume is divided into segments, and for each segment the beginning and ending densities and light values are averaged to compute a mean density and lighting value for the segment.
- Separate parameters scale the density of the smoke as it applies to its tendency to obscure things behind it, versus the ability of the dense smoke to scatter light to the viewer. This allows you to, for example, make the volume scatter much light without blocking light behind it, or to obscure the background without introducing any newly scattered light.

Listing 12.6 `smoke.sl`: a volume shader for a smoky atmosphere.

```
/*******************************************************************
 * smoke.sl
 *
 * Description:
 *    This is a volume shader for smoke.  Trapezoidal integration is
 *    used to find scattering and extinction.
 *
 * Parameters:
 *    opacdensity - overall smoke density control as it affects its ability
 *         to block light from behind it.
 *    lightdensity - smoke density control as it affects light scattering
 *         toward the viewer.
 *    integstart, integend - bounds along the viewing ray direction of the
 *         integration of atmospheric effects.
 *    stepsize - step size for integration
 *    smokefreq, smokeoctaves, smokevary - control the fBm of the noisy
 *         smoke. If either smokeoctaves or smokevary is 0, there is
 *         no noise to the smoke.
 *    scatter - when non-1, can be used to give wavelength-dependent
 *         extinction coefficients.
 *******************************************************************/

#include "noises.h"


/* For point P (we are passed both the current and shader space
 * coordinates), gather illumination from the light sources and
 * compute the smoke density at that point.  Only count lights tagged
 * with the "__foglight" parameter.
 */
void
smokedensity (point Pcur, Pshad;
              uniform float smokevary, smokefreq, smokeoctaves;
              output color Lscatter; output float smoke)
{
    Lscatter = 0;
    illuminance (Pcur) {
        extern color Cl;
        float foglight = 1;
        lightsource("__foglight",foglight);
        if (foglight > 0)
            Lscatter += Cl;
    }
    if (smokeoctaves > 0 && smokevary > 0) {
        point Psmoke = Pshad * smokefreq;
        smoke = snoise (Psmoke);
        /* Optimize: one octave only if not lit */
        if (comp(Lscatter,0)+comp(Lscatter,1)+comp(Lscatter,2) > 0.01)
            smoke += 0.5 * fBm (Psmoke*2, 0, smokeoctaves-1, 2, 0.5);      ▶
```

Listing 12.6 (continued)

```
        smoke = smoothstep(-1,1,smokevary*smoke);
    } else {
        smoke = 0.5;
    }
}


/* Return a component-by-component exp() of a color */
color colorexp (color C)
{
    return color (exp(comp(C,0)), exp(comp(C,1)), exp(comp(C,2)));
}


volume
smoke (float opacdensity = 1, lightdensity = 1;
       float integstart = 0, integend = 100;
       float stepsize = 0.1, maxsteps = 100;
       color scatter = 1;    /* for sky, try (1, 2.25, 21) */
       float smokeoctaves = 0, smokefreq = 1, smokevary = 1;)
{
    point Worigin = P - I;     /* Origin of volume ray */
    point origin = transform ("shader", Worigin);
    float dtau, last_dtau;
    color li, last_li;

    /* Integrate forwards from the start point */
    float d = integstart + random()*stepsize;
    vector IN = normalize (vtransform ("shader", I));
    vector WIN = vtransform ("shader", "current", IN);

    /* Calculate a reasonable step size */
    float end = min (length (I), integend) - 0.0001;
    float ss = min (stepsize, end-d);

    /* Get the in-scattered light and the local smoke density for the
     * beginning of the ray
     */
    smokedensity (Worigin + d*WIN, origin + d*IN,
                smokevary, smokefreq, smokeoctaves, last_li, last_dtau);
    color Cv = 0, Ov = 0;    /* color & opacity of volume that we
                                accumulate */
    while (d <= end) {
        /* Take a step and get the local scattered light and smoke
           density */
        ss = clamp (ss, 0.005, end-d);
        d += ss;
        smokedensity (Worigin + d*WIN, origin + d*IN,
                    smokevary, smokefreq, smokeoctaves, li, dtau);         ▶
```

Listing 12.6 (continued)

```
            /* Find the blocking and light-scattering contribution of
             * the portion of the volume covered by this step.
             */
            float tau = opacdensity * ss/2 * (dtau + last_dtau);
            color lighttau = lightdensity * ss/2 * (li*dtau +
                                           last_li*last_dtau);

            /* Composite with exponential extinction of background light */
            Cv += (1-Ov) * lighttau;
            Ov += (1-Ov) * (1 - colorexp (-tau*scatter));
            last_dtau = dtau;
            last_li = li;
        }

    /* Ci & Oi are the color and opacity of the background element.
     * Now Cv is the light contributed by the volume itself, and Ov is the
     * opacity of the volume, i.e. (1-Ov)*Ci is the light from the
     * background that makes it through the volume.  So just composite!
     */
    Ci = Cv + (1-Ov)*Ci;
    Oi = Ov + (1-Ov)*Oi;
}
```

- The `smokedensity` function makes two important choices. First is the scattering function. Here we just sum the `Cl` contributions from each light. Thus, we are using a simple isotropic scattering function for the volume. For a different, and possibly more physically correct, appearance, we could use a different scattering function that depended on the particle size and angle between the light and viewing directions. Second, we compute a simple `fBm` function for the smoke. Obviously, we could get a very different appearance to the smoke density by substituting a different density function.
- Setting either `smokeoctaves` or `smokevary` to 0 results in the smoke being homogeneous rather than varying spatially.

Volume shaders of this type can be very expensive. The computational expense is proportional to the number of iterations of the while loop, which is determined by the step size and the length of I. Therefore, it is important to choose your step size carefully—too large a step size will result in banding and quantization artifacts, while too small a step size results in very long render times. You will probably need to tune the step size carefully on a scene-by-scene basis.

The `smoke` shader is reasonably robust, and is used for all of the figures in Chapter 14. Chapter 15 discusses even more uses of volume shaders of this type for special effects.

12.7   Lens Flare and "Clipping Plane" Shaders

People ask all the time how to do "lens flare"—those artifacts that occur when you point a real camera at a bright light source and you can see all sorts of interreflections from inside the lens system. This is an artifact that real-life photographers and cinematographers try hard to avoid, though *very* occasionally they can be used to give a mood of extreme brightness or heat (a scene from *Lawrence of Arabia* comes to mind). For some reason, many CG artists purposely add these artifacts to many of their scenes.

If you look at real lens flare, or some of the more low-key, tasteful CG lens flare, you will find several common features:

- There will be a bright glow, or "bloom" effect, around the directly visible light source. This is assumed to be related to overexposure or saturation of the film.
- There is a "starburst" pattern and a faint "rainbow" surrounding the image of the light. In real light, these are due to diffraction effects of the camera mechanism or even your eyelashes.
- There are a number of faint circles or blotches distributed about the axis joining the center of the image and the position of the light source. These are presumably out-of-focus glints of light reflecting off of lens elements or other surfaces inside the camera itself.

Ordinary light sources don't have geometry associated with them, and even area light sources (in renderers that support them) can't account for these effects "where the lights aren't." So how do you get these effects in the lens, if there is no obvious shader attached to the light? The answer is surprisingly simple: we place a flat patch right in front of the camera, but closer than any other object—in other words, right next to the near clipping plane. This is *very* easy in *PRMan*, using the CoordSysTransform command:

```
AttributeBegin
CoordSysTransform "screen"
Surface "lensflare"
Patch "bilinear" "P" [ -2 2 0  2 2 0   -2 -2 0  2 -2 0]
AttributeEnd
```

This is of course in the World block. The CoordSysTransform command sets the active transformation to the one that matches the name of the argument, in this case "screen" space. Screen space is postperspective, so a $z = 0$ in "screen" space corresponds to being right on the near clipping plane. This postperspective space is not a big problem for *PRMan*, which works by projecting geometry into "camera" space, then eventually into "screen". This is especially convenient, since the preceding fragment places the patch right on the near clipping plane without even knowing where the near clip plane is!

Not all renderers can do this. In particular, ray tracers typically work by transforming the ray origin and direction into object space by using the *inverse* transformation, then testing the ray intersection against an object, doing calculations in object space. But in this case the ray origin is at the origin of "camera" space, and "object" space is "screen" space. Thus, we run right up against the singularity in the perspective transformation. So using CoordSysTransform with coordinate systems that contain perspective transformation is difficult for many renderers, including *BMRT*.

But all is not lost. We can still CoordSysTransform to "camera" space, then simply translate to be right on the other side of the clipping plane. For example, suppose that the near clipping plane was known to be at a distance of 0.1 from the camera. Then the following fragment would place the patch right on the other side of the plane:

```
AttributeBegin
CoordSysTransform "camera"
Translate 0 0 0.1001
Surface "lensflare"
Patch "bilinear" "P" [ -2 2 0  2 2 0   -2 -2 0  2 -2 0]
AttributeEnd
```

Notice that this is slightly less convenient than going straight to "screen" space, because you will have to know the exact value of the near clipping plane distance.

So now that we know how to place a patch in front of all other geometry, how do we write a shader to compute the lens flare but keep what's behind it visible? The basic outline of our shader is straightforward:

```
Ci = 0;
Oi = 0;
illuminance (P, vector "camera" (0,0,1), PI/2) {
    /* calculate the contribution of each source, for
     * bloom, starburst, rainbow, and spots
     */
    Ci += /* this light's contribution */
}
```

Thus, we are gathering from each light source that is visible from the camera's origin, E, and that is in the general direction that the camera is looking. We set Oi=0 because the lens flare merely *adds* light to the pixels without blocking the geometry that is behind the lens flare patch.

Because most of the effects in the shader are really happening in the 2D viewing plane rather than in 3D, we will transform both the position on the lens plane and the light positions into a common screen-like space:

```
point Pndc = (transform("NDC", P) - vector (.5, .5, 0))*2;
Pndc *= vector(aspect, 1, 0);
float dPndc = filterwidthp(Pndc);
```

The aspect is a quantity we compute from the image aspect ratio (see the final program listing for implementation). Similarly, we project the light position into the same space and also compute an attenuation based on how far outside the lens field of view the light is, the overall brightness of the light, and the angle and distance between the shading point and the light:

```
illuminance (P, vector "camera" (0,0,1), PI/2) {
    float atten = acos(zcomp(normalize(vector transform("camera",
                                                        P+L))));
    atten = 1 - smoothstep(1, 2, abs(atten)/(lensfov/2));
    float brightness = atten * intensity
                        * (comp(Cl,0)+comp(Cl,1)+comp(Cl,2))/3;
    point Plight = (transform("NDC", E+L) - vector (.5, .5, 0))*2;
    Plight *= vector(aspect, 1, 0);
    vector Lvec = Plight - Pndc;
    float angle = atan (ycomp(Lvec), xcomp(Lvec)) + PI;
    float dist = length(Lvec);
         .
         .
         .
```

The bloom effect is achieved by making a pleasing amount of light that falls off as we get farther from the light's projection position:

```
float radius = sqrt(brightness)*5*mix(.2, bloomradius, urand());
float bloom = pnoise (bloomnpoints*angle/(2*PI), bloomnpoints);
bloom = mix (0.5, bloom, bloomstarry);
bloom = mix (1, bloom, smoothstep(0, 0.5, dist/radius));
bloom = pow(1-smoothstep(0.0, radius*bloom, dist),bloomfalloff);
Cflare += bloom * (bloomintensity / intensity) / brightness;
```

We use pnoise to help give a wobbly outline to the glowing bloom. The starburst effect is just an exaggerated pnoise calculation much like we did for bloom:

```
float radius = sqrt(brightness)*5*mix(.2, starburstradius, urand());
float star = float pnoise (starburstnpoints*angle/(2*PI),
                           starburstnpoints);
star = pow(1-smoothstep(0.0, radius*star, dist), starburstfalloff);
Cflare += star * (starburstintensity / intensity) / brightness;
```

The bloom and starburst effects can be seen individually in the top of Figure 12.13. Notice that both use a function called urand. This is a function we have written that uses cellnoise to provide a repeatable random sequence. The implementation can be inspected at the top of the body of the final shader.

The rainbow effect is also not difficult, and simply uses a spline call to generate the colors (see example in Figure 12.13):

```
color rainbow (float x, dx) {
    return filteredpulse (0, 1, x, dx)
```

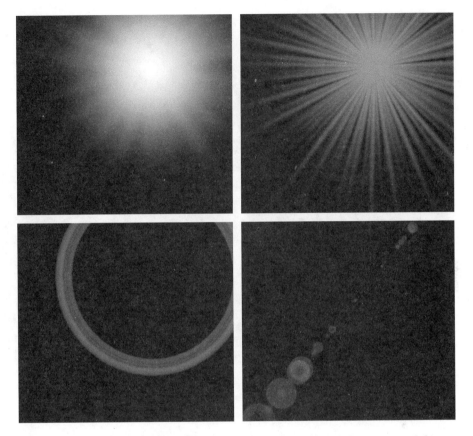

Figure 12.13 The major components of the lens flare effect: bloom (upper left), starburst (upper right), rainbow (lower left), and spots (lower right).

```
      * spline (x, color(.5,0,.5),color(.5,0,.5),color(.375,0,0.75),
              color(0,0,1),color(0,1,0),color(1,1,0),
              color(1,.5,0),color(1,0,0),color(1,0,0));
}

Cflare += brightness*(rainbowintensity / intensity)
          * rainbow((dist/rainbowradius-1)/rainbowwidth,
                  (dPndc/rainbowradius)/rainbowwidth);
```

Finally, we must make the spots. We continue using our `cellnoise`-based random number generator to lay out a large number of locations along the axis joining the image center with the light source position. For each location, we see where it is and then if we are within the spot radius we add light to make the effect. We actually implemented four kinds of spots, chosen randomly: a perfectly flat "disk," a "ring,"

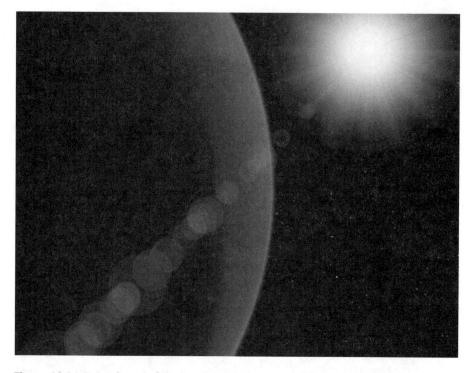

Figure 12.14 Example use of the lensflare shader. See also color plate 12.14.

a disk with a smooth outer falloff (which we call a "blot"), and a disk with less intensity in the middle (which for no apparent reason we call a "bloon"). The final shader shows the implementation of all these features and contains parameters that allow the user to choose the total number of spots as well as the relative proportions of disks, rings, blots, and bloons.

Don't spend much time trying to justify the physical processes that lie behind these effects—there really aren't any. Our shader vaguely mimics some artifacts from real lens flare but also makes up several that don't occur in real lens systems.

You should be aware that lens flare effects are a cliché (an expression that once was fresh but has become dull and stereotyped through frequent repetition). They were clever and interesting the first few times they were used, but now any clod can and does sprinkle lens flare in images where it doesn't belong. Lens flare, perhaps because it is so low-key and rare in real life but so over-the-top in CG images, can easily give a CG image a "cheesy," amateurish look. So use this shader (Listing 12.7) wisely—which means rarely, if at all, and without cranking the parameters to outrageous values. A moderately tasteful example of the final shader is shown in Figure 12.14, but frankly, even this image is pushing it.

Listing 12.7 The `lensflare.sl` shader.

```
/***************************************************************
 * lensflare.sl
 *
 * Description: This shader, when placed on a piece of geometry
 *   immediately in front of the camera, simulates lens flare.
 *   These effects happen in real cameras when the camera points
 *   toward a bright light source, resulting in interreflections
 *   within the optical elements of the lens system itself.
 *   Real lens flare is pretty plain looking and uninteresting;
 *   this shader takes some liberties but looks pretty good.
 *
 * Parameters:
 *   intensity - overall scale of intensity of all lens flare
 *           effects
 *   bloomintensity - overall intensity of the "bloom"
 *           effect. Setting this to 0 removes the bloom effect
 *           altogether.
 *   bloomradius, bloomfalloff - control the size & shape of the
 *           bloom
 *   bloomstarry, bloomnpoints - control the "starry" appearance
 *           of the bloom effect (bloomstarry=0 means perfectly
 *           round bloom)
 *   starburstintensity - overall intensity of starburst effect
 *           (0=none)
 *   starburstradius, starburstnpoints, starburstfalloff - control
 *           the size and shape of the starburst effect
 *   rainbowintensity - intensity of rainbow effect (0=none)
 *   rainbowradius, rainbowwidth - size of the rainbow
 *   nspots - number of "spots" splayed out on the axis joining
 *           the image center with the light position
 *   disky, ringy, blotty, bloony - give the relative proportions
 *           of the 4 different kinds of spots.
 *   spotintensity - overall intensity scale for the spots
 *   spotvarycolor - scale the color variation of the spots
 *   seed - random number seed for many of the computations
 *
 * WARNING: lens flare is notorious as a sign of cheesy, cheap
 *   computer graphics.  Use this effect with extreme care!
 ***************************************************************/

#include "patterns.h"

/* Helper function: compute the aspect ratio of the frame */
float aspectratio ()
{
    uniform point Pcorner0 = transform ("NDC", "screen",
            point(0,0,0));
    uniform point Pcorner1 = transform ("NDC", "screen",
            point(1,1,0));
    return (xcomp(Pcorner1)-xcomp(Pcorner0)) /
            (ycomp(Pcorner1)-ycomp(Pcorner0));
}
```

▶

Listing 12.7 (continued)

```
/* Helper function: compute the camera's diagonal field of view */
float cameradiagfov ()
{
    uniform vector corner = vector (transform("NDC","camera",
    point(1,1,0)));
    uniform float halfangle = acos (normalize(corner) .
    vector(0,0,1)); return 2*halfangle;
}


color rainbow (float x, dx)
{
#define R          color(1,0,0)
#define O          color(1,.5,0)
#define Y          color(1,1,0)
#define G          color(0,1,0)
#define B          color(0,0,1)
#define Ii         color(.375,0,0.75)
#define V          color(0.5,0,0.5)
    return filteredpulse (0, 1, x, dx) * spline (x, V,V,Ii,B,G,Y,O,R,R);
}


surface
lensflare ( float intensity = 1.0;

            float bloomintensity = 1;
            float bloomradius = 0.5;
            float bloomstarry = 0.75;
            float bloomnpoints = 25;
            float bloomfalloff = 8;

            float starburstintensity = 0.075;
            float starburstradius = 0.5;
            float starburstnpoints = 100;
            float starburstfalloff = 3;

            float rainbowintensity = 0.03;
            float rainbowradius = 0.5;
            float rainbowwidth = 0.2;

            float nspots = 50;
            float disky = 3;
            float ringy = 1;
            float blotty = 1;
            float bloony = 1;
            float spotintensity = 0.08;
            float spotvarycolor = 0.5;

            float seed = 143;
    )
```

▶

Listing 12.7 (continued)

```
{
    uniform float nrand = 0;
    uniform float urand () {
        extern uniform float nrand, seed;
        nrand += 1;
        return cellnoise(nrand, seed);
    }


    Ci = 0;
    Oi = 0;

    uniform float aspect = abs(aspectratio());
    uniform float lensfov = cameradiagfov();

    point Pndc = (transform("NDC", P) - vector (.5, .5, 0))*2;
    Pndc *= vector(aspect, 1, 0);
    float dPndc = filterwidthp(Pndc);

    illuminance (P, vector "camera" (0,0,1), PI/2) {
        float atten = acos(zcomp(normalize(vector transform("camera",
                P+L))));
        atten = 1 - smoothstep(1, 2, abs(atten)/(lensfov/2));

        float brightness = atten*intensity*(comp(Cl,0)+comp(Cl,1)+comp
                (Cl,2))/3;

        color Cflare = 0;

        nrand = 0;
        point Plight = (transform("NDC", P+L) - vector (.5, .5, 0))*2;
        Plight *= vector(aspect, 1, 0);

        vector Lvec = Plight - Pndc;
        float angle = atan (ycomp(Lvec), xcomp(Lvec)) + PI;

        /*
         * Handle the image of the lamp.  There are 3 effects:
         * the bloom, a small red ring flare, and the triple starburst.
         */
        float dist = length(Plight - Pndc);

        if (bloomintensity > 0) {
            float radius = sqrt(brightness)*5*mix(.2, bloomradius, urand());
            float bloom = pnoise (bloomnpoints*angle/(2*PI), bloomnpoints);
            bloom = mix (0.5, bloom, bloomstarry);
            bloom = mix (1, bloom, smoothstep(0, 0.5, dist/radius));
            bloom = pow(1-smoothstep(0.0, radius*bloom, dist),bloomfalloff);
            Cflare += bloom * (bloomintensity / intensity) / brightness;
        }                                                             ▶
```

Listing 12.7 (continued)

```
/* Starburst */
if (starburstintensity > 0) {
    float radius = sqrt(brightness)*5*mix(.2, starburstradius,
            urand());
    float star = float pnoise (starburstnpoints*angle/(2*PI),
                               starburstnpoints);
    star = pow(1-smoothstep(0.0, radius*star, dist),
            starburstfalloff);
    Cflare += star * (starburstintensity / intensity) / brightness;
}

/* Rainbow */
if (rainbowintensity > 0) {
    Cflare += brightness*(rainbowintensity / intensity)
        * rainbow((dist/rainbowradius-1)/rainbowwidth,
                  (dPndc/rainbowradius)/rainbowwidth);
}

/*
 * Now emit the random rings themselves
 */
vector axis = normalize(vector Plight);
uniform float i;
nrand = 20;    /* Reset on purpose! */
for (i = 0; i < nspots; i += 1) {
    uniform float alongaxis = urand();
    point cntr = point (mix(-1.7, 1.7, alongaxis) * axis);
    float axisdist = distance (cntr, Pndc);
    float radius = mix (0.04, .1,
                        pow(urand(),2)) * distance(cntr,Plight);
    color clr = Cl;
    clr *= 1 + spotvarycolor * (color cellnoise(i) - 0.5);
    float bright = 1 - (2 * radius);
    bright *= bright;

    uniform float alltypes = (disky+ringy+blotty+bloony);
    uniform float type = urand()*alltypes;

    float int = 0;
    if (type < disky) {  /* Flat disk */
        int = 1 - filterstep(radius, axisdist-dPndc/2,
                            axisdist+dPndc/2);
    } else if (type < (disky+ringy)) {  /* Ring */
        int = filteredpulse (radius, radius+0.05*axisdist,
                            axisdist, dPndc);
    } else if (type < (disky+ringy+blotty)) {  /* Soft spot */
        int = 1 - smoothstep (0, radius, axisdist);
    } else {   /* Spot with soft hole in middle */
        int = smoothstep(0, radius, axisdist) -
```

▶

Listing 12.7 (continued)

```
                        filterstep(radius, axisdist-dPndc/2,
                        axisdist+dPndc/2);
            }
            Cflare += spotintensity * bright * clr * Cs * int;
        }

        Ci += Cflare * Cl * atten;
    }

    Ci *= intensity;
}
```

So why, with all these caveats about lens flare, do we present it at all? Because (1) it shows how easy it may be in RenderMan to implement something that is nominally impossible, given the right inspiration and a little shader hackery; and (2) it shows, just in case you remain unconvinced, that there is often no need to be slavishly bound to physical processes as long as the result is coherent in a way that convinces the observer of its reality. This lens flare thus achieves photosurrealism, and we still hope to inspire others along this line.

12.8 Cartoon Shaders

We will conclude this chapter with a totally different kind of shader that produces a decidedly nonphotorealistic appearance. We will attempt to simulate a cartoony look, as you would see in a traditional cel-painted animation. This has become a popular topic lately, as most or all recent 2D cel animations incorporate 3D elements into certain sequences. The trick is to avoid a jarring juxtaposition of styles when the 3D elements are combined with the real paintings by giving the 3D elements a look similar to the 2D artwork.

The approach we will take is surely naive, and much more robust methods with more controls would be required for a final shader used in a feature film. However, our shader will do the basic job and should give a sense for the technique, and possibly serve as a starting point for a more complete implementation. In addition, Chapter 16 covers additional and more complete techniques for "nonphotorealistic" rendering.

Our simplistic approach will concentrate on two primary features of the cel painting appearance. First, we note that cel paintings do not show continuous gradation of color, as do 3D renderings. Rather, there are typically only three flat colors: specular highlights, diffusely lit, and shadowed. Second, objects and characters in cel paintings are typically given thick, dark outlines.

Figure 12.15 Working toward a cel-painting appearance. A red plastic teapot (left).
Using LocIllumGlossy and LocIllumCelDiffuse illumination models to create a "flat"
look (right).

Recall the LocIllumGlossy model that we described in Section 9.5.3. With the
parameters set correctly, this provided a specular highlight that ramped up to full
intensity quickly and was flat in the center. This will serve well as our model for
highlights in our cel-paintings. We can also construct an analogous local illumination function for diffuse light:

```
color LocIllumCelDiffuse ( normal N; )
{
    color C = 0;
    extern point P;
    illuminance (P, N, PI/2) {
        extern vector L;   extern color Cl;
        float nondiff = 0;
        lightsource ("__nondiffuse", nondiff);
        if (nondiff < 1)
            C += Cl * ((1-nondiff) * smoothstep(0,0.1,N.normalize(L)));
    }
    return C;
}
```

This LocIllumCelDiffuse function operates similarly to a standard diffuse( ),
but thresholds the light value with a smoothstep. Figure 12.15 shows a teapot
with an ordinary plastic reflection model and one lit with the LocIllumGlossy and
LocIllumCelDiffuse illumination models.

Our next, and somewhat trickier, task is to draw outlines around the silhouette
edges of the object. We will base our approach on the observation that exactly at
silhouette edges, N and I are perpendicular, and therefore the dot product of N and
I will be zero. In our first attempt, we will mix between the object color and a black
outline by simply thresholding this dot product:

```
float angle = abs(normalize(N) . normalize(I));
```

Figure 12.16 Adding outlines to our cel shader. Using `angle` only makes for uneven outlines (left). Using derivatives to make the outline widths more even (right).

```
float border = 1 - step (0.3, angle);
Ci = mix (Ci, color 0, border);
```

This produces the image in Figure 12.16 (left). As you can see, though there is clearly some outlining effect, it isn't quite right. The outlines are sometimes missing, sometimes too thick, and generally uneven. This is because where curvature is high, the value of $N \cdot I$ changes rapidly, thus making a thin sliver of the portion where it is less than the threshold. But where the curvature is low and the orientation is just right, very large portions of screen space can be below the threshold value. We will correct for this unevenness by using the derivative of `angle` to scale the angle, and also we use `filterstep` to antialias the edges of the outline (see Figure 12.16 (right)):

```
float angle = abs(normalize(N) . normalize(I));
float dangle = filterwidth(angle);
float border = 1 - filterstep (5, angle/dangle);
Ci = mix (Ci, color 0, border);
```

Listing 12.8 shows our simple yet complete implementation of a shader that simulates the cel painting appearance. Figure 12.17 shows this cel shader applied to a 3D character. As simple as this approach is, it is clear that the look is very similar to a cel painting. There are, however, several tips and obvious areas for improvement:

- You should not light such "pseudo-2D" scenes as richly as a more realistic 3D scene. Very few lights (one key, one fill, and one ambient) is plenty, and simpler lighting setups will help achieve the flat look.
- Identifying outlines by examining the dot product works reasonably well for "outside silhouettes." Interior silhouettes, folds, or other feature lines are trickier. In addition, the technique doesn't do well on polygonal or other objects that don't have rounded corners. The round corners on all objects are critical for the successful appearance of the outline method.

Figure 12.17 Our celshader applied to a previously modeled 3D character.
(© Pixar Animation Studios.) See also color plate 12.17.

Listing 12.8 `cel.sl` is a naive (but functional) shader that creates a cartoony
cel-painted appearance.

```
/******************************************************************
 * cel.sl
 *
 * Description: generate flatly shaded objects that look like cartoon
 * "cel" paintings.
 *
 * Parameters for the color and pattern:
 *
 * Parameters for illumination model:
 *    Ka, Kd, Ks, roughness - the usual meaning
 *    outlinethickness - scales the thickness of the silhouette outlines
 ******************************************************************/

#include "filterwidth.h"
#include "material.h"
```

►

Listing 12.8 (continued)

```
color LocIllumCelDiffuse ( normal N; )
{
    color C = 0;
    extern point P;
    illuminance (P, N, PI/2) {
        /* Must declare because extern L & Cl because we're in a
            function */
        extern vector L;  extern color Cl;
        float nondiff = 0;
        lightsource ("__nondiffuse", nondiff);
        if (nondiff < 1)
            C += Cl * ((1-nondiff) * smoothstep(0,0.1,N.normalize(L)));
    }
    return C;
}


color MaterialCel (normal Nf;  color Cs;
                   float Ka, Kd, Ks, roughness, specsharpness;)
{
    extern vector I;
    vector IN = normalize(I), V = -IN;
    return   Cs * (Ka*ambient() + Kd*LocIllumCelDiffuse(Nf))
            + Ks * LocIllumGlossy (Nf, V, roughness/10, specsharpness);
}

color CelOutline (normal N; float outlinethickness;)
{
    extern float du, dv;
    extern color Ci, Oi;
    extern vector I;
    float angle = abs(normalize(N) . normalize(I));
    float dangle = filterwidth(angle);
    float border = 1 - filterstep (5*outlinethickness, angle/dangle);
    Oi = mix (Oi, color 1, border);
    return mix (Ci, color 0, border);
}


surface
cel ( float Ka = 1, Kd = 1, Ks = .5, roughness = 0.25;
      float outlinethickness = 1;)
{
    normal Nf = faceforward(normalize(N),I);
    Ci = MaterialCel (Nf, Cs, Ka, Kd, Ks, roughness, 0.25);
    Oi = Os;  Ci *= Oi;
    Ci = CelOutline (N, outlinethickness);
}
```

## PART FOUR

Tricks of the Trade

13 Storytelling through Lighting, a Computer Graphics Perspective

Sharon Calahan
Pixar Animation Studios

This chapter is designed as a beginning, nontechnical discussion of how lighting in computer graphics can be used to enhance visual storytelling for cinematic purposes. It collects knowledge and principles from the disciplines of design, fine art, photography, illustration, cinematography, and the psychology of visual perception. Although much of the content of this chapter is not solely applicable to lighting on the computer, its special needs are always in mind.

13.1 Introduction

The shortage of available literature on the subject led me to write this chapter. Frequently I am asked to recommend a book or two on lighting, and although several good books are available, none are ideal. Most tend to focus on the equipment and mechanics of live-action lighting without explaining how to achieve the fundamental principles of making good imagery. The commonality between live-action lighting and computer lighting is chiefly the thought process, not the equipment. Computer tools vary with implementation, are continually evolving, and are not limited by physics. In the future, those tools will be driven by the desire to see on the screen what we are able to visualize in our minds. This chapter focuses on these thought processes, while providing not only practical information but, I hope, the inspiration and resources to continue exploring.

The term *lighting* in computer animation often includes the task of describing the surface characteristics of objects (often referred to as *shaders*), as well as compositing and the integration of special effects. Here lighting is defined more in live-action terms as the design and placement of the light sources themselves, in, however, a purely computer graphics environment.

Visual storytelling is a vast topic that reaches far beyond the realm of lighting. Most of it is not noticeable on a conscious level to the viewer but adds depth and richness to the story and the visual experience. The lighting principles and techniques presented in this chapter are discussed in isolation from other visual storytelling devices. Ideally, the lighting would be designed with these other devices in mind, but that discussion would extend far beyond the scope of this chapter.

13.2 Objectives of Lighting

When asked to explain how lighting contributes to filmmaking, I often show a completely black slide to emphasize that without light, it doesn't matter how great the composition and acting are—nothing can be seen. This is an oversimplification, but it illustrates how much control the lighting designer has in revealing or hiding what we see, and its influence on the composition of the final result.

The primary purpose of cinematic lighting is to support the story by contributing to the overall visual structure of the film. The director is the storyteller, and it is his vision that the lighting designer is attempting to reveal. To that end, it is vital to understand the story point behind each shot and how it relates to sequence and to the story as a whole. It is not enough that the lighting designer simply illuminate the scene so the viewer can see what is happening, or to make it look pretty. It is the lighting designer's task to captivate the audience by emphasizing the action and enhancing the mood.

The following lighting objectives are five of the important fundamentals of good lighting design. They are borrowed and adapted from the book *Matters of Light and Depth* by Ross Lowell.

- directing the viewer's eye
- creating depth
- conveying time of day and season
- enhancing mood, atmosphere, and drama
- revealing character personality and situation

Figure 13.1 *A Bug's Life*—Bunker with uniform lighting (top), and with controlled lighting (bottom). (© Disney Enterprises, Inc. and Pixar Animation Studios.) See also color plate 13.1.

13.3   Directing the Viewer's Eye— The Study of Composition

Light is used to illuminate the scene so that the viewer can see the action. As the example in Figure 13.1 (top) illustrates, it is possible to have too much of a good thing. With light shining from everywhere, the viewer can't make sense of anything. What is going on and where are we supposed to be looking? The primary objective of good lighting is to show the viewer where to look by enhancing what is important while minimizing what isn't (Figure 13.1, bottom). Shots are often on-screen only briefly, which means the storytelling effectiveness of a shot often depends upon how well, and how quickly, the viewer's eye is led to the key story elements.

Learning to direct the viewer's eye is essentially the study of composition. The term *composition* often causes confusion because of the many different definitions assigned to it. We will use the following definition here:

Figure 13.2 *Toy Story*—Example of how lighting can alter the composition of an image: Woody with full body lighting (left) and with a strip of light over his eyes (right). (© Disney Enterprises, Inc.)

Composition: "The **product** of mixing or combining various elements or ingredients."

The word "product" is stressed because it indicates that it is the end result that is important, not the individual parts.

Composition is therefore used to collectively describe a group of related visual principles. These principles are the criteria employed to evaluate the effectiveness of an image. They are not rules to be followed, but define a structure by which to explore creative possibilities. They describe a visual vocabulary and provide methods for breaking down a complex image into manageable characteristics for subjective analysis. Besides being of interest to artists, these principles are also an important aspect of visual perception and cognitive psychology research.

The seemingly simple act of placing lights can radically change the composition and focal point of a shot. As a simple example, compare the two images of Woody in Figure 13.2. The staging and pose of the character are exactly the same. With lighting, the overall composition has changed. In this case, the focal point remains the same but is intensified in the image on the right. As an additional result, the mood of the shot and the personality of the character are also changed.

Good lighting can make a well-composed image stunning. It can also help rescue a less-than-perfect composition. The principles of composition are the tools with which the lighting designer can analyze a scene to devise ways to accentuate what is working and to minimize what is not. They are most effective in static or slow-moving scenes. Although still applicable to action shots, other principles of camera and object motion also play a large role. Most of this discussion is beyond the scope of this chapter, but suggested reading is included in the Further Reading section.

Rather than simply refer the reader at this point to a book on composition, we include a brief discussion of the primary principles needed by the lighting designer. Although each principle relates to the others, they are presented in isolation for clarity. Combining them in fresh ways is the fun part.

13.3.1 Unity/Harmony

The name of this principle suggests that the elements of the composition appear to belong together, relate to each other, and to otherwise visually agree. Where other principles of composition break down the image into specific topics for study, the principle of unity reminds the artist to take a step back and look at the image as a whole.

Although most artists rely on intuition to decide if a composition is working, the cognitive psychologists offer a somewhat less subjective alternative. They study the eye and brain processes that lead to the artist's intuitive decisions. Cognitive psychologists have developed the Gestalt theory to help explain some of our perceptual tendencies. The word *gestalt* means "whole" or "pattern." The term is defined as "a functional unit with properties not derivable from its parts in summation." In other words, the finished whole is more meaningful than merely the sum of its discrete parts.

Gestaltists emphasize the importance of organization and patterning in enabling the viewer to perceive the whole stimulus rather than discerning it only as discrete parts. They propose a set of laws of organization that reflect how people perceive form. Without these organizational rules, our world would be visually overwhelming. They include the following:

■ The grouping principle explains a very strong visual tendency. The brain tends to group objects it sees that are in close proximity to each other into a larger unit. This is especially true with objects that share properties such as size, shape, color, or value.

   In Figure 13.3, the eye reads a field of round dots, and the brain tries to make sense out of them by grouping near ones together. The brain then recognizes the grouping as something familiar, an S shape. By doing so, it also attributes meaning to the shape. Once meaning is established, the door is open for possible psychological or emotional response.

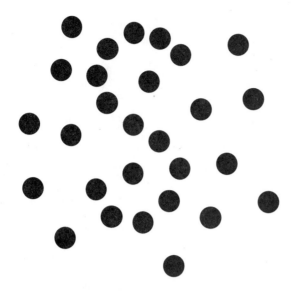

Figure 13.3 Grouping by proximity makes you recognize the S shape.

Figure 13.4 illustrates the grouping principle with shape and value. Color works as well.

- Our brains also organize our world by slicing our view up into planes as well as foreground and background layers that define positive and negative spaces.

- Another variation of the grouping principle is the perception that patterns or objects that continue in one direction, even if interrupted by another pattern, are recognized as being continuous. The brain wants to perceive a finished or whole unit even if there are gaps in it. In Figure 13.5, we visually assemble a circle and a square from the broken line segments.

- The principle of constancy describes the brain's tendency to interpret the world by comparing objects and deciding if something is the same as or different from something else it sees. It also makes comparisons to things it remembers to find relationships between what it sees with what it already knows. If a person is familiar with an object, he remembers its size, shape, and color and applies that memory when he sees that object in an unfamiliar environment. This helps him to become familiar with the new environment, instead of becoming disoriented, by relating the objects in the new environment to the known object. The familiar objects provide context for the unfamiliar ones.

By ignoring the principles of unity, an artist risks creating an image that challenges the eye to organize it, with little success. The viewer's eye will quickly tire and lose interest. Conversely, too much unity can be boring; if there is nothing to visually resolve, the eye will also quickly lose interest. By understanding how the

Figure 13.4 Geometric grouping principles based on shape and value.

Figure 13.5 The continuity principle causes you to mentally connect the segments to form a square and circle.

eye tends to group objects together, the lighting designer can help unify a disorganized or busy composition with careful shadow placement or by minimizing or emphasizing certain elements with light and color.

13.3.2 Emphasis

To direct the viewer's eye, an image needs a point of emphasis, or focal point. An image without emphasis is like wallpaper; the eye has no particular place to look and no reward for having tried. Images lit with flat, uniform lighting similarly feel drab and lifeless. By establishing the quantity, placement, and intensities of focal points, the lighting designer directs the attention of the viewers by giving them

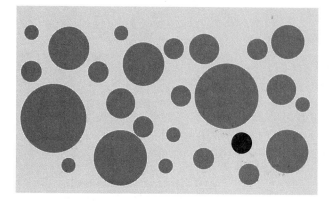

Figure 13.6 Emphasis through contrast.

something interesting to look at but without overwhelming them with too much of a good thing.

A composition may have more than one focal point, but one should dominate. The more complicated an image is, the more necessary points of emphasis are to help organize the elements. Introducing a focal point is not difficult, but it should be created with some subtlety and a sense of restraint. It must remain a part of the overall design.

By first understanding what attracts the eye, the lighting designer can then devise methods to minimize areas that distract the viewer by commanding unwanted attention and instead create more emphasis in areas that should be getting the viewer's attention.

Emphasis through Contrasts

The primary method for achieving emphasis is by establishing contrast. A focal point results when one element differs significantly from other elements. This difference interrupts the overall feeling or pattern, which automatically attracts the eye. With one dark dot among many bright ones, there is no question which dot gets noticed in Figure 13.6—the dark one, for two reasons: it has the most difference in value compared to the background, but primarily it is the only one of its type. Contrast in value (brightness/tone) is easy for the eye to see, which is why black-and-white imagery is successful despite its lack of color. It also illustrates why lighting is a major tool in the establishment of emphasis and directing the eye of the viewer.

The term *contrast* is often used to denote opposites. Black and white is a good example—it describes maximum contrast in value: black is the opposite of white. The term *affinity* is used to describe entities that are similar to each other. The colors beige and cream have great affinity in value as well as hue. The light dots in Figure 13.6 have an affinity with each other, while they also share more affinity with

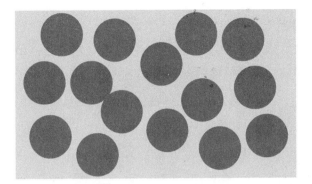

Figure 13.7 Emphasis through tangency.

the background than the dark one does. The dark dot also appears to have more energy, or visual intensity, than the bright dots. As contrast is increased, visual intensity is also increased.

In a painting, contrast describes relationships between values, colors, texture, size, depth, and rhythm. The motion picture adds not only the element of motion but also time. As in a static image, contrast or affinity can be compared within the image frame; however, the element of time allows for comparisons to be made as one shot cuts with another or from one sequence to another.

Emphasis through Tangents

Tangents, where two edges just touch each other, can produce a strong point of emphasis by creating visual tension (see Figure 13.7). The eye is not comfortable with tangent edges and wants to move them apart. With care, tangents can be created intentionally to attract viewer interest; however, most of the time they are accidental and distracting. If a tangent is creating unwanted emphasis, it is best to try to move one of the shapes. It may be necessary to move an object in the scene if it falls tangent to another object. Another potential compositional problem is an edge of a shadow or light falling tangent to an object or other geometric edge. In this case, it is preferable to move the shadow or light to avoid the tangency.

A great deal of visual tension is also created by two elements that we feel should touch. The gap in the line in Figure 13.8 attracts our eye because we want the two lines to connect. Michelangelo understood this when he painted the Sistine Chapel. Originally, he planned to have the fingers touch, but he repainted it for greater emphasis (Figure 13.8).

Emphasis through Isolation

Emphasis through isolation is a variation of the Gestalt grouping concept. When an object defies grouping, by not being near or similar to any other object, it calls

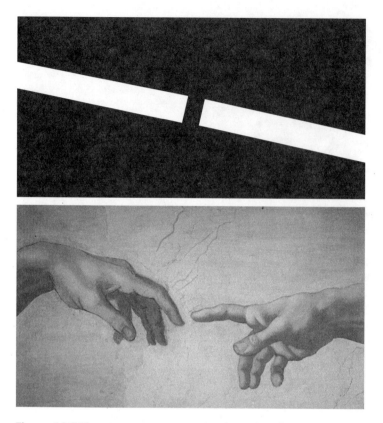

Figure 13.8 Near tangency creates visual tension, focusing our attention on the gap.

attention to itself and becomes a point of emphasis through tension. This tension is created by the feeling of unpredictability caused by the lone element not belonging to the larger group or exhibiting the expected behavior (Figure 13.9).

If this emphasis is undesirable, finding a way to link the element to the larger group may help minimize attention. Using an edge of a shadow to point to the isolated element is one way to link it to the group. N. C. Wyeth used this technique in the painting in Figure 13.10. The man's hat would create too much emphasis if it were not linked to his body by the shadow of his walking stick.

Emphasis through Linear Elements

Edges and contours do not really exist as physical entities, but are illusions created by the borders or intersections of shapes. The human eye is very sensitive to change and can find even very subtle distinctions, which it mentally connects to create an edge or contour. This connection process forces the eye to travel; it is an active

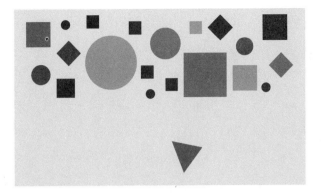

Figure 13.9 Emphasis through isolation.

Figure 13.10 N. C. Wyeth's *Blind Man with Walking Stick* uses a shadow edge to point to the man's hat in order to reduce the emphasis created by isolation.

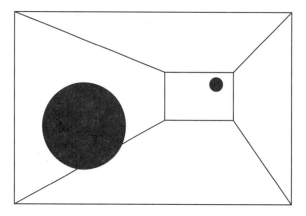

Figure 13.11 Emphasis through perspective angles.

process and is therefore dynamic. The careful placement and emphasis of edges play an important role in leading a viewer's eye through a composition, directing it to the intended subject. A practical example of how lighting can be used to control the placement and emphasis of edges might be the angle of a shadow, highlighting the edge of an object, accentuating the difference between two adjoining planes, or even deliberately allowing an edge to blend with the background.

Linear perspective is the process of taking a 3D space and projecting it onto a view plane, representing the spatial relationship of objects changing over distance, as they appear to the eye. In the CG world, the computer does this for us automatically; in the live-action world, the camera does the job. The result of either is a 2D illusion of the original 3D space. The illusion is partially maintained by lines (edges) that appear to point to one or more vanishing points. The eye travels along the edges and terminates at a vanishing point. As a result, an on-screen vanishing point creates a strong focal point and can easily lead the eye toward or away from the intended subject. If a vanishing point is creating unintended emphasis, it may be necessary to minimize it and attract the eye more strongly using another point of emphasis. In Figure 13.11, it is easy to see how strongly the eye is pulled to the shape that is near the vanishing point.

The painting in Figure 13.12 by Mary Cassatt is an interesting example of using linear elements to direct the eye. The edges of the boat bow, as well as the man's arm and oar, are used to create an artificial vanishing point to lead our eye to the intended focal point, the baby.

A line may also be implied by positioning a series of points so that the eye tends automatically to connect them. The eye has to work a little harder to make the connection, and as a result an implied line is more dynamic than an actual one. A row of ants is a nice example (see Figure 13.13). An implied line can also be created by movement. As an object travels from point A to point B, an imaginary line is created by its path. A line can also be implied by objects that create a mental connection. The eyeline of a character is a good example. If a character looks toward

Figure 13.12 Mary Cassatt's painting *The Boating Party* uses elements to direct the eye. (Photograph courtesy of the Board of Trustees, National Gallery of Art, Washington.)

an object, the viewer will also look. These lines are very dynamic because the eye and brain are working on several levels to make the connection. A subtle example of a linear element is the perceived axis through an object. A tall, thin man standing has a vertical axis, while a recumbent man has a horizontal one.

Emphasis through Shape

The brain tends to characterize edges and shapes as either rectilinear or curvilinear. Most images are not composed of strictly one or the other. By creating an image with primarily one type, the other type becomes a point of emphasis. In the simple example in Figure 13.14, the triangle stands out from the field of circles because its shape is unusual in this context. There are very few examples of perfectly straight lines in nature. This is probably why we find curvilinear shapes to be more appealing than rectilinear ones.

Shapes that enclose or frame other shapes draw and contain our eye. A subject that is staged within a door frame will attract more attention than he would if he were staged against a plain wall. A target is an exaggerated example of this visual tendency.

Figure 13.13 *A Bug's Life*—Implied line created by a row of ants. (© Disney Enterprises, Inc. and Pixar Animation Studios.) See also color plate 13.13.

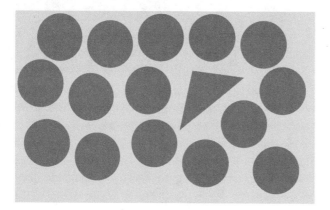

Figure 13.14 Emphasis through shape.

Emphasis through Size

Size is an obvious way to manipulate emphasis because larger objects tend to attract more attention (Figure 13.15, left). But when an object becomes large enough to break the image frame (Figure 13.15, right), our attention is directed to the smaller of the two shapes because we can see it more clearly.

Emphasis through Recognition

Humans are intrigued by other humans. When we see another person, our brains immediately begin to work to determine whether we know the person. Despite a familiar walk or physical build, we are often unsure whether we recognize someone until we see his face. If we do not recognize him, we often look anyway to become

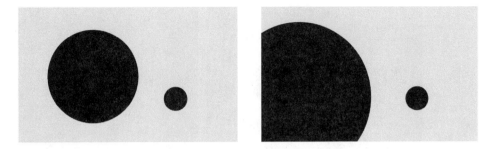

Figure 13.15 Emphasis through size.

familiar with the new person. If two characters are standing side by side, one facing the camera and the other one facing away, we will spend most of our time looking at the character whose face we can see, even if the other character has the dialog. We don't learn much from the back of someone's head. We need the mouth and especially the eyes to observe what the person might be thinking or feeling. The less we can observe, the less trusting we are of the person's intentions. Compare the two Woody images in Figure 13.16. Both are smiling the same smile, but which would you rather encounter in a dark alley late at night?

Humans have such a strong interest in themselves that they even like to attach human-like appearance, behavior, emotion, and intelligence to animals and inanimate objects. The animation business has been built around this attraction to anthropomorphosis. Talking animals are a perennial favorite, as well as classic hybrid charactacters such as mermaids, centaurs, and genies.

Emphasis through Motion

A static image has static points of emphasis and all principles of emphasis apply, but the cinematic image has the added bonus of being able to create emphasis through the illusion of motion. Motion can be implied by movement of the camera, movement of the subjects, or by redirecting the eye of the viewer from one area of the screen to another. The eye can be redirected within a single shot or across the cut from one shot to the next. An in-depth discussion of the principles of cinematic motion are beyond the scope of this chapter. Please browse the Further Reading section for suggested reading.

13.4   Creating Depth

The film medium is a 2D surface through which light is projected. Any feeling of depth, space, or volume achieved is merely an illusion. This implied depth must be created; it does not happen automatically simply because the subject matter is 3D. A 3D world can be staged and/or lit to look flat. If the major planes in the scene

Figure 13.16 *Toy Story*—Woody fully lit (left) and with his eyes in shadow (right). (© Disney Enterprises, Inc.)

are staged to be parallel to the image plane, the scene will look flat compared to one with the planes converging toward a vanishing point. Lighting can minimize or accentuate surfaces to alter the illusion of depth and volume. How the illusion of depth is handled in a film is a major component of its visual structure and style.

The painting by Berthe Morisot in Figure 13.17 (top) is a nicely composed and rendered image, however, it is staged and lit to look very flat. This creates a particular visual style. The image from *A Bug's Life* in Figure 13.17 (bottom) was staged and lit to impart as much visual depth to the image as possible for the location, which creates a very different visual style.

The motion picture image is a window into a world where viewers make intuitive comparisons to determine what they are seeing. Some of these comparisons are easy. If an object is bigger than another, it is probably nearer. If an object overlaps another, it is decidedly closer. At this point, the comparisons start to become more complicated. Does the object appear small because it is a small object or because it is far away? The brain looks for other monocular and binocular clues to establish size and distance, but the clues can be misleading. As an example, a long telephoto lens tends to condense distance, making faraway objects appear very near. Focus

Figure 13.17 An example of flat stage lighting (top) in Berthe Morisot's *The Sisters*. (Gift of Mrs. Charles S. Carstairs. Photograph © Board of Trustees, National Gallery of Art, Washington.) *A Bug's Life*—An example of deep staging and lighting (bottom). (© Disney Enterprises, Inc. and Pixar Animation Studios.) See also color plate 13.17.

and depth of field are also important clues but are dependent on the lens focal length and aperture used. Aerial perspective is helpful, but it can vary depending upon atmospheric conditions. The brain also uses the angle between a light source and where its shadow falls to help determine object-to-object proximity. The viewer uses all of these static comparisons to organize the image and to establish depth. In a motion picture shot, motion parallax due to camera or object motion is a vital depth cue.

Figure 13.18 *A Bug's Life*—Reversing the usual value cues by making more distant objects brighter. (© Disney Enterprises, Inc. and Pixar Animation Studios.) See also color plate 13.18.

13.4.1   Linear Perspective

We have already discussed linear perspective as it relates to emphasis. It is also an important element for implying depth. If all of the planes in a scene are parallel to the image plane, the scene appears very flat. Sometimes this effect is desirable if it supports the visual structure defined for the story. By rotating the planes off parallel, the plane edges converge toward one or more vanishing points. A two-point perspective appears to have more depth than one; three-point seems even deeper; beyond three points depth seems to stop accumulating.

13.4.2   Value

A bright value will attract our eye more than a darker one. This is especially true in a darkened theater because the bright value has more contrast with the surrounding environment. The darker values also tend to recede into the darkened environment, while the lighter ones tend to pop instead. Therefore, lighter values tend to feel nearer most of the time. Contrast also provides spatial cues for depth perception. Areas of greater contrast appear to advance into the foreground, while areas of lesser contrast tend to recede.

A value progression from the area nearest the camera to the area farthest away can help to exaggerate the perception of distance. A short hallway can look much longer if it is lit so that the light falls off before the end of it. Reversing this progression so that the light gets brighter as surfaces gain distance from the camera will draw the viewer into the frame. (See Figure 13.18.)

13.4.3 Color

Depth can also be enhanced with color. In general, warm colors tend to feel nearer than cool colors. One reason may be that we are familiar with the cooling effect of aerial perspective. A warm subject over a cool background will impart more apparent depth than a subject and background with the same color temperature. The reverse situation is also true, however. It is the chromatic separation of planes that increases the illusion of depth.

13.4.4 Atmosphere

The use of atmospheric effects can enhance both depth and mood. Except for a windy day or immediately following a rainstorm, some dust and water particles hang in the air that reflect, refract, and scatter light. Smoke and fog machines are heavily used in live-action cinema to heighten natural effects.

Atmospheric effects are noticeable over distance where they create aerial perspective by minimizing local color saturation and contrast. In the computer, simply adding a percentage of a fog color into the shading calculation for each pixel based upon surface distance from the camera can create aerial perspective. For more complicated, three-dimensional effects, volumetric light shaders can be used.

To create a natural-looking aerial perspective, keep in mind that atmosphere that is backlit will appear to brighten objects over distance, while frontlit atmosphere will appear to darken objects over distance. The color of the atmosphere also changes depending upon the camera angle relationship to the light source and depending upon what the atmospheric particles consist of. Dense atmosphere or fog will tend to make objects blend with the background as they recede over distance, as shown in Figure 13.19.

Atmospheric effects are usually employed to enhance the feeling of depth or space in an environment. They can also be used to limit depth if the atmosphere is thick enough to obscure objects. Limiting depth in this way can have a profound emotional effect on the viewer in the right context. Imagine yourself driving on a winding, unfamiliar road in very dense fog. How do you feel? You probably feel tense because the situation feels unpredictable. You can't see where you are, and you aren't sure where the road is going to turn or what might pop up in front of you. This feeling of apprehension adds drama to the foggy chase scene in *A Bug's Life* in which Dot is running from the grasshoppers (Figure 13.20).

Atmospheric effects are also used on a smaller local scale to create shafts of light projected through openings, which can help to impart a nice feeling of space (see Figure 13.1).

13.4.5 Resolution

Surface texture gives the audience cues as to how close they are to the object surface, because texture becomes less apparent as the object moves farther away.

Figure 13.19 Atmosphere.

Figure 13.20 *A Bug's Life*—Dot running from the grasshoppers. See also color plate 13.20.

This is one reason why sometimes you can spot a model miniature; the texture doesn't properly resolve for how far away it is supposed to be.

13.4.6   Size Relationships and Position

How objects relate to each other in apparent size gives us cues about how far away they are from us. Familiar objects provide context for unfamiliar ones. In Figure 13.21 (left), we see a variety of shapes, none of which are familiar to us. We are unable to judge how big or how near any of them are to us by comparing them to each other; thus the image has no depth. In Figure 13.21 (right), we may

Figure 13.21 Different shapes of all the same size create no feeling of depth (left). Various sizes of the same shape introduce depth (right).

Figure 13.22 *A Bug's Life*—This image is staged to remind the viewer of the true scale of tiny insects in the huge world. (© Disney Enterprises, Inc. and Pixar Animation Studios.) See also color plate 13.22.

not necessarily be familiar with the size of any particular square, but the repeating shapes tempt us to think that perhaps all of the squares are the same size at various distances away from us. By repeating the shape, we gain some familiarity with it. The illusion of forced perspective often includes this technique.

Usually the eye expects large objects that are large in frame to be nearer than the small objects. When we were working on *A Bug's Life*, we realized early on that the characters were small in an enormous world. We occasionally designed a shot to reinforce this normal indicator of scale and perspective (Figure 13.22). We also found that reversing common perspective also helped to drive home our disparity in scale, especially when the distant elements are visibly much larger than the foreground elements in the frame (Figure 13.23).

An object's size and position within the image frame imply depth. In Figure 13.24 (left), we have a large square on the left and a small one on the right. The right

Figure 13.23 *A Bug's Life*—This image emphasizes scale on the insect's level. (© Disney Enterprises, Inc. and Pixar Animation Studios.) See also color plate 13.23.

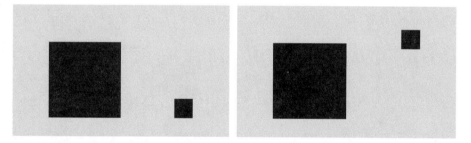

Figure 13.24 Object position in the frame can imply depth or size.

one tends to appear smaller rather than farther away because it has the same vertical position in the frame. When we move the smaller one up in the frame (Figure 13.24, right), it appears farther away rather than simply smaller. In Andrew Wyeth's painting of *Christina's World* (Figure 13.25), this visual cue is necessary to make the illusion of depth work, since it doesn't have the benefit of other cues such as aerial or linear perspective. Christina would look like a giant, or the house and barn would look like toys, if they were all on the same level in the frame.

13.4.7 Overlap

If object A occludes object B by overlapping it, then object A is decidedly nearer. This depth comparison is not at all subjective. An image that has minimal overlap will appear more flat than an image that contains many overlapping shapes.

Figure 13.25 In Andrew Wyeth's *Christina's World,* size and position of objects create depth. (Courtesy of the Museum of Modern Art, New York.)

13.4.8 Volume

An object that is lit to maximize its volume will increase the impression of depth because it appears to occupy more space than an object that is flatly lit. Compare the two images in Figure 13.26. Both are the same geometry, but one is lit to showcase the volumetric form while the other is lit to minimize it. The orange on the right is lit with very soft frontal lighting, which tends to reduce texture and volume. The orange on the left was lit from a three-quarter position with a harder light to enhance the roundness of the form and to emphasize texture.

13.4.9 Planes of Light

Most literature on live-action lighting discusses the necessity of creating planes of light, often without really explaining what that means or how to achieve it. In its simplest form, a lighting plane is essentially a collection of objects or subjects that are parallel to the camera plane and are lit as a unit to contrast with other planes. These planes can be any distance from the camera and are defined with light for the purpose of creating the illusion of depth through overlapping layers. The illusion created is limited, however, because the planes themselves mirror the image plane. Simple planes of light can be used to visually simplify and organize a busy scene (see Figure 13.27).

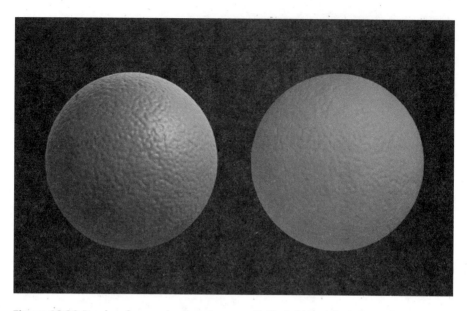

Figure 13.26 Rendered example of orange roundly lit (left) and flatly lit (right).

Figure 13.27 An example of simple planes of light in William Joyce's *Dinosaur Bob and His Adventures with the Family Lazardo*. (Copyright © 1998, 1995 by William Joyce. Used with permission of HarperCollins Publishers.)

Figure 13.28 Rendered example showing objects lit as planes of light.

In its more complicated form, objects can be lit in relationship to other objects to enhance the illusion of space. Not only is the form lit to enhance its volume, illumination and form are carefully placed so that the lights and darks create small planes within the image. In Figure 13.28 notice how each bright area is staged over a dark area and vice versa.

13.4.10 Depth of Field

Depth of field is an inherent feature of binocular eyesight, hence it feels natural in a monocular camera lens. With a live-action camera, depth of field is determined by the focal length of the lens as well as the aperture used. Each lens has its limits within which it can operate effectively. With these limits in mind, a lens is chosen depending on the story point, mood, film stock, available lighting intensity, the actor's features, and compositional reasons. The choice is a technical decision as well as an artistic one. A synthetic camera has the technical restrictions removed, which makes the choice a purely aesthetic one. This doesn't mean that the choice becomes any easier. The lens focal length can determine how the viewer interacts with the subject. Two close-ups with similar subject framing can have dissimilar effects resulting from the perspective and focal depth caused by the choice of lens. One lens can place the viewer uncomfortably close to the subject, and the other places the viewer at a more detached distance simply through depth of field. A close-up where the background is out of focus will feel more intimate than one where the background is sharp.

Figure 13.29 *Toy Story 2*—Andy's room at four different times of day, and the light color palettes for each setting. (© Disney Enterprises, Inc. and Pixar Animation Studios.) See also color plate 13.29.

13.5   Conveying Time of Day and Season

Conveying the time of day and season is important to place the story setting and to illustrate passages of time. It is also a major factor in determining the quality, quantity, motivation, direction, and color of light sources for a scene; as a result, it is also a major component in setting the mood.

Morning feels optimistic and cheerful. The day is beginning with high hopes for what it will bring. The air is fresh and you feel rested and rejuvenated. Midday is energetic and the time for getting things done. Evening is romantic, but it is also a little melancholy. The day is coming to an end, slowing down, and you are getting tired. Night is lonely and pessimistic, which is why we tend to "sleep on our problems" because they do not seem so bad the next morning. These daily cycles are repeated on a yearly scale as well; spring is a new beginning, the summers are for getting work done, autumn is the time for reflecting and taking stock, and winter is for hibernating, dormancy, and even death.

The angle and color of the light, as well as the length and color of the shadows, provide the viewer much information about the time of day. In the four examples in Figure 13.29, we see Andy's room from *Toy Story 2* at four different times of day: early morning, noon, late afternoon, and at sunset. The figure also shows the light color palettes for each setting.

13.6 Enhancing Mood, Atmosphere, and Drama

Many aspects of an image affect its mood and dramatic qualities. The sets, the costumes, the actors and their acting, the staging, the score, the weather, and the time of day are all components that can illustrate the mood of the story being told. There are also other aspects that may not be as obvious: basic shape, rhythm, balance, value, and color, as well as the style and motivation of the lighting.

13.6.1 Shape

The computer animation environment is 3D as it exists within the computer. Three-dimensional objects move and deform freely, changing shape and position, in their 3D world. And although the sculptural form and motion of the objects affect how light is reflected and shadows are cast, ultimately, it is the placement and definition of the resulting 2D shapes, within the image frame, that become the final product. Camera placement and lighting are what control this transition from the original design space to the image the audience sees projected on the screen.

Shapes supply an important emotional role within a visual structure. All shapes are based upon three simple primitives: a square, a circle, or a triangle. Each has its own inherent personality. A square is stable and solid, and implies no motion or direction. A circle is benign and friendly, also implying no motion or direction. The diagonal edges of a triangle make it an energetic and dynamic shape. Horizontal shapes imply stability, vertical lines imply potential motion, and diagonal lines imply dynamic motion and depth. When working within the rectangular cinema format, horizontal and vertical lines work as stabilizers and reduce feelings of movement because they mirror the format boundaries; thus a common camera technique to introduce a feeling of instability is to roll the camera.

A composition is primarily an arrangement of shapes. The brain not only strives to recognize shapes, it also attempts to organize them into figure and ground relationships, or positive and negative space. This happens on several levels. Just as the brain distinguishes between background and foreground planes, it also looks for positive and negative relationships within each plane. The focal points and busy areas of the plane become the positive space, while the other areas become relief for the eye, or negative space. Negative spaces are not necessarily empty flat areas, but they do not tend to attract attention. In a finely crafted image, as much care is given to the shape and placement of the negative spaces as is given to the subject itself.

A lighting designer is constantly balancing the need for readability and the need for integration. An image that has all of its shapes clearly defined is easy to understand. However, it is not as interesting as an image where shapes fall in and out of definition, by falling in and out of light and shadow. Similarly, clear definition between foreground/background and positive/negative space is easy to read but is

Figure 13.30 *Tin Toy*—An example of distortion. (© Pixar Animation Studios.)

not a particularly interesting spatial solution. It is often desirable to blend together, or integrate, the spaces in some way to avoid the harsh juxtaposition of forms, as is evident in a bad matte. The use of a similar color or value along an edge can help the eye travel more easily between the spaces. The brain is very good at recognizing shapes with a minimal amount of information, especially if this shape is already familiar to the viewer. By just hinting at a shape with a minimal amount of light, the viewer's imagination becomes engaged, and a mood of mystery and suspense is evoked.

Shape distortion can be a powerful emotional tool. The viewer is so accustomed to seeing the world in a natural fashion that when shape is distorted in an image, it signals an altered state of reality. An emotional response will range widely depending on the shape being distorted and its context. The baby in *Tin Toy* is distorted, using refraction through a cellophane wrapper, with comic relief to the plight of Tinny (Figure 13.30). In another context the same technique may be eerie and unsettling. The individual parts of the mutant toys in *Toy Story* are not themselves distorted, but in combination they represent a distorted vision of a lifelike toy. The combined effect is disturbing and repulsive, which helps us believe that they may indeed be cannibals. Alfred Hitchcock's *Vertigo* has many nice examples of using the camera to dynamically distort the environment to create an emotional response.

Figure 13.31 Degas' *Millinery Shop* illustrates repetition of shape. (Photograph courtesy of the Art Institute of Chicago.)

13.6.2   Repetition and Rhythm

The use of similarly shaped or colored elements in an image, however subtle, is a strongly unifying force, as the Gestalt grouping principle indicates. Repetition is an aspect of visual unity that is exhibited in some manner in every image. The human eye is very good at making comparisons and correcting minor differences to equate two shapes as being essentially the same. This comparison process is very dynamic as the eye jumps from one shape to another. In the Degas image (Figure 13.31), we immediately recognize the hat shapes and visually equate them. Our eye moves from one hat to the next in a circular manner around the image.

A shape or line that is repeated once has special properties. As the eye ping-pongs between the two elements, it creates a visual channel that contains the eye and directs attention to anything that happens to be within it.

A small number of repeated or similar elements become visually grouped together to form a unit. To cross the boundary from simple repetition to rhythm, a larger number of elements is required, enough elements so as to discourage grouping as a single unit, but instead several units. Groupings of three or more start to introduce rhythm, but only if they are not exactly the same. As a design principle, rhythm is based on repetition, although just because something repeats itself doesn't mean it has rhythm. Rhythm also requires variation within its repetitive groupings. Frequency and amplitude are also factors. Frequency controls the speed of repetition; amplitude controls the intensity of the repetition and the degree of variation.

Rhythm can be established using just about any type of visual element, but colors and shapes are common repetitive elements. Rhythm can be contained within a single image or introduced over time in a shot or sequence. The editorial cutting of shots introduces another type of temporal rhythm to be considered.

13.6.3 Balance

When an object is unbalanced, it looks as though it will topple over. Instinctively, the viewer wants to place it upright or straighten it. An unbalanced object can be used as a way to achieve emphasis. An entire image that is off-balance will make the viewer uncomfortable because he wants to balance it but cannot. This discomfort can be desirable if it enhances the mood or story point. By knowing ways to balance or intentionally unbalance an image, the lighting designer can affect the mood of the scene.

A measuring scale is balanced by putting equal weight on both sides. It doesn't matter how large or dense the objects placed on the scale are, they will balance as long as they have equal weight. The balancing of a composition is similar except that the unit of weight measurement is visual emphasis; therefore, the principles of emphasis and balance are closely related.

Visual balance is achieved using two equations. The first balances the image around a horizontal axis, where the two halves, top and bottom, should achieve a sense of equilibrium. Although it is desirable to have a sense of equal distribution, because of gravity, the viewer is accustomed to this horizontal axis being placed lower than the middle of the frame.

Besides helping to create a pleasing image, the top/bottom weight ratio can also have a storytelling effect. The majority of constant factors in our visual life experience tend to be horizontal in nature—the ground plane beneath our feet, the horizon in the distance, the surfaces of water. Where these horizontal divisions are, relative to where we are, tells us how tall we are, how far off the ground we might be, or whether we might bump our heads on something. Because we are accustomed to making these comparisons, the placement of a character within the image format and the angle that the camera sees him can imply the height of a character. And because we tend to associate height as a dominating physical characteristic, it can say something about the importance of the character in his current situation. For example, in one shot a short character is placed high in the frame, and in the next shot a tall character is placed low in the frame. The shorter character in the first shot feels taller and more important to us than the character who is actually taller but is visually subservient. In *A Bug's Life*, an effort was made to keep the P. T. Flea character in the lower half of the image to accentuate his stature as well as his personality.

The second equation of visual balance divides the image around a central vertical axis. The horizontal format of cinema, especially widescreen, is most affected by this left/right ratio. And with the possibilities of action entering and exiting the frame or of camera pans, tracking, and dollies, this ratio has the potential to be very dynamic.

The simplest type of left/right balance is symmetrical balance, where the two sides are mirror images of each other. Heavily used in architecture, symmetrical balance feels very formal, permanent, strong, calm, and stable. One distinct advantage of symmetry is the immediate creation and emphasis of a focal point. With two similar sides, there is an obvious visual importance to whatever element is placed on the center axis. Another asset is its ability to easily organize busy, complex elements into a coherent whole. In filmmaking, symmetrical balance is sometimes used to help portray a formal, official, or religious environment or mood.

Asymmetrical balance is more commonly used, more natural in feeling, and much more challenging to achieve. Although asymmetry appears casual and unplanned, its visual ease belies the difficulty of its creation. Balance must be achieved with dissimilar elements by manipulating the visual emphasis of each. Position in the frame is also an important factor. On a scale, a heavy weight can be balanced to a lighter one by moving the heavy weight closer to the scale center point or by moving the lighter weight further away from the center. Children are familiar with this principle as they play on the teeter-totter with their friends. This principle is also true in composition. A large element placed close to the center of the image can be balanced by a smaller element placed near the edge.

A pleasing composition evokes a sense of well-being, a feeling that everything is happy and going to stay that way. A composition that is a little unbalanced or otherwise feels awkward can create a feeling of tension and apprehension. This feeling can be useful if the intent is to build story tension or to portray the emotional state of a character. A progressive building of visual tension can foretell that something bad is going to happen whether it actually does or not. A sudden change in visual tension can accentuate the shock of a dramatic change. Sometimes the composition or lighting design will intentionally be in contradiction to the subject matter. Soft, warm, beautiful lighting can be used to light a violent, ugly subject matter. This contradiction can enhance viewer discomfort because it feels especially out of context and shocking. David Lean used this approach for a scene in *Dr. Zhivago* where innocent students are massacred by an army.

13.6.4 Lighting Style

The establishment of mood and drama through lighting is the sum of the properties of the lights themselves: their motivation, purpose, placement, direction, range, color, quality, quantity, and brightness. An infinite number of combinations of lighting properties can be created for a wide range of visual and emotional effects.

Value and Tone

Lighting styles are often described by their tonal range, which is the range of values from the darkest dark to the brightest highlight and the values in between. The character and mood of an image is dramatically affected by the range of values from light to dark and by their distribution within the frame. This decision is usually motivated by the dramatic quality of the story and can be consistent throughout the entire movie or vary widely with the location, time of day, or the emotional intent.

A light-hearted or comedic story might dictate a high-key lighting style. High-key lighting is characterized by a scene that is mostly well lit, with a lot of soft fill light and no heavy or hard shadows. The sets and costumes also tend to be light in color. This doesn't mean that there aren't any dark areas, but the overall brightness tends to be light, contrast is low, and the dark areas are soft and few. The result minimizes suspense because nothing is left to the imagination of the audience. At the other end of the spectrum is low-key lighting. In a low-key lighting situation, most of the scene is darkly lit, with the emphasis on the few areas that are brightly lit. The sets and costumes are also usually dark in color. The overall impression is dark but not murky. What is seen is equally important to what is not seen. The detail only hinted at is much richer than it would be if it were well lit. Light is used to direct the viewer's attention, the darkness to stimulate the viewer's imagination. Of course, these are the polar opposites, with many possible tonal ranges in between.

Aside from the overall brightness or darkness of the style, its contrast range can evoke mood and meaning. Unlike a low-key scene where most of the frame is dark, high-contrast scenes contain a wide range of light and dark areas with a narrow middle range of grays. A high-contrast image, with many hard edges of light and shadow, has a dramatic graphic quality and can evoke a sense of energy or unrest. A low-contrast image, composed of a range of shades of middle tonality, can convey a feeling of calmness or bleak oppression. Most images are somewhere in between.

Even before the viewer has understood the story point, the lighting style can suggest a feeling for a scene, especially in comparison to adjacent scenes. Or within a single shot, one character may be modeled in bright tones and another in shadows and dark tones to suggest their individual personalities or their emotional or dramatic situations.

A black-and-white image can often work as well as a full-color image because enough visual information exists for the viewer's imagination to fill in the missing color information. In fact, a black-and-white image can sometimes be more powerful than color precisely because it requires the use of imagination.

Color

Value and color are related to each other because the light that falls on reflective surfaces, or shines through translucent materials, produces various levels of brightness. On black-and-white film, they are reproduced as gray values. On color film, the apparent brightness is greatly influenced by the hue and saturation of the colors, but the final outcome is still a range of values. Every color has a value, but color, which is based on wavelengths of light, offers a much broader field of visual differences and contrasts.

The color of a surface is determined by how it reflects the light that illuminates it. The apparent color of a surface depends upon the lighting situation. Unfamiliar objects appear just as the eye perceives them; that is, the apparent color and value are determined by the actual wavelength of the reflected light. For familiar objects, the principle of color and brightness constancy takes effect. Here the brain uses previous experience to augment the strictly physical perception of the eye. If the color of a familiar object differs from that in memory, the brain assumes that its environment affects the color of the object. For example, if viewers see a purple apple, chances are they have never seen an actual purple apple and will assume they are viewing a red apple as seen under blue lighting or through a blue filter. The brain then evaluates the rest of the scene with that knowledge and starts to shift the overall color of the scene toward what it thinks it would look like under white light.

A color is also perceived as a certain hue, saturation, and brightness as it relates to the color next to it. A color on a neutral background may appear very different than it would in context with other colors. Similarly, two complementary colors when juxtaposed will accentuate each other and appear more intense than they would if either were placed adjacent to an analogous color. Neutral colors can be heavily influenced by a stronger color next to them; the neutral color will tend to go toward a hue that contrasts with the strong color. In other words, a gray square next to a red one will tend to go a little greenish. This is one reason why we have a relatively poor color memory; color is so heavily influenced by what is around it.

A lighting style is described as a chosen tonal range, but it also includes a color style as well. Color style is often discussed in terms of palette, consisting of hues and tones. In order to set a style, a fairly small selection of colors are chosen according to how they relate to each other. This selection, or palette, may consist of complementary colors, analogous colors, or an infinite variety of combinations. The production designer and the lighting director work together to choose a lighting palette that works well with the sets and costumes already established as well as the desired mood.

Naturalistic lighting mimics the complementary palette found in nature. The range is from yellow/purple to orange/blue to red-orange/blue-green in varying degrees of saturation. For a daytime scene, the key light is warm, simulating the sun, while the fill light is cool, simulating the natural fill of blue sky. A nighttime scene might reverse this sense with a strong blue key light acting as moonlight with a soft warm fill emanating from incandescent interior lighting. The eye is accustomed to seeing this warm-cool relationship in a wide range of color intensities. The contrast between warm and cool is minimized during the early to middle part of the day and grows as the day nears dusk as dust particles in the atmosphere filter the color of the light. A natural feeling still can be maintained even when using a strongly colored light that falls outside of this natural palette, as long as it appears to emanate from a visible practical source.

The similarity or contrast between lighting hues and saturation can help suggest the mood of the scene. Scenes that are lit with analogous colors tend to be more somber than scenes that use extremes. The colors of individual objects, sets, and costuming evoke emotional responses of their own. The combination of these elements into a whole image also presents an overall color for emotional consideration. Lighting can be used to accentuate or minimize individual areas of color as well as setting the tone for the overall scene.

The placement and intensities of the lights also have an effect on the overall color. A low-key, almost black-and-white effect can be achieved by minimizing object color saturation with the use of strong directional lighting and minimal fill. The emphasis falls on the shapes of objects rather than their surface colors.

Early man's use of color was largely symbolic and emotional, based in mysticism and religion, and not necessarily chosen for aesthetic reasons. The palette for a culture was established and adhered to within that culture and was used to identify itself by dynasty, race, tribe, or caste. Not until the Renaissance was color appreciated as an aesthetic choice.

Colors evoke physiological, psychological, and emotional responses. These responses are a reaction to associations we make with our past experiences and cultural heritage. Two people can have very different reactions to the same color, and one person can have varied reactions to the same color depending upon its context. Even so, there are enough common life experiences and contexts within which to draw some generalizations about how color affects us emotionally, especially in American culture where many colors have been stereotypically reinforced by advertising.

Colors are often referred to as being warm, cool, or neutral. Warm colors are generally agreed to be those that fall within the red-orange-yellow spectrum, and cool colors to be within the green-blue-violet range. Neutral colors are those that are near gray in saturation value. Cool hues tend to recede and induce calm. Warm hues stimulate the nervous system and raise the heartbeat. Pure, saturated colors tend to advance and excite, while duller, neutral colors tend to recede into the background.

Specific colors evoke more specific associations and responses. Red, for example, is an emotionally charged color that has many associations: anger, passion, fire, blood, violence, sunset, sex, adultery, aggression, power, creativity, embarrassment, and courage. It is also used as a universal symbol to stop or to denote when an error is encountered.

Green recalls calmer memories: nature, water, trees, mountains, meadows. It is an introspective, reserved color that evokes feelings of security, constancy, normalcy, balance, civility, and convention. It is a suburban color for active healthy people. It is the color of money. Green is generally a positive color, although it does have negative associations—we have all heard the expression "green with envy." Green lighting can look eerie, chemical, artificial, and unhealthy.

Blue can feel heavenly and religious and is associated with Western-culture weddings. It feels spacious as it reminds us of the sky and oceans. It is a rational, conservative color that symbolizes authority, loyalty, order, peace, conformity, success, caution, and patience. Blue lighting can look gloomy, electric, and cold if there is no warm light to counterbalance it.

Violet and purple have been associated with royalty since the Egyptians when only royalty was allowed to wear it. It can feel magical, exotic, sensitive, sophisticated, idealistic, and cultured.

Yellow feels sunny and happy and reminds us of summer days and flowers. It is also associated with intellect, wisdom, timidity, cowardice, and hunger. In China, yellow is considered the royal color.

Orange is the social color, full of fun and cheerfulness. It is urban and outgoing. It has also recently become known as the safety and construction color due to its visibility. It is interesting to observe how we use color by convention. For example, when you see a coffee pot with an orange top on it, you automatically know that it contains decaf coffee.

Brown is a homey and down-to-earth color, full of duty and responsibility. It is often associated with poverty and the lower class and is easily disliked. It is also associated with the past because objects tend to turn brown with time and exposure.

Pink packs more punch than other pastel colors. It can immediately portray someone as feminine, silly, delicate, floral, pampered, tender, healthy, wealthy, vain, and indulgent.

Black can look formal, elegant, sleek, and expensive. It can feel evil, empty, mysterious, anxious, and fearful. It is associated with night, death, and inevitability.

White can feel pure, virginal, innocent, classical, and youthful; but it can also feel sterile and emotionless.

Gray is the color of oppression and isolation. It can feel institutional, indifferent, sad, cold, and heartless.

A person's response to a color is immediate but is usually short-lived. After continued exposure to a color, the effect wears off or sometimes even reverses itself. It is the change from one color to another that triggers an acute response.

Researchers who study human response to color have established that people remember skin tones as being warmer or pinker than they really are. Human skin (real or computer generated) is more appealing in warm light, and we like to remember it that way. Films are usually lit and color-corrected during printing to make skin tones look "rosy," and in general, films are usually color-corrected for the skin tones rather than for other colors or objects in the scene. Overall skin tones that are colored more realistically tend to give an image a documentary feel.

Color provides context for shape. This significantly affects our emotional responses because the shape changes in meaning as it changes in color. In Figure 13.32 (left) we see a drop shape, which we recognize as a water drop because the color of it provides necessary context. The sight of it might make us feel thirsty.

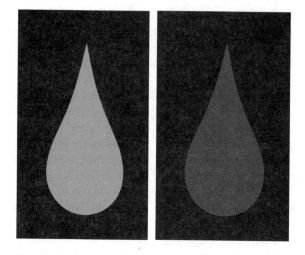

Figure 13.32 Water or blood? The same shape with different colors can evoke entirely different emotions. Color provides context for shape. See also color plate 13.32.

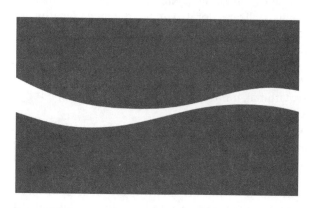

Figure 13.33 Does this combination of shape and color make you thirsty? See also color plate 13.33.

In Figure 13.32 (right) the context is changed by the red color. We recognize it as blood and feel differently about the shape.

The combination of shape and color can create strong visual symbols. The recognition of a symbol is based on whether it has any meaning to us. The meaning then triggers an emotional response, and sometimes even a physical one. The image in Figure 13.33 may make you feel thirsty.

Lighting Motivation

The style of lighting is also affected by the motivation for the illumination in the scene. Lights are characterized as being either logical or pictorial. A light is logical if it appears to be motivated by an actual source of light (practical source) that the viewer can see or is implied, such as a window or table lamp. Logical lighting, also called naturalistic, motivated, or method lighting, generally follows the natural, logically established visible sources in a scene. On the other hand, pictorial lighting generally uses lighting directions simply because they produce a pleasing picture.

Most of the time, there is a compromise between the logic of the source and the compositional requirements of the frame. Sometimes the light direction is established by what feels natural, even if the logic of the source is slightly violated. It is the overall character of the light—its color, softness, and direction—that matters. The audience will never scrutinize the exact angle and intensity of the light as long as it is not disorienting. Purely natural or physically correct lighting is often not interesting enough to create drama and captivate the audience. Pushing the limits of reality can create magic and beauty that connects the imagination with the story being told.

Practical sources that are visible to the audience need to be well placed. If there is a visible source of light within the image frame, the viewer expects the overall light direction to emanate from the source they see, even if it originated from a different source in the previous shot.

Quality of Light

The creation of varying degrees of softness and directionality are important aspects in creating mood through lighting. In addition to considering the tonality of image, lighting style is also often defined by the quality of the lights, especially the key source. The quality of a light is composed of three characteristics: the primary one is its hardness or softness, the other two are its angle of throw and its color. A soft source is diffused, which means that it scatters light in many directions and creates very soft shadows, whereas a hard source is not diffused and casts very crisp shadows. A light source, even a soft one, will become harder as it moves farther away from the subject. The apparent size of the source becomes smaller, and as its rays become more parallel, its highlights and shadows become more crisp.

In addition to the actual hardness or softness of the sources themselves, the contrast range of the resulting image also contributes to the overall feeling of hard or soft lighting. Subjects of limited tonal range, with middle tones of gray, appear softer than subjects with deep blacks and brilliant whites.

Quantity of Lights

The number of logical sources chosen will also help determine the mood of the scene. A soft one-light scene, for instance from a candle, can feel very warm and romantic. A big bank of fluorescent lights can feel sterile, cold, and overlit. There are many possibilities in between, but in general, the number of logical sources is usually kept relatively small to be able to establish overall direction.

The number of logical sources may be small even though the actual number of lights used to achieve a look may be many. This is true in live-action and even more so in synthetic lighting because no ambient or bounce lighting comes for free (unless of course a radiosity renderer is used). In general, a light should not be added to a scene without an intended purpose, and the temptation to use one light to serve two purposes should be avoided.

The number and quality of light sources also help determine the number and quality of shadows. In live-action situations, the placement and quality of the light determine the quality of the shadow. A hard or distant light will cast a crisp shadow. The softest light will not cast any shadow. The density of the shadow is determined by the amount of bounce and fill lights in the scene. In synthetic lighting, shadow direction, quality, color, and density controls can be independent of the light attributes, but they should still feel naturally motivated by the sources in the scene.

Light Type, Purpose, Placement, Direction, and Intensity

Types of Lights

Three basic types of lights are used for lighting: the spotlight, the floodlight, and the area light. The spotlight is usually focused into a narrow beam and used as a hard light source. It casts crisp shadows and a crisp bright highlight. The floodlight has a broader beam and is usually diffused and used as a softer source. It casts a soft shadow and a broader diffused highlight. An area light is either fully diffused through a diffusion material or is bounced off another surface such as a white card. It casts very faint shadows, if any.

The use of diffusion and focusing materials creates a wide range between a very soft scattered light and a very hard directional light. Light placement also affects the apparent hardness of the light, because even a soft light will appear harder as it moves farther away from its subject, as its rays become more parallel. These three types of studio lights are designed to emulate nature. Sunlight is an example of parallel rays that cast very crisp shadows. An overcast sky is an example of very diffused light casting soft shadows. And the shadow area under a clear blue sky is an example of a big area source that casts faint, very soft shadows.

Light Functions and Placement

The function of a light is independent of its type, its quality, and even its placement. A light's function is particularly meaningful for describing how it is used on a subject. For this reason, light function and placement are discussed here together.

Ambient (or base lighting). The overall brightness of the shadow areas is usually determined first by the use of base lighting. In live action this might be achieved by suspending a white cloth over the set and top-lighting it, bathing the entire set in a wash of light. In the computer this is accomplished by using a combination of an ambient light and diffuse lights. The ambient light adds a slight amount of light everywhere to prevent any absolute black areas but is extremely flat. The use of a few diffuse lights can add a little bit of directionality to ambient base lighting. A large area light would be even better yet. A radiosity renderer eliminates the need for adding a flat ambient light but does not necessarily eliminate the need for base lighting.

Key light (for modeling of surface and setting of mood). The key light is the main light striking a subject. It defines the brightness and shape and texture of the subject. As the dominant source, the placement, color, intensity, and textural quality of the key light are important attributes in setting the mood for a scene. But it is the placement of this light that most affects the mood and dramatic quality of the image by controlling the direction of the light as it strikes the subject. The direction of the light can vary the apparent shape and volume of the subject, by accentuating or minimizing certain features. This is referred to, in lighting terms, as *surface modeling*. The character of this modeling is also affected by the softness of the light and its shadows.

Although there are no hard-and-fast rules for the placement of the key light, it is conventionally placed 30–45 degrees to the side and above the subject relative to the camera axes. However, this light can be effectively placed as far back as 135 degrees from the camera as a three-quarters-back key light. Another convention is to place the key light so that it is on the opposite side of the actor's eyeline from the camera. These conventions are interesting but only serve as a loose guideline because the direction of light is usually dictated by the relationship of the subject to the motivation of the source, the chosen style of lighting, and the mood of the scene.

By controlling the direction and quality of the key light, it is possible to change the appearance of the subject as well as to suggest something about the subject's personality or dramatic situation. A beauty shot of the heroine may have a softer, more frontal key light than the key light on the villain who is chasing her.

Fill light (for subject contrast control). A fill light is a low-intensity, diffuse light used to fill in shadow areas. This light does not call attention to itself. In pure terms, it does not cast noticeable shadows, nor does it produce a noticeable or sharp specular highlight. Although a fill light can be placed almost anywhere, it is traditionally placed nearer to the camera axes than the key light. Because the fill light is often near the camera, it tends to fill in the key light shadows and reduce the surface modeling created by the key light.

The ratio of the key light plus the fill light to the fill light alone is called the *lighting ratio* and is one way of controlling the contrast range of the scene. In a high-key lighting situation, a lot of soft fill light is used to bring up the overall level of illumination. In low-key lighting situations, the fill light is often omitted.

Backlight (for separation from background and setting of mood). Also referred to as *rim*, *hair*, or *separation* lights, backlights were traditionally used in black-and-white cinematography for foreground separation. In color cinema, they are needed less for separation but are still heavily used.

A true backlight is traditionally placed behind the subject so that it is pointing directly at the camera, resulting in a thin rim of light around the edge of the subject. Backlights are also placed at higher angles to highlight hair and clothing. Back crosslighting is frequently used to put a rim on both sides of the subject. A soft backlight can look natural even if it has no obvious motivation. A hard backlight, unless a visible practical light motivates it, may look unnatural.

Backlighting is easy to achieve in live action, often with one light. However, many shading algorithms ignore light that strikes the back of an object and do not try to simulate the halo effect that results from a backlight hitting a surface that is not mirror smooth. Without special shaders that comprehend backlighting, creating this effect in CGI requires a bit of cheating and patience. It helps to have roughness controls on the specular highlight of each light source, so that the backlights can have as broad a highlight as possible. Exact light placement can be tricky to control, especially with moving or multiple characters, multiple sources, and wide-angle lenses.

Kicker (for surface modeling and character enhancement). A kicker light is an optional light usually used to define the nonkey edge of a subject. This light typically works from a three-quarters-back position and is placed nearer to the floor than the backlight. It can be soft and diffuse or hard and specular, depending on need and the intended lighting style.

A kicker light is a more general name for a variety of lights that perform slightly different functions. The three main types are a kicker, a liner, and a glow light. When used to create sheen (specular light), on a cheek for instance, they are frequently referred to as a *kicker light*. When far enough forward to contribute more diffuse light, they are sometimes referred to as a *liner light*. A glow light is a little farther forward still and is softer, nonspecular, and shadowless.

Specials (to accent an area for either subject or background). A special is any type of light that is used for background and set lighting, or for highlighting an area on the subject.

Bounce lights (to simulate radiosity effects). In the live-action world, light is often bounced off of a reflective surface onto a subject as a soft light source. In computer graphics lighting, an extra light would need to be created, and unless a radiosity renderer is used, extra lights usually need to be added to simulate the light that normally bounces off nearby surfaces. These lights are usually localized, nonspecular, low-intensity, and colored to mimic the surface they are reflecting.

Shaping and Controlling Light

Of equal importance to the placement and direction of light are shaping and controlling it—illuminating the intended subject without spilling into unwanted areas. It is sometimes also desirable to create a defined light shape, either to mimic a logical source or for dramatic or compositional purposes. Many of the techniques used to control and shape light synthetically can be similar to those of live action because the problems are also similar. These problems include controlling the light's size, shape, distribution, isolation, and coverage over distance.

It is often desirable to break up large or even surfaces with varying light and shadow. Sometimes this can be achieved with deliberate, recognizable shadows from actors or props and sets; other times, a more subtle overall variation will be appropriate. Barndoors, the four flaps attached to the sides of a light, can be used to shape and trim a source. The use of freestanding flags to block lights can be used to shape light at various distances from the source, which allows control over the hardness or softness of the shaping. A cucaloris (or cookie), a rigid board with squiggly holes cut into it, can be used in front of a light to create a more random, organic light pattern. Gobos can be used to restrict bounce light. A good computer lighting toolkit will offer a variety of light types and shapes along with sizing and soft barndoor controls. Further light shaping can be accomplished with the use of blocker flags, slides, and cookies, as well as variable light attenuation over distance.

Computer lighting has several benefits that do not exist in live action. Lights and flags can exist anywhere in space without interfering with the camera or subject. It is also possible to illuminate a subject and not have the light affect other characters or the background; negative intensity lights can be used to softly subtract illumination; and shadows can be independently colored, blurred, and given an arbitrary density value. The apparent softness of a light can be independent of its distance from the scene and resulting shadows do not necessarily have to be projected from the source point of the light.

13.7   Revealing Character Personality and Situation

The quality, color, and direction of light can give the audience impressions about the personality or character of the subject. They can also say something about the dramatic situation, or emotional state of mind, in which the subject currently finds himself. When a character is narrating a scene, he can describe his thoughts and how he sees the world; visual representation of his thoughts is not necessary. Most of the time, however, we require the use of our imagination to decipher the motivations and feelings of the characters by observing their actions, watching them emote, listening to them interact with other characters, and surveying their surroundings. It would be confusing to listen to a movie with the picture turned off; we rely so much on our vision to tell us what is happening, which is why we "watch" television or go to "see" a movie.

Visual clues are an aid for the viewer to help him understand the story more quickly or completely, getting him emotionally involved with the characters and their predicaments. Visual clues are tangible elements, such as location, sets, props, wardrobe, time of day, time of year, that are almost taken for granted but without which the viewer would have no context. Is it Elizabethan England in the dead of winter, high noon on the chaparral, or a humid summer night in New Orleans?

Besides establishing context for scenes, visual clues can also impart an emotional impression to the viewer by employing symbolism. My online computer dictionary describes symbolism as "expressing the invisible or intangible by means of visible or sensuous representations" and as "artistic imitation or invention that is a method of revealing or suggesting immaterial, ideal, or otherwise intangible truth or states." Some of this is absorbed on a conscious level (the good guys wear white hats, right?), while much of it is subliminal.

Light itself expresses symbolism—life, freedom, clarity, hope, enlightenment, truth, and guidance. Darkness represents the opposing forces. The source type can also express emotion. Candles, for instance, are associated with happy occasions such as weddings and social dinners, as well as contemplative locations such as church. They are also nostalgic because they remind us of times before electricity. Warm, soft, flickering candlelight is sensuous, flattering, seductive, and romantic. Windows and doorways represent transitions. Our hopes "fly out the window," and "opportunity knocks" on, and comes in through, the doorway. How something is portrayed relative to a subject can also have an effect. The past is "behind us," while the future is "in front of us."

Light placement and direction can impart emotional significance as well. Hard underlighting is commonly used to signify an evil or criminal character or situation. Soft underlighting can look very sensual. Lighting from directly overhead can look dreary when the subject is looking down but spiritual, uplifting, and hopeful as the subject looks up toward the light. Completely illogical lighting is often used in dream sequences or hallucinations—the more illogical, the better. The images of Woody in Figure 13.34 show that lighting can dramatically alter the form, and the resulting visual personality, of a character.

In the image of Hopper in Figure 13.35, great care was taken in staging to keep a wall of fire behind Hopper in his close-ups. This is a good example of using staging and lighting to reveal the personality of the character and to also heighten the tension of the scene.

Whether we realize it or not, we attach symbolic meanings and react emotionally to virtually everything. Some reactions are innate, others are dependent on our culture, and still others are uniquely personal. As lighting designers (and visual storytellers), we can take advantage of these emotional reactions in how we choose to portray characters in a scene. The best way to learn how to do this is to study films (with the sound off) to experience how you are emotionally affected by what you see.

Figure 13.34 *Toy Story*—Lighting direction, quality, and shaping are powerful tools to change the visual personality of a character. (© Disney Enterprises, Inc.) See also color plate 13.34.

Figure 13.35 *A Bug's Life*—An example of staging and lighting used to reveal personality of a character and to heighten tension. (© Disney Enterprises, Inc. and Pixar Animation Studios.) See also color plate 13.35.

13.8   Continuity

It would be wonderful if there were enough time to craft each shot as its own masterpiece, capable of surviving scrutiny on a gallery wall. But there isn't enough time, and sometimes it is also not appropriate. A complex composition takes time to study, and the eye can take its time meandering to various points of emphasis. A thirty-frame shot needs to direct the eye quickly. The audience does not have time to guess where to look; the shot needs to have immediate impact. Often, most of the subtleties are unnoticed.

The desire to craft each shot as a masterpiece also needs to be balanced with the necessity of a consistently lit sequence. It is very important to constantly check the lighting progress on other shots being lit in a sequence, especially if adjacent shots are being lit by other people. Lighting will inevitably and necessarily vary from shot to shot, but the overall feeling of the shot should be consistent with its sequence and especially with its adjacent shots. Sometimes this means that lights need to be brighter, darker, warmer, cooler, or even repositioned to achieve a unified feeling as camera angles change. Two characters standing side by side may even need different lighting to make it feel like they are being lit by the same source.

It is also easy to get too carried away with continuity. You can get away with more than you might think, but the only way to know for sure is to be able to view the shot in context. The computer lighting environment offers immediate feedback as well as preview and comparison capabilities not found in live action.

Another advantage the CG world has over live action is not having the physical reality of getting all of the day's shots filmed before the light changes significantly. If you have watched the film *Liar, Liar*, did you happen to notice the big time-of-day shift in the climax? Probably not. In one shot, Jim Carrey is racing down the airport runway, chasing a jet, on one of those motorized stairs, emergency crews in full pursuit. It is broad daylight. He has a crash and flies off of it. We cut to a night shot of the emergency crews attending to him. The cut feels like it has been minutes; the lighting change looks like it has been hours. Nobody notices the lighting change because we expect maybe a slight time shift, but also because it isn't really relevant to the story. The cinematographer may have been begging for another shooting day for the sake of continuity, but the producer was probably happy because the shooting stayed on schedule.

13.9 Film Considerations

Once a shot is lit on the computer, it is rendered and exposed onto film. It is then developed, printed, and projected onto the screen, sometimes with surprising results. Colors and values can sometimes change drastically. Film can only capture a small range of the available light and color gamut of the real world. Film recorders may not even be able to reach the gamut of the film stock. Video monitors vary widely and may not match the final result. However, color-matching software now exists to minimize surprises.

Although it is desirable to get as close as possible at exposure time, the printing process offers great latitude in altering overall color and density (brightness). This process is called *timing* or *grading*. The traditional lab timing is applied to individual shots over the entire image and usually cannot vary over time. It is now possible to do color timing digitally with as much control as a digital film-to-tape transfer session using a DaVinci. This will dramatically change what is possible and the speed with which it can be accomplished. It will be interesting to see how quickly this new process becomes commonplace.

If using the traditional lab timing process, it should be kept in mind that it is much easier to time a print darker than brighter. Brightening a print means that more light is pumped through the negative, which can result in a washed-out "milky" quality.

13.10 Conclusion

The primary purpose of lighting is to support the visual structure established for the story being told. The visual structure is designed top down, from the overall story arcs, the sequences and scenes, down to the individual shots. Visual "rules" for the movie are decided and implemented for all design elements, including the lighting design. Sometimes the rules are complicated, sometimes they are as simple as a particular character who is always lit with underlighting, and sometimes the established rules are intentionally ignored. Having a plan and defining a visual style is the primary outcome of preproduction.

Once a film is in production, the priority of meeting a hard deadline causes the planning processes to shift toward efficiency. Making good decisions and compromises in the heat of production is another part of the art. A good lighting designer knows how to visually reduce a complex scene so that the important story point reads instantly. A good lighting designer also knows when the band-for-the-buck has been reached where continued refinement does not aid the story.

This chapter has presented a wide range of visual tools to explore, the details of which may seem overwhelming. Observation of the physical world and the study of cinematic and artistic interpretations of it are also necessary. Experience from actual lighting shots and learning from spontaneous happy accidents are better than reading any chapter. Get out there and do it!

Further Reading

Matters of Light & Depth by Ross Lowell, 1992, Broad Street Books.
Logic & Design in Art, Science & Mathematics by Krome Barratt, 1980, Design Books.
Painting with Light by John Alton, 1995, University of California Press.
Film Lighting by Kris Malkiewicz, 1986, Prentice-Hall Press.
Cinematography, 2d ed., by Kris Malkiewicz, 1989, Simon & Schuster Inc.
Design Basics, 3d ed., by David A. Lauer, 1990, Holt, Rinehart and Winston Inc.

Psychology in Action, 2d ed., by Huffman, Vernoy, Williams, and Vernoy, 1991, John Wiley & Sons.

Elements of Film, 3d ed., by Lee R. Bobker, 1979, Harcourt Brace Jovanovich.

Introduction to Film by Robert S. Withers, 1983, Barnes & Noble Books.

Color & Human Response by Faber Birren, 1978, Van Nostrand Reinhold.

Design and Composition by Nathan Goldstein, 1989, Prentice-Hall.

Composing Pictures by Donald W. Graham, 1970, Van Nostrand Reinhold.

Film Directing Shot by Shot by Steven D. Katz, 1991, Michael Wiese Productions.

Film Directing Cinematic Motion by Steven D. Katz, 1992, Michael Wiese Productions.

By Design by Vincent LoBrutto, 1992, Praeger.

Story by Robert McKee, 1997, ReganBooks.

14 Lighting Controls for Computer Cinematography[1]

Ronen Barzel
Pixar Animation Studios

This chapter presents a practical light source model that has developed over several years in response to the needs of computer graphics film production, in particular for making CG animated films such as *Toy Story*. The model gives the CG lighting designer control over the shape, placement, and texture of lights so that the designer's real-world cinematographic talent can be applied to computer images. Chapter 13 discussed what lighting effects are desired; this chapter presents a light source implementation that allows such effects to be conveniently described.

---

[1] This chapter is adapted from Barzel (1997).

14.1   Introduction

Photorealism is an important and much-studied goal in computer graphics imagery and illumination. But photographers and cinematographers know that when it comes to lighting, realism is not the only goal.

As discussed in Chapter 13, the purposes of lighting for cinematography are to contribute to the storytelling, mood, and image composition, and to direct the viewer's eye. The "practical" light sources on a real-world movie set, such as desk or ceiling lamps, are rarely major contributors to the illumination. Instead, various types of lamps and spotlights are placed offcamera in order to create the desired illumination effect. A lighting designer will use whatever techniques, tricks, and cheats are necessary, such as suspending a cloth in front of a light to soften shadows, positioning opaque cards or graded filters to shape a light, focusing a narrow "tickler" light to get an extra highlight, or hiding a light under a desk to fill in dark areas under a character's chin.

This chapter describes a CG lighting model that provides a convenient and powerful encapsulation of control for cinematography. It was developed in response to needs and requests of lighting designers doing computer graphics film production: the features that we describe are those that have proven useful in practice, and almost all lighting effects used in *Toy Story* were achieved with the available features.

The emphasis of the model is not on realism nor on physically simulating the tools of real-world cinematography. Rather, we take advantage of various sorts of unreality available to us in the CG world in order to get the desired cinematographic effects,[2] so, although real-world effects provide motivation, our lighting model is ultimately based on effects that are useful in computer graphics.

To keep things intuitive, we'll first describe all the features of the lighting model (Section 14.2) and give the implementation notes (including a complete RenderMan shader) later on (Section 14.3). We'll also go over a few examples from *Toy Story* (Section 14.4). But remember, we talk here mostly about the *technology* of cinematography; for the *artistry* of cinematography, see Chapter 13 and its references.

14.2   The Lighting Model

Section 9.6 presented some basic light source shaders that implement a fairly limited model of lighting control. Here, we generalize and introduce controls over many more aspects of each light source: *selection, shape, shadowing, texture, dropoff, direction,* and *properties.* We describe and illustrate these capabilities in

---

[2] In fact, real-world cinematographers would doubtless use CG tricks if they could—for example, have light emanate out of nowhere, cut off a light after a certain distance, or change the direction of shadows.

Color Plates

Figure 14.15 Example 2: *Toy Story* — Use of a cookie to generate a dappled leaf effect. (© Disney Enterprises, Inc.)

Figure 14.16 Example 3: *Toy Story* — A practical light source, a flashlight, also using a cookie for the lens ring effect. (© Disney Enterprises, Inc.)

Figure 14.17 Example 4: *Toy Story* — An example of the importance of shadow placement. (© Disney Enterprises, Inc.)

Figure 14.18 Example 5: *Toy Story* — A variety of lighting technical features used. (© Disney Enterprises, Inc.)

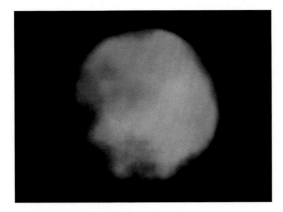

Figure 15.4 Explosion cloud.

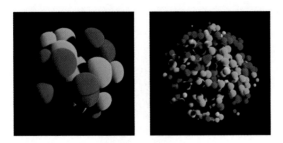

Figure 15.5 Cell Clouds.

Figure 15.11 Modeling the Eagle Nebula. An actual NASA photograph of the Eagle Nebula (top). CG models of the nebula (middle and bottom). (Top photograph courtesy of NASA. Middle and bottom images © Sony Pictures Imageworks.)

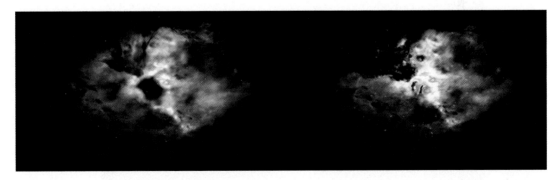

Figure 15.12 CG rendering of the Eagle Nebula. (*CONTACT* © 1997 Warner Bros. All Rights Reserved.)

Figure 15.13 CG rendering a close-up of the Eagle Nebula. (*CONTACT* © 1997 Warner Bros. All Rights Reserved.)

Figure 15.14 Rendering of the machine glow sequence. (*CONTACT* © 1997 Warner Bros. All Rights Reserved.)

20

Figure 15.15 Rendering of Saturn. (*CONTACT* © 1997 Warner Bros. All Rights Reserved.)

Figure 16.23 Escher-inspired woodblock print in two layers.

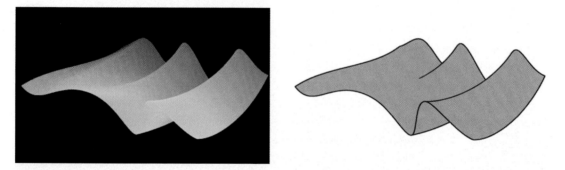

Figure 16.27 Combining three channel types into one render gives a general-purpose shader that is a good starting point for cartoon rendering.

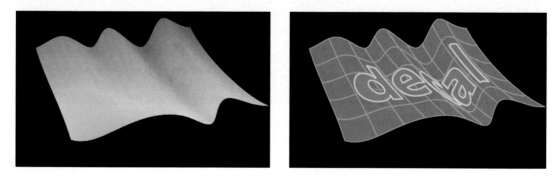

Figure 16.30 `nizid` shaded image (left) and detected image (right) with different material properties (width, color) applied to the regions.

Figure 16.31 The Giant rendered as an indexed image. (*THE IRON GIANT* © 1999 Warner Bros. All Rights Reserved.)

Fiugre 16.32 Can opener inspired by the pen-and-ink illustrations of David Macaulay.

Figure 17.3 *A Bug's Life* — Use of the "ray server." (© Disney Enterprises, Inc. and Pixar Animation Studios)

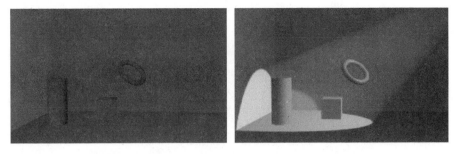

Figure 14.1 Cylinder and cube on the floor, torus in midair (left), with a conical key light (right).

Figure 14.2 Selection; same as Figure 14.1, but the torus is unaffected by the key light.

Sections 14.2.1–14.2.7. For clarity, each feature is illustrated in isolation, although the model allows them to be used in any combination. Also, we illustrate with static images, but all parameters can of course be animated.

Figure 14.1 shows a sample scene lit only by fill lights and the same scene with a simple conical key light. Fog is introduced to illustrate the effect of the light throughout space. (The fog is implemented using the technique and shader described in Section 12.6.)

14.2.1 Selection

Computer graphics lights can be enabled or disabled on a per-object basis (Figure 14.2). The ability to selectively illuminate objects in a scene is a powerful feature, which has no analog in real-world lighting. In our experience, per-object selection is used frequently, in particular to adjust illumination separately for the characters and the set.

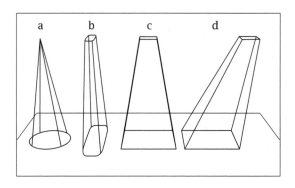

Figure 14.3 Shape; a superellipse profile is swept into a pyramid, which may be truncated or sheared.

14.2.2 Shape

A basic task of lighting is the placement and shape of light in a scene. Real-world cinematography commonly uses spotlights and barndoor (rectangular) lights to achieve desired shapes; our model provides a generalization of these.

- **Generalized cone/pyramid.** The light affects a region whose cross section is a superellipse, which is continuously variable from purely round, through rounded rectangle, to pure rectangle (Figures 14.3, 14.4). The slope of the pyramid can be varied until at the limit the sides are parallel. The pyramid may be truncated, as if it were originating from a flat lamp face, and may be sheared, for window and doorway effects (Figure 14.4).
- **Soft edges.** To soften the edge of the light, we define a boundary zone in which the light intensity drops off gradually. The width and height of the boundary zone can be adjusted separately. Thus, we have two nested pyramids: the light is at full intensity inside the inner pyramid and has no effect—that is, 0 intensity— outside the outer pyramid, with a smooth falloff between them (see Figure 14.5 and Section 14.3.1).
- **Cuton and cutoff.** The light shape can further be modified by specifying near and far truncation, again with adjustable-width smooth dropoff zones (Figure 14.6). These have no real-world physical analog but are very useful to soften a lighting setup and to keep the light from spilling onto undesired parts of the scene.

Being able to adjust the shape and edge dropoff of lights easily allows for soft lighting of a scene, faking area-light penumbra effects.[3] In the projects we have

---

[3] Being able to fake area lights in this way is important when using *PRMan* because it doesn't natively support area lights. The lack of actual area lights can manifest itself, however, in the shapes of shadows and surface highlights. Conversely, even when using *BMRT*, which does support area lights, it's still useful to have soft control over the light shape.

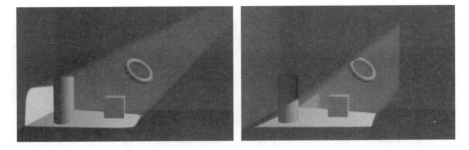

Figure 14.4 Rounded rectangle shape, as in Figure 14.3b (left); a sheared barndoor light, as in Figure 14.3d (right).

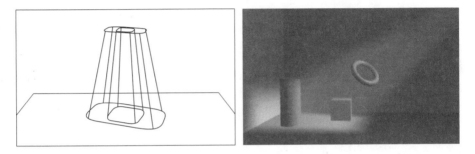

Figure 14.5 Nested pyramids define the soft edges (left); same as Figure 14.4 (left) but with soft edges (right).

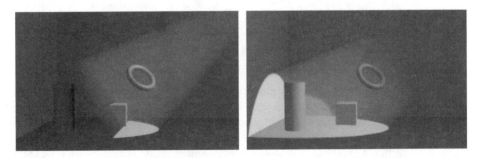

Figure 14.6 Cuton and cutoff controls: a sharp cutoff (left); a gradual cuton (right).

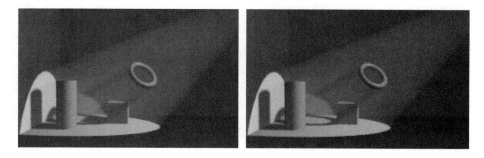

Figure 14.7 Shadow controls: applying a shadow map to the key light (left); the cube casts no shadow (right).

worked on, the majority of lights are chosen to be mostly rectangular, with large edge zones to provide smooth gradation of lighting; conical lights are used mostly if the scene includes a practical source, such as a flashlight.

The light shape can, of course, be rigidly rotated, scaled, and placed anywhere in space. This is a strength of CG lighting over real-world lights: we are not encumbered by physical structures and mechanisms that must be hidden or placed offcamera; CG lights can emanate spontaneously anywhere in space, giving the lighting designer great freedom. Finally, another choice for the shape is to have no shape at all: the light affects all of space.

14.2.3 Shadowing

Shadows and shadow placement are an important part of cinematography. Computer graphics has great freedom to control shadows for artistic effect. As you read the following discussion, it is convenient to think of shadow projection as defining a "volume of darkness" inside of which illumination is inhibited; this volume can be manipulated as an independent entity.

- **Shadow selection.** A light doesn't necessarily have to cast shadows. (For most rendering algorithms it is of course cheaper and easier *not* to cast shadows.) In Figure 14.7, the key light casts shadows, but the background fill lights do not. Shadows may also be disabled on a per-object basis, as in Figure 14.7. Thus, a difficult problem in real-world cinematography, suppressing unwanted shadows, is trivial in computer graphics.
- **Shadow direction.** The direction that shadows are cast doesn't necessarily have to follow the light—each "volume of darkness" can be aimed as needed. For example, the light in Figure 14.8 (left) is the same as in Figure 14.7, but the shadows have been shifted so that the torus casts a shadow on the cylinder. It is perhaps surprising just how far shadow directions can be shifted from true without incurring visual dissonance. "Cheating" the shadow directions can be a powerful tool for controlling image composition; in our experience, background shadows are often "cheated."

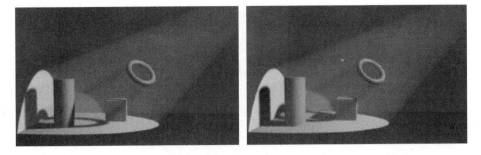

Figure 14.8 More shadow controls: cheated shadows (left); all light parameters are the same as in Figure 14.7, but the shadow directions have been cheated so that the torus slightly shadows the cylinder. Shared shadows (right); same as in Figure 14.7, but the key light shares its shadows with the fill lights.

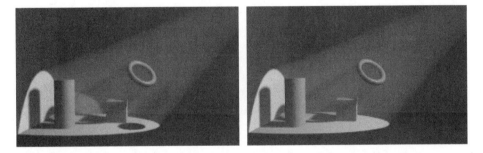

Figure 14.9 Shadow blockers (left); same as Figure 14.7, but with a blocker that casts a shadow. Shape trimming (right); same as Figure 14.7, but a large blocker has been placed just in front of the rear wall to eliminate unwanted illumination of the wall.

- **Shadow sharing.** A seemingly bizarre capability is for a light to share its shadows with other lights, as shown in Figure 14.8 (right). That is, a "volume of darkness" defined by a given light and object can inhibit illumination from other lights as well. This allows the lighting designer to strengthen shadows that might otherwise be washed out by nearby lights. The sharing technique is one we often use.
- **Fake shadows.** It is often useful to create extra shadows, to imply nonexistent offscreen objects or simply to darken a scene where needed. In real-world lighting, opaque cards can be placed in front of a light. In our model, *blockers* can similarly be defined; each is specified by a 2D superellipse that can be placed anywhere in space, as in Figure 14.9 (left). As with ordinary shadows, the direction that the blocker casts its shadows can be adjusted, and a blocker can be shared among several lights. In our experience, blockers are heavily used, sometimes several per light.

- **Shape trimming.** A blocker can be made large and placed so as to trim the shape of a light, as in Figure 14.9 (right). Animating a large blocker can be an easy way to fake a door-opening-offscreen effect.
- **Shadow softening.** To keep shadows from being too harsh, any shadow or blocker can be made translucent to only partially inhibit illumination. Shadow edges can be softened as well: for blockers, this is done via an edge-zone dropoff in the same manner as the light shape; for object shadows, the boundary of the "volume of darkness" is blurred. Finally, rather than going to black, a shadow can be assigned a color; subtle use of colored shadows can add richness to an image.

14.2.4 Texture

Just as images are used in computer graphics to create texture on surfaces, they can also be used to create texture in lights, via projection.

Cookie. A single-channel matte image can be used as a "cookie cutter," to get cross-sectional shapes other than the built-in superellipses or, more subtly, to fake complex shadows from offscreen objects (Figure 14.10, top and middle). ("Cookie" is colloquial for *cucaloris*, the technical term for an opaque card with cutouts, used to block a light.)

Slide. A full-color image yields a slide-projector effect (Figure 14.10, bottom). An unfocused projection (such as from a television set) can be achieved by applying a blur filter whose width increases as the projection distance increases.

Noise. In addition to stored image files, the light can be projected through a 2D noise function that modifies the intensity or color, yielding "dirty" lights.

As with shadows and blockers, it is possible to "cheat" the origin and direction of an image projection, to blur it, and to adjust its intensity.

14.2.5 Dropoff

The intensity of the light can vary, in the familiar manner of computer graphics lighting:

Beam distribution. Figure 14.11(left) illustrates dropoff of intensity across the beam using the usual exponentiated cosine function; however, the angle is normalized so that the intensity attenuates to 0 at the edge of the beam.

Distance falloff. Figure 14.11(right) illustrates dropoff of intensity with distance from the light source location, using the usual inverse power attenuation; to keep the intensity well-defined at the light origin, we provide a smooth clamp to a maximum intensity (see Section 14.3.2).

In our experience, choosing exponential dropoff parameters is not visually intuitive; it is often easier to have no a priori dropoff and to gradate lighting by using soft shape, cutoff, and blocker edges.

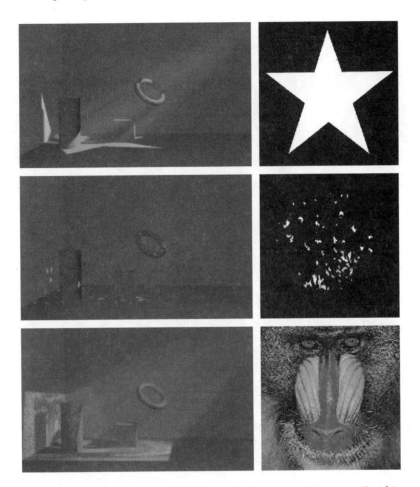

Figure 14.10 Light cookies and slides: projecting a matte image as a "cookie cutter" to get alternate light shapes (top); projecting a matte image to get simulated shadows, here for a dappled-leaf effect (middle); projecting a color image (the well-known mandrill) to get a slide effect (bottom).

14.2.6   Direction

The light ray direction has the two options common in computer graphics:

- **Radial.** The rays emanate from a point at the apex of the pyramid.
- **Parallel.** The rays are parallel to the centerline of the light pyramid, as per a very distant light.

Figure 14.12 illustrates parallel and radial rays in a light pyramid. The combination of parallel rays with widening shape yields a nonphysical, but still useful, effect: light rays are created along the edges of the shape. There are circumstances

Figure 14.11 Light distribution: intensity distribution across beam (left); intensity falloff with distance (right).

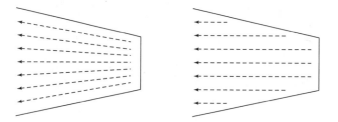

Figure 14.12 Cross section of light shape, with radial and parallel light rays.

in which it is useful to "cheat" the ray direction in other ways—for example, to have rays parallel to a direction other than the pyramid centerline or to define an arbitrary curvilinear vector field for the ray direction.

14.2.7 Properties

We have discussed where and from what direction the light reaches the surfaces in the scene. Finally, we come to the properties of the "photons" that are incident on the surfaces:

- **Intensity.** The nominal intensity of the light is specified at its origin or at a target point within the shape. This value is attenuated by the shape boundary, shadows, cookies, noise, and dropoff.
- **Color.** The color of the light is expressed as a standard three-channel RGB value, which can be filtered by a slide, noise, or colored shadow.
- **Effect.** The three standard CG illumination effects are available: ambient flat lighting, diffuse shape lighting, and specular highlighting. They may be used in combination, with a scale factor for each. (For ambient lighting, the ray direction is, of course, irrelevant.) In practice, diffuse-only lights are usually used for soft

fills (Figure 14.1), while key lights use both diffuse and specular effects. A small ambient component to a light is useful to keep regions from going completely black.

■ **Other information.** Depending on what can be supported by the surface shaders, additional information can be carried to surfaces. For example, a fourth channel of color can contain "ultraviolet" that a "fluorescent" surface will react to by self-illuminating; or we may have an identifier for each light source so that surfaces can react differently to specific lights. The usual mechanism for passing this information is the `lightsource` statement, discussed in Section 9.3.

14.3   Implementation Notes

The lighting model is implemented as a RenderMan light source shader. The programmability of shaders has been invaluable in developing and extending the model. Following the RenderMan paradigm, a light source is considered to be a functional unit: given a point on a surface anywhere in space, a light source computes the direction and color of the "photons" incident on that point due to that source.

We next describe a couple of tricky mathematical points of the implementation. Then, in Section 14.3.3, we give an example light shader implementation of the features described in this chapter.

14.3.1   Superellipses

A superellipse is a figure that varies between an ellipse and (in the limit) a rectangle, given by

$$\left(\frac{x}{a}\right)^{2/d} + \left(\frac{y}{b}\right)^{2/d} = 1,$$

where a and b are the x and y radii and d is a "roundness" parameter varying the shape from pure ellipse when $d = 1$ to a pure rectangle as $d \to 0$ (Figure 14.3). We want to soft-clip a point P to a shape specified by two nested superellipses having radii a, b and A, B. That is, given P, compute a clip factor of 1 if it is within the inner superellipse and 0 if it is outside the outer superellipse, varying smoothly values in between. We assume that the 3D point has been projected into the first quadrant of the canonical plane of the ellipse.

We express the ray through P as $\mathcal{P}(s) = sP$ and intersect it with the inner superellipse at Q and with the outer at R (see Figure 14.13). To find the points $P, Q,$ and R, we express them as

$$P = \mathcal{P}(p), \qquad Q = \mathcal{P}(q), \qquad R = \mathcal{P}(r).$$

Trivially, $p \equiv 1$. To compute q, we derive

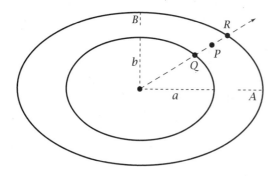

Figure 14.13 Geometry of nested superellipses.

$$\left(\frac{qP_x}{a}\right)^{2/d} + \left(\frac{qP_y}{b}\right)^{2/d} = 1$$

$$q^{2/d}\left(\left(\frac{P_x}{a}\right)\left(\frac{2}{d} + \frac{P_y}{b}\right)^{2/d}\right) = 1$$

$$q^{2/d} = \left(\left(\frac{P_x}{a}\right)\left(\frac{2}{d} + \frac{P_y}{b}\right)^{2/d}\right)^{-1}$$

$$q = \left(\left(\frac{P_x}{a}\right)^{2/d} + \left(\frac{P_y}{b}\right)^{2/d}\right)^{-d/2}$$

$$= ab\left((bP_x)^{2/d} + (aP_y)^{2d}\right)^{-d/2}$$

and, similarly, $r = AB((BP_x)^{2/d} + (AP_y)^{\frac{2}{d}})^{-d/2}$. The final clip factor is given by $1 - \mathsf{smoothstep}(q, r, p)$. For a pure rectangle, $d = 0$, we simply compose x and y clipping to compute a clip factor:

$$(1 - \mathsf{smoothstep}(a, A, P_x)) * (1 - \mathsf{smoothstep}(b, B, P_y)).$$

This gives a different falloff at the corners than the limit of the round calculation but suits our purposes.

Other falloff functions than smoothstep could be useful in some circumstances, but we have not experimented with any. It could also be useful to support asymmetric edge widths.

14.3.2 Intensity Falloff Curve

The common inverse power formula for light intensity can be expressed as

$$I(d) = K\left(\frac{L}{d}\right)^{\alpha},$$

where d is distance from the light source, α is attenuation exponent, and K is the desired intensity at a canonical distance L. This expression grows without bound as d decreases to 0 (solid line):

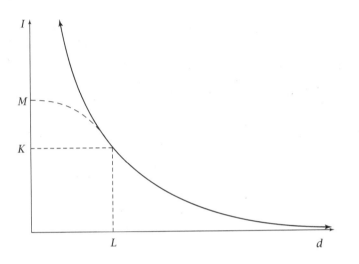

A common solution is to clamp the intensity to a maximum value; however, this yields a curve with discontinuous derivative, potentially causing Mach banding. Instead, we use a Gaussian-like curve (dashed line) when inside the canonical distance:

$$I(d) = \begin{cases} Me^{s(d/L)^{\beta}}, & d < L \\ K\left(\frac{L}{d}\right)^{\alpha}, & d > L \end{cases}$$

where $s \equiv \ln(\frac{K}{M})$ and $\beta \equiv -\frac{\alpha}{s}$ are chosen so that the two curves have matching value $I(d) = K$ and slope $I'(d) = -\frac{K\alpha}{L}$ at distance $d = L$.

14.3.3 Example Implementation in Shading Language

Listing 14.1 is an example shader implementing most of the ideas we have covered in this chapter. It was written by Larry Gritz and was used to render all of the images in this chapter so far (as well as many elsewhere in this book). Note that this shader, while functional, is designed for pedagogical purposes. The actual RenderMan code we use in production is somewhat messier, in particular because of the need to support *multiple* blockers, slides, cookies, and shadow maps per light. Such extensions to multiple instances of each kind of effect are left for you as an exercise. (*Hint*: Consider using *arrays* for such things as shadow map names, blocker positions, and so on, then looping over the elements of each array of features.)

For efficiency, if any features aren't used, we skip the corresponding steps of the computation. Also, if at any step the attenuation factor becomes 0, the remainder of the steps can be skipped.

In practice, we use shadow maps for shadow generation (Williams 1978; Reeves, Salesin, and Cook 1987), as this is the mechanism supported by *PRMan*. With shadow maps, the shadow trickery of Section 14.2.3 is straightforward: objects can be selectively included in shadow maps; shadow directions can be cheated by adjusting the shadow camera before computing the map; and shadows can be shared by referencing the same shadow map file in several lights. For other shadowing algorithms, these tricks may need to be coded into the renderer. For example, the shader listing above also supports ray-traced shadows for users who are rendering with *BMRT* (or using the ray server described in Chapter 17).

Listing 14.1 uberlight, an example shader implementing many of the lighting features discussed in this chapter.

```
/*************************************************************************
 * uberlight.sl - a light with many fun controls.
 *
 * Description:
 *    Based on Ronen Barzel's paper "Lighting Controls for Computer
 *    Cinematography" (in Journal of Graphics Tools, vol. 2, no. 1: 1-20).
 *
 * Rather than explicitly pass "from" and "to" points to indicate the
 * position and direction of the light (as spotlight does), this light
 * emits from the origin of the local light shader space and points
 * toward the +z-axis (also in shader space).  Thus, to position and
 * orient the light source, you must translate and rotate the
 * coordinate system in effect when the light source is declared.
 * Perhaps this is a new idea for some users, but it isn't really
 * hard, and it vastly simplifies the math in the shader.
 *
 * Basic color/brightness controls:
 *    intensity - overall intensity scaling of the light
 *    lightcolor - overall color filtering for the light
 *
 * Light type:
 *    lighttype - one of "spot", "omni", or "arealight".  Spot lights are
 *        those that point in a particular direction (+z in local light
 *        space, for this light).  Omni lights throw light in all
 *        directions. Area lights are emitted from actual geometry
 *        (this only works on BMRT area lights for the time being).    ▶
```

Listing 14.1 (continued)

```
* Distance shaping and falloff controls:
*   cuton, cutoff - define the depth range (z range from the origin, in
*       light coordinates) over which the light is active.  Outside
*       this range, no energy is transmitted.
*   nearedge, faredge - define the width of the transition regions
*       for the cuton and cutoff.  The transitions will be smooth.
*   falloff - defines the exponent for falloff.  A falloff of 0 (the
*       default) indicates that the light is the same brightness
*       regardless of distance from the source.  Falloff==1 indicates
*       linear (1/r) falloff, falloff==2 indicates 1/r^2 falloff
*       (which is physically correct for point-like sources, but
*       sometimes hard to use).
*   falloffdist - the distance at which the incident energy is actually
*       equal to intensity*lightcolor.  In other words, the intensity
*       is actually given by:   I = (falloffdist / distance) ^ falloff
*   maxintensity - to prevent the light from becoming unboundedly
*       large when the distance < falloffdist, the intensity is
*       smoothly clamped to this maximum value.
*   parallelrays - when 0 (the default), the light appears to emanate
*       from a single point (i.e., the rays diverge).  When nonzero,
*       the light rays are parallel, as if from an infinitely distant
*       source (like the sun).
*
* Shaping of the cross section.  The cross section of the light cone
* is actually described by a superellipse with the following
* controls:
*   shearx, sheary - define the amount of shear applied to the light
*       cone direction.  Default is 0, meaning that the center of the
*       light cone is aligned with the z-axis in local light space.
*   width, height - define the dimensions of the "barndoor" opening.
*       They are the cross-sectional dimensions at a distance of 1
*       from the light.  In other words, width==height==1 indicates a
*       90-degree cone angle for the light.
*   wedge, hedge - the amount of width and height edge fuzz,
*       respectively.  Values of 0 will make a sharp cutoff, larger
*       values (up to 1) will make the edge softer.
*   roundness - controls how rounded the corners of the superellipse
*       are.  If this value is 0, the cross section will be a perfect
*       rectangle.  If the value is 1, the cross section will be a
*       perfect ellipse.  In-between values control the roundness of
*       the corners in a fairly obvious way.
*   beamdistribution - controls intensity falloff due to angle.
*       A value of 0 (the default) means no angle falloff.  A value
*       of 1 is roughly physically correct for a spotlight and
*       corresponds to a cosine falloff.  For a BMRT area light, the
*       cosine falloff happens automatically, so 0 is the right physical
*       value to use.  In either case, you may use larger values to
*       make the spot more bright in the center than the outskirts.
*       This parameter has no effect for omni lights.                    ►
```

Listing 14.1 (continued)

```
* Cookie or slide filter:
*    slidename - if a filename is supplied, a texture lookup will be
*        done and the light emitted from the source will be filtered
*        by that color, much like a slide projector.  If you want to
*        make a texture map that simply blocks light, just make it
*        black-and-white but store it as an RGB texture.  For
*        simplicity, the shader assumes that the texture file will
*        have at least three channels.
*
* Projected noise on the light:
*    noiseamp - amplitude of the noise.  A value of 0 (the default)
*        means not to use noise.  Larger values increase the blotchiness
*        of the projected noise.
*    noisefreq - frequency of the noise.
*    noiseoffset - spatial offset of the noise.  This can be animated;
*        for example, you can use the noise to simulate the
*        attenuation of light as it passes through a window with
*        water drops dripping down it.
*
* Shadow mapped shadows.  For PRMan (and perhaps other renderers),
* shadows are mainly computed by shadow maps.  Please consult the
* PRMan documentation for more information on the meanings of these
* parameters.
*    shadowmap - the name of the texture containing the shadow map.  If
*        this value is "" (the default), no shadow map will be used.
*    shadowblur - how soft to make the shadow edge, expressed as a
*        percentage of the width of the entire shadow map.
*    shadowbias - the amount of shadow bias to add to the lookup.
*    shadownsamps - the number of samples to use.
*
* Ray-traced shadows.  These options work only for BMRT:
*    raytraceshadow - if nonzero, cast rays to see if we are in shadow.
*        The default is zero, i.e., not to try ray tracing.
*    nshadowrays - the number of rays to trace to determine shadowing.
*    shadowcheat - add this offset to the light source position.  This
*        allows you to cause the shadows to emanate as if the light
*        were someplace else but without changing the area
*        illuminated or the appearance of highlights, etc.
*
* "Fake" shadows from a blocker object.  A blocker is a superellipse
* in 3-space that effectively blocks light.  But it's not really
* geometry; the shader just does the intersection with the
* superellipse.  The blocker is defined to lie on the x-y plane of
* its own coordinate system (which obviously needs to be defined in
* the RIB file using the CoordinateSystem command).
*    blockercoords - the name of the coordinate system that defines the
*        local coordinates of the blocker.  If this is "", it indicates
*        that the shader should not use a blocker at all.
*    blockerwidth, blockerheight - define the dimensions of the blocker's
*        superellipse shape.
*    blockerwedge, blockerhedge - define the fuzzyness of the edges.   ▶
```

Listing 14.1 (continued)

```
*    blockerround - how round the corners of the blocker are (same
*        control as the "roundness" parameter that affects the light
*        cone shape).
*
* Joint shadow controls:
*    shadowcolor - shadows (i.e., those regions with "occlusion" as
*        defined by any or all of the shadow map, ray cast, or
*        blocker) don't actually have to block light.  In fact, in
*        this shader, shadowed regions actually just change the color
*        of the light to "shadowcolor".  If this color is set to
*        (0,0,0), it effectively blocks all light.  But if you set it
*        to, say, (.25,.25,.25), it will make the shadowed regions lose
*        their full brightness but not go completely dark.  Another
*        use is if you are simulating sunlight: set the lightcolor to
*        something yellowish and make the shadowcolor dark but
*        somewhat bluish.  Another effect of shadows is to set the
*        __nonspecular flag so that the shadowed regions are lit only
*        diffusely, without highlights.
*
* Other controls:
*    nonspecular - when set to 1, this light does not create
*        specular highlights!  The default is 0, which means it makes
*        highlights just fine (except for regions in shadows, as
*        explained above).  This is very handy for lights that are
*        meant to be fill lights, rather than key lights.
*        NOTE: This depends on the surface shader looking for, and
*        correctly acting upon, this parameter.  The built-in functions
*        diffuse(), specular(), and phong() all do this, for PRMan 3.5
*        and later, as well as BMRT 2.3.5 and later.  But if you write
*        your own illuminance loops in your surface shader, you've got
*        to account for it yourself. The PRMan user manual explains how
*        to do this.
*    __nondiffuse - the analog to nonspecular; if this flag is set to
*        1, this light will only cast specular highlights but not
*        diffuse light.  This is useful for making a light that only
*        makes specular highlights, without affecting the rest of the
*        illumination in the scene.  All the same caveats apply with
*        respect to the surface shader as described above for
*        nonspecular.
*    __foglight - the "noisysmoke" shader distributed with BMRT will add
*        atmospheric scattering only for those lights that have this
*        parameter set to 1 (the default).  In other words, if you use
*        this light with noisysmoke, you can set this flag to 0 to
*        make a particular light *not* cause illumination in the fog.
*        Note that the noisysmoke shader is distributed with BMRT but
*        will also work just fine with PRMan (3.7 or later).
*
* NOTE: this shader has one each of: blocker, shadow map, slide, and
* noise texture.  Some advanced users may want more than one of some or
* all of these.  It is left as an exercise for you to make such
* extensions to the shader.
*****************************************************************************
```
▶

Listing 14.1 (continued)

```
/* Comment out the following line if you do *not* wish to use BMRT and
 * PRMan together.
 */
#include "rayserver.h"


/* Superellipse soft clipping
 * Input:
 *    - point Q on the x-y plane
 *    - the equations of two superellipses (with major/minor axes given by
 *         a,b and A,B for the inner and outer ellipses, respectively)
 * Return value:
 *    - 0 if Q was inside the inner ellipse
 *    - 1 if Q was outside the outer ellipse
 *    - smoothly varying from 0 to 1 in between
 */
float
clipSuperellipse (point Q;           /* Test point on the x-y plane */
                  float a, b;        /* Inner superellipse */
                  float A, B;        /* Outer superellipse */
                  float roundness;   /* Same roundness for both ellipses */
                 )
{
    float result = 0;
    float x = abs(xcomp(Q)), y = abs(ycomp(Q));
    if (x != 0 || y != 0) {  /* avoid degenerate case */
        if (roundness < 1.0e-6) {
            /* Simpler case of a square */
            result = 1 - (1-smoothstep(a,A,x)) * (1-smoothstep(b,B,y));
        } else if (roundness > 0.9999) {
            /* Simple case of a circle */
            float re = 2;    /* roundness exponent */
            float sqr (float x) { return x*x; }
            float q = a * b / sqrt (sqr(b*x) + sqr(a*y));
            float r = A * B / sqrt (sqr(B*x) + sqr(A*y));
            result = smoothstep (q, r, 1);
        } else {
            /* Harder, rounded corner case */
            float re = 2/roundness;    /* roundness exponent */
            float q = a * b * pow (pow(b*x, re) + pow(a*y, re), -1/re);
            float r = A * B * pow (pow(B*x, re) + pow(A*y, re), -1/re);
            result = smoothstep (q, r, 1);
        }
    }
    return result;
}
```

▶

Listing 14.1 (continued)

```
/* Volumetric light shaping
 * Inputs:
 *    - the point being shaded, in the local light space
 *    - all information about the light shaping, including z smooth depth
 *      clipping, superellipse x-y shaping, and distance falloff.
 * Return value:
 *    - attenuation factor based on the falloff and shaping
 */
float
ShapeLightVolume (point PL;                         /* Point in light space */
                  string lighttype;                 /* what kind of light */
                  vector axis;                       /* light axis */
                  float znear, zfar;                 /* z clipping */
                  float nearedge, faredge;
                  float falloff, falloffdist;        /* distance falloff */
                  float maxintensity;
                  float shearx, sheary;              /* shear the direction */
                  float width, height;               /* xy superellipse */
                  float hedge, wedge, roundness;
                  float beamdistribution;            /* angle falloff */
                  )
{
    /* Examine the z depth of PL to apply the (possibly smooth) cuton and
     * cutoff.
     */
    float atten = 1;
    float PLlen = length(PL);
    float Pz;
    if (lighttype == "spot") {
        Pz = zcomp(PL);
    } else {
        /* For omni or area lights, use distance from the light */
        Pz = PLlen;
    }
    atten *= smoothstep (znear-nearedge, znear, Pz);
    atten *= 1 - smoothstep (zfar, zfar+faredge, Pz);

    /* Distance falloff */
    if (falloff != 0) {
        if (PLlen > falloffdist) {
            atten *= pow (falloffdist/PLlen, falloff);
        } else {
            float s = log (1/maxintensity);
            float beta = -falloff/s;
            atten *= (maxintensity * exp (s * pow(PLlen/falloffdist,
                        beta)));
        }
    }
```

▶

Listing 14.1 (continued)

```
        /* Clip to superellipse */
        if (lighttype != "omni" && beamdistribution > 0)
            atten *= pow (zcomp(normalize(vector PL)), beamdistribution);
        if (lighttype == "spot") {
            atten *= 1 - clipSuperellipse (PL/Pz-point(shearx,sheary,0),
                                           width, height, width+wedge,
                                           height+hedge, roundness);
        }
        return atten;
}


/* Evaluate the occlusion between two points, P1 and P2, due to a fake
 * blocker.  Return 0 if the light is totally blocked, 1 if it totally
 * gets through.
 */
float
BlockerContribution (point P1, P2;
                        string blockercoords;
                        float blockerwidth, blockerheight;
                        float blockerwedge, blockerhedge;
                        float blockerround;
                        )
{
    float unoccluded = 1;
    /* Get the surface and light positions in blocker coords */
    point Pb1 = transform (blockercoords, P1);
    point Pb2 = transform (blockercoords, P2);
    /* Blocker works only if it's straddled by ray endpoints. */
    if (zcomp(Pb2)*zcomp(Pb1) < 0) {
        vector Vlight = (Pb1 - Pb2);
        point Pplane = Pb1 - Vlight*(zcomp(Pb1)/zcomp(Vlight));
        unoccluded *= clipSuperellipse (Pplane, blockerwidth,
                                        blockerheight,
                                        blockerwidth+blockerwedge,
                                        blockerheight+blockerhedge,
                                        blockerround);
    }
    return unoccluded;
}


light uberlight (
            /* Basic intensity and color of the light */
            string lighttype = "spot";
            float intensity = 1;
            color lightcolor = color (1,1,1);
            /* Z shaping and distance falloff */
            float cuton = 0.01, cutoff = 1.0e6, nearedge = 0, faredge = 0;
            float falloff = 0, falloffdist = 1, maxintensity = 1;            ▶
```

Listing 14.1 (continued)

```
            float parallelrays = 0;
            /* xy shaping of the cross-section and angle falloff */
            float shearx = 0, sheary = 0;
            float width = 1, height = 1, wedge = .1, hedge = .1;
            float roundness = 1;
            float beamdistribution = 0;
            /* Cookie or slide to control light cross-sectional color */
            string slidename = "";
            /* Noisy light */
            float noiseamp = 0, noisefreq = 4;
            vector noiseoffset = 0;
            /* Shadow mapped shadows */
            string shadowmap = "";
            float shadowblur = 0.01, shadowbias = 0.01, shadownsamps = 16;
            color shadowcolor = 0;
            /* Ray-traced shadows */
            float raytraceshadow = 0, nshadowrays = 1;
            vector shadowcheat = vector "shader" (0,0,0);
            /* Fake blocker shadow */
            string blockercoords = "";
            float blockerwidth=1, blockerheight=1;
            float blockerwedge=.1, blockerhedge=.1, blockerround=1;
            /* Miscellaneous controls */
            float nonspecular = 0;
            output varying float __nonspecular = 0;
            output float __nondiffuse = 0;
            output float __foglight = 1; )
{
    /* For simplicity, assume that the light is at the origin of shader
     * space and aimed in the +z direction.  So to move or orient the
     * light, you transform the coordinate system in the RIB stream, prior
     * to instancing the light shader.  But that sure simplifies the
     * internals of the light shader!  Anyway, let PL be the position of
     * the surface point we're shading, expressed in the local light
     * shader coordinates.
     */
    point PL = transform ("shader", Ps);
#ifdef BMRT
    /* If it's an area light, we want the point and normal of the light
     * geometry.  If not an area light, BMRT guarantees P,N will be the
     * origin and z-axis of shader space.
     */
    point from = P;
    vector axis = normalize(N);
#else
    /* For PRMan, we've gotta do it the hard way */
    point from = point "shader" (0,0,0);
    vector axis = normalize(vector "shader" (0,0,1));
```

▶

Listing 14.1 (continued)

```
#endif
    uniform float angle;
    if (lighttype == "spot") {                      /* Spot light */
        uniform float maxradius = 1.4142136 * max(height+hedge+abs(sheary),
                                                   width+wedge+abs(shearx));
        angle = atan(maxradius);
    } else if (lighttype == "arealight") {          /* BMRT area light */
        angle = PI/2;
    } else {                                        /* Omnidirectional light */
        angle = PI;
    }
    __nonspecular = nonspecular;

    illuminate (from, axis, angle) {
        /* Accumulate attenuation of the light as it is affected by various
         * blockers and whatnot.  Start with no attenuation (i.e., a
         * multiplicative attenuation of 1).
         */
        float atten = 1.0;
        color lcol = lightcolor;

        /* Basic light shaping - the volumetric shaping is all encapsulated
         * in the ShapeLightVolume function.
         */
        atten *= ShapeLightVolume (PL, lighttype, axis, cuton, cutoff,
                                   nearedge, faredge, falloff, falloffdist,
                                   maxintensity/intensity, shearx, sheary,
                                   width, height, hedge, wedge, roundness,
                                   beamdistribution);

        /* Project a slide or use a cookie */
        if (slidename != "") {
            point Pslide = PL / point (width+wedge, height+hedge, 1);
            float zslide = zcomp(Pslide);
            float xslide = 0.5+0.5*xcomp(Pslide)/zslide;
            float yslide = 0.5-0.5*ycomp(Pslide)/zslide;
            lcol *= color texture (slidename, xslide, yslide);
        }

        /* If the volume says we aren't being lit, skip the remaining
           tests */
        if (atten > 0) {
            /* Apply noise */
            if (noiseamp > 0) {
#pragma nolint
                float n = noise (noisefreq * (PL+noiseoffset) *
                                 point(1,1,0));
                n = smoothstep (0, 1, 0.5 + noiseamp * (n-0.5));
                atten *= n;
            }
```

▶

Listing 14.1 (continued)

```
                /* Apply shadow-mapped shadows */
                float unoccluded = 1;
                if (shadowmap != "")
                    unoccluded *= 1 - shadow (shadowmap, Ps, "blur",
                                              shadowblur, "samples",
                                              shadownsamps,
                                              "bias", shadowbias);
            point shadoworigin;
            if (parallelrays == 0)
                shadoworigin = from;
            else shadoworigin = point "shader" (xcomp(PL), ycomp(PL),
                                              cuton);
#if (defined(BMRT) || defined(RAYSERVER_H))
            /* If we can, apply ray-cast shadows.  Force a ray trace if
             * we're in BMRT and the user wants a shadow map.
             */
            if (raytraceshadow != 0
#ifdef BMRT
                || shadowmap != ""
#endif
                ) {
                color vis = 0;
                uniform float i;
                for (i = 0;  i < nshadowrays;  i += 1)
                    vis += visibility (Ps, shadoworigin+shadowcheat);
                vis /= nshadowrays;
                unoccluded *= (comp(vis,0)+comp(vis,1)+comp(vis,2))/3;
            }
#endif
            /* Apply blocker fake shadows */
            if (blockercoords != "") {
                unoccluded *=
                    BlockerContribution (Ps, shadoworigin, blockercoords,
                                          blockerwidth, blockerheight,
                                          blockerwedge, blockerhedge,
                                          blockerround);
            }
            lcol = mix (shadowcolor, lcol, unoccluded);
            __nonspecular = 1 - unoccluded * (1 - __nonspecular);
        }
        Cl = (atten*intensity) * lcol;
        if (parallelrays != 0)
            L = axis * length(Ps-from);
    }
}
```

Figure 14.14 Example 1: *Toy Story*—A simple scene that illustrates the significance of light shape and placement. (© Disney Enterprises, Inc.) See also color plate 14.14.

14.4 Examples

Figures 14.14–14.18 show several *Toy Story* frames. We discuss some technical features of the lighting in each. For further discussion of the principles of cinematographic lighting, see Chapter 13.

Figure 14.14 is a simple scene that illustrates the significance of light shape and placement for image composition: The character is framed by a rectangular profile of a barndoor light. The light nominally shines through a window offscreen to the right, but the placement was chosen for visual effect, not necessarily to be consistent with the relative geometries of the window, the sun, and the bed. Notice also the soft (partial-opacity) shadows of the bed on the wall.

Figure 14.15 also uses a cookie (the same one used in Figure 14.10(middle)) to generate a dappled leaf effect. A separate cone-shaped light, with its own cookie, spotlights the area around the soldier crouching in the rear. The characters in the foreground are lit with an additional, blue light acting only on them for the blue highlights. This scene also includes a practical light, the red LED, which is used for effect but not as a key source of illumination.

Figure 14.16 features a practical light source, the flashlight, also using a cookie for the lens ring effect. The flashlight actually includes two light sources, one that illuminates the character and one used only for a fog calculation; the latter has a cutoff so that the fog doesn't obscure the character. This scene also features an

Figure 14.15 Example 2: *Toy Story*—Use of a cookie to generate a dappled leaf effect. (© Disney Enterprises, Inc.) See also color plate 14.15.

Figure 14.16 Example 3: *Toy Story*—A practical light source, a flashlight, also using a cookie for the lens ring effect. (© Disney Enterprises, Inc.) See also color plate 14.16.

Figure 14.17 Example 4: *Toy Story*—An example of the importance of shadow placement. (© Disney Enterprises, Inc.) See also color plate 14.17.

"ultraviolet" light (as described in Section 14.2.7), responsible for the blue glow of the white shirt.

Figure 14.17 illustrates the importance of shadow placement—the shadows of the milk crate were carefully adjusted so that an "X" would fall on the character's face without obscuring the eyes or mouth, because the character is speaking. Blockers were also used to darken the background, both to darken the mood and to accentuate the character's face in the foreground.

Figure 14.18 contains a variety of techniques: the key light has soft edges; the character's shadow direction is cheated for compositional effect; a light at a grazing angle from the left illuminates only the desktop, to accentuate its texture; separate lights illuminate only the character to provide extra highlighting; and a cookie is animated from one frame to the next, to provide a falling-rain effect.

Further Reading

Warn (1983) developed the cone spotlight model that has since become standard in computer graphics (as well as a simple barndoor light), "based in part on observation . . . of the studio of a professional photographer," in order to be able to create better-lit images than were available with then-standard tools. We continue in this vein, extending the model to meet increasingly ambitious cinematic lighting needs.

Figure 14.18 Example 5: *Toy Story*—A variety of lighting technical features used. (© Disney Enterprises, Inc.) See also color plate 14.18.

Doubtless others have met similar needs, but we are not aware of other published work in this area.

Our lighting model does not provide controls specifically for finite-area lights; although, as mentioned in Section 14.2.2, our light-shaping methods can to a large extent fake their soft lighting effects. For further discussion of finite-area lights, see, for example, Verbeck and Greenberg (1984) or Cook, Porter, and Carpenter (1984).

Global illumination methods can yield subtly and realistically lit images, but they typically support limited lighting controls and emphasize light from practical sources. However, the cinematographic emphasis on offcamera lighting and other trickery is not incompatible with global illumination methods. For example, Dorsey, Sillion, and Greenberg (1991) model opera lighting using offcamera lights and projected images. Gershbein, Schroder, and Hanrahan (1994) and Arvo (1995) also address textured light sources.

The task of a lighting designer can be aided by tools that speed up the process of choosing and varying lighting parameters. For example, Bass (1981) and Dorsey, Arvo, and Greenberg (1995) describe techniques to quickly recompute and redisplay images as lighting parameters change; Schoeneman, Dorsey, Smits, Arvo, and Greenberg (1993) and Kawai, Painter, and Cohen (1993) determine lighting parameters given user-specified objectives.

15 Volumetric Shaders for Visual Effects

Clint Hanson
Sony Pictures Imageworks

Traditionally, computer graphics has dealt only with surfaces rather than with volumes. Texture maps, bump maps, and surface lighting models all represent how light interacts with the "skin" of an object, but natural phenomena rarely occur just on the surface. Fire, smoke, clouds, and explosions are common examples of volumetric effects that are notorious for being difficult to produce in CG. In order to simulate them well we must represent a huge number of particles by using general models to describe the characteristics of objects smaller than the eye can see. Because these models require a volume, they can be difficult to create in a scanline renderer such as *PRMan*. Although this is never an easy task, this chapter examines directions taken on various productions that might give insights as to how volumetric effects can be produced with RenderMan.

15.1   Using Textured Geometry for Volume Effects

In production, the simplest methods for producing an effect, although not always the most elegant, can often produce results superior to realistic or complex models. There are several reasons for this. First, the more complicated a simulation is, the greater the chance that it will be hard to control. Second, the render and simulation times can be prohibitive for a more realistic model. A classic example of these trade-offs is water. Good renditions of water have been used in movies, but they often require long simulation times and lack specific control. If the director wants a wave to happen at a specific time, then with a complex simulation this might be hard to achieve. Under short production schedules, long simulation times can make it impossible to produce in time. In some cases, you must trade off some realism for timing or overall feel. Using a simple method often allows you to tweak the effect until you get both the control and the look desired.

The same principle applies to volumetric effects such as clouds or smoke. It is important to have a method for producing quick renders in order to iteratively tweak the color, form, and movement to achieve the desired look. Rendering volumes takes a lot of time, and if control over shape and movement is difficult, the end result could look worse than if a simpler method were chosen instead.

15.1.1   The Basics: Using Planes and Spheres with Projected Textures

A straightforward approach is to use ordinary geometry, such as planes and spheres, with 2D textures on their surfaces. This can produce good results under many conditions, especially when self-shadowing is not needed. Missile trails and dust clouds are two types of effects that can be produced quite quickly using these methods.

Gardner described simulating clouds using ellipsoids with 2D textures controlling their opacity (Gardner, 1984). Such textures can be applied to particle spheres trailing from an emitter on the back of a missile, for example. This simple and effective technique is a commonly used trick in effects, and its results are illustrated in Figure 15.1

Similar results can be achieved with the gcloud shader (Listing 15.1). Spheres are textured with an fBm pattern modulating opacity. The opacity also falls off with the angle of the normal relative to the viewing direction, in order to make the sharp edges of the spheres less apparent, and optionally with the age of the particle and distance from the viewer. Basic self-shadowing can be added by darkening those spheres on the opposite sides of the cylindrical trail from key light sources.

Figure 15.1 Dust clouds by Rob Bredow.

Listing 15.1 `gcloud.sl`: Fractal opacity function for a smoke puff.

```
/* gcloud - simple "Gardner cloud" shader
 *
 * Use spheres as particles for clouds -- this shader will make a nice
 * fluffy cloud appearance on them.  Fade with angle causes the edges
 * of the spheres to not be apparent.  Also includes controls for
 * falloff with distance from the camera and with age of the particle.
 */

#include "noises.h"

surface
gcloud (float Kd = 0.5;
        string shadingspace = "shader";
        /* Controls for turbulence on the sphere */
        float freq = 4, octaves = 3, lacunarity = 2, gain = 0.5;
        /* Falloff control at edge of sphere */
        float edgefalloff = 8;
        /* Falloff controls for distance from camera */
        float distfalloff = 1, mindistfalloff = 100, maxdistfalloff = 200;
        /* Falloff controls for age of particle */
        float age = 0;
        float agefalloff = 2, minagefalloff = 10, maxagefalloff = 20;
    )
{
    point Pshad = freq * transform (shadingspace, P);
    float dPshad = filterwidthp (Pshad);

    if (N.I > 0) {
        /* Back side of sphere . . . just make transparent */                ▶
```

Listing 15.1 (continued)

```
            Ci = 0;
            Oi = 0;
    } else {  /* Front side: here's where all the action is */

            /* Use fBm for texturing function */
            float opac = fBm (Pshad, dPshad, octaves, lacunarity, gain);
            opac = smoothstep (-1, 1, opac);
            /* Falloff near edge of sphere */
            opac *= pow (abs(normalize(N).normalize(I)), edgefalloff);
            /* Falloff with distance */
            float reldist = smoothstep(mindistfalloff, maxdistfalloff,
                                       length(I));
            opac *= pow (1-reldist, distfalloff);
            /* Falloff with age */
            float relage = smoothstep(minagefalloff, maxagefalloff, age);
            opac *= pow (1-relage, agefalloff);

            color Clight = 0;
            illuminance (P) {
                /* We just use isotropic scattering here, but a more
                 * physically realistic model could be used to favor
                 * front- or backscattering or any other BSDF.
                 */
                Clight += Cl;
            }
            Oi = opac * Oi;
            Ci = Kd * Oi * Cs * Clight;
    }
}
```

15.1.2 Dust Clouds

Another simple trick is to texture map the particles with real elements that have been filmed and scanned in as digital images. Using this method, the gross movement of the effect can be controlled by the particle system, while the more detailed aspect of the look is determined by the scanned elements. If you have a collection of image files representing the scanned sequence of frames of a real element, it is easy to select the right image for each frame using the format function to create a texture filename. This is illustrated in Listing 15.2. By using this technique with filmed elements of real dust and clouds, it is possible to produce very good simulations of large dust effects quickly.

There are countless ways to cheat volumetric effects. Each effect requires its own unique solution, but generally clever tricks work better than complex simulation. With that being said, we can now move on to some more interesting ways of producing volumetric effects within RenderMan.

Listing 15.2 `texdust.sl`: apply an animated texture to a sphere primitive.

```
/*  texdust - apply an animated texture to a sphere primitive.
 *
 * Params:
 *   Ka, Kd - the usual meaning
 *   falloff - controls softness of sphere edge: higher == softer
 *   texturename - base texture name: it will add ".0001.tx" for example
 *   id - a "label" for each sphere to make it easy for each to differ
 *   life - 0-1 controls the animation of the texture.  If life goes
 *          outside of the range 0-1, the texture will stop animating.
 *   maxLife - how many texture frames are there out there?
 *   texScaleU, texScaleV - U and V scale.  Use a large texture and set
 *          these scale parameters small and the shader will offset
 *          randomly into the texture differently for each sphere.
 */
surface
texdust ( float Ka = 1.0, Kd = 1.0;
          float falloff = 3;
          string texturename = "";
          float id = 1.0;
          float life = 1.0, maxLife = 70.0;
          float texScaleU = .3, texScaleV = .3; )
{
    color Ct = Cs;
    normal Nf = faceforward(normalize(N),I);
    vector V = normalize(I);

    if (texturename != "") {
        /* Assign ss and tt to be textured on the sphere and pointed at
         * the camera.  The texture will look the same from any direction
         */
        normal NN = normalize(N);
        vector Cr = V ^ NN;
        float ss = ycomp(Cr)+.5;
        float tt = xcomp(Cr)+.5;
        /* Scale and offset into the texture - randomly for each "id" */
        ss = ss * texScaleU + float cellnoise(id)*(1.0-texScaleU);
        tt = tt * texScaleV + float cellnoise(id+12)*(1.0-texScaleV);
        /* Build the texture filename and read it.  It's going to look
         * for a filename in this format: "basename.0001.tx"
         */
        string name = format("%s.%04d.tx",texturename,
                        clamp(round(life*maxLife)+1.0,1,maxLife));
        Ct = color texture(name,ss,tt);
    }

    /* Shade it */
    Oi = Os * pow(abs(Nf . V),falloff) * Ct;
    Ci = Oi * Cs * (Ka*ambient() + Kd*diffuse(Nf));
}
```

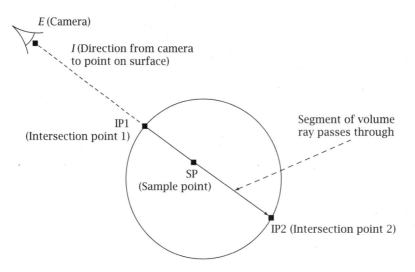

Figure 15.2 Volumetric effects step through the interior or a region of space intersected by the viewing ray.

15.2 Ray Marching Techniques

A more complex and expensive technique is to evaluate the cloud density throughout the volume using ray marching techniques. We can use Shading Language to build a simple ray marcher, similar to that presented in Section 12.6. The following pseudocode illustrates the basic starting point of the idea:

> Calculate segment to ray trace through.
> Set starting point
> **while** (current point is behind final point)
>   Call density function
>   Calculate light hitting point
>   Update current color total and opacity total
>   Calculate next sample point along ray using specified step size
> **end**
> Set surface Ci/Oi

First, we must figure out the volume to trace through. The solution to this problem is to build shaders with inherent knowledge of the geometry they are bound to. As a simple example, we will assume that we are using a sphere. As shown in Figure 15.2, given the P, E, and I variables available from the surface shader of the sphere, it is straightforward to determine the points at which the sphere is intersected by the incident ray I. The segment between the two intersection points defines the volume inside the sphere that the ray passes through.

We already know that the point we are shading, P, is an intersection of the sphere and the ray with origin E and direction I. From there we can calculate the other end point by using the `raysphere` function presented in Chapter 9.

15.2.1 Hypertexture Clouds

Once we have determined the basic segment to trace through, we need to think about generating the pattern we want inside the sphere—that is, our density function and color. For the cloud shader example we will use the `fBm` function described in Chapter 10. This seems to produce a very soft and detailed 3D fractal pattern. The cost is high for this function, as it uses `noise()` many times to calculate the hypertexture. For simplicity, we will use a constant color for the cloud.

While stepping through the ray, we sample the density and color functions. As mentioned in Perlin and Hoffert (1989), we base the strength of the density on the step size, so that when one changes the step size of the ray marcher, the image retains the same look.

We will also randomize the starting sample point of the ray march. The benefit of doing this is that your eye tends to notice the noise created by this less than the alternative quantization artifacts resulting from large discrete steps. This addition and the preceding formula allow you to produce quick test renders of what the final image will look like by rendering test images with large step sizes. The resulting test images will be noisy but will retain the same overall character as if you had used a small step size.

As the shader steps along the ray, it calculates the current running opacity total and the current color total. We use basic compositing and Blinn's model of low-albedo atmospheric scattering. If the clouds produced are thin and do not self-shadow significantly, then we can stop here, merely varying the color function to get a wide variety of interesting images.

However, more realistic-looking clouds need self-shadowing. The expense of this is great, but if you have the means, the results can be much more interesting. Self-shadowing of the volume is achieved by casting a shadow ray back to the light for each sample. Each shadow ray itself marches from the sample point to the light position, calculating an opacity total along the shadow ray and using this as a multiplier for the total light reaching the sample point. This is illustrated by Listing 15.3, which is simply the `smoke` shader presented in Section 12.6 modified to work within a sphere rather than as an atmosphere, and to have the volume self-shadow as we described. An enhanced version of this technique was used to produce the images in Figure 15.3.

Figure 15.3 also includes some images of very dense clouds. To get backlighting effects, we add a light directly behind the clouds, and to get explosion-type effects, we place a light inside the cloud volume. You'll notice in Figure 15.4 that the denser areas of the cloud block light more, producing a nice effect that would be hard to get otherwise.

Listing 15.3 shadowedclouds.sl a self-shadowing volume cloud shader.

```
/* shadowedclouds - self-shadowing volumetric clouds
 *
 * Params:
 *    Ka, Kd - the usual meaning
 *    radius - object space radius of the sphere in which the volume resides
 *    opacdensity - overall smoke density control as it affects its ability
 *             to block light from behind it.
 *    lightdensity - smoke density control as it affects light scattering
 *             toward the viewer.
 *    shadowdensity - smoke density control as it affects its ability to
 *             shadow iteself.
 *    stepsize - step size for integration
 *    shadstepsize - step size for self-shadowing ray marching
 *    noisefreq - frequency of the noise field that makes the volume
 */


#include "noises.h"
#include "filterwidth.h"
#include "raysphere.h"


float volumedensity (point Pobj;  float radius, noisefreq, stepsize;)
{
    float density = 0.5 + 0.5 * fBm(Pobj*noisefreq, stepsize*noisefreq,
                              7, 2, 0.65);
    /* Increase Contrast */
    density = pow(clamp(density,0,1), 7.28);
    /* Fade At Edges Of Sphere */
    density *= 1 - smoothstep (0.8, 1, length(Pobj)/radius);
    return density;
}


color volumecolor (point Pobj)
{
    return color 1;  /* Trivial function - white clouds */
}


float volumeshadow (point Pobj; vector Lobj;
                    float radius, density, noisefreq, stepsize)
{
    float Oi = 0;
    float Llen = length(Lobj);
    vector Iobj = normalize(Lobj);
    float t0, t1;
    float hits = raysphere (Pobj, Lobj, radius, 1.0e-4, t0, t1);
    float end = (hits > 0) ? t0 : 0;  /* distance to march */
    end = min (end, Llen);
    float d = 0;
```

►

Listing 15.3 (continued)

```
    float ss = min (stepsize, end-d);
    float last_dtau = volumedensity (Pobj, radius, noisefreq, stepsize);
    while (d <= end) {
        /* Take a step and get the scattered light and density */
        ss = clamp (ss, 0.005, end-d);
        d += ss;
        float dtau = volumedensity (Pobj + d*Iobj, radius, noisefreq,
                                    stepsize);
        float tau = density * ss/2 * (dtau + last_dtau);
        Oi += (1-Oi) * (1 - exp(-tau));
        last_dtau = dtau;
    }
    return Oi;
}


color volumelight (point Pcur, Pobj;
                   float radius, density, noisefreq, stepsize)
{
    color Lscatter = 0;
    illuminance (Pcur) {
        extern color Cl;
        extern vector L;
        color Cscat = Cl;
        if (density > 0)
            Cscat *= 1 - volumeshadow (Pobj, vtransform("object",L),
                                       radius, density, noisefreq,
                                       stepsize);
        Lscatter += Cscat;
    }
    return Lscatter * volumecolor(Pobj);
}


surface
shadowedclouds (float Ka = 0.127, Kd = 1;
                float radius = 10.0;
                float opacdensity = 1, lightdensity = 1, shadowdensity = 1;
                float stepsize = 0.1, shadstepsize = 0.5;
                float noisefreq = 2.0;)
{
    Ci = Oi = 0;
    /* Do not shade the front of the sphere -- only the back! */
    if (N.I > 0) {
        /* Find the segment to trace through.  The far endpoint is simply
         * P.  The other endpoint can be found by ray tracing against the
         * sphere (in the opposite direction).
         */
        point  Pobj = transform ("object", P);
        vector Iobj = normalize (vtransform ("object", I));
        float t0, t1;
```

▶

Listing 15.3 (continued)

```
      float hits = raysphere (Pobj, -Iobj, radius, 1.0e-4, t0, t1);
      float end = (hits > 0) ? t0 : 0;  /* distance to march */
      point origin = Pobj - t0*Iobj;
      point Worigin = transform ("object", "current", origin);

      /* Integrate forwards from the start point */
      float d = random()*stepsize;

      /* Calculate a reasonable step size */
      float ss = min (stepsize, end-d);

      point Psamp = origin + d*Iobj;
      float last_dtau = volumedensity (Psamp, radius, noisefreq,
                                        stepsize);
      color last_li = volumelight (transform ("object", "current",
                              Psamp), Psamp, radius, shadowdensity,
                              noisefreq, shadstepsize);
      while (d <= end) {
          /* Take a step and get the scattered light and density */
          ss = clamp (ss, 0.005, end-d);
          d += ss;
          /* Get the scattered light and density */
          Psamp = origin + d*Iobj;
          float dtau = volumedensity (Psamp, radius, noisefreq, stepsize);
          color li = volumelight (transform ("object", "current", Psamp),
                          Psamp, radius, shadowdensity,
                          noisefreq, shadstepsize);

          float tau = opacdensity * ss/2 * (dtau + last_dtau);
          color lighttau = lightdensity * ss/2 * (li*dtau +
                                            last_li*last_dtau);

          /* Composite with exponential extinction of background light */
          Ci += (1-Oi) * lighttau;
          Oi += (1-Oi) * (1 - exp(-tau));
          last_dtau = dtau;
          last_li = li;
      }
  }
}
```

Finally, there is no limit to what type of density functions you can place in the cloud shader. As an example, Listing 15.4 gives alternative implementations of density_func and color_func. Placing the voronoi_f1_3d of Section 10.5 into the density function allows us to make images like those shown in Figure 15.5. Neat effects can be created by modifying the space of the sample point before passing it into the voronoi_f1_3d function.

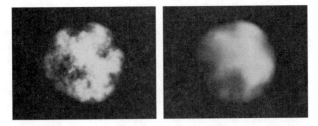

Basic unshadowed clouds.

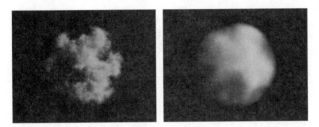

Same as above, but shadowed.

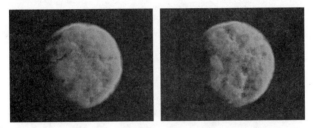

Dense clouds.

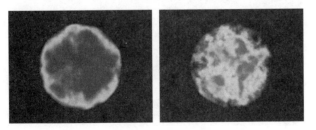

By placing lights behind the volume you can acheive
very nice backlighting effects.

Figure 15.3 Basic cloud effects.

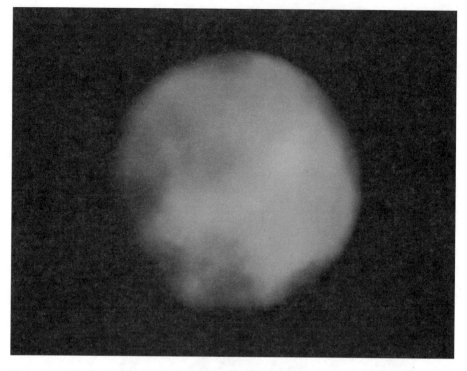

Figure 15.4 Explosion cloud. See also color plate 15.4.

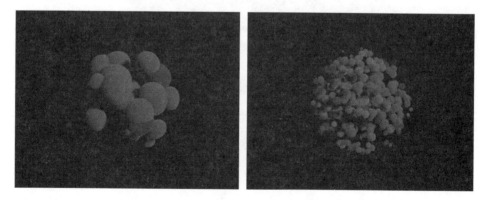

Figure 15.5 Cell clouds. See also color plate 15.5.

Listing 15.4 Alternative density and color functions resulting in "cell clouds."

```
float volumedensity (point Pobj;  float radius, noisefreq, stepsize;
                     output point cellcenter)
{
    float density;
    voronoi_f1_3d (Pobj*noisefreq, 1, density, cellcenter);
    density = 1 - density;
    /* Increase Contrast */
    density = pow(clamp(density,0,1), 7.28);
    /* Fade At Edges Of Sphere */
    density *= 1 - smoothstep (0.8, 1, length(Pobj)/radius);
    return density;
}


color volumecolor (point Pcenter)
{
    return color "hsv" (cellnoise(Pcenter), 1, 1);
}


/* We then replace calls to:
 *      den = volumedensity (Pobj, radius, noisefreq, stepsize);
 * with:
 *      point cellcenter;
 *      den = volumedensity (Pobj, radius, noisefreq, stepsize, cellcenter);
 *
 * and replace:
 *      volumecolor(Pobj)
 * with:
 *      volumecolor(cellcenter)
 */
```

15.2.2 Solid Hypertextures

Logically, if you can produce clouds it shouldn't be that hard to produce solids using the same basic idea. We use the same basic model Perlin presented in Perlin and Hoffert (1989), which assumes that a solid surface exists wherever the density function is at a particular value, as illustrated in Figure 15.6. We begin with the following algorithm:

> Calculate segment to ray trace through.
> Set starting point
> **while** (current point is behind final point)
>   Call density function
>   Calculate normal
>   Calculate shading based on normal

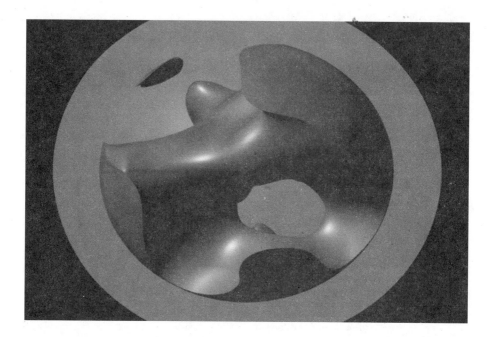

Figure 15.6 Rendering with the solid shader.

      Update current color total and opacity total
      Calculate next sample point along ray using specified step size
end
Set surface Ci/Oi

The basic addition to the original algorithm is the inclusion of a normal calculation for each point along the ray. We can obtain a normal for the "surface" by calculating the gradient of the density field. This gradient can be approximated numerically by:

```
normal compute_normal (point sampleP; float den)
{
    normal norm;
    norm = normal ( density_func(sampleP - vector (0.001,0,0)) - den,
                    density_func(sampleP - vector (0,0.001,0)) - den,
                    density_func(sampleP - vector (0,0,0.001)) - den );
    return normalize(norm);
}
```

The parameter `samplePoint` is the current sample point we wish to obtain a normal for, and the `den` parameter is the previously calculated density at that sample point.

This trick works rather well, but there are several pitfalls that should be pointed out. The first is that if you are using a density function with discontinuities (abrupt changes in otherwise smooth transitions between the values of your density function), then it is best to try to pull the discontinuities out for this normal calculation; otherwise, the results will not be what you expect.

In the solid shader example, I really wanted a density function that changes from 0.0 to 1.0 instantly, creating a discontinuity in the density function. To ensure that the normal calculated is correct, I remove this discontinuity from the density function that the `calculate_normal` function uses. This works great and solves the problem fairly easily. A second tip is that at the boundary of the shape you are tracing through, you will want to use the normal of the surface geometry; otherwise, you will probably get unwanted normal directions at the boundary edges. One final tip is to use `smoothstep` to transition between those discontinuities in your density function. This will also help to eliminate unwanted aliasing artifacts.

We can modify `shadowedclouds` shader to produce a solid volume (see Listing 15.5). This shader runs a great deal faster than the cloud shader simply because the ray does not have to be traced through the entire volume (it can stop when the "surface" is detected). Also, we can skip normal calculations when the density is zero, because no light will be reflected there anyway. In the case of the solid shader, it is silly to trace through the solid to calculate the self-shadowing because shadow maps were designed specifically for this case. Lastly, don't forget that the `diffuse()` and `specular()` functions given by RenderMan return light arriving at P, so we need to calculate the diffuse lighting ourselves and use the `specularbrdf()` function for specular lighting calculations.

15.2.3   Flying through Volumes and Combining Volumes of Basic Shapes

It is possible to fly through the cloud shader. Simply modify the use of `raysphere` to take into consideration the case where the camera is inside the sphere. This is the reason we are shading the backside of the sphere—so that if the camera enters the sphere itself, the volumetric effect will continue to work. Using this technique, you can create animations of cloud fly-throughs. However, the expense is high because as you get closer to the volume, your step size must decrease in order that it not be apparent that the pixel-to-pixel spacing is vastly smaller than the depth spacing of the volume samples. The ability to fly through the volume opens the door to many more possible uses of the shader. Note that you will want to set up a clipping plane in the shader in order to fade the density function off close to the camera. This will create a more expected rate of change when flying through cloud volumes. The example picture in Figure 15.7 was taken from within the volume of such an inside–the–sphere cloud shader.

It is also possible to combine solid volumetric shapes to form more complex shapes (transparent textures are a lot more difficult to join). With solid textures,

Listing 15.5 hypertexture: using gradients to make the cloud surface solid.

```
/* hypertexture - self-shadowing solid clouds
 *
 * Params:
 *    Ka, Kd, Ks - the usual meaning
 *    radius - object space radius of the sphere in which the volume resides
 *    opacdensity - overall smoke density control as it affects its ability
 *            to block light from behind it.
 *    lightdensity - smoke density control as it affects light scattering
 *            toward the viewer.
 *    shadowdensity - smoke density control as it affects its ability to
 *            shadow iteself.
 *    stepsize - step size for integration
 *    shadstepsize - step size for self-shadowing ray marching
 *    noisefreq - frequency of the noise field that makes the volume
 *    thresh - threshold value for the solid boundary of the hypertexture
 */


#include "noises.h"
#include "filterwidth.h"
#include "raysphere.h"


float volumedensity (point Pobj;  float radius, noisefreq, stepsize;)
{
    float density = 0.5 + 0.5 * fBm(Pobj*noisefreq, stepsize*noisefreq,
                                    3, 2, 0.6);
    /* Fade At Edges Of Sphere */
    density *= 1 - smoothstep (0.8, 1, length(Pobj)/radius);
    return density;
}


color volumecolor (point Pobj; float stepsize)
{
#pragma nolint 2
    return color (0.5 + 0.5*filteredsnoise(Pobj, stepsize), 0.75,
                  0.5 + 0.5*filteredsnoise(Pobj-10, stepsize));
}


float volumeshadow (point Pobj; vector Lobj;
                    float radius, density, noisefreq, stepsize, thresh)
{
    float Oi = 0;
    float Llen = length(Lobj);
    vector Iobj = normalize(Lobj);
    float t0, t1;
    float hits = raysphere (Pobj, Lobj, radius, 1.0e-4, t0, t1);
    float end = (hits > 0) ? t0 : 0;   /* distance to march *
```

▶

Listing 15.5 (continued)

```
    end = min (end, Llen);
    float d = 0;
    float ss = min (stepsize, end-d);
    float last_dtau = volumedensity (Pobj, radius, noisefreq, stepsize);
    last_dtau = smoothstep (thresh, thresh+0.01, last_dtau);
    while (d <= end  &&  Oi < 0.999) {
        /* Take a step and get the scattered light and density */
        ss = clamp (ss, 0.005, end-d);
        d += ss;
        float dtau = volumedensity (Pobj + d*Iobj, radius, noisefreq,
                                    stepsize);
        dtau = smoothstep (thresh, thresh+0.01, dtau);
        float tau = density * ss/2 * (dtau + last_dtau);
        Oi += (1-Oi) * (1 - exp(-tau));
        last_dtau = dtau;
    }
    return Oi;
}


normal compute_normal (point P; float den, noisefreq, sphererad,
                       stepsize)
{
    float density (point p) {
        extern float noisefreq, sphererad, stepsize;
        return volumedensity (p, sphererad, noisefreq, stepsize);
    }

    normal norm;
    if (length(P) > sphererad - 0.0051)
        norm = normal P;
    else
        norm = normal (density(P + vector (stepsize/10, 0, 0)) - den,
                       density(P + vector (0, stepsize/10, 0)) - den,
                       density(P + vector (0, 0, stepsize/10)) - den );
    return normalize(norm);
}


color volumelight (point Pcur, Pobj;
                   vector Icur;
                   float density_here, Kd, Ks;
                   float radius, density, noisefreq, stepsize, thresh)
{
    normal N = compute_normal (Pobj, density_here,
                               noisefreq, radius, stepsize);
    N = faceforward (ntransform ("object", "current", N), Icur);
    N = normalize(N);
    color Lscatter = 0;
    vector V = -normalize(Icur);
```

▶

Listing 15.5 (continued)

```
    illuminance (Pcur) {
        extern color Cl;
        extern vector L;
        color Cscat = Cl;
        if (density > 0)
            Cscat *= 1 - volumeshadow (Pobj, vtransform("object",L), radius,
                                       density, noisefreq, stepsize, thresh);
        vector LN = normalize(L);
        vector H = normalize (LN + V);
        Lscatter += Kd * Cscat * max (LN . N, 0)
                    + Ks * Cscat * specularbrdf (LN, N, V, 0.1);
    }
    return Lscatter * volumecolor(Pobj, stepsize);
}



surface
hypertexture (float Ka = 0.127, Kd = 1, Ks = 0.3;
              float radius = 10.0;
              float opacdensity = 1, lightdensity = 1, shadowdensity = 1;
              float stepsize = 0.1, shadstepsize = 0.5;
              float noisefreq = 2.0;
              float thresh = 0.5;)
{
    Ci = Oi = 0;
    /* Do not shade the front of the sphere -- only the back! */
    if (N.I > 0) {
        /* Find the segment to trace through.  The far endpoint is simply
         * P.  The other endpoint can be found by ray tracing against the
         * sphere (in the opposite direction).
         */
        point  Pobj = transform ("object", P);
        vector Iobj = normalize (vtransform ("object", I));
        float t0, t1;
        float hits = raysphere (Pobj, -Iobj, radius, 1.0e-4, t0, t1);
        float end = (hits > 0) ? t0 : 0;   /* distance to march */
        point origin = Pobj - t0*Iobj;
        point Worigin = transform ("object", "current", origin);

        /* Integrate forwards from the start point */
        float d = random()*stepsize;

        /* Calculate a reasonable step size */
        float ss = min (stepsize, end-d);
```

▶

Listing 15.5 (continued)

```
point Psamp = origin + d*Iobj;
float last_dtau = volumedensity (Psamp, radius, noisefreq,stepsize);
color last_li = volumelight (transform ("object", "current", Psamp),
                             Psamp, I, last_dtau, Kd, Ks,
                             radius, shadowdensity,
                             noisefreq, shadstepsize, thresh);
/* Sharpen at boundary */
last_dtau = smoothstep (thresh, thresh+0.01, last_dtau);

while (d <= end && (comp(Oi,0)<0.1 || comp(Oi,1)<1 || comp(Oi,2)<1))
{
    /* Take a step and get the scattered light and density */
    ss = clamp (ss, 0.005, end-d);
    d += ss;
    /* Get the scattered light and density */
    Psamp = origin + d*Iobj;
    float dtau = volumedensity (Psamp, radius, noisefreq, stepsize);
    color li = 0;
    if (dtau > thresh)
        li = volumelight (transform ("object", "current", Psamp),
                          Psamp, I, dtau, Kd, Ks, radius,
                          shadowdensity, noisefreq, shadstepsize,
                          thresh);
    dtau = smoothstep (thresh, thresh+0.01, dtau);

    float tau = opacdensity * ss/2 * (dtau + last_dtau);
    color lighttau = lightdensity * ss/2 * (li*dtau +
                                            last_li*last_dtau);
    lighttau = lightdensity * (li + last_li)/2;
    float alpha = 1 - exp(-tau);

    /* Composite with exponential extinction of background light */
    Ci += (1-Oi) * lighttau * alpha;
    Oi += (1-Oi) * alpha;
    last_dtau = dtau;
    last_li = li;
}
}
}
```

you will want to draw the frontside of the object if objects overlap, or you will get unwanted results. You can build up more complex objects using primitives in this way for use with this volume technique, as the example image in Figure 15.8 illustrates.

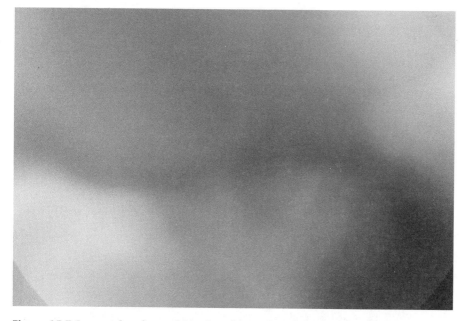

Figure 15.7 Image taken from within the volume of a sphere cloud shader.

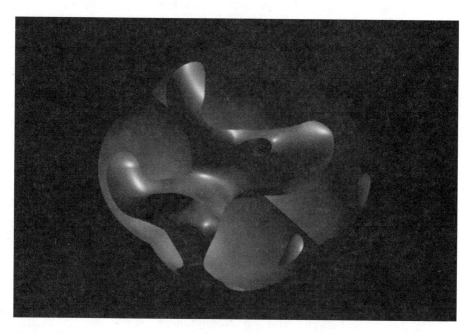

Figure 15.8 Overlapping solid hypertextures.

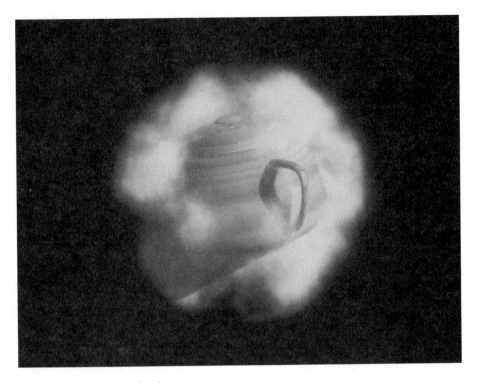

Figure 15.9 Teapot in clouds.

15.2.4   Holding Out Volumes with Depth Maps

Sometimes we want to embed a solid object in a volume, as illustrated in Figure 15.9. When marching through an object, as we do in shadowclouds, RenderMan does not directly provide us with z-depth values for other objects. But we can get them simply by using shadow maps. We can render a shadow map from the camera's view and incorporate a shadow( ) call in the surface shader to check if the current point is in shadow. If the shadow( ) call indicates we are in shadow from the camera depth view, then we set its opacity and color to 0, or just stop tracing the ray after this point.

15.3   In the Real World (Volumetric Effects for Production)

This section describes the process behind creating several of the CG effects shots in *Contact*, with an emphasis on atmospheric and volumetric effects. Specifically, we address the opening shot, which begins the movie, and the machine glow sequence, which occurs just before Ellie is hurled through space by the machine.

Contact was a production that had a great number of diverse CG effects shots. The opening shot was conceived halfway through production and was originally planned to be 90 seconds long. By the end of the show, in order to impress upon the audience the awe and immensity of space, the shot had grown to 3 minutes and 27 seconds of full film-resolution CG animation. When we began the opening shot, half the show's production schedule was behind us and the artwork for the shot had not been worked on yet. Initial efforts for the opening shot revolved around gathering existing astrophotographs from NASA, Hubble Space Telescope pictures, and generating images from within our own art department. Long-time concept artists for Carl Sagan, Jon Lomberg and Don Davis, also provided initial reference images. Robert Zemekis, Ken Ralston, and Stephen Rosenbaum chose from the best of these reference images, and sequence supervisor Jay Redd modeled and choreographed a 3D animatic wireframe pull-out of our universe using accurate scale.

At this point, I started work on the Eagle Nebula and during the rest of the production the shots I worked on in some way or another involved volumetric effects. In this section I would like to share some of the wisdom we gained while creating these shots.

15.3.1 Opening Shot

When I first joined the opening shot team I was excited about the possibilities, until they assigned me the Eagle Nebula and dropped stacks of reference photos on my desk, all depicting nebulous volumes of stellar gas being lit by the hundreds of stars around it and buried within it. I have to admit it wasn't until several weeks later that it really hit me how hard it was to do lit gas in the time frame we had for the shot. As you can see by the Hubble Space Telescope image (Figure 15.10), the task was a little daunting.

We began with the ray marching idea of the previous section. We progressed pretty far before hitting several roadblocks, mainly related to controlling the shape of the noise. After struggling for a while, we chose a particle approach instead, for several reasons.

First, it is common to come up with a brilliant method for doing an effect beautifully only to have the director request changes to several parts of the image, all of which you have almost no control over with the method you are using. Noise is notoriously difficult to control in a precise way—like taking away this cloud piece or toning down this area of the pillar—but particles allow this kind of control naturally.

The second major reason we went with particles was the fact that we knew we would be able to make it work, and with the ray marching method there were simply too many unknowns at that time. With the deadline approaching, we had no leeway for taking a blind alley and having nothing to show the director at the end.

Figure 15.10 Hubble telescope image of the Eagle Nebula. (Image courtesy of NASA.)

Finally, the techniques to compute volumetric lit gas take far too long to render with the detail we needed for this scene. In the beginning of the shot, we pass very close to one of the pillars, and by the end of the shot we translate out until we can see the whole of the nebula. This is the worst case, going from very high detail close in to a very wide shot where that detail cannot still exist without aliasing. With the ray marching method, we were scared that the rendering times would be unmanageable. We also knew we would need to render the shot many times before we got the look the director wanted.

15.3.2   The Eagle: How We Did It

Rik Stringfellow, then senior technical director at Sony Imageworks, and I achieved the Eagle Nebula effect using the following method.

First, we broke the gas down into three major sections: the three main pillars of dense stellar gas, the inner gas surrounding those pillars, and the far-reaching oyster-shell-shaped nebulous cloud surrounding the other two elements.

For the main pillars we used tens of thousands of spheres, each with a cloud shader similar to that in Listing 15.1. We built a model around the volume of the inner pillars (see Figure 15.11) and then shot sphere particles into the center of those pillars using Houdini's particle system. We managed this by emitting particles from all points on the tessellated geometry in the direction of their inverted normals (i.e., into the inside of the volume of the three pillars).

We tried to keep the shaders for the particles as simple as possible. We basically used a glow shader with turbulence functions to add variation to the color of the surface. We added in the ability to light this gas as well as controls for the detail level, color, density, and antialiasing of the gas. Because we needed to fly through the volume of gas, and we didn't want the gas to suddenly pop on-screen, we faded the opacity on with distance from the camera to produce a feeling that the gas was slowly building up. The stars were done by building lights with carefully controlled attenuation. To get some level of shadowing, we used attenuation away from the light sources, darkened particles based on which side of the pillar they were emitted from, and used 2D compositing tricks. All of this helped add to the dense feeling of the gas when we had passed the pillars and were viewing them from far away.

For the inner gas, we used even more spheres, all with the same basic shader used for the pillars, and varied the density of the spheres throughout the volume. This seemed to work well, producing random spots of dense dark matter that had a much more natural placement than if we had placed those dense spots by hand. But we did add and remove some dark matter by hand, just as we predicted we would need to do.

We built the shape of the outer gas by emitting particle spheres around basic geometry, which was actually never included in the final render. Then we modified the shaders to take a percentage of their color values from projection lights in the scene. In this way we could more easily approach the general color and look of the reference photos we had. A simple texture map would not have produced the perspective shift that helps to sell the scale of the shot. The addition of noise, in addition to the projected color, helped to break up any streaking that might have occurred had we used only the projected maps for color. The outer gas by itself, as included in the composite for the film, is shown in Figure 15.12.

We have found that the general technique of combining painted and procedural textures works extremely well. To achieve the overall look of the Eagle Nebula would have taken a lot longer had we used procedural methods alone. In addition, this technique gave us some fine control over the color of the scene very rapidly. It is faster and easier to predict the result of modifying colors in 2D than it is with purely procedural color changes. We also added procedurally defined stars within the gas. Finally, an extra layer of dark matter on the outside of the shell helped to achieve some of the backlit effect in the overhanging lip of the outer shell of stellar gas. Rik Stringfellow composited the elements together to form the

Figure 15.11 Modeling the Eagle Nebula. An actual NASA photograph of the Eagle Nebula (top). CG models of the nebula (middle and bottom). (Top photograph courtesy of NASA. Middle and bottom images Sony Pictures Imageworks, Inc. © 1997). See also color plate 15.11.

Figure 15.12 CG rendering of the Eagle Nebula. (*CONTACT* © 1997 Warner Bros., a division of Time Warner Entertainment Company L.P. All Rights Reserved.) See also color plate 15.12.

Figure 15.13 CG rendering a close-up of the Eagle Nebula. (*CONTACT* © 1997 Warner Bros., a division of Time Warner Entertainment Company L.P. All Rights Reserved.) See also color plate 15.13.

finished look, and Jay Redd composited the Eagle into the Milky Way (see Figure 15.13).

15.3.3 Machine Glow Sequence

The ray marching technique we had originally planned for the Eagle Nebula (before switching to the particle method) eventually paid off, though, because we were able to use the shader in another sequence to produce electrical-like effects around the core of the machine. Laurence Treweek expanded the basic ray marching shader to produce the effect of the machine glow. The electrical pattern inside the volume was produced by using spherical coordinates to create a 3D texture function that, when animated, moved inwards toward the center of the sphere. This created the chaotic turbulent core as seen in the movie (Figure 15.14). We used the shadow map technique to make the machine look like it was embedded inside the gas, as described in Section 15.2.4.

15.3.4 Saturn

The last shot I'd like to discuss is the effect produced for Saturn's rings that also appeared in the opening shot (Figure 15.15). Rodney Iwashina created the CG effects for this shot using Houdini and RenderMan. The Saturn rings used a number of elements. The long shots showed the rings looking like rings. This was done with simple geometry but with a shader that varied the opacity according to the various belts that make up Saturn's rings. These values were taken from the specs of the actual rings. Different shaders were applied to the top and bottom rings to account for the fact that the rings looked quite different depending on whether you were looking at the top at a grazing angle to the Sun or looking at the bottom with the Sun backlighting the ice particles that make up the rings.

There were about 40,000 large ice "rocks" instanced with the Houdini particle system with procedurally varying sizes and a displacement shader to put mid- and high-frequency detail in them. The surface shader was fairly simple, coloring them dark against the backlit small ice particles. The small ice particles that gave the rings the volumetric feel used a lot of stacked planes, approximating a ray march or discrete sampling of continuous noise space. About eight octaves of fBm with sharpened high frequencies gave the rings their gritty look. The "God rays" were created by some judicious tweaking with moire patterns, and the lighting was given a falloff based on the angle of the Sun object behind the planes and the I vector.

15.4 Conclusion

Realistic rendering of volumetric gases and clouds is not usually justified. Particles and stacking planes can often work faster and provide more control over important aspects like overall shape and motion. However, each new show raises the bar, and it won't be long before fully shadowed volumetric effects are the norm rather than the exception in visual effects. The ray marching technique really is at its best when no self-shadowing is needed (for example, flames for jet engines).

You should not underestimate the power and convenience of texture maps. Although it is a joy to write beautiful algorithms to describe a scene, if a texture map can be used, the result is more controllable and much faster to produce and change in 2D.

It is possible to expand on the basic volume shader idea to use depth maps, or to write plug-ins to Pixar's RenderMan to define volumes and include voxel intersection for faster density function integrations. Refraction is also not difficult to add, but when doing so it is important to do your specular calculations only at the surface of your solid.

Figure 15.14 Rendering of the machine glow sequence. (*CONTACT* © 1997 Warner Bros., a division of Time Warner Entertainment Company L.P. All Rights Reserved.) See also color plate 15.14.

Figure 15.15 Rendering of Saturn. (*CONTACT* © 1997 Warner Bros., a division of Time Warner Entertainment Company L.P. All Rights Reserved.) See also color plate 15.15.

16 Nonphotorealistic Rendering with RenderMan

Scott Johnston
Fleeting Image Animation

16.1 Introduction

Photorealism is a recent phenomenon. Before the invention of the camera, artists drew, painted, carved, and printed their impressions of the world; many did not aggressively pursue realism and quite often purposely avoided it. Defining nonphotorealism is a daunting task: there is photorealism and there is "everything else." The term *nonphotorealism* itself implies a bias toward photorealism—other imagery is not described by what it is, but by what it is not.

Nonphotorealistic rendering is a rapidly growing subgenre of computer graphics. In addition to synthesizing the photographic process, there is a trend among digital artists to imitate other media. Recent work on painterly rendering (Meier, 1996), pen-and-ink illustration (Winkenbach and Salesin, 1994), and watercolor (Curtis, Anderson, Seims, Fleisher, and Salesin 1997) shows an interest not in "nonphotorealism," but in expression in other media.

Most CG research in the past decade has focused on photorealism, with the implicit belief that the process of achieving this goal will deliver the tools required to reproduce any look. Several fundamental concepts were introduced that do aid in the exploration of nonphotorealistic looks, and tools designed to produce photorealistic effects can be successfully tailored to create a variety of other looks. In addition, information encoded with these tools can provide temporal coherence, allowing the production of effects in animation that would be impossible to achieve with traditional techniques.

The pursuit of other techniques never went away, as the use of CG within traditional animation demonstrates, but was overshadowed by the progress in photorealism. Technology has begun to allow artists to succeed in the quest for realism; that people are turning to alternatives is further proof of this achievement.

The examples presented here are by no means exhaustive but illustrate how RenderMan can be used to implement and augment the design of alternative styles.

16.1.1   *Meta*-realism

The primary goal of a technical director is to incorporate CG elements seamlessly into the context of a film. This context consists of two elements: the world within the film and the filmmaking process through which the material is presented. The TD must accurately model not only content in the world but also the method (and artifacts) of its presentation.

Photorealism generally refers to live-action film realism. In addition to matching the lighting and texture of the live-action subject, getting an effect to work within the world of a film requires the incorporation of the properties of the film process: motion blur, film grain, lens flares, camera jars, and other properties of filmmaking, whether intentional or accidental. These visual traits make a live-action film "feel" like a film. The audience has learned to expect them, and although it is possible to create imagery without some of these artifacts, viewers are less willing to accept the result as real, especially in the context of material that exhibits these artifacts.

In live-action filmmaking, the more realistic something appears, the more believable it becomes. The process and artifacts are made as transparent as possible. Unfortunately, the audience's technical sophistication matures over time. The bar on film realism keeps being raised—along with the budget. In nonphotorealistic media, like animation, the process is never transparent. The methods and their artifacts create the content rather than record it. Making something believable does not mean making it real. If story and emotion are expressed believably, they will feel real. This freedom from the restrictions of realism is part of what makes animation timeless.

The aim of cartoon realism is to integrate CG with the rest of the elements and "really look like a cartoon." The production designer and art director define "reality" for a particular film. It may be photo-, crayon-, watercolor- or Lego-, but whatever -realism it is, to preserve the illusion, artists must strive to present the style believably and not unintentionally break from the design.

The wildebeest stampede in *The Lion King* is an example of a nonphotoreal element integrated into the environment of the film. (The stampede was done with RenderMan plus an inking method that was a precursor to what is presented later in this chapter.) The CG characters were animated and visually treated like their 2D counterparts; the camera moves maintained the 2D multiplane pan style of the rest of the film.

In *Beauty and the Beast*, the ballroom scene was designed to break the visual style of the film. The sequence is a high point in the film—the characters fall in love. The emotion of the moment is enhanced by the visual clarity of a more realistic environment. (The ballroom was all RenderMan with a lot of `noise()` layered like paint on a background, displacement maps for most ornamentation detail, passing a stationary "eye" to lock some highlights to surfaces independent of the camera motion, and some beautiful 2D character animation by James Baxter.)

Pixar's films make use of many live-action-film visual traits, but like all aspects of good animation, these cues are studied, exaggerated, and caricatured.

16.1.2   Flat Media

A subset of nonphotorealistic rendering research has been on synthesizing "flat media." These are canvas- or paper-based techniques, like drawing, painting, pen-and-ink illustration, engraving, and woodblock printing. In the context of these media, a "stroke" is generalized to mean an agent acting on a medium. It can include charcoal, paint, carved grooves, or watercolor as applied to board, canvas, wood, paper, cel, and so on.

Previous work on representational nonphotorealistic computer graphics can be traced as far back as Peter Foldes' *Hunger* in 1974. Current nonphotoreal rendering is predominantly derived from Perlin (1985), Saito and Takahashi (1990), and Haeberli (1990). Recent work by Curtis, Anderson, Seims, Fleischer, and Salesin (1997), Winkenbach and Salesin (1994), and Wood, Finkelstein, Hughes, Thayer, and Salesin (1997) explore several aspects of rendering flat media.

Some of the ideas presented here are extensions to research that occurred during the early development of Disney's *Fantasia 2000*. Barbara Meier's "Painterly Rendering for Animation" is a superb account of that work (Meier, 1996).

Hand-crafted flat media share several intrinsic properties that must be mimicked to represent the styles believably. The following is a summary of these properties and the problems they present for synthetic image construction. These problems are often compounded when the technique is animated. The remainder of the chapter presents methods for applying these properties with RenderMan.

16.1.3   Nonideal Camera Models

Accurate perspective is a choice. Lens exaggeration, noncentered perspective, multipoint perspective, and panoramas are common outside of photorealism. Having the center of perspective exactly in the center of an image is rare. Perspective constantly changes in a scene with a moving 3D camera; this is often undesirable in nonphotorealistic animation.

16.1.4 Applied in the Image Plane

In flat media, the stroke is applied directly onto the image plane. Placing an image of a painting in perspective is very different from painting an image in perspective. Texture mapping reveals the photoreal underpinnings of a renderer; when mapped onto a surface, a texture gives objects a "gift-wrapped" look.

The surface of the medium may have a texture, like canvas or paper tooth, which exists in the image plane and affects the strokes.

16.1.5 Coloring outside the Lines

Objects extend past their borders, blending into adjoining regions. All the objects in a scene are built from the same basic building blocks—the "strokes" of the media—creating a cohesive image. Object boundaries can be ambiguous. They are not explicit, but are implied in the way the artist manipulates the medium: color, stroke direction, brush style, size, and so on.

16.1.6 Space Filling

Most natural media examples fill the canvas. If too few strokes are used on a surface, the result will be sparse. Some painters solve this by underpainting with large brush strokes, then layering smaller strokes over them to pull out details. Alternatively, more brush strokes can be used to cover larger areas, and fewer strokes on smaller areas.

16.1.7 Level of Detail

Distant objects are rendered with less detail than near objects. Meier points out that artists also use level of detail to focus a viewer toward a point of interest, "simplifying unimportant details." Simply scaling a technique down, even when properly antialiased, is not always correct. In flat media, the detail on a surface needs to be thinned out as it recedes, not just filtered. In etching or pen-and-ink illustration, for example, the lines have a minimum practical size. Fewer strokes are used on a midground object than on a near one, with little or no detail on a distant object.

The traditional method for level of detail is through changes in geometry. As shown with antialiasing, however, far and near surfaces can also be rendered differently. This idea can be explored with traditional texture mapping by creating a set of images with progressively "thinned" detail and substituting the lower-detail images for the lower-resolution mip-maps. Figure 16.1 shows three texture sources. The first has complete detail, the second a simplified representation of that detail, and the third no detail. When a mip-map is created with larger resolution images from the first image, and smaller resolution images from the second and third im-

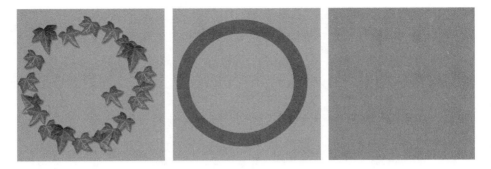

Figure 16.1 A texture painted at three levels of detail.

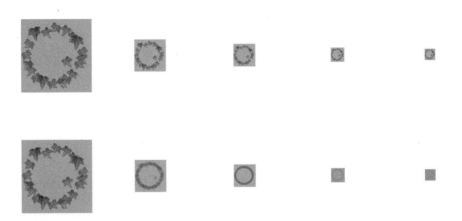

Figure 16.2 A patch normally filters the texture as it gets smaller (upper) while a level-of-detail texture transitions between high and low detail over the same range (lower).

ages, the texturing process will adjust the level of detail as well as provide filtering. Figure 16.2 shows a square at different sizes. The top row has an unmodified mip-map and the lower row a mip-map with level-of-detail substitutions. Figure 16.3 shows a plane in perspective. The "traditional" texture to the left gets muddy in the distance, whereas in the image on the right, the texture vanishes after being simplified. The first transition point has been exaggerated toward the viewer for illustrative purposes.

Creating a level-of-detail mip-map for *BMRT* is simple. Use `mkmip` to create mip-maps for each of the level-of-detail images. Then use `tiffsplit` to break them into component images. Select a level of detail for each layer and build a new mip-map with `tiffcp`.

Figure 16.3 Receding patch without (left) and with (right) level-of-detail texture.

16.1.8 Spatio-temporal Coherence

Temporal coherence is not a problem for still imagery, but is important in animation. As objects move, the media should move with them. When an effect is applied without tracking, objects appear to move behind the effect and are obscured by it. This is known as the "shower door" problem. Changes to the level of detail on moving objects must also be achieved coherently.

16.1.9 Energy/Entropy

Handcrafted media are imperfect. Although coherence is important, if the style is too rigidly locked, it will not feel organic. Conversely, if changes occur too quickly, the result becomes distracting noise. An artist's natural variance strikes a balance between freneticism and sterile order. Serendipity introduces surprising imperfections that become features at the artist's discretion.

Energy in animation is also controlled in other ways: properly timed character animation uses both ones and twos to control the energy in the animation, not just to save drawings. With properly charted slow-out and slow-in, a move can be made languid or given more snap. (A full discourse on animation is outside the scope of this book. Please see the bibliography at the end of this chapter.) Independent animators working in alternative media have used in-camera dissolves to save drawing time and soften the transitions between images. Quick morphs between frames is a newer variation of this technique. In both cases, it is done to control the energy of the medium.

16.1.10 Color, Lighting/Anti-lighting, Layering

The discussions on lighting and color in Chapters 10 and 12 apply directly to nonphotorealistic rendering. Color and light can also be used in more abstract ways. Both are built up in layers—not just in the composition of separate objects, but to construct an object. Shifts in color can replace value changes. For example, the shadowed side of an object may be a different hue rather than just a darker value, allowing warm light with cool shadows or cool light with warm shadows. Emotion can directly dictate color. Underpainting in a complementary color helps lift subsequent layers. Anti-lighting—using lights with negative intensities to cast darkness—can pull color out of a layer.

16.2   Alternate Camera Models

Nonideal camera models are common in flat media but can be used with any rendering technique. In a simple camera model, the camera's view of a scene is centered on the z-axis. This model is limited, as the following examples illustrate:

- The bellows of a professional large-format camera can be adjusted so that the lens is not parallel to the film plane, giving a photographer more control on the perspective of an image.
- Architectural renderings often employ one-, two-, or three-point perspective.
- Animation backgrounds contain complex multipoint perspective views of an environment; local regions appear correct and a 2D camera move over the image gives the illusion of a 3D camera move without the distortion of constantly changing perspective.

Figure 16.4 is a layout from Walt Disney Pictures' *The Prince and the Pauper* (1990). The shot opens on the left side of the painting, looking up into the sky past a bell tower, and pans down (right) until we're looking out over the city, towards Goofy's hovel. This scene was my introduction to multipoint perspective: I was asked to make it snow in the scene—towards the camera at the head of the shot and down and away at the tail. At the time, I approximated the pan with an animating 3D camera.

RenderMan offers several solutions to extend the camera model, providing tools that can more accurately re-create nonideal situations like this one.

16.2.1   Off-Center Perspective

Camera moves do not have to be 3D. Traditional animation camera mechanics consist of 2D and multiplane moves. In RenderMan, the `ScreenWindow` API call can be used to construct 2D moves over a scene without changing the camera position, thus preserving the perspective.

It is useful to view the camera model as being split between 3D and 2D. The 3D portion establishes the overall layout of a scene, including the projection from 3D to 2D. The 2D portion operates on the image plane to select a region of interest. The 3D camera can remain fixed even if the 2D view changes over time.

Figure 16.4 Multipoint perspective with 2D camera mechanics from Walt Disney Pictures' *The Prince and the Pauper*. (© Disney Enterprises, Inc.)

Setting the `ScreenWindow` away from the image plane origin offsets the view, moving away from perspective center. One limitation of `ScreenWindow` is that it cannot be rotated; instead, the camera must be rotated to align the desired view with the x- and y-axes. Rotating the camera around the z-axis has no effect on the perspective, just on the orientation.

16.2.2 Affine Cameras

Perspective and orthographic projections can be modified by the composition of a camera matrix to position the camera in the world (or, rather, to position the world in front of the camera). Multipoint perspective can be achieved by building a sequence of matrix transformations onto the camera, but this can be unintuitive. It is often more useful to manipulate the camera matrix directly.

Designers often want to indicate exactly where vanishing points belong. A quick refresher on affine matrices shows how easily this is accomplished within Render-Man.

Perspective Axes

Given a transformation matrix M:

$$M = \begin{bmatrix} m_{00} & m_{01} & m_{02} & m_{03} \\ m_{10} & m_{11} & m_{12} & m_{13} \\ m_{20} & m_{21} & m_{22} & m_{23} \\ m_{30} & m_{31} & m_{32} & m_{33} \end{bmatrix}$$

A point P will transform to: $P' = [P_x\ P_y\ P_z\ 1]M$. For example, the origin $(0,0,0)$ will transform to

$$P' = [0\ 0\ 0\ 1]M$$
$$= [m_{30}\ m_{31}\ m_{32}\ m_{33}]$$

This projects to the point

$$\left(\frac{m_{30}}{m_{33}}, \frac{m_{31}}{m_{33}}, \frac{m_{32}}{m_{33}} \right)$$

To force the origin O to project to a point (O_x, O_y, O_z), the last row of the matrix can be set to:

$$[m_{30}\ m_{31}\ m_{32}\ m_{33}] = [O_x\ O_y\ O_z\ 1]$$

or, more generally,

$$[m_{30}\ m_{31}\ m_{32}\ m_{33}] = [(O_x O_w)\ (O_y O_w)\ (O_z O_w)\ O_w]$$

where O_w is some nonzero scale factor.

Similarly, for a point with a very large P_x,

$$P' = \lim_{P_x \to \infty} ([P_x\ P_y\ P_z\ 1]M)$$
$$= [(P_x m_{00})\ (P_x m_{01})\ (P_x m_{02})\ (P_x m_{03})]$$

which projects to

$$\left(\frac{P_x m_{00}}{P_x m_{03}}, \frac{P_x m_{01}}{P_x m_{03}}, \frac{P_x m_{02}}{P_x m_{03}} \right)$$
$$= \left(\frac{m_{00}}{m_{03}}, \frac{m_{01}}{m_{03}}, \frac{m_{02}}{m_{03}} \right)$$

Therefore, a vanishing point for the X-axis at (X_x, X_y, X_z) is defined by:

$$[m_{00}\ m_{01}\ m_{02}\ m_{03}] = [(X_x X_w)\ (X_y X_w)\ (X_z X_w)\ X_w]$$

where X_w is a nonzero scale factor.

A general solution to three-point perspective of the three major axes to points $P_x = (X_x, X_y, X_z)$, $P_y = (Y_x, Y_y, Y_z)$, and $P_z = (Z_x, Z_y, Z_z)$ with the origin at $P_o = (O_x, O_y, O_z)$ is

$$M = \begin{bmatrix} (X_x X_w) & (X_y X_w) & (X_z X_w) & X_w \\ (Y_x Y_w) & (Y_y Y_w) & (Y_z Y_w) & Y_w \\ (Z_x Z_w) & (Z_y Z_w) & (Z_z Z_w) & Z_w \\ (O_x O_w) & (O_y O_w) & (O_z O_w) & O_w \end{bmatrix}$$

The four scale factors, $[X_w, Y_w, Z_w, O_w]$ control how quickly each axis converges to its vanishing point. The first three affect only their own axis, while O_w simultaneously scales all three axes.

Orthographic Axes

In the standard perspective matrix, the x- and y-axes remain orthographic, and the perspective divide occurs along z. In our general scheme, any of the three major axes, N, can be made orthographic by substituting its row with

$$[((N_x - O_x)N_w) \; ((N_y - O_y)N_w) \; ((N_z - O_z)N_w) \; 0]$$

Notice that the orthographic axes are vectors relative to the transformed origin. Additional affine transformations can be composed with this scheme to reorient objects in relation to the vanishing axes.

In RenderMan, a call to `Projection "orthographic"` followed by a `Transform` matrix as just described sets a multipoint perspective. (See Figure 16.5.) Care must be taken when setting the `ScreenWindow` and the z-values of the transform to ensure proper boundaries and reliable depth information.

16.2.3 Area Cameras

Using a surface to drive a camera as opposed to a pinhole is analogous to using a patch as a light source rather than a point. I call this family of imaging tools *area cameras*.

Placing a flat patch just past the near clipping plane or just in advance of the far clipping plane and extending it to the boundaries of the image can lead to several useful tricks. Shaders on these patches are referred to as "clip plane" shaders.

In implementations of RenderMan that support the `trace()` call, like *BMRT*, one interesting use of a near-clip shader is to override the camera model completely, allowing for complex nonideal cameras within RenderMan.

In 1997, Wood, Finkelstein, Hughes, Thayer, and Salesin described a technique for stitching together a series of images from a moving camera to create a multipoint perspective. Inspecting the resulting image reveals that every point is a view *from* somewhere *to* somewhere—with a map of these Ps and Is, a simple nonideal camera shader can be written for a near clip plane surface to trace a multipoint perspective lens in one pass through a renderer. There are at least three ways to derive nonideal camera maps:

- analytically in a procedural shader
- from a texture map image
- from reference geometry

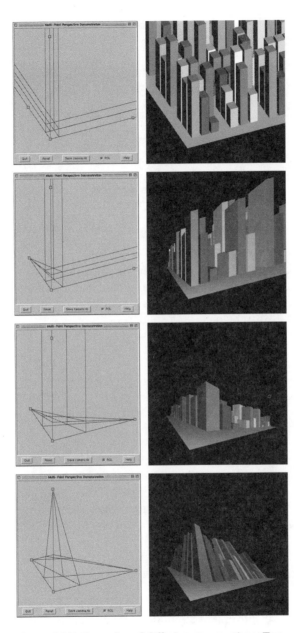

Figure 16.5 Examples of differing perspectives. Top to bottom: orthographic axes; single-point perspective; two-point perspective; three-point perspective.

Figure 16.6 A 180-degree spherical lens rendered with `panorama.sl`.

Procedural Lenses

Shaders mimicking fish-eye, cylindrical, and hemispherical lenses are straightforward to write parametrically. Listing 16.1 shows a sample panoramic shader capable of reproducing a variety of lenses. Figure 16.6 is a 180-degree spherical panorama of a cubescape generated with the `panorama` shader.

Texture-Mapped Lenses

The multipoint perspective implementation suggested by Wood et al. can be extended to create texture-map images. For each frame to be stitched together, images that contain the world-space positions and eye positions are also rendered. As the main images are stitched together, these additional images are stitched in the same manner and can aid in the correlation step. The result can be used in a shader to render the scene from the vantage point of the multipoint perspective camera.

Texture maps can be derived for other purposes as well. Omnimax introduces distortion in the image as it is projected onto a curved screen. Some compensation for this warp can be handled through image processing prior to recording an image. With a nonideal lens, the inverse of this distortion can be modeled in a texture map and used to render "predistorted" imagery.

Reference Geometry Lenses

The most interesting method of generating nonideal lenses is with reference geometry. The flat film plane is a convenient simplification of the eye. When an image is projected onto the retina, it forms a patch that is a section of a sphere whose normals all point through a common focal point. (Okay, so this isn't exactly how the eye works either, but the image is useful.) This patch can be built and placed in a scene as the reference geometry for a clip-plane patch. (See Figure 16.7.) A shader can use the lens by calling `trace(Pref, Nref)`. Nonideal cameras are created by changing the reference geometry.

> **Listing 16.1** panorama shader captures a panorama around the y-axis from a location in world space.

```
/*
 * Procedural lens to capture a panorama around the y-axis
 * from a location in world space.
 *
 * This can mimic both cylindrical (spherical = 0.)
 * and spherical (spherical = 1., ymax == ymin)
 * panoramic lenses.
 *
 * To avoid intersecting the scene, the point P is
 * cast from the axis rather than the surface of
 * the cylinder or sphere.
 *
 * The theta angles select a range of angles around
 * the y-axis, which span [0, 1] in s.
 *
 * The fovy angles set the "field of view" in the y-direction.
 * For example, a fovylo = -15; fovyhi = 15 sets a centered
 * field of view of 30 degrees.
 *
 * When usendc is set, the parametric coordinates are overridden
 * by screen-filling normalized device coordinates, allowing
 * any clip-plane object to look through the lens.
 *
 */
surface
panorama ( float usendc = 0;
           float spherical = 0;
           float thetamin = 0.;
           float thetamax = 360.;
           float ymin = 0.;
           float ymax = 10.;
           float worldx = 0.;
           float worldz = 0.;
           float fovylo = 0;
           float fovyhi = 0;      )
{
    varying float ss = s;
    varying float tt = t;

    if (usendc != 0.0) {
        varying point P2 = transform("NDC", P);
        ss = xcomp(P2);
        tt = 1. - ycomp(P2);
    }
    varying float theta = radians(thetamin + ss * (thetamax - thetamin));
    varying float angley;
    if (spherical != 0.0) {
        angley = radians(fovylo + (fovyhi - fovylo) * tt);
```

▶

Listing 16.1 (continued)

```
    } else {
        uniform float sfovylo = sin(radians(fovylo));
        uniform float sfovyhi = sin(radians(fovyhi));
        varying float sfovyt = sfovylo + (sfovyhi - sfovylo) * tt;
        angley = asin(sfovyt);
    }

    varying float sy = sin(angley);
    varying float cy = cos(angley);
    varying vector It = vector "world" ( cos(theta) * cy, sy, sin(theta)
                                                             * cy);
    varying point Pt = point "world" ( worldx, ymin + tt * (ymax - ymin),
                                                             worldz);

    Ci = trace(Pt, It);
    Oi = Os;
    Ci *= Oi;
}
```

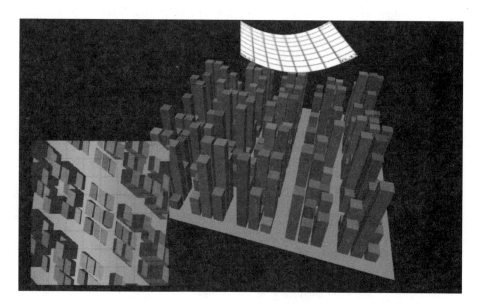

Figure 16.7 Simple scene with reference geometry visible. Inset: view through area camera.

Surrounding a scene with a cylinder with normals pointing in produces something akin to a Cyberware scanner—a form of "slit-scan" camera. A more general "slit-scan" camera can be generated where the u-direction of the reference geometry travels along a film-plane-tangent curve and the v-direction is a circular arc for a desired vertical field of view. A way of building this reference geometry is to generate two curves through a scene. The first represents the location of the camera, and the second a point of interest. A patch can be constructed such that u travels along the first curve, and the patch normals across v at any given u pass through the second curve at u.

An alternative to using the normal of the reference surface for the incident vector is to construct two reference geometry patches: the first is a "point-of-interest" surface, as above, and the second an eye-reference patch that can be compressed in one parametric dimension to form a curve. The incident vector is defined by vector (Pref–Eref).

Listing 16.2 is a shader that uses reference geometry as a lens. The geometry is transformed into the scene to a user-specified coordinate system. When establishing an area camera, building the scene with the geometry visible is helpful. A named coordinate system at the location of the visible geometry allows the shader to properly place the reference patch.

The clip-plane patch does not have to be a screen-filling rectangle. The solution in Wood, Finkelstein, Hughes, Thayer, and Salesin (1997) indicates that a curved planar patch on the image plane reduces the distortion of the resulting image. For a given camera path, finding a clip-plane patch that minimizes distortion is an area for future research.

The trace() call returns no opacity information. A second pass with all geometry shaded with a white matte shader will generate an alpha channel.

Listing 16.2 areacam produces an image using reference geometry for lens shape.

```
/*
 * areacam.sl
 *
 * View a scene through a nonideal lens specified as
 * reference geometry for a clip-plane surface.
 *
 * Parameters:
 *    space - the name of the space that Pref/Eref are expressed in
 *    Pref - reference position of the lens
 *    Eref - optional eye reference geometry
 *    use_Eref - when nonzero, use the Eref geometry; otherwise just
 *           use the normal of the lens reference geometry
 */
```

▶

Listing 16.2 (continued)

```
surface
areacam (string space = "world";
         varying point Pref = point -1e10;
         varying point Eref = point -1e10;
         uniform float use_Eref = 0;)
{
    varying point Pobj = transform ("object", Pref);
    varying point Pareacam = transform (space, "current", Pobj);
    varying vector Iareacam;
    if (use_Eref != 0.) {
        /* Look from the eye through the reference geometry */
        varying point Eobj = transform("object", Eref);
        varying point Eareacam = transform(space, "current", Eobj);
        Iareacam = Pareacam - Eareacam;
    } else {
        /* Look through the reference geometry from the visible side */
        Iareacam = -calculatenormal(Pareacam);
    }

    Oi = 1;
    Ci = trace(Pareacam, Iareacam);
}
```

16.3 Shading Nonphotorealistically

Techniques developed by Curtis, Salesin, Haeberli, and others often involve highly interactive user processes or specialized renderers that allow each to be suited to a specific task but require longer development time and potentially difficult integration with production pipelines. RenderMan's flexible Shading Language provides a foundation for implementing aspects of these techniques in a framework that accommodates existing production methods.

There are two principal ways RenderMan can be used to generate nonphotoreal imagery:

- **Direct**: nonphotorealistic images are produced directly by RenderMan.
- **Indirect**: RenderMan is used to create a control image, or a set of control images, that are passed to a secondary renderer to generate the final image.

Both methods are useful; using one over the other depends on the specific application. The following two sections present examples of direct and indirect nonphotorealistic techniques.

16.3.1   Direct Rendering with RenderMan

Material presented in previous chapters shows how shaders can build layers of complexity into a texture incrementally. Some of the issues in nonphotorealistic rendering can be addressed directly using the same techniques.

The shader described next addresses the remaining issues. Although the example can be applied directly to imitate woodblock printing, pen-and-ink illustration, etching, and engraving, the principles extend to other families of nonphotorealistic media.

Woodblock Printing, Engraving, and Pen-and-Ink Illustration

In woodblock, engraving, and pen-and-ink illustration, line quality is consistent. As an object's apparent size changes, by advancing, receding, or scaling, the line density should be adjusted—a far or small object should be drawn with fewer lines than a near or large object. Similarly, a surface that pinches together should have fewer lines in the pinched area and more lines in the stretched area. To work in animation, these changes should evolve over time coherently—having a new solution for each frame would cause undesirable strobing.

The image plane is filled by lines that define the surfaces. Lighting is accomplished by one of two methods: for pen-and-ink illustration, the density of lines varies as a function of image intensity, but the individual line widths remain constant. This can be accomplished by layering lines over one another, often at opposing angles to create cross-hatching. For engraving and woodblock printing, the line density remains uniform, but the width of the line varies according to image intensity. (See Figure 16.8.)

Engraving and printing involve carving grooves into metal or wood, inking the surface, and pressing it onto paper to print a mirror image. Often, more than one block is used for a single output image, with different elements of the image on each block. These layers can be printed with different-colored inks to create multitonal imagery. Alternatively, a single ink can be used and the resulting image handtinted. The contours of the grooves in a woodcut are often designed to accentuate features of the surface being described. The width and spacing of the grooves can be used to control tonality, or perceived value. (The width is usually controlled by the depth of the chisel marks.)

Following contours makes synthesis fairly natural, because the isoparametric curves of surface patches often follow these features (or, at least, a simple transform of the parametric coordinate system does). The shader solution involves developing a space-filling parametric surface texture.

Simple Stripes

A simple, naive method for striping an object is to use mod(). For example, stripes running along the v direction of a patch can be shaded by

Figure 16.8 Engraving of Brahma head from Temple Phnom-Boc (and detail), Paris, 1880 (from L. Delaporte, "Voyage au Cambodge," Libraire Ch. Delagrave, p. 341).

Figure 16.9 The simple stripe function.

```
sawtooth = mod(u * frequency, 1);
triangle = abs(2.0 * sawtooth - 1.0);
square = filterstep(duty, triangle);
```

This first defines a sawtooth wave of a specified frequency along the u-direction. The sawtooth is converted to a triangle wave and then to a square wave with a given duty cycle. As the triangle wave's value rises above the duty-cycle value, the step function will trigger.

As shown in Figure 16.9, this function provides uniform striping when applied to a simple patch. When applied to an object with nonuniform geometry, the stripes become nonuniform as well. Where the object pinches together, as at the top of the sphere, the stripes become narrower, and where the object is wider, around its equator, the stripes are wider. As an object changes size, so do the stripe details. The smaller sphere has the same features, just smaller.

Figure 16.10 Toward uniform line density.

Uniform Line Density

To achieve consistent line spacing and width, the stripe frequency is modified based on the size of the object—increased where the surface is stretched, for more stripes, and decreased where it is pinched, for fewer.

RenderMan provides derivatives across surfaces, and length(dPdu) is a good measure of how stretched or pinched a surface is in the direction normal to the stripes. The length(dPdu) is visualized in Figure 16.10 (left). The value in this image is proportional to the length of the derivative in the u direction. Because the length variation is continuous across v, directly modulating the frequency of the stripes by this value produces a continuously changing frequency, which is difficult to control and therefore undesirable (Figure 16.10, center). To compensate for this, rather than modulate the frequency continuously, adjust the frequency in discrete steps following a simple rule: every time the length(dPdu) doubles, use twice as many stripes (as in Figure 16.10, right):

```
logdp = log(length(dp),2);        /* Log base 2 of length(dp) */
ilogdp = floor(logdp);            /* Floor to discretize */
stripes = pow(2,ilogdp);          /* Restore multiplier */
sawtooth = mod(u * stripes * frequency, 1);
```

Normalize Line Width

The discrete stepping introduces some undesirable artifacts (jumps) in the width of the lines. This can be corrected by tapering the duty cycle across the transition from one frequency to the next.

```
transition = logdp - ilogdp;
```

The transition variable will vary from 0.0 to 1.0 in the interval between discrete frequency jumps. Because the frequency doubles at each transition, this can be used to halve the duty cycle across the region (see Figure 16.11).

```
square = filterstep(duty*(1 - transition/2), triangle);
```

Figure 16.11 Tapering by changing duty cycle.

Figure 16.12 Detail reduces as size reduces.

As with the pinching and stretching, when the object changes size, the length of the derivative will scale, and thus the amount of striping will change. Because of the discrete steps, the frequency changes will be coherent over time—new stripes appear to "draw on" or "erase off" in between other stripes as they spread and contract. The overall density remains uniform, as shown in Figure 16.12.

Coherent Frequency Adjustment

If the frequency is changed over time, the stripes slide across the surface, as seen in Figure 16.13. By moving the frequency term inside the log function, frequency adjustments react the same as scale adjustments—as existing lines thin and separate, new lines are added in between (see Figure 16.14).

Screen Space Attenuation

This procedural surface texture compensates for stretching and pinching of the object and the overall object size but is still being computed on a 3D object in world space. The detail would still be maintained as an object recedes in space. Also, towards the edge of the sphere, where the surface bends away from the viewer, the apparent frequency increases.

Figure 16.13 Frequency changes cause stripe sliding on the surface.

Figure 16.14 Frequency inside log function.

Figure 16.15 Visualizing the dp variable.

To mimic a natural technique, the shader needs to be modified to work relative to the canvas in screen space. An approximate solution is to transform the derivative into screen space and clamp it in z.

```
dp = dpscale * vtransform ("screen", dPdu);
setzcomp(dp, 0.0); /* Normal dropoff compensation */
```

In the image in Figure 16.15, where the value indicates the length of dp, the edges become darker as the normal falls off. The dpscale factor helps to balance the magnitudes of dp and dPdu. Now as an object advances or recedes, or as a surface

Figure 16.16 Line-width compensation as normal drops off.

Figure 16.17 Grooves with tapered tips.

drops away from the viewer, the screen space derivative will scale and shrink and thus the frequency will adjust to attempt to maintain uniform line widths (see Figure 16.16).

Tapered Tips

The frequency transition of lines is still abrupt. This may be appropriate for thin-line pen-and-ink illustration, but for woodcut printing and engraving, an adaptation of how the "transition" variable is used gives a better appearance.

If the triangle wave is representative of grooves cutting into wood, adding a new line between two others should be accomplished by slowly chiseling to a desired depth, not by abruptly starting a new groove. The following code increases the frequency across transitions by continuously narrowing the peaks and raising the valleys into a new set of peaks.

```
transtriangle = abs((1 + transition) * triangle - transition);
square = filterstep(duty, transtriangle);
```

The grooves now have shallower entry and exit points, as seen in Figure 16.17.

Figure 16.18 Tapering by changing duty cycle.

Figure 16.19 Angle adjustment.

Space-Filling Algorithm

Looking down at the sphere and modifying the duty cycle shows the space-filling nature of the resulting procedural texture (see Figure 16.18).

Angle

This development is not restricted to isoparametric lines in u and v. The parametric coordinate system can also be rotated, as long as the derivatives are also rotated (see examples in Figure 16.19).

Lighting

Thus far, we've been keeping the frequency and duty cycle consistent. Lighting computations can be used to modulate these to create a variety of effects. For pen-and-ink, the frequency would also be modulated by lighting intensity; duty-cycle tapering can be used to maintain constant width. For woodblock printing, the duty cycle is the measure of how wide or narrow the lines appear and can be made directly proportional to desired intensity. (See Figure 16.20.) A simple lighting equation is sufficient.

```
diffuzeC = Ka * ambient() + Kd * diffuse(faceforward(normalize(N),I));
diffuze = (comp(diffuzeC,0)+comp(diffuzeC,1)+comp(diffuzeC,2))/3.0;
/* Straight average here. Luminance can also be used. */
```

Figure 16.20 Intensity as duty-cycle step threshold.

Although the lighting can be adjusted for different layers, it is useful to have a separate linear scaling term so that different features can be pulled from the same lighting condition.

```
diffuze = (diffuze - lo)/(hi - lo);
```

This replaces, or modulates, the duty-cycle.

```
square = filterstep(duty * diffuze, triangle);
/* usually want duty = 1.0 now. */
```

Layers

Postprocess compositing can be used to "print" a set of render layers into a final image (see Figure 16.21). Some layers, particularly light area crosshatches, can be used for "anti-lighting," erasing from the underlying layers rather than being composed with them.

When rendering multiple passes for multiple layers, complex lighting can be computed in a separate pass and stored as a texture map. Subsequent levels will not have to compute the lighting and, in fact, can have all lights turned off.

To use a preexisting render, the diffuze term is evaluated via a texture lookup in "NDC" space.

```
if (mapname != "") {
    Pndc = transform("NDC", P);
    screenx = xcomp(Pndc);
    screeny = ycomp(Pndc);
    diffuze = float texture(mapname[0], screenx, screeny);
}
```

An added benefit to rendering intensity in a separate pass is that the image resolution of the lighting pass can be significantly smaller than the striping passes. When computed at the same resolution, high-frequency lighting information, such as a hard shadow edge, can cause abrupt changes in line width. In woodblock printing, we want to soften these transitions while maintaining high-contrast lines. A smaller intensity map with texture filtering accomplishes this.

Figure 16.21 Compositing layers.

Figure 16.22 Stochastic adjustments to the pattern.

Figure 16.23 Escher-inspired woodblock print in two layers. See also color plate 16.23.

Stochastic Adjustments

Noise can be used to make the effect more natural. The line width can be adjusted and lines made to stipple slightly by adding noise to the diffuze term as a function of the parameter normal to the striping direction (Figure 16.22, left). To be accurate, the noise frequency should be adjusted so that the frequency of the stipple shifts between octaves of noise as the apparent frequency in this direction changes. In practice, this isn't always necessary.

The peaks of our triangle waves can also be adjusted within a stripe to jiggle the stripes across the surface. In this case, their width is maintained, but the placement of the visible portion of the stripe is moved in the direction normal to the stripe (Figure 16.22, right, and Figure 16.23). The final shader is given in Listing 16.3.

Listing 16.3 woodblockprint shader makes images that look like woodblock prints.

```
/*
 * woodblockprint.sl -- surface shader for carved woodblock printing
 *
 * (c) Copyright 1998 by Fleeting Image Animation, Inc.
 * All rights reserved.
 *
 * Permission is hereby granted, without written agreement and without
 * license or royalty fees, to use, copy, modify, and distribute this
 * software and for any purpose, provided that the above copyright
 * notice appears in all copies of this software.
 *
 * Author: Scott F. Johnston
 *
 */
surface
woodblockprint ( float freq = 2;
                 float duty = 0.50;
                 float normal_dropoff = 1.0;
                 float dpscale = 0.1;
                 color stripe_color = 0;
                 float Ka = 0.2;
                 float Kd = 0.8;
                 float lo = 0.0;
                 float hi = 1.0;
                 string mapname = "";
                 float aspect = 1.0; )
{
    color diffuzeC;
    float diffuze;

    point Pscreen = transform("screen", P);
    vector dp = dpscale * vtransform("screen", dPdv);
    setzcomp(dp, 0);

    float lendp = mix (length(dp), length(dPdv), normal_dropoff);

    float logdp = log(freq * lendp)/log(2);
    float ilogdp = floor(logdp);
    float stripes = pow(2,ilogdp);

    float sawtooth = mod(v * stripes, 1);
    float triangle = abs(2.0 * sawtooth - 1.0);
    float transition = logdp - ilogdp;
    float transtriangle = abs((1 + transition) * triangle - transition);

    if (mapname != "") {
        float screenx = xcomp(Pscreen) / aspect;
        float screeny = ycomp(Pscreen);
```

▶

Listing 16.3 (continued)

```
        screenx = 0.5 * (screenx + 1.0);
        screeny = 1.0 - 0.5 * (screeny + 1.0);
        diffuze = float texture(mapname[0], screenx, screeny);
    } else {
        diffuzeC = Ka * ambient() + Kd * diffuse(faceforward
                                        (normalize(N),I));
        diffuze = (comp(diffuzeC,0) + comp(diffuzeC,1) + comp
                    (diffuzeC,2))/3.0;
    }
    diffuze = (diffuze - lo)/(hi - lo);

    float square = filterstep(duty * diffuze, transtriangle);

    color CC = mix(Cs, stripe_color, square);

    Oi = Os;
    Ci = Os * CC;
}
```

Animation

The noise functions can be kept fixed, for locked frame-to-frame coherence, but in animation it can be more natural to allow them to vary over time. Offsets to the noise functions can either be random, causing new stippling and jiggling for each frame, or can be evolved over time, producing a smoother, continuous variation.

16.4 Indirect Rendering with RenderMan

Ken Perlin described a pixel stream editor (PSE) in "An Image Synthesizer" in 1985. By prerendering a suite of images he showed how postprocessing in 2D image space could be used to create a wide variety of effects. Because most flat media are generated in 2D, his framework is a good one to adopt when synthesizing flat techniques. In his initial PSE, Perlin constrained the computation to local pixel information, allowing for simple parallelization of the algorithm but limiting it as well. Most compositing suites include operators that work across regions of pixels, not just current pixels.

To generalize Perlin's ideas is to recognize that images are an efficient means of storing information needed for secondary processes. TDs know this from utilizing texture and displacement maps. The correlation between the source images and the final result can be less distinct with nonphotoreal processes.

Working in a layered 2D painter's algorithm space can avoid the "gift-wrap" problems of textures. Haeberli and Meier both exploit this aspect in their work.

Haeberli's paint-by-numbers showed that Perlin-style image buffers could be used to control aspects of his painting system; Meier made extensive use of RenderMan-generated control images to drive different aspects of the Painterly Rendering system. The fundamental idea behind these systems is the use of 3D information from a 3D rendering system applied to a destination image using 2D manipulation. This split takes some baggage out of the 3D portion, making it more efficient.

One of Perlin's most important insights is the benefit of a system's ability to defer art-direction decisions until postproduction. In a production environment, changes will always be made down the line. Anticipating changes and providing a venue for them can increase throughput.

The work of Saito and Takahashi, which built on Perlin's ideas, evolved into the cartoon shaders used by several major animation studios.

16.4.1   Rendering Traditional "Ink and Paint" Cel-Animation

Chapter 12 presented a one-pass shader solution that can be convincing for some geometry in some stand-alone applications. However, when integrating traditional and computer-generated artwork, it is important to match the traditional methods more closely.

Background

Historically, once an animator's drawings were cleaned up, a transparent piece of acetate (cel) was placed over the line artwork and the image was traced onto the cel by hand in colored ink (later, by a Xerox camera). The inked cel would be flipped over, and the backside would be painted. When viewed from the front, this simple process kept the integrity of the line and gave the paint a uniform appearance.

The introduction of CGI into this process meant using hidden-line algorithms to generate vector representations of the imagery, plotting the result on animation paper, and sending it through the Xerox camera to be transferred to cel and painted by hand. This process was used in Disney features from *The Great Mouse Detective* (1986) to *The Little Mermaid* (1989) and in several shorts. It was also used at other studios in films like Bill Kroyer's *Technological Threat* (1988).

After the conversion to digital ink and paint processes, plotting and printing computer-generated line artwork was still necessary to provide reference material to traditional animators, but the final imagery could be transferred digitally to the backend of the production system.

Digital Process

In the digital process, each cel can be thought of as the composite of an ink layer and a paint layer. Drawn artwork is scanned as an ink layer. Digital inkers tint the scanned lines, and the paint layer is filled using the ink layer as boundaries for the paint. One restriction imposed on the cleaned-up artwork is that shapes must be closed-off regions to prevent the paint from "spilling" out; hand painting could accommodate a looser line. Additional layers mask the ink and paint layers to provide cel-to-cel or cel-to-background registration.

Commercial animation packages often provide both hidden-line and hidden-surface renderers as separate processes, making it difficult to guarantee alignment between the resulting output. The features available in combination are restricted to those common to both methods.

In 1990, Saito and Takahashi published "Comprehensible Rendering of 3-D Shapes," which laid the groundwork for a unification of hidden-line and hidden-surface rendering algorithms. They presented a method for image enhancement using 2D image processing rather than 3D analytic tools. The benefits of using an image-based hidden-line solution include being able to use the same production pipeline for both line and rendered art, and accurate registration between different renders—the *exact* same camera, lights, and geometry can be used. Surface renderers provide additional tools that enhance hidden-line rendering but would be prohibitively difficult to include in analytical hidden-line algorithms. Most notable is the TD's ability to use procedural and image-based shaders to define edges and the ability to use displacement.

RenderMan provides an excellent environment for generating the source images. Many of the shaders are simple and efficient. Users who want to create more than three channels in one pass can extend RenderMan in ways that accommodate this or just run multiple passes through the renderer. In addition, recent releases of *PRMan* support the simultaneous output of multiple data channels (see the *PRMan User Manual* for details).

Cartoon Shaders Redux

Limitations and restrictions of the `cel` cartoon shader previously presented in Section 12.8 include

- The `cel` shader darkens the inside of edges of objects, but true ink lines "overdraw" the object.
- Boundary edges are not detected between adjoining surfaces.
- Application of `cel` is limited to curved surfaces.
- The `cel` shader does not have enough control over ink parameters.
- Rendering a single image incorporating tones and highlights limits postproduction flexibility.

A cartoon rendering environment consists of five steps: prerendering a set of control images, edge detection of desired features, edge classification to associate ink properties with the edges, rendering edges with "ink" properties, and final image construction suitable for compositing with other elements.

Edge Detection

Although prerendering is the first step in the process, understanding how edge detection works will establish the goals for the prerender shaders. There are two

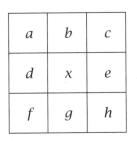

Figure 16.24 Neighboring pixels.

principal types of edges: feature edges and silhouette or profile edges. Feature edges are lines that exist on an object. They are formed by the boundaries between surfaces and by texture detail applied to a surface. Silhouette edges do not naturally exist on the surface, but are created at a boundary where a surface bends away from the viewer. Internal silhouette edges of self-occluding concave objects are the most difficult to detect.

The edge detector is an image filter designed to detect feature and silhouette edges. Each channel of a source image provides separate information to the detector; multiple channels can be combined to pass vector data. Rather than hard code which channels contain what information, or train an edge detector to specific types of data, it is best to keep the detector general and have a TD select which algorithms to use on which channels. For simple geometry and scenes, 8-bit channels may suffice, but better accuracy is achieved with higher bit-depths.

The information in the channels can represent continuous or discrete data. Care must be taken to ensure that discrete channel data are not filtered by the renderer.

Feature Edges

The simplest edge method is not to detect an edge but to pass rendered edge information through to a channel of the output. This can be helpful for texture mapping linear features on an object—draw the feature on the object and pass that channel unmodified through the edge detector. Without a pass-through mechanism, edge detectors are likely to trace around these features, doubling up the lines.

Saito shows us that identifying discontinuities in the image and turning them into visible edges can be accomplished by looking at a pixel and its neighbors (see Figure 16.24 for neighbor labeling). Boundary edges are quickly detected with a discrete surface identifier channel by looking for any change between a pixel and its neighbors. For example, if each surface patch is given a unique "blue" value, the boundaries between the surfaces are given by any discontinuity in the blue channel (see Figure 16.25). Two ways of computing this are to decide how different a pixel is from its neighbors or how similar. The first method peaks on a solo pixel surrounded by unlike neighbors:

```
count = (a!=x)+(b!=x)+(c!=x)+(d!=x)+(e!=x)+(f!=x)+(g!=x)+(h!=x);
edge = count/8.0;
```

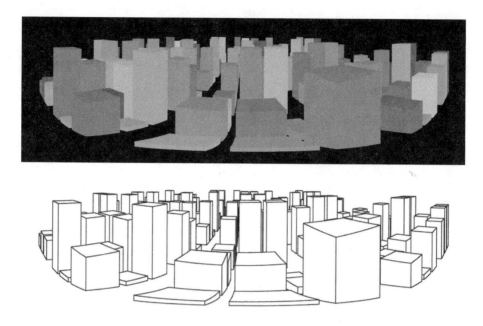

Figure 16.25 Constant shaded image (top) has a different color for each face. Detecting any change in color produces clean edges (bottom).

However, an edge will most likely share four neighbors. The number of "same-valued" neighbors with a bias for expected edges is

```
count = (a==x)+(b==x)+(c==x)+(d==x)+(e==x)+(f==x)+(g==x)+(h==x);
bias = 4;
edge = 1.0 - abs(count - bias)/bias;
```

If all the neighbors are the same (count = 8), the pixel is entirely within a region and our edge prediction is 0. If all the neighbors are different, the center pixel is suspect, and we presume the solo pixel is a noisy aberration.

This method detects silhouette edges between dissimilar objects and can also be used to generate feature edges within an object, such as isoparametric lines.

Silhouette Edges

Internal silhouette edges of self-occluding objects, including convex curved surfaces, can be detected by looking at first- and second-order discontinuities of continuous tone data. Saito recommends (and I concur) Sobel's method for first-order differentiation:

```
edge = (abs(a + 2*b + c - f - 2*g - h) +
        abs(c + 2*e + h - a - 2*d - f))/6.0;
```

Figure 16.26 Attempts at edge detection.

And for second-order:

```
edge = (8*x - a - b - c - d - e - f - g - h)/8;
edge = abs(edge); /* If you don't care about the sign. */
```

Saito continues his detection process with a normalizing step to improve the quality of the line, which may be necessary if the result of the edge detector is going to be used directly. However, if the process is part of a larger pipeline, simple thresholding during edge classification may suffice.

Prerender

The source images form a collection of information about the objects in the scene. Writing shaders that take advantage of the properties of the edge detector need not be complicated. Because no single channel will detect all edge conditions, if one method works for an edge, trying to coerce another method into detecting the same edge is unnecessary.

Wherever possible, detecting edges using a discrete channel is recommended, as it is both quick and robust. In the simplest cases, the constant surface shader can be applied to a scene where every distinct region is given a different color. Figure 16.26 (left) shows that edge detection of a `constant` shader image will not pick up internal silhouette edges, and the front and back of a surface will not be distinct. As in Figure 16.26 (middle), the front and back sides of an object can be shaded separately by comparing N to faceforward(N,I). The sign of (N . faceforward(N,I)) will be different for each side. In Figure 16.26 (right), first-order differentiation of a "normal" image is good for detecting internal silhouette edges. Normals can be encoded by

```
surface N ( string space = "camera" )
{
    normal Nspc = 0.5 * (1.0 + normalize(ntransform(space, N)));
    Ci = color (Nspc);
    Oi = 1;
}
```

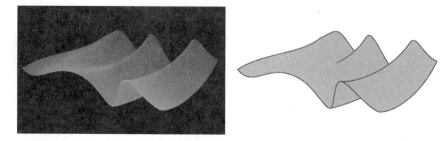

Figure 16.27 Combining three channel types into one render gives a general-purpose shader that is a good starting point for cartoon rendering. See also color plate 16.27.

Normals on a distant object are likely to change more per pixel than near objects, triggering the edge detector to "muddy" the distant object with ink. A depth-based dampening on the magnitude of the normal can control this.

If devoting three channels to the normal is undesirable, a single channel containing the normal dotted with the eye vector is almost as good:

```
varying float ni;
ni = N.I;
ni = (ni * ni)/(N.N * I.I);
ni = 1. - sqrt(ni);
```

This is an inverted variation of *PRMan*'s `defaultsurface.sl` shader.

To gain the most resolution in a depth image, each surface can have local `near` and `far` parameters. The boundaries between objects will be determined by a separate, discrete channel; having this data tunable for each object can aid in extracting internal silhouettes (see Figure 16.27).

```
zee = 1. - clamp((depth(P) - near)/(far - near), 0., 1.);
```

More complex regionalization can be written into the shader to create additional feature lines. A decal can be added by switching region IDs when a map crosses a threshold. (See Figure 16.28.)

```
id = region_id;
if (mapname != "") {
  float decal = float texture(mapname[0], t, s);
  if (decal > 0.5)
    id = decal_id;
}
```

Any continuous tone data can be quantized and placed in a discrete-detection channel for contour lines. This includes generating isoparametric lines by quantizing in the (s,t) parametric space. (See Figure 16.29.) It is insufficient to simply

Figure 16.28 Texture image used to
change region IDs.

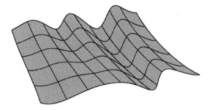

Figure 16.29 Parametric texture
generated isoparametric lines.

alternate between two region IDs "checkerboard-style" if a surface is concave. Instead, each block is given a unique region ID.

```
float scheck = floor(s * sfreq);
float tcheck = floor(t * tfreq);
float check = scheck + sfreq * tcheck;
if (faceforward(N,I) . N > 0.0) {
  id = region_id + check;                /* One set of IDs for
                                            the front */
} else {
  id = region_id + check + sfreq * tfreq; /* and another set for
                                             the back. */
}
```

The three channels of ni, depth (z), and object id can be combined into a
single RGB image file, as done by the nizid shader of Listing 16.4. (See Figure
16.30.) Channels containing discrete information, like surface identifiers, cannot
be antialiased. To compensate for aliasing, prerender at higher resolution and

Listing 16.4 nizid shader creates a reference image that encodes N.I, camera depth, and object ID in the red, green, and blue channels of the image.

```
/*
 * nizid : General-purpose prerender shader for cartoon rendering.
 *
 *    red   -- ni (normal dotted with I for silhouette detection.)
 *    green -- z (depth for silhouette detection and edge classification.)
 *    blue  -- id (unique region ID for feature edge detection.)
 *
 * Uses two region IDs. (front, back)
 */

surface
nizid ( float near = 0.;
        float far = 1.;
        float region_id = 1.;    /* Starting ID number for surface. */
        float region_one = 255.; /* Set to 65535 during 16-bpp renders. */
     )
{
    varying float ni;
    varying float zee;
    varying float id;

    ni = N.I;
    ni = (ni * ni)/(N.N * I.I);
    ni = 1. - sqrt(ni);

    zee = 1. - clamp((depth(P) - near)/(far - near), 0., 1.);

    if (faceforward(N,I) . N >= 0.0) { /* Give front/back different IDs */
        id = region_id;
    } else {
        id = region_id + 1.;
    }

    Ci = color "rgb" (ni, zee, id/region_one);
    Oi = 1.0;
}
```

filter down the final output image. Disable dithering, jittering, motion blur, and supersampling, set Exposure 1 1, and set PixelFilter "box" 1 1.

Edge Classification

While edge detection is about locating pixels at edge boundaries, edge classification is about associating material properties to the detected edges. Only in rare instances can the result of edge detection be used directly. Usually, edge properties, such as width and color, need to be associated with the edges and used to derive a

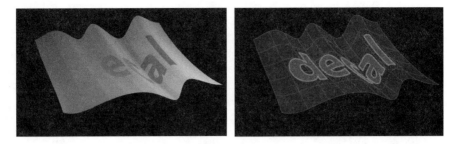

Figure 16.30 `nizid` shaded image (left) and detected image (right) with different material properties (width, color) applied to the regions. See also color plate 16.30.

final output image. Varying properties are stored in image buffers, and uniform properties are indexed from tables.

Any two regions coming together can form an edge. Cataloging material properties for all combinations of regions for all surfaces is unwieldy. It is easier to associate edge properties with regions. During edge detection, pixels are tagged on both sides of an edge, which can leave ambiguity over which region's material properties should be used. Averaging the properties is an option, but in most instances, choosing one set over another is preferable.

Edge classification is trivial for external silhouette edges and feature edges drawn within a single surface: all the edge pixels belong to the nearest underlying surface region. The boundary between two regions is more difficult to classify. Classifying by depth, with the closer surface winning, works for disconnected surfaces. One modeling trick is to build surfaces with important features riding slightly above the underlying geometry. For connected regions, the depth differences are negligible. Giving each region a priority rating to bias the edge classification toward "important" regions is effective. In implementation, neighboring pixels are compared and the pixel becomes associated with the highest-priority region. None of these solutions is perfect, and in animation, edges can still "pop" from one classification to another.

Ink Rendering

Rendering the final image is accomplished by stepping through a classified-edge image and, wherever an edge is detected, painting with an appropriate brush into a destination buffer. The width, color, and texture of the brush can be stored as parameters indexed for the object or by data encoded in image buffers. Stochastic variation can be added during the edge rendering to make the result appear more natural. In addition to simple ink lines, more complex brush methods, like those used by Haeberli and Meier, can be used to generate a variety of styles.

Production Considerations

In a studio production environment, it is inefficient to rerender complex geometry for changes in color. In traditional ink and paint, the art director works with the color models department to determine which colors will be used in the different regions of the character on a scene-by-scene basis. Palettes of these colors are then given to the ink and paint department.

With computer-based ink and paint systems, this process can be reversed. Rather than store the actual color in the painted cel, each region is filled with an index number that refers to an entry in a color palette. A rough "painter's palette" with exaggerated colors makes the painting process more efficient. ·The art director associates final colors with the palette after the painting is complete.

Ink and paint index images can be conveniently stored in a color image file. The red channel stores the coverage of the ink line (0 == transparent, 1 == opaque). This continuous data is either scanned or rendered and includes the proper texture or "tooth" of a drawn line. The green channel contains color-index data for the ink. Wherever the ink value in the red channel is nonzero, the green channel contains an index to a color palette entry for the ink. The blue channel contains a paint palette color index.

A problem with color-index images is that each pixel is either one color or another—the images are highly aliased. Two things compensate for this problem: The first is to work with source images that are larger than the output resolution, as previously discussed. Second, the ink's value is antialiased and, when composited over the paint, opaque ink will mask the aliased paint boundaries.

Image Construction

An indexed ink and paint image can be converted into a full-color image for use in compositing:

```
color src, dst, ink, paint;
paint = palettecolor(src.b); /* RGBA with premultiplied alpha */
ink = palettecolor(src.g);   /* RGBA with premultiplied alpha */
dst = src.r * ink + (1. - ink.a * src.r) * paint;
```

Creating a new destination image for a different set of palette colors is a quick process. Adding a "node" to most compositing software to allow an indexed cel image with an associated palette is straightforward.

Figure 16.31 shows an image from Warner Bros. Feature Animation's *The Iron Giant*. The Giant was rendered as an indexed image with a method similar to the one we have described. The art director color-styled the Giant with the traditional characters on a scene-by-scene basis after rendering.

Figure 16.31 The Giant rendered as an indexed image. (*THE IRON GIANT* © 1999 Warner Bros. All Rights Reserved.) See also color plate 16.31.

16.5 Conclusion

The woodblock shader introduces concepts for creating a space-filling texture with coherent level-of-detail changes and includes adjustments to make the effect appear to be drawn in the image plane. This striping provides a basic framework for other stroke methods. Knowing where the strokes are placed and controlling their density allows a TD to focus on rendering the strokes in a chosen style and building up layers into a final image.

Cartoon rendering addresses the image-plane considerations by using Render-Man as a preprocess to other imaging techniques. This allows for "coloring outside the lines" and is the basis for even more flexibility in stroke brush application.

These methods are complementary and can be used in combination to create a diverse range of nonphotorealistic styles (see Figure 16.32).

Further Reading

Cassidy J. Curtis, Sean E. Anderson, Joshua E. Seims, Kurt W. Fleischer, and David H. Salesin, "Computer-Generated Watercolor." *Computer Graphics (Proc. SIGGRAPH 97)*, p. 421–430, 1997.

Paul Haeberli, "Paint by Numbers: Abstract Image Representations." *Computer Graphics (Proc. SIGGRAPH 90)*, pp. 207–214, 1990.

Barbara J. Meier, "Painterly Rendering for Animation." *Computer Graphics (Proc. SIGGRAPH 96)*, pp. 477–484, 1996.

Figure 16.32 Can opener inspired by the pen-and-ink illustrations of David Macaulay. See also color plate 16.32.

Victor Ostromoukhov and Roger D. Hersch, "Artistic Screening." *Computer Graphics (Proc. SIGGRAPH 95)*, pp. 219–228, 1995.

Ken Perlin, "An Image Synthesizer." In *Computer Graphics (SIGGRAPH 1985 Conf. Proc.)*, pp. 287–296, 1985.

Takafumi Saito and Tokiichiro Takahashi, "Comprehensible Rendering of 3-D Shapes." *Computer Graphics (Proc. SIGGRAPH 90)*, pp. 197–206, 1990.

Steve Upstill, *The RenderMan Companion*. Reading, MA: Addison-Wesley Publishing Company, 1990.

Georges Winkenbach and David H. Salesin, "Computer-Generated Pen-and-Ink Illustration." *Computer Graphics (Proc. SIGGRAPH 94)*, pp. 91–100, 1994.

Georges Winkenbach and David H. Salesin, "Rendering Parametric Surfaces in Pen and Ink." *Computer Graphics (Proc. SIGGRAPH 96)*, pp. 469–476, 1996.

D. N. Wood, A. Finkelstein, J. F. Hughes, C. E. Thayer, and D. H. Salesin, "Multiperspective Panoramas for Cel Animation." In *Computer Graphics (SIGGRAPH 1997 Conf. Proc.)*, pp. 243–250, 1997.

17 Ray Tracing in *PRMan*

(with a little help from BMRT)

This chapter explains how to get *PRMan* to render scenes with ray-traced shadows, reflections, and refractions, using *BMRT* as an "oracle" to provide answers to computations that *PRMan* cannot solve. We describe a method of stitching the two renderers together using a Unix pipe, allowing each renderer to perform the tasks that it does best.

17.1   Introduction

PhotoRealistic RenderMan has a Shading Language function called `trace()`, but because there is no ability in *PRMan* to compute global visibility, the `trace()` function always returns 0.0 (black). There is no way to ask for any other global visibility information in *PRMan*. Though *PRMan* often can fake reflections and shadows with texture mapping, there are limitations:

- Environment-mapped reflections are only "correct" from a single point. Environ-ment mapping a large reflective object has errors (which, to be fair, are often very hard to spot).
- Mutually reflective or self-reflective objects are a big pain in *PRMan*, if not im-possible.
- Environment and shadow maps require multiple rendering passes and can re-quire TD time to set up properly.
- Dealing with shadow maps—selecting resolution, bias, blur, and so on—can be time-consuming and still show artifacts in the shadows. Also, shadows cannot motion blur in *PRMan* and cannot correctly handle opacity (or color) changes in the object casting a shadow.
- Refraction is nearly impossible to do correctly, because even when environment mapping is acceptable, *PRMan* cannot tell the direction that a ray exits a refrac-tive object, since the "backside" is not available for ray tracing.

The *Blue Moon Rendering Tools*, or *BMRT* for short, contains a renderer, *rendrib*, that is fully compliant with the RenderMan specification and supports ray tracing, radiosity, area lights, volumes, and so on (Gritz and Hahn, 1996). It can compute ray-traced reflections, shadows, and so on, but is much slower and requires more memory than *PRMan* for geometry that doesn't require these special features.

Both renderers share much of their input—by being RenderMan-compliant, they both read the same geometry description (RIB) and shader source code files. (The compatibility is limited to areas dictated by the RenderMan Interface Specification. The two renderers each have different formats for stored texture maps and com-piled shaders and support different feature subsets of the spec.) It's tempting to want to combine the effects of the two renderers, using each for those effects that it achieves well. Several strategies come to mind:

1. Choosing one renderer or the other based on the project, sequence, or shot. Perhaps a strategy might be to use *PRMan* most of the time and *BMRT* if you need radiosity or ray tracing.
2. Rendering different objects (or layered elements) with different renderers, then compositing them together to form final frames.
3. Rendering different lighting layers with different renderers, then adding them together. For example, you might render base color with *PRMan* but do an "area light pass" (or radiosity, or whatever) in *BMRT*.

All of these approaches have difficulties (though all have been done). Strategy 1 may force you to choose a slow renderer for everything, just because you need a little ray tracing. There may also be problems matching the exact look from shot to shot, if you are liberally switching between the two renderers. Strategies 2 and 3 have potential problems with "registration," or alignment, of the images computed by the renderers. Also, Strategy 3 can be very costly, as it involves renders with each renderer.

The attraction of using the two renderers together, exploiting the respective strengths of both programs while avoiding undue expense, is alluring. We have developed a method of stitching the two programs together.

17.2   Background: DSO Shadeops in *PRMan*

RenderMan Shading Language has always had a rich library of built-in functions (sometimes called *shadeops*) already known to the Shading Language compiler and implemented as part of the run-time shader interpreter in the renderer. This built-in function library includes math operations (sin, sqrt, etc.), vector and matrix operations, coordinate transformations, and so on. It has also been possible to write functions in Shading Language itself (in the case of *PRMan*, this ability was greatly enhanced with the new compiler included with release 3.7). However, defining functions in SL itself has several limitations.

PRMan 3.8 introduced "DSO Shadeops." This feature allows you to write Shading Language functions in C or C++ as dynamic shared objects, or DSOs. DSOs, also sometimes called *shared libraries* or *DLLs*, are a way of packaging up code and data in such a way that they can be linked to a program at *run-time*, as opposed to the usual practice of linking all library functions to the executable at *compile time*. This change in binding time allows you to alter a program's available code base at a much later date and often by the user rather than the program author. Writing new shadeops in C and linking them as DSOs has many advantages over writing functions in Shading Language, including

- The resulting object code from a DSO shadeop is shared among all its uses in a renderer. In contrast, compiled shader function code is expanded in-line into the object code every place the function is called and thus is not shared among its uses, let alone among separate shaders that call the same function.
- DSO shadeops are compiled to optimized machine code, whereas shader functions are interpreted at run-time. Although *PRMan* has a very efficient interpreter, it is definitely slower than native machine code.
- DSO shadeops can call library functions from the standard C library or from other third-party libraries.
- Whereas ordinary shader functions are restricted to operations and data structures available in the Shading Language, DSO shadeops can do anything you might normally do in a C program. Examples include creating complex data structures or reading external files (other than textures and shadows). For example, implementing an alternative noise() function that needs a stored table to be efficient would be exceptionally difficult in Shading Language but very easy as a DSO shadeop.

DSO shadeops also have several limitations that you should be aware of:

- DSO shadeops only have access to information passed to them as parameters. They have no knowledge of "global" shader variables such as P, parameters to the shader, or any other renderer state. If you need to access global variables or shader parameters or locals, you must pass them as parameters.
- DSO shadeops act strictly as point processes. They possess no knowledge of the topology of the surface, derivatives, or the nature of surface grids (in the case of a REYES renderer like *PRMan*). If you want to take derivatives, for example, you need to take them in the shader and pass them as parameters to your DSO shadeop.
- DSO shadeops cannot call other built-in shadeops or any other internal entry points to the renderer itself.

Further details about DSO shadeops, including exactly how to write them, are well beyond the scope of this chapter. For more information, please see the *Photo-Realistic RenderMan User Manual*.

17.3   A Ray Server

So *PRMan* 3.8 and later has a magic back door to the shading system. One thing it's good for is to make certain common operations much faster, by compiling them to machine code. But it also has the ability to allow us to write functions that would not be expressible in Shading Language at all—for example, file I/O, process control or system calls, constructing complex data structures, and so on.

How far can we push this idea? Is there some implementation of trace() that we can write as a DSO that will work? Yes! The central idea is to render using *PRMan* but implement trace() as a call to *BMRT*. In this sense, we would be using *BMRT* as an oracle, or a "ray server," that could answer the questions that *PRMan* needs help with but let *PRMan* do the rest of the hard work (see Figure 17.1).

We defined a "ray server protocol" as follows. The client opens a pipe to the server, then writes a series of queries to the pipe. Every query begins with a two-byte header. The first byte is the number of floats in the postheader part of the query. The second byte is one of 't', 'v', 'h', or 'f', which indicates the type of query ("trace," "visibility," "hittest," or "fulltrace," respectively). (By the time you read this, it's possible that there will be more query types. Please consult the current *BMRT* documentation for more information.) Following this is the data for the particular type of query. The server computes the answer and sends the correct answer data back over the pipe to the client. The data formats for the queries and answers are given in the C header file shown in Listing 17.6. The meanings of the data will be apparent after reading the Shading Language API in Section 17.4.

By an astonishing coincidence, *BMRT* (release 2.3.6 and later) has such a ray server mode, triggered by the command line option -rayserver. When in this mode, instead of rendering the frame and writing an image file, *BMRT* reads the scene file,

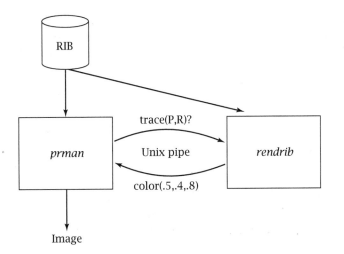

Figure 17.1 Block diagram of the "ray server."

but it just waits for the ray queries to come over stdin. When such queries are received, *BMRT* computes the results of the query and returns the data to stdout.

The *PRMan* side is a DSO that, when called, runs *rendrib* and opens a pipe to its process. Thereafter, calls to the new functions make ray queries over the pipe, then wait for the results.

17.4   New Functionality

This hybrid scheme effectively adds six new functions that you can call from your shaders:

color trace (point from; vector dir)

> Traces a ray from position from in the direction of vector dir. The return value is the incoming light from that direction.

color visibility (point p1, p2)

> Forces a visibility (shadow) check between two arbitrary points, returning the spectral visibility between them. If there is no geometry between the two points, the return value will be (1,1,1). If fully opaque geometry is between the two points, the return value will be (0,0,0). Partially opaque occluders will result in the return of a partial transmission value.

> An example use of this function would be to make an explicit shadow check in a light source shader, rather than to mark lights as casting shadows in the RIB

stream. The `uberlight` shader described in Chapter 14 uses the `visibility` function to implement shadows when using *BMRT* alone or when using the ray server functionality. While it is also possible in *BMRT* to have shadows cast automatically (by setting a particular `Attribute`), it is often more convenient to have shadows directly controlled in the light source, much as shadow map access is directly controlled by the lights.

```
float rayhittest (point from; vector dir;
    output point Ph; output vector Nh)
```

Probes geometry from point `from` looking in direction `dir`. If no geometry is hit by the ray probe, the return value will be very large (1e38). If geometry is encountered, the position and normal of the geometry hit will be stored in `Ph` and `Nh`, respectively, and the return value will be the distance to the geometry.

```
float fulltrace (point pos; vector dir;
    output color hitcolor; output float hitdist;
    output point Phit; output vector Nhit;
    output point Pmiss; output vector Rmiss)
```

Traces a ray from `pos` in the direction `dir`. If any object is hit by the ray, then `hitdist` will be set to the distance of the nearest object hit by the ray, `Phit` and `Nhit` will be set to the "world" space position and surface normal of that nearest object at the intersection point, and `hitcolor` will be set to the light color arriving from the ray (just like the return value of `trace`).

If no object is hit by the ray, then `hitdist` will be set to 1.0e38, and `hitcolor` will be set to (0,0,0).

If any ray (including subsequent rays traced through glass, for example) ever misses all objects entirely, then `Pmiss` and `Rmiss` will be set to the "world" space position and direction of the deepest ray that failed to hit any objects, and the return value of this function will be the depth of the ray that missed. If no ray misses (i.e., some ray eventually hits a nonreflective, nonrefractive object), then the return value of this function will be zero. An example use of this functionality would be to combine ray tracing of near objects with an environment map of far objects:

```
missdepth = fulltrace (P, R, C, d, Phit, Nhit, Pmiss, Rmiss);
if (missdepth > 0)
    C += environment ("foo.env", Rmiss) / missdepth;
```

This code fragment traces a ray (for example, through glass). If the ray emerging from the far side of the glass misses all objects, it adds in a contribution from an environment map, scaled so that the more layers of glass it went through, the dimmer it will be.

float isshadowray ()

> Returns 1 if this shader is being executed in order to evaluate the transparency of a surface for the purpose of a shadow ray. If the shader is instead being evaluated for visible appearance, this function will return 0. This function can be used to alter the behavior of a shader so that it does one thing in the case of visibility rays, and something else in the case of shadow rays. See Sherstyuk (1996) for a discussion of applications.

float raylevel ()

> Returns the level of the ray that caused this shader to be executed. A return value of 0 indicates that this shader is being executed on a camera (eye) ray; of 1, that it is the result of a single reflection or refraction; and so on. This allows you to customize the behavior of a shader based on its depth in the reflection/refraction tree.

17.5   Ray Tracing for Reflections and Refractions

Typically, you will want to ray trace in the *mirror direction*—that is, the perfect reflection of the incident direction I from a surface with orientation given by the surface normal N. Shading Language provides a built-in function reflect() that computes this mirror direction. Thus, naive ray tracing can be accomplished as follows:

```
/* Get a forward-facing normal */
normal Nf = normalize (faceforward (N, I));
/* Calculate the mirror direction */
vector R = normalize (reflect (I, N));
/* Trace a reflection ray */
color Crefl = trace (P, R);
```

One problem with ray tracing is that it is fundamentally a *point sampling* process. In other words, it is sampling a direction exactly, which has the tendency to alias. We can remedy this with *stochastic supersampling*, which is the process of spawning and averaging several jittered rays as an estimate of a true solid angle reflectance. Listing 17.1 presents the RayTrace() function, which performs stochastic super-sampling, with user control over the number of rays spawned, the amount of jitter, and an additional additive blur. The base spread of the jittered rays is computed by taking derivatives of the reflection direction and of P. Note that this function uses the new fulltrace() routine.

There's something subtle going on in RayTrace: we pass in a Kr value, but we don't multiply the result of the ray tracing by this value. We are assuming that whatever routine calls RayTrace will do this scaling, but we are nonetheless passing Kr in order to avoid spawning rays for parts of the surface that are not reflective

Listing 17.1 RayTrace() function spawns traced rays, with control over
blurriness, number of samples, and jittering.

```
/* RayTrace() - A fancy ray trace routine.  Sample over the surface
 * element and over the varying ray spread due to surface curvature.
 * An ordinary call to trace would point sample the environment in a
 * very simplistic way.  This function takes the size of the surface
 * facet and curvature of the surface into account, and lets you
 * sample the space with multiple rays.
 * Inputs:
 *    P - surface position
 *    Rdir - the unit-length reflection direction
 *    blur - reflection blurriness; 0 = sharp reflection
 *    jitter - 1 = fully jitter the ray directions, 0 = no jitter.
 *    nsamples - number of rays.  Larger numbers will have less noise but
 *         will be more expensive.
 * Return value: the average of the trace calls.
 *
 * Warning!!! This function takes derivatives. This can cause trouble if
 * called inside a loop or varying conditional!  Be cautious.
 */
color
RayTrace (point P;  vector Rdir;  float Kr, blur, jitter;
          uniform float nsamples;  output float alpha;)
{
    float rand () {
        extern float jitter;
        return (raylevel()==0) ? (0.5 + jitter * (float random() - 0.5))
        : 0.5;
    }
    extern float du, dv;
    color C, Ct;
    float hitdist; point Phit, Pmiss;  vector Nhit, Rmiss;
    float bluramt = blur + filterwidthp(Rdir);
    uniform float nrays = (raylevel() == 0 ? max(1,ceil(sqrt(nsamples)))
                          : 1);
    vector Tu = Du(P) * (1.5 * du); /* overblur just a tad... */
    vector Tv = Dv(P) * (1.5 * dv);
    if (Kr < 0.0001) {
        C = 0;
    } else if (bluramt > 0 || nrays > 1) {
        /* Construct orthogonal components to Rdir */
        vector uoffset = blur * normalize (vector
                                           (zcomp(Rdir) - ycomp(Rdir),
                                            xcomp(Rdir) - zcomp(Rdir),
                                            ycomp(Rdir) - xcomp(Rdir)));
        vector voffset = Rdir ^ uoffset;
        uniform float i, j;
        C = 0;  alpha = 0;
        for (i = 0;  i < nrays;  i += 1) {
            for (j = 0;  j < nrays;  j += 1) {                        ▶
```

Listing 17.1 (continued)

```
                    /* Add a random offset to the smooth reflection vector */
                    vector R = Rdir + ((i + rand())/nrays - 0.5) * uoffset +
                                      ((j + rand())/nrays - 0.5) * voffset;
                    R = normalize(R);
                    point Pray = P +  ((j + rand())/nrays - 0.5) * Tu +
                                      ((i + rand())/nrays - 0.5) * Tv;
                    fulltrace (P, R, Ct, hitdist, Phit, Nhit, Pmiss, Rmiss);
                    C += Ct;
                    alpha += 1 - step(1.0e10,hitdist);
                }
            }
        uniform float totrays = nrays*nrays;
        C /= totrays;     alpha /= totrays;
    } else {
        /* No blur or curvature, just do a simple trace */
        fulltrace (P, Rdir, C, hitdist, Phit, Nhit, Pmiss, Rmiss);
        alpha = 1 - step(1.0e10,hitdist);
    }
    return C;
}
```

(thus saving the time that would be wasted if we traced the rays only to multiply their result by zero). Furthermore, we are careful to place this conditional *after* the calculation of derivatives, to avoid any artifacts.

Now we can rewrite the SampleEnvironment function from Section 9.2.4 to incorporate ray tracing, in addition to reflection and environment mapping. This is illustrated in Listing 17.2. Using these new definitions, shaders that previously used environment and reflection mapping, like the shinymetal shader of Listing 9.8, can use ray tracing simply by being recompiled without modification. Aha! Now you should realize why, way back in Section 9.2.4, we passed Kr into SampleEnvironment rather than having the calling routine do the scaling—it was all so that we could have that value around in order to cull traced rays that would not otherwise contribute to the image.

Notice that SampleEnvironment uses the alpha value returned by RayTrace to effectively composite the ray-traced results atop the environment or reflection map. By doing this, we can ray trace against close objects but use environment maps for more static distant objects, or ray trace against CG objects but still have live-action background environments. Also notice that the blur parameter that we send to RayTrace is actually sqrt(blur). This is purely an empirical result; the author found that this sqrt factor caused the apparent blur of the ray tracing to more closely match that of environment mapping.

Finally, Listing 17.3 presents the shader source code for ray-traced glass, making use of the functions we have presented.

Listing 17.2 Modified `SampleEnvironment` function that can make calls to any of `Environment`, `ReflMap`, or `RayTrace` as needed.

```
#define ENVPARAMS \
        envname, envspace, envrad, rayjitter, raysamples

#define DECLARE_ENVPARAMS                                       \
        string envname, envspace;                               \
        uniform float envrad, rayjitter, raysamples

#define DECLARE_DEFAULTED_ENVPARAMS                                      \
        string envname = "", envspace = "world";                        \
        uniform float envrad = 100, rayjitter = 0, raysamples = 1


color
SampleEnvironment (point P; vector R; float Kr, blur; DECLARE_ENVPARAMS;)
{
    color C = 0;
    float alpha;
    if (envname != "") {
        if (envspace == "NDC")
            C = ReflMap (envname, P, blur, alpha);
        else
            C = Environment (envname, envspace, envrad, P, R, blur, alpha);
    }
#if (defined(BMRT) || defined(RAYSERVER_H))
    color Cray = RayTrace (P, R, Kr, sqrt(blur), rayjitter,
                            raysamples, alpha);
    C = Cray + (1-alpha) * C;
#endif
    return Kr*C;
}
```

Listing 17.3 `glass.sl`—a surface shader that uses ray tracing for accurate refraction.

```
/**********************************************************************
 * glass.sl -- Shiny reflective & refractive glass, using ray tracing.
 *
 * Description:
 *   Makes semitransparent glass, using ray tracing to calculate
 *   reflections and refractions of the environment.
 *
 * Parameters:
 *   Ka, Kd, Ks, roughness, specularcolor - the usual meaning
 *   Kr - coefficient for mirror-like reflections of environment
 *   blur - how blurry are the reflections? (0 = perfectly sharp)    ▶
```

Listing 17.3 (continued)

```
*    envname, envspace, envrad - controls for using environment maps
*    rayjitter, raysamples - ray tracing controls for reflection
*    Kt - coefficient for refracted transmission
*    transmitcolor - color of the glass
*    refrblur - how blurry are the refractions? (0 = perfectly sharp)
*    eta - the coefficient of refraction of the glass
*    reflrayjitter, refrraysamples - ray tracing controls for refraction
************************************************************************/

#include "rayserver.h"
#include "material.h"


surface
glass ( float Ka = 0.2, Kd = 0, Ks = 0.5, roughness = 0.05;
        color specularcolor = 1;
        float Kr = 1, reflblur = 0;
        DECLARE_DEFAULTED_ENVPARAMS;
        float Kt = 1, refrblur = 0, eta = 1.5;
        color transmitcolor = 1;
        float refrrayjitter = 0, refrraysamples = 1; )
{
    vector IN = normalize (I);
    normal Nf = faceforward (normalize(N), I);

    /* Compute the reflection & refraction directions and amounts */
    vector Rfldir, Rfrdir;   /* Smooth reflection/refraction directions */
    float kr, kt;
    fresnel (IN, Nf, (I.N < 0) ? 1.0/eta : eta, kr, kt, Rfldir, Rfrdir);
    kt = 1-kr;   /* Physically incorrect, but portable */
    kr *= Kr;
    kt *= Kt;

    /* Calculate the reflection & refraction color */
    color Crefl = SampleEnvironment (P, normalize(Rfldir), kr, reflblur,
                                ENVPARAMS);
    color Crefr = SampleEnvironment (P, normalize(Rfrdir), kt, refrblur,
                                envname, envspace, envrad,
                                refrrayjitter, refrraysamples);

    Oi = 1;
    Ci = Cs * (Ka*ambient() + Kd*diffuse(Nf)) +
         specularcolor * (Crefl + Ks*LocIllumGlossy(Nf,-IN,roughness,0.5)) +
         transmitcolor * Crefr;
}
```

17.6   Using the Ray Server

Using the ray server is straightforward:

1. Use these functions in your shaders. In any shader that uses the functions, you should:

   `#include "rayserver.h"`

   If you inspect `rayserver.h` (Listing 17.4), you'll see that the functions we have described are really macros. When compiling with *BMRT's* compiler, the functions are unchanged (all six are actually implemented in *BMRT*). But when compiling with *PRMan's* compiler, the macros transform their arguments to world space and call a function called `rayserver()`.

2. Compile the shaders with both *BMRT* and *PRMan's* shader compilers. When compiling for *PRMan*, make sure that the DSO `rayserver.so` is in your include path.

3. Instead of rendering the RIB file with `prman`, run the `frankenrender` script:

   `frankenrender teapots.rib`

   This is a Perl script, shown in Listing 17.5. By default (as used above), it causes both renderers to read the same RIB file(s). Inspection of the script will reveal that there are options to specify different RIB files for each renderer, so that, for example, you can ray trace only a small subset of the scene.

That's it!

17.6.1   Results

Figure 17.2 shows an example image rendered with *PRMan*, unassisted, and with the ray server. The left image makes calls to `trace()` for reflections, but of course this does nothing in *PRMan*. On the right is the same RIB file, with the same shaders, taking advantage of the ray server we have described. This picture was rendered by *PRMan* (mostly) but using the "ray server" instead of shadow or environment maps.

We used the ray server technique to ray trace the glass bottles appearing in 15 shots of *A Bug's Life*. Figure 17.3 shows four example frames from the film. The ray tracer knew about the bottle, the seeds, and the rocks next to the bottle. For rays that missed those objects, the glass shader "filled in the blanks" with environment map lookups. This kept the memory use of the ray tracer to a minimum, as it would have been prohibitively expensive for the ray tracer to have known about the entire huge scene from *A Bug's Life*. (Remember that it's much easier for *PRMan* to handle such large scenes because it can throw out geometry that isn't seen. The ray tracer cannot do that, since you never know if a reflection ray might hit those objects!)

Note that *all* other objects with reflection or refraction in *A Bug's Life* (as well as all reflective or refractive objects in our other films) were done with standard-issue

---

Listing 17.4 `rayserver.h`: the SL header file for using the ray server.

```
/* rayserver.h - Shading Language (PRMan side) include file for ray server.
 *
 * These macros translate calls to trace(), visibility(), and
 * rayhittest() into calls to rayserver().  Each generates different
 * numbers of args, allowing rayserver() to be polymorphic.
 *
 * It is assumed that the rayserver() function itself is implemented
 * as a DSO shadeop.  (See docs for PRMan 3.8 or later.)
 *
 * Note that the ray server expects its data in world space.
 *
 * Author: Larry Gritz (gritzl@acm.org)
 *
 * Reference:
 *    Gritz, Larry, "Ray Tracing in PRMan (with a little help from
 *    BMRT)".  Appeared in: Apodaca and Gritz, eds., "Advanced
 *    RenderMan: Beyond the Companion," SIGGRAPH '98 course notes
 *    (Course #11), July 20, 1998.
 */

#ifndef RAYSERVER_H
#define RAYSERVER_H

#ifndef BMRT

/* PRMan side only -- BMRT already knows these functions */

#define worldp(p) transform("world",p)
#define worldv(v) vtransform("world",v)

#define trace(p,d) rayserver(worldp(p), worldv(d))

#define visibility(from,to) rayserver(worldp(from), worldp(to))

#define rayhittest(p,d,phit,nhit) \
        rayserver(worldp(p), worldv(d), phit,nhit)

#define fulltrace(p,d,chit,hitdist,phit,nhit,pmiss,rmiss) \
        rayserver(worldp(p),worldv(d),chit,hitdist,phit,nhit,pmiss,rmiss)

float raylevel () { return 0; }
float isshadowray () { return 0; }

#endif

#endif
```

Listing 17.5 frankenrender: the Perl script that drives the *PRMan/BMRT* combo.

```perl
#!/usr/local/bin/perl
# N.B. Change the above path if your site keeps perl someplace different!
#
# frankenrender renderer script
#
# This script drives the hybrid renderer that results when using
# the "ray server" -- the scheme where PRMan uses BMRT to return ray
# tracing results.  The rayserver DSO will launch BMRT using the
# environment variable RAYSERVER.  The purpose of this script is mainly
# to set that variable correctly.
#
# Usage: frankenrender file1 file2 ...
#        frankenrender [commonfiles] [-bmrt bmrtfiles] [-prman prmanfiles]
#
# For the first usage above, this script will set up RAYSERVER and call
# prman so that both renderers see exactly the same geometry and scene.
#
# If you want each renderer to see a different scene, then the second
# usage is preferred.  Using the -bmrt or -prman flag designates
# subsequent files as applying to only one renderer or the other.
# File names that appear prior to either -bmrt or -prman will be sent
# to both renderers.
#
# Author:  Larry Gritz (gritzl@acm.org)
#

$forbmrt = 1;
$forprman = 1;
$bmrtargs = "";
$prmanargs = "";

$servercmd = "rendrib -rayserver ";

for ($i = 0;  $i <= $#ARGV;  $i = $i + 1) {
    if ($ARGV[$i] eq "-rayserver") {
        $i = $i + 1;
        $servercmd = $ARGV[$i];
        next;
    } elsif ($ARGV[$i] eq "-bmrt") {
        $forbmrt = 1;
        $forprman = 0;
        next;
    } elsif ($ARGV[$i] eq "-prman") {
        $forbmrt = 0;
        $forprman = 1;
        next;
    }
```

▶

Listing 17.5 (continued)

```
    if ($forprman) {
        $prmanargs = "$prmanargs $ARGV[$i] ";
    }
    if ($forbmrt) {
        $bmrtargs = "$bmrtargs $ARGV[$i] ";
    }
}

# print "prmanargs: $prmanargs \nbmrtargs: $bmrtargs\n";

$ENV{RAYSERVER} = "$servercmd $bmrtargs";

#print "RAYSERVER = \"$ENV{RAYSERVER}\"\n";
'prman $prmanargs';
```

Figure 17.2 Using the ray server. *PRMan* only (left); *PRMan* and *BMRT* work together (right).

PRMan environment maps, without any ray tracing. Ray tracing is expensive and rarely necessary, but for those few effects in which you really need it, this technique just might do the trick.

17.6.2   Pros and Cons

The big advantage of this technique is that you can render most of your scene with *PRMan*, using *BMRT* for tracing individual rays on selected objects or calculating shadows for selected lights. This is much faster than rendering in *BMRT*, particularly if you only tell the ray tracer about the subset of the scene that you want in the shadows or reflections. The following effects are trivial to produce using this scheme, with no setup time or multipass rendering needed:

Figure 17.3 *A Bug's Life*—Use of the "ray server." (© Disney Enterprises, Inc. and Pixar Animation Studios.) See also color plate 17.3.

- Ray-cast shadows, including shadows that correctly respond to color and opacity of occluding objects. Moving objects can cast correct motion-blurred shadows.
- Correct reflections, including motion blur.
- Real refraction for glass, water, and so on.
- Mutual reflection of objects, self-reflection (seeing parts of an object in its reflection), and refraction of objects with internal structure (such as grain inside a bottle). These are the effects that are prohibitively difficult or impossible to do with environment maps.

The big disadvantage is that it requires two renderers running at the same time, each with the entire scene loaded. This can be alleviated somewhat by reducing the scene that the ray tracer sees, or by telling the ray tracer to use a significantly reduced tessellation rate, and so on. But still, it's a significant memory hit compared to running *PRMan* alone.

All of the usual considerations about compatibility between the two renderers apply. Be particularly aware of new *PRMan* primitives and SL features not currently supported by *BMRT*, texture file format differences and results of `noise()` functions.

17.7   Implementation Notes

This section lists the source code to several components of the ray server for those curious about exactly how it works. You should feel free to skip this section—none of the information in the source is necessary to use the ray server effectively, and current releases of *BMRT* come with these components included and precompiled.

Listing 17.4 lists the Shading Language include file that declares the new routines. This is the file that you must `#include` in any *PRMan* shaders that you want to be able to call the ray tracing routines.

Listing 17.5 is the `frankenrender` script that drives the combined renderers, substituting for an ordinary invocation of `prman` or `render`. Because there is no way for the `rayserver` DSO shadeop to know which program to invoke as the ray server or which RIB files *PRMan* was instructed to render, one of the main tasks of `frankenrender` is to pass the appropriate information to the DSO. It does this through an environment variable that is read in by the `rayserver` DSO (see Listing 17.7).

Listing 17.6 defines the data exchanged between the client and server—that is, the ray server communication protocol. Listing 17.7 is the implementation of the ray server DSO shadeop.

Further Reading

Recursive ray tracing was introduced in Whitted (1980). The use of jittered rays to antialias and simulate blurry reflections was detailed in Cook, Porter, and Carpenter (1984) and Cook (1986).

Some of *BMRT's* algorithms are detailed in Gritz and Hahn (1996).

Listing 17.6 `rayquery.h`: the C header file defining the ray server queries and answers.

```c
/* rayquery.h - protocol definition for ray servers
 *
 * The ray server protocol consists of the following:
 * - Client opens a pipe to rendrib with the -rayserver option, then
 *   writes a series of queries to the pipe.
 * - Each query consists of:
 *   1. Client sends an RSQueryHeader to server. This specifies the size
 *      of the postheader query (expressed in number of *floats*), and
 *      a character telling the query type.
 *   2. Client sends an RS*Query, depending on the query type.
 *   3. Server sends back an RS*Answer, depending on the query type.
 * - When finished, client closes the pipes, thus terminating rendrib.
 */

typedef struct {
    unsigned char querysize;    /* Size of postheader query (in floats) */
    unsigned char querytype;    /* One of 't' 'v' 'h' 'f' */
} RSQueryHeader;


typedef struct {
    RtPoint raypos, raydir;
    float raytime, raylod, unused[4];
} RSTraceQuery;

typedef struct {
    RtColor hitcolor;
    float unused[1];
} RSTraceAnswer;


typedef struct {
    RtPoint P0, P1;
    float raytime, raylod, unused[4];
} RSVisibilityQuery;

typedef struct {
    RtColor hitcolor;
} RSVisibilityAnswer;


typedef struct {
    RtPoint raypos, raydir;
    float raytime, raylod, unused[4];
} RSHittestQuery;

typedef struct {
    float hitdist;
    RtPoint Phit, Nhit;
} RSHittestAnswer;
```

►

Listing 17.6 (continued)

```c
typedef struct {
    RtPoint raypos, raydir;
    float raytime, raylod, unused[8];
} RSFulltraceQuery;

typedef struct {
    float result;
    RtColor hitcolor;
    float dist;
    RtPoint Phit, Nhit, Pmiss, Rmiss;
    float unused[3];
} RSFulltraceAnswer;
```

Listing 17.7 rayserver.c is the implementation of the ray server DSO shadeop.

```c
/* rayserver.c - implements the ray server protocol -- client side.
 * When one of the ray server functions is called, open a pipe to a ray
 * server program, and transmit queries using a ray server protocol.
 *
 * Compile me like this (on SGI):
 *     cc -mips3 -n32 -c rayserver.c
 *     ld -shared -o rayserver.so rayserver.o
 */

#include <stdio.h>
#include <string.h>
#include <stdlib.h>
#include <unistd.h>
#include <signal.h>
#include <alloca.h>
#include <sys/types.h>
#include <sys/stat.h>
#include <fcntl.h>

#include "ri.h"
#include "shadeop.h"
#include "rayquery.h"

SHADEOP_TABLE(rayserver) = {
    { "color rayserver_trace (point, vector)",
                "rayserver_init", "rayserver_cleanup" },
    { "color rayserver_visibility (point, point)",
                "rayserver_init", "rayserver_cleanup" },
    { "float rayserver_rayhittest (point, vector, point, vector)",
                "rayserver_init", "rayserver_cleanup" },
```
►

Listing 17.7 (continued)

```
        { "float rayserver_fulltrace (point, vector, color, float, point,
                                    vector, point, vector)",
                "rayserver_init", "rayserver_cleanup" },
        { "" }
};


/* shortcuts for manipulating 3-vectors efficiently */
typedef struct { RtPoint v; } VECTOR_STRUCT;
#define vcopy(a,b) *((VECTOR_STRUCT *)(a)) = *((VECTOR_STRUCT *)(b))
#define vset(a,v) (a)[0] = v, (a)[1] = v, (a)[2] = v


typedef struct {
    int initialized;
    FILE *in;
    int pipe[2];
    int jitter_times;
    int capturefile;
} RS_DATA;


static RS_DATA rs_data = { 0 } ;


float raytime (void)
{
    if (rs_data.jitter_times)
        return drand48();
    else return 0.0f;
}


SHADEOP (rayserver_trace)
{
    RSTraceQuery query;
    RSTraceAnswer answer;
    char buf[2];

    if (! rs_data.initialized) {
        vset ((float *)argv[0], 0.0f);
        return 0;
    }
    buf[0] = sizeof(query)/sizeof(float);  buf[1] = 't';
    write (rs_data.pipe[1], buf, 2);
    if (rs_data.capturefile)
        write (rs_data.capturefile, buf, 2);
    vcopy (query.raypos, (float *)argv[1]);
    vcopy (query.raydir, (float *)argv[2]);
```

▶

Listing 17.7 (continued)

```
    query.raytime = raytime();
    query.raylod = 0.5f;
    write (rs_data.pipe[1], &query, sizeof(query));
    if (rs_data.capturefile)
        write (rs_data.capturefile, &query, sizeof(query));
    read (rs_data.pipe[0], &answer, sizeof(answer));
    vcopy ((float *)argv[0], answer.hitcolor);
    return 0;
}


SHADEOP (rayserver_visibility)
{
    RSVisibilityQuery query;
    char buf[2];

    if (! rs_data.initialized) {
        vset ((float *)argv[0], 1.0f);
        return 0;
    }
    buf[0] = sizeof(query)/sizeof(float);  buf[1] = 'v';
    write (rs_data.pipe[1], buf, 2);
    if (rs_data.capturefile)
        write (rs_data.capturefile, buf, 2);
    vcopy (query.P0, (float *)argv[1]);
    vcopy (query.P1, (float *)argv[2]);
    query.raytime = raytime();  /* time */
    query.raylod = 0.5f;  /* detail */
    write (rs_data.pipe[1], &query, sizeof(query));
    if (rs_data.capturefile)
        write (rs_data.capturefile, &query, sizeof(query));
    read (rs_data.pipe[0], (float *)argv[0], sizeof(RtColor));
    return 0;
}


SHADEOP (rayserver_rayhittest)
{
    RSHittestQuery query;
    RSHittestAnswer answer;
    char buf[2];

    if (! rs_data.initialized) {
        *((float *)argv[0]) = RI_INFINITY;
        vset ((float *)argv[3], 0.0f);  vset ((float *)argv[4], 0.0f);
        return 0;
    }
    buf[0] = 12;  buf[1] = 'h';
    write (rs_data.pipe[1], buf, 2);
```

▶

Listing 17.7 (continued)

```
    if (rs_data.capturefile)
        write (rs_data.capturefile, buf, 2);
    vcopy (query.raypos, (float *)argv[1]);
    vcopy (query.raydir, (float *)argv[2]);
    query.raytime = raytime();  /* time */
    query.raylod = 0.5f;  /* detail */
    write (rs_data.pipe[1], &query, sizeof(query));
    if (rs_data.capturefile)
        write (rs_data.capturefile, &query, sizeof(query));
    read (rs_data.pipe[0], &answer, sizeof(answer));
    *((float *)argv[0]) = answer.hitdist;
    vcopy ((float *)argv[3], answer.Phit);
    vcopy ((float *)argv[4], answer.Nhit);
    return 0;
}


SHADEOP (rayserver_fulltrace)
{
    RSFulltraceQuery query;
    RSFulltraceAnswer answer;
    float *result = (float *)argv[0];
    float *hitcolor  = (float *)argv[3];
    float *hitdist  = (float *)argv[4];
    float *Phit = (float *)argv[5];
    float *Nhit = (float *)argv[6];
    float *Pmiss = (float *)argv[7];
    float *Rmiss = (float *)argv[8];
    char buf[2];

    if (! rs_data.initialized) {
        result[0] = 0;
        vset (hitcolor, 0.0f);
        hitdist[0] = RI_INFINITY;
        vcopy (Pmiss, (float *)argv[1]);  vcopy (Rmiss, (float *)argv[2]);
        return 0;
    }
    buf[0] = sizeof(query)/sizeof(float);  buf[1] = 'f';
    write (rs_data.pipe[1], buf, 2);
    if (rs_data.capturefile)
        write (rs_data.capturefile, buf, 2);
    memset (&query, 0, sizeof(query));
    vcopy (query.raypos, (float *)argv[1]);
    vcopy (query.raydir, (float *)argv[2]);
    query.raytime = raytime();  /* time */
    query.raylod = 0.5f;  /* detail */
    write (rs_data.pipe[1], &query, sizeof(query));
    if (rs_data.capturefile)
        write (rs_data.capturefile, &query, sizeof(query));           ▶
```

Listing 17.7 (continued)

```c
    read (rs_data.pipe[0], &answer, sizeof(answer));
    *result = answer.result;
    vcopy (hitcolor, answer.hitcolor);
    *hitdist = answer.dist;
    vcopy (Phit, answer.Phit);
    vcopy (Nhit, answer.Nhit);
    vcopy (Pmiss, answer.Pmiss);
    vcopy (Rmiss, answer.Rmiss);
    return 0;
}


static void sig_pipe (int signo)
{
    fprintf (stderr, "SIGPIPE caught\n");
    exit(1);
}


static int popen2 (char *cmd, int fd[2])
{
    int fd1[2], fd2[2];
    int pid;

    if (signal(SIGPIPE, sig_pipe) == SIG_ERR) {
        fprintf (stderr, "signal error\n");   return -1;
    }
    if (pipe(fd1) < 0 || pipe(fd2) < 0) {
        fprintf (stderr, "pipe error\n");   return -1;
    }
    if ((pid = fork()) < 0) {
        fprintf (stderr, "fork error\n");   return -1;
    } else if (pid > 0) {
        /* Parent */
        close (fd1[0]);
        close (fd2[1]);
        fd[0] = fd2[0];
        fd[1] = fd1[1];
        sleep (1);
        return 0;
    } else {
        /* Child */
        char *argv[100];
        int i, a;
        char *command = alloca(strlen(cmd)+2);
        strcpy (command, cmd);
        a = 0;
        cmd = command;
        argv[a++] = cmd;
```

▶

Listing 17.7 (continued)

```
            while (*cmd && *cmd != ' ') ++cmd;
            if (*cmd)
                *cmd++ = 0;
            while (*cmd) {
                while (*cmd == ' ') ++cmd;
                argv[a++] = cmd;
                while (*cmd && *cmd != ' ') ++cmd;
                if (*cmd)
                    *cmd++ = 0;
            }
            argv[a] = NULL;
            close (fd1[1]);
            close (fd2[0]);
            if (fd1[0] != STDIN_FILENO) {
                if (dup2(fd1[0], STDIN_FILENO) != STDIN_FILENO) {
                    fprintf (stderr, "dup2 error to stdin\n");
                    close (fd1[0]);
                }
            }
            if (fd2[1] != STDOUT_FILENO) {
                if (dup2(fd2[1], STDOUT_FILENO) != STDOUT_FILENO) {
                    fprintf (stderr, "dup2 error to stdout\n");
                    close (fd2[1]);
                }
            }
            if (execvp (command, argv) < 0) {
                fprintf (stderr, "execl error\n");
                return -1;
            }
        }
    return 0;
}


SHADEOP_INIT (rayserver_init)
{
    char *servername, *jitterval, *stash_filename;
    int len;

    if (rs_data.initialized)
        return NULL;

    servername = getenv ("RAYSERVER");
    if (! servername)
        return NULL;        /* Could not find name of server */     ▶
```

Listing 17.7 (continued)

```c
    len = strlen (servername) + 2;
    if (popen2 (servername, rs_data.pipe)) {
        fprintf (stderr, "Error opening pipe to "%s"\n", servername);
        return NULL;      /* Could not open pipe */
    }

    rs_data.in = fdopen (rs_data.pipe[0], "r");
    setlinebuf (rs_data.in);

    jitterval = getenv ("RAYSERVER_JITTER_TIMES");
    if (jitterval)
        rs_data.jitter_times = atoi(jitterval);

    stash_filename = getenv ("RAYSERVER_CAPTURE");
    if (stash_filename)
        rs_data.capturefile = open (stash_filename,
                                O_WRONLY|O_CREAT|O_TRUNC, exit 0777);
    else rs_data.capturefile = 0;

    rs_data.initialized = 1;
    return NULL;
}


SHADEOP_CLEANUP (rayserver_cleanup)
{
    if (rs_data.initialized) {
        close (rs_data.pipe[0]);
        close (rs_data.pipe[1]);
        if (rs_data.capturefile)
            close (rs_data.capturefile);
        rs_data.initialized = 0;
    }
}
```

Afterword

And now the story will be told. Just where did the goofy name RenderMan come from anyway? Does it have anything to do with the comic book character Superman? And why the ridiculous embedded capital M?

In the very beginning, in the early 1980s, when Ed Catmull first brought a bunch of folks together to create the Computer Division of Lucasfilm, the goal was to computerize the special effects industry in three ways: replace the optical film printer by a digital compositing system; replace the physical film editing station by digital off-line editing; and replace traditional miniature effects by computer-generated animation. In those days, when the fastest computer generally available was a VAX 11/780, it was clear that special-purpose hardware was required for these tasks. So the Computer Division undertook three hardware projects: the Pixar-2D, the EditDroid, and the ambitious Pixar-3D.

The Pixar-2D was an image processing engine, which eventually came to be sold by the name of Pixar Image Computer. The central processor, known as the Chap (Levinthal and Porter, 1984), was a four-way parallel SIMD engine for working on four-channel RGBA images. The software that was written for the machine included an implementation of the Porter/Duff compositing algebra (Porter and Duff, 1984), and a layered photograph retouching and paint program similar to what eventually became *Adobe Photoshop*.

The EditDroid was the one of the first off-line editing systems. Filmmakers would transfer their film onto videodisks and create the edit lists that showed which takes were to be used in which sequence to create the final film. The EditDroid was eventually spun off into another company, known as the DroidWorks, but the technology didn't mature until the advent of the Avid Digital Editing system.

The Pixar-3D was a giant image synthesis hardware pipeline, designed by Adam Levinthal, Jeff Mock, Mark Leather, and Lane Molpus. The software prototype of this rendering pipeline, developed by Loren Carpenter and Rob Cook, was given the name Reyes by Loren, which stood for "renders everything you ever saw" (but was also the name of a local national park). It became relatively successful even on the slow VAX computers. The "Genesis Effect" sequence in *Star Trek: The Wrath of Khan* was done with an early version of the software, and the stained-glass man sequence in *Young Sherlock Holmes* demonstrated both motion blur and depth of field for the first time. This special effect proved that computer animation could be seamlessly integrated into live-action footage.

Pixar was spun off from Lucasfilm in 1986, thanks to the beneficence (and not-insignificant cash outlay) of Steve Jobs, and contained the Image Computer product team, the backbone and central focus of the young company, the animation R&D group, which continued to make short-subject CG animations, and the graphics R&D group, which continued to pursue Reyes.

The Pixar-3D hardware project was eventually renamed the "Reyes Machine," and the hardware team and their software partners Jim Lawson, Pat Hanrahan, and Sam Leffler set out to design and build this machine. The Reyes Machine was an expensive piece of hardware, with a series of special-purpose boards that each accomplished one part of the Reyes rendering pipeline. Most were programmable to a certain extent, and the first of these to proceed to a completed prototype was the filtering/pixel reconstruction board, which was a parallel array of Transputer processors. The Transputer was a CPU designed in the UK in the late 1980s, which had extremely high floating-point performance and had parallelism and message-passing hardware built into the chip (quite unique at the time).

It was not long before the team recognized that the filter board design was so general, and the Transputer CPU so powerful, that the entire software Reyes implementation could be run on the Transputer array, creating a rendering machine that was significantly cheaper than the original Reyes Machine design.

Thus was born the RM-1 Project, a single-board implementation of the Reyes Machine, whose goal was to produce a piece of special-purpose rendering hardware that was small enough and cheap enough to sell but powerful enough to significantly outperform any other "general-purpose" computer that was available in the same price range. It might not be as fast as the true Reyes Machine, but it would be much more cost-effective. Pat Hanrahan realized that, in the face of this oft-changing hardware architecture, a standard interface to rendering hardware, like Silicon Graphics had to their hardware, was a good idea. So he started design work, at first with SGI and later without them, on the next-generation GL, called the "Rendering Interface," or RI.

At some point during the design and building of the RM-1, Pat and Jeff noted that "one day" the Transputer would be so powerful that a single chip would do the work that the entire Reyes Machine was originally designed to do. You could imagine a small box with a single CPU and some superhigh-density memory running Reyes. It would render in real time and generate video that you'd pipe directly to video eyeglasses. It would be small enough to carry around on your belt the way you carry a Sony WalkMan. It would be a *Render*-Man.

After that, the "RM" in RM-1 was simply understood to mean RenderMan, and Pixar undertook to start selling these RenderMan-1 boxes to anyone who needed high-speed rendering services: at the time pretty much Industrial Light and Magic, although we thought others might enter the business soon. One of the keys to gaining market acceptance was to promote the new Rendering Interface as the "industry standard for high-end rendering." We put together a little advisory group of about 20 big-name companies in the computer graphics industry to announce that we were all agreeing that RI was the PostScript of 3D.

There was only one snag. Steve Jobs felt that the name "Rendering Interface" was just not snazzy enough. We needed a cool name to rally support around. What about that "RenderMan" name? That was definitely memorable and cool. Let's just put that on the front cover of the document instead of Rendering Interface. Yes, *RenderMan* it is: RenderMan Interface, RenderMan-1 hardware, RenderMan Toolkit software.

And so it was.

Sadly, the hardware never made it out of beta test. Pixar made one short using it (*Tin Toy*), and ILM made a small amount of footage for a ride film, but it was killed by the inexorable march of Moore's law and the intrinsic unsupportability of special-purpose hardware over the long haul. The Image Computer died, too, and the focus of the company shifted to software sales and to the wildly successful animation production group. And although *the* RenderMan never came to be, the software that spawned the idea lives on and has made computer graphics a household word.

Oh, and the fact that at the launch of the beta RM-1 hardware we all had blue, long-sleeve T-shirts with little red capes silk-screened on the back, and a red and yellow emblem on the front that was an R inside of a five-sided shield? Never mind.

Glossary

Aliasing. Undesirable image artifacts related to the rendering process inadequately sampling and representing high frequencies in the image.

Alpha. An extra channel in an image giving a measure of *coverage* of a pixel, to aid in image compositing. An alpha of 1.0 means fully opaque; 0.0 means fully transparent.

Anisotropic. Something that has a directional dependence. When talking about surface reflectivity, it refers to a BRDF that depends on the rotational orientation of a surface, as well as the angles of the incoming and outgoing light.

Antialiasing. Ways of combating aliasing artifacts. Generally encompasses capturing geometric edges without "jaggies," motion blur, or depth of field, and otherwise adequately sampling high frequencies in the image.

API. Applications Programming Interface. An API is a set of data types and procedures that define the public interface to a library or program.

Archive. The word that the *RenderMan Interface Specification* uses to denote RIB metafiles, because they were originally designed for archival purposes.

Artifact. A visible imperfection in a computer graphics image, particularly one that betrays the fact that the image is CG and is not a real photograph or physical artwork. Aliasing, polygonal silhouettes, oversimplistic shading, and Mach bands are typical examples of artifacts.

Associated alpha. For pixels represented by RGB and alpha (coverage), the practice of *pre-multiplying* the RGB values by the alpha values. This makes the computations for image compositing simpler.

Attribute. In RI/RIB, attributes are properties that apply to individual geometric primitives. Examples of attributes include color, opacity, shader assignments, sidedness, orientation, and so on.

Back facing. Surfaces whose surface normals face away from the camera viewpoint.

Blinn's law. The observation, common in the early days of CGI but first published by Jim Blinn, that an artist is willing to wait a fixed amount of time for an image to render, and that faster hardware simply results in more complex images that take the same amount of time to render.

Blue Moon Rendering Tools (*BMRT*). A shareware, RenderMan-compliant renderer that can do ray tracing and radiosity.

BRDF. Bidirectional reflectance distribution function. A BRDF is a formula whose inputs are the incoming (L) and outgoing (V) directions on a surface, and its output is the portion of light coming from L that is scattered toward V. A BRDF is the heart of a *local illumination model*.

CGI. Computer graphics imagery, especially computer graphics imagery that is produced for use in motion pictures (such as for special effects).

Constant primitive variables. In RIB, those variables that are specified with a single value for the entire geometric primitive.

Convolution. A mathematical operation that combines two functions (or waveforms) together. Used, for example, in filtering, in order to weight samples by their importance as represented by the shape of the filter kernel. It is typically visualized by *sliding* one waveform past the other.

Cucaloris. Often called a "cookie" for short, a light-blocking card (or image file) that controls the cross-sectional shape of a spotlight.

Depth of field. The property of physical cameras that only a limited range of distances can be in focus at any one time. Also, any rendering calculation that takes this property into account.

Displacement bound. Extra space added to the bounding box of an object to account for the fact that displacement might make the primitive "poke out" of the original bounds.

Displacement shading. Allowing user-supplied programs or shaders to alter surface geometry to add fine detail.

Fill light. A dim, nonspecular light that fills in areas of a scene not illuminated by a key light.

Front facing. Surfaces whose surface normals face toward the camera viewpoint.

Gamma correction. A scaling of the values in an image to compensate for the property of all physical display devices that they react to input values in a nonlinear way.

General polygon. In RenderMan, any polygon that is either concave, or has holes, or both.

Geometric primitive. An individual piece of geometry, such as a sphere, polygon, NURBS mesh, and so on.

Global illumination. Calculation of how light affects an entire scene, especially the contribution of light reflected between surfaces (as opposed to coming straight from a light source).

Global variable. In Shading Language, any of the built-in variables describing the shading situation, for example, P, N, u, and so on.

Isotropic. Means "the same in all directions." When referring to surface reflectivity, it means a BRDF that depends only on the angles of the incoming and outgoing light relative to the surface normal, without regard to the rotational orientation of the surface about its normal.

Key light. A major source of illumination in a scene, usually resulting in hard shadows and specular highlights.

Local illumination model. A formula that, given the directions and intensities of light impinging on a surface, computes the amount of light scattered away from the surface in a particular direction (such as toward the camera). Synonyms: local Reflection Model, BRDF.

Local reflection model. Same as **local illumination model**.

Mach bands. Dark and light stripes that seem to appear alongside the intersection of two regions of different value (brightness), but are not actually there, caused by a physchophysical response of the human visual system, which is trying to accentuate such edges.

Metafile. A file that records a sequence of commands that were (and can be again) sent through a procedural interface. Specifically, RIB is a metafile for commands sent through the RI procedural API.

Mip-map. Short for "multiple-image pyramid." A texture map for which the results of filtering the texture with a series of larger and larger filters (typically sized in powers of two) have been precalculated and stored with the map, in order to speed render-time texture access.

Modeler. A program that allows users to specify the shape of geometric objects, and to place objects, lights, and cameras in a virtual scene.

Moore's law. The observation that computing power (as measured by the time it takes to perform certain fixed benchmark calculations on new computers) increases exponentially over time, and that historically it has doubled every 18 months or so over a very long time span. Contrast with **Blinn's law**.

Motion blur. The property of physical cameras that objects that move relative to the camera leave a streak in photographs, proportional to the length of time the camera shutter is open. Also, any rendering calculation that takes this property into account.

Option. In RI/RIB, options are properties that apply to the scene or image as a whole (as opposed to applying to individual geometric primitives). Examples of options include image resolution, color depth, and projection type.

Parameter list. An arbitrary-length list of name-value pairs that provide the parameter data for open-ended API calls in RenderMan. Each name is a string, and each value is an array of data whose length is dependent on the API call and the storage class associated with the name.

Parametric coordinates. The (typically) two values that uniquely specify a point on a parametric surface, such as a NURBS or a quadric primitive.

PhotoRealistic RenderMan. The name of Pixar's rendering product, a specific renderer that is compliant with the RenderMan standard and is widely used for feature-film animation and visual effects.

Primitive variables. Data attached to a geometric primitive (per primitive, facet, corner, or vertex), interpolated by the renderer, and that can be accessed in a shader.

PRMan. *PhotoRealistic RenderMan.*

Procedural primitive. A geometric primitive that is specified not by providing a large array of precomputed vertex data, but rather by running a program that takes parameters such as the object's screen location and size, and that generates a specific array of vertex data that is optimized for use at that location and size.

Projection. A transformation that "flattens" space by removing one dimension, for example, converting points in a 3D space into positions on a 2D object (such as a plane or the surface of a sphere).

Radiosity. A global illumination method involving solution by finite element methods. Radiosity solutions usually make the assumption that all surfaces are perfectly diffuse. Sometimes "radiosity" refers colloquially to any global illumination algorithm.

Ray casting. A method of global visibility determination that computes the intersection of viewing "rays" with scene geometry for any purpose.

Ray tracing. A method of rendering that solves hidden surfaces, shadows, and reflections by computing the intersection of viewing "rays" and scene geometry.

Reference geometry. A description of geometry in a canonical pose. As the "real" geometry is deformed by animation, the reference geometry can be used for shading calculations to ensure that any patterns computed by the shader will stick to the surface as it deforms.

Renderer. A program that takes a description of a scene (camera, objects, materials, lights) and produces an image.

RenderMan. A standard for describing scenes to high-quality renderers. Also colloquially refers to *PRMan*.

Reyes. The name of the rendering algorithm used by the *PRMan* renderer ("renders everything you ever saw"). Reyes is a type of scanline rendering method.

RIB file. Short for "RenderMan Interface Bytestream." The metafile format for the RenderMan API.

Scanline rendering. A family of rendering methods that involve projecting geometry into screen space and handling geometric primitives in image order.

Shadeop. Short for *shading operation*, shadeops are the built-in operators and functions in Shading Language (in other words, the operators and functions that the SL compiler already knows about).

Shader. A computer program, written in RenderMan Shading Language, that describes the appearance of a surface, light, or volume.

Shading Language. A computer language, loosely based on C, for expressing shading and lighting calculations to RenderMan-compliant renderers.

Shading rate. The area on a surface (expressed in square pixels) for which each shader calculation is representative. Smaller values for the shading rate imply that each sample is used for a smaller screen area, therefore more total shading calculations will be performed (with the expected increase in cost). Larger values for the shading rate will result in fewer total invocations of the shader, thus rendering in less time and memory, but with lower image fidelity.

SL. Shading Language.

Space. A short synonym for "coordinate system."

Stochastic sampling. A particular method of antialiasing that involves point sampling with an irregular pattern. Replaces aliasing artifacts with high-frequency noise, which is often less objectionable.

Storage class. Refers to the type of interpolation and amount of data for primitive variables or Shading Language variables. Primitive variables may have a storage class of **constant**, **uniform**, **varying**, or **vertex**. Shading Language variables may only be **uniform** or **varying**.

Story point. The single simple idea that the director of a film is trying to get across in a scene, usually a piece of the plot or a facet of character development.

Superwhite. A color that is too bright to be displayed on a physical display device. Also, RGB values that are "greater than 1.0," and therefore have this property.

TD. Short for **technical director**.

Technical director. At a production studio, the personnel who are responsible for creating geometric models, writing shaders, lighting shots, and other technical tasks. The exact job description varies from studio to studio, but generally these are the people who are responsible for the "look" of a film (as opposed to the motion or the artistic design), and are thus the primary users of image rendering software.

Texture mapping. Taking colors (or other data) from a stored image file and applying the pattern to a surface to give added detail.

Translucency. The property of some thin surfaces that allows some light to pass through them but scatters the light sufficiently that the viewer cannot see a clear image of what is behind the object. Leaves, lamp shades, and draperies are examples of objects that are translucent.

Transparency. The property of some surfaces to transmit light with minimal scattering, allowing the viewer to see a more or less clear image of what is behind the surface. Ordinary window glass is an example of a transparent surface.

Uniform primitive variables. In RIB, those variables that are specified per facet or subpatch and are constant across each facet.

Uniform shader variables. In Shading Language, those variables or parameters that can take on only one value at a time, all over the surface (as opposed to **varying shader variables**). Uniform SL variables use less storage and are less expensive computationally than varying quantities.

Varying primitive variables. In RIB, those variables that are specified per *facet or subpatch corner* and are linearly interpolated across each facet or subpatch.

Varying shader variables. In Shading Language, those variables or parameters that may take on different values at different points on the surface. Varying SL variables use more storage and are more computationally expensive than uniform quantities.

Vertex primitive variables. In RIB, those variables that are specified once per control vertex and are interpolated using the same method as the surface positions (i.e., just like "P"). Vertex primitive variables will be considered varying in a shader.

Wavelength-dependent. Any quantity or calculation whose value varies at different wavelengths of light (at different spectral colors).

Bibliography

Arvo, J. (1995). Applications of irradiance tensors to the simulation of nonlambertian phenomena. In R. Cook (ed.), *SIGGRAPH 95 Conference Proceedings*, Annual Conference Series, ACM SIGGRAPH, Addison Wesley, pp. 335-342. Held in Los Angeles, California, August 6-11, 1995.

Barzel, R. (1997). Lighting controls for computer cinematography, *Journal of Graphics Tools* 2(1): 1-20. ISSN 1086-7651.

Bass, D. H. (1981). Using the video lookup table for reflectivity calculations: specific techniques and graphic results, *Computer Graphics and Image Processing* 17: 249-261.

Blinn, J. F. (1977). Models of light reflection for computer synthesized pictures, *Computer Graphics (SIGGRAPH '77 Proceedings)*, Vol. 11, pp. 192-198.

Blinn, J. F. (1978). Simulation of wrinkled surfaces, *Computer Graphics (SIGGRAPH '78 Proceedings)*, Vol. 12, pp. 286-292.

Blinn, J. F. (1982). Light reflection functions for simulation of clouds and dusty surfaces, *Computer Graphics (SIGGRPAH '82 Proceedings)*, Vol. 16, pp. 21-29.

Blinn, J. F. (1985). The ancient Chinese art of Chi-Ting, *ACM SIGGRAPH '85 Course Notes #12 (Image Rendering Tricks)*, ACM SIGGRAPH.

Blinn, J. F., and Newell, M. E. (1976). Texture and reflection in computer generated images, *Communications of the ACM* 19: 542-546.

Catmull, E. E. (1974). *A Subdivision Algorithm for Computer Display of Curved Surfaces*, Ph.D. thesis, Dept. of Computer Science, University of Utah.

Cook, R. L. (1984). Shade trees. In H. Christiansen (ed.), *Computer Graphics (SIGGRAPH '84 Proceedings)*, Vol. 18, pp. 223-231.

Cook, R. L. (1986). Stochastic sampling in computer graphics, *ACM Transactions on Graphics* 5(1): 51-72.

Cook, R. L., Carpenter, L., and Catmull, E. (1987). The Reyes image rendering architecture. In M. C. Stone (ed.), *Computer Graphics (SIGGRAPH '87 Proceedings)*, pp. 95-102.

Cook, R. L., Porter, T., and Carpenter, L. (1984). Distributed ray tracing, *Computer Graphics (SIGGRAPH '84 Proceedings)*, Vol. 18, pp. 137-145.

Cook, R. L., and Torrance, K. E. (1981). A reflectance model for computer graphics, *Computer Graphics (SIGGRPAH '81 Proceedings)*, Vol. 15, pp. 307-316.

Cook, R. L., and Torrance, K. E. (1982). A reflectance model for computer graphics, *ACM Transactions on Graphics* 1(1): 7-24.

Curtis, C. J., Anderson, S. E., Seims, J. E., Fleischer, K. W., and Salesin, D. H. (1997). Computer-generated watercolor. In T. Whitted (ed.), *SIGGRAPH 97 Conference Proceedings*, Annual Conference Series, ACM SIGGRAPH, Addison-Wesley, pp. 421-430. ISBN 0-89791-896-7.

DeRose, T., Kass, M., and Truong, T. (1998). Subdivision surfaces in character animation. In M. Cohen (ed.), *SIGGRAPH 98 Conference Proceedings*, Annual Conference Series, ACM SIGGRAPH, Addison-Wesley, pp. 85–94. ISBN 0-89791-999-8.

Disney/Pixar (1995). *Toy Story*, computer-animated film.

Dorsey, J., Arvo, J., and Greenberg, D. (1995). Interactive design of complex time dependent lighting, *IEEE Computer Graphics and Applications* **15**(2): 26–36.

Dorsey, J. O., Sillion, F. X., and Greenberg, D. P. (1991). Design and simulation of opera lighting and projection effects. In T. W. Sederberg (ed.), *Computer Graphics (SIGGRAPH '91 Proceedings)*, Vol. 25, pp. 41–50.

Ebert, D., Musgrave, K., Peachey, D., Perlin, K. and Worley (1998). *Texturing and Modeling: A Procedural Approach* (2nd ed.), Academic Press, San Diego, CA. ISBN 0-12-228730-4.

Egerton, P. A., and Hall, W. S. (1998). *Computer Graphics: Mathematical First Steps*, Prentice-Hall, Hemel Hempstead, England.

Farin, G. (1990). *Curves and Surfaces for Computer Aided Geometric Design*, Academic Press, San Diego, CA.

Farin, G. (1995). *NURB Curves and Surfaces*, A K Peters, Ltd., Wellesley, MA.

Foley, J. D., van Dam, A., Feiner, S. K., and Hughes, J. F. (1990). *Computer Graphics, Principles and Practice*, 2nd ed., Addison-Wesley, Reading, MA. (Overview of research to date.)

Gardner, G. Y. (1984). Simulation of natural scenes using textured quadric surfaces. In H. Christiansen (ed.), *Computer Graphics (SIGGRAPH '84 Proceedings)*, Vol. 18, pp. 11–20.

Gershbein, R., Schroder, P., and Hanrahan, P. (1994). Textures and radiosity: Controlling emission and reflection from texture maps, *Technical Report CS-TR-449-94*, Princeton University.

Glassner, A. S. (1989). *An Introduction to Ray Tracing*, Academic Press, San Diego, CA.

Glassner, A. S. (1995). *Principles of Digital Image Synthesis*, Morgan Kaufmann Publishers, Inc., San Francisco.

Goldman, D. B. (1997). Fake fur rendering. In T. Whitted (ed.), *SIGGRAPH 97 Conference Proceedings*, Annual Conference Series, ACM SIGGRAPH, Addison-Wesley, pp. 127–134. ISBN 0-89791-896-7.

Gondek, J. S., Meyer, G. W., and Newman, J. G. (1994). Wavelength dependent reflectance functions. In A. Glassner (ed.), *Proceedings of SIGGRAPH '94* (Orlando, Florida, July 24–29, 1994), Computer Graphics Proceedings, Annual Conference Series, ACM SIGGRAPH, ACM Press, pp. 213–220. ISBN 0-89791-667-0.

Gonick, L., and Huffman, A. (1992). *The Cartoon Guide to Physics*, Harper/Perennial Library, New York.

Greene, N. (1986a). Applications of world projections. In M. Green (ed.), *Proceedings of Graphics Interface '86*, pp. 108–114.

Greene, N. (1986b). Environment mapping and other applications of world projections, *IEEE Computer Graphics and Applications* **6**(11): 21–29.

Gritz, L., and Hahn, J. K. (1996). BMRT: A global illumination implementation of the RenderMan standard, *Journal of Graphics Tools* **1**(3): 29–47. ISSN 1086-7651.

Haeberli, P. E. (1990). Paint by numbers: Abstract image representations. In F. Baskett (ed.), *Computer Graphics (SIGGRAPH '90 Proceedings)*, Vol. 24, pp. 207–214.

Hall, R. (1986). A characterization of illumination models and shading techniques, *The Visual Computer* **2**(5): 268–277.

Hall, R. (1989). *Illumination and Color in Computer Generated Imagery*, Springer-Verlag, New York. (Includes C code for radiosity algorithms.)

Hanrahan, P., and Krueger, W. (1993). Reflection from layered surfaces due to subsurface scattering. In J. T. Kajiya (ed.), *Computer Graphics (SIGGRAPH '93 Proceedings)*, Vol. 27, pp. 165-174.

Hanrahan, P., and Lawson, J. (1990). A language for shading and lighting calculations. In F. Baskett (ed.), *Computer Graphics (SIGGRAPH '90 Proceedings)*, Vol. 24, pp. 289-298.

He, X. D., Torrance, K. E., Sillion, F. X., and Greenberg, D. P. (1991). A comprehensive physical model for light reflection. In T. W. Sederberg (ed.), *Computer Graphics (SIGGRAPH '91 Proceedings)*, Vol. 25, pp. 175-186.

Heckbert, P. S. (1986). Survey of texture mapping, *IEEE Computer Graphics and Applications* **6**(11): 56-67.

Kajiya, J. T. (1985). Anisotropic reflection models. *In* B. A. Barsky (ed.), *Computer Graphics (SIGGRAPH '85 Proceedings)*, Vol. 19, pp. 15-21.

Kawai, J. K., Painter, J. S., and Cohen, M. F. (1993). Radioptimization—goal based rendering, *Computer Graphics Proceedings, Annual Conference Series, 1993*, pp. 147-154.

Lafortune, E. P. F., Foo, S.-C., Torrance, K. E., and Greenberg, D. P. (1997). Non-linear approximation of reflectance functions. In T. Whitted (ed.), *SIGGRAPH 97 Conference Proceedings*, Annual Conference Series, ACM SIGGRAPH, Addison-Wesley, pp. 117-a126. ISBN 0-89791-896-7.

Levinthal, A., and Porter, T. (1984). Chap—a SIMD graphics processor. In H. Christiansen (ed.), *Computer Graphics (SIGGRAPH '84 Proceedings)*, Vol. 18, pp. 77-82.

Lewis, J.-P. (1989). Algorithms for solid noise synthesis. In J. Lane (ed.), *Computer Graphics (SIGGRAPH '89 Proceedings)*, Vol. 23, pp. 263-270.

Lynch, D. K., and Livingston, W. (1995). *Color and Light in Nature*, Cambridge University Press, Cambridge, England.

Meier, B. J. (1996). Painterly rendering for animation. In H. Rushmeier (ed.), *SIGGRAPH 96 Conference Proceedings*, Annual Conference Series, ACM SIGGRAPH, Addison-Wesley, pp. 477-484. Held in New Orleans, Louisiana, August 4-9, 1996.

Minnaert, M. G. J. (1993). *Light and Color in the Outdoors*, Springer-Verlag New York.

Nakamae, E., Kaneda, K., Okamoto, T., and Nishita, T. (1990). A lighting model aiming at drive simulators. In F. Baskett (ed.), *Computer Graphics (SIGGRAPH '90 Proceedings)*, Vol. 24, pp. 395-404.

Oren, M., and Nayar, S. K. (1994). Generalization of lambert's reflectance model. In A. Glassner (ed.), *Proceedings of SIGGRAPH '94* (Orlando, Florida, July 24-29, 1994), Computer Graphics Proceedings, Annual Conference Series, ACM SIGGRAPH, ACM Press, pp. 239-246. ISBN 0-89791-667-0.

Perlin, K. (1985). An image synthesizer. In B. A. Barsky (ed.), *Computer Graphics (SIGGRAPH '85 Proceedings)*, Vol. 19, pp. 287-296.

Perlin, K., and Hoffert, E. M. (1989). Hypertexture. In J. Lane (ed.), *Computer Graphics (SIGGRAPH '89 Proceedings)*, Vol. 23, pp. 253-262.

Phong, B.-T. (1975). Illumination for computer generated pictures, *Communications of the ACM* **18**(6): 311-317.

Piegl, L., and Tiller, W. (1995). *The NURBS Book*, Springer-Verlag Berlin.

Pixar (1989). *The RenderMan Interface, Version 3.1*, Pixar.

Pixar (1997). *Geri's Game*, computer-animated short film.

Porter, T., and Duff, T. (1984). Compositing digital images. In H. Christiansen (ed.), *Computer Graphics (SIGGRAPH '84 Proceedings)*, Vol. 18, pp. 253-259.

Poulin, P., and Fournier, A. (1990). A model for anisotropic reflection. In F. Baskett (ed.), *Computer Graphics (SIGGRAPH '90 Proceedings)*, Vol. 24, pp. 273-282.

Reeves, W. T., and Blau, R. (1985). Approximate and probabilistic algorithms for shading and rendering structured particle systems. In B. A. Barsky (ed.), *Computer Graphics (SIGGRAPH '85 Proceedings)*, Vol. 19, pp. 313-322.

Reeves, W. T., Salesin, D. H., and Cook, R. L. (1987). Rendering antialiased shadows with depth maps. In M. C. Stone (ed.), *Computer Graphics (SIGGRAPH '87 Proceedings)*, Vol. 21, pp. 283-291.

Rogers, D., and Adams, J. A. (1989). *Mathematical Elements for Computer Graphics* (2nd ed.), McGraw-Hill, New York.

Saito, T., and Takahashi, T. (1990). Comprehensible rendering of 3-D shapes. In F. Baskett (ed.), *Computer Graphics (SIGGRAPH '90 Proceedings)*, Vol. 24, pp. 197-206.

Schlick, C. (1993). A customizable reflectance model for everyday rendering. In M. F. Cohen, C. Puech, and F. Sillion (eds.), *Fourth Eurographics Workshop on Rendering*, Eurographics, pp. 73-84. Held in Paris, France, June 14-16, 1993.

Schoeneman, C., Dorsey, J., Smits, B., Arvo, J., and Greenberg, D. (1993). Painting with light, *Computer Graphics Proceedings, Annual Conference Series, 1993*, pp. 143-146.

Sherstyuk, A. (1996). Ray tracing with selective visibility, *Journal of Graphics Tools* 1(4): 41-46. ISSN 1086-7651.

Smits, B. E., and Meyer, G. M. (1989). Newton colors: Simulating interference phenomena in realistic image synthesis, *Proceedings of Eurographics Workshop on Photosimulation, Realism and Physics in Computer Graphics,* Eurographics, pp. 185-194. Held in Rennes, France, June 1990.

Thompson, S. P., and Gardner, M. (1998). *Calculus Made Easy*, St. Martin's Press, New York.

Upstill, S. (1990). *The RenderMan Companion: A Programmer's Guide to Realistic Computer Graphics*, Addison-Wesley, Reading, MA.

Verbeck, C. P., and Greenberg, D. P. (1984). A comprehensive light source description for computer graphics, *IEEE Computer Graphics and Applications* 4(7): 66-75.

Ward, G. J. (1992). Measuring and modeling anisotropic reflection. In E. E. Catmull (ed.), *Computer Graphics (SIGGRAPH '92 Proceedings)*, Vol. 26, pp. 265-272.

Warn, D. R. (1983). Lighting controls for synthetic images, *Computer Graphics (SIGGRAPH '83 Proceedings)*, Vol. 17, pp. 13-21.

Watt, A., and Watt, M. (1992). *Advanced Animation and Rendering Techniques: Theory and Practice*, Addison-Wesley Publishing Company, New York.

Westin, S. H., Arvo, J. R., and Torrance, K. E. (1992). Predicting reflectance functions from complex surfaces. In E. E. Catmull (ed.), *Computer Graphics (SIGGRAPH '92 Proceedings)*, Vol. 26, pp. 255-264.

Whitted, T. (1980). An improved illumination model for shaded display, *Communications of the ACM* **23**(6): 343-349.

Whitted, T., and Cook, R. L. (1985). A comprehensive shading model, *SIGGRAPH '85 Image Rendering Tricks* seminar notes.

Whitted, T., and Cook, R. L. (1988). A comprehensive shading model. In K. I. Joy, C. W. Grant, N. L. Max, and L. Hatfield (eds.), *Tutorial: Computer Graphics: Image Synthesis*, Computer Society Press, pp. 232-243.

Williams, L. (1978). Casting curved shadows on curved surfaces, *Computer Graphics (SIGGRAPH '78 Proceedings)*, Vol. 12, pp. 270-274.

Winkenbach, G., and Salesin, D. H. (1994). Computer-generated pen-and-ink illustration. In A. Glassner (ed.), *Proceedings of SIGGRAPH '94* (Orlando, Florida, July 24–29, 1994), Computer Graphics Proceedings, Annual Conference Series, ACM SIGGRAPH, ACM Press, pp. 91–100. ISBN 0-89791-667-0.

Wolberg, G. (1990). *Digital Image Warping*, IEEE Computer Society Press, Los Alamitos, CA.

Wood, D. N., Finkelstein, A., Hughes, J. F., Thayer, C. E., and Salesin, D. H. (1997). Multiperspective panoramas for cel animation. In T. Whitted (ed.), *SIGGRAPH 97 Conference Proceedings*, Annual Conference Series, ACM SIGGRAPH, Addison-Wesley, pp. 243–250. ISBN 0-89791-896-7.

Worley, S. P. (1996). A cellular texture basis function. In H. Rushmeier (ed.), *SIGGRAPH 96 Conference Proceedings*, Annual Conference Series, ACM SIGGRAPH, Addison-Wesley, pp. 291–294. Held in New Orleans, Louisiana, August 4–9, 1996.

Index

About the Authors

Anthony A. (Tony) Apodaca is Director of Graphics R&D at Pixar Animation Studios, co-creator of the RenderMan specification, and lead engineer of *PhotoRealistic RenderMan*. His film credits include *Tin Toy*, *Knick-knack*, *Toy Story*, and *A Bug's Life*. Tony has been at Pixar since 1986 and holds an MEng degree in computer and systems engineering from Rensselaer Polytechnic Institute. In March 1993, Tony and five other engineers received a Scientific and Technical Academy Award from the Academy of Motion Picture Arts and Sciences for work on *PhotoRealistic RenderMan*.

Larry Gritz works in the Graphics R&D group at Pixar, where since 1995 he has been one of the senior engineers of Pixar's rendering technology, including *PhotoRealistic RenderMan*, as well as performing occasional stints as a technical director. His film credits include *Toy Story*, *Geri's Game*, *A Bug's Life*, and *Toy Story 2*. Larry's research interests include global illumination, shading languages and systems, and rendering of hideously complex scenes. Prior to joining Pixar, Larry wrote the *Blue Moon Rendering Tools (BMRT),* the most widely used RenderMan implementation other than *PRMan*. Larry holds a BS in computer science from Cornell University, and MS and PhD degrees in computer science from George Washington University.

Ronen Barzel currently works in the Studio Tools R&D group at Pixar Animation Studios. He worked on the production of *Toy Story*, building models, lighting, and developing software. He holds a BS in math and physics and an MS in computer science from Brown University and a PhD in computer science from the California Institute of Technology. He authored *Physically Based Modeling for Computer Graphics: A Structured Approach* (Academic Press, 1992) and is editor-in-chief of the *Journal of Graphics Tools*.

Sharon Calahan has been a member of the technical team at Pixar since 1994, and was the Creative Lighting Supervisor for *Toy Story* and Director of Photography for *A Bug's Life* and the upcoming *Toy Story 2*. Her background and education in art and design led her into advertising, broadcast TV, video production, and eventually computer animation. With a focus on lighting direction, Sharon has worked in computer animation for over 14 years.

Clint Hanson received his B. Mathematics from the University of Waterloo in 1993. After that he worked at Vertigo Technologies Inc. for three years, where he developed 3D software tools that were used in conjunction with *PhotoRealistic Render-Man.* He is currently working at Sony Pictures Imageworks in Los Angeles on the upcoming *Stuart Little.* His list of movie credits includes *Contact*, *Escape from L.A.*, *The Postman, Mortal Kombat,* and *The Santa Clause.*

Scott Johnston founded Fleeting Image Animation, Inc. in 1997 to develop and produce animation integrating traditional and computer-generated techniques. Prior to this, Scott worked at Walt Disney Feature Animation, where he was a principal designer of the ballroom sequence in *Beauty and the Beast* and was CGI Supervisor for *The Lion King.* Scott recently completed *The Iron Giant* for Warner Brothers Feature Animation, where he served as Artistic Coordinator.